NORTHERN SPAIN

*'I   any bar or café you could see an old sailor delicately
sipp i   ng his camomile tea next to a young mother, baby under
he   arm, stopping in for a beer break during her shopping;
walking into any of them can be an adventure.'*

Dana Facaros & Michael Pauls

About the Guide

The full-colour introduction gives the authors' overview of the country, together with suggested itineraries and a regional 'where to go' map and feature to help you plan your trip.

Illuminating and entertaining cultural chapters on local history, culture, food, wine and everyday life give you a rich flavour of the country.

Planning Your Trip starts with the basics of when to go, getting there and getting around, coupled with other useful information, including a section for disabled travellers. The Practical A–Z deals with all the essential information and contact details that you may need while you are away.

The regional chapters are arranged in a loose touring order, with plenty of public transport and driving information. The author's top 'Don't Miss' ⭐ sights are highlighted at the start of each chapter.

A language and pronunciation guide, a glossary of cultural terms, ideas for further reading and a comprehensive index can be found at the end of the book.

Although everything we list in this guide is personally recommended, our authors inevitably have their own favourite places to eat and stay. Whenever you see this Author's Choice ⭐ icon beside a listing, you will know that it is a little bit out of the ordinary.

Hotel Price Guide

Luxury	€€€€€	over €200
Very Expensive	€€€€	€160–200
Expensive	€€€	€120–160
Moderate	€€	€80–120
Inexpensive	€	under €80

Restaurant Price Guide

Expensive	€€€€	over €45
Moderate	€€	€25–45
Inexpensive	€	under €25

About the Authors

Dana Facaros and Michael Pauls have written over 30 books for Cadogan Guides. They have lived all over Europe with their son and daughter, and are currently ensconced in a old farmhouse in southwestern France with a large collection of tame and wild animals.

7th Edition published 2011

01 INTRODUCING NORTHERN SPAIN

The north is the alternative Spain, the 'Green Spain', where all national stereotypes collapse, or at least those stereotypes we acquire on the Med. Northern landscapes can be just as spectacular, and beaches just as plentiful, with blue and emerald colours in the ocean and along the estuaries that bite into the coast; and the mountains – the western Pyrenees, the Cordillera Cantábrica and the Picos de Europa – are endearingly lovely and inviting to linger and walk in, unlike much of the austere, dry *meseta* to the south. Here are sheep in the meadows, cows in the corn and storks on every spire – the biggest colony of these, over a hundred, live atop Calahorra cathedral.

The northwest of the country is as rich and lush as the rest of Spain is traditionally hard and dry; here you'll find Spain's finest cheer: Galician seafood, La Rioja wine, Asturian cider, Cantabrian cheese, Navarrese garden vegetables, Castilian suckling pig and roast lamb, and the chefs with the best reputation for putting it all together – the Basques. Of course much of the north's luxuriance comes from the fact that no matter how Eliza Doolittle pronounces it, the rain in Spain does not fall mainly in the plain, but rather right on its head.

Northern Spain has the knack of acquiring a plethora of 'firsts' and then discreetly retiring into the background. The earliest settlers in Iberia found it convivial and left one of the world's great Palaeolithic masterpieces, at Altamira; the Basques, the oldest race in Europe, found it just as cosy and have called it home almost since the beginning of time. After the conquest of the Moors, the embryo of modern Spain, its architecture and language – Castilian – were formed in the mountains of Asturias and crystallized in

Previous page: Playa de San Lorenzo, Gijón
Above, from top: Mogrovejo village, Cantabria; Hórreo (granary), Galicia

Above: Crucifix at Cabo Finisterre, Galicia

Opposite page: Saja Valley, Cantabria

Burgos. With the discovery of the relics of St James in Galicia, the northwest became the forerunner of European tourism, inventing the pilgrimage to Santiago de Compostela, now in its second millennium.

Even though Spain's centre of gravity gradually moved south to Madrid, the cities and countryside of the north have been adorned with a generous helping of magnificent architectural treasures, from the Visigothic to the most florid Baroque, not to mention a few works by the great Catalan Modernista master Antoni Gaudí.

The Spaniards, especially the Madrileños, have in the past few decades guarded the northwest as a secret for themselves, although they only come in July and August, when it rains less. But even then you have to look hard to find beaches blighted by Benidormish excess (Laredo and Zarautz are the only ones that come close); tourism in northern Spain is more low-key, and by the nature of its short 'season' is probably destined to remain so.

To let the threat of a shower or two keep you away would be to miss out on the best preserved and most idiosyncratic corners of old Europe, a place that has kept a sense of place in the face of creeping homogeneity, one full of unexpected pleasures: a Roman bridge over a brook or a medieval one over a river, the fishmarket in A Coruña, a tableland in northern Castile abruptly cut away by a canyon filled with eagles, a spontaneous party that lasts until dawn in an outdoor *sidreria*, old women herding their cows home by twilight, the walls of stained glass in León, a Basque tug-of-war match, and a sunset at Finisterre, the end of the world.

Where to Go

Below: Vineyards,
La Rioja
Opposite page:
Cathedral, Burgos,
Old Castile and Léon

From the Pyrenees to Galicia's Atlantic seaboard, our guide covers the northern sliver of Spain, broadly tracking the westward progress of the ancient pilgrimage route to Santiago de Compostela.

Navarra, where we begin, spills down from the Pyrenees in lush valleys of pine and beech forest. It is here that we pick up the pilgrimage trail down towards Pamplona, a city speared with narrow lanes through which bulls charge and crowds jeer during the world-famous madness of the *Los Sanfermines* festival. Beyond the barren plains south of Pamplona are the fertile banks of the River Ebro in La Rioja, a region pinstriped with vineyards.

The Basque Lands (Euskadi) are home to the oldest and proudest race in Europe. Among its features are the remote, unpronounceable villages of the Pyrenean lowlands, the golden bay of Donostia-San Sebastián and Bilbao's dazzling Guggenheim museum – worldwide symbol of urban regeneration. Inland is stylish Vitoria-Gasteiz, which hosts the six-day *Fiesta de la Virgen Blanca*, with parties till dawn.

In the following chapter, we move from the rural idyll of **Cantabria**, where a common sight is a clog-clad farmer's wife driving home an ox-cart piled high with grass – Cantabria has the highest density of cows in Europe – to the peak-packed **Picos de Europa**, a haven for hikers and the most beautiful mountains in Spain. Cantabria is also

home to the caves of Altamira, decorated in prehistoric times with exuberant works of artistic genius.

Then there is the rugged beauty of **Asturias**, its coastline studded with beaches, its tumbling mountain rapids and gentle lowland streams teeming with trout, salmon and eel; if you're lucky you might just catch a glimpse of the elusive Cantabrian bear. Inland, around Oviedo, you'll find a scattering of unusual pre-Romanesque churches, which have stood proud since the 9th century and are now protected by UNESCO.

Old Castile and León comprise the rolling scrub-pocked plains of the *meseta*, a land of hamlets and the most tortuous stretch of the Camino de Santiago. We track down ancient hermitages in the Valley of Silence, and describe the diaphanous beauty of Gothic cathedrals in Burgos and León, built half of stone, half of light and air.

Galicia, Spain's sea-battered northwest corner, is a place of its own, for many years removed from the mainstream of Spanish life and history. Its estuaries (*rías*) offer up a feast of sea creatures, which Galician cooks whip up in a thousand different ways, while its jagged shoreline (the 'coast of death') presents coves, cliffs and sandy beaches to explore. Moss-stained Santiago de Compostela, the original European tourist destination, is the culmination of the pilgrim's journey, and the tail end of our guide.

Chapter Divisions

FRANCE

Santander

09 CANTABRIA & THE PICOS DE EUROPA p.183

Picos de Europa

CANTABRIA

San Sebastián (Donostia)

Hondarribia

VIZCAYA

EUSKADI

Bilbao (Bilbo)

08 THE BASQUE LANDS (EUSKADI) p.127

Vitoria (Gasteiz)

ALAVA

Pamplona (Iruña)

NAVARRA

11 OLD CASTILE & LEÓN p.243

BURGOS

Burgos

PALENCIA

LA RIOJA

07 NAVARRA & LA RIOJA p.79

ZARAGOZA

VALLADOLID

SORIA

SEGOVIA

Above, from top: Playa El Silencio, Cudillero, Asturias; Playa de La Concha, Donostia-San Sebastián, Euskadi

Coasting Along

This is Spain, so the coasts all have names – from the Costa Vasca along the Bay of Biscay, to the Costa Verde of Asturias, to the wild Costa de la Muerte in the far west of Galicia. But the names only begin to hint at the extraordinary beauty, variety and sheer lushness of these Atlantic shores.

Unlike on Spain's Mediterranean *costas*, which were almost deserted until the mid-20th century when Europe en masse discovered an uncontrollable longing to bake by the sea, the towns here have plenty of history and little room for dense crops of tower blocks. In northern Spain, you can instead swan around gilded Belle Epoque resorts, beginning with Donostia-San Sebastián and Santander. You can indulge in a dazzling array of exotic seafood in colourful fishing ports tucked along the jigsaw estuaries. You can laze on golden crescents of sand in Asturias and Cantabria – the season is short, but you'll have mostly Spaniards for company. Or you can take long walks along Galicia's savage Rías Altas, where wild horses roam the 2,000ft cliffs of San Andrés de Teixido and the ocean crashes against the world's end of Finisterre.

Surf and Turf, *Viñő* and *Sidra*

The seafood in Northern Spain is the stuff of legend, served as tapas or *pintxos* in a corner bar, or exquisitely prepared by one of several Michelin-starred chefs in Donostia-San Sebastián. There are people who visit Galicia just for the shellfish – not only its fat and justly famous scallops, but also delicacies such as *santiaguiños* and *zamburiñas* that are found only in the *rías*. Inland, look for lamb, dried hams, sausages, rich stews and soups, tasty green peppers and the mighty cheeses from the mountains.

La Rioja, of course, produces Northern Spain's best-known red wine, while the white *txakoli* from the Basque lands and Galicia's Ribeiro are the perfect accompaniment to all that seafood. And in Asturias, don't miss the *sidra*: cider poured with effervescent panache at arm's length. It's an acquired taste – give it a chance and don't give up after the first swallow.

Above, from top: wine barrels, La Rioja; Asturian sidra (cider); pulpo a feira (octopus), Galicia

Above: Picos de Europa, Asturias and Cantabria

Opposite page: Forest of Irati, Navarra

Attitudes to Altitudes

Northern Spain's spinal ridge of mountains that rise to the high plains of Castile may not be the country's highest peaks, but they would win any Iberian mountain beauty contest hands down, and they are bursting with variety. Start with the Pyrenees of Navarra, where the pass at Roncesvalles is the classic entry point of pilgrims wending their way to Compostela and where numinous mountain sanctuaries, lost in deep forests, have a fairytale quality. The arid Bárdenas Reales near Tudela look like something out of the Wild West, and look nothing like the rolling vine-clad hills of La Rioja. In Euskadi and Cantabria, the hills are emerald-green, while heart-stoppingly sheer gorges mark the frontiers of Old Castile, including the majestic eagle-haunted canyons of the Ebro. West of Léon, ancient Roman gold mines, orchards and medieval hermitages await in the isolated mountains of El Bierzo.

Last but hardly least, Asturias and Cantabria share the fabled Picos de Europa, with their stunning cluster of limestone peaks that were designated Spain's very first national park – a top destination for trekking, canyoning, mountain-biking, rock-climbing, canoeing, and sighting rare flora and fauna (including brown bears).

Urban Legends

Spaniards are among the most urbane people on earth, and Northern Spain's cities count among its greatest attractions, packed full of character and unique sights, and citizens intent on getting the most out of life. Some towns, such as the lovely granite Santiago de Compostela, have hosted visitors for over a thousand years, while once-industrial,

Above, from top:
Arcaded square, León,
Old Castile and León;
Arco de Santa María,
Burgos, Old Castile
and León

Opposite page:
Guggenheim Museum,
Bilbao

hardworking Bilbao with its titanium-clad Guggenheim Museum has firmly taken its place in the vanguard of 21st-century city-break chic. Burgos and León hold dazzling concentrations of architecture and art, and slightly dour Pamplona is synonymous with one of Europe's wildest parties in its July running of the bulls.

A Coruña, nicknamed 'Crystal City' for its seafront façade of glass galleries, is a lively, salty mix of pleasure and business. But lesser-known cities such as Oviedo, Pontevedra and Vitoria-Gasteiz throw up more than their share of surprises, too, and, being in Spain, concentrate more bustle and fun in their cores than many much larger cities in Northern Europe.

Above: Gaudí's El Capricho, Comillas, Cantabria

Opposite page, from top: Cathedral, Logroño, La Rioja; Gaudí's Casa de Los Botines, León, Old Castile and Léon; Cathedral, Santiago de Compostela, Galicia

Green Spain, Surprising Spain

It does rain in Spain, but unlike the song it's along the Atlantic coast rather than mainly on the plain – parts of the region are so green that they could be in Ireland (traditionally compared to Galicia) or Wales (traditionally compared to Asturias).

But northern Spain also has attractions you'll find nowhere else, attractions that go back beyond the night of time. It was a favourite dinosaur stomping ground – La Rioja Baja has Europe's greatest collection of fossilized footprints – and our ancestors found it congenial enough, leaving the oldest humanoid fossils yet found in Western Europe in Atapuerca near Burgos; over a million years later their descendants decorated the beautiful Palaeolithic caves at Altamira and the Cueva de Santimamiñe. The world's oldest continuous working lighthouse, the 2nd-century Torre de Hércules, still guides ships at A Coruña. Then there's the Virgin Mary's stone boat at Muxía, the Emir's emerald at Roncesvalles and some modern surprises: Gaudí's green and gold tower house at Comillas and his Bishop's Palace at Astorga, Frank Gehry's Guggenheim Museum and Philippe Starck's Alhóndiga in Bilbao, and the flash new designer *bodegas* in Rioja Alavesa around Laguardia built by Gehry and other leading architects – plus one in Haro by Zaha Hadid.

Itineraries

The Road to Compostela: Two Weeks by Car

Day 1 Crossing the traditional Valcarlos Pass in the Pyrenees, visit **Roncesvalles** and its Colegiata then continue to **Pamplona** to visit the cathedral complex and the Museo de Navarra.

Day 2 Drive west to the medieval villages of **Puente la Reina**, **Cirauqui** and **Estella**, the latter famous for its lovely churches, its medieval bridge, the 12th-century Palace of the Kings of Navarre and the monastery of Irache. Stay overnight in Estella.

Day 3 Pop into the churches of **Viana** and La Rioja's capital **Logroño**, and visit at least one *bodega*, before continuing west to **Navarrete** and **Nájera**; take in the monastery of Santa María la Real and its royal pantheon. Sleep in Nájera.

Day 4 Detour south to visit **San Millán de la Cogolla** and the 9th-century Monasterio de Suso. Then go west to **Santo Domingo de la Calzada** (the famous 'chicken church') and **San Juan de Ortega**. Overnight in Burgos.

Day 5 In **Burgos**, see the cathedral, the Monasterio de Las Huelgas and the Cartuja de Miraflores. Stay a second night here.

Day 6 The villages on the plain each have something to see: **Sasamón**, **Hornillos del Camino**, **Castrojerez**, **Boadillo del Camino**. Overnight in **Frómista**, home to the 'perfect Romanesque church'.

Day 7 Today you will head for the Templar town of **Villalcázar de Sirga**, the curious churches of Carrión de los Condes, and for a change, a 3rd-century Roman villa at **Quintanilla de la Cueza**. Overnight in Sahagún.

Day 8 See the *mudéjar* masterpieces of **Sahagún**; the 10th-century San Miguel de Escalada, then head for Léon to sleep.

Day 9 Spend the day in **Léon**, especially the cathedral and the Real Colegiata de San Isidoro, which has the finest Romanesque frescoes in Spain.

Day 10 Drive west to **Astorga** to see the cathedral and Gaudí's Bishop's Palace, and the pretty villages of **Castrillo de los Polvarares** and **Rabanal del Camino**. Overnight in **Ponferrada**.

Day 11 Visit charming **Villafranca del Bierzo** and enter Galicia at mountaintop **O Cebreiro** with its 9th-century church of Santa María; visit **Samos** and the Benedictine Abadía de San Xulián. **Sarriá** is a good place to stay overnight.

Day 12 **Portmarín**, **Vilar de Donas**, and **Melide** are the final stops on the way to Santiago de Compostela.

Days 13–14 **Santiago de Compostela**: the end of the journey for pilgrims and for you.

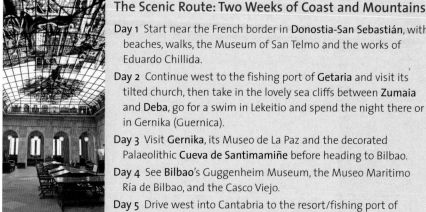

Above: Casa de Juntas, Gernika, Euskadi

Below: Fuente Dé cable car, Cantabria; Harbour, Llanes, Cantabria

The Scenic Route: Two Weeks of Coast and Mountains

Day 1 Start near the French border in **Donostia-San Sebastián**, with beaches, walks, the Museum of San Telmo and the works of Eduardo Chillida.

Day 2 Continue west to the fishing port of **Getaria** and visit its tilted church, then take in the lovely sea cliffs between **Zumaia** and **Deba**, go for a swim in Lekeitio and spend the night there or in Gernika (Guernica).

Day 3 Visit **Gernika**, its Museo de La Paz and the decorated Palaeolithic **Cueva de Santimamiñe** before heading to Bilbao.

Day 4 See **Bilbao**'s Guggenheim Museum, the Museo Maritimo Ría de Bilbao, and the Casco Viejo.

Day 5 Drive west into Cantabria to the resort/fishing port of **Castro Urdiales**, then carry on to **Santander** and spend the night, with a possible visit to the caves of **Puente Viesgo**.

Day 6 West to **Santillana del Mar**, 'the most beautiful village in Spain', and the Altamira Caves museum, then to **Comillas** to see Gaudí's El Capricho and spend the night.

Days 7–9 Head for **San Vicente de la Barquera** and **Unquera**, then turn south through the Desfiladero de la Hermida into the **Picos de Europa**. From **Potes** take the spectacular cable car from **Fuente Dé** up to the Mirador del Cable; go hiking; buy cheese in **Arenas de Cabrales**; visit the lakes of **La Ercina** and **Enol**, and squeeze into the narrow **Desfiladero de los Beyos**.

Day 10 Now you are on the **Costa Verde**, with golden beaches at **Llanes** and **Ribadesella**. Sup away an evening in a *chigre* (cider bar) and sleep overnight in **Villaviciosa**.

Day 11 Dip inland to **Oviedo** to see its cathedral and famous pre-Romanesque churches; in the afternoon continue west into Galicia, to the wild cliffs and beaches of **As Mariñas de Lugo**. Overnight in **Viveiro**.

Day 12 Continue west to the pretty fishing village of **O Barqueiro** and the gorgeous beach at **Bares**, and the cliffs and dunes, beaches and lagoons along the coast to **Ferrol**; visit medieval **Pontedeume** and then spend the night in **A Coruña**.

Day 13 Head south along the Costa da Morte, visiting its dolmens and **Finisterre**, and admire the strange Celtic souvenirs along the Ría de Muros y Noia. Eat peppers in **Padrón**, and spend the night in the pretty granite town of **Pontevedra**.

Day 14 Head to **Vigo** for a seafood lunch, or take a picnic out for a lazy day on the **Islas Cíes**.

CONTENTS

18

Maps and Plans

Contents

History

02

25,000 BC–AD 409

In which a cultural early bird slows down and gets carved up for lunch by Romans and Carthaginians

Along with southwestern France, this corner of Spain can claim itself as home to the world's oldest known culture. About 25,000 BC, in the Palaeolithic age, the peninsula's many caves began to fill up with Palaeospaniards (or perhaps the ancestors of the Basques, *see* p.129), living well enough off herds of bison and deer to create impressive works of art on cave walls from Cantabria to the western Pyrenees and Périgord. Scholars generally divide these people into the earlier Aurignacian and later Magdalenian cultures. The latter reached their height around 15,000 BC and created some of the Stone Age's finest art, notably in the caves of Altamira near Santander.

It's a long, dull stretch from the Palaeolithic masters to the next interesting period in Europe, the Neolithic age. Neolithic culture, with settled farming, trade and megalithic building, may have come to Spain as early as 5500 BC, and it enjoyed a long and relatively peaceful reign over the peninsula, lasting until roughly 2000 BC. This culture, extending from Spain to Scandinavia, distinguished itself by creating Europe's first architecture, with its dolmens, other burial chambers, standing stones and stone circles. Neolithic peoples, though probably a matriarchal society, were sailors and traders, and liked to live near the coasts, including the northern coasts; large concentrations of megalithic monuments are found in the Basque country and Galicia. The latter seems to have been unusually prosperous: dolmen burials here included plenty of gold jewellery, rare for the time.

About 2000 BC, many of the peoples of Iberia learned the use of bronze and started using it to make weapons, while spending their spare time building fortresses to protect the bronze. In an Iberia increasingly turned towards the Mediterranean, the northern coast seems to have been spared most of this progress, however, and people carried on in their sweet old Neolithic way. About 800 BC, the native Iberians were joined by other peoples, notably the Celts from over the Pyrenees. These got along well enough with the Iberians; in many cases they gradually merged with some tribes, creating a new people, the Celtiberians, who occupied much of the centre and north of the peninsula. The heritage of the Celts everywhere is the *castro*, or, as it is called in France and sometimes here too, the *oppidum*. Astérix's lot didn't care much for towns, but wherever there was some trade to be conducted, or treasure to be guarded, the Celts would have a sort of tiny urban centre, perched on a hilltop and surrounded by walls – more a castle than a town.

Meanwhile, the Phoenicians were making their presence felt in the south. Their traders and colonists began taking over parts of coastal Andalucía around 1200 BC, but evidence is lacking and it remains an open question just how much time the Phoenicians spent in the north. Several of the port towns have a height called *Atalaya*, believed to be a Phoenician word meaning 'tower', while *Spain* is another Phoenician word, meaning 'land of rabbits'. We can imagine that the northern coast was part of a fairly busy trade route, monopolized by Phoenician ships, bringing tin from Cornwall to make bronze in the Mediterranean – the Phoenicians were understandably secretive about the world they discovered outside the Pillars of Hercules, and they probably made up all the stories of sea monsters and suchlike to scare off potential competitors.

Overlordship of Iberia fell to Rome in 202 BC, the big prize for the victory over Hannibal and Carthage in the Second Punic War. But, just as the Carthaginians had never really controlled the wild northwest, Roman rule here was mostly a vain boast for another two centuries. The Romans found the region inhabited by a people they called the *Vascones*, the Basques, and further west the Celtiberian *Cantabri*, *Asturi* and *Gallæci*. Unlike the Carthaginians, the Romans couldn't bear a messy map, and they spent those two centuries methodically grinding down Celtiberians and Basques alike. One highlight of the endless campaigns was the epic siege of Numancia, a Celtiberian stronghold in what is now northern Castile (near Soria). After beating off Roman attacks for 19 years, the Numancians escaped the dishonour of final defeat by burning the town with themselves inside it.

To subdue Spain, Rome had to send its best – Cato, Pompey, Caesar and Augustus were all commanders in the Spanish conquest – and in some isolated areas the job was not finished until 20 BC. The rest of Spain had metal ores to make it worth the trouble, and even in the far northwest Rome probably broke even, thanks to the gold mines of El Bierzo. Only a few towns were founded: *Pallantia* (Palencia) was probably the biggest, followed by *Clunia* (an abandoned site near Aranda de Duero), *Pompaelo* (Pamplona), *Asturica Augusta* (Astorga), *Brigantium* (A Coruña), and *Lucus Augusti* (Lugo). Nor did the Romans break the bank building roads here, although the most important one, linking Zaragoza to León, would one day become the pilgrimage route of the *camino de Santiago*. No town ever managed a population of more than about five thousand. So while the rest of Spain got a good washing and a Latin grammar to study, the peoples of the north were pretty much left alone. Compared to the rest of the western Empire, relatively few wealthy villas have been discovered here, a sign that the Roman élite barely penetrated the region.

Throughout most of the imperial era, the north was a forgotten corner of the province of *Tarracona*, with its capital on the Mediterranean, modern Tarragona. In one of the reforms of Diocletian this sprawling province was split up, the far western part gaining the name of *Gallaecia* after its Gaulish inhabitants – the future Galicia. Christianity spread quickly in Spain, at least among the officials and landlords in the south, so much so that the peninsula held its first Church council in 313. The only representative from the north was the bishop of a little town called *Lanobriga* (León).

409–711

In which the northwest dozes fitfully through a depressing parade of barbarian hordes

The first Germans had found their way into Iberia during the great barbarian raid of the 260s, though the legions gradually recovered and threw them out again. When the Rhine frontier collapsed in 407, some of the Germans storming westward were probably already thinking of Spain. Vandals, Alans and Suevi all made it over the pass at Roncesvalles by 409, and they separately ranged the peninsula looking for land and swag. To try and restore order, what was left of the Empire sent in another horde, the Visigoths, as allies to sort their cousins out. They smashed the Alans and Vandals, but let the Suevi keep the remote northwest. Rome, now worrying that the cure might be worse than the disease, talked the Visigoths into crossing the Pyrenees again to have some fun in southern Gaul. In the resulting vacuum, a new horde of Vandals (the Siling Vandals) broke in in 422. They did what Vandals will do, seven years of it, before crossing the Straits of Gibraltar in search of richer lands and towns in Africa.

That left the field clear for the Suevi (or Swabians – their stay-at-home relations gave the name to a region of southwestern Germany). Under their chief Rechila, they made a little kingdom for themselves, centred at Astorga, and by 448 they controlled much of the peninsula. In 456, however, the Visigoths came back and defeated them near Astorga, bottling the remnant up in remote Galicia. The Visigoths thought they were just adding some Iberian possessions to their kingdom of southern Gaul – but, when the Franks in turn defeated them at the great Battle of Vouillé in 507 and chased them over the Pyrenees, they found themselves in a position they would have to be content with – as rulers of Spain.

As Teutonic barbarians go, the Visigoths were a cut above the rest. They did not drink out of skulls, like the Lombards, or smear bear grease all over their bodies, like the Franks. The line of their kings went back to Alaric I, the Goth who had sacked Rome. For the next two centuries, the Visigoths ruled their Spanish kingdom from Toledo, building churches and inventing a rather blunt code of laws in vulgar Latin; in the northwest, they engaged in endless desultory fighting with the Suevi until 585, when the great King Leovigild finally put an end to their kingdom.

Meanwhile, up in their mountains, the Basques lapsed into *de facto* independence, meeting in democratic assembly around the oak of Gernika to make their own laws. They were expanding in all directions, and were especially present in what is now Navarra – peacefully colonizing lands wasted by too many hard times and too many armies. The kings sent frequent expeditions north to try and squeeze some tribute money out of them, with occasional success. Asturias and Galicia proved just as hard to control, and the Visigothic kingdom probably had no more influence here than the Romans had.

711–800

In the middle of the Dark Ages, Spanish history records one of its most frantic centuries ever

At the dawn of the 8th century, it seemed that the Visigothic kingdom had truly established itself: a stable state by the standards of the time, with a strong Church and some modest cultural achievements (in architecture and literature especially, Spain was more than holding its own). In fact, riven with clan feuds and religious bigotry, the kingdom was a plum waiting to be picked. Of all the luck, this happened to be the first century of Islam, with explosive bursts of the Arab armies across the Middle East and North Africa. After they had digested North Africa, Spain was the only place to go on Islam's western front, and the first small force under Tariq ibn-Ziyad landed at Gibraltar in 711. The last Visigothic king, Roderick, was defeated and killed in a great battle near Toledo, and within three years the Muslims were in control of the entire peninsula – except, as you might have guessed by now, parts of the north.

The Arabs surged across the Pyrenees, only to be defeated and driven back by the Franks at Poitiers in 732, but what really kept them from consolidating their hold over northwest Spain was a short but intense revolt of the Muslim Berber troops in 740 against their Arab leaders. To hear the Spaniards tell the story, though, the turning of the tide came with a legendary prince of Asturias named Pelayo, who defeated the Moors at the 'Battle of Covadonga' in 718 and kept Asturias free and Christian. Now, there seems to have really been a historic Pelayo, a Visigothic baron, but no reliable record of such a battle is preserved anywhere, and Asturias, like the rest of the region, was still largely pagan. Spanish history and national mythology were becoming inextricably intertwined; a little inconsequential skirmish in the mountains that Iberia's new masters didn't even notice would some day, in retrospect, appear as the beginning of a national history. Nearly 40 years after the Battle of Covadonga, the *Chronicle of 754*, written by a Christian in al-Andalus, does not mention either the battle or the new Christian 'kingdom' in the north.

Later legends in Cantabria and Asturias spoke of the 'Foramontanos', who fled into the mountains from the Moors and 'returned to repopulate Castile'. And it seems likely that a number of die-hard Visigothic nobles took refuge up in the more inaccessible parts of Asturias. But the romantic legend of the last few defenders of the faith, heroically holed up in the Asturian mountains – the seed from which Spain would grow – is only partially true. The records say that, only four years after the invasion began, the Moors were pretty much in control of Asturias and most of the rest of the northwest. Gijón, on the coast, fell to the Muslims in 715 and had an Arab governor for years afterwards, as did Pamplona. Galicia too was in Arab hands for some time.

While all this was happening, other neglected fringes of the Iberian world were beginning their careers, including the little state of Navarra. Pamplona freed itself from Muslim rule in the Berber revolt of 740, and the Basques were independent once again. Once again, though, they had to fight to stay that way. After beating the Moors at Poitiers, the self-confident Franks soon came over the Pyrenees looking for new lands to conquer. One of their raids gave birth to the famous legend of Roland and Oliver, the famous knights of Charlemagne who perished at the hands of the Basques in an ambush at the pass of Roncesvalles in 778.

800–1000

The northern mountain boys tweak the moustaches of a powerful Emirate and then found some kingdoms

The endless conquests and confusions of the 8th century set the pattern for centuries of Spain's history to come. The new Emirate of al-Andalus developed a policy of insulating itself from the wild north by a band of marches – no-man's-lands with military governors. At the beginning, these included what is now León, Castile and much of Aragón. The emirs might raid them every few years, but they could not keep Christian settlers from gradually filling in the empty spaces, laying the groundwork for the Reconquista.

While the Emirate (Caliphate after 929) was developing a brilliant Spanish-Muslim civilization in the middle of the Dark Ages, the northern kingdom was prospering and growing too, while economically and culturally drawing closer to Christian Europe. Not only was Asturias slowly and gradually expanding, but new centres of power appeared as well. In 800, the year Charlemagne was proclaimed emperor, the first written mention is made of the County of Castile, the 'Land of Castles'. The north may not have been so backward at all, comparatively speaking. The sophisticated and urbanized society of al-Andalus had a constant need for raw materials and food, and it spread prosperity and learning beyond its borders. One of the surprises of the Christian north was its pre-Romanesque architecture, as expressed in the famous 9th- and 10th-century churches around Asturias and Cantabria, built at a time when the rest of Europe was hardly building anything in stone. Design and clothing, however, were still heavily influenced by the latest fashions in Moorish Córdoba, Granada and Seville, and such educated princes as there were would more likely know Arabic than Latin.

In the 9th century, Muslim al-Andalus entered the golden age of its prosperity and power. Campaigns against the Christians in the north were frequent though inconclusive: Pamplona was taken again in 842, and León in 848, but neither could be held for long. Under ineffectual caliphs such as Abd Allah, the late 9th century was a time of civil strife and confusion in the south, and it permitted the new kingdom of Asturias to take its first steps on the way to the Reconquista – the retaking of all Iberia for Christianity that had already been predicted, against all odds, in a Christian work called *The Prophetic Chronicle*.

Christians began to resettle and hold lands south of the Cantabrian mountains; they also managed to found or refound a number of towns in the no-man's-land of the Duero Valley, notably Burgos (884). The reign of Alfonso III (866–910) was a watershed for the northerners, in which they pushed their boundaries into Portugal and resettled much of northern Castile (for convenience's sake, historians call Asturias the 'Kingdom of León', after that city was taken in 913, though, interestingly, for centuries the kingdom had no name at all, and such kings as could write would sign documents simply *Yo, el Rey*).

As for the Basques, by 824 Pamplona had chased the Franks out once and for all, forming the county of Navarra under a leader named Jimeno Aritza and his descendants. The Basques seem to have got on well enough with the Moors, and were often in alliance with them against the famous clan of the Banu Qasi – renegade Visigoths who had turned Muslim, and who held Zaragoza and much of Aragón not for the Emirate, but for themselves. Later, Basques would provide many of the favourite women in the palace harem at Córdoba, and consequently more than a few of the emirs were at least half Basque.

The reign of Abd ar-Rahman III (912–961), who declared himself caliph, marked the high point of the power of al-Andalus, and a setback for the northerners, though the caliph could do little to stop the resettlement of the new northern lands. Abd ar-Rahman's notable contemporary in the north was Fernán González, *El Buen Conde*, the 'Good Count' of Castile (923–970), who despite continuous war with the Moors made his land into a kingdom independent of Asturias. More troubles for the north came with the rule in al-Andalus of al-Mansur, 'the Victorious', an ambitious vizier who had locked away the weak young caliph Hisham II in the palace at Córdoba and pulled all the strings himself. Al-Mansur defeated the Asturians and sacked León in 988, and Burgos in 1000. He forced most of the northerners to pay tribute, and on one raid his armies even occupied Santiago de Compostela, carrying off the church bells as a prize for the Great Mosque of Córdoba.

1000–1218
The northerners persist, and find that constant bellicosity brings big rewards

The Muslims definitely still held the real power in the peninsula, but the same al-Mansur who had won so many battles for them was unwittingly to be the downfall of the caliphate. By assuming personal power, he removed the main prop of the legitimacy of the state. When he died, his sons attempted to carry on in his place, leading to a revolution in 1009 that put an end to the political unity of al-Andalus forever, leaving a collection of small states quarrelling amongst themselves. That was all the opportunity the warriors of the north needed. Especially under Alfonso VI (1065–1109) they extended their boundaries ever farther; Alfonso crowned a long string of victories with the capture of Toledo in 1085, securing permanent control of the central *meseta*. Alfonso was the first Castilian king to mint coins (instead of using Moorish currency); he collected tribute money from the little kings of al-Andalus, and he began calling himself 'Emperor of All Spain', but he never would have done it without the help of the Castilian adventurer El Cid, Rodrigo Díaz de Vivar.

The new millennium had definitely got off to an auspicious start for Christian Spain. But for a while it looked as if the big victor among the Christian states would be little Navarra. Still Basque but becoming increasingly hispanicized and feudalized, Navarra had reached its zenith under Sancho el Mayor (1000–35), capturing all of La Rioja and even much of Castile. But, like so many of the transient empires formed in the free-for-all of the Reconquista, Sancho's proved to be only a house of cards, and Alfonso VI cut Navarra down to size in the 1070s. In fact, every Christian state was taking advantage of al-Andalus's disarray to expand its boundaries: León/Castile (united by marriage), Navarra, Portugal and Aragón. Aragón and León/Castile eventually emerged as the main rivals for dominance in the new Spain that was growing. Under Alfonso I, *El Batallador*, Aragón emerged as a major power; in the 1110s Alfonso briefly controlled parts of Castile, including Burgos.

The new states could afford such rivalry; the new frontier life created by conditions on the *meseta* gave the Christians one particular military advantage: a class of hard men doing well enough to afford heavy armour and a horse. The

Spanish cavalry was small in number, but they could cover ground quickly, raid everywhere and often carry the day in pitched battles against Moorish forces that were numerically superior. Another advantage was the spirit of the Crusader, both in reinforcing morale and attracting fresh blood; early on, the popes had declared Spain a legitimate sphere of Crusading activity, as much as was the Holy Land.

Al-Andalus, however, was not finished yet. Before the Christians could completely swallow it up, the various little states were swept away by the new Almoravid (Murabit) empire. Originally an Islamic fundamentalist movement among the Berbers, dominated by a few powerful tribes, this grew into an emirate that controlled all of Morocco. After the fall of Toledo the Almoravids were invited into Spain, where they stopped the Christian tide – and added al-Andalus to their dominions. They lasted until 1147, falling into decay and being replaced by a nearly identical African sectarian empire, that of the Almohads (Muwahhid).

Although Muslim art and culture continued to shine, the Almohads suffered the same decay of reforming zeal as had the Almoravids, once introduced to the pleasures of Córdoba and Seville. The great disaster for al-Andalus came in 1212: the Battle of Las Navas de Tolosa, where a Christian alliance led by Alfonso VIII of Castile destroyed the Almohad power forever. The great cities of the south were gobbled up soon after, leaving the Muslims only the little kingdom of Granada, which held out by careful diplomacy and heavy tributes until 1492. Six years after Las Navas de Tolosa, in 1218, León and Castile merged once and for all under Ferdinand III el Santo.

1218–1516

In which medieval Spain creates a fat and happy civilization, and pride goes before a fall

It's the great historical paradox of the Reconquista, one of the examples of Cervantean irony that Spain is always bountiful in providing: the northwest, previously little more relevant to Spain's history than Novgorod or Baluchistan, suddenly takes centre stage in creating a new Spain, and then, with success, finds itself left behind on the periphery again with nothing to do. After Las Navas de Tolosa, all the money was to be made in the centre and south, in New Castile around Madrid, and in al-Andalus – now Spanish Andalucía.

Castile had tripled in size, and its kings, now by far the most dangerous ones on the chessboard, began spending much more of their time in central towns such as Toledo and Valladolid, and less in León or Burgos. For simple geographical reasons, the northwest would never be the real heartland of a nation. But for the time being it managed to share fully in Western Europe's blossoming during the 12th and 13th centuries.

Particularly striking was the growth of towns. Trade came back in the Atlantic in a big way, for the first time since the Romans, and little ports from A Coruña to San Sebastián reawakened from 600 years' slumber. Increasingly, they sent wool to England, France and Flanders. That was the big-money commodity of the age, and the northern plains were perfectly suited for raising sheep. Run under a sophisticated sort of royal co-operative called the *mesta*, this trade fuelled most of medieval Castile's remarkable prosperity, and the annual fair at Medina del Campo became one of the biggest in Europe. Many of the northern cities at least doubled in size in the 12th century, the biggest boom in all history for places such as León and Burgos. Though doomed never to make a role for themselves as capitals or great trade centres, both these cities took advantage of the good times to create notable monuments, including the finest Gothic cathedrals in Spain. León began its one in 1205, and Burgos followed in 1221.

With money came increasing power for the growing towns, and nearly all of them in this period were able to gain a high degree of independence from the kings, bishops or nobles who had formerly bossed them around. All over Spain, the towns were organizing themselves into *comunes*, as in the rest of Europe. A good example of the new type of medieval *comune* is Vitoria-Gasteiz, founded by King Alfonso VI of Navarra in 1181, soon after he had conquered the territory from Castile. Alfonso wanted a loyal town to consolidate his hold, and to keep the new settlers' loyalty he granted it a charter of *fueros* (literally 'outsides', or exceptions to royal law) that gave the town rights of self-government and exemptions from some taxes and feudal responsibilities. This story was repeated literally hundreds of times across Christian Spain.

The *fueros* gave Spain a less oppressive government than most countries. They were made possible by the good example of the Basques. It was a good time for this incurably industrious people too, as they began to turn their talents to the sea. In 1296 a kind of Hanseatic league of Basque ports was founded, the Hermandad de las Marismas; shipping Vizcaya's iron and Castile's wool northwards, the Hermandad grew to control a disproportionate share of the Atlantic trade. But, as in Navarra, the Basque language and culture were being pushed further into the background, in a world increasingly dominated by Spanish-speaking nobles and merchants. Navarra, condemned by geography to lose out in the Reconquista land grab, was now in full decline. French involvement in the kingdom dated from 1284, when an heiress of the kingdom, Juana I, married King Philip the Fair of France. Members of the Capetian dynasty ruled Navarra as a quaint Pyrenean Ruritania from then on.

Throughout the 14th and 15th centuries, the peninsula occupied itself with consolidating the gains of the Reconquista and trying to make some sense out of all the commotion that had occurred. Burgos and León got their tremendous cathedrals finished, but economically and culturally the northwest was increasingly left on the periphery of a Spain that was growing very large and complex. And already, some of the forces that would make this Spain go to pieces were in their larval forms – the big winners of the Reconquista, a bloated nobility and a dangerous but morally decayed Church, both exempt from taxes and loaded with privileges. On the whole, the experience of the Reconquista coarsened the life of Castile, creating a pirate ethos where honest labour was scorned, and wealth and honour were things to be snatched from one's neighbours.

The climax of unification came in 1469 with the marriage of *los Reyes Católicos*, Ferdinand of Aragón and Isabel of Castile. Under their reign Spain's borders were rounded out. Not only did they finally conquer the kingdom of Granada, the last remnant of al-Andalus, but Ferdinand's campaigns put an end to that medieval relic up north, the kingdom of Navarra. Spain was also embarking on its career as a grand imperialist, invading Italy and colonizing the Americas. All this cost a good deal of money, which Ferdinand and Isabel's ministers extorted out of the towns and cities of Castile. They whittled away at the communal lands and the *fueros*, and towns that had run their own affairs for centuries now found their assets carved up little by little among the crown and the local nobles. The religious bigotry of the 'Catholic Kings', Isabel in particular, put a perverse twist on Spanish life that was to last a long time. Under their reign the Inquisition was reintroduced, and the Jews expelled.

1516–1931
The north's history is dissolved into that of united Spain, and it isn't a pretty story

Worse was still to come. Whatever cash and valuables were left in Old Castile were soon relentlessly sucked out by Ferdinand and Isabel's grandson, the Habsburg Carlos I. Better known to history as Charles V, his title as Holy Roman Emperor, this rapacious megalomaniac gained the throne by declaring the rightful queen, his mother Juana, insane, and locking her up in a windowless cell for the next 40 years. Charles and his Flemish minions then started squeezing Spain dry, to raise the gargantuan bribes that were necessary for an Imperial election in those days (even though there were only seven voters!). To accomplish the looting of his new country, Charles rescinded or ignored most of the remaining municipal *fueros*, wrecked the trade fairs and invented new taxes everywhere. The church and nobles jumped in for a share of the spoils, and Spain embarked on a rather remarkable and ultimately successful attempt to destroy its own economy.

A national financial collapse came in 1519, and an outraged Castile finally rose up in rebellion. The Comunero Revolt, a brave last attempt of the *comunes* to defend their purses and their liberties, began in 1520 and quickly spread through the towns of Old Castile. Charles' foreign troops put it down the following year, and although the king took a conciliatory line towards the rebels there was no doubt now about who was boss. Castile was finished, its trade ruined and its once-thriving towns condemned to be the backwater relics they remain today.

Ripping out the heart of his country meant relatively little to Charles, who now had gold and silver flowing in from America to finance his endless aggressions across Europe. For a final note on one of history's bigger rotters, we see Charles after his abdication in 1556, living in a monastery at Yuste, in Extremadura, praying for his soul and gorging himself continually on eel pies. His favourite recreation in the later days was rehearsing his funeral, and at one practice session he caught a chill and died.

For Spain, still worse was yet to come. Under Charles's neurotic son Philip II, Spain reached the height of its book- and heretic-burning frenzy, while the economy stayed wrecked and military defeats piled up on every side. A particular blow against the northwest, motivated by corrupt ministers, was Philip's decision in 1573 to allow Seville to monopolize trade with the New World. The northern ports dwindled, and all the poor souls whose prospects had been ruined even had to find their way to the south to catch a boat just to emigrate.

This state of affairs lasted until 1788, by which time the northern towns had already undergone a steep decline along with the rest of Spain. Nevertheless, the northwest found ways to wring a penny from the Americas. The enterprising Basques, for example, created the Compañia Guipúzcana de Caracas, which wangled a monopoly over the chocolate trade and brought a lot of money home to the Basque country. For generations, Basques and Spaniards alike contributed their share to Spain's colonial adventures. Sons who went overseas to make their fortunes were called *indianos* – and *indianos*, or *casas de indianos*, is also the name for the houses built by the lucky ones who came home well off; you'll see them everywhere in the northwest, as early as 1650 and as late as 1920.

If little good happened in these centuries, at least the north was usually spared the curse of armies and wars. That is, until Napoleon crossed the Pyrenees in 1808. French occupation led to a spontaneous national revolt – the Spaniards call it their 'War of Independence'. The British pitched in to fight their mutual nemesis, at first catastrophically as their army under Sir John Moore, pursued by Maréchal Soult, beat a desperate retreat across the northwest to flee from A Coruña. When the British returned under Wellington, it was their turn to chase the French from Cádiz to Paris, the result as much a disaster for Napoleon as his winter in Moscow. Wellington is well remembered by the Spanish for kicking the French out (they made him a duke too), but his boys dealt with conquered land far worse than Napoleon or any contemporary army would have dreamed, distinguishing them-selves notably at the sack of San Sebastián. The French had been content with simply looting all the gold crucifixes and a lot of bad paintings.

But as the great chef Escoffier later expressed it, the only worthwhile thing France got out of the Peninsular War was the recipe for pheasant *à la Alcántara*. That did not stop the French from sending their army down again in 1823, with the blessing of the English and Austrians, to stamp out a democratic revolt against the despotic Bourbons. Nineteenth-century Spain became quite a wild place, often the very image of the banana republics that had just gained their independence from it in Latin America. The Basques, especially those of Navarra, did their best to keep the pot boiling. Supporting the claims of the pretender Don Carlos, they sided with the Church and reactionaries in the Carlist Wars of 1833–39 and 1872–6. Many Carlists only took up the cause in defence of what was left of their *fueros*, which liberal reformers in Madrid were trying to abolish. The generals of Isabel II put down both revolts, though there were some close moments, as in the Second Carlist War when the insurgents briefly besieged Bilbao.

Isabel II presided over the confusing height of the banana monarchy where rival generals and politicians could compete for her favours while issuing *pronuncia-mientos* and plotting backstage coups. But, while the country as a whole was becoming an increasingly inconsequential backwater in Europe, some signs of life were stirring in unlikely places – not in the moribund Castilian centre, but on the periphery. Along with the Catalans, the Basques were doing their best to give the country a boost into the Industrial Revolution. Bilbao became a noisy boom town around its ironworks and shipyards, while a small echo was heard from tiny Asturias, which grew into Spain's most important mining region.

1931–the Present

The northerners choose sides, fight it out, and most finally conclude that pluralism isn't so bad after all

Along with industrialization came political change. The Basque Nationalist Party, or PNV, appeared to speak up for Basque concerns at the Cortes in Madrid, while Asturias with its strong unions became increasingly radicalized. The boom years of the First World War, provided by Spain's neutrality, were followed by a steep depression that brought social problems to a head, especially after the Second Republic was proclaimed in 1931. One famous event of the time, a prelude to the Civil War, was the bloody revolt of the Asturian miners in 1934, crushed by army troops under a general named Franco.

When the Civil War broke out in July 1936, the Basques and Asturians sided enthusiastically with the Republic, while Old Castile supported Franco. Until the end of the war the Nationalists kept their capital at Burgos. Most Galicians took the Nationalist side too – Franco was after all a native son, from Ferrol – and so did the Navarrese, whose politics still revolved around Carlism. Franco's armies soon reduced Republican territory in the northwest to a chain of small pockets along the coast. The Basques held out until 1937, when they succumbed to a campaign distinguished by the terror bombing of Guernica, performed by Franco's Nazi allies.

After the war the Basques suffered more than anyone for their loyalty to the Republic. As in Catalunya, the government suppressed even the casual use of the native language, forbade most festivals and cultural manifestations, and sent thousands of intellectuals to prison or into exile. State industrial schemes were consciously planned in a way to bring in large numbers of Spanish job-seekers to dilute the Basque population. The Basque response was the growth of the terrorist organization ETA, beginning in the 1950s. As the only active resistance to the dictatorship, ETA attracted widespread sympathy within Spain and elsewhere, especially in 1973 when they blew the car of Franco's hand-picked successor, Admiral Carrero Blanco, over the roof of a Madrid church.

In striking contrast, plenty of Navarrese, mostly Carlists, found posts in Franco's army and government until the end of the regime in 1975 (the Spanish fascists even borrowed the Carlists' yoke-and-arrows symbol for their own party). There are Carlists to be found even today, although the current pretender, Prince Hugo de Borbón, has tacitly acknowledged King Juan Carlos by paying him a social visit. Navarra remains the most politically reactionary part of Spain, maybe of all Europe; Pamplona, its bright and prosperous capital, is the mecca of Opus Dei, the shadowy Catholic organization that in Franco's later years attempted to gain control of the Spanish government by insinuating its members into high positions.

In Galicia, Cantabria and Castile, politics remain quietly Neanderthal; these are the only parts of Spain where you're still likely to see statues and streets named after Nationalist heroes. Santander only dismantled its statue of Franco in 2008.

Since the restoration of democracy in 1977, the most dramatic change in Spain has been the reversal of centuries of centralization, with the creation of autonomous regional governments throughout the country, including Galicia, Asturias, Cantabria, the Basque Country (Euskadi), Navarra and Old Castile – the latter the only part of Spain where a majority didn't actually want autonomy, and had it forced upon them by Madrid. The Basques got a special autonomy statute, and have made the most of it, with their own schools, television and police force. This wasn't enough for the die-hards of ETA, who still demand total independence, and who have continued their murders and bombing campaigns, almost always in other parts of Spain. The surprise truce declared in September 1998 brought 15 months of peace to Spain and the Basque lands, during which it was hoped that a peaceful solution could be found. Unfortunately, ETA found its marginalization in peace worse than the disgust it inspired when it was active, and in December 1999 the organization resumed the terror. The most spectacular loser in the May 2001 regional elections was Euskal Herritarok (ETA's political wing), which lost half of its 14 seats. Indeed, the record turnout of nearly 80 per cent of eligible voters gave a clear message to the rest of Spain: nationalism yes, terrorism no.

The message seemed to fall on deaf ears when, two days after the election, Basque journalist and anti-violence campaigner Gorka Landaburu lost part of his hand when a packet bomb sent to his home exploded. Then, in August of the same year, a municipal councillor in Leiza died when a bomb exploded beneath his van. Ten hours later an officer with the Basque police force was shot dead with a sub-machine gun as he parked his car in Tolosa. A further deadly attack took place in Madrid with the car bomb assassination of a national police office. A subsequent poll showed that terrorism had moved even further ahead of unemployment as the main concern of Spaniards.

Until the summer of 2002, most ETA attacks had taken place either in the capital or the Basque country. Tourism seemed to be the target that year when, during the height of the season, two car bombs exploded in Fuengirola on the Costa del Sol and a few weeks later in a resort near Alicante, resulting in the death of a child. The Spanish government responded definitively on 26 July by applying the newly devised 'Ley de Partidos' to Batasuna, the political wing of ETA, effectively making the party illegal, on the grounds of its 'carrying out politics in connivance with terror' and 'encouraging generalized intimidation' among other points.
The group's offices were closed by the Basque police and its accounts frozen. Meanwhile the party moved to Bayonne, France, where it is registered as an 'association'. In a further development approximately three months later, the president of the (recognized) Basque government, Juan José Ibarretxe, put an end to the political ambiguity in the region and placed his cards clearly on the table, proposing that the European Union grant the Basque Country the status of free state, associated to Spain with shared sovereignty – a plan that no one except the Basques takes seriously. This was still a key issue in the Basque elections of April 2005, which Ibarretxe's party won – but only just. They lost their overall majority, and much of their bargaining power with it.

Meanwhile, José Maria Aznar's hardline Partido Popular (PP or People's Party) was ousted from government in the dramatic Spanish general election of 2004, when the Spanish people expressed their anger at the PP's deliberate attempts to implicate ETA in the terrible bombings at Madrid train stations on 11th March 2004, in which almost 200 people were killed. The attacks were claimed by Islamic fundamentalists in retaliation for Spanish involvement in the Iraq war (opposed by more than 90 per cent of Spaniards). In early 2005, the new Socialist (PSOE) goverment under José Luís Rodríguez Zapatero promised to open peace talks with ETA if the group laid down its arms, but the announcement was followed by a series of car bombings in Madrid. These were widely perceived to be a gesture of defiance from ETA, and the government responded by arresting Arnaldo Otegi, the leader of the (still outlawed) Batasuna party, and by threatening to limit some areas of the Basque Country's current autonomy. Fragile hopes for peace were raised when ETA declared a 'permanent' ceasefire on March 2006, and a few months later Zapatero's government showed signs that it was prepared to sit and talk with the armed separatists. But the sceptics were proved right when on December 30th ETA detonated a van bomb in a car park building at the Madrid Barajas international airport, killing two men. Although Zapatero discontinued talks immediately, it wasn't until June 2007 that ETA formally announced the end of the 'permanent' ceasefire. In 2008 and 2009, ETA attempted to put a popular spin on its ongoing struggle, drawing comparisons with independence movements in other parts of Europe such as Scotland and Kosovo, but the organisation was badly damaged by a series of high-profile arrests of some of its most senior members.

With its leadership in disarray, and links with political parties severed, ETA finally declared a new ceasefire on 5 September 2010. This was followed in January 2011 with a statement promising that the ceasefire would be 'permanent, general and verifiable'. However, most Spaniards remain sceptical that this third ceasefire will endure and some fear that it will split ETA into two groups, with hardliners continuing to use armed struggle along the lines of the Real IRA. The Spanish Supreme Court banned Sortu, a Basque nationalist political party, soon after it was established in February 2011, even though Sortu's manifesto specifically condemned politically motivated violence. The Basque reaction was mixed: some felt that Sortu was only the lastest incarnation of Batasuna, but most believed that a political party that promoted non-violent strategies should be supported. Indeed, the new party **Bildu** ('gather' in Basque), which was quickly established in the wake of Sortu's demise, made an impressive showing at the Basque elections in 2011.

As Euskadi looks to the future, however, the most promising story is not this relic of a troubled past, but the surprising rebirth of Bilbao as a symbol of the Basques' prosperity. Long known only for industrial obsolescence and rust, the city has pulled itself up with such projects as Frank Gehry's Guggenheim Museum, Philippe Starck's arts centre (the Alhóndiga), and and a huge riverfront redevelopment plan; in just a couple of decades Bilbao has emerged from nowhere to become one of the most exciting cities in Spain, and the showcase for a small, ancient nation that in the past has always been able to absorb new ideas, innovate and prosper. The Basques, in spite of their troubles, seem poised to do it again.

Topics

03

The Pilgrimage to Santiago

The Official History

No saint on the calendar has as many names as Spain's patron – Iago, Diego, Jaime, Jacques, Jacobus, Santiago or, in English, James the Greater. James the fisherman was one of the first disciples chosen by Jesus, who nicknamed him Boanerges, 'the son of thunder', after his booming voice. After the Crucifixion, he seems to have been a rather ineffectual proselytizer for the faith; in the year AD 44 Herod Agrippa in Caesarea beheaded him and threw his body to the dogs.

But Spain had another task in store for James: nothing less than posthumously leading a 700-year-old crusade against the peninsula's infidels.

In fact, the evidence suggests that it was really the French who put him up to it: the first mention of the Apostle's relics in Spain appears in an 830 annexe to the *Martirologio de Florus*, written in 806 in Lyon; after the fright of 732, when the Moors invaded as far as Poitiers and settled a good portion of France's Mediterranean coast, the French were ready to pull out all the stops to encourage their old Christian neighbours to rally and defeat the heathen. A new history of James emerged, one with links to Spain. First, before his martyrdom, he went to Zaragoza to convert the Spaniards and failed. Second, after his martyrdom, two of his disciples piously gathered his remains and sailed off with them in a stone boat (faith works wonders). The destination was Iria Flavia in remote Galicia, and the disciples buried Boanerges in the nearby cemetery of Compostela. In 814, a shower of shooting stars guided a hermit shepherd named Pelayo to the site of James's tomb; the bones were 'authenticated' by Bishop Theodomir. Another legend identifies Charlemagne (who died in 814) with the discovery of James's relics: in the Emperor's tomb at Aachen you can see the 'Vision of Charlemagne', with a scene of the Milky Way, the Via Lactea, a common name for the pilgrims' road.

In 844, not long after the discovery of the relics, James was called into active duty in the battle of Clavijo, appearing on a white horse to help Ramiro I of Asturias defeat the Moors. This new role as Santiago Matamoros, the 'Moor-Slayer', was a great morale-booster for the forces of the Reconquista, who made 'Santiago!' their battle cry. In the churches along the *camino*, James is portrayed either as a humble pilgrim himself or as a mighty warrior trampling the Moors underfoot. Ramiro was so pleased by his divine assistance that he made a pledge, the *voto de Santiago*, which ordained an annual property tax for St James's church at Compostela.

Never mind that the bones, the battle and the *voto* were as bogus as each other; the story struck deep spiritual, poetic and political chords that fitted perfectly with the great cultural awakening of the 10th and 11th centuries. The medieval belief that a few holy bones or teeth could serve as a hotline to heaven made the discovery essential. After all, the Moors had some powerful juju of their own: an arm of the Prophet Mohammed in the Great Mosque of Córdoba (possession of it was Abd ar-Rahman's justification for declaring himself caliph in 929). Another factor in the early 9th century was the Church's need for a focal point to assert its doctrinal control over the newborn kingdoms of Spain, especially over the Celts in Galicia, stubborn followers of the Gnostic Priscilian heresy (*see* p.313). A third factor must have been the desire to reintegrate Spain into Europe – and what better way to do it than to increase human, commercial and cultural traffic over the Pyrenees? Pilgrimages to Jerusalem and Rome were already in vogue; after the long centuries of the Dark Ages, the Church was keen on re-establishing contacts across the old Roman Empire that it had inherited for Christianity.

The French were the great promoters of the Camino de Santiago (the Way to Santiago), so great in fact that the most commonly tramped route became known as the *camino francés*. The first official pilgrim was Gotescalco, bishop of Le Puy, in 950; others followed, including Mozarab Christians (those living under Moorish rule) from Andalucía, who emigrated north and put themselves under the protection of Santiago, founding some of the first churches and monasteries along the road in the province of León.

In the next century, especially once the frontier with the Moors was firmly pushed back to the south bank of the Duero, the French monks of the reforming abbey of Cluny did more than anyone to popularize the pilgrimage, setting up sister houses and hospitals along the way. Nor were the early Spanish kings slow to pick up on the commercial potential of the road: Sancho the Great of Navarra and Alfonso VI of Castile founded a number of religious houses and institutions along the way and invited down French settlers to help run them. It was at this time too that the French stuck another oar in with their *Chanson de Roland*, which made Charlemagne something of a proto-pilgrim, although his adventure into Pamplona happened decades before the discovery of James's relics.

The 12th century witnessed a veritable boom along the *camino francés*: the arrival of new monastic and military orders, including the Templars, Hospitallers and Knights of Santiago, who all vowed to defend the pilgrim from dangers en route. In 1130, the Abbey of Cluny commissioned Aymery Picaud, a priest from Poitou, to write the *Codex Calixtinus*, the world's first travel guide, chock-full of prejudices and practical advice for pilgrims: he describes the four main roads through France and gives tips on where not to drink the water, where to find the best lodging, where to be on guard against 'false pilgrims' who came not to atone for crimes but to commit them. The final bonus for Santiago de Compostela came in 1189, when Pope Alexander III declared it a Holy City on equal footing with Jerusalem and Rome, offering a plenary indulgence – a full remission from Purgatory – to pilgrims on Holy Years (if you're planning a trip, the next will be 2021; other years you'll only get half time off). The favourite song they would sing along the way was the *Ultreya*:

Dum Pater familias, rex universorum
donaret provincias ius apostolorum
Jacobus Hispanias lux ilustrat morum
Primus ex apostolis, martyr Jerosolimis
Jacobus egregio, sacre et martyrio.
Herru Sanctiagu, grot Santiagu
e ultreia e suseia, Deus adiuva nos

(Our father, King of the Universe/Concede the land to apostolic right/Santiago of Spain is the light illuminating tradition/First among the Apostles, martyr of Jerusalem/Distinguished Santiago, holy and martyred/Lord Santiago, Great Santiago!/And Forward! and Onward! God help us!)

The Tour St-Jacques in Paris was a traditional rallying point for groups of pilgrims (there was more safety in numbers); from there the return journey was 1,280km (800 miles) and took a minimum of four months on foot. It was not something to go into lightly, but for many it was more than an act of faith, a chance to get out and see the world. By the time of Aymery Picaud, the French had been joined by pilgrims from across Europe. Many were ill (hence the large number of hospitals), hoping to complete the pilgrimage before they died. Not a few were thieves, murderers and delinquents condemned by the judge to make the journey for penance. Sometimes dangerous cons had to do it in chains. To keep them from cheating or stealing someone else's indulgence (the Compostellana certificate), pilgrims had to have their documents stamped by the clergy at various points along the route, just as they do today (as a nice touch, the old stamps and seals have recently been revived).

An estimated half-million people a year made the trek in the Middle Ages (out of a European population of about 60 million) and, even in the 18th century, the so-called century of Enlightenment, the pass at Roncesvalles still counted 30,000 pilgrims a year. But in the 19th century numbers fell dramatically; most of the monasteries and churches were closed for ever with the confiscation of church lands in 1837, and many were converted into stables or simply pillaged for their building stone. In the 1970s, just when it seemed as defunct as a dodo, the pilgrimage made a remarkable revival, owing to a number of factors – the modern world's disillusionment with conventional religion; the search for something beyond what over-organized day-to-day life and church attendance can offer, and, more prosaically, the growth of ecological and alternative tourism. In 1982 John Paul II became the first pope ever to visit Santiago; in 1985, UNESCO declared it the 'Foremost Cultural Route in Europe', helping to fund the restoration of some of the Romanesque churches that punctuate the trail. Although modern roads have changed the face of the pilgrimage for ever, efforts have been made to create alternative paths for pedestrians, marked every 500m with a stylized scallop shell, and new inexpensive *hostales* have sprouted along the way for walkers or cyclists. The pilgrims' quest is back in business.

The Field of the Star

In the Middle Ages it took real courage to leave home and make such an arduous, perilous journey west to Finisterre; back then, as today, there was more to it than just picking up an indulgence to deposit as credit in the Bank of Grace. The pilgrimage was one of the few opportunities for the average Middle Ager to attain a consciousness and understanding beyond the strict limits of Church dogma. All the humbuggery over the 'discovery' of the Apostle's relics in the far northwest corner of Spain would never have caught the popular imagination so powerfully had it not been for the deep mythopoeic resonances already present; especially for the Celts, the far west was the abode of souls that pass on. It was an ancient Indo-European belief that a star appears in the Milky Way whenever a mortal is born, and shoots towards the west when they die, towards the realm of the dead in, as for example the Celts conceived it, the Castle of the Goddess Arianhrod (the constellation Corona Borealis). Similarly, according to Plato, the dead go to the

celestial west, to the spot where the Milky Way meets the circle of the Zodiac –
towards the real 'Compostela' (*campus stellae in finis terrae*), the 'field of the star at
the world's end'. To make the journey to the end of the world *while still alive* was
to come to terms with our ultimate destiny, to vanquish and harrow hell, to
understand the mystery in a unique way with both body and mind. There were
certainly plenty of miracles and mysteries for the pilgrims to ponder as they
followed the setting sun, both in legends and in the subject matter chosen by the
sculptors who decorated the portals and capitals of the churches along the way.
Much of their symbolism is enigmatic in the extreme. With the destruction,
deterioration and ham-handed restoration of so many pilgrim churches and
hospitals, many important clues left by the itinerant guilds of builders were lost,
but the remains include Celtic and other pagan symbols, man-eating lions, eagles
and snakes, two-headed monsters, jovial eroticism, labyrinths, figures from the
Zodiac or from the 'labours of the months', and much more, along with a wide
range of orthodox and unorthodox depictions of scenes from scripture.

Aymery Picaud's *Codex Calixtinus* divided the *camino francés* into 13 days or
stages. Some are rather long hauls, possible only with a fresh horse; others are
short and walkable. Some of the stages are to famous towns like León and Burgos;
others to dusty one-horse nowheres, apparently chosen arbitrarily, which existed
on their reputation only as long as the *Codex Calixtinus* was consulted. The number
13 has its own deep resonance, going back to the proto-pilgrimages of ancient
Egypt, when a journey down the Nile was a living re-enactment of the journey
made by an Egyptian after death. Egypt itself was a metaphor for the heavens,
while the Nile was divided into 12 parts representing the Zodiac, as a lunar year is
12 or 13 months. As if to prove that such ideas reached Spain, a curious 9th-
century BC Egyptian alabaster burial urn, found at Almuñécar and displayed in the
Casa Castril in Granada, has hieroglyphs that suggest such a pilgrimage:

> I have arrived from my foreign land. I have passed through countries and have
> heard about your being, you of the primordial state of the two lands, you who
> have engendered what exists. In you your two eyes shine. Your Word is the way
> of life that gives breath to all throats. Now I am in the horizon, flooded by the
> happiness of the harija oases, and I speak to it like a friend. In me there is a source
> of health, of life, beyond your shores.

The Wild Goose Chase

One theory has it that the Goose Game, a favourite children's pastime in Spain
and most continental countries, is a playful memory of the pilgrimage, the
medieval path of initiation. The Goose Game first became popular at the time of
Philip II, the age when anything faintly outside church dogma was likely to lead to
an auto-da-fé. In the Goose Game, the board has a path of 63 squares set in a spiral,
leading inwards to the goal, with a picture of a goose in the centre. Twelve of the
63 squares also have pictures of geese, which are invariably good to land on;
another six have obstacles (the bridge, the inn, the well, the labyrinth, the prison,
and death, usually represented by a skull). Players roll dice to move their markers
around the board.

A number of writers on Compostela, beginning with Louis Charpentier who wrote *The Mystery of Compostela* (1973), have remarked on the persistency of the word 'goose' in the place names along the Camino de Santiago. *Oca* is Spanish for goose, *Ganso* is the Visigothic German, *Anser* the Latin, and a look at the map reveals that northwest Spain has far more than its share of goosey names: El Ganso, the Montes de Oca, Rio Oja, Puerto de la Oca, the river Anso.

Goosiness permeates the other side of the Pyrenees too. In France, *dévider les jars*, 'to spin the ganders', meant to speak in argot, the secret language of the builders' confraternities. The mysterious, now vanished Agotes (or Cagots in French), an outcast race who lived on either side of the Navarrese Pyrenees, were often forced to wear a goose foot around their necks. The Basques had a race of lovely, goose-footed fairies, the *laminak*, and Toulouse was the home of the famous Visigothic queen Ranachilde, wife of Theodoric II. Better known as *la reine pédauque*, the 'goose foot', her story inspired the legend of goose-footed Berthe, Charlemagne's mum, a rather domestic queen who told children stories by her spinning wheel (French fairytales customarily begin with 'In the time when good Queen Berthe spun...'). Andrew Lang found the first reference to Mother Goose, *La Mère d'Oye*, in 1650.

So why choose, of all God's creatures, a goose as the key? One guess is that the goose is only a European adaptation of the Egyptian ibis, the bird sacred to Isis that destroyed the eggs of the Nile crocodile and annually battled winged serpents from Arabia (geese are pretty handy with serpents too, as every farmer knows). The figure of Isis distantly haunts the whole *camino*, which is littered with miraculous, usually dark-faced statues of the Virgin, her Christian equivalent. The Universal Way to Compostela, the Milky Way, the Starry Stairway to Heaven, was a path of initiation into the mysteries of life and death and unity of all things. A wild goose chase, for those who understood the cosmic joke. Why else would the figures Master Mateo carved on the cathedral of Santiago laugh so merrily?

Pilgrim Facts

To be considered a pilgrim you have three choices of transport: foot, horse or bicycle.

On foot, if you're reasonably fit and can clock up 30km (19 miles) a day, expect a journey of six weeks from Roncesvalles to Santiago; to enjoy the experience and take in all the monuments along or just off the way, give yourself two months. To get the Compostela certificate in Santiago (and the time off Purgatory that goes with it), genuine pilgrims are expected to bring a letter of accreditation from their parish priest, from one of the world-wide confraternities, including the **Confraternity of Saint James UK** (for members only), c/o Marion Marples, 27 Blackfriars Rd, London, SE1 8 NY, *www.csj.org.uk*. The 'credential letter' (*credencial* in Spanish) must be stamped along the way in order for pilgrims to qualify for the Compostela certificate (you must complete 100km on foot, or 200km by bicycle). The credential letter also entitles you to stay free or very cheaply in the *refugios* run by towns, churches or monasteries along the way, although the accommodation is often little more than a place to lay a sleeping bag; note that they can have fairly early curfews. The footpath is well marked, though bear in mind that in most parts of the trip, especially in Castilla y León, you won't have a footpath at all, but a dusty verge along a busy highway. July and August may have the best weather for the trip, but also bring the most traffic.

Spanish organizations devoted to helping pilgrims and answering questions include the **Federación Española de Asociaciones de Amigos del Camino de Santiago**, C/Ruavieja 3, Logroño-La Rioja, t 941 24 56 74, *www.caminosantiago.org*. There are numerous useful websites, including *www.jacobeo.net* (Spanish only), *www.csj.org.uk* (in English), and *www.americanpilgrims.com* (in English). Spanish tourist offices can also provide basic information.

To the insufficiently pious, the real revelation of the pilgrimage is that, when you get to the end, there's simply nothing there – just a corpse that could be a mythical character's or anybody's. In the Goose Game, square number 58, on the brink of the goal, is the skull, and if you land there, you're dead and have to start again from the beginning. To those who see the pilgrimage as containing a secret teaching for a few, that's just the point. Once you have made it to Santiago de Compostela, it would hardly make sense not to go all the way to land's end. It isn't far, and the trail meets the sea at Noia, a place that was a holy site long before Compostela, with Neolithic dolmens, and a churchyard full of mysterious tombstones from the Middle Ages, carved with signs and motifs that no one has ever explained.

Roland the Rotter

All over the Pyrenees, you'll find memories of Roland – from the *Brèche de Roland* in the High Pyrenees, hewn with a mighty stroke of his sword Durandal, to a menhir on Mt Aralar that he tossed like Obélix. From here, his fame spread across Europe, remembered in everything from Ariosto's Renaissance epic *Orlando Furioso* to the ancient, mysterious statue of 'Roland the Giant' in front of Bremen city hall.

But who is this Roland really? Outside of the *Chanson de Roland*, information is scarce. The chronicler Eginhardt, writing *c.* 830, mentions a certain Roland, Duke of the Marches of Brittany, who perished in Charles the Great's famous ambush in the Pyrenees in 778, without according him any particular importance. Two hundred years later this obscure incident had blossomed into one of the great epics of medieval Europe. Here is the mighty hero, with his wise friend and companion-in-arms Oliver. Here is the most puissant knight in the army of his uncle Charlemagne, come down from the north to crusade against the heathen Muslims of Spain. Charlemagne sweeps all before him, occupying many lands south of the Pyrenees and burning Pamplona to the ground before coming to grief at an unsuccessful siege of Zaragoza. On their return, Roland and Oliver and the peers of the rearguard are trapped at the pass of Roncesvalles, thanks to a tip from Roland's jealous stepfather Ganelon. Numberless hordes of paynims overwhelm the French; though outnumbered, they cut down Saracens by the thousands, like General Custer or John Wayne against the savage Injuns. Finally Roland, cut with a thousand wounds, smites his sword Durandal against the rock, meaning to keep it from the hands of the infidels (although in the *Chanson* he ends up heaving it in the air, whereupon it finally ends up stuck in the cliff at Rocamadour, a major French site on the pilgrims' road). He then sounds his horn Oliphant to warn Charlemagne, who alas is too far away to rescue them, puffing so hard that he blows his brains out as Michael and Gabriel appear to escort his soul to heaven, the archetypal warrior victorious in defeat. History says it wasn't a Muslim horde at all, but rather the Navarrese Basques who did Roland in. And why shouldn't they get their revenge on these uncouth Franks who were devastating their land, trying to force this democratic nation to kneel before some crowned foreign thug who called himself their king?

How this affair metamorphosed into an epic at the turn of the millennium or how the caterpillar Roland of history re-emerged as the mythological butterfly in the *Chanson* is murky, but as with most epics it involved a modicum of propaganda.

The immediate source of the *Chanson* is said to have been a famous vision of Roland given to an 11th-century archbishop of Pamplona, which transformed Basque farmers into infidel knights (just in time for the Crusades). For the French there was another bonus: glorification of Carolingian imperialism provided poetic justification for the expansionist dreams of the Capetian kings.

Of Racial Purity and Pork

Spanish history is shot through with tragicomic implosions. One of the most destructive was the mania for *limpieza de sangre* (purity of blood), a doctrine that so undermined the national economy in the 15th–17th centuries that all the loot from the Americas couldn't patch the gaping wound. Purity of blood meant pure Christian ancestry, something probably only a few Asturian and Basque hillbillies could claim with a clear conscience. But as the Reconquista swept south, Castile, more than any of the other kingdoms of the northwest, began to define itself as a nation by religious segregation. Many Jews and Moors tried to conform by converting and, although at first they were accepted without stigma, bigotry raised its ugly head in the 1400s, just as the Christians achieved total control.

The Jews were the first to go. In Spain since the Diaspora, they were an educated and useful minority, many of them doctors and moneylenders (two of the few professions they were allowed to exercise). They were the subject of the first 'purity of blood' law, the 1449 Toledo decree, issued in spite of opposition from the king of Castile and the pope: 'We declare that the so-called *conversos*, offspring of perverse Jewish ancestors, must be held by law to be infamous and ignominious, unfit and unworthy to hold any public office or benefice within the city of Toledo.' Many cities followed suit. In 1480, Isabel and Ferdinand refounded the Inquisition to institutionalize discrimination against *conversos*: any of them suspected of backsliding in the faith – or often anyone merely accused of it – would have their property confiscated by the state, and would probably be burned at the stake. In 1492, Isabel celebrated the conquest of Granada by booting the Jews out of Spain. The kings of Navarra took them under their wing, at least until 1514, when Navarra itself was gobbled up by Ferdinand. Not satisfied with this, the Inquisition after 1530 began posting in the cathedrals the names of everyone who had any dealings at all with the Holy Office, so that people suspected of 'tainted blood' could always be readily identified – and not hired for any important post. In response, books of family trees were published, to prove one's own purity or to disparage someone else's. *Limpieza de sangre* contributed more than anything to the prevailing atmosphere in 16th-century Spain, which could be described as raging, surreal paranoia. The economic result was more concrete: by bankrupting and expelling the Jews and *conversos*, the perennially broke kings of Spain had to borrow money from Genoese bankers at calamitous rates. The annual silver fleet from the Americas would sail into Seville only to be sucked up whole by the Italians.

Muslims who refused to convert were given their walking papers in 1502. Those who did convert, the *moriscos*, were robbed and booted out a century later. The *moriscos* were excellent farmers, experts in irrigation, and willing to perform jobs no pure-blooded Spaniard would touch. Although the usual mafia of aristocrats, especially the Count of Lerma, picked up a tidy bundle from the sale of their confiscated lands, the *moriscos'* departure left many parts of Spain not far from Skid Row. Philip III, imbecile spawn of many generations of Habsburg family incest, was the king who allowed the *moriscos* to be put out. Philip, incidentally, died from sitting too close to the fire – so weighty was his concept of his own nobility that he couldn't imagine getting up and moving away from the flames on his own.

The blood obsession was becoming increasingly kinky. In Spain, a true aristocrat would bleed 'blue', while his younger brothers, poor *hidalgos* (and Christ himself, profusely, in a thousand horror-show Spanish statues) bled red, and everyone else bled 'plain blood' unless they were Moors, Jews or Lutheran heretics, whose blood was said to be 'black'. The *hidalgos* (from *hijo de algo*, 'son of somebody'), once the backbone of medieval Castile, were by now a mentally deranged caste of haughty layabouts. Located at the bottom of the noble ladder, with neither land nor vassals, they came to be the class most obsessed with blood and honour. It was their sole capital, all that they had from the ancestors who achieved the Reconquista. Some of them went to America as *conquistadores*, but most stayed, impoverished and futile like Don Quixote, guarding the iron-bound coffers where they kept their letters patent, attesting to their arms, rank, and privileges that exempted them from direct taxation and debtors' prison, all the time depriving Spain of productive men and poisoning society with their attitude.

> *My father was afflicted by a disgrace which he passed on to all his sons like original sin. He was a hidalgo. This is not unlike being a poet, for there are few hidalgos who escape perpetual poverty and continuous hunger. He possessed letters patent of his nobility so ancient that even he was unable to read them, and no one cared to touch them for fear of getting their fingers greasy from the bedraggled knots and ribbons of the tattered parchments. Even the mice took care not to gnaw them lest they were stricken with sterility.*
> Estebanillo González (1646)

Short of resorting to being bled to see what colour of *sangre* leaked out, there were two sure-fire ways to tell a true Christian Spaniard: he hardly ever washed ('the odour of sanctity'), and he ate lots of pork. Bathing was Jewish, Moorish and effeminate: one of the first acts of Isabel and Ferdinand after the conquest of Granada was to close the baths. If a suspect hadn't bathed, the second test was to offer him a bit of pig meat. Now this was perhaps a more honest vetting; Spain has been known for pork since ancient times; and even a historian like Diodorus Siculus could rave about Iberian 'hams transcendently superlative' in the 1st century AD.

We can suppose that making the pig into a badge of the True Faith could not happen without some distortion of the national psyche. Pigs and Spanish strangeness went hand in hand, sometimes in uncanny ways. Extremadura was long Spain's hog heaven, and the best, most exquisite porkers there were fed on vipers. Like so many *conquistadores*, the great, unspeakable Pizarro came from there; he was suckled by a sow, and started his career as a swineherd. The Spanish national psychosis of the old days, a witches' brew of *limpieza de sangre*, lust for gold, vicious imperialism, hatred and bigotry, found its reflection in the kitchen, in an obsession with pork that can be disconcerting, even today.

The Spanish Distemper

Home on the Range

If you want to see the best-preserved early medieval frescoes in Spain, you'll have to go to Gaceo, a dusty nowhere off the road from Vitoria to Pamplona. It's an unpromising spot, but, if you can find the man with the key, there is a wonderful cartoon vision of heaven and hell – a rare relic from a lost world. So often in Spain, the real treasures are hidden in out-of-the-way places. Gaceo is a somewhat special case – a Roman road, later the Camino Real (now buried beneath the E5/E80 motorway), once ran through it. Still, it would be only natural to ask why such a huge expenditure, by medieval standards, of money and talent should have been lavished on tiny Gaceo. That question itself is a key to understanding Spain.

All over Castile, in scores of cities and even villages, you will sense there were great expectations long ago, and greater disappointments afterwards. A dusty hamlet will sport an arcaded Plaza Mayor that never quite grew into a stone one like Vitoria's or Madrid's. Similarities with provincial American towns are obvious: a half-built feeling, streets ludicrously too wide for the traffic, laid out anticipating a boom that never came, and a couple of Plateresque palaces, sticking out from the humble tile roofs like the grand Victorian business blocks amidst the car parks of wasted American city centres. Like America, and unlike any European country save Russia, Spain has a heritage as a frontier society. Nearly every valley and plain south of the Cordillera Cantábrica knows a history of reconquest from the Moors and Christian resettlement. Romans, Vandals, Alans, Suevi, Byzantines, Franks, Visigoths and Arabs had all done their part to make Spain's central plateau into an empty wasteland. From the 800s, when the Asturians and others began to cross the mountains, to the final victory over the heathen Moor in 1492, the wave of the Reconquista spread gradually southwards; at one time every part of it was the scene of pioneers reclaiming land and founding villages and towns. And, as in the American West, the money that fuelled the expansion came largely from livestock – sheep, not cows. The biggest ranchers were the *hidalgos*, and they dominated frontier political life by influence and force; the towns found themselves constantly on the defensive against the *hidalgos*' attempted land grabs and extortions.

Few frontier expansions in history ever came off quite like this one, though. The people that started America's push west arrived logically from behind the frontier; many of Spain's, bizarrely enough, came from beyond it. The northwest was hardly overflowing with population at the beginning of the Reconquista, and the numbers were largely supplied by Mozarab Christians from Muslim-ruled Spain, from al-Andalus, looking for free land and a Christian atmosphere. Few facts were ever recorded about this trickling exodus, but it is reasonable to assume that Mozarabs with the gumption to pack up and move into the lonesome *meseta* were also likely to be the most fanatical supporters of Christianity and the new Christian states. And, instead of half-naked Indians without towns or technology, the heathen enemy of the new Spanish frontiersmen happened to be probably the most delightful and sophisticated civilization in the Western world, led by caliphs whose greatest joys were writing lyrical poetry and planting pleasure gardens with tinkling fountains. Such irony can weigh on a nation's soul.

The pioneer warriors of the north had a secret weapon in their fight against the Moors – utter ruthlessness. Organized in highly mobile raiding parties, they could extort tributes from the Muslim lands simply by threatening to girdle their irreplaceable olive trees. Destroying crops and villages was another key tactic. The Christians expanded their boundaries by making the lands beyond uninhabitable. It all worked brilliantly, and behind the lines the new Spain gradually took shape. What happened in the end to all hopes of the frontiersmen can be read in Spain's sad history. The boom did come, fitfully and unequally, but nearly every village and town of Castile enjoyed at least a few decades of dizzying prosperity, enough to at least begin some grandiose projects. The woebegone church at Villalcázar de Sirga comes to mind. Santa María looks to have been planned to match the size of Burgos cathedral, and thrown up in a hurry. Sadly it never got more than a third finished, and today the dust blows around it. As always, after the boom came the bust, and what a bust it was. Castile has been busted ever since.

El Cid Campeador

In the Spanish pantheon El Cid Campeador comes in a close second to Santiago himself, but, unlike Arthur, Siegfried, Roland and other heroes of national medieval epics, the Cid, Rodrigo Díaz de Vivar (1043–99), was entirely flesh and blood. Born in Vivar near Burgos, his unique title is derived from the Arabic *sayyidi* ('my lord'), and *Campeador*, which means 'Battler'. His fame spread widely among both Moors and Christians (in his career he served both Alfonso VI of Castile and the Emir of Zaragoza); even before his death, ballads celebrated his prowess. The greatest achievement of his life, the capture of Valencia from the Moors in 1095, took place when he was already 52 years old. Through modern eyes Rodrigo was little better than a gangster, but for the warrior class of the Reconquista he served as a model of virtue – fearless, with an exaggerated sense of honour, devoutly Catholic yet wholly pragmatic, a generous conqueror, devoted to his family, who paid his debts and always kept his word. The Cid was the perfect man for his time, living in the frontier society among Christians, Moors and Jews, where a king's powers were limited, and the main issues of the day were the simple pleasures of turf and booty.

For all that, 'O Born in a Happy Hour' – Rodrigo's other nickname – would not have had such a long shelf life, inspiring such diverse spirits as Corneille and Hollywood (where he was played, inevitably, by Charlton Heston), if there weren't something more to his character. This comes through in the epic *Poem of the Cid*, composed around 1140, less than half a century after his death. For 500 years the actual poem was lost, until 1779 when the royal librarian, through some literary detective work, located a copy from 1307, appropriately enough in Vivar, the Cid's home town. Not a single ounce of the magic or marvellous touches the text; the Rodrigo Díaz who emerges lies and cheats, but has a rustic sense of humour and a certain generous charm, always ready to praise another, happy to have his wife and daughters present to watch him 'earn his bread' fighting the Moors. You can't help liking the guy. His saga, though somewhat repetitive to read, is also the first known example of the Spanish gift for realism that would reach its climax in Cervantes' *Don Quixote*. Actually, even more realism would have been in order, for life on the frontier was not always the stuff of poetry.

Reconquista Man

Here he comes. Slouching in a rough woollen tunic, García Gómez is riding out of the sorrowful wilderness of the Cantabrian mountains and into history. García Gómez may look the Arkansawyer redneck of the American frontier, the sort that proverbially 'never had nothin', never learned nothin', and don't want nothin'', but he is a man on the make. He's got himself an iron sword, while his daddy had to get by with a big stick that he cut himself, like Little John – he carried it around, and anyone that gave him any lip was likely to get a taste of it with iron; such encounters are fewer but a little more dangerous. Of course being a Castilian, he is a *hidalgo*, really *hijo de algo*, a 'son of somebody'; we're all *muy noble y muy leal*, ain't we, boys? At least as much as the big shot who owns the castle – he just came and nicked it from the former proprietor. Nicked his wife too.

The first thing to do is clear some land. And as you can see from the Castilian landscape today, there was something in García Gómez that didn't love trees. They used to say that a squirrel could go from Portugal to the Pyrenees, if he wanted, without touching ground. Juan José and his sons will do their best to blot out the offending forests, and the *coup de grâce* will be administered by the Habsburgs, who as we remember were always building armadas, and also creaming the profits off the timber trade for themselves and sending them home to Germany. Next thing to do is wrestle all the stones out of the fields, and build a dry-stone house. Piece of cake. In a generation or two, with a lot of luck and an eye constantly on the main chance, the family will be able to afford a little showplace – one of the hundreds of rude hilltop castles that gave Castile its name.

Unlike the settlers of the American West, García Gómez did not come over the mountains with his Bible in his hand. He couldn't really read it, and anyhow the Church doesn't exactly hand them out – a little later, when Ferdinand and Isabel bring in the Inquisition, a man could get himself incinerated just for reading one in Spanish. It might give him ideas. But García Gómez is content to let the learned clerics tell him what to believe. The mysteries of faith, all conducted in Latin of course, are too subtle for him, and the Church supplies the insistent propaganda that shapes his life: the triumph of the only faith over the godless Moors and Jews. Every now and then, fire-eating preachers like St Peter Martyr do the circuit, rousing the fools in the towns against the heathens, and our man will ride into town for the show; afterwards the good townspeople usually let off some steam, and any resident heathens are happy to escape with their lives. The towns are mostly of the one-horse variety (León, the biggest, counted a thousand souls at most in the early 11th century, maybe ten times that while they were building their cathedral) and they are not there to show a Gómez a good time. They're full of suspicious monks, merchants and officials, and, though they'd usually let him through the gate when he and the town weren't feuding, García Gómez hardly ever has reason to go.

Status in this neck of the woods is a horse. Being able to afford one of these most prized commodities secures García Gómez's position as one of the mounted warriors in the local count's retinue, ready to form an army for the king or a springtime expedition south to fight the Moors and grab some booty. A horse is the most significant investment the average man can have, but the men of the Reconquista know how to make it pay. Then as now, Arabian blood was prized most of all – it was mainly through Spain that Arabian horses first came into Europe. The profits to buy the beast come from sheep. Gómez has a nice little spread, and a village of malodorous tenant farmers to kick in a little rent. They pay taxes and tithes, as do the townspeople. Gómez, being a *hidalgo*, does not.

Keep your eye on this boy, for he is blessed by the gods. Tucked away on a peninsula at the extremity of Europe, the *hidalgo* has nobody to bang away against except the hapless Moors, and eventually he will have all their land and goods. By 1500, flushed with ill-gotten wealth, he will be troubling the peace of Europe, and soon after he and his sword will be tramping around the Andes, up into Kansas and down the Amazon. And finally, before he rides off into the sunset he will burn himself out completely, tilting at windmills on the plains of La Mancha.

The Saving Grace

For all the sound and fury of the Reconquista, all the waste and futility, was anything left that would last? There are people capable of conjuring up beauty and delight in any age, and at the beginning of the Middle Ages Europe had the cash to do it in stone for the first time since the late Roman Empire. 'So it was,' wrote an 11th-century chronicler, 'as though the world had shaken herself and cast off her old age, and were clothing herself everywhere in a white garment of churches.' Spain shared fully in this flowering of Romanesque architecture and art; indeed the little Christian kingdoms of the north were the unlikely vanguard of the movement.

Where did the Romanesque come from? Unlike most parts of western Europe, northern Spain had very few Roman buildings left to serve as models. But from scattered examples around Europe and the Middle East it is easy to see a continuous progression everywhere, from late Roman architecture through the Dark Ages. The real homeland of Romanesque seems to be Syria, where Greek Christians built elegant basilican churches with plenty of rounded arches, windows and blind arcading up until the 7th-century Muslim conquest. Syrian monks, including most likely the architects and painters, spread across Christendom after that as refugees, taking the style with them. In this age buildings of any kind are few, and records almost non-existent, and, while early Romanesque works in Armenia, northern Italy and Asturias may show some striking similarities, it is impossible to say too much about how they got that way. Europe's first Romanesque churches appeared in the hills of Asturias in the 9th century, practically the only important architecture anywhere in Europe from that dark time. These showed classical elements, pediments, columns and arches, as well as considerable borrowings from the Muslim south: notably delicate double windows called *ajimeces*, divided by a column, and horseshoe arches, a native Spanish style that the Moors had adapted from the Visigoths.

In the sudden, explosive burst of energy and economic expansion after the magic year 1000, the impulse to build and create spread across Europe; in Spain, as elsewhere, the Romanesque churches were the symbol of the new civilization that had emerged from the chrysalis of the Dark Ages. One of the oldest Asturian buildings, San Miguel de Lillo at Oviedo, has carvings of what seems to be a circus scene, setting the tone for the wild imaginative freedom that characterizes all

Romanesque art. The greatest charms of most churches are the carved portals, capitals and cloisters, on which you will see not only scriptural scenes, but legions of fantastical monsters, legendary heroes from Hercules to Roland, mermaids, farting monks, droll-looking insects, intricate floral designs and arabesques, demons, house cats, camels and leopards, spirals, labyrinths, hunting scenes, whales – everything in God's good creation, along with many things God never thought of, boiling up from the depths of the medieval unconscious. Unlike every age of religious art that followed, the Romanesque was never constrained by any narrow Church dogma; perhaps the most striking example is the number of frankly erotic scenes, as on the portal of the country church at Cervatos in Cantabria. Anything at all that could be experienced, or imagined, was a fit subject to decorate the House of God.

Expressive freedom in the Romanesque was hardly limited to stone-carving. The buildings themselves show a wide variety of ideas. Every province of Europe had its own distinct style and, within each, builders were often free to follow their fancy; eccentricities in northern Spain range from the octagonal churches at Eunate and Torres del Río in Navarra, modelled after the Holy Sepulchre in Jerusalem (these were either built or inspired by the Templars), to the outlandish Santa María del Sar at Santiago, built with the columns and walls of the nave tilted precariously outwards, or the Basque church of San Miguel de Arratxinaga in Markina, built over a huge dolmen – many early churches, most perhaps, replaced pre-Christian holy sites. What ties all the disparate Romanesque works together is a simple theory of proportion. Instead of the classical 'orders', medieval builders employed a new system of sacred architecture based on constructive geometry. Anyone with a mathematical bent will enjoy looking over the buildings, seeing how every point in them can be proved with a compass and straightedge, just as their builders designed them. Later ages of religious building may be more showy, more technically sophisticated, but none has the same hold over the imagination. The Romanesque is the art of springtime, of a new world where rules were few and fancy could wander where it liked.

The pilgrimage trail to Santiago is also a pilgrimage through some of medieval Europe's finest creations, from rustic one-aisled village churches to the great basilica of Santiago de Compostela, the biggest and most ambitious Romanesque work in Spain. Some of the other major attractions include Santo Domingo de Silos, south of Burgos, with the most beautiful Romanesque cloister in Spain; Estella, with a wealth of Romanesque buildings; San Martín at Frómista, west of Burgos; and the remote area called the 'Románico Palatino', north of Frómista, with one of the biggest concentrations of Romanesque country churches in Europe.

Food and
Drink

04

Fish Soup and Pig's Ear

The massive influx of tourists has had its effect on Spanish kitchens, but so has the Spaniards' own increased prosperity and, perhaps most significantly, the new federalism. Each region, each town even, has come to feel a new interest and pride in the things that set it apart, and food is definitely one of them. Northern Spain, with its markedly different personalities, is a special treat in this regard.

Seafood is undoubtedly the star of the show in the areas along the northern coast. The Atlantic has much more and better seafood than has the Mediterranean, and the ardent fishermen of this region are perfectly positioned to nab the best of it. They have plenty of practice cooking the stuff – archaeologists have found remains of sea urchins in settlements 10,000 years old. The bounty of the sea finds expression in famous **fish soups**, from the western *caldereta Asturiana* to the Basque *ttoro*, and there are any number of prized delicacies in every region: surprising things, such as *kokotxas*, 'cheeks' of the hake, or the Galician *vieiras de Santiago*, scallops cooked with almonds. On the whole, though, Spaniards try to keep their seafood simple. Galicians like to cook fish with potatoes and garlic; Basques do it with simple garlic and parsley sauces.

By popular acclaim, the champion cooks of northern Spain – really of all Spain – are the **Basques**, who coincidentally are also the most legendary eaters. Like the Greeks, the well-travelled Basques take their culinary skill with them everywhere. Basque restaurants turn up in unlikely places all over France, and it isn't unusual to drive through a dusty, one-horse town out in the American West where the only restaurant serves up good Basque home cooking.

Marseille may have its *bouillabaisse*, among a score of other exotic and treasured fish stews of southern Europe, but the Basques stoutly maintain their version, called *ttoro* (pronounced *tioro*), is the king of them all; naturally there is a solemn confraternity of the finest *ttoro* chefs. A proper one requires a pound of mussels and a mess of crayfish and congers, as well as the head of a codfish and three different kinds of other fish. Basque cuisine relishes imaginative yet simple sauces, including the legendary *pil pil* (originally named for the sound it made while frying), where somehow olive oil, garlic, and chillies magically meld with the cooking juices of salt cod. Another delight is fresh tuna cooked with tomatoes, garlic, aubergine and spices and *chipirones* (squid) – reputedly the only kind in the world that are all black, and better than they sound.

Each Basque chef knows how to work wonders with elvers (*angulas* or *txitxardin*) in garlic sauce, salmon and the famous *txangurro* – spider crab, flaked, seasoned, stuffed and served in its own shell. Gourmets especially recommend *kokotxas a la Donostiarra*, hake cheeks with a garlic and parsley green sauce, clams and slightly piquant red *guindilla* peppers. These peppers are another icon of the Basque kitchen; housewives still hang strings of them on the walls of their houses for drying (and for decoration). Peppers turn up everywhere: in omelettes, in sauces for seafood, or in the common stewed chicken. Basques like to wash it down with *txakoli*, a tangy green wine produced on the coast with just a modicum of sunlight.

The **Galicians** too have their talents in the kitchen, with the best of the best seafood, including some delicacies found nowhere else in the world. Throughout

Spain, Gallego restaurants command as much respect as Basque. The estuaries are rich in an extraordinary array of seafood, from the famous scallops of Santiago and lobster to some creatures unique to Galicia such as *zamburiñas* scallops, lobster-like *santiaguiños*, and ugly *percebes*, that have no names in English. Quantity is matched by quality: Galician seafood is considered the best in the world and preparation is kept as simple as possible. Another favourite served in every town are *empanadas*, large flat flaky pies filled with eels or lamprey (the most sought-after; try it before you knock it), sardines, tuna, pork, or veal. Turnip greens (*grelos*) are a staple, especially in *caldo gallego*, a broth that also features turnips and white beans; in winter, the heartier *lacón con grelos*, pork shoulder with greens, sausages and potatoes, holds pride of place. Galicia produces Spain's best veal and good cheeses, such as Roquefort-like *cabrales* and *gamonedo*, both mainly from cow's milk mixed with smaller quantities of ewe's or goat's milk; birch-smoked pear-shaped San Simón; or mild, soft *ulloa* or *paiego*. A tapas meal to make a Gallego weep includes grilled sardines, *pulpo gallego* (tender octopus with peppers and paprika), *zamburiñas* (intensely flavoured clams), roasted small green peppers (*pimientas de Padrón*), with chewy hunks of bread and lightly salted breast-shaped *tetilla* cheese, washed down with white Ribeira wine. For dessert try *tarta de Santiago* (almond tart) and, to top it all off, a glass of Galician fire water, *aguardiente* – served at night after a meal to ward off evil spirits – properly burned (*queimada*), with lemon peel and sugar.

Inland, though you'll still find plenty of seafood, the cuisine is an entirely different world. Cooking can be heavy, almost medieval, with plenty of roasts and chops, stews and game dishes – partridge and pheasant are special favourites. Local dishes include *chuletas de cordero a la navarra* (lamb chops), *truchas con jamón* (trout stuffed with ham) or, for something out of the ordinary, *liebres con chocolate* (hare with chocolate), washed down by the good strong wines from Tudela and Estella. **Asturias** and **Cantabria** are the dairylands of Spain, and produce a number of cheeses, notably the Cabrales of Asturias, made from cow's, sheep's and goat's milk all mixed together. Asturias has its famous dishes too, including hake in *sidra* (the ubiquitous local cider) or *fabada*, a mess of beans usually served with pork.

You would do well to sharpen your taste for **pork** before venturing into **Castile**. Here not much of the pig gets thrown away. Besides the famous ham, the bacon, chops and such, Castilians take what's left to make endless sausages, smoked sausages, blood sausages, tripes and puddings. Castilians make the somewhat extravagant claim that pork 'spiritualizes the stomach' (back in the days of the Reconquista and Inquisition, eating it also confirmed one's status as a Christian), and the less expensive pig parts are the staple of cooking; big chunks of pig meat get thrown into all the heavy stews and casseroles that Castilians love. The apotheosis of the porker in Spain is *cochinillo asado*, roast suckling pig, and its capital is Segovia, where top *asadores* wear medals and cover their restaurant walls with parchment certificates that look like papal bulls, proclaiming their culinary achievements. *Cochinillo* can be a genuine treat, though from here the attractive-ness of the cuisine drops off rather sharply. Another favourite is the famous *botillo* of El Bierzo (*botillo del Bierzo*), which can include minced pork, sausages, fat, lips and ears. Wrap all this up in a pig's intestine, hang it in the chimney for two or three months, and there you are.

One of the symptoms of pork abuse is a permanent craving for **pulses** on the side. Red beans, white beans, chickpeas and lentils, the Spaniards' real staples are all those spirit-laden dried delights that Pythagoras and other philosophers warned us against (of course any Pythagoreans in Spain would have been tidied away by the Inquisition long ago). The 'musical fruit' adds much to the, let us say, expansive nature of much traditional cooking, as in the countryman's *olla podrida*, praised by Cervantes, or the 'Maragato stew' with chickpeas, pig's ears and trotters, and a few inches of blood sausage. Pork and beans is wagon cooking, the simple food of pioneers – pig-farming pioneers – and the presence of such a humble cuisine is another of the curious phenomena bobbing in the wake of Spain's curious history. It is the cuisine of the frontier experience.

Rioja, *Sidra* and Other Tipples

There are 55 areas in Spain under the control of the Instituto Nacional de Denominaciones de Origen (INDO), which acts as a guide to the consumer and keeps a strict eye on the quality of Spanish wine (DO, or *denominación de origen*, is the same as French AOC).

La Rioja is the best known and richest area for wine in Spain, producing a great range from young whites to heavy, fruity reds; it is divided into several sub-districts; east of Logroño, there is an extension of the La Rioja wine belt in Navarra. Rioja tastes like no other wine: soft, warm, mellow, full-bodied, with a distinct vanilla bouquet; its *vino de gran reserva* spends three years ageing in American oak barrels, and then another year in bottles, before release to the public. The Phoenicians introduced the first vines which, after the various invasions, were replanted under the auspices of the Church; the first law concerning wine was decreed by Bishop Abilio in the 9th century. The arrival of masses of thirsty pilgrims proved a big boost to business, much as mass tourism would do in the 1960s and 1970s.

Despite a long pedigree, the Rioja we drink today dates from the 1860s, when growers from Bordeaux, their own vineyards wiped out by phylloxera, brought their techniques south of the border and wrought immense improvements on the native varieties. By the time the plague reached La Rioja in 1899, the owners were prepared for it with disease-resistant stock. During the First World War, when the vineyards of Champagne were badly damaged, the French returned to buy up *bodegas*, sticking French labels on the bottles and trucking them over the Pyrenees. Rioja finally received the respect it deserved after Franco passed on to the great fascist parade ground in the sky. In the last few decades, *bodegas* have attracted buyers from around the world and prices have skyrocketed.

La Rioja's growing area covers 64,000 hectares, comprising three zones: **Rioja Alta**, home of the best red and white wines, followed by **Rioja Alavesa** (on the left bank of the Ebro in the Basque province of Álava) known for its lighter, perfumed wines, and the decidedly more arid **Rioja Baja**, where the wines are coarse and mostly used for blending – a common practice in La Rioja. The varieties used for the reds are mostly spicy, fruity *tempranillo* (covering some 30,000 hectares alone), followed by *garnacha tinta* (a third of the red production, a good alcohol booster) with smaller portions of *graciano* (for the bouquet) and high-tannin *mazuelo* (for acidity and tone). Traditional Rioja whites are relatively unknown but are excellent, golden and vanilla-scented like the reds: *viura* grapes are the dominant grape, with smaller doses of *malvasía* and *garnacha blanca*.

Unlike French wines, Riojas are never sold until they're ready to drink (although of course you can keep the better wines even longer). DOC rules specify that La Rioja's Gran Reserva, which accounts for only three per cent of the production, spends a minimum of two years maturing in American oak barrels (six months for whites and rosés) then four more in the *bodega* before it's sold. *Reservas* (six per cent of the production) spend at least one year in oak and three in the *bodega*. *Crianzas* (30 per cent of the production) spend at least a year in the barrel and another in the bottle. The other 61 per cent of La Rioja is *sin crianza* and labelled CVC (*conjunto de varias cosechas*, 'combination of various vintages'); this includes the new young white wines and light reds (*claretes*) fermented at cool temperatures in stainless steel vats, skipping the oak barrels altogether and losing most of the vanilla tones.

Of course you'll find plenty of other Spanish wines in the region. **Euskadi** is known for its very palatable young 'green' wine called **txacoli** (in 1994 made a *denominación de origen*), which is poured into the glass with bravura from a height, like cider. *Txakoli* is made along the coast, around Getaria and Zarautz, as well as in small regions in Vizcaya and Álava provinces. In addition, there is a small, recently declared DO region around **León, El Bierzo**, with light and fruity reds (Casar de Valdaiga is a good one). **Galicia**'s excellent **Ribeíro** (west of Ourense), made from aromatic albarino grapes, resembles the delicate *vinho verde* of neighbouring Portugal; other good wines from the region are **Rías Baixas** (areas on the coast near Pontevedra, and south of Vigo on the Portuguese border) and **Valdeorros** (east of Ourense) – pleasant, light vintages that complement the regional dishes, seafood in particular.

Much of the inexpensive wine sold throughout the country comes from **La Mancha** or the neighbouring **Valdepeñas** DO regions. And then there is **Jerez**, or what we in English call **sherry**. When a Spaniard invites you to *tomar una copa* (glass) it will nearly always be filled with this Andalucían sunshine. It comes in a wide range of varieties: *manzanillas* are very dry, *fino* is dry, light and young (the most famous is Tío Pepe); *amontillados* are a bit sweeter and rich; *olorosos* are very sweet dessert sherries, and can be either brown, cream or *amoroso*.

North of the Cordillera Cantábrica in **Asturias**, where apples grow better than vines, they produce hard **cider**, or *sidra*, which can come as a shock to the taste buds for the first five minutes, then it goes down just fine. Cider means as much to Asturians as milk to babies; Basques are fond of good hard cider too. They claim to have taught the more famous cider-makers of Normandy and Asturias their secrets, and, back in the 1500s, Basque fishermen used to trade the stuff with the American Indians for furs.

Spanish **brandy** (mostly from Jerez too) is excellent; the two most popular brands, 103 (very light in colour) and Soberano, are both drunk extensively by Spanish labourers and postmen at about 7am (they throw a shot into their breakfast coffee and call it a *carajillo*). **Anís** (sweet or dry) is also quite popular. **Sangría** is the famous summertime punch of red wine, brandy, mineral water, orange and lemon with ice, but beware – it's rarely made very well, even when you can find it. Each region has its wine and liqueur specialities and nearly every monastery in Spain seems to make some kind of herbal potion or digestive liqueur that tastes more or less like cough syrup. In the Basque country, look for **Izarra**, a potent mix of Pyrenean herbs with exotic spices, which comes in either green or the less potent yellow; for something more unusual you can top off your meal with a tipple of deadly Basque hooch, *patxaran* (sloe brandy).

Practicalities

Learning to Eat the Spanish Way

Going to Spain, you may have to learn to eat all over again; dining is a much more complex affair here than in many countries. The essential fact to learn is that Spaniards like to eat all day long – this scheme spreads the gratification evenly through the day, and it facilitates digestion, which in Spain can be problematic. Give it some consideration. Start out with a big coffee, a *doble*, and a pastry (mostly poor French clones, with extra sugar) or find a progressive-looking bar where you might find a more fitting breakfast – a glass of wine or brandy, and a salami sandwich or *pincho*, or a glazed American doughnut. These bars will be around all day, their piles of treats under the glass cases on the bar growing by the hour, an eternal alternative to a heavy sit-down dinner. Ask around for the one that does seafood tapas. As if the bars weren't enough, there are *pastelerías* in the towns with all sorts of savoury pastries, *merenderos* (snack stands) in the countryside, and ice cream everywhere – you will never be more than a hundred feet from ice cream in a Spanish town. For a mid-morning or mid-afternoon energizer, there are sweet 'n' greasy *churros* (those inscrutable fried things that look like garden slugs) sold in bars and *churrerías*, dipped in thick cups of rich chocolate, for most non-Spaniards a once-in-a-lifetime gut-gurgling experience.

The best **restaurants** are almost always those specializing in regional cuisine, though at the upmarket end of the scale you'll find plenty of new restaurants with innovative dishes heavily influenced by what the Basques call their *cocina nueva* – as with French *nouvelle cuisine*, expect a lot of surprising combinations, peculiar sauces and an obsession with appearances. There are still thousands of old-fashioned restaurants around – and many of the sort that travellers have been complaining about for centuries; Spanish cooking still usually comes a bit on the heavy side. The worst offenders are often those with the little flags and ten-language menus in the most touristy areas, and in general you'd do better to buy some bread, Cabrales cheese and a bottle of Rioja red and have a picnic. But the regions along the northern coast have a repertoire of traditional dishes as gratifying as any in the country, and seafood is undoubtedly the star of the show.

In any coastal town or village, the best seafood restaurants will be around the harbour. The fancier ones will post set menus, while at the rest you'll find only a chalkboard with prices listed for a plate of grilled fish, or prawns or whatever else came in that day. It's a convivial arrangement; just choose a plate, or negotiate a full dinner with the waiter. Don't expect seafood to be a bargain, though; a plate of prawns in garlic all by itself usually costs about €8–10.

If you dine where the locals do you'll be assured of a good deal if not necessarily a good meal. Almost every restaurant offers a *menú del día*, or a *menú turístico*, featuring an appetizer, a main course, dessert, bread and drink at a set price, always a certain percentage lower than if you had ordered the items *à la carte*. These are always posted outside the restaurant; decide what you want before going in if it's a set-price menu, because these bargains are hardly ever listed on the menu the waiter gives you at the table. Unless it's explicitly written on the bill (*la cuenta*), service is not included in the total, so tip accordingly. Spaniards will just round up the bill by a few euros – 10 per cent is considered ludicrous, and 3–5 per cent is generous – but in tourist areas there are different expectations of visitors.

If you are travelling on a budget you may want to eat one of your meals a day at a tapas bar or *tasca*. **Tapas** (*caxuelitas* in Basque, though this is very unusual) means 'lids', and they started out as little saucers of goodies served on top of a drink. They have evolved over the years to form a main part of the world's greatest snack culture. Bars that specialize in them have platter after platter of delectable titbits, from shellfish to slices of omelette or mushrooms baked in garlic or vegetables in vinaigrette or stews. All you have to do is pick out what looks best and order a *porción* (an hors-d'œuvre) or a *ración* (a big helping) if it looks really good. It's hard to generalize about prices, but on average €15–20 of tapas and wine or beer will really fill you up. You can always save money in bars by standing up; sit at that charming table on the terrace and you'll find prices can jump considerably.

Another advantage of tapas is that they're available at what most Americans or Britons would consider normal **dining hours**. Spaniards are notoriously late diners; in the morning it's a coffee and roll grabbed at the bar, a huge meal at around 2 or 3pm, then after work at 8pm a few tapas at the bar to hold them over until supper at 10 or 11pm. After living in Spain for a few months this makes perfect sense, but it's exasperating to the average visitor. On the coasts, restaurants tend to open earlier to accommodate foreigners (some as early as 5pm) but you may as well do as the Spaniards do. Galicians are the early diners of Spain (8 or 9pm); Basques do it from 9 to 11 – if you can find a restaurant at all. In quieter non-touristy areas they will be inconspicuous and few. Just ask someone, and you will find a nice **comedor** with home cooking tucked in a back room behind a bar – if you hadn't asked you never would have found it. Such *comedores* (literally, dining rooms), where the food and décor are usually equally drab but cheap, are common everywhere, along with *cafeterías*, those places that feature photographs of their *platos combinados* (combination plates) to eliminate any language problem. Dinner will go for between €15 and €20, and you'll find as many good ones as real stinkers. **Asadores** are restaurants that specialize in roast meat or fish; **marisquerías** serve only fish and shellfish. Visit one in the countryside on a Sunday lunchtime when all the Spanish families go out to eat and make merry.

There are also many Chinese restaurants in Spain which are rarely good but usually inexpensive, and American fast-food outlets in the big cities and resort areas; while Italian restaurants are 98 per cent dismal in Spain, you can usually get a reasonable pizza. Don't neglect the rapidly disappearing shacks on the beach – they often serve up barbecued sardines that are out of this world. **Vegetarians** are catered for in the cities, which always manage to come up with one or two veggie restaurants, usually rather good ones too. In the countryside and away from the main resorts, proper vegetarians and vegans will find it hard going, though tapas make it easier to get your nutrition than in some other southern European countries. Navarra, perhaps the best producer of fruit and vegetables in Spain, is particularly good for veggies. Fish-eaters will manage just about everywhere.

What to Drink Where

No matter how much other costs have risen in Spain, **wine** has remained refreshingly inexpensive by northern European or American standards. What's more, the north produces much of Spain's best – the famous reds of La Rioja and a number of good whites from Galicia. A restaurant's *vino del lugar* or *vino de la casa* is always your least expensive option while dining out; it usually comes out of a barrel or glass jug and may be a surprise either way. Anyone with more than a passing interest in wine will want to visit a *bodega* or two. A good place to start would be Haro, the growing and marketing centre for the wines of Rioja Alta, with a clutch of *bodegas* near the train station (*see* p.124).

Northern Spain is not all wine, though. One bottle of Asturian **cider**, or *sidra*, is usually enough if you mean to do any walking afterwards; if not, the ritual of drinking it can make your evening. In any proper restaurant the waiter will hold the bottle over his head and pour it into a pint glass held behind his hip. The ones with the most *duende* do it without looking, splashing the stuff all over you, the floor, themselves, and people at three or four adjacent tables. This is done to air the stuff out; for the same reason they never put more than an inch in the glass, but it's a point of honour among them never to let your glass stay empty longer than fifteen seconds. In most bars they'll just leave the bottle (green, without a label and returnable) on the table and let you try it yourself. *Sidrerías* are the social centres of every Asturian town and village (there are also quite a few in Euskadi); to find one just follow your nose. In summer they migrate out on to the streets, and whole families gab around them until one in the morning, with small children bicycling between the tables.

Many Spaniards prefer **beer**, which is generally nondescript. The most popular brand is San Miguel, but try Mahou Five Star if you see it. Imported whisky and other **spirits** are pretty inexpensive, though even cheaper are the versions Spain bottles itself, which may come close to your home favourites.

Coffee, **tea**, all the international **soft drink** brands and the locally made Kas round off the average café fare. Spanish coffee is good and strong and if you want a lot of it order a *doble*; one of those will keep you awake even through the guided tour of a Bourbon palace. In summer look for the bars that make *blanco y negros* – coffee and ice cream treats that quickly become addictive in the hot sun. Ground almonds whipped to create *horchata de chufa* are also refreshing in summer.

Spanish Menu Reader

Entremeses (Hors d'œuvres)
aceitunas olives
ancas de rana frogs' legs
caldo broth
gambas pil pil shrimp in hot garlic sauce
gazpacho cold soup
huevos al plato fried eggs
huevos de flamenco baked eggs in tomato sauce
huevos revueltos scrambled eggs
sopa de ajo garlic soup
sopa de arroz rice soup
sopa de espárragos asparagus soup
sopa de fideos noodle soup
sopa de garbanzos chickpea soup
sopa de lentejas lentil soup
sopa de verduras vegetable soup
tortilla Spanish omelette, with potatoes
tortilla a la francesa French omelette

Pescados (Fish)
acedías small plaice
adobo fish marinated in white wine
almejas clams
anchoas anchovies
anguilas eels
angulas baby eels (elvers)
ástaco crayfish
atún tuna fish
bacalao codfish (usually dried)
besugo sea bream
bogavante lobster
bonito tunny
boquerones anchovies
caballa mackerel
calamares squid
cangrejo crab
centolo spider crab
chanquetes whitebait
chipirones baby squid
  ...en su tinta ...in its own ink
chirlas baby clams
cocochas hake cheeks
dorado sea bass
escabeche pickled or marinated fish
gambas prawns (shrimps)
langosta lobster
langostinos giant prawns
lenguado sole
lubina sea bass
mariscos shellfish
mejillones mussels
merluza hake
mero grouper
navajas razor-shell clams
ostras oysters
pejesapo monkfish
percebes barnacles
pescadilla whiting
pez espada swordfish
platija plaice
pulpo octopus
rape monkfish
raya skate
rodaballo turbot
salmón salmon
salmonete red mullet
sardinas sardines
trucha trout
ttoro Basque fish stew
veneras scallops
zarzuela fish stew

Carnes y Aves (Meat and Fowl)
  Note: *cazuelas, cocidos, estofados, guisados, fabadas* and *potajes* are all kinds of stew.

albóndigas meatballs
asado roast
bistec beefsteak
buey ox
callos tripe
cerdo pork
chorizo spiced sausage
chuletas chops
cochinillo suckling pig
cola de toro see under 'rabo'
conejo rabbit
corazón heart
cordero lamb
faisán pheasant
fiambres cold meats
filete fillet
hígado liver
jabalí wild boar
jamón de Bayonne cured ham
jamón de York baked ham
jamón iberico cured ham
jamón serrano raw cured ham
lengua tongue
liebre hare
lomo pork loin
morcilla blood sausage
paloma pigeon
pato duck
pavo turkey
perdiz partridge
pinchitos spicy mini-kebabs
pollo chicken
rabo/cola de toro bull's tail with onions and tomatoes
riñones kidneys
salchicha sausage
salchichón salami
sesos brains
solomillo sirloin steak
ternera veal

Verduras y Legumbres (Vegetables)
ajo garlic
alcachofa artichoke
apio celery
arroz rice
   ...a la marinera with saffron and seafood
berenjena aubergine (eggplant)
cebolla onion
champiñones mushrooms
col, repollo cabbage
coliflor cauliflower
endibia endive (chicory)
ensalada salad
espárragos asparagus
espinacas spinach
garbanzos chickpeas (garbanzo beans)
judías (verdes) French beans
lechuga lettuce
lentejas lentils
patatas potatoes
   ...fritas/salteadas ...fried/sautéed
   ...al horno ...baked
pepino cucumber
pimiento pepper
puerro leek
remolacha beetroot (beet)
setas Spanish mushrooms
zanahoria carrot

Frutas y Nueces (Fruit and Nuts)
albaricoque apricot
almendras almonds
avelanas hazelnuts
cacahuetes peanuts
castañas chestnuts
cerezas cherries
ciruelas plums
ciruelas pasas prunes
dátiles dates
durazno nectarine
frambuesas raspberries
fresas strawberries
fruta de la pasión passion fruit
granada pomegranate
grosellas redcurrants
grosellas o casis blackcurrants
higos figs
lima lime
limón lemon
mandarina mandarin
mango mango
manzana apple
melocotón peach
melón melon
membrillo quince
moras blackberries
naranja orange
nueces walnuts
pera pear

picotas black cherries
piña pineapple
plátano banana
pomelo grapefruit
sandía watermelon
uvas grapes

Postres (Desserts)
arroz con leche rice pudding
bizcocho/pastel/torta cake
blanco y negro ice cream and coffee float
canutillos rolls of flaky pastry filled with
   custard
flan crème caramel
galletas biscuits (cookies)
helado ice cream
pantxineta almondy *gâteau basque* filled
   with cream or cherry jam
pasteles pastries
queso cheese
requesón cottage cheese
tarta de frutas fruit pie
turrón nougat

Miscellaneous
aceite oil
arroz rice
azúcar sugar
ensalada salad
huevos eggs
mantequilla butter
pan bread
pimienta pepper
sal salt
vinagre vinegar

Bebidas (Drinks)
agua con hielo water with ice
agua mineral mineral water
   ...sin/con gas ...still/sparkling
batido de leche milkshake
botella (media) bottle (half)
brandy brandy
café (con leche) coffee (with milk)
caña draught (beer)
cava Spanish champagne
cerveza beer
chocolate caliente/hecho hot chocolate
dulce sweet (wine)
granizado slush, iced squash
hielo ice
leche milk
seco dry
semi-seco semi-dry
spumoso sparkling (wine)
té (con limón) tea (with lemon)
vaso glass
vino (tinto, rosado, blanco) wine (red,
   rosé, white)
zumo de manzana/naranja apple/orange juice

Planning
Your Trip

05

When to Go

Climate

You have just one guess to figure out what makes the north coast of Spain so luxuriantly green. The Cordillera Cantábrica stops all the weather fronts coming over the Atlantic and squeezes out all the precipitation; the coast gets between three and four inches of rain in August – and the real rainy season doesn't start until September. Galicia seems to get a bit less rain than the coastal regions to the east, and the high Castilian plains are climatically another world – hot and dry most of the year, chilly and strange in winter. La Rioja enjoys a more reasonable climate between the two extremes, which is very good for the vines. For the coast as a whole, rain is spread around the calendar; plenty of it falls from September to January, with July the most reliable month (only an inch or two, if you're lucky). The rain champion is the Basque coast, which can get seven or eight feet a year, as much as Wales or the west of Ireland.

Spring and summer are the best times to visit; winter can be pleasant, though damp and chilly. Most Spanish homes – and hotel rooms – are not made for the winter. High season is between June and September, when the ocean is warm enough for water sports, and the fiesta calendar is in full swing.

Festivals

One of the most spiritually deadening aspects of Francoism was the banning of many local and regional fiestas in Spain. These are now celebrated with gusto, and if you can arrange your trip to include one or two you'll be guaranteed an unforgettable holiday. The big holidays celebrated throughout Spain are *Corpus Christi* in late May or early June; Holy Week (*Semana Santa*), the

week preceding Easter; 15 August (the Assumption of the Virgin); and 25 July (the feast day of Spain's patron, Santiago). No matter where you are, there are bound to be fireworks or processions on these dates, especially for *Semana Santa* and *Corpus Christi*.

Many village patronal fiestas feature *romerías* (pilgrimages) up to a venerated shrine. Getting there is half the fun, with everyone in local costume, riding on horseback or driving covered wagons full of picnic supplies. Music, dancing, food, wine and fireworks are all necessary ingredients of a proper fiesta, while the bigger ones often include bullfights, funfairs, circuses and competitions. In the Basque lands and Navarra, summer fiestas often feature a loose bull or two stampeding through the streets – an *encierro*. 'Giants' (10ft-tall dummies of Ferdinand and Isabel and a Moor) and 'fatheads' (comical or grotesque caricatures) pirouette through the throngs.

The Calendar of Events opposite is by no means complete: during the summer every village has its own special fiesta.

Tourist Information

After receiving millions of tourists each year for the last four decades, no country has more information offices, or more helpful ones, or more intelligent brochures and detailed maps. Every city will have an office, and you will almost always find someone who speaks English except in rural areas. Sometimes they'll be less helpful in the big cities in the summer. More often, though, you'll be surprised at how well they know the details of accommodation and transportation. Many large cities also maintain municipal tourist offices, though they're not as well equipped as those run by the Ministry of Tourism, better known as *Turismo*. Opening hours for most offices are Monday to Friday, 9.30–1.30 and 4–7.

Nearly all the provinces in Northern Spain have websites for everything you might want to see and do; some are more informative than others. Try: *www.bilbao.net*, *www. infoasturias.com*, *www.navarra.es*, *www. spain.info*, *www.euskadi.net/turismo*, *www.liebanaypicosdeeuropa.com*, *www. turgalicia.es*, *www.turismodecantabria.com*.

Average Maximum Temperatures °C/°F

	Jan	April	July	Oct
San Sebastián	15/58	27/81	34/93	24/75
A Coruña	16/61	25/77	27/81	26/79

Average Monthly Rainfall mm/in

	Jan	April	July	Oct
San Sebastián	142/5.5	84/3.3	92/3.6	142/5.5
A Coruña	125/4.9	78/3	35/1.4	135/5.3

Calendar of Events

Note that many of these dates are subject to change (to fit weekends, etc.); a call ahead to the tourist office is always a good idea.

January

6 *Los Reyes* (the Three Kings or Magi) procession, Baiona (Pontevedra).

15 *San Mauro*, big fiesta with fireworks, Villanova de Arousa (Pontevedra).

19–20 St Sebastian's Day, *Tamborrada*, when scores of drum corps bang their way through the streets, followed by feasting, Donostia-San Sebastián (Guipúzcoa).

22 Fiesta, San Vicente de la Barquera (Cantabria).

Third Sun *San Vicente*, bachelors' party, Los Arcos (Navarra).

Last Mon and Tues *Zanpantzar*, pre-Christian dances of the *joaldunaks*, with pointed hats, sheepskins and big bells, Ituren and Zubieta (Navarra).

28 *San Tirso*, with dances and the burning of a papier-mâché *falla*, Villafranca del Bierzo (León).

30 *San Lesmes*, patron saint of Burgos.

February

Carnival A big affair everywhere in Spain. Some of the biggest celebrations are in Bilbao, Donostia-San Sebastián, Vitoria-Gasteiz and Tolosa (with a *pelota* championship). The entire week before Lent, Asturias puts on the biggest show in the northwest: at Avilés on Saturday and Tuesday; at Gijón on Monday; and in Oviedo on Tuesday, or Mardi Gras, the day before Ash Wednesday.

Every Sun Horse-racing in Donostia-San Sebastián.

March

Two Sundays after 4th *Javierada*, two important pilgrimages for St Francis Xavier, Javier (Navarra).

March–April

Palm Sunday Procession at Monte San Tecla, A Garda (Pontevedra).

Semana Santa (Easter/Holy Week) In the north, it's the Castilians who really get into the processions, especially at León and Covarrubias (Burgos). Good Friday brings *Los Picaos*, medieval-style self-flagellants, San Vicente de la Sonsierra (La Rioja); Descent from the Cross, Vivero (Lugo); mystery plays, Balsameda (Vizcaya), processions in Hondarribia and Segura (Guipúzcoa). In Avilés (Asturias), Easter and Easter Monday are celebrated with the *Fiesta del Bollo*, with folklore groups, cake-eating and regattas.

First Sun after Easter *Fiesta de San Telmo*, including bull-running on the beach, Zumaia (Guipúzcoa); San Vicente de Barquera's *La Folia*, where the sailors transport an image of the Virgin at night in an illuminated maritime procession (Cantabria).

April

2nd Sun after Easter *Fiesta de San Isidoro*, León.

2nd Mon after Easter *Fiesta de San Telmo*, Tui (Pontevedra).

19 *Fiesta de Santísimo Cristo*, Finisterre.

End April Wine Festival, Ribadavia (Ourense).

May

First weekend *Día de las Almadías*: rafts are built and floated downriver to commemorate the ancient method of log transport, followed by picnics in the Irati and Salazar Valleys (Navarra).

10–15 Saint's day and parades, Santo Domingo de la Calzada (La Rioja).

22 *Santa Rita*, Vilagarcía de Arousa (Pontevedra).

23 Anniversary of the Battle of Clavijo (La Rioja).

Corpus Christi Usually falls at the end of May or early June (Thursday after Trinity Sunday), initiating four days of festivities. Also, *Procesión del Olé*, with dances, Frómista (Palencia); flower carpets in the streets, Ponteareas (Pontevedra). On the first day after Corpus Christi, *Los Corpillos* dances and celebrations at Las Huelgas, Burgos; Maragato festivals, Astorga (León) and surrounding areas.

June

11 *San Bernabé*, with the distribution of grilled fish, Logroño (La Rioja).

12 *San Juan*, with *encierros*, giants and Maragato bagpipers, Sahagún (León).

21–24 *La Magdalena*, with Basque sports, Bermeo (Vizcaya), followed by a nautical *romería* to the isle of Izaro; *San Juan*, bonfires and fishwives' festivities in Laredo (Cantabria); for midsummer's day, 'bonfires of San Juan' in many Basque villages; León celebrates St John's Day with parties and bullfights; bonfire in Plaza Alfonso II, Oviedo (Asturias).

24 *Fiesta de San Juan*, Laguardia (Álava); *Vueltas de San Juan*, Nájera (La Rioja).

26 *Fiesta de San Pelayo*, Zarautz (Guipúzcoa).

End of June *San Felices de Bilibio*, pilgrimage and drunken 'wine battles', Haro (La Rioja);

La Semana Gastronómica, Donostia-San Sebastián; *La Amuravela*, satirical poems on the year's events in the local dialect and lots of drink, Cudillero (Asturias).

29 *Fiesta de San Pedro*, Orio and Zumaia (Guipúzcoa); wine battle, Haro (La Rioja); beginning of two weeks of International Folklore *Feria*, Burgos, San Pedro.

30 *Fiesta de San Marcial*, Irún (Guipúzcoa); *El Coso Blanco*, processions and fireworks, Castro Urdiales (Cantabria).

July

All month International Jazz Festival, the biggest in Spain, Donostia-San Sebastián.

All month Santander holds its International Music Festival.

First Sun *Rapa das Bestas* (Gallego wild horse round-ups, races and shearings), Viveiro and San Lorenzo de Sabucedo (Lugo). At La Estrada (Pontevedra), another *Rapa das Bestas*, with big festivities from Sat till Mon.

5–9 Getxo Jazz Festival, both international and national bands, Getxo (Vizcaya).

7–14 Famous running of the bulls and mad party for *San Fermín*, Pamplona (Navarra).

11 *San Benitiño de Lérez*, with river races and pageantry, Pontevedra (Galicia).

13 *Tributo de las Tres Vacas*, Piedra de San Martín, French mayors from the Baretous valley give Spanish mayors from the Roncal valley a tribute of three cows, renew their peace vows and name the keepers who will watch the common grazing land.

15 'Catch the goose' and other country fair-type festivities and humour, Comillas (Cantabria); Avilés (Asturias) has dances, entertainment and bullfights.

16 *Virgen del Carmen* with boat processions, Muros and Concubión (A Coruña).

Third week Jazz festival, Vitoria-Gasteiz (Álava).

Second fortnight International horse-racing competition, Donostia-San Sebastián.

Last half Historical sound and light pageant, Nájera (La Rioja).

22 Boat races, Basque sports and dancing, Bermeo (Vizcaya); *Fiesta de Santa María Magdalena*, Rentería (Guipúzcoa); fiesta with the dance of the *Zancos*, down the streets and steps on stilts, Anguiano (La Rioja).

24–30 *Santa Ana*, music and dancing for a week, Tudela (Navarra).

25 **Santiago de Compostela**, great celebrations for Santiago – national offering to the saint, the swinging of the *botafumeiro*, burning of a

cardboard replica of Córdoba's Mezquita, fireworks and more; *Romería de Saniaguiño do Monte*, with bagpipes and a sardine and pepper feast, Padrón (A Coruña); shepherds' festival, Cangas de Onís (Asturias). Also Vitoria and Bilbao's saint's day, Santiago.

Last Sun *Fiesta de la Playa*, Langosteira (Finisterre); *Fiesta de los Vaqueros*, La Braña de Aristébano, by Luarca (Asturias).

29 *Fiesta de San Pedro*, Mundaka (Vizcaya); *Vaqueiro* festival, mock wedding and dances, Luarca (Asturias); pilgrimage made in coffins by people who narrowly escaped death the year before, Santa María de Ribarteme (Pontevedra).

31 *Fiesta de San Ignacio*, Getxo (Vizcaya) and Azpeitia (Guipúzcoa).

August

3–9 Ancient fiesta, with giants, and the only *encierro* in Spain where women can run with the bulls, Estella (Navarra); Basque sport finals, Biarritz (Pays Basque).

First Sat Great kayak race on the Río Sella, Arriondas-Ribadesella (Asturias).

First Sun Asturias Day celebrations, with lots of folklore, Gijón. Festival of Albariño wine, Cambados (Pontevedra); Santa Cruz, Ribadeo (Lugo).

4–10 Giants, music, bonfires and more, for the *Virgen Blanca* – one of Spain's best parties (*see* p.176), Vitoria-Gasteiz (Álava).

6 *Fiesta de San Salvador*, Getaria (Guipúzcoa).

9–11 *San Lorenzo* festivities, folklore and kayaking, Foz (Lugo).

10 *San Juan Dantzak*, procession and traditional dancing, Berástegui (Guipúzcoa); International Celtic Music Festival, Cudillero.

Second Sun Mountain Day folklore, song contests, Cabezón de la Sal (Cantabria); octopus-eating festival and bagpipe music, Carballino (Ourense); *romería* to the Ermita de Oca, Villafranca de Montes de Oca (La Rioja).

15 *Zikiro-Jatea* festival in Zugurramurdi (Navarra) with a popular picnic held in the caves on the 17th.

15–16 *Fiesta de San Rocco*, Gernika (Vizcaya); on the Saturday after the 15th, Bilbao starts its *Aste Nagustia* or *Semana Grande* ('Great Week'), with Basque sports and races; a week-long international fireworks festival starts in Donostia-San Sebastián (Guipúzcoa); Assumption of the Virgin and San Roque festivities at Sada (A Coruña), with a big sardine roast; bagpipes and ancient dances, Llanes (Asturias); *El Rosario*, fisherman's fiesta, Luarca (Asturias).

15–19 Battle of flowers, Betanzos (A Coruña).

20 Running of the bulls, Tafalla.

26 *Festa da Istoria*, Ribadavia (Ourense); the whole village celebrates its origins with street pageantry and markets.

Last week Cider festival with free tasting and pouring competitions, Gijón (Asturias).

Last Sun Pilgrimage and music, Vivero (Lugo); *encierro*, Calahorra (La Rioja).

31 St Ignacio de Loyola Day, Loiola (Guipúzcoa); Battle of Flowers, Laredo (Cantabria).

September

First week Basque food festival, Donostia-San Sebastián (Guipúzcoa).

1–8 Festival with Basque 'goose games', a contest between boatmen to pull the head off a goose with a greased neck, Lekeitio (Vizcaya).

6–10 *Fiestas del Portal*, Ribadavia (Ourense).

7–8 *Encierro*, Ampuero (Cantabria).

7–10 Pilgrimage of *Nostra Señora da Barca*, Muxia (A Coruña).

2nd week Basque games, Zarautz (Guipúzcoa).

8 *Fiesta de la Virgen de Guadalupe*, Fuenterrabía (Guipúzcoa); Virgin's birthday, celebrations in many places; *Fiesta de la Virgen de la Encina*, Ponferrada (León); pilgrimage at Cebreiro (Lugo); *San Andreu*, Cervo (Lugo).

8–10 *Fiesta de Santa Eufemia*, Bermeo (Vizcaya).

12 International Film Festival, Donostia-San Sebastián.

14 Festival, Altsasu (Navarra).

16 Folk festival, Llanes (Asturias).

19 Vendimia wine festival of La Rioja, Logroño.

Second fortnight *Quincena Musicale*, classical music fortnight in Donostia-San Sebastián.

Third weekend Americas Day, celebrating the many immigrants to the Americas from Asturias, Oviedo.

29 *Fiesta de San Miguel*, Oñati (Guipúzcoa); traditional Basque dancing, Markina (Vizcaya).

Last weekend San Cosme y San Damián, with antique dances, Covarrubias (Burgos).

October

First Sun *Las Cantaderas*, with medieval song and a sacred dance, León.

13 *Fiesta de San Fausto*, Durango (Vizcaya).

Second Sun Shellfish festival, O Grove (Pontevedra).

18–20 *As San Lucas*, big horse fair dating from the Middle Ages, Mondoñedo (Lugo).

November

19 *Fiesta de San Andrés*, Estella (Navarra).

Last Sun Oyster festival, Arcade (Pontevedra).

December

13 *Santa Lucia* fair, Zumárraga (Guipúzcoa).

Last week *O Feitoman*, handicrafts fair, Vigo (Pontevedra); *Olentzero* processions in many Basque villages.

31 The 'National Offering to the Apostle' – a major religious ceremony with the *botafumeiro*, Santiago de Compostela.

Spanish National Tourist Offices

UK: 6th floor, 64 North Row, London W1K 7D, t 00 800 10 10 50 50, *www.spain.info/en_GB*.

USA: Water Tower Place, Suite 915 East, 845 North Michigan Avenue, Chicago, Illinois 60611, t (312) 642 1992, *www.okspain.org*; 8383 Wilshire Blvd, Suite 960, Beverly Hills, California 90211, t (323) 658 7188; 666 Fifth Avenue, New York, NY 10103, t (212) 265 8822; 1395 Brickell Avenue, Miami, Florida 33131, t (305) 358 1992.

Canada: 2 Bloor St West, Suite 3402, Toronto, Ontario, M4W 3E2, t (416) 961 3131, *www.spain.info/ca*.

Japan: Daini Toranomon Denki Building, 6F, 3-1-10 Toranomon, Minato Ku, Tokyo 105-0001, t + 81 (3) 3432 6141, *www.spain.info/jp*.

Provides information for Australian and New Zealand nationals as well as Japanese.

Embassies and Consulates

Foreign Embassies, etc. in Spain

UK: Alameda Urquijo 2, Bilbao, t 94 415 76 00, *www.ukinspain.com*.

Ireland: C/Elcano 5, Bilbao, t 94 423 04 14.

USA: C/Serrano 75, Madrid, t 91 587 22 00. Consulate: Paseo de la Castellana 52, *www.embusa.es*.

Canada: C/Núñez de Balboa 35, Madrid, t 91 423 32 50, *www.canadainternational.gc.ca*.

Spanish Embassies, etc. Abroad

UK: 20 Draycott Place, London SW3 2RZ, t (020) 7589 8989; 1a Brook House, 70 Spring Gardens, Manchester M2 2BQ, t (0161) 236

1262; 63 North Castle Street, Edinburgh EH2 3LJ, **t** (0131) 220 1843.

Ireland: 17a Merlyn Park, Ballsbridge, Dublin 4, **t** (01) 269 1640.

USA: 31 St James Ave, Suite 905, Boston, MA 02116, **t** (617) 536 2506; 180 North Michigan Avenue, Chicago, IL 60601, **t** (312) 782 4588; 2655 Le Jeune Road, 203 Coral Gables, Miami, FL, **t** (305) 446 5511; 5055 Wilshire Blvd, Suite 960 Los Angeles, CA 90036, **t** (323) 938 0158; 150 East 58th Street, New York, NY 10155, **t** (212) 355 4080; 2375 Pennyslvania Avenue NW, Washington, DC 20009, **t** (202) 728 2330.

Canada: 1 West Mount Square, Montreal H3Z 2P9, **t** (514) 935 5235; 200 Front Street, Toronto, Ontario, **t** (416) 977 1661.

Entry Formalities

Passports and Visas

Holders of EU, US, Canadian, Australian and New Zealand passports do not need a visa to enter Spain for stays of up to three months; most other nationals do.

If you intend staying longer in Spain, you should report to the Foreign Nationals Office (*oficina de extranjeros*). Non-EU citizens should apply for a resident's card (*tarjeta de residente comunitario*). EU citizens will be issued with a printed Residence Certificate stating name, address, nationality, NIE number (*Número de Identificación Extranjeros*) and date of registration. Non-EU citizens had best apply for an extended visa at home, a complicated procedure requiring proof of income, etc. You can't get a *tarjeta* without this visa.

Customs

Duty-free allowances have been abolished within the EU. **EU nationals** over the age of 17 can now import a limitless amount of goods for their personal use. For travellers coming from **outside the EU**, the duty-free limits are one litre of spirits or two litres of liquors (port, sherry or champagne), plus two litres of wine and 200 cigarettes. Much larger quantities – up to 10 litres of spirits, 90 litres of wine, 110 litres of beer and 3,200 cigarettes – bought locally and provided you are travelling between EU countries, can be taken through customs if you can prove that they are for private consumption only.

Residents of the USA may each take home US$400-worth of foreign goods without attracting duty, including the tobacco and alcohol allowance. Canadians can bring home $300 worth of goods in a year, plus their tobacco and alcohol allowances.

Disability Organizations

Spain

ECOM, Gran Vía 562, Barcelona, **t** 93 451 55 50, *www.ecom.es*. A federation of private Spanish organizations that offer services for disabled people.

ONCE (Organización Nacional de Ciegos de España), C/José Ortega y Gasset 18, **t** 91 577 37 56, *www.once.es*. Association for the blind.

UK

Access Travel, 6 The Hillock, Astley, Lancashire M29 7GW, **t** (01942) 88 88 44, *www.access-travel.co.uk*. Travel agent for disabled people.

Tourism for All, Hawkins Suite, Enham Place, Enham Alamein, Andover, Hants SP11 6JS, **t** 0845 124 9971, *www.holidaycare.org.uk*.

RADAR (Royal Association for Disability and Rehabilitation), Unit 12, City Forum, 250 City Road, London EC1V 8AF, **t** (020) 7250 3222, *www.radar.org.uk*. Open Mon–Fri 10–4.

RNIB (Royal National Institute of the Blind), 105 Judd Street, London WC1H 9NE, **t** 0845 766 9999, *www.rnib.org.uk*.

USA

Alternative Leisure Co., 165 Middlesex Turnpike, Suite 206, Bedford, MA 01730, USA **t** (718) 275 0023, *www.alctrips.com*. Organizes vacations abroad for disabled people.

American Foundation for the Blind, 2 Penn Plaza, Suite 1102, New York, NY 10121, **t** (212) 502 7600, or **t** 800 232 5463, *www.afb.org*.

Mobility International USA, 132 Broadway, Suite 343, Eugene, OR 97440, **t** (541) 343 1284, *www.miusa.org*. International educational exchange programmes and volunteer service overseas for the disabled.

SATH (Society for Accessible Travel and Hospitality), 347 5th Ave, Suite 610, New York, NY 10016, **t** (212) 447 7284, *www.sath.org*. Travel and access information; also details other access resources on the web.

Disabled Travellers

Eurotunnel is a good way to travel to northern Spain by car from the UK, since passengers are allowed to stay in their vehicles. By train, **Eurostar** gives wheelchair passengers first-class travel for second-class fares. Most **ferry** companies will offer special facilities if contacted beforehand. Vehicles fitted to accommodate disabilities pay reduced tolls on *autoroutes* through France.

Once you arrive, the facilities for disabled travellers are limited. Spanish public transport is not particularly wheelchair-friendly, though the rail operator RENFE usually provides wheelchairs at main city stations, and many trains are slowly being upgraded to provide accessible services (lift access to platforms, etc.). The Spanish Tourist Office has compiled a fact sheet and can give general information on accessible accommodation; more useful is the official Spanish hotel guide (*Guía Oficial de Hoteles*), published annually, which covers hotels throughout the country (available in most bookshops, €14). For wheelchair-accessible beaches, see *www.esplaya.com*.

Insurance and EHIC Cards

No inoculations are required to enter Spain, though it never hurts to check that your tetanus jab is up to date.

Citizens of the EU are entitled to a certain amount of free medical care in EU countries if they have a free **European Health Insurance Card** or **EHIC** (available online at *www.dh. gov.uk/travellers*, or *www.ehic.org.uk*, or by calling **t** 0845 605 0707, or by post using the forms available from post offices). You will need a card for every family member.

If you need urgent medical treatment while in Spain, ensure that you are taken to a public hospital or clinic and show your EHIC card on arrival. Private healthcare is not covered by the EHIC card. Note that dentistry, even emergency dentistry, is not covered by the reciprocal agreements. Canadians, US citizens and those of other nations should check their individual health policies.

As an alternative, consider a **travel insurance** policy covering theft and losses and offering 100 per cent medical refund plus repatriation costs if necessary; check to see if it covers extra expenses if you get bogged down in airport or train strikes. Beware that accidents resulting from sports are rarely covered by ordinary insurance. Make sure you save all doctor's and pharmacy receipts, plus police reports for thefts.

Maps

Cartography has been an art in Spain since the 12th-century Catalans charted their Mediterranean Empire in Europe's first great school of map-making. The tourist offices give out detailed maps of every town. Unfortunately, for rural areas you will not find the detail you need for serious exploration of the countryside, and Spanish signposting isn't all it could be.

The maps available in Britain and America aren't very good, and you won't find much better general maps in Spain. On most, the road system in particular will be out of date, thanks to Spain's ambitious road improvement programmes. Topographical maps for hikers and mountaineers can be obtained from **CNIG** (Centro Nacional de Información Geográfica), part of the Instituto Geográfico Nacional (IGN). There are shops in all provincial capitals, and their maps are usually available in larger bookshops. You can buy maps and travel books online from the Spanish travel bookshop **Altaïr**, *www.altair.es*.

If in the UK, visit **Stanfords** at 12 Long Acre, WC2, for the biggest selection, or you can buy online at *www.stanfords.co.uk*.

Money and Banks

The currency of Spain is the **euro**. Coins are issued in denominations of 1, 2, 5, 10, 20 and 50 cents, and 1 and 2 euros. Notes are issued in denominations of 5, 10, 20, 50, 100, 200 and 500 euros. For the latest **exchange rates**, check out *www.xe.com*.

Traveller's cheques are the safest way to carry money. Major international **credit cards** are widely used in Spain, although American Express is often not accepted and Diners' Club cards almost never. For purchases, you will have to show some ID (a passport or identity card) when using a card. Smaller hotels, *pensiones*, restaurants, bars and cafés, particularly in rural areas, won't accept credit cards. Museums and sights still almost never have credit card facilities.

Cash withdrawals in euros can be made from bank and post office automatic cash machines (**ATMs**) using your PIN; the specific cards accepted are marked on each machine, and all give instructions in English. Credit card companies charge a fee for cash, but exchange rates are often better than banks.

Most banks will change **traveller's cheques** and cash, and are open Mon–Fri 9–2; a few open late (until 4pm) on Thursday afternoons. Pre-paid holiday cards have become popular, but shop around before you purchase as fees and charges vary widely. You can usually change money at travel agencies, fancy hotels, restaurants, stations and big department stores like El Corte Inglés. Exchange rates vary, and nearly all take a commission of varying proportions. Beware of private exchange offices in tourist areas, which can be a rip-off despite the 'no commission' sign.

Getting There
By Air

There is an astounding variety of flight options to Spain these days, especially from the **UK**. A high-season **scheduled** return costs from around £80 on a no-frills carrier, and up to around £200 on a national airline. However, even British Airways and Iberia offer special deals. No matter how you go, you can always save by booking in advance.

There are international **airports** in Bilbao, Santander, Santiago de Compostela and Asturias/Oviedo, and smaller airports that receive internal flights in San Sebastián, A Coruña, Pamplona, Vitoria, Vigo and Hondarribia.

British Airways has a daily flight to Bilbao from London Heathrow (code-sharing with Iberia).

easyJet operates daily flights to Bilbao from London Stansted (twice daily in summer) and a daily flight to Asturias; they also have a

Airline Carriers

UK

British Airways, t 0844 493 0787, *www.ba.com*.
easyJet, t 0843 104 5000, *www.easyjet.com*.
Iberia, t 08706 090 500, *www.iberia.com*.
Ryanair, t 0871 246 0000, *www.ryanair.com*.
Vueling, t 0906 754 7541, *www.vueling.com*.

USA and Canada

Air Canada, t 1-888 247 2262, *www.aircanada.ca*.
American Airlines, t 1-800 433 7300, *www.aa.com*.
British Airways, t 1-800 247 9297, *www.ba.com*.
Continental Airlines, t 1-800 231 0856, *www.continental.com*.
Delta, t 1-800 221 1212, *www.delta.com*.
Iberia, t 1-800 772 4642, *www.iberia.com*.
United Airlines, t 1-800 864 8331, *www.ual.com*.

Discounts and Special Deals

The best deals are almost always available online, particularly if you book well in advance. Check the small print, particularly 'administration fees', before booking.

Useful **websites** include: *ww.skyscanner.com*; *www.momondo.com*; *www.justfares.com*;
www.flyaow.com; *www.air-fare.com*; *www.cheapflights.com*; *www.expedia.com*; *www.travelocity.com*; *www.orbitz.com*; *www.priceline.com* (bid for low-cost airline tickets and hotels); *www.smartertravel.com*; *www.sidestep.com*.

UK and Ireland

CIE Tours International, Ireland **t** (01) 703 1888, *www.cietours.ie*.
Flightbookers, UK **t** 0821 223 5000, *www.ebookers.com*.
Trailfinders, UK **t** 08450 58 58 58, *www.trailfinders.com*.
Joe Walsh Tours, Ireland **t** (01) 241 0800, *www.joewalshtours.ie*.

USA and Canada

Air Brokers International, USA **t** 800 883 3273, *www.airbrokers.com*.
Last Minute Travel Club, USA **t** 1-888 868 7722, Canada **t** 877 970 3500, *www.lastminuteclub.com*. Payment of an annual membership fee gets you cheap standby deals; there are also special rates for the major car rental companies in Europe, and train tickets.
Club ABC Tours, 200 Broadacres Drive, Bloomfield, NJ 07003, **t** 1-888 868 7722, *www.clubabc.com*.

www.traveldiscounts.com. Members get special discount rates on flights, hotels and tours.
www.orbitz.com. Cheap flights, hotels and car rental companies.

Student Discounts

Students and under-26s are eligible for considerable reductions on flights, train fares, admission fees to museums, concerts and more. Agencies specializing in youth travel can help you apply for the correct ID cards.

Europe Student Travel, 6 Campden Street, London W8, **t** (020) 7727 7647.

STA Travel, *www.sta-travel.com*/*www.statravel. co.uk*. Has over 450 branches in countries all over the world, including more than 50 in the UK. Check the website, or call intersales: UK **t** 0871 230 0040; USA **t** 1-800 781 4040.

Travel Cuts, 187 College St, Toronto, Ontario M5T 1P7, **t** 1-866 246 9762, *www.travelcuts.com*. Canada's largest student travel specialist.

USIT, Aston Quay, Dublin 2, **t** (01) 602 1906, *www.usit.ie*. Also: Belfast, **t** (028) 903 27111; Cork, **t** (021) 427 0900; Galway, **t** (091) 565 177; Limerick, **t** (061) 415 064; Waterford, **t** (051) 351 762.

service from Manchester to Bilbao (three days a week).

Iberia flies direct to Bilbao from London Heathrow daily, and to Bilbao via Barcelona or Madrid from Manchester. There are connections with major UK cities via London Heathrow. Also direct flights to Santiago de Compostela and to Santander, Vitoria-Gasteiz, Pamplona, Vigo, Donostia-San Sebastián and A Coruña (via Madrid or Barcelona).

Ryanair has flights to Santander, Vitoria and Santiago de Compostela from London Stansted.

Vueling fly from London Heathrow to Bilbao, and offer summer-only services to A Coruña and Vigo.

There are no direct flights to northern Spain from the **USA and Canada**, but numerous carriers fly direct to Madrid, Barcelona and Paris. A high-season return will cost around US$1,100–2,000. Alternatively, it may be cheaper to fly to London and pick up an onward flight to Spain from there, especially off-season (October–April).

By Train

Travelling by high-speed train makes an attractive alternative to flying from the UK. **Eurostar** departs from London St Pancras with direct connections to Paris (Gare du Nord; 2hrs 15mins) and Lille (1hr 40mins). Fares are cheaper if booked in advance and/or include a Saturday night away. You must check in at least 30mins before departure or you will not be allowed on the train. Prices

range from around £55 (more than 21 days in advance) to £300 for a standard return.

Once you reach Paris or Lille, France's high-speed **TGVs** (*trains à grande vitesse*) shoot along at an average of 180mph, when they're not breaking world records. From London to Bilbao or Donostia-San Sebastián it's a full day's trip, changing trains in Paris and usually at Bordeaux or Hendaye in the small hours of the morning. For Bilbao you will have to change at Donostia-San Sebastián for the slow but scenic **EuskoTren** service, which takes 2½ hours. The TGV service from Paris to Bordeaux can cut some hours off the trip if the schedule works for you. Another option is to take a direct train from Paris to Vitoria-Gasteiz, and take a bus or local train from there. Spain is currently expanding its high-speed AVE network, which will cut travel times considerably (the completion date is currently 2020, although some sections will open from 2013).

If you plan to take some long train journeys, it may be worth investing in a **rail pass**. The good-value **Inter-Rail Global Pass**, *www.interrail.net* (for European residents of at least six months) offers 15 days', 22 days' or one month's unlimited travel in Europe, plus discounts on trains to cross-Channel ferry terminals, and returns on Eurostar from £59. Inter-Rail cards are not valid on UK trains. You can also get an **Inter-Rail One Country Pass** for three days (£169, under-26s £114) or eight days (£229, under 26s £173).

Visitors from North America have a wide choice of passes, including **Eurailpass**, **Europass** and **France 'n' Spain Pass**, which can all be purchased in the USA. A one-month

Eurailpass costs around $995/1,110 for those aged under/over 26 years. There are also **Senior Passes** for the over-60s.

Note that rail passes are not valid on Spain's numerous narrow-gauge (FEVE) lines; you will also have to pay supplements for any kind of express train. For information on Spanish trains, see p.67.

For long-distance train travel, **bicycles** need to be transported separately and must be registered and insured. They can be delivered to your destination, though this may take several days. On Eurostar you need to check in your bike at least 24 hours before you travel, or wait 24 hours at the other end. For more details, call **t** 08705 186 186.

Rail Europe books all services, including Eurostar and French Motorail (trains that carry your car), and sells passes.

Rail Europe (UK), 1 Lower Regent St, London SW1Y 4XT, **t** 08448 484 064, www.raileurope.co.uk.

Rail Europe (USA), **t** 1-800 622 8600; Canada **t** 1-800 361 7245, www.raileurope.com.

Eurostar, t 08705 186 186, www.eurostar.com.

By Coach

Eurolines offers departures several times a week in the summer (once a week out of season) from London to Spain (although most require a change, usually in Paris or Tours), along the east coast as far as Alicante, or to Algeciras via Donostia-San Sebastián and Burgos. From either Donostia-San Sebastián or Burgos, it will be easy to find further connections to any other town in the northwest. The journey time from London to Donostia-San Sebastián is 22 hours. The fare goes from £99–149 return, or to Vitoria-Gasteiz and Burgos from £85–120.

There are discounts for anyone under 26, senior citizens and children under 12. The national coach companies operate services that connect with the local bus system.

Eurolines, t 08717 818181, www.eurolines.com.

By Sea

The ferry port is at Santurzi, 13km from the centre of Bilbao. Brittany Ferries runs from Portsmouth to Bilbao.

Ferry Companies

Brittany Ferries, t 0871 244 0744, www.brittany-ferries.co.uk. Ferries from Portsmouth to Bilbao; fares vary throughout the year. A high-season return for two adults, two children and a car in an outside 4-berth cabin currently costs £748. From Portsmouth, they also operate services to Santander, Caen, Cherbourg, Roscoff and St Malo; from Plymouth, there are services to Santander and to St Malo.

Eurotunnel, t 08443 35 35 35, www.eurotunnel.com. Operates the shuttle through the Channel Tunnel, Folkestone to Calais.

DFDS Ferries, t (020) 8127 8303, www.dfdsseaways.com. Dover to Dunkirk.

P&O Ferries, t 08716 642 121, www.poferries.com. Dover to Calais; Hull to Rotterdam or Zeebrugge.

Seafrance, t 0871 423 7119, www.seafrance.co.uk. Dover to Calais.

If you prefer to cross the Channel to France, it is cheapest by ferry from Dover, but quickest via the Channel Tunnel. For ferries, check out www.directferries.co.uk, and try price-comparison websites such as www.ferrysmart.co.uk and www.ferrybooker.com.

By Car

From the UK via France you have a choice of routes. If you get a ferry (see above) or the Eurotunnel train (see below) to Calais, you may face going through or around Paris on the abominable périphérique, a task best tackled either side of rush hour. To avoid this, you can get a ferry from Portsmouth to Cherbourg, Caen, Roscoff or St-Malo (see above). From any of these ports, the most direct route takes you to Bordeaux down the western coast of France, past Biarritz to the border at Irún and on to Donostia-San Sebastián and Bilbao. For something different, opt for one of the routes the pilgrims to Santiago followed over the Pyrenees, through Somport-Canfranc (down the N134/E7/N330 south of Pau) or the classic route through Roncesvalles (on the D933 from St-Jean-Pied-de-Port) – you can get warmed up for Spain by inspecting the French Basque country along the way.

You may find it less tiring to take the ferry from Plymouth to Santander, which cuts out

Drivers' Clubs

For more information on driving abroad, contact the AA, RAC or, in the USA, the AAA:

AA, t 0870 600 0371, *www.theaa.com.*

RAC, t 0870 572 2722, *www.rac.co.uk.*

AAA (USA), **t** 800 222 4357, *www.aaa.com.*

driving through France and saves expensive *autoroute* tolls.

Eurotunnel trains carry cars and their passengers through the Channel Tunnel from Folkestone to Calais on a simple drive-on, drive-off system (journey time 35mins). Payment is made at toll booths (which accept cash, cheques or credit cards). Prepaid tickets and booked spaces are available, but at off-peak times you can just turn up and take the next available service. Eurotunnel runs 24 hours a day, all year round, with a service at least once an hour through the night. Return fares range from around £84 (5-day return fare) to £398 (fully flexible return fare).

Drivers must carry **registration** and **insurance** papers. If you're coming from the UK or Ireland, the dip of the **headlights** must be adjusted to the right (you can buy patches to stick on headlights). Carrying a **warning triangle** is mandatory, and it should be placed 50m (55 yards) behind the car if you have a breakdown. **Seat belts** are also mandatory; in addition, all cars in France and Spain are required to have rear seat belts and these must be worn by rear seat passengers. Drivers with a valid **photo licence** from the EU , Canada, the USA or Australia don't need an international licence for Spain or France.

Eurotunnel, info and bookings **t** 08443 35 35 35, *www.eurotunnel.com.*

Getting Around

If you're using public transport, there is usually an even choice between the bus and train. Buses are usually cheaper, and often faster, and are often the only way to reach smaller towns and villages. However, for long distances, trains are usually faster. High-speed services throughout Spain are being substantially improved, and the government aims to bring all provincial cities within three hours' train journey of the capital by 2020.

By Train

Democracy in Spain has made the trains run on time, but western Europe's most eccentric railway, RENFE, still has a way to go. The problem isn't the trains themselves – they're almost always clean and comfortable, and do their best to keep to the schedules – but that the RENFE network remains phenomenally complex.

There are basically four kinds of train service: the high-speed inter-city AVE trains (Alto Velocidad Española, which means Spanish High Speed); fast inter-city services with a bewildering variety of names including Talgo, Alvia, Estrella and Diurno; the slower and less expensive *regionales*, which link major towns and cities; and *cercanías*, which are local services connected to a major hub like Bilbao.

To add to the confusion, northern Spain has two private narrow-gauge railway lines: in Euskadi, the **EuskoTren** (Basque Railways) connects Bilbao and Donostia-San Sebastián by way of Zarautz and Zumaia; and **FEVE** has tracks along the north coast of Spain connecting Bilbao to Oviedo via Santander. Both these lines show off rural Spanish life and scenery at their best. See 'Rail Excursions', overleaf. Passes are not valid.

Every variety of train has different services and a different price – yet the system is efficient, albeit confusing for the visitor. There are **discounts** for children, large families, senior citizens and regular travellers. If you buy a single ticket, hang on to it, because if you decide to return you are still elegible for a discount. The under-26s in possession of a *tarjeta joven* (youth card) issued in Spain or abroad are elegible for discounts.

Every city has a RENFE travel office in the centre, and you can make good use of these for information and tickets. Always buy tickets in advance if you can; one of RENFE's little tricks is to close station ticket-windows 10 minutes before your train arrives. You can also book tickets online, or by telephone.

RENFE, t 902 320 320, *www.renfe.com* (website has timetables, types of ticket available and fares, also in English). For international trains, visit *www.elipsos.com.*

Rail Excursions

FEVE has inaugurated a series of special trains designed to attract tourists. One of these, the luxurious **Transcantábrica**, takes in some of the loveliest parts of northern Spain, including the Picos de Europa; see *www.eltranscantabricoclasico.com*. For other FEVE rail tours, including the week-long **El Expresso de la Roble** tours (two in Galicia, and one in Castile-Léon), see *www.elexpresodelarobla.com*.

The **EuskoTren** narrow-gauge line maintains an electric train from the 1920s with wooden carriages, and runs it in summer for excursions around Donostia-San Sebastián; ask at the EuskoTren station there for details.

By Bus

Like the trains, buses in Spain are cheap by northern European standards. Usually, whether you go by train or bus will depend on simple convenience: in some places the train station is a long way from the centre; in others the bus station is out of town. Small towns and villages can normally be reached by bus only through their provincial capitals.

With literally hundreds of companies providing services all over Spain, expect confusion. Most bus stations have an information point (although it is unlikely you will find an English-speaker) which will provide you with schedules and fare information. Buy tickets from the window dedicated to the company providing the service. Tourist offices are the best sources of information.

By City Bus and Taxi

Every Spanish city has a perfectly adequate system of public transport. You won't need to make much use of it, though, for even in the bigger cities nearly all attractions are within walking distance.

City buses usually cost around €1, and if you intend using them often there are books of tickets called *bono-Bús* or *abonamiento*, or *tarjeta* cards to punch on entry, available cheaper from tobacconists (*estancos*). Bus drivers will give change (although most will only accept notes up to the value of €10). In most cities, the entire route will be displayed on the signs at each bus stop (*parada*).

Taxis are cheap enough for the Spaniards to use them regularly on their shopping trips. The average fare for a ride within a city will be €10–15. Taxis are metered and the drivers are usually quite honest; they are entitled to certain surcharges (for luggage, night or holiday trips, to the train or airport, etc.), and if you cross the city limits they can usually charge double the fare shown. It's rarely hard to hail a cab from the street, and there will always be a few around the stations. If you get stuck where there is none, or in a small village, call information (t 11811 is just one of the numbers in Spain for directory enquiries) for the number of a radio taxi. If you call a radio taxi, be aware that the fare will start as the taxi-driver makes his way to you.

By Car

This is probably the most pleasurable way of getting about, though the convenience is balanced by a considerable cost. **Petrol** is less expensive in Spain than most places in Europe but not by much. In cities, **parking** is often difficult; another problem is that only a few hotels – the more expensive ones – have garages or any sort of parking.

Spain's **highway network** is good, and many major cities are now linked by motorways (called *autovías* or, if a toll is charged, *autopistas*) or dual carriageways. The government has invested a considerable sum on a full-scale motorway system, including one following the entire length of the northern coast. Oviedo sits at a motorway hub, which links it with Bilbao to the east, and León and Madrid to the south, with another motorway linking A Coruña and Vigo with Oporto and Lisbon. In some rural areas in western Asturias or Galicia, the road will suddenly disappear, leaving you stranded on a hellish road little better than a mule track, crammed with heavy trucks. The other motorist's nightmare is the Bilbao area; even if you're passing through, you'll probably get lost among the endless roadworks and bizarre topography. Be warned that tolls on the motorways (*autopistas*) are sheer highway robbery.

See p.67 for **driving regulations** in Spain. The **speed limit** in Spain is 120kph (75mph) on the *autopistas*, and 100kph (62mph) on all other national highways unless marked.

Car Hire Companies

Auto Europe, UK t 0800 223 5555, USA t 1-800 223 5555, Spain t 900 801 879, *www.autoeurope.com.*

Atesa, Spain t 902 100 101, *www.atesa.es.*

Avis, UK t 0844 581 0147, Spain t 94 427 57 60, *www.avis.com.*

Budget, UK t 08701 56 56 56, USA t 800 527 0700, Spain t 902 112 585, *www.budget.com.*

Europcar, UK t 08706 075 000, USA t 877 940 6900, Spain t 902 105 055, *www.europcar.com.*

Hertz, in UK t 08708 44 88 44, Spain t 91 749 77 78, *www.hertz.com.*

Holiday Autos, UK t 0870 400 4461, Spain t 902 887 210, *www.holidayautos.com.*

Car Hire

This is slightly cheaper in **Spain** than elsewhere in Europe. Most of the big inter-national companies are expensive, but budget firms like Auto Europe, Holiday Autos and Atesa offer cheaper rates. Prices for the smallest cars begin at about €300 (£260) per week with unlimited mileage, but full insur-ance can add considerably to the costs. Small local firms can sometimes offer a better deal, but should be treated with some caution.

Car hire can also be booked through most of the airlines when you purchase your ticket. This is often the cheapest option.

Check out rental prices on price comparison websites such as *www.comparecarhire.co.uk*, but carefully check hidden charges.

By Bicycle

Cycling is taken extremely seriously in Spain but you don't often see people using a bike as a form of transport. This is changing slowly, and some cities, particularly Bilbao, are laying out new bike lanes and even operate a city-wide bike rental scheme. But cycling is still most widely practiced by Lycra-clad enthusiasts pedalling furiously up the steepest of hills on weekends, causing dire traffic hazards while they strive to reach the standards set by Miguel Indurain and Carlos Sastre, former winners of the Tour de France. In summer the moderate climate of the Basque lands, Cantabria, Asturias and Galicia, plus their greenery and network of coastal secondary roads, make them perfect spots for cycling. It's probably the current transport of choice among pilgrims to Santiago; pedalling across the frying pan of northern Castile in August is, appropriately, a lot like purgatory.

The main towns and holiday centres always seem to have at least one shop that hires out mountain bikes (BTT in Spanish) or touring/racing bikes; local tourist offices have lists. Do take into account how fit you are. Wear a helmet.

Maps and information are available from the following federations and clubs:

Real Federación Española de Ciclismo, C/Ferraz 16, 28008 Madrid, t 91 540 08 41, *www.rfec.com.*

Cyclists' Touring Club, Parklands, Railton Rd, Guildford, Surrey, t 0844 736 8450, *www.ctc.org.uk.*

On Foot

Spain has a network of long-distance paths, the *Gran Recorridos*, but they are often poorly marked on the ground, the guides which cover them are usually out-of-date, and the paths are not marked on most maps.

Hitchhiking involves a long wait; few Spaniards ever do it and it is not recom-mended.

If you are planning on following some or all of the pilgrimage route of the Camino de Santiago, *see* pp.34–9.

Where to Stay

Hotels in Spain are no longer the bargains they once were. However, overall rates are still pretty reasonable, and there are still some great deals to be found. For those travelling on a tight budget, there are plenty of *hostales* (generally one- or two-star places), rooms over bars, and rooms in private homes. Room prices must be posted in hotel

Accommodation Price Ranges

Note that prices listed here and elsewhere in this book are for a double room in high season.

luxury	€€€€€	over €200
very expensive	€€€€	€160–200
expensive	€€€	€120–160
moderate	€€	€80–120
inexpensive	€	under €80

lobbies and in rooms, and if there's a problem you can ask for the complaints book (*Libro de Reclamaciones*).

The prices given in this guide do not include **VAT** (IVA), charged at 8 per cent. **Prices** for single rooms will average about 60 per cent of a double, while triples or an extra bed are around 35 per cent more. Within the price ranges shown, the most expensive are likely to be in the big cities, while the cheapest are in provincial towns or villages.

If you're travelling around a lot, a good investment would be the government publication *Guía de Hoteles*, a great fat book with every classified hotel and *hostal* in Spain, available in most bookshops (€14). The government also publishes similar guides to holiday flats (*apartamentos turísticos*) and campsites. Local tourist offices have complete accommodation lists.

Paradores

The government, in its plan to develop tourism in the 1950s, started this nationwide chain of classy hotels to draw attention to little-visited areas. They restored old palaces, castles and monasteries for the purpose, furnished them with antiques and installed fine restaurants featuring local specialities.

Paradores for many people are one of the best reasons for visiting Spain. Not all are historic landmarks; in resort areas, they are as likely to be cleanly designed modern buildings, usually in a good location with a pool and some sports facilities. As their popularity has increased, so have their prices; in most cases both the rooms and the restaurant will be the most expensive in town, though most offer substantial off-season discounts.

Parador Booking

Spain: Head office, C/Requena 3, 28013 Madrid **t** 91 516 66 66.
UK: Keytel International, 156 Blackfriars Rd, London SE1 8EN, **t** (020) 7953 3020, *www.keytel.co.uk*.
USA: Marketing Ahead Inc., 381 Park Avenue, South Suite 718, New York, NY 10016, **t** 800 223 1356, *www.marketingahead.com*.

More information is available online at *www.parador.es*. Look out for special offers.

There are also discounts for the over-55s and the under-35s (but these must be booked in advance, see under 'Offers and Promotions' at *www.parador.es*). There is also a good-value pass called the Five-night Card, offering five nights in any *parador* for a discounted price. Note that you will have to book months in advance for the most popular *paradores*, including the famous one in the Hostal dos Reis Católicos in Santiago de Compostela.

Hoteles

Hoteles (H) are rated from one to five stars, according to the services they offer. These are the most expensive places, and even a one-star hotel will be a comfortable, middle-range establishment. Many of the more expensive hotels have some rooms available at prices lower than those listed; you'll have to ask. You can often get discounts in the off season but will be charged higher rates during big festivals. If you want to attend any of these big events, be sure to book as far in advance as possible.

Hostales, Pensiones and Fondas

Hostales (Hs) are rated with from one to three stars. *Pensiones* and *fondas* no longer have an official category, but many establishments still bear the name. Like *hostales*, these are usually more modest places, often a floor in an apartment block; a two-star *hostal* is roughly equivalent to a one-star hotel, but not always. A few may require full- or half-board in high season. *Hostales* and *pensiones* with one or two stars will often have cheaper rooms without private baths.

You can also ask in bars or at the tourist office for unidentified *casas particulares*, private houses with a room or two. In fact, in most towns and resorts you will not have to look at all. Someone will probably find you in the bus or train station, and ask if you need a room. Almost all of these will be pleasant enough. Prices are usually negotiable (before you are taken to the place). Always make sure the location suits you – 'five minutes away' can mean five minutes on foot or in a car. In many villages these rooms will be the only accommodation on offer, but they're usually clean. In cities, the best places to look are right in the centre, not around the stations. Some may ask you to pay a day in advance.

Alternative Accommodation

Youth hostels exist in Spain, but they're rarely worth the trouble. Most are open only in summer, there are the usual inconveniences and silly rules, often they're in out-of-the-way locations – and they can be block-booked by schools. You're better off with the inexpensive *hostales*.

Ask at the local tourist office for rooms that might be available in **university halls**.

If you fancy some tranquillity, several **monasteries and convents** welcome guests. Accommodation and meals are simple and guests can usually take part in the religious ceremonies. We've listed some in the text; for others, ask for details at local tourist offices.

Camping

Campsites are rated from one to three stars, depending on their facilities. As well as the ones listed in the official government handbook, there are always others, rather primitive, that are unlisted. Facilities in most first-class sites include shops, restaurants, bars, laundries, hot showers, first aid, swimming pools, phones and, occasionally, a tennis court. Caravans (trailers) converge on all the more developed sites, but, if you just want to pitch your little tent or sleep out in some quiet field, ask around in the bars or at likely farms. Camping is forbidden in many forested areas because of the danger of fire, as well as on the beaches. If you're doing some hiking, bring a sleeping bag and stay in the *refugios* along the major trails. The government handbook *Guía Oficial de Campings*, published by Turespaña, can be found in most bookstores and at tourist offices. See also *www.spain.info*.

FEECPV (**Federación Española de Empresarios de Campings y Parques de Vacaciones**), C/Valderribas 48, 1°C, 28007 Madrid, **t** 91 448 12 34, *www.fedcamping.com*.

Private Accommodation, Self-Catering and *Casas Rurales*

With the rise in hotel prices, staying in private homes has become an increasingly popular way of holidaying in Spain. *Casas rurales*, rural accommodation in farms or country houses, has become extremely popular and is a wonderful way to enjoy the spectacular countryside of northern Spain. Some are rented whole, while others offer B&B accommodation. Some even offer special activities such as cheese-making. Some provincial tourist offices have full lists of *casas rurales* and other self-catering properties. This type of accommodation is also called *Agriturismo*, or *Turismo Rural*, or in Basque (wait for it) *Nekazalturismoa*. Kitchen facilities may or may not be available, and prices generally fall in the range of €40–80 per day for a double room. A very useful website is *www.toprural. com*, which lists all kinds of rural accommodation throughout Spain and is also in English. You can also contact the following:

Asociacion Nekazalturismoa, Edificio Kursaal, Av. de Zurriola 1, Donostia-San Sebastián **t** 902 130 031, *www.nekatur.net*.

Agroturismo de Navarra, C/ José Manuel Martínez de Irujo San Pedro 4, 31173 Izane (Cendea de Olzo), **t** 94 817 67 74, *www. agroturismosnavarra.com*.

There are numerous private firms offering all sorts of different types of self-catering accommodation. See the box below for some of the many travel operators who arrange self-catering holidays in the north of Spain.

Tour Operators

In the UK

Alternative Travel Group, 274 Banbury Road, Oxford OX2 7GH, **t** (01865) 315 678, *www.atg-oxford.co.uk*. Pilgrimages to Compostela on foot, and also other walking tours.

Arblaster & Clarke Wine Tours, Cedar Court, 5 College Street, Petersfield, Hants GU31 4AE,

t (01730) 263 111, *www.winetours.co.uk*. Tours to the Rioja region, escorted by a wine expert, with lunches and visits to *bodegas*.

Exsus Travel, 23 Heddon Street, London W1B 4BQ, **t** (020) 7292 5050, *www.exsus.com*. Tailor-made tours of the Basque region.

Explore Worldwide Ltd, Nelson House, 55 Victoria Rd, Farnborough, Hants GU14 7PA, **t** 0870 333 4001, *www.explore.co.uk*. Exploratory holidays and treks in the Picos de Europa.

Martin Randall, Voysey House, Barley Mow Passage, London W4 4GF, t (020) 8742 3355, www.martinrandall.com. Lecturer-accompanied cultural tours.

Page & Moy, Compass House, Rockingham Rd, Market Harborough, Leicestershire LE16 7QD, t 0800 043 0234/t (0116) 217 8005, www.page-moy.com. Cultural guided tours.

Pico Verde, 792 Wilmslow Road, Didsbury, Manchester M20 6UG, t (0161) 773 5335, www.picoverde.com. Walking holidays in northern Spain, including the Atlantic Pyrenees.

Plantagenet Tours, 85 The Grove, Moordown, Bournemouth BH9 2TY, t (01202) 521 895. Historical tour every spring of Castile, Galicia and Asturias.

Prospect Cultural Tours, 79 William St, Herne Bay, Kent CT6 5NR, t (01227) 743 307, www.prospecttours.com. Music and art tours.

Pyrenean Experience, UK t (0121) 711 3428, www.pyreneanexperience.com. Beginners' Spanish and walking holidays, painting and tailor-made holidays in the Spanish Pyrenees.

Ramblers Holidays, Lemsford Hill, Lemsford, Welwyn Garden City AL8 7TR, t (01707) 331 133, www.ramblersholidays.co.uk. Walking tours.

Sherpa Expeditions, 131a Heston Road, Hounslow, Middlesex TW5 0RD, t (020) 8577 2717, www.sherpaexpeditions.com. Guided walks in the Picos de Europa.

The following companies organize group/individual walking tours/pilgrimages to Santiago de Compostela: www.saranjan.com; www.experienceplus.com; www.petersway.com; www.easyridertours.com/walking.html.

In the USA

NRCSA (National Registration Center for Study Abroad), PO Box 1393, Milwaukee, WI 53201, t (414) 278 0631, www.nrcsa.com. Language and cultural courses, Donostia-San Sebastián.

Wilderness Travel, 1102 9th Street, Berkeley, CA 94710, t 800 368 2794, www.wilderness travel.com. Hiking in the Basque country.

In Spain

Euro Adventures, C/Velázquez Moreno 9, Vigo, Pontevedra, Galicia, t 98 622 13 99, www.euroadventures.net. Gastronomic tours, walking tours, and tailor-made holidays.

Tenedor, PO Box 5070, San Sebastián, t 94 331 39 29, www.tenedortours.com. A superb range of cultural (art, food, wine and architecture) tours of the Basque country and Northern Spain, lasting from one to 13 days in length.

Totally Spain, Barrio Zoña, 39193 Castillo, Cantabria; Spain t 94 263 73 58, UK t 0871 666 0214, USA t (561) 828 0238, www.totallyspain.com. Tailor-made and themed holidays in Bilbao and the Spanish Basque lands, as well as tours and city breaks.

Self-catering Accommodation

In the UK

Casas Cantábricas, 31 Arbury Road, Cambridge, CB4 2JB, t (01223) 328 721, www.casas.co.uk. Holiday houses and small hotels.

Hoseasons, Manor Court, Bignor, Pulborough, West Sussex, RH20 1QD, t 08448 471 356, www.hoseasons.co.uk. Village and rural accommodation.

Keytel International, 156 Blackfriars Rd, London SE1 8EN, t (020) 7953 3020, www.keytel.co.uk..

Secret Destinations, Aztec House 137 Molesley Ave, West Molesley, Surrey KT8 2RY, t (020) 89 41 6588, www.secretdestinations.com. Self-catering and hotels along the coast, in mountain villages and in the cities.

In the USA

EC Tours, 12500 Riverside Drive, Suite 206, Toluca Lake, CA 91602, t 800 388 0877, www.ectours.com. Flights and accommodation in villas and apartments as well as hotels.

Interhome USA, t 1-800 882 6864, www.interhomeusa.com. Rental properties all over the world with a selection in Northern Spain.

Practical A–Z

06

Imperial–Metric Conversions

Length (multiply by)
Inches to centimetres: 2.54
Centimetres to inches: 0.39
Feet to metres: 0.3
Metres to feet: 3.28
Yards to metres: 0.91
Metres to yards: 1.1
Miles to kilometres: 1.61
Kilometres to miles: 0.62

Area (multiply by)
Inches square to centimetres square: 6.45
Centimetres square to inches square: 0.15
Feet square to metres square: 0.09
Metres square to feet square: 10.76
Miles square to kilometres square: 2.59
Kilometres square to miles square: 0.39
Acres to hectares: 0.40
Hectares to acres: 2.47

Weight (multiply by)
Ounces to grams: 28.35
Grams to ounces: 0.035
Pounds to kilograms: 0.45
Kilograms to pounds: 2.2
Stones to kilograms: 6.35
Kilograms to stones: 0.16
Tons (UK) to kilograms: 1,016
Kilograms to tons (UK): 0.0009
1 UK ton (2,240lbs) = 1.12 US tonnes (2,000lbs)

Volume (multiply by)
Pints (UK) to litres: 0.57
Litres to pints (UK): 1.76
Quarts (UK) to litres: 1.13
Litres to quarts (UK): 0.88
Gallons (UK) to litres: 4.55
Litres to gallons (UK): 0.22
1 UK pint/quart/gallon = 1.2 US pints/quarts/gallons

Temperature
Celsius to Fahrenheit: multiply by 1.8 then add 32

Fahrenheit to Celsius: subtract 32 then multiply by 0.55

Spain Information

Time Differences
Spain: + 1hr GMT; + 6hrs EST
Daylight saving from last weekend in March to end of October

Dialling Codes
Note: to dial within Spain and within a province, include the area code (9X).
Spain country code 34
To Spain from: UK, Ireland, New Zealand 00 / USA, Canada 011 / Australia 0011; then dial 34 and the full number
From Spain to: UK 00 44; Ireland 00 353; USA, Canada 001; Australia 00 61; New Zealand 00 64; then the number without the initial zero
Directory enquiries: 11811
International directory enquiries: 176

Emergency Numbers
General EU emergency number: 112
Police: 112 or 091 (national)/092 (local)
Ambulance: 112 or 061
Fire: 112 or 080

Embassy Numbers in Spain
UK: 94 415 76 00 (Bilbao); **Ireland** 94 423 04 14 (Bilbao); **USA:** 91 587 22 00 (Madrid); **Canada** 91 423 32 50 (Madrid); **Australia** 91 353 66 00 (Madrid); **New Zealand** 91 523 02 26 (Madrid)

Shoe Sizes

Europe	UK	USA
35	2½ / 3	4
36	3 / 3½	4½ / 5
37	4	5½ / 6
38	5	6½
39	5½ / 6	7 / 7½
40	6 / 6½	8 / 8½
41	7	9 / 9½
42	8	9½ / 10
43	9	10½
44	9½ / 10	11
45	10½	12

Women's Clothing

Europe	UK	USA
34	6	2
36	8	4
38	10	6
40	12	8
42	14	10
44	16	12

Crime and the Police

General emergency number t 112

Crime is not really a big problem in Spain, and Spaniards talk about it perhaps more than is warranted. Pickpocketing and robbing parked cars are the specialities; except for some quarters of the largest cities, walking around at night is no problem.

Note that in Spain less than 8 grams of marijuana is legal; anything else may easily earn you the traditional 'six years and a day'. In Galicia, the traditional smuggling business has created a growing drug problem at home, along with some fierce vigilante efforts by locals to stop it.

There are several species of police, and their authority varies with the area. Franco's old goon squad, the *Policía Armada*, was reformed and relatively demilitarized into the *Policía Nacional*, known as 'chocolate drops' for their brown uniforms. Nowadays they wear blue and white, and their duties seem to consist largely of driving around and drinking coffee. The *Policía Municipal* (*Udaltzainzoa* in Basque) in some towns do control crime, while in others they are limited to directing traffic. Mostly in rural areas you will see the *Guardia Civil*, with green uniforms. The *Guardia* is now most conspicuous as a highway patrol, assisting motorists and handing out tickets. Most traffic violations are payable on the spot; the traffic cops have a reputation for upright honesty. The Basques don't want anything to do with any of these and have set up their own police force, the *Ertzantza*. You'll see them looking dapper in their red berets, waiting by the roadsides for motorists in a barely legal hurry.

Report thefts (called making a *denuncia*) to the nearest police station: the reward is the bit of paper you need for an insurance claim. You can also call t 902 102 112. If your passport is stolen, contact the police and your nearest consulate for emergency travel documents.

Eating Out

Spaniards are notoriously late diners. In the morning it's a coffee and a roll grabbed at the bar, followed by a huge meal at around 2 or 3pm, then after work at 8pm a few tapas at the bar to hold them over until supper at

Restaurant Price Categories

Price categories in the 'Eating Out' sections throughout this book indicate the cost of a three course meal with wine for one person. The set menus can drop prices considerably.

expensive	€€€	over €45
moderate	€€	€25–45
inexpensive	€	under €25

10pm. On the coasts, restaurants tend to open earlier to accommodate foreigners (some as early as 5pm), while Galicians are the early diners of Spain (8 or 9pm); Basques do it from 9 to 11.

In non-touristy Spanish areas, restaurants are inconspicuous and few. Just ask someone, and you will find a nice *comedor* with home cooking tucked in a back room behind a bar. If you dine where the locals do, you'll be assured of a good deal if not necessarily a good meal. Almost every restaurant offers a *menú del día* (usually only available at weekdays) or a *menú turístico*, featuring an appetizer, a main course, dessert, bread and drink at a set price. Unless it's explicitly written on the bill (*la cuenta*), service is not included in the total, so **tip** accordingly.

Since a 2011 extension to the ban on smoking in public spaces, restaurants are now **non-smoking**.

A wide array of snacking establishments will help fill in the gaps in your day, wherever you are. **Bars** and **cafés** collect much of the Spaniards' leisure time. They are wonderful institutions, where you can eat breakfast or linger over a glass of beer until four in the morning. Some have music – jazz, rock or flamenco; some have great snacks, or *tapas*, some have games or pinball machines. Some bars put on Parisian airs; others, including the *chigres* (another word for *sidrerías* in Asturias) are resolutely proletarian. Many night-time bars and clubs are totally invisible in the day, exploding into blue-light noise palaces punctually at midnight until 6am. This is the twilight world of *la marcha*, the all-night pub crawl of Madrid and Barcelona that finds a reflection in any Spanish city, especially if it has a university. Cities that can nourish a proper *marcha* include Santander, San Sebastián, Oviedo, Santiago, A Coruña, Pontevedra, Pamplona and León, while Burgos and Vigo are a little too staid to try.

For further information about eating and drinking in Spain, including local specialities and wines and a menu decoder, *see* the **Food and Drink** chapter, pp.47–56.

Electricity

The current is 225 AC/220V, the same as most of Europe. North Americans will need converters, and the British will need the usual two-pin adapters for the different plugs. Adapters and converters are sold in department stores and electrical shops.

Health and Emergencies

General emergency number t 112

The tap water in Spain is safe to drink, but at the slightest twinge of queasiness switch to the bottled stuff.

Citizens of the EU are entitled to a certain amount of free medical care in EU countries if they have a European Health Insurance Card (EHIC). *See* **Planning Your Trip**, p.63.

In an emergency ask to be taken to the nearest *hospital de la seguridad social*.

Tourist offices can supply lists of local English-speaking doctors, but, if it's not an emergency, before resorting to a *médico* and his fat fee (ask at the tourist office for a list of English-speaking doctors), go to a pharmacy and tell them your woes; Spanish *farmacéuticos* are highly skilled.

Internet

Getting online is easy in **Spain**. WiFi is widely available in most hotels and some cafés (curiously, smaller establishments rarely charge for use, while the big hotels can charge up to €25 for 24 hours). Some cities, including Bilbao, have introduced free WiFi hotspots (check the website, *www.bilbao.net*, which lists the locations in English).

Every city of any size has a few *cibers*, as the Spanish call their Internet cafés. Even the most unlikely and out-of-the-way one-horse towns sometimes have Internet facilities. The average cost in cities is around €2.50 per hour, rising to an inflated €4 in places like Zarautz.

Most hotels have their own websites with online booking.

National Holidays

Everything closes on:

1 January New Year's Day
6 January Epiphany
Holy Thursday (March/April)
Good Friday (March/April)
Easter Sunday (March/April)
1 May Labour Day
Corpus Christi (May/June)
25 July *Santiago Apóstol*: St James' Day
15 August *Asunción*: Assumption
12 October *Día de la Hispanidad*: Columbus Day
1 November *Todos los Santos*: All Saints' Day
6 December *Día de la Constitución*: Constitution Day
8 December *Immaculada Concepción*: Immaculate Conception
25 December *Navidad*: Christmas Day

Opening Hours, Museums and National Holidays

Shops usually open at 10am, boutiques an hour or so later. Spaniards take their main meal at 2pm and, except in larger cities, most shops close for 2–3 hours in the afternoon, from 1pm or 2pm. In the evening, most establishments stay open until 7 or 8pm.

Most **banks** are open Mon–Fri 9–2. A few open until 4pm on Thursdays.

Main **post office** opening hours are Mon–Fri 8.30–8.30, Sat 9.30–1, but smaller branches may open only in the morning. Many post offices close early in summer.

Museums and historical sites tend to follow shop hours, though they are shorter in winter. Nearly all close on Mondays. Seldom-visited sites have a raffish disregard for their official hours. Don't be discouraged: bang on doors and ask around. We've done our best to include opening hours in the text, but they are liable to change. Most close on national holidays and give discounts if you have a student ID card, or are an EU citizen under 18 or over 65 years old; most charge admission.

Most of the less important **churches** are always closed. If you're determined to see one, it will never be hard to find the *sacristán*, or caretaker. Usually they live close by and will be glad to show you around for a tip. Don't be surprised when cathedrals and famous churches charge for admission – just consider the cost of upkeep.

Post Offices

Every city in Spain, regardless of size, seems to have one **post office** (*correos*) and no more. They will often be crowded, but unless you have packages to send you may never need visit one: most tobacconists sell **stamps** (*sellos*) and they'll usually know the correct postage for whatever you're sending. Send everything by air mail (*por avión*) and don't send postcards unless you don't care when they arrive. **Post boxes** are bright yellow. Don't confuse post offices with the *Caja Postal*, the postal savings banks.

Sports and Activities

Football has pride of place in the Spanish heart, and Athletic Club de Bilbao is one of only three teams (the others are Real Madrid and Barcelona) never to have been relegated from La Liga. **Bullfighting** and **cycling** vie for second place; all are regularly shown on television.

Bullfighting

The *corrida* is still big in parts of Northern Spain, although its popularity has waned considerably in the last decades. A recent poll showed that less than 10 per cent of Spaniards were in favour of bullfighting, and in Catalunya it has now been completely banned on the grounds of cruelty. In Spanish newspapers, you will not find accounts of the bullfights (*corridas*) on the sports pages: you should look in the 'arts and culture' section, for that is how Spain has always thought of this spectacle. If you choose to attend, be aware that tickets can be astronomically expensive and hard to come by. Prices vary according to the sun – the most expensive seats are entirely in the shade.

Bull-running

The biggest and most famous bull-running festival is **Los Sanfermines** in Pamplona (*see* pp.93–4), but bull-running is also a highlight of plenty of local festivals in the smaller villages of central Navarra. The custom dates back to the times when herds of cattle were chased down from their summer pastures in the mountains, a hair-raising journey which now takes place in the village streets. The most popular *encierros* outside Pamplona take place in Tudela (last week of July), Pilón (last week of August), Tafalla (20 August) and Sangüesa (mid-September).

Cycling

See 'Getting Around', p.69.

Fishing and Hunting

Fishing and hunting are long-standing Spanish obsessions, and you'll need to get a licence for both. **Freshwater fishing permits** (*permisos de pesca*) are issued from the Consejería de Agricultura y Pesca (Agriculture and Fishing Council), which has an office in each of the the provincial capital cities. A **maritime recreational fishing licence** (1st and 3rd class) is required for fishing from the shore or from a boat near the coast; get it from the Delegación Provincial de la Consejería de Agricultura y Pesca, which also has an office in each provincial capital city (tourist offices can provide addresses). **Deep-sea** fishermen need to obtain a **five-year licence** from the provincial Comandancias de Marina.

Spanish Fishing Federation (Federación Española de Pesca y Casting), Navas de Tolosa 3, 28013 Madrid, t 91 532 83 52, *www.fepyc.es*.

Directorate General of Sea Fishing (Subsecretaria de la Marina Mercante), Ministerio de Comercio, Calle Ruíz de Alarcón 1, Madrid. Information on the best fishing waters and boat rentals.

You may bring sporting guns to Spain, but you must declare them on arrival and present a valid firearms certificate with a Spanish translation bearing a consulate stamp. Hunters (boar and deer are the big game, with quail, hare, partridges and pigeons, and ducks and geese along the coasts in the winter) are obliged to get a **licence** (*permiso de caza*) from the local autonomous community, presenting passports and insurance.

Spanish Hunting Federation (Federación Española de Caza), C/ Francos Rodríguez 70, 28039 Madrid, t 91 311 14 11, *www.fedecaza.com*.

Golf

English settlers built Spain's first golf course at the Rio Tinto mines in Andalucía in the 19th century, and since the advent of Severiano Ballesteros Spaniards too have gone nuts for the game. The sunny, warm winters, combined with greens of international tournament standard, attract golfing enthusiasts from all over the world throughout the year. Most places hire out clubs. Green fees have taken a leap in recent years, however, and even the humblest clubs will charge at least €20. Many hotels cater specifically for the golfer and there are numerous golf-package tour operators.

Royal Spanish Golf Federation (Real Federación Española de Golf), C/Arroyo del Monte 5, 28035 Madrid, t 91 555 26 82, *www.rfegolf.es.*

Hiking and Mountaineering

Spain's sierras attract thousands of hikers and mountaineers. The Picos de Europa and the Pyrenees are by far the most popular, though there are also some lovely hikes in El Bierzo of western León and Os Ancares of eastern Galicia. *See* pp.71–2 for tour operators who organize walking holidays.

The tourist office or the Spanish Mountaineering Federation provide a list of *refugios*, which offer mountain shelter in many places. Some are well equipped and can supply food. Most, however, do not, so take your own sleeping bags, cooking equipment and food with you. Hiking boots are essential, as is a detailed map of the area, issued by the Instituto Geográfico Nacional, or the Servicio Geográfico Ejército.

Spanish Hiking and Mountaineering Federation (Federación Española de Deportes de Montaña y Escalada), C/Floridablanca 84, Barcelona, t 93 426 42 67, *www.fedme.es.*

Tennis

There is as much fervour in Spain for tennis as for golf, inspired by champions such as Rafael Nadal who currently holds ten Grand Slam titles. Every resort hotel has its own courts; municipal ones tend to be rare.

Royal Spanish Tennis Federation, Avenida Diagonal 618, 08021 Barcelona, t 93 200 53 55, *www.rfet.es.*

Telephones

Calls within **Spain** are expensive (25–80 cents for a short local call), and overseas calls from Spain are among the most expensive in Europe: calls to the UK cost about €1 a minute, to the USA substantially more. Most tobacconists sell PIN-**phonecards** that make international phone calls much cheaper.

Public **phone booths** have instructions in English and accept phonecards, available from news stands, tobacconists and post offices. Most will also take credit cards and a few still accept coins. In every big city in Spain, there are also **calling centres** (*locutorios*) where you telephone from a metered booth. These offer cheap international calls, but national calls are expensive. They can usually be found around bus and train stations. Expect to pay a big surcharge if you make any calls from your hotel.

For directory enquiries, dial t 11811.

Telephone codes have now been incorporated into the telephone numbers. All numbers in this guide are listed as they must be dialled. If you're ringing from abroad, the code for Spain is 34 followed by the number. For international calls from Spain, dial t 00, wait for the higher tone and then dial the country code and the rest of the number (omitting the zero in any area code).

Time

Spain is one hour ahead of UK time and six hours ahead of North American EST. Summer time runs from the last Sunday in March to the last Sunday in October.

Toilets

Apart from bus and train stations, public facilities are rare in Spain. On the other hand, every bar on every corner has a toilet; just ask for *los servicios* and take your own toilet paper.

Navarra and La Rioja

Europe's traditional front door to Spain, Navarra combines a sizeable, often nationalistic Basque minority up in the misty western Pyrenees with a conservative, non-Basque Navarrese majority tending the sunny vineyards and gardens of the Ebro valley flatlands to the south. The combination hasn't always been comfortable, and only now that much of the population has abandoned the countryside have tensions between the two groups loosened up.

As everyone must know by now, much of this 'loosening up' is concentrated in Pamplona, the capital both groups share, into an ecstatic week-long bacchanalia of inebriated recklessness, bull running and partying known as Los Sanfermines.

Roads from Navarra – most importantly, the Camino de Santiago – flow naturally southwest into the autonomous comunidad of La Rioja, celebrated far out of proportion to its size for its red wine with the distinctive vanilla flavour.

07

Don't miss

⭐ **Running the bulls**
Pamplona **p.90**

⭐ **The atmospheric 'town of the star'**
Estella **p.107**

⭐ **Striking Wild West scenery**
Bardenas Reales **p.103**

⭐ **Chickens in church**
Santo Domingo de la Calzada **p.122**

⭐ **Wine *bodegas***
Rioja Alta **p.124**

See map overleaf

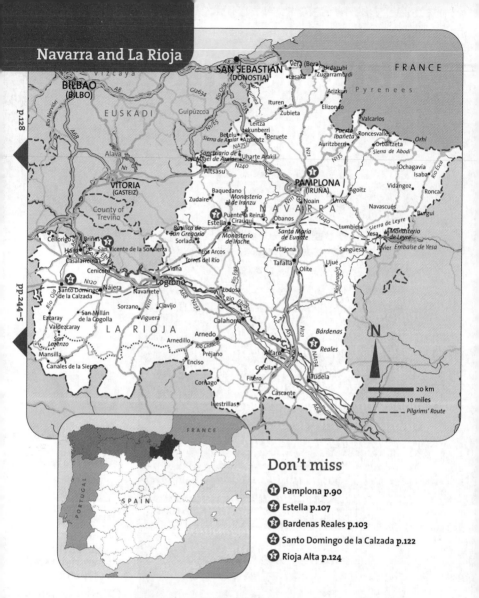

Don't miss

Navarra: A Potted History

To understand the standoffish, weird James Dean role Navarra traditionally plays, you need a bit of Spanish history, which is full of the phrase 'except Navarra'. Even in 'the nation of nations' the region has stood apart ever since 605, when the Franks tried to harness it as part of the Duchy of Vasconia, a huge, untenable territory that extended from the Garonne to the Ebro. Charlemagne himself came down in 778, either to discipline the unruly duchy or to force it to join his fight against the Moors, and after razing the walls of Pamplona he went stumping back to

France – except for his rear guard, which the furious Basques of Pamplona ambushed in 778 at the pass of Roncesvalles.

Charlemagne taught the Navarrese that owing nothing to nobody was the way to go, and within a few years of his passing they created the independent kingdom of Navarra. Its most talented king, Sancho III 'the Great' (1004–34), firmly established the *camino francés* through Navarra and controlled much of French Basque country and Galicia, and pocketed Castile and León after the death of its last count, setting up his son Ferdinand I as the first to take the title of 'King of the Spains'. The centre was too precocious to hold, and by the time of Sancho IV (1054–76) Navarra was once again a fierce rival of Castile, but it avoided entanglements – marital or martial – by playing the French card. 'The Flea between Two Monkeys', as it became known, was ruled by three different French dynasties between 1234 and 1512, when Ferdinand the Catholic slyly demanded that Navarra let his armies march through to France. His demand, as he'd anticipated, was refused, and he used the refusal as an excuse to grab Navarra south of the Pyrenees. France was left with only Basse-Navarre, a thimble-sized realm but one that gave her a long line of kings, with the accession of Henri IV (1589–1610). Ferdinand kept the Navarrese happy by maintaining their *fueros* (or privileges), which in practice gave the region an independence enjoyed by no other in Spain; it was ruled by a viceroy, minted its own coins and had its own government. Napoleonic and Liberal attempts to do away with the *fueros* in the cause of central unity turned the Navarrese into fierce reactionaries and the most ardent of Carlists (supporters of the pretender Charles III). In the 1930s Navarra rejected the Republic's offer of autonomy; instead, the Navarrese Carlist *requetés* in their distinctive red berets became some of Franco's best troops, fighting for their old privileges and Catholicism – just as the Basques were, only on the Republican side. Franco rewarded Navarra by leaving the *fueros* intact, making it the only autonomous region in Spain until his death.

Approaches from France: Down the Valleys of the Pyrenees

The Navarrese Pyrenees don't win altitude records, but they're green, wooded and shot through with legends, many lingering in the mists around Roncesvalles, for centuries the pass most favoured by French pilgrims to Santiago. Much of Navarra's Basque population is concentrated in the three valleys of Roncal, Salazar and Baztán, where seemingly every house in every hamlet is emblazoned with a coat of arms – for the Basques have traditionally considered themselves all equal and all noble.

The Eastern Valleys: Valles del Roncal and de Salazar

Like many Pyrenean valleys, for centuries the Roncal was so remote that the central authorities were content to let it run its own show. Time has changed a few things: timber logged on its thickly forested slopes now travels by truck instead of careering down the Esca river, and the valley's renowned sheep's cheese, *queso de Roncal*, is now made in a factory (but according to farm traditions). Mist often envelops **Isaba**, the Valle del Roncal's biggest town, gathered under its fortress-church of San Cipriano (1540). Every 13 July since 1375, at stone frontier-marker no.262, the mayor of Isaba and his colleagues don traditional costume, march up to meet their counterparts from the Vallée de Barétous in France, and ask them three times for the 'Tribute of the Three Cows' in exchange for the right to graze their herds in the Valle del Roncal in August – something both sides used to kill for before the annual tribute was agreed on. Isaba provides an excellent base for exploring the magnificent mountain scenery: hike up the region's highest peaks, **Pic d'Anie** (8,200ft/2,500m) and **Mesa de los Tres Reyes** (7,900ft/2,408m), or take the most beautiful walk of all, into the Parque Natural Pirenáico to the **Refugio de Belagua**, set in a stunning glacial amphitheatre.

Refugio de
Belagua
t 94 839 40 02

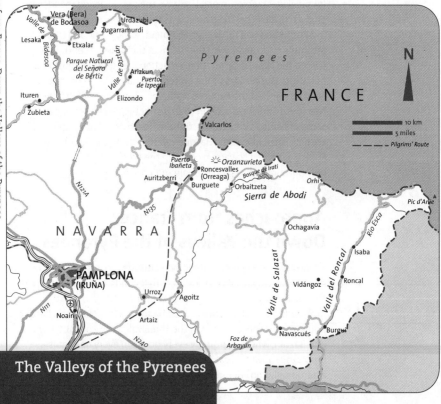

The Valleys of the Pyrenees

Getting to and around the Eastern Valleys

There are no **trains** here, and in most cases the **buses** from Pamplona go only once a day; there is usually no service on Sundays.

La Tafallesa (t 94 870 09 79) buses go to the Valle del Roncal, with stops at Burgui, Roncal, Urzainqui and Uztárroz. For a **taxi** in the valley, call Vidángoz t 94 847 70 13.

Artieda (t 94 830 35 70) operates the service to Roncesvalles, and **Conda** (t 902 422 242) runs buses to the Valles de Salazar and Aezkoa, including Ochagavía and Orbaitzeta. **La Baztanesa** (t 94 858 01 29) serves the Valle de Baztán.

Casa-Museo Julián Gayarre
www.julian gayarre.com; open April–Sept Tues–Sun 11.30–1.30 and 5–7; Oct–Mar Sat–Sun 11.30–1.30 and 4–6; adm

Roncal, once the capital of the valley, is a pretty village in the midst of pine forests. The great, amiable Basque tenor Julián Gayarre (1844–90) was born here and lies buried in a suitably high-operatic tomb just outside town; the **Casa-Museo Julián Gayarre** contains costumes and photos from his glory days. **Burgui**, south, has a Roman bridge and two roads that cut over to the Valle de Salazar: an easy one westward to Navascués and a narrow one northward by way of the remote village of Vidángoz.

The sparsely populated **Valle de Salazar** is much less visited but just as lovely, a-bubble with trout streams, beech forests and old white stone Basque *caserones*, or mansions, with their pompous coats of arms. The best of them line the riverfront and cobbled lanes in **Ochagavía** (Otsagabia), the local metropolis and another good base for walks. An easy one is up to the 13th-century chapel of **Santa María de Muskilda**, topped by an unusual square tower with a round roof: its *romería* (pilgrimage) on 8 September is celebrated with some of Navarra's most ancient dances.

To the north, a road twists through the Sierra de Abodi to the snow-white hermitage of **Nuestra Señora de las Nieves** (1954): from here, trails of varying length and difficulty lead into the vast beech and ancient yew **Forest of Irati** (Bosque de Irati), the largest primeval forest in Spain, with majestic Mount Orhi (6,618ft/ 2,017m) as a backdrop. This is one of the richest wildlife habitats in the Pyrenees, full of red squirrels, deer and wild boar, with lesser populations of wildcat and beech marten. The area also contains a couple of real rarities: the white-backed woodpecker, found only where there are plenty of insect-ridden beech trees, and the endemic Pyrenean desman, an aquatic shrew with a nose like a dragon's snout. Besides the usual Basque fairy folk, the forest is haunted by a rather unexpected ghost: that of Jeanne d'Albret, queen of French Navarre and mother of Henri IV, a nasty, die-hard Protestant fanatic. Poisoned in 1572, Jeanne tours her old domain on windy nights with an escort of lovely Basque *lamiaks*, the mischievous nymphs with whom she never would have been caught dead while still alive. On the other side of the forest, the picturesque village of **Orbaitzeta** makes a good base; nearby, a dolmen called **Azpegi I** is surrounded by a circle of 123 stones.

In the south of the valley, the spectacular 1,000ft sheer-sided limestone gorge, the **Foz de Arbayún**, extends for 10km below the road, home to Spain's largest colonies of rare griffon vultures (*buitres leonados*), with their 8ft wing span, and an assortment of smaller eagles; you can nearly always spot them floating around the roadside belvedere between Navascués and Lumbier. Man-made wonders Leyre and Sangüesa are just south (*see* pp.98–100).

⭐ Casa Tetxe >>

ⓘ **Roncal** >
Centro Interpretación de la Naturaleza,
t 94 847 52 56,
www.roncal.es

ⓘ **Ochagavía** >>
Centro Interpretación de la Naturaleza, on the main road, opposite the river, t 94 889 06 41,
www.ochagavia.com

Where to Stay and Eat in the Eastern Valleys

Navarra as a whole has made efforts to improve the provision of reasonably priced accommodation in rural areas. Traditional houses have been restored as *casas rurales*, or bed and breakfasts: many are listed online at *www.turismonavarra.es*.

Valle del Roncal ✉ 31680

There are several *casas rurales* in and around Roncal: visit the website *www.roncal-salazar.com* (Spanish only) or contact the tourist office. The website *www.toprural.com* is available in several languages. Most accommodation here is concentrated in Isaba, the largest village.

***Isaba, C/Bormapea 51, Isaba, t 94 889 30 00, *www.isabaha.com* (€€). A modern 'apart-hotel', offering apartments with kitchenettes for 2–4 people, a daily cleaning service, and breakfast buffet. Ideal for families.

Pensión Txiki, C/Mendigatxa 17, Isaba, t 94 889 31 18, *www.pensiontxiki.com* (€). Plain rooms in a pretty, white-washed building in the centre of the village. The traditional restaurant (€) serves good local cuisine.

*Hs Lola, C/Mendigatxa, Isaba, t 94 889 30 12, *www.hostal-lola.com* (€). Welcoming little place with comfy rooms, flower-filled balconies, and a decent restaurant.

*Hotel Ezkaurre, C/Garagardoia 14, Isaba, t 94 889 33 03, *http://hotelezkaurre.es* (€€–€).This classic mountain *hostal* has basic rooms and a sitting room with fireplace. Serves dinners to non-guests during the summer months.

Casa Estanislao, C/Izarjentea, Isaba, t 94 889 34 50, *http://casaestanislao.*

com (€). *Pintxos, regional dishes, platos combinados,* and set menus.

*Hs Zaltua, C/Castillo 23, Roncal, t 94 847 50 08 (€). A friendly whitewashed *hostal* with simple rooms and a lovely dining room.

Casa Tetxe, C/Iriondoa 63, Roncal, t 94 847 50 98 (€). A charming *casa rural* in a traditional stone-built house, with B&B accommodation and a small organic farm. Meals are served with two days' notice.

Ochagavía ✉ 31680

Most accommodation in the Salazar valley is in *casas rurales*.

Auñamendi, Plaza Gurpide 1, t 94 889 01 89, *www.hostalauniamendi.com* (€€–€). As well as offering rooms, this place serves good local cuisine. *Closed mid-Sept–mid-Oct.*

**Hs Salazar, C/Mayor s/n, Oronz, t 94 889 00 53, *www.hostalsalazar.com* (€). Traditional chalet-style hotel just south of Ochagavía, with an outdoor Jacuzzi and pretty views.

*Hs Orialde, C/Urrutia 6, t 94 889 07 42, *www.hostalorialde.com* (€). A welcoming 12-room inn in a former farmhouse by the river.

Casa Ballent, t 94 889 03 73 (€). One of the best, with just three cosy bedrooms, a welcoming owner and views from the terrace over the Pyrenees and the vegetable patch.

Casa Sarbide I and **II**, t 94 889 03 42, *www.casasarbide.com* (€). A guest room with private bathroom and lots of character, and a *casa rural* for four.

Orbaitzeta ✉ 31670

There are no hotels here, and only a handful of *casas rurales*.

Casa Sastrarena, C/San Juan, t 94 876 60 93 (€). Offers rooms with private bath and a pretty garden .

Roncesvalles (Orreaga)

Of all the passes over the Pyrenees, introverted Roncesvalles ('Bramble Valley') is the most renowned, thanks to the *camino francés* to Compostela (*see* pp.34–8). French pilgrims would mumble verses from the *Chanson de Roland* as they paid their respects to the sites associated with Charlemagne and his nephew Roland (*see* **Topics**, pp.39–40), then say their first prayer to another gallant knight, Santiago. From Roncesvalles' Colegiata it's 781km to Santiago, a distance the fittest pilgrims could cover in 20 days.

Not so long ago the Colegiata had a sad, has-been look. Although in the 18th century Roncesvalles still counted 30,000 passing pilgrims a year, numbers fell dramatically in the 19th century. Most of the monasteries and churches along the route were closed forever with the national confiscation of church lands in 1837; many were converted into stables or pillaged for their building stone. By the 1970s, the medieval floods of pilgrims had dried to a trickle of eccentrics. But just when it seemed that the pilgrimage was ready to be pushed into Europe's closet of forgotten traditions, it came roaring back. A number of factors seem to be involved – modern disillusionment with conventional religion, the restless search for something beyond the routine of over-organized day-to-day lives and, more prosaically, the growth of ecological and alternative tourism. In 1982, John Paul II became the first pope ever to visit Santiago, followed in 2010 by Benedict XVI; in 1985, UNESCO declared this the 'Foremost Cultural Route in Europe', helping to fund the restoration of the churches that punctuate the trail. Although modern roads have changed the face of the *camino francés* for ever, efforts have been made to create alternative paths for pedestrians, marked with scallop shells, and *hostales* have sprouted along the way. The pilgrims' quest is back in business; it has even been the subject of a 2011 Hollywood movie, *The Way*.

The three main pilgrims' routes through France converged at St-Jean-Pied-de-Port and then continued up to the busy frontier town of **Valcarlos**, the 'carlos' in its name referring to Charlemagne, who was camped here when he heard the dying Roland's horn blast. From here, the road winds up through lush greenery to Roncesvalles, where the 12th-century church of **Sancti Spiritus** (the 'Silo de Charlemagne') is said to have been first built as Roland's tomb. According to legend, by the time the emperor arrived, not only were Roland and the peers dead, but so were all the Saracens; since he couldn't tell who was who (poor Charlemagne – his legends always make him seem as thick as a pudding), he asked heaven for a sign that he should make sure he gave all the Franks a Christian burial, and all at once the Christian corpses looked up to heaven, with red roses sprouting from their lips. Equally unlucky pilgrims were laid in the 7th-century **ossuary** underneath the

Santiago
*open summer daily
10–2 and 3.30–7; winter
except Jan daily 10–2
and 3.30–5; Jan Thurs–
Tues 10.30–2.30, closed
Wed; adm*

church; according to Aymery Picaud (*see* p.37), many were done in by 'false pilgrims', mostly locals. Adjacent, the tiny church of **Santiago** is a plain Gothic chapel from the 13th century.

Set back from the road, at the foot of the pass, the **Colegiata de Roncesvalles** is a French-style Gothic church consecrated in 1219, which replaced the first Colegiata, built up at Puerto Ibañeta in 1112 and abandoned by the frostbitten monks after five ghastly winters. What was originally the front of the Colegiata caved in under the snow in 1600 (hence the incongruous corrugated zinc roof on the rest) and was replaced by a **cloister**, from where you can pop into the 14th-century chapterhouse to see the stained glass (1960) showing a scene from the 1212 Battle of Las Navas de Tolosa, where Sancho VII 'the Strong' led the Navarrese to their great victory over the Moors. The chains in the chapel are among those that bound 10,000 slaves at the ankle and wrist, forming a human shield around the emir's tent, a scurvy tactic that failed to prevent the Christians from leaping over and carrying off the tent as booty. The chapterhouse holds the **tomb of Sancho the Strong**. Apparently, in life the king was exactly as tall as his 7ft 4in effigy: pilgrims used to think that his battle maces, now in the museum, belonged to Roland. Sancho financed the Colegiata, which over time has been stripped of its costly gifts, with the exception of a much-revered 13th-century image of the Virgin under her baldachin. Its jumbled, anachronistic, pious legend goes that after the battle at the pass, Charlemagne founded a monastery up at Ibañeta. When the Moors poured through to attack France in 732, the monks hid the statue, and it remained hidden until 1130, when the hiding place was revealed to a Basque shepherd by a red stag with a star shimmering between its antlers.

Museum
*open daily 10–2
and 3.30–7; adm*

The fascinating **museum** contains such medieval treasures as the emerald which fell from the emir's turban when giant King Sancho burst into his tent at Las Navas de Tolosa; an 11th-century pyx, or golden box used to hold the Host; and a reliquary of gold and enamel (*c.* 1350) called 'Charlemagne's chessboard' for its 32 little cases, each designed to hold a saintly fingertip or tooth. Among the paintings there's an excellent 15th-century Flemish triptych and a *Holy Family* by Morales, and two books on Confucianism, purchased in India in the time of St Francis Xavier.

An easy and beautiful path from the monastery leads up to the **Puerto Ibañeta** (3,150ft/960m), from where the Basques, hidden on Mounts Astobizkar and Orzanzurieta, dropped boulders on the heads of the Franks. A modern chapel replaces the monastery of San Salvador, where the monks would toll a bell to guide pilgrims through the mists and snowstorms. Heading south, the pretty villages of **Auritz (Burguete)** and **Auritzberri (Espinal)** were the pilgrims' next stops and are still good places to stay.

Where to Stay and Eat in Roncesvalles

Roncesvalles >
Antiguo Molino,
t 94 876 03 01,
oit.roncesvalles@
cfnavarra.es,
www.roncesvalles.es

Roncesvalles ✉ 31650

If you have no luck at any of the places listed below, then try one of several *casas rurales* in the vicinity.

Hs Loizu, Avda Roncesvalles 7, in Auritz (3km from Roncesvalles), **t 94 876 00 08, *www.loizu.com* (€€). A pretty, two-hundred-year-old hotel-restaurant with plenty of atmosphere.

Hostal Burguete, C/Única s/n, Auritz, **t 94 876 00 05, *www.hotelburguete.com* (€). Whenever Hemingway decamped to the Pyrenees, he stayed here. Though its elegance is mostly faded, this antique-bedecked old place is still a great choice for slumming it in style.

*Hs Casa Sabina, t 94 876 00 12, *www.casasabina.es* (€). By the monastery, with four pleasant rooms and good Navarrese cooking. They also run the equally lovely but more upmarket **Hotel Roncesvalles** (€€).

Hs La Posada, t 94 876 02 25, *www.laposadaderoncesvalles.com* (€). Charming, with spacious rooms in the Colegiata, and a fine **restaurant (€€) in the medieval inn which formerly served the pilgrims.

Western Valleys: Valle de Baztán and Valle de Bidasoa

Frequent rains off the Atlantic make these valleys so lush that they're called the 'Switzerland of Navarra'. Both are dotted with well-preserved, unspoiled white Basque villages, trout streams and quietly beautiful scenery. One of the best-known smugglers' routes ran from the caves of Sare, just over the border in France, to the caves of Zugarramurdi; it still makes a pretty and easy walk today.

But what **Zugarramurdi** is most famous for is its role as the Salem of the Basque lands. The **Valle de Baztán** once had Spain's largest Agote population (*see* p.99) and perhaps not entirely coincidentally a supposed colony of witches in the early 17th century, based in Zugarramurdi, 'the Hill of Elms', a pretty place just in from the French frontier. As in Salem, the witchcraft scare began with the dubious confessions of a young woman in 1608, and spread like wildfire from denunciation to denunciation in a kind of mass hysteria. It wasn't long before 10 witches had confessed to a whole slew of heinous crimes, taking responsibility for nearly every

Museo de las Brujas
C/Behitiko karrika 22,
t 94 859 90 04;
mid-July–mid-Sept
Tues–Sun 11–7.30;
mid-Sept–mid-July
Wed–Fri 11–6.30,
Sat–Sun 11–7; adm

death and trouble in Zugarramurdi that had occurred over the past 50 years. According to Basque law, they were tried and pardoned. Then the Inquisition, based in Logroño, got wind of it. Thirty-one hapless souls, mostly women and children, were arrested and 'put to the question' in 1609; of those condemned, 13 died under torture, and six, who refused to confess, survived to be burned alive at an *auto-da-fé*. Another 11 were burned the following year. That year, the Inquisition claimed to have discovered 1,590 witches in Navarra alone. No one really knows how many died. The village's **Museo de las Brujas**, in a restored hospital, tells their tale.

Cuevas de Zugarramurdi
www.turismo
zugarramurdi.com,
t 94 859 91 70;
open summer daily
9–dusk; adm

Just outside the village, carved out of the mountain by the *Infernuko Erreka* ('Hell's Stream'), the vast **Cuevas de Zugarramurdi** were the scene of black sabbaths, or *akelarres*, in which the participants smeared themselves with an unguent made of human brains and bones – mixed with belladonna, toads, salamanders and snakes – and flew through the night to join in outrageous orgies with a Satanic black billy goat, *akerbeltz* – at least according to the confessions extracted by the Inquisitors.

Basque witchcraft enjoyed a revival in the post-Franco 1970s, when the cult was seen either as a feminist revolt against an oppressive male-dominated society and religion, or as an instance of pocket survivals of the old pagan beliefs, demonized by the Church, perhaps even practised as underground rituals of Basque solidarity. Whatever the case, the inhabitants of Zugarramurdi have decided that it was all a splendid excuse for a hugely popular *Sorginak Besta* (Fiesta of Witches), to dress up and party on the Saturday closest to the summer solstice, and thousands still gather in the caves for an old-fashioned re-enactment of an *akelarre*, complete with all kinds of philtres and magic potions. Even older magic was built into the **cromlechs**, dedicated to the Basque goddess Mari, reached by a path from the village. There are other caves, including the lovely stalactite **Cuevas de Urdax** just south at Urdazubi/Urdax, where fish-tailed *lamiaks* once frolicked in the stream, or perhaps still do when no one's looking.

Cuevas de Urdax
t 94 859 92 41,
www.cuevasurdax.com;
guided tours run Jan–Feb
Sat–Sun 11am–2pm;
Mar–June daily 10–5;
July–Aug daily 10–7;
Sept–Oct 10–6; Nov–Dec
Tues–Sun 11–6; adm

Elizondo, one of the prettiest villages in the Baztán valley, has several historic houses: those along the river are especially impressive. **Arizkun**, 7km northeast, has the fortified stone house of one of Spain's busiest *conquistadores*, Pedro de Úrsua, leader of the search for El Dorado up the Amazon in 1560 when he was killed by rebel leader Lope de Aguirre. The parish church has a striking Baroque façade. Further north, a road turns east to France by way of the spectacular **Izpegui pass**.

Izpegui pass
accessible in
summer only

Navarra's westernmost Pyrenean valley, the **Valle de Bidasoa**, embraces streams filled with salmon and trout and, more prosaically, the main San Sebastián–Pamplona road. Bus services in the area offer a chance to visit charming old Basque villages such as **Bera (Vera) de Bidasoa**, only a couple of miles from the French frontier, with the former summer home of Basque novelist and doctor Pío Baroja (1872–1956). A member of the Generation of '98, Baroja was a firm supporter of the Republic from the beginning (*Memorias de un hombre de acción*), but he was also fascinated by Basque witchcraft, and made it a feature of one of his novels, *La Dama de Urtubi*. **Lesaka**, equally pretty, claims one of the best-preserved fortified feudal houses in Navarra.

Tiny **Etxalar (Echalar)**, a hamlet that time forgot, is on a stream on the pretty, seldom-used road to Zugarramurdi – seldom used except in October, during the annual wild pigeon and woodcock holocaust. The church at Etxalar is surrounded by 100 Basque funerary steles with their distinctive solar symbol discs.

Parque Natural del Señorío de Bértiz

t 94 859 24 21, www. parquedebertiz.es; open summer daily 10–8; winter daily 10–6

Farther south, the **Parque Natural del Señorío de Bértiz**, a former private estate, has foot, bicycle and riding paths through thousands of acres of oak, beech and chestnut forests; the gardens near the manor boast over 120 species of exotic trees. Note the coat of arms of the lord of Bértiz, showing a mermaid holding a mirror and comb; Charles III ordered her to be placed there in 1421 in honour of his ambassador, Micheto de Bértiz.

Two villages just west of here, **Zubieta** and **Ituren**, are famous for a late-January ritual ushering in spring that could have been invented by Dr Seuss: young unmarried men and boys (starting as young as five) called *joaldunaks* dress up in dunce's caps and lacy smocks or sheepskins and fasten a pair of copper *polunpaks* (giant bells) to their backs with an intricate network of laces. Thus arrayed, for two days the *joaldunaks* make a *zanpantzar*, a group of 20 or so, who dance and march from village to village across the frosty land, their *polunpaks* clanging with deep resonance.

 Elizondo »
Palacio de Arizkunenea, t 94 858 12 79

Sports and Activities in the Western Valleys

The old **smugglers' path** to Sare is easy to follow and waymarked with silhouettes of the little Basque horse, the *pottok*.

Orbela, at the Albergue Beintza, Beintza-Labaien ✉ 31753, t 94 845 00 14, *orbela@alberguesnavarra.com*. Treks, mountain-biking and potholing.

BKZ, at the Albergue Bertiz Aterpea in Narbarte, t 94 859 23 22, *bkz@ navarraaventura.com*. White-water rafting and canoeing trips at all levels.

★ **Casa Rural Urruska ›**

Where to Stay and Eat in the Western Valleys

Zugarramurdi ✉ 31710

Alzatenea, C/Basaburua 3, t 948 59 91 87 (€). Charming restaurant: roast meats cooked over a wood fire.

 Zugarramurdi ›
in the Museo de las Brujas, t 94 859 90 04, www.turismo zugarramurdi.com

Urdazubi ✉ 31711

Hostal Irigoienea, C/Salvador, t 94 859 92 67, *www.irigoienea.com* (€€). This old, whitewashed Navarrese farmhouse furnished with a handful of antiques is a charming place to stay.

Restaurante La Koska, C/San Salvador, 4, t 94 859 90 42, (€€). Traditional Navarra fare is served in this long-established, family-run restaurant. *Closed Mon, and mid-Dec to mid-Jan.*

Elizondo ✉ 31700

Señorío de Ursúa, Caserio Ikazatea, Arizkun, t 94 845 35 00, *www. hotelursua.com* (€€). Sumptuous rooms and a fine restaurant in this beautifully renovated 17th-century Basque farmhouse.

★★★Baztán, on the main road, t 94 858 00 50, *www.hotelbaztan.com* (€€). Modern, with panoramic views, two pools (one for children) and a garden.

★★Hs Saskaitz, C/M. Azpilijueta 10, t 94 858 04 88, *hotelelizondo@ biazpe.net* (€€€–€€). Cosy and calm, despite being in the centre of town.

Casa Rural Urruska, 10km away in Barrio de Bearzún, t 94 845 21 06, *www.urruska.com* (€€). This B&B is a real charmer. Simple but solid home cooking is served, and kids can help feed the livestock and collect eggs.

Casa Galartza, C/Santiago 1, t 94 858 01 01 (€). A rival to Roncal's offerings, this haven of traditional Baztánian cuisine and cheese serves tender lamb chops and local vegetables.

Bera (Vera) de Bidasoa ✉ 31780

Hotel Churrut, Plaza de los Fueros 2, t 94 862 55 40, *www.hotelchurrut.com* (€€). A chic rural hotel, with antique-filled rooms in a rosy-pink 18th-century building surrounded by woods and gardens. It also has great restaurants.

Pamplona (Iruña)

 Pamplona

Whether you call it Pamplona, the town founded by Pompey in 75 BC, or by its older name of Iruña, which means simply 'the city' in Basque, the capital of Navarra sits on a strategic 1,400ft pimple on the beautiful fertile plain, its existence as inevitable as its nickname, the 'Gateway of Spain'. For a few years in the 730s, the Arabs used it in reverse, as the gateway to France, until their dreams of Europe were hammered at Poitiers.

Over the next decades, the Basques regained control of Pamplona, clobbered Charlemagne after he burnt their walls, and set up their own king. In 918 the Moors came back and razed Pamplona to the ground again. To encourage rebuilding, Sancho the Great invited his subjects over the Pyrenees, in what is now Basse-Navarre, to come and start trades in what became the two new districts of Pamplona, San Cernín and San Nicolás. The fact that the three districts of the city were practically independent and had their own privileges led to violent rivalry between them, so much so that in 1521 the French, coming to the rescue of the French Navarrese, unsuccessfully besieged Pamplona in an effort to regain San Cernín and San Nicolás. Wounded while fighting for Castile was a certain Captain Iñigo López de Recalde (or Loyola), who got religion in a militant way and founded the Jesuits (*see* p.149).

Pamplona seems to have been naturally conducive to that sort of thing, with a reputation for being crazily austere, brooding and puritanical. To anyone who knows the city only for throwing the wildest party in Europe, this comes as a shock of *desfase*, or maladjustment, a word that means (and gleefully celebrates) the unresolved contradictions that coexist in post-Franco Spain. Stern Catholicism is part of the city's fabric. 'From the top to the bottom of Pamplonese society, I have found the whole place poisoned by clerical alkaloid,' grumped Miguel de Unamuno. 'One drop in the eye is enough to infect you forever.' In the 1950s, the shadowy Opus Dei, Christianity's conservative fifth column, chose Pamplona to build their Universidad de Navarra, their most important educational institution in Spain, especially since the late Pope John Paul II's beatification of the founder, Josemaría Escrivá. Today, the head prelate of the order is a Basque, Bishop Javier Echevarría. In the 1960s, Pamplona's new tennis club still built separate swimming pools for men and women. Fifty years on, the city prides itself on having set up Spain's first shelter for battered women, the first city workshops for training disadvantaged youths and the first urban recycling programme. It is also the seat of the Udako Euskal Unibertsitaea (Basque Summer University), which has led the way in higher education in Euskera and has promoted the printing of over 180 university textbooks in Basque. 'Pamplona is a city that

Getting to and around Pamplona

By Air

Pamplona's **airport** (t 91 321 10 00, *www.aena.es*) is 6km south of the city, with regular connections to Madrid and Barcelona. The cheapest way to get to the airport is to take no.16 bus opposite the bus station, which drops you 800m from the airport.

By Train

The RENFE **train station** (t 902 320 320, *www.renfe.com*) is 2km out of town on Avda San Jorge. Local bus nos.9 and 3 link it to the centre.

By Bus

The **bus station** (t 902 023 651, *www.estaciondeautobusesdepamplona.com*) is in town, near the citadel, at C/Yanguas y Miranda 2. Besides provincial connections, there are several buses daily to Vitoria-Gasteiz, Bilbao, Donostia-San Sebastián and Zaragoza. There are fewer services at weekends, particularly on Sundays. Local bus timetables are available at *www.mcp.es* (Spanish only).

gives much more than it promises,' said Victor Hugo. It certainly will if you come in the second week of July for *Los Sanfermines*, but expect it also to take your money, your sleep and a lifetime's supply of adrenaline.

A Walk through the Casco Viejo

Pamplona was squeezed into a tight girdle of walls until the early 1900s, when the city spread in all directions and accumulated around 185,000 inhabitants in the process. But for all its 20th-century flab the vital organs in the historic Casco Viejo remain intact, curled tightly around the city's heart, the spacious **Plaza del Castillo**. Off the southwest corner extends the **Paseo de Sarasate**, populated by stone kings and queens and the overwrought **Monumento a los Fueros**, erected by popular subscription after Madrid tried to mess with Navarra's privileges back in 1893. The bronze allegory of Navarra holds a copy of the *Ley Foral*, or *Fueros'* Law, surrounded by the broken chains from the Battle of Las Navas de Tolosa, symbolizing freedom; these also feature on Navarra's coat of arms. Historical frescoes decorate the neoclassical **Palacio de Navarra** at one end of the Paseo; its archives contain one of the best caches of medieval documents in Spain and the garden boasts a massive sequoia.

Off the eastern end of Plaza del Castillo, the narrow streets jammed with shops and bars were once the **Judería**, where Pamplona's Jews, 'a gentle and reasonable race' according to the king of Navarra, lived unmolested until Navarra was gobbled up by the intolerant, Inquisitor-infested Spain of Ferdinand and Isabel. Behind these, tucked up near the ramparts, the gracious 14th–15th-century Gothic **cathedral** hides behind a dull neoclassical façade, slapped on in the 18th century by a misguided do-gooder; a shame, because the original front, according to travellers' descriptions, was as lusty as the one at Cervatos (*see* pp.197–8).

Cathedral
cathedral open
Mon–Sat 10–7, Sun 10–2
and 6.30–9; **museum**
open mid-Mar–mid-Oct
Mon–Sat 10–7, mid-
Oct–mid-Mar Mon–Sat
10–5; adm, includes
Museo Diocesano

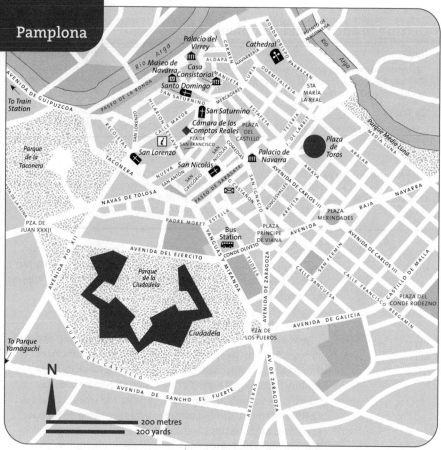

When completed, this was the second-largest cathedral in Spain after León's, and suitable shelter for the beautiful alabaster tombs of the cathedral's sponsors, big-nosed Charles III 'the Noble' and his big-nosed queen Leonora de Trastámara, sculpted in the 15th century by Jean de Lomme of Tournai. The kings of Navarra were crowned before the Romanesque statue of Santa María La Real, carved and gilded in silver in the 12th century, who peers out from beneath a spidery neo-Gothic canopy in the presbytery. The delicacy of the Gothic **cloister** (1280–1472) approaches gossamer in stone and reaches a climax of decorative bravura in the justly named **Puerta Preciosa** (1350–60), carved with a superb *Dormition of the Virgin*. The **Museo Diocesano** occupies the kitchen and refectory where pilgrims once dined; the refectory is filled with sweet-faced 12th–15th-century carvings of the Madonna and Child, while the kitchen is remarkable for its enormous chimneys. The Cillería contains two remarkable reliquaries – the 1258 *Relicario del Santo Sepulcro* and the 1401 *Relicario del Lignum Crucis*, adorned with precious stones.

The narrow old lanes around the cathedral belong to the **Navarrería**, the original Basque quarter, populated in the Middle Ages by cathedral-builders and farmers who tilled the bishop's lands. Here, on the promontory of the Rincón del Caballo Blanco, you'll find the most impressive segment of the surviving **walls** built by Philip II, with a reputation for impregnability so powerful that no one challenged it until the French tried to hole up here against Wellington; the views stretch for miles over the plain. Just west, the 12th-century **Palacio del Virrey** started out as the royal palace: restored and strikingly expanded by Rafael Moneo, it is now the Royal and General Archive of Navarra.

Past the attractive **Portal de Zumalacárregui** (16th-century, but renamed after the heroic Carlist general who died at the siege of Bilbao), the **Museo de Navarra** occupies a huge 16th-century hospital and contains everything from Navarrese prehistory to contemporary art, with Roman mosaics, Gothic wall paintings, carved capitals from Pamplona's original Romanesque cathedral (minus the naughty bits), an ivory coffret from Leyre made in Córdoba in the 11th century and a fine portrait of the *Marqués de San Adrián* by Goya. A pretty courtyard with Roman mosaics offers views of a stretch of the old city walls. Just below the museum, wooden barricades remind you that this is the beginning of the *encierro*; the bulls leave their corral near Plaza Santo Domingo and head up C/Mercaderes and C/Estafeta. Follow their route and you'll come to Plaza Consistorial and the colourful Baroque **Casa Consistorial**, topped with jaunty allegorical figures. Pamplona's nobles built their finest escutcheoned palaces just off this square, along C/Zapatería and C/Mayor. Plazas de Consejo and San Francisco, set diagonally opposite each other, are also worth a look, the latter with a Modernista (Art Nouveau) hotel converted into a bank. Nearby in C/Ansoleaga, the well-preserved Gothic **Cámara de los Comptos Reales**, the king's mint in the 12th century, has a magnificent porch opening on to a vault and patio.

Museo de Navarra
t 94 842 64 92, www.navarra.es; open Tues–Sat 9.30–2 and 5–7, Sun and hols 11–2; closed Mon; adm

Cámara de los Comptos Reales
open Mon–Fri 8–3

07 Navarra and La Rioja | Pamplona (Iruña)

Pamplona's Annual Meltdown: *Los Sanfermines*

Before Hemingway there was Fermín, son of a Roman senator and first bishop of Pamplona. His family had been converted by San Saturnino (or Sernin, or Cernín) of Toulouse, who was martyred by being dragged by a bull. Fermín, for his part, travelled as a missionary to the Gauls and was beheaded in Amiens. Some time between then and 1324, when Pamplona held its first fiesta, Fermín decided to take bullfighters under his saintly cape; by 1591 his festival had found its current dates and form. Although it's the insanely dangerous running of the bulls that has made *Los Sanfermines* world-famous, this is only a tiny portion of the nine days of non-stop revelling when 'Pamplona becomes the world capital of happiness', a state of hyper-bliss fuelled by three million litres of alcohol.

There is some order to the madness. The *Sanfermines* officially start at noon on 6 July, when thousands of Navarrese in their festival attire (white shirts and white trousers or skirts, red sashes and red bandanas) gather in front of the town hall to hold their bandanas aloft as a rocket called *El Chupinazo* is fired off the balcony and a city councillor cries in Spanish and Basque: 'People of

Pamplona! Long live San Fermín!' The city explodes with a mighty roar, while popping tens of thousands of champagne corks (and smashing the bottles on the pavement).

In the afternoon, the giants and big heads (*gigantes y cabezudos*) – as essential to the fiesta as the bulls – leave their 'home' in the bus station. The eight 13ft plaster giants supported by dancers date from 1860 and represent kings and queens, whirling and swirling to the minuet, their sweeping skirts flowing in the air. They are accompanied by the *cabezudos* and *kilikis*, big-headed figures in tricorn hats, with names like Napoleon and Patata, who wallop children on the head with foam rubber balls tied to bats. This is also the prerogative of the *zaldikos*, the colourfully dressed men wearing cardboard horses around their waists; all are accompanied by dancers, *txistularis* and *gaiteros*.

At four o'clock a massive scrum, the *Riau Riau*, begins when members of the Corporación de San Fermín dressed in all their finery try to proceed 400m down the Calle Mayor to the chapel of San Fermín at San Lorenzo for vespers, but everyone else tries to prevent them in a gung ho defiance of authority, to the extent that it's often late at night before the Corporación achieves its goal. The mayor of Pamplona has tried for several years to ban the chaotic *Riau Riau*, but it seems to be unbannable. After a first night of carousing and dancing in the streets, the dawn of 7 July and every following day is welcomed with the *dianas*, a city-wide wake-up call performed on screeching pipes.

The *encierro*, or *zezenketa*, the running of the bulls, begins daily at 8am, but, if you want a good place to watch, wedge yourself into a spot along the route – Cuesta de San Domingo, Mercaderes and Estafeta – at least an hour earlier. Before running, the locals sing a hymn to Fermín and arm themselves with a rolled-up newspaper to distract the bull's attention, since the animals – 1,200lbs of muscle and fury – charge at the nearest moving object, ideally at a flung newspaper instead of a falling runner. A rocket goes up as the first bull leaves the corral; a second rocket means that all are released, and a third signals that all have made it to the bullring – on a good run the whole *encierro* only lasts three minutes. The most dangerous moments are when the runners and bulls have to squeeze into the runway of the bullring, or when a bull gets loose from his fellows and panics. People get trampled and gored every year; if you run you can hedge your bets by running on weekdays, when it's less crowded, and by avoiding the *toros* of the Salvador Guardiola ranch, which have the most bloodstained record.

The spirit of abandon is so infectious that, even if you come determined not to run, you may find yourself joining in on a self-destructive spur of the moment. Women do defy the authorities and run, although the police try to pull them out. During the *encierro* the lower seats of the bullring are free (again, arrive early), except on Sunday; from here you can watch the bulls and runners pile in and, afterwards, more fun and games as heifers with padded horns are released on the crowd in the ring. The traditional breakfast is huge (bull stews, lamb's sweetbreads, ham and eggs in tomato sauce, washed down with gallons of chilled rosé and *patxaran*).

The bullfights themselves take place daily at 6.30 in the evening – tickets sell out with the speed of lightning and are usually only available from scalpers. The *sombra* seats are for serious aficionados, while members of the *peñas* (clubs devoted to making noise and in general being as obnoxious as possible) fill up the *sol* seats and create a parallel fiesta if the action in the ring isn't up to snuff, or create pandemonium if it is. Afternoons also see other bull sports that are bloodless (for the bull, at any rate): the dodging, swerving *concurso de recortadores* and leaping *corrida vasca-landesa*. Between the bullfights there are concerts, Navarrese dance (*jotas*) and Basque dances, processions of the relics of San Fermín, parades and activities for young children and senior citizens. At night, fireworks burst over the citadel and the *toro de fuego*, or 'fire bull', carried by a runner and spitting fireworks, chases children down the route of the *encierro*. Then there's the midnight *El Estruendo de Irún*, led by an enormous drum called the *bomba*, in which hundreds of people – just about anyone who can lay their hands on anything that makes a sound – gather and let loose in an ear-bashing sonic disorder.

At midnight on 14 July, Pamplona winds down to an exhausted, nostalgic finale, a ceremony known as the *Pobre de mí*; everyone gathers in front of the town hall (or in the Plaza del Castillo for the livelier, unofficial ceremony), with a candle and sings: 'Poor me, poor me, another San Fermín has come to an end.' As the clock strikes 12 everyone removes their red scarves and agrees, like Hemingway, that it was 'a damned fine show' and promises to do better and worse next year. Die-hards party on until 8am the next day, and perform one last feat, the *encierro de la villavesa*: the bulls are all dead so they run in front of a bus.

**San Saturnino/
San Nicolás/
San Lorenzo**
*all churches open
roughly 8.30–12
and 6.30–7.30*

The not always tremendously popular *francos* invited to Pamplona by Sancho the Great lived just to the east in their two rival quarters named after, and defended by, 13th-century churches that doubled as fortresses when their fellow citizens went on the warpath. These are **San Saturnino** (or San Cernín) in C/San Saturnino and **San Nicolás** in lively, bar-lined C/San Nicolás; a plaque by the former marks the site where the first Pamplonans were converted by San Saturnino. To the west, **San Lorenzo** is best known for its chapel dedicated to San Fermín, built by the city in 1717, where his bust reliquary quietly resides 51 weeks of the year, presiding over weddings; so many Pamplonese want to be married under his protective eye that there's a two-year waiting list.

Pamplona is well endowed with parks. The oldest, the French-style **Parque de la Taconera**, closes the west end of the Casco Viejo and has one of the city's nicest cafés, the **Vienés**. Just south, the star-shaped **Ciudadela**, built on the orders of Philip II, now has a green park inside and outside the steep walls. The immaculate **Parque Yamaguchi** is named after Pamplona's Japanese 'twin' and has a neat Japanese garden complete with lakeside wooden house for the tea ceremony. Also here is one of Pamplona's newer attractions, a tall, fat red and blue tower containing the **Planetario**.

Planetario
*t 94 826 26 28, www.
pamplonetario.org;
open Aug–Sept Mon–
Sat 11–1.30 and 5–8;
Oct–June Mon 9.30–
1.30, Tues–Fri 9.30–1.30
and 4–7.30, Sat 11 –1.30
and 5–8.30; closed Sun
and July; adm*

The city's prettiest garden, **Parque Media Luna**, lines the river east of the city and has a path ending at the medieval bridge, the **Puente de Magdalena**, used by the pilgrims. The park in front of the **Plaza de Toros** was renamed Paseo Hemingway and has a grizzled bust of the writer whose novel *The Sun Also Rises* (1926) made Pamplona a household name.

Museo Oteiza
*t 94 833 20 74,
www.museooteiza.org;
open Oct–May Tues–Fri
10–3, Sat–Sun and hols
11–7; June–Sept
Tues–Sun 11–7;
adm, free on Fri*

The influential sculptor Jorge Oteiza (1908–2003) is remembered in the **Museo Oteiza**, close to the village of Navarra de Alzuza. The museum, in a bold, boxy building by Francisco Sáenz de Oiza which links to the sculptor's home, and includes more than 1,600 pieces.

ⓘ **Pamplona >**
*C/Eslava 1, Plaza
San Francisco,
t 84 842 04 20, oit.
pamplona@navarra.es*

Tourist Information in Pamplona

For up-to-date info on *Los Sanfermines*, see *www. sanfermin.com*.

Cultural/historical walking tours: The tourist office runs themed tours of the city, including tapas and wine-tasting tour and night tours. See *www.turismodepamplona.com*, or ask at the tourist office. Other tour companies include **Incoming, t** 94 822 15 06, *www.incomingnavarra.net*, who offer a range of tours in Pamplona and around.

Post office: Paseo de Sarasate 9, t 94 820 72 17.

Internet access: The city provides free WiFi at hotspots throughout the city, including the Parque de la Ciudadela. For a cybercafé, try **Kuria Net**, C/Curia 15, t 94 822 30 77.

Markets in Pamplona

Mercado de Santo Domingo, next to the town hall in Plaza de los Burgos. The oldest and most popular produce market in the city (*Mon–Sat*).

Mercadillo de Landaben, Polígono Landaben. This Sunday-morning open-air market (*not July and Aug*) has everything to buy, from clothes to fruit.

07

Navarra and La Rioja | Pamplona (Iruña)

Where to Stay in Pamplona

Pamplona ✉ 31300

During *Los Sanfermines*, hotel prices double and often triple, supplemented by scores of overpriced rooms in *casas particulares*, advertised weeks ahead in the local newspaper, *Diario de Navarra*. If you end up sleeping outside, any of the gardens along the walls or river are preferable to the noisy, filthy, vomit-filled citadel. Keep a close eye on your belongings (petty criminals, unfortunately, go into overdrive along with everyone else during the fiesta) and check in what you don't need at the *consigna* in Plaza San Francisco, next to the tourist office; everyone else does too, so get there early. Campsites are set up outside the city, including some with pre-erected tents (see *www.thefanatics.com*). If you stay outside Pamplona and drive into town, beware that theft from cars is widespread.Cheaper *hostales* and *pensiones* are mostly on C/San Gregorio and C/San Nicolás.

 Hostal Navarra >>

⭐ La Perla >

★★★★★La Perla, Plaza del Castillo, **t** 94 822 30 00, *www.granhotellaperla.com* (€€€€€–€€€). Hemingway always stayed at this, Pamplona's oldest hotel, with its high ceilings and plaster mouldings, lavishly restored and reopened as a luxury hotel a few years ago. Woody Allen counts among its more recent celebrity guests.

★★★★Hotel Palacio Guendulain, C/Zapatería 53, **t** 94 822 55 22, *www.palacioguendulain.com* (€€€€–€€€). A luxury hotel in a sumptuously restored 18th-century palace, with a fine restaurant, and a garden with a collection of vintage cars. Bedrooms are classically elegant.

★★★★Alma Pamplona, Beloso Baja, **t** 948 29 33 80, *www.almapamplona. com* (€€€€–€€€). Bold, contemporary architecture and 21st-century design meet in this smart hotel on the edge of the city. It has a gym, spa, and restaurant.

★★★★Iruña Palace Los Tres Reyes, C/de la Taconera, **t** 94 822 66 00, *www. hotel3reyes.com* (€€€). Conveniently located a short walk from the old town, this big modern hotel pampers its well-heeled guests with every possible convenience, including an indoor heated pool and tennis.

★★★Yoldi, Avda San Ignacio 11, **t** 94 822 48 00, *www.hotelyoldi.com* (€€). A bland, modern business hotel that offers great weekend deals.

★★★NH El Toro, Berrioplano (5km from Pamplona on the Guipúzcoa road), **t** 94 830 22 11, *www-nh-hotels.es* (€€). Quiet rooms in a traditional-style stone mansion, overlooking a statue group of the *encierro*.

Casa Otano, San Nicolás 5, **t** 94 822 50 95, *www.casaotano.com* (€). Popular for years for its nice rooms with baths, and a good, inexpensive bar-restaurant. Discounts for pilgrims.

★★Hostal Navarra, C/Tudela 9, **t** 94 822 51 64, *www.hostalnavarra.com* (€). Next to the bus station, this offers immaculate cream-painted rooms with sage-green furnishings and all the conveniences. Five minutes' walk from the Casco Viejo.

★Castillo de Javier, San Nicolás, 50–52, **t** 94 820 30 40, *www.hotelcastillo dejavier.com* (€). A delightful and well-priced hotel in a central location. Rooms are stylish, comfortable and clean. The street-side rooms can get noisy, so, if you are a light sleeper, insist on a back room.

★★Hotel Eslava, Plaza Virgen de la O, **t** 94 822 22 70, *www.hotel-eslava.com* (€). A modest, family-run hotel tucked next to the old city walls, with clean, simple rooms and park views.

Mesón del Barro, C/Acella 2, **t** 92 825 63 66, *www.mesondelbarro.com* (€). Good-value rooms, with or without bath, above a restaurant close to the Parque Yamaguchi. They also offer self-catering apartments.

★★★Hs Bearán, San Nicolás 25, **t** 94 822 34 28, *www.hostalbearan.com* (€). The doubles here come with baths, TV, and air-conditioning.

Pensión Sarasate, Paseo Sarasate 30, **t** 94 822 30 84 (€). Small and personal; the decent but unspectacular rooms all have a private bath.

Ezcaba, **t** 94 833 03 15, *www. campingezcaba.com*. A good campsite, 7km north of the city and linked by a bicycle path.

Eating Out in Pamplona

Josetxo ❯

Josetxo, Plaza Príncipe de Viana 1, **t** 94 822 20 97, *www.restaurante josetxo.com* (€€€). A local gourmet institution in Pamplona for more than half a century, serving contemporary updates of classic Navarrese cuisine. Try the artichokes with crayfish or the venison with a nut sauce. *Closed Sun and Aug.*

Alhambra, C/Francisco Bergamín 7, **t** 94 824 50 07, *www.restaurante alhambra.es* (€€€). Look out for the more imaginative dishes at this fashionable place, a favourite with local gourmets: potatoes stuffed with truffles and scampi. *Closed Sun and mid-July–early Aug.*

Rodero, C/Emilio Arrieta 3, **t** 94 822 80 35, *www.restauranterodero.com* (€€€). One of the best restaurants in the city, serving modern variations on Navarrese, Basque and French recipes prepared with the finest seasonal ingredients. Try the Baztán suckling pig with honey, pumpkin seeds and kumquat. *Closed Sun.*

Enekorri, C/Tudela 14, **t** 94 823 25 47, *www.enekorri.com* (€€€). Stylish, contemporary restaurant serving exciting modern Navarrese cuisine.

Casa Manolo, C/García Castañón 12, **t** 94 822 51 02, *www.restaurantecasa manolo.com* (€€). Traditional, good value and welcoming, with a range of set menus offering fine local cuisine.

Bodegón Sarria, C/Estafeta 50, **t** 94 822 77 13, *www.bodegonsarria.com* (€€). Fronted by a wonderful old bar (with some of the best tapas in town) with black and white pictures of Hemingway and bulls on the walls, the restaurant here dishes up solid traditional fare.

El Merca'o ❯

El Merca'o, C/Tafalla 5–7, **t** 94 829 25 88, *www.elmercao.com* (€€). Stunning designer restaurant and bar, with superb *pintxos*, stellar contemporary cuisine and award-winning service.

Erburu, C/San Lorenzo 15, **t** 94 822 51 69 (€€–€). This is a quiet, wooden-beamed retreat in the middle of a buzzy bar-lined street. It serves tapas, traditional Navarrese dishes, and a good range of wines. *Closed Mon..*

Baserri, C/San Nicolás 32, **t** 94 822 20 21, *www.restaurantebaserri.com* (€€). Hard to beat for *cocina en miniatura*; this restaurant's fine creations have repeatedly walked away with the top honours at Pamplona's annual *Concurso de Pintxos*.

San Fermín, C/San Nicolás 44, **t** 94 822 21 91, *www.restaurantesanfermin.com* (€€). This is one of the best places to try Navarra's famous vegetables, all freshly prepared. They also offer tasty meat and fish, and there's a lunch menu for €12. *Closed Mon.*

Sarasate, C/San Nicolás 19, **t** 94 822 57 27 (€€). Come here for the best vegetarian meals in Pamplona. *Closed Sun and evenings, except Fri and Sat.*

Tapas/*Pintxos* in Pamplona

As well as elegant cafés, Pamplona had some 700 bars at the last count, or one for every 280 inhabitants – many of whom seem to be always in them day and night.

Bar Chelsy, C/Iturrama 20, **t** 94 825 28 30. An unassuming spot which is nonetheless one of the very best tapas bars in northern Spain, with scores of awards to prove it.

Café Iruña, Plaza del Castillo 44, *www.cafeiruna.com*. A famous 1888 Modernista place, with etched glass and chandeliers. It also boasts a wonderful summer terrace.

Mesón del Caballo Blanco, Rincón del Caballo Blanco (behind the cathedral), C/Redín s/n, **t** 94 821 15 04 An atmospheric old stone house with the best summer terrace in the city and a cosy fireplace in winter. Outdoor concerts in summer.

Café Roch, C/Comedias 6. One of the oldest cafés in the city, this is small, lively and usually packed; try the house special, pepper croquettes.

Letyana, Travesía de Bayona 2. Excellent, award-winning *pintxos*, and a great atmosphere.

El Molino, Avda Bayona 13. A much-loved classic, with fabulous *pintxos* and a regular crowd of locals.

Fitero, C/Estafeta 58. This is the best tapas bar on legendary Estafeta, with an array of mouthwatering *pintxos*.

East of Pamplona: Sangüesa, Javier and Leyre

Pilgrims to Santiago from Mediterranean lands would cross the Pyrenees at Somport in Aragón and enter Navarra at Sangüesa, home of one of the very best Romanesque churches and one of the craziest palaces in all Spain; but these days, if the wind's wrong, the pong of the nearby paper mill hurries visitors along. Note that if you go by bus from Pamplona there are only three a day.

Agoitz (Aoiz)

The area due east of Pamplona, crossed by the Río Irati, gets few tourists, but, if you're driving, the undulating landscapes and nearly deserted villages make an interesting alternative to the more direct N240 to Sangüesa. Agoiz itself has fine old houses, a medieval bridge and the 15th-century **San Miguel Arcángel**, worth a look for its excellent *retablo mayor* (1580) by Basque master Juan de Achieta and for its unusual 12th-century painted stone font. Romanesque connoisseurs should go out of their way to **Artaiz**, a tiny blip to the southwest (due south of Urroz), where the church of **San Martín** has the finest sculpture in rural Navarra.

Sangüesa

Sangüesa was a direct product of the pilgrimage, purposely moved from its original hilltop location in the 11th century to the spot where the road crosses the Río Aragón. In 1122, Alfonso el Batallador, king of neighbouring Aragón, sent down a colony of *francos* to augment Sangüesa's population, and 10 years after that ordered the Knights of St John to build a church well worth stopping for: **Santa María la Real**. This possesses one of the most intriguing and extraordinary portals anywhere, so strange that some writers believe that its symbols (knotted labyrinths, mermaids, two-headed beasts symbolizing duality, etc.) were sculpted by Agotes (*see* box, opposite), or by a brotherhood of artists, into something deeper than orthodox Catholicism. Even the damned are laughing in the *Last Judgement* on the tympanum, presided over by a Christ in Majesty with a secret smile. Below, the elongated figures on the jambs show stylistic similarities to Chartres cathedral, although again the subjects are unusual: on the left the three Marys (the Virgin, Mary Magdalene and Mary Salome, mother of St James), on the right Peter, Paul and Judas, hanged, with the inscription *Judas Mercator*. The upper half of the portal is by another hand altogether, crossed by two tiers of Apostles of near-Egyptian rigidity and another Christ in Majesty. If the church is open, ask the sacristan to show you the capitals in the apse, hidden behind the Flemish Renaissance *retablo*, and note

Getting East from Pamplona

Around three **buses** a day are run by **La Veloz Sangüesina, t** 94 887 02 09, from Pamplona to Sangüesa.

---

the well in the corner. Walk around to see the beautiful carved corbels on the apse and the octagonal tower.

When Aragón and Navarra went their separate ways, the kings of Navarra made Sangüesa one of their several residences. Its arcaded Rúa Mayor is lined with palaces, including the **Casa Consistorial**, built over the old royal patio of arms, today a leafy square; behind this is the austere 12th-century, twin-towered **Palacio del Príncipe de Viana**. The 12th-century **church of Santiago** has a huge battlemented tower and carved capitals, and conserves a large stone statue of St James, discovered buried under the floor in 1965. The slightly later, Gothic **San Salvador** has a pentagonal tower and a huge porch, sheltering a carved portal; its Plateresque choir stalls come from Leyre. Just around the corner, in C/Alfonso el Batallador, the brick **Palacio Vallesantoro** catches the eye with its corkscrew Baroque portal and the most extraordinary wooden eaves in Spain, carved with a phantasmagorical menagerie.

Javier and Leyre

Sangüesa is the base for visiting two of Navarra's holy sites. **Javier**, 13km away, is topped by a picturesque if over-restored

Europe's Untouchables: the Agotes

Some of Europe's best-known outcasts, the Agotes (Cagotes in French) lived in the valleys of Navarra and especially across the Pyrenees in Basse Navarre and Gascony. Apartheid-style laws forced them to live separately and only marry other Agotes; to enter church only by a certain door and hear Mass in a special corner; to dress differently, with a goose foot sewn on to the backs of their coats; and to play castanets at all crossroads and other public places to warn passers-by of their presence. Trades were forbidden them – except building and carpentry, a craft they excelled at to the extent that they were often called 'the Master Carpenters' instead of Agotes.

Guesses as to who the Agotes actually were and how they came to be pariahs vary in the extreme: some say they were dwarves, or albinos covered with a blond down, or Visigoths who failed to give up their Arian heresies and took refuge in the mountains when the Moors invaded. A strong tradition linking the Agotes to leprosy suggests that they were descended from a colony sent to live up in the remote valleys; but leprosy is not hereditary, and the Agotes who lived in Sangüesa and other towns were not lepers, although the stigma may have remained. In the Middle Ages, their ranks may have been swollen by all the loose ends of Europe who landed up along the road to Santiago. Or it may have been that the Agotes were only symbolic lepers, kept at a distance for the stigma of their heresies (curiously, they were also Crestias, or Christians, as if emphasizing that they were still, really, in the fold). This heresy may have been a highly contagious kind of universal mysticism practised by the Templars or the Order of the Knights of St Lazarus, an order founded in the East before the Templars and devoted to the care of lepers, using Lazarus as their symbol of death within life.

Whatever the real reason for their pariah status, it was forgotten by the 16th century, when the fed-up Agotes petitioned the pope to give them the same rights as other citizens. The pope agreed, but it was only in the 20th century, after a long civil rights struggle, that the Agotes were fully integrated into society, intermarrying with non-Agotes and vanishing without trace.

Javier castle
t 94 888 40 24, www.
santuariodejavier.org;
open for guided visits
daily 10–1.30 and
3.30–6.30; adm

battlemented **castle**, the birthplace in 1506 of Francisco de Javier (Xavier), Jesuit apostle of Japan and the Indies. Although the castle is now a Jesuit college, you can take the tour and learn a lot, about both St Francis and castles. Perhaps most fascinating is the fresco of the *Dance of Death*, a grim reminder that the Pyrenees were especially hard hit by the plague.

Just north of Javier, at **Yesa**, the Río Aragón has been dammed to form the vast **Yesa Reservoir**. A road from Yesa leads up into the Sierra de Leyre and to the **Monasterio de San Salvador de Leyre**. Its foundation pre-dates the Moors, and in the 8th century its most famous abbot, San Virila, so constantly prayed to heaven for a peek into infinity that he was granted his wish, by the lovely warbling of a bird. To the abbot, the vision was a sublime moment, but when he went down to tell his monks about it he found that his eternal second had lasted 300 years. Leyre essentially dates from the 11th century, when Sancho the Great reformed the rule according to that of Cluny and declared it 'the centre and heart of my realm'. The first kings of Navarra were buried there, and the abbot of Leyre served as the bishop of Pamplona. Abandoned in the 19th century, the monastery was reoccupied in 1950 by the Benedictines, who began a restoration programme that unfortunately obscures much of the older building. Visits begin in the startling, 11th-century crypt, where the first impression is that the church is sinking into the ground. The columns are runty little stubs of columns of unequal height weighed down by heavy block capitals, carved with simple geometric designs that stand at about chest level. The chancel above was consecrated in 1057 and supplemented two centuries later with a single-aisled nave; the effect is harmonious, light and austere, providing the perfect setting for the Benedictines' beautiful 7th-century **Gregorian chant**, still sung at matins and vespers. The bones of the first 10 kings of Navarra lie in a simple wooden casket behind a fine grille; the 13th-century statue of the Virgin of Leyre sits on the altar. The west portal, the **Porta Speciosa**, is finely carved with a mix of saints and monsters.

Monasterio de San Salvador de Leyre
t 94 888 41 50;
www.hotelhospederia
deleyre.com; open
Mar–Oct Mon–Fri
10.15–2 and 3.30–7; Sat
and Sun 10.15–2 and
4–7; Nov–Feb Mon–Fri
10.15–2 and 3.30–6; Sat
and Sun 10.15–2 and
4–6.30; adm

Gregorian chant
t 94 888 41 50;
call to confirm times,
but usually daily 7 pm
and 9.15pm, plus at
noon on Sun and
special feast days

It's a 10-minute walk up to the **Fountain of San Virila** for the magnificent view of the artificial lake and the Navarrese countryside that the abbot contemplated during his prayers, although the warbling birds have been replaced by hang-gliding Spaniards. Nature is a big attraction in eastern Navarra. The Sierra de Leyre divides the Roncal and Salazar valleys (*see* pp.82–4), but there are two splendid gorges quite close at hand. The **Foz de Lumbier**, formed by the Irati river, has a pleasant riverside trail, and is a breeding site for griffon vultures. The even more spectacular, sheer-sided, 6km **Foz de Arbayún** (*see* p.84) lies further to the north along the Río Salazar, with more griffon and a few Egyptian vultures; both gorges are accessible from Lumbier.

Where to Stay and Eat East of Pamplona

Aoiz >
C/Nueva 22,
t 94 8 33 60 05,
www.aoiz.es

Xabier >>

Sangüesa >
C/Mayor 2, t 94 887
14 11, www.sanguesa.es

Aoiz (Agoitz) ✉ 31430

*Hs Beti Jai, C/Santa Águeda 2,
t 94 833 60 52, *www.beti-jai.com* (€).
A rural delight, with classically
decorated rooms, an excellent
restaurant (€€), and a traditional
café-bar for drinks and tapas.

Sangüesa ✉ 31400

**Yamaguchi, on the road to Javier,
t 94 887 01 27, *www.hotelyamaguchi.*
com (€€). A modern hotel with a pool,
frontón, and a pleasant restaurant.

**Hostal Rural JP, Avda Padres
Raimondo Lumbier 3, **t** 94 887 16 93,
www.hotelruraljp.com (€). A handful
of basic but spotless rooms and a
café-bar They also rent apartments.

Mediavilla, C/Alfonso El Batallador 15,
t 94 887 02 12 (€). A Basque *asador*
serving delicious charcoal-grilled fish
and meat with local wine. *Closed Mon.*

Javier/Leyre ✉ 31411

****Hotel Señorio de Monjardín,
Ctra de Leyre 4, **t** 94 888 41 88,
www.hotelsenoriodemonjardin.com
(€€). Large, modern hotel, 3km
from Leyre on the N240, with some
luxurious suites and a restaurant
featuring Navarrese cuisine and
game dishes.

***Xabier, Plaza de Javier, **t** 94 888
40 06, *www.hotelxabier.com* (€€).
You can stay and eat next to the
castle at this charming, historic
hotel-restaurant, with balconies
peeking through the ivy.

**El Mesón, t 94 888 40 35, *www.*
hotelmeson.com (€€). Also next to the
castle; pretty, but rather more basic.
Closed mid-Dec–mid-Feb.

**Hospedería de Leyre, t 94 888 40 11,
www.hotelhospederiadeleyre.com (€€).
This charming former pilgrims' *hostal*
at Leyre is the perfect antidote to
stress; its restaurant specializes in
traditional Navarrese cuisine.

South of Pamplona to Tudela

The green Basque hills are a distant memory south of Pamplona;
here the skies are bright and clear, the land arid and toasted
golden brown after the winter rains, except for the green swaths of
vineyards in La Ribera, cradle of Navarra's finest, freshest rosés.

Tafalla and Olite

In the 17th century, a Dutchman named E. Cock described Tafalla
and Olite as the 'flowers of Navarra'. Old **Tafalla** has wilted a bit
over the centuries and grass grows between the cobbles, but it still
has an impressive Plaza Mayor and claims one of the finest and
biggest *retablos* in the north: a masterpiece by Basque artist Juan
de Ancheta tucked away in the austere church of **Santa María**.

Northwest of Tafalla, **Artajona** has the air of an abandoned stage
set: majestic medieval walls with startlingly intact crenellated
towers defend little more than the 13th-century fortress church of
San Saturnino. The Hispano-Flemish *retablo mayor* dates from 1515.
This is the second church on the site. Artajona's walls, redone in
the 14th century, were first built between 1085 and 1103 by the
Templars and canons of St-Sernin (San Saturnino) of Toulouse.

Near Artajona, the **Ermita de la Virgen** shelters a bronze and
enamel 13th-century Virgin holding a bouquet of roses. There are
two megalithic gallery tombs nearby.

Getting around South of Pamplona

Trains linking Pamplona and Zaragoza call at Tafalla, Olite and Tudela. **Conda buses** (t 94 822 10 26, *www.conda.es*) stop at Tafalla, Olite and Tudela on the way to Zaragoza. Hire a **bicycle** or mountain bike from **Chiqui-bike** in Tudela and Arguedas (for the Bardenas Reales), t 94 882 52 01, *www.chiquibike.com*.

Palacio Real de Olite
open July and Aug daily 10–8; spring and autumn daily 10–7; winter daily 10–6; adm

Olite (Erriberri), south of Tafalla, is a fabulous medieval town dwarfed by its bewitching, lofty-towered **Palacio Real de Olite**, built for the king of Navarra in 1407. Each of its 15 towers and turrets has its own character, and restorers have made the whole thing seem startlingly new. Inside, the décor is *mudéjar*; hanging gardens were suspended from the great arches of the terraces, and there was a *leonera*, or lion pit, and a very busy set of dungeons; the Navarrese royal families led messy, frustrated lives. At night the whole complex is illuminated with a golden light, creating a striking backdrop to performances in the summer Festival of Navarra.

Santa María la Real
open daily 9.30–12 and 5–8

San Pedro
open daily 9.30–12 and 5–8

The castle's Gothic chapel, **Santa María la Real**, has a gorgeous 13th-century façade, and the Romanesque church of **San Pedro** has an octagonal tower and portal adorned with two large stone eagles, one devouring the hare it has captured (symbolizing force) and the other, more friendly, representing gentleness.

Eastwards, the village of **San Martín de Unx** has a superb crypt under its 12th-century church. From here a by-road branches south for the spectacular medieval village of **Ujué**, set on a hill corrugated with terraces, where a shepherd, directed by a dove (*ujué*), found the statue of the black Virgin now housed in the powerful 13th-century Romanesque-Gothic church of **Santa María**. The doorway has finely carved scenes of the Last Supper and the Journey of the Magi, and the altar preserves the heart of King Charles II of Navarra. Every year since 1043, on the first Sunday after St Mark's day (25 April), the Virgin has been the object of a solemn pilgrimage that departs from Tafalla at 2am.

Tudela

Founded by the Moors, Tudela, the second city of Navarra and capital of La Ribera region, was the last town in Navarra to submit to Ferdinand the Catholic, and it did so most unwillingly. Before the big bigot, Tudela had always made a point of welcoming Jews, Moors and heretics expelled from Castile or persecuted by the Inquisition, and it was no accident that its tolerant environment nurtured three of Spain's top medieval writers: Benjamin of Tudela, the great traveller and chronicler (1127–73); the poet Judah Ha-Levi of the same period; and doctor Miguel Servet (1511–53), one of the first to write on the circulation of the blood. Head straight for the picturesque, labyrinthine Moorish-Jewish kernel, around the elegant 17th-century **Plaza de los Fueros**; the decorations on the façades recall its use as a bullring in the 18th and 19th centuries.

Cathedral
open Tues–Sat 9–1
and 4–7, Sun and
Mon 9–1; adm

The Gothic **cathedral** was built over the town's Great Mosque in the 12th century and topped with a pretty 17th-century tower. It has three decorated doorways, and the delightful choir, behind its Renaissance grille, is considered the finest Flamboyant Gothic work in Navarra, carved with geometric flora, fauna and fantasy motifs; note, under the main chair, the figures of two crows picking out the eyes of a man – the dean who commissioned the work but refused to pay the sculptors the agreed price. The main altar has a beautiful Hispano-Flemish *retablo* painted by Pedro Díaz de Oviedo, and yet more chains from Las Navas de Tolosa. There's an ornate Gothic *retablo* of Santa Caterina and a chapel of Santa Ana, patroness of Tudela, with a cupola that approaches Baroque orgasm. The cool, plant-filled 13th-century cloister, with twin and triple columns, has capitals on the Life of Jesus and other New Testament stories, while the Escuela de Cristo, off the east end of the cloister, has *mudéjar* paintings and decorations. The square is pedestrianized and filled with a sea of café tables.

Among the best palaces are the 16th-century **Casa del Almirante**, near the cathedral, and, in the C/de Magallón, the lovely Renaissance **Palace of the Marqués de San Adrián**. An irregular, 17-arched, 13th-century bridge spanning the Ebro still takes much of Tudela's traffic, with help from an ultramodern suspension bridge.

Around Tudela: Desert, Water and Wine

 Bardenas Reales
www.bardenas reales.es; open 8am–1hr before dusk;
visitor centre: *north of Tudela, just off the NA-134, Ctra del Polígono de Tiro, Km.6,* **t** *94 883 03 08,* *turismo@ bardenasreales.es*

Just east of Tudela is a striking desert straight out of the American Far West known as the **Bardenas Reales**, where erosion has sculpted steep tabletops, weird wrinkled hills and rocks balanced on pyramids. You might recognize it, since it's a popular location for everything from Bond films to pop videos. The best way to see it (and not get lost) is by the GR13 walking path, which crosses its northern extent from the Ermita de Nuestro Señoro del Yugo. An easier way, however, is to go on an organized excursion, by horse, mountain bike or 4x4 (*see* box, overleaf).

South of Tudela, **Cascante** is known for its wines and the lofty church of the **Virgen del Romero** (Our Lady of the Rosemary Bush), built in the 17th century and reached by way of an arcaded walkway from the village below. The small spa town of **Fitero** (the waters are used in treating tuberculosis) grew up around the 11th-century Cistercian monastery of **Santa María la Real**, whose abbot, San Raimundo, founded the famous Order of the Knights of Calatrava in 1158. Don't miss the Romanesque Sala Capitular, a monumental *retablo* from the 16th century, the 18th-century chapel of the Virgen de la Barda and, among the treasures, a 10th-century ivory coffer from the workshop of the Caliph of Córdoba. **Cintruénigo** and **Corella**, just north, are important producers of DO Navarra wine, with a good dozen *bodegas* in the environs.

Market Days
South of Pamplona

Tafalla: Fri, Plaza Navarra.
Olite: Wed, Paseo del Portal.
Fitero: Tues and Fri, Plaza San Raimundo.

Sports and Activities
South of Pamplona

A number of firms offer excursions into the Bardenas Reales, in a 4x4 or on horseback. For more info, see *www.bardenasreales.com*, which has a list of tour operators. Turismo Bardenas *www.turismobardenas.com*, **t** 94 841 23 96, brings together professional guides offering a range of different tours, including wine and gourmet tours; active tours (4x4, quad biking, horse-riding and hiking).

Where to Stay and Eat
South of Pamplona

Tafalla ✉ 31300

Hs Tafalla, on the Zaragoza road, **t 94 870 03 00, *www.hostaltafalla.com* (€€–€). Modern roadside hotel. The food is delicious, especially when the dishes involve asparagus, lamb and hake.

Túbal, Plaza de Navarra 6, **t** 94 870 08 52, *www.restaurantetubal.com* (€€€–€€). Chef Atxen Jiménez draws in diners from Pamplona and beyond with her variations on classic Navarrese themes. Book well in advance. *Closed Mon and late Aug.*

Olite ✉ 31390

***Parador de Olite, Plaza de los Teobaldos 2, **t** 94 874 00 00, *www.parador.es* (€€€). Next to the castle of Carlos III in the converted 13th-century Castillo de los Teobaldos. A garden, air-conditioning and beautiful furnishings make castle-dwelling a delight, as do Navarrese gourmet treats in the dining room.

La Joyosa Guarda, C/de los Medios 23, **t** 94 874 13 03, *www.lajoyosaguarda.com* (€€€). Stylish country hotel in a renovated mansion, with a mix of antiques and contemporary

(i) **Tudela >>**
*C/Juicio 4, **t** 94 884 80 58, www.tudela.es; exhibitions on local interests*

(★) **Restaurante 33**
>

(i) **Olite >**
*Plaza de los Teobaldos 10, **t** 94 874 17 03, www.olite.es*

furnishings and a very elegant restaurant.

Casa Zanito, Rúa Revillas 16, **t 94 874 00 02, *www.casazanito.com* (€€). A modern hotel in a historic building with cheerful rooms and excellent meals, based on market availability.

Hotel Merindad de Olite, Rúa de la Judería 11, **t 94 874 07 35, *www.hotel-merindaddeolite.com* (€€–€). In a restored old building, incorporating part of the 12th-century walls.

Ujué ✉ 31390

Casa El Chofer I and **II**, **t** 94 873 90 11 (€). Simple rooms in a charming old house, plus a cottage to rent.

Mesón las Torres, **t** 94 873 90 52, *www.mesonlastorres.com* (€€). Has long been the place to eat, with Navarrese treats and Ujué's special *migas*, once a shepherd's dish.

Tudela ✉ 31500

*Hs Nueva Parrilla, C/Carlos III el Noble 6, **t** 94 882 24 00 (€€–€). Friendly, basic; functional rooms.

Hs Remigio, C/Gaztambide 4, **t 94 882 08 50, *www.hostalremigio.com* (€). Rustically decorated *hostal*, not far from the Plaza de Fueros.

Restaurante 33, C/Capuchinos 7, **t** 948 82 76 06, *www.restaurante33.com* (€€€). Widely regarded as the best in Navarra when it comes to local produce – they even offer a *menú* entirely of vegetable dishes. Carnivores will be more than satisfied with slow-roast kid and country stews.

Casa Ignacio, C/Cortaderos 2, **t** 94 882 10 21 (€€). Long-established favourite: try the famous *menestra de verduras*: asparagus, artichokes, peas, celery and lettuce. *Closed Mon eve.*

La Estrella, C/Carnicerías 14, **t** 94 882 18 58 (€). Serves up good home cooking and wonderful *pintxos*. *Closed Sun eve and 2 wks in Sept.*

Cintruénigo ✉ 31592

Hotel Restaurante Maher, C/La Ribera 19, **t** 94 881 11 50, *www.hotelmaher.com* (€€€). One of Navarra's best restaurants. Delicious Navarrese dishes with an imaginative *nouvelle cuisine* touch.

Getting around Northwest of Pamplona

Most Pamplona–Altsasu **trains** stop at Uharte Arakil.
Daily **buses** go to Lekunberri and Aldatz from Pamplona (**La Muguiroarra**, **t** 94 850 40 66)

Northwest of Pamplona: Aralar and San Miguel in Excelsis

Sanctuario de San Miguel in Excelsis
open daily 9.30–8

Navarra's magic mountain, **Aralar**, now a natural park, is a favourite spot for a picnic or Sunday hike from Pamplona, gracefully wooded with beech, rowan and hawthorn groves. It has been sacred to the Basques since Neolithic times, when they erected 30 dolmens and menhirs in the yew groves around Putxerri. On top is Navarra's holy of holies, the **Sanctuario de San Miguel in Excelsis**, on a panoramic south–north road (NA751) that climbs over Aralar between Huarte Arakil and Lekunberri. The gloomy stone chapel built by the count of Goñi was consecrated in 1098. Traditionally guarded by mastiffs, the chapel has had an empty air ever since French Basques plundered it in 1797, when they knocked off St Michael's head (or so say apologists who find the crystal head too weird); the hands of the desecrators were chopped off before they were put to death, and nailed over the chapel door. You can see the chains worn by Teodosio de Goñi (*see* below) and the hole through which the dragon appeared. A high-tech alarm system protects the recently stolen and recovered enamelled Byzantine *retablo*, showing the Virgin on a rainbow in a mandorla with the Christ Child; the only comparable work in Europe is the great altarpiece in St Mark's in Venice. Tentatively

(Side margin, vertical text) **07** | **Navarra and La Rioja** | Northwest of Pamplona: Aralar and San Miguel in Excelsis

The Knight, the Dragon and the Archangel

In the 9th century, Count Teodosio de Goñi went off to fight the Saracens with his Visigothic overlord King Witiza. He was returning home when he met a hermit (the devil in disguise) who warned him that his wife was unfaithful. Seething with rage, the knight stormed into his castle, saw two forms lying in his bed and without hesitation slew them both (this was endemic in the Middle Ages; the same thing happened to St Julian the Hospitaller). When Teodosio ran out he met his wife returning from Mass, who told him, to his horror, that she had given his own aged parents the bed. Horrified, Teodosio went to Rome to ask the pope what penance he could possibly do to redeem his soul, and after three nights the pope had a dream that he should wear heavy chains in solitude until God showed his forgiveness by breaking them.

Binding himself in chains, Teodosio went up to the top of Mount Aralar and lived as a hermit for years. One day, when he was sitting next to a cave, a scaly green dragon emerged, smoke billowing from its nostrils. Teodosio implored the aid of St Michael, who suddenly appeared with his sword in hand and spoke to the dragon in perfect Basque: '*Nor Jaunggoitkoa bezaka?*' ('Who is stronger than God?'). The dragon slunk back into its cave and the archangel struck off the knight's chains and left a statue of himself – an angelic figure with a large cross on its head and an empty glass case where the face ought to be. Every year between March and August the figure goes on a fertility-blessing tour through a hundred Navarra villages; and on Corpus Christi pilgrims walk or cycle up to the chapel.

Where to Stay and Eat Northwest of Pamplona

ⓘ Lekunberri >
Plazaola 21,
t 94 850 72 04,
www.lekunberri.net

Lekunberri ✉ 31870

**Hs Ayestarán I and II, C/Aralar 22, t 94 850 41 27, *www.hotelayestaran. com* (€€). A pleasant, old-fashioned atmosphere, with tennis, children's leisure facilities, a swimming pool and garden, and tasty local food. *Closed Oct–Mar.*

Hostal Elosta, C/Alde Zaharra 44, t 94 860 48 15 or t 626 177 915, *www. hostalelosta.com* (€). Seven simple rooms above a country café-bar in a traditional building in the old quarter.

Asador Epeleta, Aralar s/n, t 94 850 43 57, *www.asadorepeleta.com* (€€–€). Possibly the finest roast meats in Northern Spain, along with seafood. Book well in advance. *Closed Mon, second fortnight of June.*

Venta Muguiro, Autopista A15 (exit 123), t 94 850 41 02 (€). Old-fashioned 19th-century inn, with country cooking, including sturdy local stews and grills, and plenty of atmosphere.

dated 1028, it was probably originally stolen from Constantinople by a Crusader and sold to Sancho the Great.

In art, heaven's *generalísimo* is often shown with a spear, not slaying so much as *transfixing* dragons to the earth. A recurrent theme in the endless mysticism surrounding St Michael has it that his cult took over ancient religious centres concerned with water sources and underground streams (and, if you like, 'telluric forces' within the earth); the act of fixing the 'dragon' symbolizes the capture and manipulation of these forces. Sure enough, the Sierra de Aralar is so karstic as to be practically hollow: under the sanctuary there's an immense subterranean river that makes moaning dragonish sounds, feeding an icy lake in a domed cavern.

Around Aralar

Beigorri
www.beigorri
aventura.com; check
opening times on the
website; adm;
not suitable for
children under 8

Peru-Harri
open Sat–Sun
10.30–2.30; adm

Of the villages under the mountain **Lekunberri** is the most orientated to tourism; among its newest attractions is the **Beigorri** forest adventure park. **Leitza**, just north, is a prettier choice, besides being the home of Basque legend Iñaki Perurena, the *arrejazotzale* or champion heavy-stone weightlifter. Along with his son Iñaki, also a stone-lifter, he has established a museum, **Peru-Harri**, with a park full of sculptures and a traditional *caserío* displaying photographs and Basque sport memorabilia. **Zudaire**, south of Aralar, is the head town in a broken terrain called **Las Améscoas**, the refuge of the Carlists and delight of speleologists: most of the caves are located above Zudaire around **Baquedano**.

Southwest of Pamplona: The Camino de Santiago

Few places in Europe can boast such a concentration of medieval curiosities as this stretch of the famous road (*see* pp.34–8), where the mystic syncretism of Jews, Knights Templars, pagans and pilgrims was expressed in monuments with secret messages.

Getting along the Camino de Santiago

La Estellesa buses (t 94 832 65 09, *www.laestellesa.com*) from Pamplona stop at Puente la Reina and Estella (with a neo-Moorish station), en route to Logroño; timetables at *www.autobusesdenavarra.com*. For **guided tours** in the Estella region – everything from cultural tours to active pursuits such as pot-holing, climbing, and cycling, see the website *www.turismotierraestella.com*.

From Pamplona to Estella

A short turn off the N111 (about 15km from Pamplona) leads to the old village of **Obanos**, and 1.6km beyond that village to a lonely field and **Santa María de Eunate**, a striking 12th-century church built by the Templars. The Templars often built their chapels as octagons, but this one was purposely made irregular and is surrounded by a unique 33-arched octagonal cloister – hence its name 'Eunate' ('the hundred doors'). Many knights were buried here, and it's likely that its peculiar structure had deep significance in the Templars' initiatory rites. There are only a few carved capitals – some little monsters, and pomegranates on the portal, which, oddly, faces north. During the church's restoration, scallop shells were discovered along with the tombs – the church also served as a mortuary chapel for pilgrims. The lack of a central keystone supporting the eight ribs inside hints that Arab architects were involved in the building.

> **Santa María de Eunate**
> *open July–Sept Tues–Sun 10.30–1.30 and 5–8; Mar–June and Oct Tues–Sun 10.30–1.30 and 4–7; Jan–Feb and Nov Tues–Sun 10.30–2.30; closed Mon and Dec*

The *camino francés* from Roncesvalles (*see* p.85) and the *camino aragonés* converged at the 11th-century bridge in pretty **Puente la Reina**, which hasn't changed much since the day when pilgrims marched down the sombre Rúa Mayor, where many houses preserve their coats of arms. The pilgrims traditionally entered Puente la Reina through the arch of another Templar foundation, **El Crucifijo**, a church with scallops and Celtic interlaced designs on the portal and two naves. The smaller one was added to house a powerful 14th-century German crucifix left by a pilgrim. Towards the bridge, the church of **Santiago** has a Moorish-style lobed portal and, inside, two excellent polychrome 14th-century statues.

From Puente la Reina, the path (although not the road) continues up to atmospheric old **Cirauqui** propped on its hill. The ancient road to the west of Cirauqui, paved with Roman stones, pre-dates even the pilgrims.

Estella (Lizarra): The Town of the Star

> **Estella**

A stop at Estella, known as Estella la Bella for its beauty, was much looked forward to by the pilgrims. It owes its foundation in 1090 to a convenient miracle: nightly showers of shooting stars, which always fell on the same place on a hill, intrigued some shepherds, who investigated and found a cave hidden by thorns, sheltering a statue of the Virgin. Returning from the siege of Toledo the same year, King Sancho Ramírez founded Estella on the opposite bank of the Río Ega from the old settlement of Lizarra (coincidentally the Basque word for 'star') and populated it with *francos*, or freemen: artisans, merchants and others who owed allegiance to no feudal lord (although, confusingly, most of these *francos* were also Franks from Gascony, who fought in the Reconquista for pay or for piety's sake). Thanks to them, Estella has numerous fine medieval buildings; if many have been cropped, thank the Grand Inquisitor of Castile, Cardinal Cisneros, whose troops literally cut Navarra down to size in 1512 for Ferdinand the Catholic. The most exciting time to visit Estella is the Friday before the first Sunday in August, when it holds the only *encierro* where women are welcome to join in the run.

The arcaded **Plaza Fueros** is the town's bustling main square, full of terrace cafés and overlooked by the Gothic church of **San Juan**, with a dour early 20th-century façade and bells which ring ear-splittingly on the hour. To the west is the **Basílica de Nuestra Señora de Puy**, a must on the pious pilgrim route, being built on the point where the stars fell on Navarra. The 14th-century Virgin is still there, but the old basilica was replaced in 1951 with a concrete and glass star-shaped church, and a *mirador* offering lovely views across the old town. South of Plaza Fueros, the highlight for art pilgrims is the 12th-century **San Miguel**, the parish church of the *francos*, set on a craggy rock atop its original set of steps (which lead up from C/Chapitel). March right up them for the magnificent portal, where Christ in Majesty holds pride of place among angels, Evangelists and the Elders of the Apocalypse. On the left, St Michael pins the dragon and weighs souls; on the right, an angel shows the empty tomb to the three Marys. The top, sadly, fell to the Cardinal's tower-bashing squad, but the brackets are good, especially the man-eating wolf. Near San Miguel you'll find a faithful 19th-century copy of Estella's **medieval bridge**, which pilgrims crossed to the Lizarra side to visit the 12th-century **San Sepolcro**, with a fascinating façade added in 1328 but again truncated by Cisneros. The tympanum has an animated Last Supper, Crucifixion, Resurrection and what looks to be the Harrowing of Hell; statues of the 12 Apostles flank the door; one of them appears to be holding a stack of pancakes. To the right of the bridge is the piquant centre of old Lizarra, with churches and palaces bearing proud coats of arms, most now occupied by antiques shops, along Calle de la Rúa ('street of the street'). The finest palace is the Plateresque **Casa Fray Diego**, now used as the Casa de Cultura.

Casa Fray Diego
*open Tues–Fri
6.30pm–8.30pm, Sat
12–2 and 6.30–8.30,
Sun 12–2; closed Mon*

Off to the left was the **Judería**, or ghetto, its 12th-century synagogue converted into **Santa María de Jus del Castillo**, where the apse is decorated with a rich assortment of Romanesque modillions. The church is dwarfed by the adjacent 13th-century, austere **monastery of Santo Domingo**, now a retirement home.

Further up, near the new bridge, a 16th-century fountain under a canopy of linden trees in **Plaza de San Martín** is a delightful place.

San Pedro de la Rúa
open for mass or guided visits only; see tourist office

A curving flight of stairs leads up to the 12th-century **San Pedro de la Rúa**, defended by a skyscraper bell tower. The Moorish-inspired foiled arch of the portal is crowned by a relief of St James in a boat with stars. Inside, the church has its share of curiosities: a unique column made of three interlaced 'serpents', and the black *Virgen de la O*, a cult figure of the masons, who left their marks all over the church. The Baroque chapel to the left houses St Andrew's shoulderblade; the story goes that the bishop of Patras took it with him for good luck while making the pilgrimage in 1270. Luck failed him in Estella, where he died and was buried in San Pedro's cloister, along with his relic. The holy shoulderblade wasn't going to have any of this and made itself known by a curious light that appeared over the tomb; in 1626, the day when Andrew was proclaimed patron of Estella, a burning vision of his X-shaped cross hovered over the church. Of the cloister, only two galleries survive, reconstructed after the castle above was blown up in 1572 and crashed down on top of it. The twisted column is a copy of a famous one in Santo Domingo de Silos in Burgos.

Over the years, Estella became a favourite residence of the kings, whose 12th-century **Palacio de los Reyes de Navarra**, opposite San Pedro, is one of the best-preserved civic buildings from the period. Prominent at street level, a capital bears the oldest known depiction of Roland (*see* pp.38–9), clad in scaly armour, fighting the equally scaly giant Ferragut; further up, another capital shows a scene of devils and animal musicians, including a donkey playing a harp. The palace now houses the **Museo Gustavo de Maeztú**, devoted to works by Estella's best-known painter (1887–1947).

Museo Gustavo de Maeztú
t 94 854 60 37; open Tues–Sat 11–1 and 5–7, Sun 11–1.30; closed Mon

Around Estella

Estella is an important producer of DO Navarra wine, and the most interesting *bodega* to visit just happens to be the Benedictine **Monasterio de Irache**, 2km south at Ayegui. First recorded in 958, it later received a generous endowment from Sancho the Great, who helped finance one of the very first pilgrims' hospitals here. In 1569, Philip II moved the university of theology here from Sahagún (near León), where it remained, enjoying the same privileges as Salamanca, until it closed down with the expropriation of monasteries in 1824.

Monasterio de Irache
monastery open summer Tues 10–1.30, Wed–Fri 10–1.30 and 5–7, Sat–Sun 9–1.30 and 4–7; winter Tues 10–1.30, Wed–Sun 10–1.30 and 4.30–6; closed Mon; wine museum open Sat–Sun 10–2 and 4–8

The complex is a handsome mix behind an eclectic façade. The entrance is through an elegant Plateresque door, leading into an austerely beautiful Romanesque church with three apses under a Renaissance dome; the church is stripped of centuries' encrustation of altarpieces. The small wine museum preserves Irache's 1,000-year-old custom of offering free drinks to pilgrims.

Monasterio de Santa María de Iranzu
open summer daily 10–2 and 4–8; winter daily 10–2 and 4–6; adm; to arrange guided visits call t 94 852 00 47

Twelve kilometres up the San Sebastián road in Abarzuza, the **Monasterio de Santa María de Iranzu** was founded in the 11th century by Cistercians, who chose to live in a dramatic ravine true to their preference for wild, remote settings. It was recently restored by the government of Navarra and given to the Theatine order. The monks will show you the Romanesque-Gothic cloister with a hexagonal fountain, the medieval kitchen, and church.

South of Estella on the Ebro, **Lodosa** is famous for its red peppers, *pimientos del piquillo*, which are dried in long garlands over the white façades of the houses.

Los Arcos, Sorlada and Torres del Río

After Estella, the pilgrims walked to **Los Arcos**, where, tucked off the N111, there is an arcaded *plaza* and a 16th-century church, **Santa María**, with a pretty cathedral-size Gothic cloister, carved choir stalls and frantic Baroque *retablos*. Seven kilometres north of Los Arcos at **Sorlada**, a grand 18th-century Baroque basilica belongs to **San Gregorio Ostiense**, a once immensely popular saint who lost much of his influence to modern fertilizers. His story is told in the basilica's naïve paintings: back in 1039 locusts plagued the region so badly that a group of farmers walked to Rome and asked the pope for help. The pope had a dream that Cardinal Gregory of Ostia was the man for the job, and off he was sent to Navarra, where he preached and dispersed the locusts, an exertion that killed him after five years. He was buried at Sorlada and forgotten, until a light redirected farmers to his tomb. Remembering his good juju against the locusts (and their ancestral Celtic head cult), they would cart his skull reliquary around their fields, pouring water through the hole which made it into 'holy Gregory water'. Philip II had gallons of it sent down to water the orchards of the Escorial. Farming is so big here that you can take an **agricultural tour** of the local *bodegas*, ostrich farm, preserve-makers and distilleries.

Agricultural tour
t 94 864 00 21, Los Arcos tourist office

West of Los Arcos, **Torres del Río** has a striking, tall octagonal church, **Santo Sepolcro**, built in the late 12th or early 13th centuries by the Knights of the Holy Sepulchre, or some say the Templars; like **Santa María de Eunate** (*see* p.107) it may have been a mortuary chapel for pilgrims.

Viana: where Cesare Borgia Bit the Dust

Viana, the pilgrims' last stop in Navarra, fits a lot of monumentality into a small space. Founded by King Sancho VII 'the Strong' in 1219 to defend his frontier with Castile, it became the hereditary principality of the heir to the throne of Navarra in 1423. Although its once-proud castle fell to Cardinal Cisneros' demolition programme, nobles and courtly hangers-on stayed on and built themselves splendid mansions with big coats of arms, the elegant 17th-century **Casa Consistorial**, crowned with an escutcheon the

The Last Days of Cesare Borgia

How did Pope Alexander VI's son and Machiavelli's hero end up in Viana? With the papacy and central Italy in his pocket by 1502, married to Charlotte, sister of the king of Navarre and supported by France, Cesare had embarked on a brilliant career as a ruthless Renaissance prince-assassin. When his father pulled the rug out from under him by dying suddenly in 1503, Cesare himself was too ill to get to the Vatican and influence the conclave to elect a Borgia candidate; according to Machiavelli's *The Prince*, it was the only political mistake he ever made. It proved to be fatal. Once Julius II, arch-enemy of the Borgias, was elected in late 1503, Cesare's conquests in Italy were frittered away in anarchy; the French turned against him, and he went from being on top of the world to a man whose life was in danger. He fled to Aragón, cradle of the Borgias, only to be imprisoned by Ferdinand. The still-independent kingdom of Navarra proved to be his refuge, and he died in a skirmish in Viana, fighting Castilian rebels.

size of an asteroid, and the 13th–14th-century church of **Santa María**, hidden by a magnificent concave Renaissance façade based on a triumphal arch, with a coffered ceiling designed and carved by Juan de Goyaz (1549). Inside, the Gothic interior is quite airy and lovely, culminating in an intricate gilded Baroque *retablo*. The façade could be considered the tombstone of Cesare Borgia (1475–1507, *see* box), whose memorial, all that is left of his desecrated remains, lies buried under the marker in front of the church.

Where to Stay and Eat on the Camino de Santiago

(i) **Puente la Reina** >
C/Mayor 105, t 94 834 08 45, www.puentela reina-gares.es

(i) **Los Arcos** >>
in the Ayuntamiento, Plaza de los Fueros 1, t 94 864 00 21

(i) **Estella** >
C/San Nicolás 1, t 94 855 63 01, www.turismotierra estella.com

(i) **Viana** >>
Bajos Ayuntamiento, t 94 844 63 02

Puente la Reina ✉ 31100

**Hotel El Peregrino, on the Pamplona road, t 94 834 00 75, www.hotelelperegrino.com (€€€). This stone and timber place isn't as old as it looks, but it has luxurious rooms, a pool, and a fine restaurant.

Hotel Rural Bidean, C/Mayor 20, t 94 834 11 56, www.bidean.com (€€). A pretty stone building with a cosy, country atmosphere.

Estella ✉ 31200

****Hospederia Chapitel, C/Chapitel 1, t 94 855 10 90, http://hospederia chapitel.com (€€). Opened in 2011, this is a very comfortable choice, right in the heart of the old quarter.

*Hotel Yerri, Avenida Yerri 35, t 94 854 60 34, www.hotelyerri.es (€€–€). Modern, well-equipped if rather bland establishment, next to the bullring.

*Pensión San Andrés, Plaza Santiago 58, t 94 855 41 88 (€). Excellent value, clean and central, with family-size rooms overlooking the square.

*Hs Cristina, C/Baja Navarra 1, t 94 855 07 72 (€). Simple, clean and central.

La Navarra, C/Gustavo de Maeztú 16, t 94 855 00 40 (€€). A good bet, perhaps more for its medieval atmosphere than food, which is good if a bit pricy. *Closed Sun eve and Mon.*

Restaurante Richard, Avda Yerri, 10, t 94 855 13 16, www.barrestaurante richard.com (€€). Traditional cooking using fresh local produce. *Closed Mon and first week Sept.*

Los Arcos ✉ 31210

**Hotel Mónaco, Pza del Coso 1, t 94 864 00 00, www.hotelmonaco.es (€). Modest, with clean, modern rooms at a good price.

**Hs Ezequiel, C/La Serna, t 94 864 01 07, www.hostalezequiel.com (€). A friendly, family-run hotel, with large restaurant/bar.

Viana ✉ 31230

Hôtel Casa Armendariz, C/Navarro Villoslada 19, t 94 864 50 78 (€). A cosy little spot in the centre of town; traditional and modern cuisine in their *sidreria* (€€–€).

Borgia, C/Serapio Urra 1, t 94 864 57 81 (€€). A classic, serving modern interpretation of traditional Navarrese specialities, all prepared with the freshest local produce. The cellar is excellent. *Closed Sun and Aug.*

La Rioja

La Rioja may be named after the river Oja, one of the seven tributaries of the Ebro, but to most people it means wine, wine and more wine. The banks of the Ebro are frilly with vineyards and pinstriped with rows of garden vegetables on the flat, fertile plains of Rioja Baja around Calahorra. In the Sierra de la Demanda in the southwest, mountains are high enough to ski down; in the gullies of Rioja Baja, dinosaurs once made the earth tremble. Wedged up against the Ebro between Navarra and Castile, which once so hotly contested its fields and vineyards, the *comunidad* of La Rioja is now the smallest autonomous region in Spain (5,000 sq km) – not that there is any distinctive Riojan language or race, although in the 11th century a king, one of the four sons of Sancho the Great of Navarra, sat in Nájera. This was a brief period of independence, when Riojans began the history of Castilian Spanish as a written and poetic language and contributed to the invention of Santiago.

Logroño

More than half of all the 250,000 Riojans live in Logroño, their shiny, up-to-date capital famous not only for wine but also coffee caramels. It began under the Visigoths as Gronio, 'The Ford', but really bloomed only with the advent of the pilgrimage, when a stone bridge was built over the Ebro by San Juan de Ortega, one of La Rioja's two building saints. A prosperous modern agricultural centre, it nonetheless contains a pleasant little historic centre huddled around the graceful cathedral.

Logroño is a big long sausage of a town, but the interesting bits are concentrated in a small area near the Ebro. Barely an arch survives of San Juan's first bridge, which was replaced in the 1800s by the **Puente de Hierro**, or iron bridge. Just off this the pilgrims would pass in front of the 16th-century fountain and lofty Gothic **Santiago**, the oldest church in town. This was rebuilt in 1500, with a single nave a startling 53ft wide and still standing, in spite of the fact that its architect had no confidence in his handiwork and left town as soon as it was completed. It has a Renaissance *retablo*, and at the front a mighty 18th-century statue of Santiago Matamoros ('St James Moor-killer') who rides a steed with *cojones* as big as beach balls. The sculptor of the equestrian statue of General Espartero (in Logroño's central park, the **Espolón**) took them into consideration and equipped the mortal general's mortal horse a few degrees less generously.

The skyline of Logroño is stabbed by church towers, including two slender 18th-century Churrigueresque towers by Martín de Beratúa that frame the magnificent Baroque façade of the

Santa María de la Redonda

open Mon–Sat 8–1 and 6.30–8.45, Sun 9–2 and 6.30–8.45

cathedral, **Santa María de la Redonda** in Plaza del Mercado, a front that belies the Gothic-inspired gloom inside; the rotundity of its name (the first Romanesque church was octagonal) is recalled in an exuberant round rococo altar. Near here, in a high-security strongbox, is the *Tabla de Calvario*, supposedly painted by Michelangelo for his friend and muse Vittoria Colonna. Logroño's most distinctive landmark is its nubby pyramidal 'Needle', the 149ft 13th-century spire atop the lantern of **Santa María de Palacio**, in C/Marqués de San Nicolás, a church said to have been founded by no one less than Emperor Constantine. If it's open, pop in to see the Renaissance choir stalls, the 13th-century *Nuestra Señora de la Antigua*, and what remains of the Gothic cloister. Another tower, brick 11th-century *mudéjar* this time, looks over **San Bartolomé** with a ruggedly carved, time-blackened 14th-century Gothic façade; the smooth white interior has lovely shallow choir vaults.

Museo de La Rioja

www.larioja.org; check whether it has reopened at the tourist office

Bodegas Marqués de Murrieta

Ctra de Zaragoza, Km.5, t 94 127 13 70, www.marquesde murrieta.com

The 17th-century **Palacio del General Espartero** in Plaza San Agustín now holds the **Museo de La Rioja**, full of art from disappeared churches (14th-century painting from San Millán and *San Francisco with Brother Lion* by El Greco) and Flemish coffers. Unfortunately, it has been closed for some years, and its future is uncertain. There are a number of wine cellars in the area, including **Bodegas Marqués de Murrieta**, at Ygay, founded in 1852 and famous for its 35–40-year-old Gran Reservas, and the striking **Bodegas Juan Alcorta**, designed by Ignacio Quemada.

Getting around Logroño

Several **trains** a day link Haro, Logroño and Calahorra on the Bilbao–Zaragoza route. The RENFE station (with a left luggage office) is at Plaza de Europa: **t** 902 320 320, or *www.renfe.com*.

Logroño's **bus** links are faster and more frequent than train services. Several buses a day run to Burgos (via the towns on the pilgrims' route), Zaragoza, Vitoria, Pamplona and Rioja's villages. In Logroño the bus station is at Avda de España 1, **t** 94 123 59 83.

Car hire: Atesa, Avda Lope de Vega, 31, **t** 94 124 29 29, *www.atesa.es*; **Ebrorent**, Siete Infantes de Lara, 16 bajo, **t** 94 128 60 73.

Taxis: Radio Taxi: t 94 122 21 22; **Tele Taxi: t** 94 150 50 50 .

Markets in Logroño

Logroño: country produce, Mercado del Campo, Marqués de la Enseñada 52, Tues and Fri 8–2.

Where to Stay in Logroño

(i) Logroño >
C/Portales 50,
t 94 127 33 53,
www.logroturismo.org
(for city information) or
www.lariojaturismo.
com (covers all tourist
offices in La Rioja)

Logroño ✉ 26000

Logroño has a surprising number of luxury modern hotels, but few of them possess much charm.

****AC La Rioja, C/Madre de Dios 21, **t** 94 127 23 50, *www.ac-hotels.com* (€€€). A modern hotel on the edge of the old city, geared towards business travellers, with every necessary convenience, including a pool.

****Carlton Rioja, Gran Vía del Rey Juan Carlos I 5, **t** 94 124 21 00, *www.hotel-carltonlogrono.com* (€€€–€€). Glassy modern block on the edge of the Casco Antiguo.

***Hotel Portales, C/Portales 85, **t** 94 150 27 94, *www.hotelportales.es* (€€). Bright rooms with red walls add warmth to this modern hotel. Centrally located, close to the tapas bars. Check offers even in summer.

***Hotel Marqués de Vallejo, Marqués de Vallejo 8, **t** 94 124 83 33, *www. hotelmarquesdevallejo.com* (€€). A handsome place near the cathedral, with a sleek contemporary interior hiding behind a historic façade.

***Ciudad de Logroño, C/Menéndez Pelayo 7, **t** 94 125 02 44, *www.hotel-ciudaddelogrono.com* (€€). Central, modern and comfortable, renovated in 2010, with views over a park.

***Hotel Murrieta, Marqués de Murrieta 1, **t** 94 122 41 50, *www.hotel-murrietalogrono.com* (€€–€). A bland, modern hotel, but central and offering guests free Internet access.

Hostal Niza, C/Capitán Gallarza 13, **t** 94 120 60 44, *www.hostalniza.com* (€). Brightly painted, if small, rooms next to buzzy C/Laurel amid the bustle of the *casco viejo*.

Pensión Cinco Villas, C/Labradores 21, 2nd floor, **t 665 978 575, *www. pensioncincovillas.es* (€). Modest, but attractively priced *pensión* about a ten-minute walk to the old city.

Eating Out in Logroño

For tapas, try the celebrated C/Laurel, which has about 200 bars each serving a different speciality.

El Cachetero, C/Laurel 3, **t** 94 122 84 63, *www.cachetero.com* (€€€–€€). A popular choice for four generations, Logroño's best restaurant serves mouthwatering Basque anchovies and local delicacies such as pigs' trotters stuffed with mushrooms, capers and paté; book ahead.

El Rincón del Vino, Marqués de San Nicolás 136, **t** 94 120 53 92, *www. rinconesdelvino.com* (€€). As well as a vast selection of the promised *vino*, they have a fine *asador* serving delicacies like sirloin steak (*chuletón*) with wild mushroom stuffing. *Closed Sun eve, Mon and Aug.*

Entrevinos, C/Juan Lobo 1, **t** 94 125 66 35, *www.entrevinosrestaurante.com* (€€). An elegant modern eaterie, serving superb local cuisine and fine wines at suprisingly reasonable prices.

Avenida 21, Avda Portugal 21, **t** 94 122 86 02, *www.restaurante-avenida21.es* (€). Traditional, with brick vaults and stone walls, serving delicious local dishes accompanied by an excellent wine selection.

Calahorra and La Rioja Baja

Down the Ebro, east of Logroño, La Rioja Baja is flat, fertile, well watered and endowed with a sunny Mediterranean climate. Olive oil and wine are the two mainstays of the economy, with the kinds of peppers the Spanish devour by the kilo coming in a close third.

Calahorra

Despite its down-at-heel appearance, Calahorra has an interesting history. In fact, it has been inhabited for so long (since Palaeolithic times) that St Jerome speculated that it was founded by Tubal, grandson of Noah. It first makes history as Kalauria, an important Celtiberian fortress town under Carthaginian sway that, thanks to the Ebro, traded with the Greek colonies on the Mediterranean coast. In 187 BC the town was grabbed by Rome and renamed Calagurris; then, in a dispute between Pompey and Sertorius in AD 72, it held out against Pompey until all its defenders were dead through starvation. The Romans rebuilt it, and Calahorra returned the favour by giving Rome Marcus Fabius Quintilian (42–118), the first salaried professor of rhetoric in Rome and author of *Institutio Oratoria*, the empire's textbook on the fine art of talking. In the Middle Ages Calahorra was a prize craved by both Aragón and Castile; in a famous incident in the romance of *Las Mocedades del Cid* (and in the film *El Cid*, 1961, starring Charlton Heston), the Cid fought one-to-one for the city against Aragón's champion, vowing to lose not only the town but his head if he were defeated, but gaining both Calahorra and the hand of his beloved Ximena if he won. Which of course he did.

Calahorra has been an episcopal see since the 5th century, but the **cathedral** has been fussed with frequently. Behind a fruity, floral neoclassical façade pasted on in 1700, the nave with graceful star vaulting is a product of 1485. The furnishings are equally eclectic: the Gothic *Cristo de la Pelota*, 'Christ of the ball', is part of a Deposition from the Cross, the alabaster statues of the saints are 17th-century, and there are paintings attributed to Titian and Zurbarán. The Plateresque cloister houses the **Museo Diocesano** with a 12th-century bible and a 15th-century Custodia called *El Ciprés*, donated by Henri IV. Just over the Río Cidacos, note the 13-spout fountain. Near the cathedral, the church of Santiago and its *retablo* of St James is considered the finest neoclassical work in La Rioja. Nearby, the **Museo Municipal**'s archaeological collection stars the serene Roman bust of the Dama Calagurritana, symbol of the city (the same building houses the tourist information office). Just north of this, the church of **San Andrés** has a Gothic portal illustrating the triumph over paganism, and the **Arco del Planillo** is the only gateway surviving from the Roman walls of Calagurris.

Cathedral
*t 94 113 00 98,
www.catedral
calahorra.org;
open summer daily
9–1 and 5–7.30; winter
daily 9–1 and 4–6.30;
adm; call in advance to
visit the Museo
Diocesano*

Museo Municipal
*open Tues–Sat 12–2
and 6–9, Sun 10–2;
closed Mon*

East of Calahorra: the Alhama Valley

Down the Ebro holding down the east end of La Rioja, **Alfaro** was known as Ilurcis in the 5th century BC but kept its Arab name even after the Reconquista. Its chief monument is the enormous twin-towered **Colegiata de San Miguel**, built in the 16th and 17th centuries and reminiscent of colonial churches in South America. The Colegiata's chief claim to fame is, it has more stork nests on its generous roof than any other in Spain, a colony of some 250 birds.

Colegiata de San Miguel
t 94 118 01 33

Further south, **Cervera del Río Alhama** long had an Arab majority and still has a Moorish feel to it: villagers speak *cerverano* (the town website, *www.riojainternet.com/cervera*, has a great little dictionary), with hundreds of words that are a last relic of the lost language of the Mozarabs, or Christians living in Moorish Spain. Between **Aguilar del Río Alhama** and **Inestrillas**, the Celtiberians, fleeing after the conquest by Mantis Acidinus (181 BC), holed up from the Romans for a hundred years at **Contrebia Leucada**, built on terraces, defended on one side by the river and the others by a vast ditch. It is a rare surviving example of Celtiberian town planning and water systems, and is currently being excavated.

La Rioja's Dinosaurs

Museo de Calzado
Factoria Callaghan, Avenida de la Industria s/n; t 94 138 00 05

South of Calahorra, **Arnedo** is a shoe-making town with a **Museo de Calzado** (shoe museum) to prove it. Every 27 September the town's patron saints Cosme and Damián are honoured in the usual Spanish effigy procession, only here the parade is combined with a scrum: villagers from Navarra come in to attack the procession and make three bold attempts to make off with the saints' statues, claiming that the Riojans stole them centuries ago.

South of Arnedo, **Arnedillo** has been La Rioja's most important spa since 1847. This is all recent history compared to the main attraction in these parts. 'When there is no trace of Spielberg left,' reads the tourist brochure, 'the dinosaur tracks will still be here.' Take that, Hollywood! La Rioja Baja has 5,000 footprints – Europe's largest concentration of dinosaur tracks, or ichnites as they're called – dating back 120 million years to when La Rioja was lush, warm and wet and the denizens of the Cretaceous (post-Jurassic) period stomped through the marshes. Somehow conditions for preserving their prints in these broken hills were better than most places. In the Middle Ages, the ichnites were said to be the hoof marks of Santiago's horse or prints left by giant chickens that lived in the time of the Moors. The best places to find them are in **Préjano** just east of Arnedillo and the Los Cayos gully at **Cornago**. **Enciso** has the largest number, especially at the Valdecevillo bed, and also houses the **Museo Palontológico**, a significant collection of prehistoric relics. Other sites are just north in **Munilla** in a gully called Peñaportillo; **Igea** has more tracks and petrified plants.

Museo Palontológico
www.dinosaurios-lariga.org; open summer daily 11–2 and 5–8; winter Mon–Sat 11–2 and 3–6, Sun 11–2; adm

ⓘ **Arnedo »**
*Palacio de la
Baronesa, C/Carrera 9,
t 94 138 39 88,
www.arnedo.com*

ⓘ **Calahorra »**
*C/Ángel Olivan 8,
t 94 114 63 98,
www.ayto-calahorra.es*

Markets in La Rioja Baja

Calahorra: Pza del Raso, Thurs.
Alfaro: Fri.
Cervera de Río Alhama: Fri.
Arnedo: Mon and Tues.

Where to Stay and Eat in La Rioja Baja

Calahorra ✉ 26500

****Parador de Calahorra, t 94 113 03 58, *www.parador.es* (€€€). A modern, red-brick *parador* near the scanty Roman ruins of Calagurris, with fine views, smart rooms and air-conditioning. It has a good restaurant serving regional cuisine.

Chef Nino, C/Padre Lúcas 2, **t 94 113 31 04 (€€). A modest hotel; the owners are also behind the best restaurant in town (found at C/Basconia 1).

Casa Mateo, Pza del Raso 15, **t** 94 113 00 09 (€€). Delicious fresh produce, including the local vegetables for which the region is famed.

La Taberna de la Cuarta Esquina, Ctra Esquinas 16, **t** 94 113 43 55 (€€). Calahorra's best-known restaurant is justly renowned for its well-prepared fish, game and vegetable dishes and reasonably priced wines.

Arnedo ✉ 26580

***Victoria, Pso de la Constitución 97, **t** 94 138 01 00, *www.hvictoria.com* (€€€). Modern and comfortable, offering good value with a pool.

***Molino de Cidacos, Ctra de Arnedo Km.14, Arnedillo (14km from Arnedo), **t** 94 139 40 63, *www.pegarrido.com* (€€€). A lovingly restored 17th-century flour mill; one of the prettiest hotels.

Virrey, Pso de la Constitución 27, **t 94 138 01 50, *www.hvirrey.com* (€€€). Ultra-modern façade; one of the few hotels in the *comunidad* with facilities for the disabled. Also has a restaurant.

Hospedería Las Pedrolas, Plaza Félix Merino 16, Arnedillo, **t 94 139 44 01, *www.laspedrolas.com* (€€). An enchanting and stylish little inn in a whitewashed 18th-century building next to the church.

Enciso ✉ 26580

Posada de Santa Rita, Ctra de Soria 7, **t** 94 139 60 71, *www.posadasantarita.es* (€). This little red 19th-century house is cosy, with a small library devoted to dinosaurs.

La Fábrica de Harinas, Ctra de Soria 10, **t** 94 139 60 51 (€). Offers delicious meals based on game dishes, served in an atmospheric old flour mill.

South of Logroño: Into the Sierra

Dry history and misty legend are often one and the same in the three-digit years in northwest Spain. Although the western bit of La Rioja was reconquered by Alfonso I of Asturias back in the 8th century, the Christians' hold on the land was tenuous and often lost for long periods to the Moors, whose caliph made the Christians pay a tribute of a hundred maidens into their harem in return for the right to worship. This humiliating loss of young womanhood was the source of the legendary Battle of Clavijo, where Santiago Matamoros made his famous début on his white horse to lead Ramiro and the Christians to victory. In gratitude, Ramiro decided to donate to Santiago a measure of wine and wheat for every *yugada* of land he reconquered, in a document known as the *Voto de Santiago* dated May 844 – a 13th-century forgery by the monks of guess where. The hamlet of **Clavijo** is on a dead-end road south of Logroño under a rocky outcrop and a ruined castle, with crenellations that look like a witch's teeth. The end of the tribute is celebrated on the third Sunday in May in the village of **Sorzano**, just west of the N111, when a hundred girls dressed in white make a pilgrimage to the Hermitage del Roble. The N111 ascends through the forested **Valley of Iregua**, which narrows between the sheer cliffs and buttes of the Sierra de Cameros, dotted with old, now partly abandoned villages of shepherds, who still follow the old transhumance paths to Extremadura in the winter. There are especially lovely views of the square-cut natural gorge, the Peñas de Islallana, and the Vega del Iregua below it from the heights of **Viguera**.

The Pilgrim Route West of Logroño

Beyond Logroño, the segment of the Camino de Santiago that crosses La Rioja is short, but choice and full of interest.

Navarrete

Eleven kilometres west of Logroño, Navarrete is known for its ceramics and rosé wine. In the Middle Ages it made pilgrims comfortable in its hospital of San Juan de Arce. Of this, only the gate survives, doing duty as the entrance to the cemetery. The older houses in Navarrete look narrow and poky but are actually quite spacious (owing to a tax on façade sizes). The 16th-century church of the **Asunción**, sometimes attributed to Philip II's architect Juan de Herrera, contains an elaborate Churrigueresque *retablo* and a triptych (in the sacristy) by Rembrandt's student Adriaen Ysenbrandt.

Nájera: the Residence of Kings

Arabic Náxara, or 'between two hills', Nájera is a bustling furniture-making town with an illustrious pedigree. It straddles both banks of the trout-filled Najerilla, where the Moorish giant Ferragut was defending the bridge like the troll in *The Three Billy Goats Gruff* when Charlemagne's knights tried to cross it. Ferragut picked them up by the armour and gathered them under his arm – at least until Roland arrived on the scene and gave him what for.

After the Moors flattened Pamplona in 918, the kings of Navarra chose to live in Nájera, mainly to keep an eye on the ambitious upstart kingdom of Castile. The first *Rex Hispaniorum*, Sancho III the Great (1004–35) held his court in both Nájera and Pamplona; in 1020 he diverted the Camino de Santiago to pass through Nájera's centre, assuring it of a good income. When he divided his kingdom between his sons, one took Pamplona and another, García III, made Nájera his capital and reconquered Rioja Baja. His grandsons were squeezed by these two medieval powerhouses, and in 1076 Nájera was snatched by Alfonso VI of Castile and the Cid. The Cid's daughter, Doña Elvira, made a happy second marriage with the son of the last king of Nájera, and their son, García V, became king of Navarra in 1134.

In 1052 García III was hunting on the banks of the Najerilla when he saw a dove fly past over the thick woods on a hill. He sent his falcon after it and followed the birds through the trees into a cave, from which a bright light emanated; inside he found the dove and falcon cooing side by side and a statue of the Virgin and Child, a jar of fresh lilies, a lamp and a bell. To celebrate the miracle, García founded an order of knights, the Caballeros de la Terraza ('Knights of the Jar' – a mystic receptacle like the Holy Grail) and the church, which was rebuilt in the 15th century as the monastery of **Santa María la Real** and restored after 1895 by the Franciscans. The entrance is through a beautiful Flamboyant Gothic door, the **Portal of Charles V**, crowned with the emperor's coat of arms. Through here waits the serene and lovely Gothic-Plateresque **Claustro de los Caballeros**, with 24 arches half-veiled by intricate sculpted screens carved to imitate lace: no two are alike. Cloister chapels hold the elegant effigy tomb of a 13th-century Queen of Portugal. From here a Plateresque walnut door leads into the solemn 15th-century **church**. The original Flemish *retablo mayor* was sold for a piece of bread when the monastery was dissolved in 1835, but the 17th-century wowser in its place still holds the miraculous 11th-century statue of Santa María la Real. Originally she wore a large ruby. This was pinched by Pedro the Cruel in 1367 to pay the Black Prince and the English for whipping the French-supported army of his brother Enrique de Trastámara in a battle near Nájera. The ruby now glows on the State Crown of England, but it cost the Black Prince his life – from a Spanish fever.

Near the high altar are the **tombs** of the Dukes of Nájera, King Ferdinand of Aragón's right-hand men, who gave Ignatius of Loyola his first job as a soldier. At the entrance of the holy cave are 16th-century tombs of the 10th–12th-century dynasties of Pamplona and Nájera, among them the original sarcophagus of Sancho III's 21-year-old wife Blanca. This is the finest Romanesque Spanish tomb to come down to us. Behind the kings is the **holy cave**; up the spiral stair is the remarkable Isabelline Gothic choir (1493–95), believed to have been carved by Jewish *conversos* (note the Hebrew letters on chair 23), a masterpiece of grace, detail and fantasy. The armour-clad King García figures on the main chair and Gothic paintings of kings and queens around the top create a charming *trompe l'œil* effect. History buffs may want to check out the town's **Museo Najarillense** on Plaza de Nájero in the centre.

Just outside Nájera, hill-top **Tricio** was an important Roman town known as Tritium Megalon. Its small mortuary temple was converted wholesale in 1181 into the **Basilica Santa María de Arcos**

Santa María la Real
t 94 136 10 83, www.santamarialareal.net; open summer Tues–Sat 10–1 and 4–7, Sun 10–12.30 and 4–6; winter Tues–Sat 10–1 and 4–5.30, Sun 10–12.30 and 4–5.30; closed Mon; adm

Museo Najarillense
open July–Sept Mon–Sat 11–2 and 5–8, Sun 11–2; Oct–June Tues–Sat 11–2 and 5–8, Sun 11–2, closed Mon; adm

Basilica Santa María de Arcos
open before and after mass

to house a miraculous dark-skinned statue of the Virgin; mellow Roman columns support Visigothic arches covered with Baroque stuccoes that at first glance seem to be made of white icing. Traces of Romanesque paintings (the only ones found so far in La Rioja) remain on the walls.

San Millán de la Cogolla: Yuso and Suso

From Nájera it's 17km south into the Sierra de la Demanda and San Millán de la Cogolla, a village that grew up around two ancient monasteries, Yuso ('The Lower' in old Castilian) and Suso ('The Upper'); *Cogolla* was a nickname for the monks' habit. San Millán (473–574) spent much of his 101 years living in the caves on the hill, his sanctity attracting numerous male and female anchorites.

In the 7th century the anchorites built the first monastery at **Suso**, signposted up a 2km narrow road, and soon became known for their literary efforts when the 7th-century monk San Baudelio wrote the *Life of San Millán*. Carved out of a wooded hill, the shadowy little church has a cloister at the entrance, containing the tombs of three queens of Navarra and those of the Seven Infantes de Lara and their tutor Nuño Salido, who met a tragic end after a game played at their uncle's wedding went wrong and a member of the bride's family was accidentally killed. Poet Gonzalo de Berceo loved to sit and write in the Visigothic portico. The church was heavily damaged by al-Mansur in the Reconquista and rebuilt in the 10th and 11th centuries, with Romanesque arches on one end and Mozarabic and Visigothic down the second aisle. Because of the lack of security, Suso's treasures – notably its golden Flemish diptych – have been removed.

Even the 11th-century tomb with its recumbent alabaster effigy of San Millán is empty, not due to any 20th-century security precautions, but rather because in 1053 King García III decided that San Millán's relics belonged in Nájera. The bones were loaded on to a cart, but the oxen, once they reached the bottom of the hill, refused to budge another inch. Realizing that 'the saint didn't want to leave his lands', García built a new, more splendid, monastery on the spot where the oxen stopped. This is **Yuso**, known as the 'Escorial of La Rioja' after it was rebuilt on a grand scale in the 16th century, its main entrance crowned by an equestrian relief of San Millán in the guise of Santiago Matamoros.

In the Middle Ages Yuso continued Suso's reputation as a literary centre: the monastery is proudest of its one anonymous monk who, in the 10th century, was writing a commentary in the margins of his Latin text or, to be precise, on folio 72 of the *Emilian 60 Codex*, when for 43 words he lapsed into the vernacular – the first known use of Castilian. It's engraved on stone along with other exhibits (mostly portraits of kings) in the **Salón de Reyes**.

Suso monastery
open summer Tues–Sun 10–1.30 and 4–6.30; winter Tues–Sun 9.30–1.30 and 3.30–6.30; closed Mon; adm

Yuso monastery
www.monasteriode yuso.org; open summer daily 10.30–1.30 and 4–6.30; winter Tues–Sun 10–1 and 4–6, closed Mon; adm

The Cradle of Spanish

When the Arabs invaded Iberia, the Christians who fled into the mountainous regions of the north were isolated for several centuries. Latin-speakers and Visigoths found themselves among pagan speakers of Iberia's pre-Roman languages, cut off from the Moors and from each other. Several languages developed in addition to the Stone Age tongue of the Basques: Catalan, Gallego, Babel and Aragonese. From Babel, the first language of the Reconquista, evolved the tongue that would dominate: Castilian, or *castellano*, or what most people know simply as Spanish.

The predominance of Castilian owes as much to Castile's conquering role in history as to the fact that the language is one of the most efficient means of communication ever devised. The Visigoths endowed it with aspirates and a stricter framework than any other Romance language, 'a dry, harsh, stone-cracking tongue', according to V.S. Pritchett, 'a sort of desert Latin chipped off at the edges by its lipped consonants and dry-throated gutturals...and each word is as distinct and hard as a pebble.' It was the first modern language to have a grammar written for it. When a copy was presented to Queen Isabel in 1492, she understandably asked what it was for. 'Your Majesty,' replied a perceptive bishop, 'language is the perfect instrument of empire.'

In the centuries to come, this concise, flexible and expressive language would prove just that: an instrument that would contribute more to Spanish unity than any laws or institutions, while spreading itself effortlessly over much of the New World. In 1870, the aforementioned Emilian gloss long held in Yuso was carted off to the Royal Academy of History in Madrid, and La Rioja still wants it back.

But Yuso has another feather in its cap: Gonzalo de Berceo, the shepherd-priest born in the nearby village of Berceo in 1198 and educated as a choirboy at San Millán, who took Castilian out of the margins and made it into poetry. Gonzalo's verses on the lives of local saints have a simple, sweet quality and, as befits a good Riojan, were inspired by a draught of wine.

Interestingly, Yuso also has the first known example of written Basque; both languages were current in medieval La Rioja.

The Renaissance church has weighty ogival vaulting and a 16th-century *retablo* on the life of San Millán; you can learn more about him in the paintings along the upper cloister, built in 1572. The library has hundreds of old codices and manuscripts, if not the precious Emilian gloss, while the small **museum** contains Yuso's prizes: the ornate wooden reliquary chests of San Millán and San Felices de Bilibio, commissioned in 1063, originally covered with ivory plates, gold and precious jewels. They were stripped of their gold and jewels by Napoleon's plundering troops, who fortunately had no eye for medieval ivories.

There are two other important religious houses in the vicinity. Just north of San Millán and Berceo, **Santa María de Cañas** was founded in 1169 and has a fine tall Gothic church with two floors of windows filling the nave with light. Off the cloister, the chapter-house has the superb 14th-century tomb of the abbess-daughter of the founder, Doña Urraca López de Haro. The nuns have long been famous for engraved ceramic work.

Monasterio de Valvanera
*www.valvanera.com;
open daily 9–7;
double rooms available
(€€–€) as well as a good
menú del día*

South of San Millán, 15km from Anguiano in the verdant foothills of the Sierra de la Demanda, the 12th-century Benedictine **Monasterio de Valvanera** was built to shelter its much-venerated Virgin, the patroness of La Rioja, discovered in a hollow tree by a thief named Nuño who became a saint. On her knee baby Jesus in regal robes is turned to the left, to avert his gaze, they say, ever since a couple fornicated in the church, a sin that led the monks to erect a circle of white crosses, which no woman was allowed to cross, around the church. Other works of art were pillaged by the French or lost when the monks abandoned the monastery in 1839. They returned in 1885 and have been distilling their herbal Valvanera liqueur ever since, plucking the herbs according to the phases of the moon.

Santo Domingo de la Calzada and its Chickens

🅐 Santo Domingo de la Calzada

As they made their way across La Rioja, pilgrims especially looked forward to Santo Domingo de la Calzada, a delightful walled village, now famous for its *muebles* (furniture) but that owes its name and existence to the first road saint. Born a shepherd, Domingo (1019–1109) applied for a monkish career at Valvanera and San Millán. Rejected, he devoted his life to building bridges and making the pilgrims' way easier, clearing paths with a magic sickle just like a druid, making him the patron saint of engineers and public works, hence *de la Calzada* ('of the causeway'). His village grew up by a complex of his works: a long stone bridge over the Río Oja, a hospital (now a *refugio*), a guesthouse (now a *parador*) and a church. The local people call him their *abuelito*, or little grandfather. His church, now the **Catedral de Santo Domingo**, was founded on land donated in 1098 by King Alfonso VI. Reconstruction began in 1158 and took centuries to finish: the first tower was destroyed by lightning in 1450; the second one, completed in 1750, sagged menacingly, and was torn down in 1760; the third, 243ft high, freestanding and neoclassical to match the façade, was built by Basque tower-master Martín de Beratúa in 1762 on boggy ground, shored up with sand, limestone and a ton of cow horns.

Catedral de Santo Domingo
t 94 134 00 33; open summer daily 9–7.10, winter daily 10–7.10; adm, includes adm to cloister and museum; guided visits are available

The Gothic interior is simple but lavishly decorated, but what everyone remembers best are the rooster and hen, cackling in their own late Gothic henhouse. Their presence recalls the miracle that took place in Santo Domingo's *hostal*: a handsome 18-year-old German pilgrim named Hugonell, travelling with his parents, refused the advances of the maid, who avenged herself by planting a silver goblet in his pack and accusing him of theft. Hugonell was summarily hanged by the judge while his parents sadly continued to Compostela. On the way back, they passed the gallows and were amazed to find their son still alive, telling them it was a miracle of Santo Domingo. They hurried to the judge and told him; the judge, about to dig into a pair of roast fowl, laughed and said their son was as alive as the birds on his table, upon which both came to life and flew away. Since then, a white hen and cock have been kept in the church, and are replaced every month; pilgrims would take one of their feathers and stick it in their hats for good luck. Under the window you can even see a piece of the gallows.

Opposite the henhouse is the magnificent tomb of Santo Domingo, designed by Felipe de Vigarni (1517–29); the saint's recumbent statue suggests he could be a starter in heaven's basketball league. On the high altar, the huge Plateresque *retablo* (1540) is the last and best work of Damián Forment, one of Spain's finest Renaissance painters. The carved choir is another excellent, detailed Plateresque work (1530s), decorated with painted scenes on the life of St Domingo, while the chapels are equally beautiful and ornate, especially the screen of the Capilla de la Magdalena. The Gothic-*mudéjar* cloister is now used as a **museum** (same hours as cathedral).

Outside the cathedral, take a look at its ornate Romanesque **apse**, at the nearby walls, erected by Pedro the Cruel, and at the arcaded *plaza*, with a stately 16th-century **Casa Consistorial**. At the west end of town, the Renaissance **Convento de San Francisco** was built by Philip II's favourite architect, Juan de Herrera, to house the elaborate tomb of the king's confessor, Fray Bernardo de Fresneda.

South of Santo Domingo, the most dramatic of La Rioja's seven valleys, the Oja, slices through the lofty Sierra de la Demanda up to the handsome stone village of **Ezcaray**. Ezcaray made its fortune on merino wool but now serves as a centre for mountain excursions, with the ski resort of **Valdezcaray** on Mount San Lorenzo (7,451ft), and picnic tables in the beech and pine forests. Don't miss a trip up to the **Ermita de la Virgen de Allende**, site of recent archaeological digs and where some delightful paintings by a well-meaning artist show St Michael dressed up like an 18th-century *generalísimo*, his avenging sword replaced by a harquebus. The Virgin is celebrated on 24 and 25 September, with traditional dances and parades and a pilgrimage to the hermitage.

Valdezcaray
ski info:
www.valdezcaray.es

> 07 Navarra and La Rioja | La Rioja: The Pilgrim Route West of Logroño

Where to Stay and Eat West of Logroño

(i) **Nájera** >
C/Constantino Garrán 8, t 94 136 00 41, www.aytonajera.es

(i) **Santo Domingo** >>
C/Mayor 70, t 94 134 00 33, www.santodomingodela calzada.org

(i) **San Millán**
Monasterio de Yuso, t 94 137 32 59

Nájera ✉ 26300

****Hostería Monasterio de San Millán**, t 94 137 32 77, *www.sanmillan. com* (€€€). In the monastery itself, with comfortable rooms and a good restaurant.

San Fernando, Pso San Julián 1, t 94 136 37 00, *www.sanmillan.com* (€€–€). A modern hotel on the Najerilla river with a restaurant.

Hs Hispano, La Cepa 2, t 94 136 36 15, *www.hostalhispanonajera.com* (€). A simple but good choice, with clean, old-fashioned rooms.

La Parra (*casa rural*), La Canal 4, Camprovín (8km from Nájera), t 94

136 16 11 (€). Simple B&B in a prettily restored stone house.

El Mono, C/Mayor 43, t 94 136 30 28 (€€). A favourite for local dishes like roast lamb, or leek and prawn tart. Buzzy bar at the entrance.

Los Parrales, C/Mayor 52, t 94 136 37 35 (€). A few doors down, this family-run restaurant has an excellent, good-value menu, plus a summer terrace.

Santo Domingo ✉ 26250

****Parador de Santo Domingo de la Calzada**, Pza del Santo 3, t 94 134 03 00, *www.parador.es* (€€€). This elegant *parador* occupies the pilgrim's *hostal* built by Santo Domingo.

Hospedería Cistercense, C/Pinar 2, t 94 134 07 00, *www.cister-lacalzada. com* (€€–€). A pleasant guesthouse run by Cistercian nuns, with a separate *albergue* for pilgrims.

Los Caballeros, C/Mayor 56, t 94 134 27 89 (€€). Tasty local dishes in rustic surroundings; try the pig's trotters (*manitas de cerdo a la riojana*).

El Rincón de Emilio, Pza de Bonifacio Gil 7, t 94 134 09 90, *www.rincondeemilio.com* (€€). Well-known place specializing in regional cuisine. It does a great set menu with local produce.

Ezcaray ✉ 26280

***Echaurren, C/Héroes del Alcázar 2, t 94 135 40 47, *www.echaurren.com* (€€€). Since the beginning of the 20th

century, this has been the place to sleep and eat; recently it has been renovated. It's usually essential to book a table at the hotel's restaurant (€€€), known for its spectacular, contemporary cuisine.

**Iguareña, C/Lamberto Felipe Muñoz 14, t 94 135 41 44, *www.hoteliguarena.com* (€€). A good choice; quiet, with a moderately priced Basque restaurant.

Casa Masip, Avda Academia Militar 6, t 94 135 4327, *ww.restaurantecasamasip.com* (€€). An elegantly restored 150-year-old townhouse, with a good restaurant and plenty of charm.

 Ezcaray ›
C/Sagastia 1, t 94 135 46 79, www.ezcaray.org

Wine Towns in La Rioja Alta

To the north along the Ebro lies the Rioja Alta, a lush region of abrupt natural features rising above rolling hills, carpeted with vineyards and roads lined with brash spanking new **wine** *bodegas* that speak of La Rioja's rising reputation.

⭐ **Rioja Alta**
bodegas

Haro

Bodegas Bilbaínas
Barrio de la Estación 3, t 94 131 01 47, *www.bodegasbilbainas.com*

Bodegas Roda
t 94 130 30 01; *www.roda.es*

CVNE
t 94 130 48 00, *www.cvne.com*

López de Heredia
t 94 131 02 44, *www.lopezdeheredia.com*

Rioja Alta
Avda Vizcaya, t 94 131 03 46, *www.riojalta.com*

Federico Paternina
Avda de Santo Domingo 1, t 94 131 05 50, *www.paternina.com*

Martínez Lacuesta Hnos
C/Ventilla 71, t 94 131 00 50, *www.martinezlacuesta.com*

At the confluence of the Ebro and Tirón, Haro is a working wine town built around a large arcaded square. Its chief monuments are a handful of noble houses, the attractive **Casa Consistorial** (1775) and the 16th-century church of **Santo Tomás** up in Plaza Iglesia, bearing a handsome, recently restored Plateresque façade with sculpture and reliefs in several registers, paid for by the Condestables de Castilla.

Haro is the growing and marketing centre for the wines of Rioja Alta, with a clutch of ***bodegas*** near the train station. While most *bodegas* welcome visitors, they usually require advance notice (the tourist office has a useful booklet listing them all). An exception is **Bodegas Bilbaínas**, with a pretty façade in *azulejos*, usually open mornings and late afternoons. Nearby, you'll find one of the newer – and among the most praised – wine-producers: **Bodegas Roda**. Along Costa del Vino, you'll find the celebrated cellars of the CUNE, or **CVNE**, home of a fine bubbly; Chilean-owned **López de Heredia**, makers of one of the best Riojas, Viña Tondonia and with a tasting pavilion designed by award-winning architect Zaha Hadid; and the vast, French-founded **Rioja Alta**, with 25,000 barrels. The even larger **Federico Paternina**, founded in 1896 by the Plaza de Toros, houses four million bottles, and welcomes visitors daily except for Mondays. Another, **Martínez Lacuesta Hnos**, is in the old gas company that became obsolete back in 1891, when Haro became the first city in Spain to have public electric street lighting. Among

Selección Vinos de Rioja
Pza Paz 5,
t 94 130 30 17

Wine Museum
Avda Bretón de los Herreros 4, t 94 131 05 47; open Tues–Fri 10–2 and 4–8, Sat and Sun 10–8; adm, free on Wed

the shops, **Selección Vinos de Rioja** offers tastings and a wide variety of different Riojas.

Since 1892, Haro's **Estación Enológica** (just behind the bus station) has tested new wine-making techniques and varieties; its excellent **Wine Museum** offers detailed explanations of the latest high-tech processes used in La Rioja. For a far less serious initiation, or rather baptism, in Rioja, come on 29 July when San Felices is celebrated with a Batalla del Vino. Everyone dresses in white and, after the Mass, fortified with *zurracapote* (Rioja sangría, made with red wine, citrus fruit and cinnamon) and armed with every conceivable squirter, splasher and sprayer, opposing groups douse one another with 100,000 litres of wine. This Dionysian free-for-all takes place 3km from Haro at the **Peña de Bilibio**, below the striking rock formation and pass of the **Conchas de Haro**, 'the Shells of Haro', where Felices, a hermit-follower of San Millán, lived in a cave. A 10th-century church and the ruins of a Roman town, Castrum Bilibium, or Haro la Vieja, were discovered under the rocks.

Around Haro: the Sonsierra

There aren't many landmarks around Haro, but a handful of villages are worth a look if you're trawling about looking for that perfect bottle. A good place to start is the Sonsierra, a pocket of La Rioja on the left bank of the Ebro. **Briñas**, just north of Haro, has a number of noble escutcheoned manors left over from the days when it was the playground of the Haro nobility. These days wine is the be-all and end-all; there's even a *bodega* under the church.

Don't confuse Briñas with **Briones** further south, where there is a nubbly church tower and a bridge to **San Vicente de la Sonsierra**, a village best known in La Rioja since 1499 for its Guild of Flagellants, Los Picaos, headquartered at **Ermita de Vera Cruz**. During Holy Week, clad in anonymous hoods, the Picaos whip themselves across the shoulders, then pique the bruises with wax balls full of crystal splinters until the blood runs.

Casa Encantada
t 94 132 24 36; open June–Sept Tues–Sun 11–2 and 6–9; May–Oct, Tues–Sat 11–2 and 4–6, Sun 11–2; closed Mon; adm

Bodegón de la Real Divisa
t 94 125 81 33

Marqués de Riscal
t 94 160 60 00, www. marquesderiscal.com

The **Casa Encantada** ('Enchanted House'), in the Baroque Palacio del Marqués de San Nicolás, has reconstructions of traditional Riojana homes and workshops. Just outside San Vicente, the curious 12th-century Romanesque church **Santa María de la Piscina** was founded by Ramiro Sanchez, son-in-law of the Cid, who allegedly brought back a piece of the True Cross from the Crusades. Over the door there's a shield carved with mysterious numbers and symbols. Paintings inside represent the *piscina probática* (waters of the flock) of Jerusalem and the Holy Grail. Just east, **Abalos** has one of the oldest cellars in Spain, the **Bodegón de la Real Divisa**, owned by descendants of the Cid, and a 16th-century church, **San Esteban Protomártir**, decorated with dragons. In **Elciego**, 9km southeast of Abalos, you'll find the *bodega* of the **Marqués de Riscal**, a famous producer who helped establish the reputation of Riojas in the 19th century. Some 30,000 barrels sit in the cellars here, a few for as long as 50 years. An added attraction is the complex designed by Frank Gehry, architect of the Guggenheim Museum in Bilbao. Gehry has once again used titanium for the undulating roof of the building, which houses a shop, museum and Basque restaurant and a luxury hotel (*see* below).

Back on the south bank of the Ebro, **Cenicero** is another important wine town which has proudly borne the sobriquet 'the Humanitarian' since the 1920s, when the inhabitants went out of their way to care for victims of a train wreck. It has some of Rioja's grandest *bodegas*: ultra-modern **Berberana**, and **Amezola de la Mora**, on the San Asensio road, a fine example of old *bodega* architecture, ideal for its *crianzas* and *reservas*. West of Haro, **Sajazarra** boasts a 13th-century castle, and **Cellórigo**, 'the Pulpit of La Rioja', has views as far as Logroño and an 11th-century castle under the pointed crags of Peña Lengua. **Casalarreina** is a little Renaissance hamlet around the Renaissance convent of La Piedad (1508); 2km west in **Cihuri** the Río Tirón is crossed by a pretty Roman bridge.

Berberana
t 94 145 31 00,
www.berberana.com

Amezola de la Mora
t 94 145 45 32,
www.bodegas amezola.net

Markets in Rioja Alta

Haro: Tues and Sat, Arco de S. Bárbara.

Where to Stay and Eat in Rioja Alta

(i) **Haro** >
Plaza Monseñor Florentino Rodriguez,
t 94 130 33 66,
www.haroturismo.org

(★) **Casa de Legarda** >>

Haro ✉ 26200

***Hospederia Señorio de Casalarreina, Plaza Santo Domingo de Gúzman 6, Casalarreina (5km from Haro), t 94 132 47 30 (€€€€). A charming rural hotel in part of the 16th-century monastery, with luxurious rooms and a pool.

****Los Agustinos, Plaza de San Agustín 2, t 94 131 13 08, *www. hotellosagustinos.com* (€€€). Superbly restored, occupying a former Augustinian monastery that later served as a prison. Fabulous restaurant, **Las Deulas** (€€€).

*Hs Aragón, C/La Vega 9, t 94 131 00 04 (€). Basic, but centrally located.

Beethoven I and II, C/Santo Tomás 3–5 and Plaza de la Iglesia 8, t 94 131 11 81 (€€). Traditional dishes at these neighbouring establishments.

San Asensio ✉ 26340

Hotel La Capellania, C/La Cruz 14, San Asensio, t 94 145 76 60, *www.hotel capellania.com* (€€). A lovely boutique hotel, located 15km south of Haro.

Casa Marisa, C/Las Cuevas 19, t 94 145 76 21, *www.casamarisa.es* (€).An original contemporary hotel, with designer rooms and bargain prices.

Briñas ✉ 26200

***Hospedería Señorio de Briñas, Travesía de la Calle Real 3, t 94 030 42 24 (€€). A carefully restored mini-palace, decorated with antiques.

Casa de Legarda, C/ Real 11, t 94 131 21 34, *www.casadelegarda.com*(€€). A rural hotel 3km from Briñas in a 17th-century townhouse, with beamed ceilings and a restaurant down the street.

Elciego ✉ 01340

Hotel Marqués de Riscal, Calle Torrea 1, t 94 518 08 80, *www. starwoodhotels.com* (€€€€€). The owners asked Frank Gehry to design a 'chateau for the 21st century' but even they couldn't have envisaged this futuristic construction with its glittering titanium exterior. Even if you can't stay (and there are special deals if you plan way in advance), you can savour some of the surreal ambience at the fine gourmet restaurant.

The Basque Lands (Euskadi)

When it isn't raining, Euskadi is one of the most charming corners of Spain – rural for the most part, lush and green, crisscrossed by a network of mountain streams that meander every which way through steep, narrow valleys in their search for the sea. Great stone country houses resembling Swiss chalets dot the hillsides and riverbanks – though the next valley over may have a grotty little town gathered about a mill. Spain's industrial revolution began in Euskadi, and even today the three Basque provinces are among the most industrialized and wealthy in Spain.

08

Don't miss

⭐ The *Fiesta de la Virgen Blanca*
Vitoria-Gasteiz **p.175**

⭐ Glorious Gothic frescoes
Gaceo **p.181**

⭐ A titanium wonder
Guggenheim Museum, Bilbao **p.167**

⭐ Colourful fishing villages
Getaria and Mundaka **pp.151 and 157**

⭐ *Belle époque* elegance and New Basque cuisine
Donostia-San Sebastián **p.138**

See map overleaf

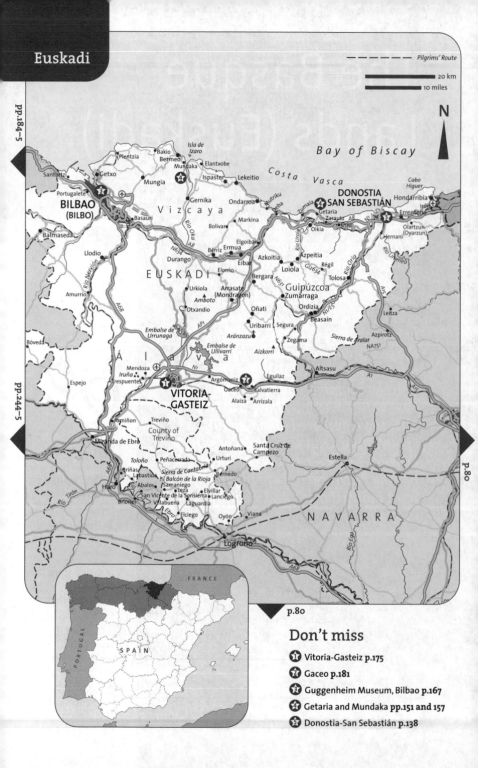

- - - - Pilgrims' Route

20 km
10 miles

N

Bay of Biscay

Costa Vasca

Isla de Izaro

Plentzia
Bakio
Bermeo
Mundaka
Elantxobe
Ispaster
Lekeitio

Santurtzi
Getxo
Mungia

Portugalete
BILBAO (BILBO)
Basauri

Balmaseda

V i z c a y a

Ondarroa
Mutriku
Deba
Zumaia
Getaria
Zarautz
Cabo Higuer
Hondarribia
Irun
Olartzun (Oyartzun)
Errentería
DONOSTIA SAN SEBASTIÁN
Oikia

Gernika
Bolívar
Markina

Llodio

N624
Durango
Berriz
Ermua
Elgoibar
Eibar
Azkoitia
Loiola
Régil
Azpeitia
Tolosa
Hernani

Amurrio

E U S K A D I
Elorrio
Bergara
Urkiola
Arrasate (Mondragón)
Amboto
Otxandio
Oñati
Uribarri
Segura
Zegama
Aizkorri

Río Urumea

Leitza

Bóveda

Embalse de Urrunaga
Aránzazu
Embalse de Ullíbarri

G u i p ú z c o a
Zumárraga
Ordizia
Beasain

Sierra de Aralar
Azpirotz
NA751

Espejo

Á L A V A
Mendoza
Iruña
Trespuentes
Argómaniz
Eguílaz
Altsasu

N1

VITORIA-GASTEIZ
Gaceo
Alaiza
Salvatierra
Arrizala

Armiñón
Treviño
County of Treviño

Antoñana
Urturi
Santa Cruz de Campezo

Estella

Toloño
Peñacerrada
Sierra de Cantabria
Balcón de la Rioja
Bernedo

Briñas
Labastida
Samaniego
Abalos
San Vicente de la Sonsierra
Villabuena
Laguardia
Elvillar
Lanciego

Haro
Briones
Leza
Elciego
Oyón
Viana

N A V A R R A

Logroño

Río Ebro
Río Tirón
Río Ega

A68

FRANCE

PORTUGAL
SPAIN

p.80

Don't miss

- **1** Vitoria-Gasteiz **p.175**
- **2** Gaceo **p.181**
- **3** Guggenheim Museum, Bilbao **p.167**
- **4** Getaria and Mundaka **pp.151 and 157**
- **5** Donostia-San Sebastián **p.138**

pp.184–5

pp.244–5

p.80

Euskadi

The Basque lands, known in the Basque language as 'Euskadi' ('Collection of Basques'), contain, according to the autonomy agreement of 1981, the three provinces of Vizcaya, Guipúzcoa and Álava. To the Basques themselves, however, 'Euskadi' means all lands inhabited by Basques – the 'Seven Provinces' that include Labourd, Haute-Navarre and the Soule in France, and northern Navarra.

Note that both the Spanish and Basque names for towns and provinces are official, and both are used on road signs. Increasingly, Basque names take precedence, while others have combined both in their official names, such as Donostia-San Sebastián and Vitoria-Gasteiz.

In most places in Euskadi, industry and finance seem remote. Basque nationalism, on the other hand, is ever-present; every bridge, underpass, and *pelota* court has been painted with the Basque flag and slogans of the Euskadi Ta Askatsuna ('Freedom for Basques'), the notorious ETA, the small but violent minority that has given this ancient people a bad press.

An Introduction to the Basques

Nomansland, the territory of the Basques, in a region called Cornucopia, where the vines are tied up with sausages. And in those parts there was a mountain made entirely of grated Parmesan cheese on whose slopes there were people who spent their whole time making macaroni and ravioli.

Boccaccio,
The Decameron, VIII

When did the inhabitants of Basqueland become Basques? Wild stories like Boccaccio's have often been told about the Basques and their inscrutable ways, but the conclusions reached by many scholars are almost as hard to believe. It seems likely that the Basques are no less than the aborigines of Europe, the descendants of Cro-Magnon hunter-gatherers and painters, having survived in their secluded valleys during the great Indo-European migrations of peoples from the east thousands of years ago. This theory has had a big boost from the discovery that the Basques have the highest proportion of type O blood in the world, as do other people pushed long ago into Europe's corners – the Irish, the Scots, and the Cretans. Yet even more peculiarly, the Basques also have the world's highest incidence of Rh negative blood, a factor characteristic of the indigenous prehistoric European race. Other clues are the slight but telling physical differences between the Basques and their neighbours: they have long noses and long earlobes, are bigger and stronger, and the distinct shape of their skulls is matched only by those of their ancestors, buried under dolmens in 2000 BC.

One doesn't visit the Basque country to see the sights, which are few and far between. The real attraction is the Basques themselves, a taciturn though likeable lot, and their distinctive culture and way of life. The setting also helps to make the trip worthwhile: emerald landscapes well tended by the same people for millennia.

History

'The Basques are like good women; they have no history.' So runs the old saying. Another of their jokes is that, when God created the first man, he got the bones from a Basque graveyard. No one knows for sure just how far back they go – only that someone, incredibly, must have been around even before them. For the areas around the Pyrenees are one of the oldest inhabited places on earth, and one of the cradles of human culture. The first European yet discovered, 'Tautavel Man', parked his carcass in a cave at the western end of the chain some 450,000 years ago. Traces of habitation in the Basque lands go back at least 100,000 years, and somebody was painting pictures on cave walls as early as 35,000 BC. While the most famous examples yet discovered are in southwestern France and Cantabria, the Cro-Magnons in the Basque provinces were no slouches, as the painted caves at Santimamiña and elsewhere show. Genetic research, perhaps less subjective than phrenology, has confirmed a unique persistence of the European Palaeolithic DNA markers in the ethnic Basque population. Even the Basque language, with no known relatives, offers its hints of extreme antiquity; practically every word for common tools, for instance, comes from the ancient root *haiz*, meaning stone, even *haiztur*, scissors.

Sheep, not native to Basqueland, arrived around 5000 BC, followed by horses and cattle, part of the Neolithic agricultural and cultural revolution that spread across western Europe. Today scholars believe that those with farming know-how migrated slowly out of Turkey, and hunter-gatherer traditions slowly disappeared through intermarriage. This is when the ancestors of the Basques remained aloof. But, if they didn't mingle, they did learn agriculture, the domestication of animals, and building – their lasting monuments include dolmens, tumuli and menhirs.

About 800 BC, Celtic peoples started moving through the region, probably intermarrying with the original people as well as conquering them. Again the ancestors of the Basques for some reason remained unassimilated while picking up tips from the newcomers, on metalworking and cultivating wheat. When the Romans came, they found a nation they called the Aquitanians or Vascones, speaking a non-Indo-European language and occupying much of the land between the Ebro and the Garonne.

The Romans never really exercised much control over the Basques' mountain fastnesses, and the Visigoths and Franks who followed found the Basques a permanent headache. Charlemagne pacified the inhabitants of the plains by 781, but the mountain Basques held out, and taught the aggressive emperor a costly lesson in the legendary battle of Roncesvalles (*see* pp.39–40). As the medieval states that claimed Basque property – Navarra, Asturias/Castilla, England, Béarn and France – grew in wealth and power, however, there was increasingly little chance that an event like Roncesvalles could be repeated. This was a world dominated by a feudal aristocracy, one made up of foreigners, the descendants of Germanic invaders and Roman landowners, and with such bossy

Folklore and Culture

The Basques are not alone. In fact, their long intimacy with their land has forced them to share it with an unreasonably large number of gods, demons, spirits and fairies, creatures of one of the richest mythologies of Europe.

Many tales are connected to the dolmens and other Neolithic monuments that grow so thickly on the mountains here; often their names connect them to **Mari**, the ancient Basque great goddess. The dolmens were built by the *jentillak*, the race of giants that once lived side by side with the Basques. The *jentillak*, often a great help to their neighbours, invented metallurgy and the saw, and introduced the growing of wheat. One day a strange storm cloud appeared from the east, and the wisest of the *jentillak* recognized it as an omen and interpreted it as the end of their age. The giants marched off into the earth, under a dolmen still visible in the Arratzaran valley in Navarra. One was left behind, named Olentzero, and he explained to the Basques: 'Kixmi [Jesus] is born and this means the end of our race.' Olentzero lives on today, as the jolly fat doll or straw figure seen prominently in the Basques' celebrations of Christmas and New Year's Day, the leader of all the processions. You will find Olentzero in Basque homes and even in the churches, often bearing an unusual resemblance to the Michelin man; he'll probably be surrounded by food because, of course, being one of the *jentillak*, Olentzero likes to eat all day. Other familiar creatures include the *laminak*, originally small female fairies with a capacity to help or harm, now a sort of leprechaun, who get blamed for everything that goes wrong. And where mythology fades off into nursery-lore, we have the '**man with the sack**' who comes to carry off naughty children, and a large bestiary with jokes like the elusive *dahu*, a kind of lizard with legs that are shorter on one side – the better to walk the mountain slopes.

Along with the myths goes a remarkable body of pre-Christian religious survivals, including rituals that lasted well into the 20th century; many old Basques in isolated villages can remember festivals with midsummer bonfires in their childhood, and in some villages the custom is coming back, just as it is in the Catalan Pyrenees. (Any excuse for a party!)

Basques are passionately fond of **music**, whether it's choral music at mass (which they do extremely well), Basque rock (rare, fortunately), or traditional tunes played by village bands. Dozens of traditional dances are still current, and small groups in many villages keep them up; you'll have a chance to see them at any village fête – especially in Guipúzcoa, where you can tour the villages on a Sunday morning and usually find a couple with traditional dances going on in the square. Traditional Basque instruments include the *txistu*, a three-holed flute played with one hand, the other hand beating the rhythm on the tambour; another is the *dultzaina*, a primitive bagpipe. When they're in the mood, the Basques dance some of the most furiously athletic dances in the world, especially the *Bolant Dantza* ('Flying Dance') or *La Espata Dantza* ('Sword Dance').

The real monument of Euskadi is the *etxe*, a word that means much more to a Basque than just 'house'. Set on its own on the velvet hillsides, the traditional Basque farmhouse is one of the most distinctive characteristics of the whole region: pretty, simple, functional and nearly always painted white, they are usually two storeys high, with a distinctive long, low gable along the façade. The upper section often has half-timbering and shutters – trimmed, of course, with green and *rouge basque*. Most *etxes* face east, towards the rising sun. In the old days, it was the heads of households who met to make laws at the assemblies, and it is common to find families whose home has been on the same site for over a thousand years. The **cemeteries** have been around even longer. Basques have distinctive 'discoidal' or round-headed tombstones. Archaeologists have dug up models 4,500 years old, and they've been using the same style ever since. The earliest ones often had human figures, sun symbols or other symbols carved on them; since the coming of Christianity the stones usually show crosses. You will see them in any churchyard, usually turned south so that the sun shines on the carved face all day.

neighbours that it is not surprising the Basques never coalesced into a nation. The Basques at this time were practically invisible, their language merely the patois of countrymen, and nobody paid much attention to them. All through the Middle Ages, the Basque boundaries shrank gradually but inexorably as the natives were either pushed out or assimilated by Spaniards, Gascons and Catalans. Many place names, especially in the eastern Pyrenees, give clues of a Basque origin, but by the 1300s the Basque lands had contracted roughly within the boundaries they retain today.

Despite the decline, the Basques survived as a nation throughout. When they finally did agree to recognize the suzerainty of Castilla it was on their own terms, retaining *fueros* (privileges) and ancient laws, one of which was that every king, once crowned, should come to Gernika and swear under the sacred oak tree to uphold their laws. Since then, Basques have always played an important role in Spanish affairs, far out of proportion to their numbers. They were great sailors and explorers, shipbuilders and whalers, *conquistadores* and pirates, and nowadays they run most of Spain's banks. The Basques organized the first whale fishery, in the Middle Ages. At first they only took whales that came too close to the shore, but as the whales got wise the Basques began chasing them farther out to sea. The Basques claim they landed in the Americas long before Columbus (who took a Basque pilot along); Basque sailors helped the English conquer Wales, built the Spanish Armada, and founded a number of Spanish colonies, including the Philippines, as well as cities like Buenos Aires. The *conquistadores* Lope de Aguirre and Pedro de Ursúa were Basques; and the Basque captain Sebastián Elcano became the first man to sail around the world. Two of Spain's most important saints, St Ignatius of Loyola and St Francis Xavier, were also Basque.

In the 19th century, the Basque lands suffered as much as any other part of France or Spain from rural poverty and depopulation. Young Basques from the mountain uplands went in great numbers to the Americas, especially to Argentina and the United States, where the Basque connection goes back to the 1,500 sailors who came to join Lafayette and fight for American independence. Simón Bolívar, liberator of Venezuela and Colombia, was of Basque descent. In the bayous of Louisiana and east Texas, and on the Argentine pampas, Basques became some of the first cowboys in the 1840s, setting the model and contributing much to the image (*lariat*, among other cowboy terms, is a Basque word, and exotic cinema locales such as Durango, Colorado and Laredo, Texas were named after Basque villages). Later in the century they moved further west, taking lonely jobs as shepherds in the Rockies. There are still large Basque communities in Idaho, Utah, California and other states.

Throughout history, the Basques have wanted only to be left alone, and they always support any politics that promise to uphold their ancient rights and liberties. In modern times, this has meant adventures with both the far right and the far left. In the 19th century, when progress meant doing away with quaint relics like Basque culture and *fueros*, the Basques remembered their pious nature and took the side of Fernando VII's reactionary brother Don Carlos in the second Carlist war (1876), and lost the *fueros* as a result. At the same time Euskadi, with its iron deposits and port towns, began to industrialize, and, while many prospered, the majority of workers, seeing their traditional society threatened on all sides, flocked to the banner of Basque nationalism.

Nationalism is hardly a recent phenomenon. It started in the 18th century, with a community of liberal bourgeois in Bilbao and the other outward-looking port cities; these supported Enlightenment thinkers such as Manuel de Larramendi, who developed a concept of Basque nationhood based on language and tradition. Throughout the 19th century, nationalist thought and the development of Basque culture proceeded apace in Spain, while, at least on the political side, it ran into a stone wall in the much more repressive

Basque Diversions

Basques definitely know how to eat. Go into a village restaurant at 9am on a market day, and watch the boys tuck into their three-course breakfasts – soup, tons of meat, fish and potatoes, with a gallon or so of wine for each. Fortunately for them, the Basques also know how to cook. Their distinctive and world-renowned cuisine will be one of the delights of your visit to the Basque Country (*see* p.48).

The real national sport, of course, is smuggling sheep over the border. But the Basques love to play, and over the millennia they have evolved a number of outlandish games that are unique in the world. Many of these are based on pure brute strength, a major element of the national mystique. Even today, especially strong, tall people are said to be descendants of the *jentillak*. One can imagine them, back in the mists of time, impressing each other by carrying around boulders – because that's what they do today, in a number of events generally called the ***harri altxatzea***, literally 'stone-lifting'. In one, contestants see how many times they can lift a 500lb stone in five minutes; in others, they roll boulders around their shoulders. Related to this is the ***untziketariak***, in which we see how fast a Basque can run with 100lb weights in each hand. They're fond of the **tug-of-war** too; they probably invented it. You will also see them at the village festivals pulling loaded wagons, racing with 200lb sacks on their shoulders, or chopping huge tree trunks against the clock. Don't fool with these people.

The miracle is that at the same time they could develop a sport like ***pelota***, the world's fastest ball game. Few sports in the world can offer an image as beautiful and memorable as the *pelotari* in his traditional loose, pure white costume, chasing down the ball with a long, curving *chistera*. Pelota takes a wide variety of forms, but the basic element is always the ball: a hard core, wrapped tightly with string and covered with hide – like a baseball, only smaller and with much more bounce; in a serious match it can reach speeds of 150mph. The oldest form of the game is *rebot*, played without a wall. This is done bare-handed; other versions, played in an outdoor *frontón*, may be bare-handed, with a leather glove (*pasaka* or *joko garbi*), or with the *chistera*, made of leather and osier, which enables a player to scoop up the ball and fling it back in the same motion.

Whatever the game, it usually requires teams of two players each. The ground in front of the wall is marked off in *cuadros* every 4m from it; to be in, a ball bounced off the wall must hit between the 4th and 7th *cuadros*, if it is not returned on the fly. Games are usually to 35 points. Every Basque village has a *frontón*, usually right in the centre. On some village churches from as far back as the 1600s, you can see how the architects left one smooth, blank wall to accommodate the game. It may also be played in a covered court, or on one with another wall on the left side, a ***jaï-alaï***, when the game is called *cesta punta*, the fastest and most furious form of *pelota*. Thanks to Basque immigrants this is now a popular sport around the Caribbean and in some areas of the USA.

climate of France. French Euskadi thus became a sideshow to main events, while in Spain the PNV, the first Basque nationalist party, controlled a majority of the region's parliamentary seats from 1917 on. In 1931, when supporters of a republic offered the Basques autonomy in exchange for support, they jumped at the chance, despite reservations about the new Second Republic's secularism. When the Civil War broke out, they remained loyal to the Republic and even the priests fought side by side with the 'Reds'. To break their spirit, the German Condor Legion practised the world's first saturation bombing of a civilian target at Gernika (see p.155).

Franco later took special pains to single out the Basques for reprisals of all kinds, outlawing their language and running the region as a police state, so that even the thousands of Castilians who immigrated to Euskadi to work in the factories felt oppressed enough to sympathize with Basque nationalist goals. Franco's rule was a catastrophe for the Basques: there were over 100,000 prisoners and 200,000 exiles after the Civil War, including the entire intelligentsia and political leadership. Resistance groups did not start forming until 1952, and Francoist repression determined the equally poisonous nature of the antidote. ETA (Euskadi Ta Askatsuna) was founded in 1959. Its bombing campaign near the end of Franco's reign was singularly effective – notably when they blew the car carrying Franco's anointed successor, Admiral Carrero Blanco, over the roof of a Madrid church.

The repression of the Basques during the Franco years caused the Spanish state to lose any claims to legitimacy in the eyes of many, and, when called upon to ratify the new constitution in 1978, most Basques abstained from the ballot box; those who voted, voted no. Although they regarded the autonomy imposed on them as second rate, they have made the best of it, and today Euskadi has the greatest autonomy of any region in Spain. Taxes are collected by local governments, and local rule covers education, culture, industry, health services, police, agriculture and fishing, etc. Most parents, even Spanish ones, choose to have their children educated in Basque and Spanish.

Terrorist ETA has gone steadily downhill since a series of high-profile arrests in 2008 and 2009 lopped off much of its leadership . Widespread disgust with terror tactics has made ETA fall out of favour, which perhaps contributed to the declaration of a ceasefire in late 2010. Nonetheless, support for a totally independent Euskadi remains considerable: a 2007 study found that 70 per cent of Basques would like a referendum on independence. Most people, however, are in no hurry for it, and would rather see independence brought about as part of a peaceful and evolutionary process.

Language

Speaking the local language is an art! The Basques point out with great pride that their language is not only Europe's oldest, but also the most difficult; the only language ever found to have any similarity to it is Berber. There are four distinct dialects, and in each the grammar is Kafkaesque, to put it mildly. Verbs, for example, can vary according to the gender of the person you are addressing. The vast number of grammatical tenses includes not only a subjunctive, but two different potentials, an eventual, and a hypothetical. But grammatical complexity permits beauty and economy; you can express anything in Basque in fewer words than in most other languages.

Basque is maddeningly, spectacularly indirect. For example, 'I am spinning', comes out as '*Iruten ari nuzu*', or literally, 'In the act of spinning doing you have me.' Or try out this proverb: '*Izan gabe eman dezakegun gauza bakarra da zoriona*'...'Having without, give (*Izan gabe eman*) we can (*dezakegun*), one thing only is (*gauza bakarra da*), happiness (*zoriona*)' – 'Happiness is the only thing we can give without having it.' Pronunciation, thank heavens, is not such a problem; it's phonetic, and there are only a few letters you need to know: *e* as long *a*; *u* as *oo*; *j* as *ee*; *s* as something halfway between *s* and *sh*; *tz* or *z* as *s*; and *x* as *sh*. Pronounce all the vowels, and don't make any soft consonant sounds.

Peculiarities of the language include the habit of doubling words for stress, unknown to any European tongue but common among the Polynesians, and some entertaining onomatopoeia. In Basque, something very hot is *bero-bero*, and when a Basque walks on all fours it is called *hitipiti-hatapata*. Looking at a menu in a Basque restaurant (they have the best cuisine in Spain, so you'll want to do this often), you may well be *keko-meko* (undecided); if you choose *birristi-barrasta* (carelessly), you might get *ttattu* (little cat), a supposed speciality in Bilbao in the 19th century. Basques can put it away; other Spaniards accuse them of *mauka-mauka* (gluttony). Like eskimos, who know no generic word for 'ice', the Basques have no word for 'tree' or 'animal'. And being democratic folk, there's no word for 'king' either – they had to borrow one from the French and Spanish potentates they were forced to pay taxes to.

Owing to the severe cultural oppression under Franco, the percentage of Basque speakers is higher on the French side, according to a recent survey: 64 per cent in Basse-Navarre, 55.5 per cent in the Soule and Labourd, as opposed to 49 per cent in Guipúzcoa, 31 per cent in Vizcaya, 11 per cent in Navarra, and 14 per cent in Álava. However, for the first time, the numbers are rising on the Spanish side in a revival that has touched all aspects of Basque culture. In Euskadi, the language is now mandatory in school, and in the past decade or so 100,000 adults have learned to speak it.

A Basque Outline

Very few Basque words have made it into English, although one, 'silhouette', is derived in a r
roundabout way from a Basque word, *zuleta*, which means 'many holes'. The surname Zul
Zuloeta was probably given to a family who lived among the holes, or caves. One bran
family in France adopted the spelling Silhouette. Their most famous member, Etienne
(1709–67), was a writer and politician who held the powerful post of controller-ger
good at it and didn't keep his office long, and his meagre policies cast but a shadow
explanation), although others say Silhouette himself liked to draw portraits in o
on the walls of his château.

Basque TV and radio are broadcast on both sides of the border; there are Basque newspapers, including *Gara* and *Berria*, and over 1,000 books of all kinds published annually, a remarkable statistic for a population of only a million potential readers: one novel, *Obabakoak* (1989), by Basqueland's best-known living writer, Bernardo Atxaga, is the first ever to be translated into English. Equally encouraging is the continuing popularity of the *bertsular* poets (often scarcely literate shepherds) who have memorized a vast repertoire of traditional pieces and are especially skilled at complex improvisions at festivals and competitions.

Along the Coast: France to Donostia-San Sebastián

If you are driving in from France, there is a choice of routes: the A8 (also signposted, confusingly, as the E5/E70 and E80) motorway, which is expensive though occasionally dramatic, or the old routes through Hendaye and Hondarribia.

Hondarribia (**Fuenterrabía** in Spanish) gets overlooked with all the border confusion, but this is one of the most agreeable destinations on the coast; the village glows with colour – in its brightly painted houses, especially along Calle San Nicolás, or Calle Pampinot, in its flower-loaded balconies and in its fishing fleet that has taken on France in the EU's battles over fishing rights. The town has had its share of sieges – you can still see the ancient walls and a **castle** of Charles V, now a *parador* – and every summer sees an invasion of French tourists. In the evening, head out towards the lighthouse on **Cabo Higuer** – the northeasternmost corner of Spain – for views of the sunset over the bay.

Irún, on the French border, is inland on the Bidasoa. It was bombed to bits by Franco and his German friends in the Civil War and has little to recommend it. Further inland you can climb Monte **San Marcial** for a memorable view over the Bay of Biscay (there is a road to the top), or else flee the bustling coast for the serene Valley **of Oiartzun** (**Oyarzun**), one of Euskadi's rural beauty spots, with the pretty villages of **Oiartzun** (**Oyarzun**), **Lesaka** and **Vera de Bid**

etting to and from Bilbao

lies 10km north of the city centre in Loui and is the busiest in northern Spain, with
m London, Dublin, Paris, Brussels, Frankfurt, Munich and Milan, and most airports in
ion, **t** 91 321 10 00, *www.aena.es*). A **taxi** into Bilbao costs around €20–25. There is also an
no. 3247, **t** 902 222 265), which runs roughly every 20mins from 6.20am to midnight to
h a metro connection) with stops at Gran Vía 79, and Alameda Recalde 11 (note that
ort runs roughly every 20mins from 5.20am to 10pm). A train line is under

By Ferry

Brittany Ferries operate a twice-weekly service from Portsmouth to Bilbao, which arrives in the suburb of Santurtzi, 13km from the centre of town. There is an information and booking office at Muelle Vizkaya, Espigón 3, **t** 94 236 0611.

By Train

Bilbao has several train lines and about a dozen stations, although as a non-suburban commuter you ave to be aware of only three of them.

The main **RENFE** station, **Estación de Abando** (**t** 902 320 320, *www.renfe.es* for information), on Plaza Circular, has connections to France, Madrid, Barcelona and Galicia. Next to Abando, at C/Bailén 2, facing the river with a colourful tiled front, is the **Estación de Santander** (**t** 94 423 22 66, *www.feve.es*), also known as **La Concordia**, where scenic, narrow-gauge **FEVE** trains set off for Santander and Oviedo.

The pretty little **Estación de Atxuri**, at C/Atxuri 6 in the Casco Viejo, is used by the Basque regional line, **EuskoTren**, **t** 902 543 210, *www.euskotren.es*, running slow but scenic services to San Sebastián by way of Durango, Zarautz and Zumaia. A separate line serves Gernika, Mundaka and Bermeo.

By Bus

All inter-city bus lines arrive and depart from **Termibús** (**t** 94 439 5077, *www.termibus.es*) near San Mamés stadium. There are hourly services to San Sebastián, Vitoria and Santander, and several buses a day to Pamplona, Madrid, Barcelona, Galicia and Castilla-León. **BizkaiBus** (**t** 902 222 265, *www.bizkaia.net*) serves destinations within Vizcaya, including Durango, Gernika and the coastal villages, from a separate terminal on Paseo del Arenal, near the Casco Viejo.

Alhóndiga, into a superb arts and leisure centre (2010). These are just the latest of a long string of celebrity architects associated with the city: the metro, with sleek modern stations, was designed by Sir Norman Foster and completed in 1995, and the airport got an elegant new terminal designed by Santiago Calatrava in 2000. The port has been given a boost as part of a vast harbour expansion project which includes a striking conference centre and auditorium, the Palacio Euskalduna (1999), and an excellent Maritime Museum (2004). Further upriver, Zaha Hadid has come up with an ambitious plan for the regeneration of the Zorrozaurre neighbourhood. Bilbao is shaping up to be one of the cities of Europe's future.

The Casco Viejo

The Casco Viejo, the centre of the city from the 15th to the 19th century, is a small, snug region on the east bank of the Nervión; tucked out of the way across the Puente del Arenal from the bustling centre, it remains the city's heart. The bridge leaves you in **Plaza de Arriaga**, known familiarly as **El Arenal** from the sand flats

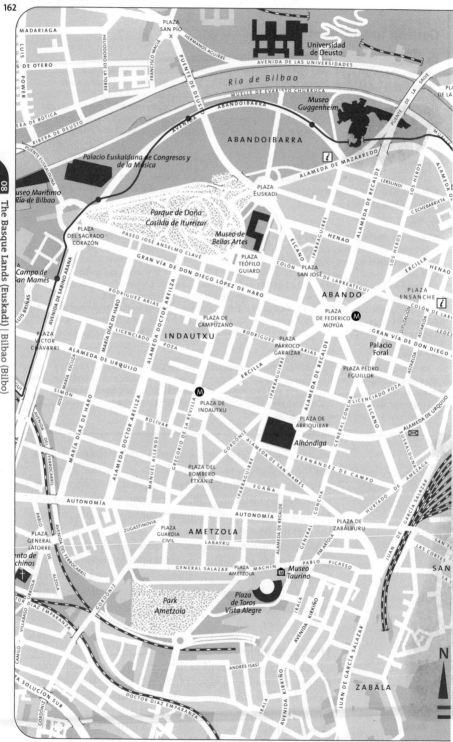

MADARIAGA

LUIS

S DE OTERO

POWER

ERA DE BOTICA

RIBERA DE DEUSTO

PUENTE EUSKALDUNA

HELIODORO DE LA TORRE

FRANCISCO MACÍA

PLAZA
SAN PÍO
X

HERMANOS AGUIRRE

PUENTE DE DEUSTO

AVENIDA

Universidad
de Deusto

AVENIDA DE LAS UNIVERSIDADES

Ría de Bilbao

MUELLE DE EVARISTO CHURRUCA

ABANDOIBARRA

Museo
Guggenheim

PUENTE DE LA SALVE

PLA
DE LA

M

ABANDOIBARRA

i

ALAMEDA DE MAZARREDO

Palacio Euskalduna de Congresos y
de la Música

Museo Marítimo
Ría de Bilbao

ALAMEDA DE RECALDE

LERSUNDI

LOS HEROS

C ECHEBARRIETA

ALAMEDA DE

PLAZA
DEL SAGRADO
CORAZÓN

PASEO JOSÉ ANSELMO CLAVÉ

PLAZA
EUSKADI

Parque de Doña
Casilda de Iturrizar

Museo de
Bellas Artes

HENAO

LOS HEROS

Campo de
San Mamés

LUIS BRIÑAS

AVENIDA DE SABINO ARANA

RODRÍGUEZ ARIAS

GRAN VÍA DE DON DIEGO LÓPEZ DE HARO

PLAZA
TEÓFILO
GUIARD

ELCANO

COLÓN

PLAZA
SAN JOSÉ DE LARREATEGUI

ABANDO

ERCILLA

HENAO

PLAZA
ENSANCHE

i

TUI

MARÍA DÍAZ DE HARO

LICENCIADO

ALAMEDA DOCTOR AREILZA

INDAUTXU

PLAZA DE
CAMPUZANO

POZA

RODRÍGUEZ

PLAZA
PÁRROCO
GARAIZAR

ARIAS

PLAZA
DE FEDERICO
MOYÚA

M

DIPUTACIÓN

COLÓN DE LARI

GRAN VÍA DE DON DIEGO

ASTARLOA

LEDES

ASTARLOA

Palacio
Foral

PLAZA
VÍCTOR
CHÁVARRI

ALAMEDA DE URQUIJO

ERCILLA

ALAMEDA DE RECALDE

IPARRAGUIRRE

PLAZA PEDRO
EGUILLOR

LICENCIADO POZA

ELCANO

ALAMEDA DE URQUIJO

JOSÉ MARÍA ESCUZA

SIMÓN

MARÍA DÍAZ DE HARO

ALAMEDA DOCTOR AREILZA

BOLÍVAR

GREGORIO DE LA REVILLA

M

PLAZA DE
INDAUTXU

GORDÓNIZ

ALAMEDA DE SAN MAMÉS

PLAZA DE
ARRIQUIBAR

Alhóndiga

GENERAL CONCHA

EUSKALDUNA

AMEZAGA

AVENIDA DEL FERROCARRIL

MANUEL ALLENDE

PLAZA DEL
BOMBERO
ETXANIZ

IPARRAGUIRRE

EGAÑA

FERNÁNDEZ DE CAMPO

HURTADO DE

AUTONOMÍA

AUTONOMÍA

PLAZA DE
ZABÁLBURU

AVENIDA DEL FERROCARRIL

PABLO

ZUGASTINOVIA

PLAZA
GUARDIA
CIVIL

AMETZOLA

LABAYRU

ALAMEDA DE RECALDE

GENERAL

CONCHA

PM ARTOLA

JUAN DE GARCÍA SALAZAR

SAN FE

LAS CORTES

PLAZA
GENERAL
LATORRE

ALZOLA

nto de
chinos

GENERAL SALAZAR

PLAZA MACHÍN
AMETZOLA

PABLO

PICASSO

Museo
Taurino

M

SAN

LA C

VILLARÓS EMPARANZA

CAMILO

GORDÓNIZ

Park
Ametzola

Plaza
de Toros
Vista Alegre

IRALA

KIRKIÑO

AVENIDA

JUAN DE GARCÍA SALAZAR

ANDRÉS ISASI

TA SOLUCIÓN SUR

GORDÓNIZ

DOCTOR DÍAZ EMPARANZA

IRALA

KIRKIÑO

AVENIDA

ZABALA

N

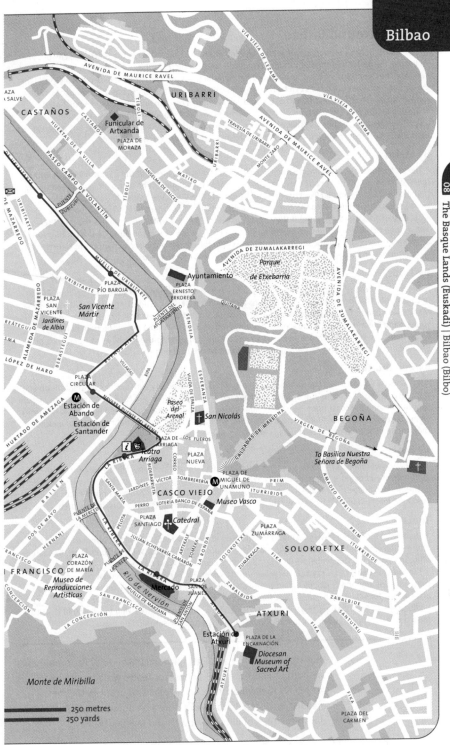

250 metres
250 yards

Getting around Bilbao

Nearly all of Bilbao's attractions are within walking distance of each other in the centre; the city bus line (**Bilbobus**), the metro and the shiny modern tram will take you there if you're elsewhere. There is a card available, the **Creditrans**, which offers reduced fares on the bus, tram and metro services (it is also valid for the airport bus). Creditrans fares can be bought at machines in metro stations, bus and tram stops, or at some tobacconists. Cards cost €5, €10 or €15, and can be topped up with any amount once purchased.

The **BilbaoCard** provides low fares on city transport as well as discounts to museums, shops, restaurants, leisure facilities and shows. Cards cost €6 (1 day), €10 (2 days) and €12 (3 days). Buy online at *www2.bilbao.net/bilbaoturismo/ingles*, at Bilbao tourist offices (*see* p.172) or the airport.

By Metro

The metro consists of two lines: a main line (L1) from Etxebarri to Plentzia, and a branch line (L2), which splits off at Sarriko to head up the left bank of the river to Portulaguete. The metro offers the easiest way to the beaches at Getxo and Plentzia; there are stations at the Casco Viejo, Abando (for long-distance trains), Plaza Moyúa (closest to the Guggenheim), Indautxu and San Mamés (for Termibús). A single ride costs €1.45–1.70 depending on the distance travelled, or 72–96 cents with Creditrans (see above). There is also a €4.50 ticket which offers unlimited metro travel for one day, or you can buy a Creditrans card (see above). Metro services run about every 2 minutes within the centre, and every 30 minutes to Plentzia.

For information call t 94 425 40 25, or visit the website *www.metrobilbao.net*.

By Tram

The modern tram system, the **EuskoTran**, t 902 543 210, *www.euskotren.es*, fills the last gap in inner Bilbao's public transport network. The line runs alongside the Nervión, connecting Estación Atxuri with San Mamés via Abando, the Guggenheim and Abandoibarra. Single tickets cost €1.35 (67 cents per journey if you're using Creditrans), and there's also a one-day card offering unlimited use of the tram network for €3.85. Trams run every 10 minutes and you can buy tickets from easy-to-use machines at tram stops, or use the Creditrans card (*see* above). Date-stamp your ticket before boarding.

By Bus and Taxi

It is unlikely you will need the local **bus** service in this pocket-sized city with such an efficient metro and tram service. The local buses, run by Bilbobus, have red and white stripes and each stop has a route map. To continue around the coast from Plentzia without your own transport, take a taxi to Mungia (€15–20) from where buses go to Bermeo. **Taxis** in Bilbao are white with a red stripe. A green light on the roof indicates they are free. For a **radio taxi**, call t 94 444 88 88 or t 94 410 21 21.

By Boat

Bilboats, *www.bilboats.com*, t 644 442 055 (mobile), offer one- and two-hour sightseeing trips with multilingual audioguides along the River Nervión; the longer trip goes out to sea. Boats depart from next to the city hall bridge (Puente del Ayuntamiento), one bridge south of the Zubizuri bridge. Prices are €10 for adults for the one-hour trip, €16 for the two-hour trip, with discounts for seniors and children.

Tours

The tourist office offers two **walking tours**, one around the Casco Viejo (departures from the tourist information office at the Teatro Arriaga) and the other around the Ensanche (departures from the tourist office in front of the Guggenheim). Both last around 1½ hours and cost €4.50.

The **Bus Turistikoa**, t 696 429 848, *www.busturistikoa.com*, is a hop-on hop-off tourist bus which has thirteen stops around the city, including the Casco Viejo and the Guggenheim. Tickets are valid 24 hours and cost €12 for adults, with concessions for seniors, students and children (under-6s are free).

Bilbao Paso a Paso, t 94 415 38 92, *www.bilbaopasoapaso.com*, organizes walking tours around the city, guided visits of the Guggenheim, tastings, and special trips into the surrounding hills.

---

that stood here long ago. Fittingly for a Basque city, its monuments are both musical: the opera house, or **Teatro Arriaga**, and a glorious Art Nouveau **pavilion** in steel and glass. Adjacent to the Arenal is arcaded, enclosed **Plaza Nueva**, now a bit down-at-heel, but in its day the symbol of Bilbao's growth and prosperity.

Museo Vasco
Plaza Miguel de Unamuno 4, www. euskal-museoa.org; open Tues–Sat 11–5, Sun 11–2; closed Mon; adm

Philosopher Miguel de Unamuno was born on nearby Calle La Ronda, not far from the **Museo Vasco**. Located in an old Jesuit cloister, this offers for your perusal a scale-model of Vizcaya, a reconstruction of the rooms of the consulate, the old merchants' organization, as well as tools, model ships and Basque gravestones. In the middle of the cloister, the ancient Idolo de Mikeldi is the museum's treasure – it looks like a primitive depiction of the cow that jumped over the moon.

Around the back of the museum, the **Catedral de Santiago** sends its graceful spire up over the centre of the Casco Viejo. Begun in the 1200s, most of this understated but elegant grey stone church is 14th–15th-century Gothic (though the façade was added in the 1880s). It matches its setting perfectly; everything to the south is the calm grey world of the 'Seven Streets' (*Siete Calles*), the core of Bilbao when it was still a village. All the colour and animation is concentrated in the 1929 **Mercado de la Ribera** on the river front, the largest covered market in Spain.

Diocesan Museum of Sacred Art
9 Plaza de la Encarnación, www. eleizmuseoa.com; open Tues–Sat 10.30–1.30 and 4–7, Sun 10.30–1.30; closed Mon; adm

Nearby, the **Diocesan Museum of Sacred Art**, occupying the former Convento de la Encarnación, displays over eight centuries' worth of religious art and finery: vestments of gold brocade and embroidery, glittering silverware, and sculptures and paintings.

The Seven Streets being closely hemmed in by cliffs, Bilbao's centre spread over the bridge as the city grew, while garden suburbs were on the cliffs. Behind the large church of **San Nicolás**, off El Arenal, an elevator ascends to the upper town, from where it's a short walk to the Viscayans' holy shrine, the 16th-century **Basílica de Begoña** with its unusual (later) spire. Inside, there is a venerated statue of the Virgin and huge paintings by Luca Giordano, who was very popular in his day. There are fine views.

The Ensanche

Nobody in the 19th century had a sharper sense of urban design than the Spaniards, and wherever a town had money to do something big, the results were impressive. Like Barcelona, Bilbao in its industrial boom years had to face exponential population growth, and its mayors chose to plan for it instead of just letting things happen. The area across the river from Bilbao, the '**Anteiglesia de Abando**', was mostly farmland in the 1870s when the city annexed it. A trio of planners, Severino de Achúcarro, Pablo de Alzola and Ernest Hoffmeyer, got the job of laying out the streets for what came to be known as the **Ensanche**, or 'Extension', and they came up with a simple-looking but ingenious plan, with diagonal boulevards dividing up the broad loop of the river like orange segments.

The Ensanche begins across from El Arenal; just over the bridge from the old town, a statue of Bilbao's founder, Diego López de Haro, looks benignly over the massive banks and circling traffic in

08 The Basque Lands (Euskadi) | Bilbao (Bilbo)

the **Plaza Circular**. This has become the business centre of the city, with the big grey skyscraper of the Banco Bilbao Vizcaya, built in the 1960s, to remind us who is the leading force in the city's destiny today. The RENFE station occupies one corner of the square; you'll have to walk around behind it on the river front to see one of the city's industrial age landmarks: the tiny **Bilbao– Santander rail station**, a charming Art Nouveau work with a wrought iron and tile façade, designed by Severino de Achúcarro.

South of the stations, Plaza Zabálburu marks the beginning of Bilbao's less salubrious quarters. On the cusp lie the **Vista Alegre** bull ring and the **Museo Taurino**, which holds mementos from three centuries of bullfighting history.

From Plaza Circular, the main boulevard of the Ensanche extends westwards: the **Gran Vía de Don Diego López de Haro**. A block to the north, the façade of the **Corte Inglés** department store is one vast high relief mural evoking the industry and history of Bilbao. The centre of the Ensanche scheme is **Plaza de Federico Moyúa**, better known as La Elíptica. The **Hotel Carlton** here, still one of the city's posh establishments, served as the seat of the Basque government under the Republic and during the Civil War. Three blocks south, along Alameda Recalde, is the city's biggest new landmark, the **Alhóndiga**, a huge wine warehouse from 1909 which occupies an entire block of the Ensanche. After languishing empty for decades, it has been spectacularly transformed into an arts and leisure complex by Philippe Starck. The central atrium is supported by a forest of columns, each different – one is Chinese laqueur red, with gold dragons, while another is a fat Baroque swirl of white marble – and lit by a huge virtual 'sun'. There's an exhibition space, a cinema, library, gym, a clutch of restaurants and cafés, and a wonderful glass-bottomed **swimming pool** with a sun terrace.

From La Elíptica, C/Elcano takes you to the **Museo de Bellas Artes**. This contains one of the best fine art collections in Spain, ranging from Flemish paintings (Metsys' *The Money Changers* is one of the best) to Spanish masters like Velázquez, El Greco, Zurbarán and Goya, to modern art by Picasso, Gauguin, Léger and the American Impressionist Mary Cassatt, and efforts by 19th- and 20th-century Basques. The beautiful **Parque de Doña Casilda Iturrizar** next to the museum is an agreeable place to spend an hour or two, with a lagoon, and a light-and-colour 'Cybernetic Fountain'.

Museo Taurino de Bilbao
www.plazatoros bilbao.com; open April–Oct Mon–Thurs 10.30–1 and 4–6, Fri 10.30–1; Nov–Mar Mon–Fri 10–2; adm

Alhóndiga
Plaza Arriquibar 4, t 94 401 40 14,; information on events at www.alhondiga bilbao.com

Museo de Bellas Artes
Plaza del Museo 2, t 94 439 60 60 www.museobilbao.com; open Tues–Sun 10–8; closed Mon; adm; for guided tours (also in English), held on Sun at 12pm, call t 94 439 61 37 or see website

Along the Nervión

When Bilbao's urban planners embarked on post-industrial regeneration in the late 1980s it was inevitable that the riverbank would be the project's lynchpin. The significance of the Nervión (which becomes the Ría de Bilbao) to Bilbao is as much symbolic as practical; for years it has been synonymous in Spain with massive

Hotel Miro ›

Expensive (€€€)

****Hotel Miro**, Alameda Mazarredo, 77, **t** 94 661 18 80, *www.mirohotel bilbao.com*. Very close to the Guggenheim, this intimate boutique hotel has sleekly designed rooms, a small spa, and delightful staff.

****Hesperia Bilbao**, Campo Volantín 28, **t** 94 405 11 00; *www.hesperia-bilbao.es*. It's difficult to miss the multicoloured window panes of this designer hotel, which is located next to Santiago Calatrava's footbridge over the Nervión River.

****Hotel Indautxu**, Plaza del Bombero Etxaniz, **t** 94 444 00 04, *www.hotelindautxu.com*. This giant glass cube attached to a traditional Bilbaíno townhouse has all the comforts in a good, quiet location. The house restaurant, **Etxaniz**, is excellent.

*****Carlton**, Plaza de Federico Moyúa 2, **t** 94 416 22 00, *www.aranzazu-hoteles.com*. This plush 19th-century hotel has lodged famous bullfighters, along with Hemingway, Ava Gardner and Lauren Bacall.

Moderate (€€)

****NH Villa**, Gran Vía 87, **t** 94 441 60 00, *www.nh-hoteles.es*. Modern, chain hotel with plush rooms near the Guggenheim. Great weekend deals.

****Best Western Hotel Conde Duque**, Paseo Campo de Volantín 22, **t** 94 44560 00, *www.bestwestern hotelcondeduque.com*. Another reliable chain, with good-value spacious rooms in a convenient central location.

Inexpensive (€)

***Hotel Ripa**, C/Ripa 3, **t** 94 423 96 77, *www.hotel-ripa.com*. On the riverfront opposite the Casco Viejo; nice, renovated rooms with balconies overlooking the old opera house.

Arriaga Suites, Bidebarrieta 3, **t** 635 707 247, *www.arriagasuites.com*. This charming option in the Casco Viejo has six spacious, brightly decorated suites, with small fridge and microwaves. One of the historic centre's best deals.

Hostal Begoña ›

****Hostal Begoña**, C/Amistad, 2, **t** 94 423 0134, *www.hostalbegona bilbao.com*. An intimate choice in a boarding house founded in the 1920s, now renovated in bright colours that come straight out of an Almodóvar film. Also has family rooms.

****Hostal Iturrienea Ostatua**, C/Santa María 14, **t** 94 416 15 00. A nice choice in the Casco Viejo; simple rooms are furnished with a mix of antique and new pieces, while flowering plants trail from the balconies. You can't miss its brightly painted façade.

***Sirimiri**, Pza de la Encarnación 3, **t** 94 433 07 59, *www.hotelsirimiri.com*. A peachy little hotel that offers a comfortable, reasonably priced option, situated on a pretty square near the old church of San Antón and Atxuri train station. Small gym and sauna.

***Pension Central**, Alameda Recalde, 35a, 1°, **t** 94 410 63 39, *www.hostal central.com*. The price is fair for the modern, clean rooms with internet access. Just off Moyúa square.

***Hostal Estrella**, C/María Muñoz 6, **t** 94 416 40 66. Refurbished, clean and bright *hostal* near the cathedral. Like most *hostales* in the Casco Viejo, it can be a bit noisy.

Hotel Artetxe, Carretera Enékuri-Artxanda Km.7, **t** 94 474 77 80, *www.hotelartetxe.com*. A traditional Basque house on a hill above the city with charming rooms and fabulous views. Best if you have your own transport. Good restaurant, and they also rent apartments in an annexe.

Pension Mendez I and II, Santa María 13, fourth floor (Pension I) and first floor (Pension II), **t** 94 416 03 64, *www.pensionmendez.com*. The rooms are rather small but clean and painted an elegant turquoise blue. You pay more for the Pension II because it's on the first floor and rooms have baths and TV. The higher options (fourth floor) come with shared baths.

Getxo ✉ 48990

****Ercilla Embarcadero**, Avda Zugazarte 51, **t** 94 480 31 00, *www.hotelembarcadero.com* (€€€€). A sumptuous hotel in a traditional Basque villa set amid landscaped gardens on the riverfront, with striking 1920s-style design.

***Gran Hotel**, C/María Díaz de Haro 2, Portugalete, **t** 94 401 48 00, *www.granhotelpuentecolgante.com* (€€€). Across from the great Getxo neighbourhood, this is a plush hotel situated in an historical building at the foot of the Vizcaya Bridge.

Artaza, Avda Los Chopos 12, Neguri, t 94 491 28 52, *www.hotelartaza.com* (€€€). Elegant comfort in a refined mansion surrounded by tranquil parkland, near Neguri metro station.

Eating Out in Bilbao

Donostia-San Sebastián might get all the fanfare, but you can eat as well in Bilbao. For the purest Basque cuisine, look for the strangest names.

Expensive (€€€)

Zortziko, Alameda de Mazarredo 17, t 94 423 97 43, *www.zortiko.es*. Splurge at this spectacular restaurant, in an historic building. The lunch menu is a relative bargain. *Closed Sun, Mon eve.*

Bermeo, C/Ercilla 37 (Hotel Ercilla), t 94 470 57 00. This offers a delicate blend of new and old Basque cuisine in sumptuous surroundings. *Closed Sat lunch, Sun eve.*

Guría, Gran Vía 66, t 94 441 57 80, *www.restauranteguria.com*. Old favourite serving traditional Basque fare since 1920. *Closed Sun eve.*

Mina, Muelle Marzana, t 94 479 59 38, *http://restaurantemina.es*. This serves spectacular New Basque cooking including fabulous desserts, served in a set menu which changes daily. *Closed Sun eve, Mon, Tues.*

Nerua, Guggenheim Museum, t 94 423 93 33, *www.nerua.com*. Book weeks in advance for a table at this light-filled restaurant. Superb, incredibly technical yet flavoursome cuisine by award-winning young chef Josean Martínez Alija. Go for the *menú de degustación* (€75). *Closed Sun eve, Mon, and Tues eves.*

Yandiola, Alhóndiga, t 94 413 36 36, *www.yandiola.com*. The most upmarket of the three restaurants in the Alhóndiga; refined dishes from Ricard Perez in a plush dining room designed by Philippe Starck. Follow up with drinks on the roof terrace.

Azurmendi, Barrio Leguina, Larrabetzu (10km east of Bilbao), t 94 455 88 66, *www.azurmendi.es*. Extraordinarily inventive cuisine by top chef Eneko Atxa, who has two Michelin stars, in a theatrical restaurant which combines rusticity with contemporary design. Don't miss his signature 'reverse egg', in which the yolk is replaced with black truffle. *Closed Sun, Mon eve.*

Moderate (€€)

Metro-Moyúa, C/Gran Vía 40, t 94 424 92 73, *www.metromoyua.com*. Elegant restaurant that serves good Basque cooking; popular at lunchtime thanks to the well-priced set menu.

Bascook, Barroeta Aldamar 8, t 94 400 99 77, *www.bascook.com*. Hidden away in a cleverly renovated old salt warehouse, Bascook serves imaginative Basque dishes designed to share, with the emphasis on the freshest local produce. A gem.

La Gallina Ciega, C/Máximo Aguirre 2, t 94 442 39 43. A tiny, eclectically decorated bar with utterly charming hosts, this serves superb lunches at the single, carved wooden table. There's no menu – you'll be served whatever looked good at the market that morning – but it's always excellent. Book months in advance.

Inexpensive (€)

Saibigain, Barrencalle Barrena, 16, t 94 415 01 23. Well established since the 1950s; with a cheap *menú del día* and a bar full of *pintxos*. *Closed Sun.*

Café Iruña, Berastegui Kalea 5, t 94 423 70 21. This turn-of-the 20th-century café serves a good set lunch menu at €13.75, or €16.50 at weekends.

Tapas/*Pintxos*

One of the city's greatest pleasures is the *txikiteo*, the ritual bar crawl, selecting titbits from the groaning bar tops. Many of the city's finest restaurants also serve *pintxos* at the bar, a great way to taste some of the best cuisine in the city.

Bitoque de Albia, C/Alameda Masaredo 6, t 94 423 65 45. The creator of some of the best *pintxos* in the Basque lands is Englishman Darran Williamson, whose exquisite miniature creations include baby squid ravioli in its own ink.

Víctor Montes, Plaza Nueva 8, t 94 415 70 67. A *belle époque* classic: restaurant upstairs, tapas bar downstairs. *Closed Sun eve.*

Berton, C/Jardines 11, t 94 416 70 35. Filled with locals at weekends;

 ⭐ **Bitoque de Albia >>**

Gazeo (Gaceo) and Alaiza

There aren't a lot of sights here, but for anyone interested in things medieval the province offers something truly outstanding – and almost totally unknown outside the area. The minuscule village of **Gazeo** (Gaceo), on the N1 east of Vitoria, offers nothing less than one of the finest ensembles of Gothic fresco painting anywhere in Europe. The frescoes are in the simple church of **San Martín de Tours**; covered in plaster, they were not rediscovered until 1966. Research places these works some time between about 1325 and 1450. The style, a bit archaic with its Romanesque attention to flowing draperies, is distinctive enough for scholars to speculate about an obscure 'Basque-Navarrese' school of artists, perhaps centred in Vitoria. A Byzantine influence is also strongly present, though details like the gnarled, rugged cross are uniquely Spanish (such a cross was the symbol of the 19th-century Carlist rebels). Thanks to the plaster, most of the paintings are well preserved, though oddly enough many of the faces have vanished. True fresco work requires that the plaster underneath the paintings, applied fresh each morning for an artist's day's work, be absolutely right. The secrets were just being rediscovered in the 14th century in Italy; artists elsewhere hadn't got it quite right.

 San Martín de Tours
guided tours available through Tour Agurain; for details call **t** *94 531 25 35 or* **t** *608 90 16 70*

Gazeo is not such an illogical spot for art as it seems. The modern highway that connects Vitoria to Burgos and Pamplona roughly follows the course of the main Roman road into the north. Enough of this survived in medieval times to keep it an important route, heavily used by pilgrims on their way to Santiago de Compostela. It may well have been that the village was a popular pilgrim stop, and some pious gentleman or lady paid for the paintings.

The figures around the *Trinity* on the apse seem to be arranged to represent the commemoration of All Saints' Day. On the right, note the conspicuous figures of St Michael and Abraham, gathering the fortunate to his bosom. The choir vault too is entirely covered in frescoes, stock images from the life of Christ divided by charming borders of *trompe l'œil* designs and fantasy architecture. At the bottom right is something no medieval mural picture book could be without: the souls of the damned getting variously swallowed up in the mouth of hell or cooked in a big pot.

While you're out in Gazeo, carry on a little further and see some quite different paintings at another tiny hamlet, **Alaiza** (from the A1/E5/E80 motorway, take the A3100 south from Salvatierra). The **Iglesia de la Asunción** here is a barn-like 13th-century building; it too has a painted apse and choir, but the contrast with Gazeo's is like day with night. Instead of flowing Gothic draperies, Alaiza has one-colour cartoons so weird and primitive they might have been done by a Palaeolithic cave artist on a bad day. The central work, on the apse, shows soldiers besieging a castle, while on the choir vault and walls bizarre hooded figures joust, murder or indulge in bodily functions. There is an inscription underneath in Gothic letters, but no one has ever managed to decipher it.

The closest village in this region, **Salvatierra**, is a pleasant place of warm stone near two of Euskadi's best dolmens – **Aizkomendi** at Eguilaz, in a little roadside park off the N1/E5, and **Sorginetxe** in Arrizala. North of Vitoria, the biggest features on the landscape are the dams and lakes of **Urrunaga** and **Ullívarri**. Farther north, on the road to Durango, **Otxandio** was the original Basque iron town, commemorated by a statue of the god Vulcan in the main square.

South of Vitoria: The Ebro Valley

Some of the best Rioja vines actually come from the province of Álava, a region known as **La Rioja Alavesa**, along the Ebro river facing the real La Rioja. Perched high over the river, the key wine town here is walled medieval **Laguardia (Biasteri)** where you can learn all about local wines and their production at **La Casa del Vino**, and visit more *bodegas*, including the wave-shaped cedar and glass **Ysios Bodega** designed by Santiago Calatrava. Don't miss the 14th-century apostles carved in the portal of Laguardia's Gothic **Santa María de los Reyes**. Near Laguardia, an Iron Age village is still being excavated: the **Poblado de la Hoya**. You can stroll around part of the site and visit the adjacent small **museum**.

As for the **County of Treviño**, though this forgotten fief looks strangely compelling on the map, in reality there's plenty of oak woods and good farmland, but unhappily no greater attractions.

Poblado de la Hoya Museum
t 94 518 19 18/t 94 562 11 22; open May–Oct Tues–Fri 11–2 and 4–8, Sat 11–3, Sun 10–2; Nov–April Tues–Sat 11–3, Sun 10–2; closed Mon

Where to Stay and Eat in Álava Province

⭐ **Hotel Castillo El Collado >>**

Argómaniz ✉ 01192

***Parador de Argómaniz, Ctra N1 Km. 363, t 94 529 32 00, *www.parador.es* (€€€). Some rooms are in the original 17th-century mansion. Tiny Argómaniz is 10km east of Vitoria, near the paintings of Gazeo. Great restaurant.

ⓘ **Laguardia >**
Palacio Samaniego, Plaza de San Juan, t 94 560 08 45, www.laguardia-alava.com

Laguardia ✉ 01300

Hospederia de los Parajes, C/Mayor, 48, t 94 562 11 30, *www.hospederia delosparajes.com* (€€€€–€€€) Chic and charm is the order of the day here, and a pair of fine restaurants to boot.

**Posada Mayor de Migueloa, C/Mayor de Migueloa 20, t 94 562 11 75, *www.mayordemigueloa.com* (€€€). In a 17th-century mansion with antique furnishings; has an excellent restaurant (€€€) and wine cellar.

**Antigua Bodega de D. Cosme Palacio, Ctra Elciego, t 94 562 11 95 (€€). Delightful little hotel with a fine restaurant in the original *bodega*.

Hotel Castillo El Collado, Paseo El Collado, t 94 562 12 00, *www.hotel collado.com* (€€). A 1920s palace full of antiques and a welcoming owner. The restaurant (€€) serves Basque and Navarrese dishes.

*Pachico Martínez, C/Sancho Abarca 20, t 94 160 00 09, *www.pachico.com* (€€). A two-centuries-old *posada*.

*Marixa, C/Sancho Abarca 8, t 94 560 01 65, *www.hotelmarixa.com* (€€). The best dining in town, with air-conditioning and expensive meals.

****Hotel Viura, C/Mayor, Vilabuena de Álava, t 94 560 90 00, *www. hotelviura.com* (€€). Spectacular contemporary design hotel in a medieval village west of Laguardia with views over the wine country. Good restaurant, and wine tours.

Cantabria
and the Picos de Europa

Spain's steep emerald-green dairy-land, Cantabria is wedged between the extraordinary Picos de Europa, the Cordillera Cantábrica and a coastline of scenic beaches. Santander, the capital and only large city, is a major summer resort but, while there are a handful of other tourist spots, much of Cantabria is serenely rural, claiming to have the highest density of cows in Europe. The majority of the bovine population lives indoors, and in the evening a common sight is the farmer or his wife, often wearing wooden clogs, driving home an ox-cart laden with grass that they have cut from their several Lilliputian plots of land scattered over the hills. On rainy winter evenings in the more remote areas they gather to hear the strains of the *rabel*, a three-stringed instrument from the Moors, made only of wood cut by the light of a full moon.

09

Don't miss

⭐ **Palaeolithic masterpieces**
Altamira p.201

⭐ **Catalan Modernista architechure**
Comillas p.202

⭐ **An aristocratic village**
Santillana del Mar p.199

⭐ **Dramatic gorges and monasteries**
Picos de Europa p.206

⭐ **Erotic medieval church carvings**
Colegiata, Cervatos p.197

See map overleaf

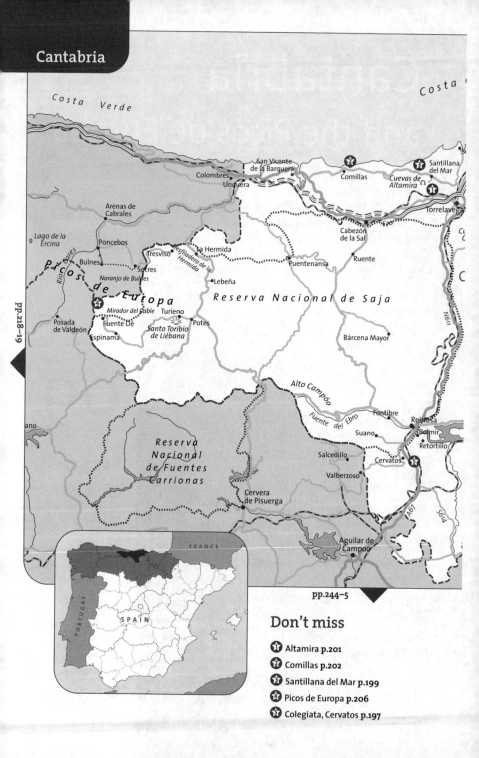

Cantabria

Costa Verde
Costa

Don't miss

⭐ Altamira p.201
⭐ Comillas p.202
⭐ Santillana del Mar p.199
⭐ Picos de Europa p.206
⭐ Colegiata, Cervatos p.197

p.128

pp.244–5

pp.244–5

Humanity has found Cantabria to its liking literally since its first cows, or prehistoric aurochs, came home some 38,000 years ago. It has Spain's greatest concentration of Upper Palaeolithic cave art, from indecipherable scratches to the masterpieces in Altamira. Back in the Iron Age, just before the arrival of the Romans, the Cantabrians carved star reliefs on large stone discs that still mystify everybody: were they part of a Celtic astral cult, remembered from the primordial night in the pilgrimage to Compostela, the Field of the Star?

Like La Rioja, Cantabria historically considered itself part of greater Castile. When the government was dividing up Spain into autonomous regions, the devolutionists feared that, if La Rioja and Cantabria were added to the new region of Castilla y León, they would feel insignificant and peripheral and liable to be lured by the wily Basques into joining Euskadi. A provision in the constitution allows Cantabria and La Rioja to change their minds and join Castilla y León if they care to, but so far autonomy suits them just fine.

Note that although areas of the **Picos de Europa** are in Asturias and León, for convenience the whole mountain range is grouped together in this chapter.

Eastern Cantabria

Bilbao to Santander: The Costa Esmeralda

If this eastern stretch of coast is all you see of Cantabria, you may think what you have just read about rural serenity is pure fiction. This seems to be the busiest coast in all northern Spain in the summer and especially at the weekend, when half of Bilbao is out here looking for a bit of beach; they all seem to end up on the endless sweep of sand at Laredo.

Castro Urdiales

Just half an hour west of Bilbao, Castro Urdiales is one of Cantabria's most scenic fishing ports, endowed with a beach and seafood restaurants that draw hordes of *bilbaínos* every summer weekend. Magdalenian-era graffiti, discovered in the 1960s in a cave near the Plaza de Toros, dates Castro Urdiales' first inhabitants back to 12,000 BC. In ancient times, the Romans muscled in on the native Cantabrians to found Flavióbriga, located where the castle stands today.

A stronghold of the Templars in the Middle Ages, the town declined in the 14th century as Pedro I and Enrique II de Trastámara fought for this stretch of coast. It suffered even more grievously in 1813 when the French punished Castro's resistance in the War of Independence by burning most of it to the ground. Only a few streets near the harbour escaped the flames, beyond the 18th-century **Ayuntamiento**, at the top of the Paseo Marítimo.

From here, walk up to the fortress-like church of **Santa María de la Asunción**, a magnificent Gothic temple with massive buttresses and pinnacles. Constructed almost entirely in the 13th century, its Templar touches are most obvious in the unusual symbolism of

Santa María de la Asunción
open June–Sept daily 10–1.30 and 4–7.30; Oct–May daily 4–6 only

Getting around the Costa Esmeralda

The two daily FEVE **trains** between Santander and Bilbao stop at Treto (5km from Laredo), departing from Santander's Plaza de las Estaciones s/n, **t** 90 224 02 02.

Several Turytrans **buses** a day run along the coast between Santander and Bilbao; from Santander they also depart from Plaza de las Estaciones s/n, **t** 90 242 22 42.

the figures carved in the lovely frieze wrapped around the top of the church – rabbits kissing oxen, dragons devouring serpents devouring birds and more, although to see them properly you'll need binoculars. Inside there's a 13th-century sculpture, the *Virgen Blanca*, and a series of Gothic woodcarvings. You can also see the Santa Cruz, or 'Holy Cross', the Christian standard at the battle of Las Navas de Tolosa (1212). A Roman milestone remains in place in front of the church, while over the striking Roman/medieval bridge most of the walls of Castro's pentagonal **Templar castle** have survived and now shelter a lighthouse.

Castro Urdiales' beach, **Playa Brazomar**, is at the other end of town, and fills up so quickly that an artificial beach, the **Playa de Ostende**, was created at the western end of town. If you want a top-to-toe tan, there's also a naturist beach just outside town at **El Pocillo** (but you have to scramble down the cliffs). The best beach, however, is 8km west up at **Islares**, a small village with a magnificent strand of sand under the cliffs, interspersed with shallow lagoons ideal for young children. Just west of Islares, at **Oriñón**, there's another beach worth stopping for, and a campsite.

Laredo

Cantabria's biggest resort has little in common with its name-sake on the Río Grande. The scenery in fact isn't too different, but on its streets there is hardly a cowboy alive or dead to be seen. This Laredo does have an old town, hidden somewhere among the *urbanizaciones*, but you'll remember it mostly as a haphazard Legoland of modern apartments with a frightening dearth of shops, restaurants and bars.

Laredo was the Roman Portus Luliobrigensium, the place where the Romans finally subdued the last die-hard Celtiberians in a great sea battle. The medieval **Puebla Vieja** over the harbour was walled in by Alfonso VIII of Castile to safeguard the region from pirates; its 13th-century church of **Santa María de la Asunción** has five naves (rare for the period) and curiously carved capitals. In the sacristy note the two eagle-shaped lecterns, donated by Charles V, who landed here on his way to his retirement at Yuste. The late-Renaissance **Ayuntamiento** in Plaza Cachupín is said to mark the location of the harbour quay that the megalomaniac Emperor actually stepped on; behind it is the attractive tiled market building erected in 1902. Not really glossy or chic, Laredo especially attracts families, who cover its splendid beach and fill the scores of cafés, bars and discos in the Puebla Vieja. *Urbanizaciones* have almost reached the tip of Laredo's wide, sheltered pride and joy: **Playa de Salvé**, a gentle 5km-long crescent of sand.

From Laredo to Santander

West of Laredo the beaches continue: **Santoña** is another fishing-port resort and home town of Juan de la Cosa (b. 1460), the cartographer who accompanied Columbus on his second voyage to America (1493) and is remembered with a suitably large monument. Santoña also claims that its shipbuilders made the *Santa María* for Columbus.

Another lovely area, **Noja**, has another stretch of fine, sandy beaches and a considerable villa and apartment *urbanización* along the shore – which seems to grow daily. Local legend says that the village takes its name from Noah, whose ark, they say, washed up on one of the mountains nearby.

The rest of the way to Santander there are plenty of unexploited beaches, reachable on back roads off the main coastal route: the **Playas de Arnuero**, near the lighthouse at Cape Ajo, and the **Playas de Barayo**, west of Ajo.

Markets on the Costa Esmeralda

Castro Urdiales: Thurs.
Laredo: Mercado Municipal, daily except Sun.

Where to Stay and Eat on the Costa Esmeralda

(i) **Castro Urdiales >**
Avda de la Constitución 1, t 94 287 15 12, www.castro-urdiales.net

Castro Urdiales ✉ 39700

****Las Rocas, Paseo de la Playa s/n, t 94 286 04 00, *www.lasrocashotel.com* (€€€€). This luxurious, tranquil place overlooks the beach. Prices outside August are cheaper (€€€).

***Miramar, Avda de la Playa 1, t 94 286 02 04, *www.miramardecastro.com* (€€€–€€). A smart, modern hotel right on the beach with attentive service.

***Hostal Vista Alegre, Brazomar, t 94 286 01 50 (€). A reasonable cheap option on the edge of town, although without much charm. There is a restaurant and free parking.

**La Sota, C/La Correría 1, t 94 287 11 88 (€). Central, attractive *pensión* with sea views from most rooms.

**La Llosa de Sámano, Barrio de Sámano, t 94 287 40 24, *www.lallosadesamano.com* (€). Pretty stone villa with its own garden in a lush valley a few kilometres out of town, offering B&B accommodation in immaculate rooms. Enchanting hosts.

El Segoviano, C/La Correría 19, t 94 286 18 59 (€€). A very good, traditional *mesón*, with wooden beams and stone arches. Come here for roast suckling pig or a seafood grill.

Mesón El Marinero, Correría 23 (in the Casa de los Chelines, by the port), t 94 286 00 05, *www.mesonmarinero.com* (€). The place to go for tapas, with a huge selection and plenty of atmosphere. There's also a good restaurant, although it's probably a tad overpriced.

La Fuente, C/ Nuestra Señora 8, t 94 278 21 91 (€). This local favourite has won awards for its melt-in-the-mouth *tortilla*, but serves plenty of other delicious titbits too.

El Faro de Castro, La Plazuela 1, t 94 286 72 32 (€). A good tapas place with tables by the harbour. Locals flock here for the fried *calamares*.

Islares ✉ 39798

Hs Arenillas, **t 94 287 09 00 (€).
A quie *hostal* near the beach.

Camping Playa Arenillas, Ctra
Bilbao–Santander, **t** 94 286 31 52,
www.camping playaarenillas.com (€).
A large and comfortable campsite
near the beach. *Closed Oct–Mar.*

ⓘ **Laredo** ›
*Alameda de Miramar
s/n,* **t** *94 261 10 96,
www.laredo.es*

ⓘ **Santoña**
Palacio Manzanedo,
t *94 266 00 66,
www.aytosantona.org*

ⓘ **Noja**
Avda del Ris 79–81,
t *94 263 15 16*

Laredo ✉ 39770

****Parador de Limpias, Fuente del
Amor s/n, Limpias, **t** 94 262 89 00,
limpias@parador.es (€€€€). Located
10km from Laredo and on the FEVE
line, in a 19th-century palace
surrounded by extensive parkland.
Gym, tennis and pool.

***Miramar, Alto de Laredo s/n, **t** 94
261 03 67, *www.hmiramarlaredo.com*
(€€€–€€). Modern, mid-size, with huge
windows to take in the huge sea views.

Montecristo, C/Calvo Sotelo 2, **t 94
260 57 00 (€€). One of the better
mid-priced beach hotels in town.
Open mid-May–mid-Sept.

**Hotel Cortijo, C/González Gallego 3,
t 94 260 56 00 (€€). Slightly dated
décor, but a good location; ask for a
room with a terrace to enjoy the view.

Posada La Torre de la Quintana,
Barrio de Hazas 25, Liendo (7km from
Laredo), **t** 94 267 74 39 (€€–€). A 15th-
century country inn (*posada*) in a 15th-
with stone walls and wooden beams.

*Pensión Salomón, C/Menéndez
Pelayo 11, **t** 94 260 50 81 (€). With immaculate rooms and wooden floors,
this is the best deal in the centre.

Casa Felipe, Travesía José Antonio 5,
t 94 260 32 12 (€€). Deliciously
fresh seafood and shellfish and a
wonderful range of local cheeses.

La Casona, C/Raimundo Revilla 11,
t 94 260 65 85 (€). A classic for tapas;
also serves good home-cooking.

Eastern Cantabria: Inland

This corner of the *comunidad* can offer absolutely nothing but
scenery, but it is some of the sweetest and greenest cow country
you'll ever see. The villages are tiny and the roads little more than
paved mule tracks, meandering exasperatingly up and down the
mountains, in and out of the eternal fog and mists. Almost all the
houses are the lovely traditional Cantabrian type, with carved and
painted wooden balconies on the front.

El Hombre Pez

In Liérganes (*see* overleaf), you might note the unusual name of the main street, the Paseo del
Hombre Pez, which commemorates a wonderfully strange story from the 1700s. The 'Fish Man' was a
native of this village, Francisco de la Vega Casar, who went off to Bilbao to work as a carpenter. One
day he went out for a bathe in the river and never returned; his friends and family assumed he'd
drowned. Nine years later some fishermen trawling in the Bay of Cádiz, way down in Andalucía, pulled
up their nets and found an odd sort of fish inside, a damp and chilly man with scales covering most of
his body. When they brought him back to Cádiz, a Cantabrian who had known him recognized him by a
birthmark. The fish-man had lost the power of speech, but he understood enough to agree that he was
in fact Francisco de la Vega Casar of Liérganes. He lived on land for nine more years, and it seems that
he was exploited as a curiosity. De la Vega stayed chilly and damp until the end, and never accepted
any food but raw fish. Needless to say, the people who were looking after him never let him get
anywhere near the water. One day he simply slipped away and was never seen again.

Now, all this happened in the middle of the Age of Enlightenment, and Spain was full of learned
sceptics, including the famous writer Fray Benito Feijóo, who couldn't let a chance like this slip by
without looking into the common belief in the miraculous. The Hombre Pez's career was thoroughly
investigated and plenty of witnesses confirmed all the details of the case. So did it really happen, or
was it simply one of the most successful carnival tricks of all time?

(i) **Liérganes >>**
Pso del Hombre Pez,
t 94 252 80 21, www.
aytolierganes.com

Markets in Inland Eastern Cantabria

Solares: Wed.

Where to Stay and Eat in Inland Eastern Cantabria

Villar ✉ 39806

Posada la Lastría, Villar, t 94 263 91 26, *www.larastria.com* (€). Lovely *casa rural* in a century-old stone house in the green Soba valley: choose from B&B in one of the charming rooms or a rent a small apartment. Plenty of fishing, walking, rafting and riding in the area.

Liérganes ✉ 39800

***Gran Hotel Balneario, C/José Antonio s/n, t 94 252 80 11, *www. grupocastelar.com* (€€€). The most luxurious of the spa hotels, with every modern facility.

***Posada del Sauce, C/José Antonio s/n, t 94 252 80 23, *www.grupocastelar. com* (€€€). A century-old stone inn with attractively decorated rooms, a pool and a good restaurant.

***Casona El Arral, C/Convento 1, t 94 252 84 75, *www.casonaelarral. com* (€€€). A charmingly converted 19th-century mansion surrounded by gardens on the river.

**El Cantábrico, Pso del Hombre Pez 8, t 94 252 80 48 (€€€–€€). A modern and relatively luxurious place.

Small Nowheres and Secret Caves

South of Laredo the N629 for Burgos heads into the rugged and empty valley of the Soba. Near Ampuero you can visit one of the major sanctuaries of Cantabria, **Nuestra Señora de la Bien Aparecida**, a 17th-century chapel commemorating a miraculous appearance of the Virgin. Near **Ramales de la Victoria**, on the borders of Euskadi, there are a number of Palaeolithic painted caves, although only the **Cueva de Covalanas** is open to the public.

Cueva de Covalanas
open summer roughly 10–8; winter Wed–Sun 10–2; times vary according to season, arrange a visit through the tourist office on t 94 264 65 04; adm

The area directly south of Santander is an odd region. Once it was one of the biggest mining areas in the north, but it is finally being allowed to recuperate; there are mineral springs everywhere, and a small, modern spa resort, **Liérganes**, the biggest village in the area.

Santander

The capital of Cantabria, Santander has a lot in common with San Sebastián – a large city beautifully situated on a protected bay, popularized by royalty as a summer resort. The story has it that Queen Isabel II first came down in the 1860s in the hope that the sea air would help with a bad dose of the clap (which she probably got from General O'Donnell, the prime minister, or another up-and-coming politician). Again, after the First World War, it was *the* fashionable place to go for Madrileños, especially with the founding of an international summer university (named after Menéndez Pelayo, Santander's favourite son and Spain's greatest antiquarian), offering holidaymakers highbrow culture to complement its wide beaches. Still, despite this and its widely

Getting to and around Santander

By Air

Santander's **airport** is 7km away at Maliaño, with connections to Barcelona, Madrid and other Spanish cities with Iberia (**t** 902 400 500, *www.iberia.com*) and to London Stansted and 20 other cities in Spain and Europe with Ryanair (**t** 94 220 24 12, *www.ryanair.com*). Airport buses leave from the bus station in Santander roughly every 30mins, 6.30am–10.45pm, and return from the airport roughly every 30mins, 6.40am–11pm. There are also direct buses from the airport to Bilbao, Gijón, Oviedo and other destinations. Airport information *www.aena.es*, **t** 91 321 10 00.

By Ferry

From Santander, **Brittany Ferries** sail to Plymouth (once a week) and Portsmouth (twice a week) between mid-March and mid-November. For information in Santander, call **t** 902 108 147, *www.brittanyferries.es*, or visit the ticket office at the Estación Marítima.

By Train

The train stations are both on Plaza de las Estaciones s/n. **RENFE**, **t** 902 320 320 for information, has connections with Madrid, Palencia, Reinosa, Segovia and Valladolid. The narrow-gauge **FEVE**, **t** 94 209 51 11, *www.feve.es*, has trains to Bilbao, Oviedo, Torrelavega and Unquera; unfortunately they miss out the coastal towns east of Santander, which are served instead by buses.

By Bus

The central bus station is conveniently opposite the train stations on Navas de Tolosa, **t** 94 221 19 95, *www.transportedecantabria.es/web/guest/home*. The biggest operator here is **Alsa** (*www.alsa.es*) which runs services to Burgos, Madrid, Bilbao, Zarautz, Donostia-San Sebastián, Llanes, Oviedo, Gijón, Vitoria-Gasteiz and Pamplona as well as nearly all the coastal towns and resorts.

The main line up into the Picos de Europa is **Palomera**, (*www.autobusespalomera.com*, **t** 94 288 06 11) with runs to Potes and Fuente Dé. Within Santander itself there are frequent buses and trams (nos.1, 2 and 7) that run from the centre to El Sardinero, just 20 minutes away.

By Tourist Bus

Theres's a hop-on, hop-off tourist bus service (**Bus Turístico**) with audioguide commentary around the Casco Viejo and along the seafront which runs from July to mid-October. Tickets cost €15 for adults, with reductions for children; see *www.santandertour.com*.

By Metro and Tram

Santander is currently constructing a new public transport network which will eventually comprise two metro lines, two tram lines and a funicular. The funicular opened in 2008, and the rest of the network is slated for completion in 2013.

By Boat

Los Reginas, *www.losreginas.com*, runs a year-round ferry service around the bay to Pedreña and Somo. In summer, there is a beach service, plus several excursions including a trip in a glass-bottomed boat. The information booth is next to the Palacete del Embarcadero in the port.

By Taxi

For a radio taxi, call **t** 94 233 33 33, and **t** 94 236 91 91.

---

acclaimed International Music Festival in August, Santander lacks the excitement and *joie de vivre* of Donostia-San Sebastián.

On the other hand, Santander has been a great town for disasters. Two of the most recent were the explosion of a ship full of dynamite in 1893, killing 500 and clearing most of the harbour area, and the fire of 1941, which started in the Archbishop's Palace and destroyed most of the old centre. No city in northern Spain shows a more striking split personality. At the centre it's a gritty,

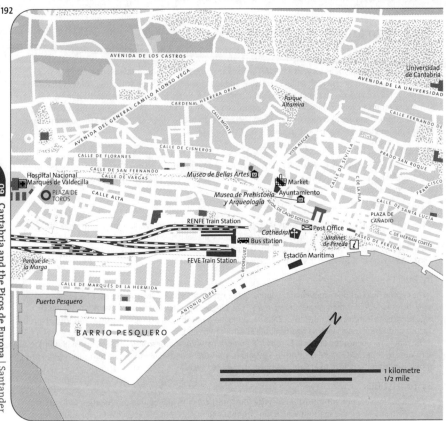

workaday town rather like Bilbao without the smokestacks, but stray a few streets to the other side of the peninsula and you'll be in what seems to be a Belle Époque dream resort, casino and all. The Santander of the festivals shows a bright and modern face to the world, but it was also the last place in Spain to have a public statue of Franco (finally dismantled in 2008), and some grey streets are still named after Nationalist hoodlums of the Civil War.

The Cathedral and Museums

Cathedral
C/Casmiro Sainz 4; open
Mon–Fri 10–1 and
4–7.30, Sat 10–1 and
4.30–8, Sun 8–2

In the centre, next to the Diputación Regional, Santander's much-altered and rebuilt **cathedral** is interesting mostly for its early Gothic crypt; this now forms the separate church of **Santísimo Cristo**, where a glass floor has been installed over the remains of a Roman building.

Santísimo Cristo
open June–Sept daily
8–1 and 4–8; Oct–May
daily 8–1 and 5–8

**Museo de
Bellas Artes**
C/Rubio 6; open
summer Mon–Fri 11.15–1
and 5.30–9, Sat 10.30–1;
winter Mon–Fri 10.15–1
and 5.30–9, Sat 10–1

The best parts of old Santander lie to the north of the fishing port and the railway station, across the main Avda Calvo Sotelo. Near the Ayuntamiento, the **Museo de Bellas Artes** has, besides a contemporary art collection of dubious merit, a good Zurbarán and several Goyas, including a portrait of Ferdinand VII, commissioned by the city to flatter the king.

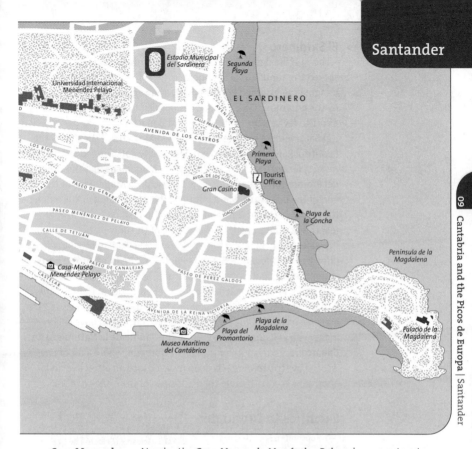

Estadio Municipal
del Sardinero

Segunda
Playa

EL SARDINERO

Universidad Internacional
Menéndez Pelayo

AVENIDA DE LOS CASTROS

CALLE PALENCIA

Primera
Playa

Tourist
Office

Gran Casino

AVDA. DE LOS HOTELES

JOAQUÍN COSTA

Playa de
la Concha

LOS RÍOS

PALAZUELOS

PASEO DE GENERAL DÁVILA

PASEO MENÉNDEZ DE PELAYO

CALLE DE TETUÁN

Peninsula de la
Magdalena

PASEO DE CANALEJAS

Casa-Museo
Menéndez Pelayo

CASTELAR

PASEO DE PÉREZ GALDÓS

REINA VICTORIA

AVENIDA DE LA REINA VICTORIA

Playa de la
Magdalena

Museo Marítimo
del Cantábrico

Playa del
Promontorio

Palacio de la
Magdalena

Santander

09 Cantabria and the Picos de Europa | Santander

**Casa Museo de
Menéndez Pelayo**
*open Mon–Fri 9.30–
11.30, guided tours
available*

**Museo de
Prehistoria y
Arqueología**
*check with tourist office
for opening times*

**Museo Marítimo
del Cantábrico**
*open May–mid-Sept
daily 10–9;
mid-Sept–April daily
10–7; adm*

Nearby, the **Casa Museo de Menéndez Pelayo** has an extensive collection of books, many of them by great Catalan writers, which were donated to the city by the scholar himself. Behind the Ayuntamiento, the iron and glass **Mercado de la Esperanza (market)** is the most colourful sight in Santander, especially the pride of the town: the glorious fish market. Another market, the **Mercado del Este** (just behind the Paseo de la Pereda gardens), is being turned into the new home of the **Museo de Prehistoria y Arqueología**, which was closed for years pending the construction of the future Museo de Cantabrica (still only at the planning stage after more than a decade of debate). The museum's exhibits are devoted to Cantabria's prehistoric cave-dwellers, including tools, reproductions of their art, and two disc-shaped star tombstones the size of tractor tyres made just before the Roman conquest, discovered in the valley of the Buelna.

On the way out to the beaches, Avenida Reina Victoria passes Santander's modern **Museo Marítimo del Cantábrico**, which has an array of model ships, exhibits on the local maritime tradition and an aquarium.

El Sardinero

The 1941 fire destroyed most of Santander's character but it spared the suburb of **El Sardinero**, with its fine twin beaches, imaginatively named **Primera** (First) and **Segunda** (Second), backed by the enormous Belle Époque **casino**, elegantly refurbished in an effort to revive some of the city's lost panache.

El Sardinero is separated from the working end of the city by the beautiful **Peninsula de la Magdalena**, a city park fringed by two more splendid beaches, the **Playa de la Magdalena** and the **Playa del Promontorio**. The Tudor-style **Palacio de la Magdalena** at the end of the peninsula was a gift from the city to Alfonso XIII; when the king accepted it, Santander's return to fashion as a summer resort was guaranteed. Today it is part of the university.

Besides the beaches in the city, there are several miles of golden dunes across the bay at **Somo**, **El Puntal** and **Pedrena**, linked every 15 minutes by boat from the centre of town; **Playa las Atenas** nearby is a naturist beach. Just west of Santander at Liencres, there is another fine and very popular beach, **Valdearenas**, a huge expanse of sand bordered by pine woods. And if you have children in tow you will probably be visiting the **Parque de la Naturaleza de Cabárceno**, 10km south of the city at **Obregón**, where a bit of land wasted by strip mining has been recycled into an attractive and enormous zoo, with more than 400 species from ape to zebra.

Parque de la Naturaleza de Cabárceno
*www.parquede cabarceno.com;
open summer daily
9.30–7; winter daily
9.30–6; adm*

Facilities in Santander

The **post office** is on the corner of Avda Alfonso XIII and C/Calvo Sotelo. **Ciberlope**, C/Lope de Vega 14, t 94 203 79 10, offers Internet access.

Markets in Santander

Plaza de la Esperanza behind the Ayuntamiento on Tues, Wed, Fri and Sat for food; Mon and Thurs for clothes; in Plaza de México on Mon, Wed, Fri and Sat for food; Tues and Fri for clothes (by the bullring at the end of Calle de San Fernando).

Shopping in Santander

Santander is a good city for shopping and it is very easy to while away an afternoon strolling along streets such as C/San Francisco in the city centre and others in the vicinity.
Lucio Herrezuelo, C/Calvo Sotelo 23, *www.lucioherrezuelo.com.*

A good place for quality shoes and leather goods.
El Oso Goloso, C/Calderón de La Barca 19. Gourmet deli selling goodies like chestnuts and goat's cheese.
La Ruta del Vino, C/Arrabal 18. A wide selection of wines and liqueurs.
Librería Estudio, C/Calvo Sotelo 21. A good selection of maps and books, including walking guides to the Picos de Europa. Several branches.

Where to Stay in Santander

Santander ✉ 39000

July to September are the busy (and expensive) months here, especially the first two, when the music festival and International University are in full swing. Prices are as high as in Donostia-San Sebastián, though there are plenty of *casas particulares* to preserve your budget.

ⓘ Santander >>
Regional: Plaza de Velarde 5,
t 94 231 07 08

Municipal: Jardines de Pereda (in the city centre, facing the port),
t 94 220 30 00,
www.ayto-santander.es;
at the beach in El Sardinero, t 94 274 04 14; and in the bus station opposite the train stations on Navas de Tolosa; they offer free guided walking tours

Luxury (€€€€€)

Santander's most elegant hotels are all found on the back side of town by the beaches. There are countless chain hotels, with lots of amenities but little charm, but they do offer low-season bargains, so check online.

*****Hotel Real, Pso de Pérez Galdós 28, **t** 94 227 25 50, *www.hotelreal.es*. A lovely Belle Époque-style hotel located near the Playa de la Magdalena offering marvellous bay views, fine rooms and a well-kept garden. Drops a category or two out of season.

****Hotel Bahía, Avda de Alfonso XIII 6, **t** 94 220 50 00, *www.hotelbahia santander.com*. Stately modern hotel towering like a lighthouse between the old town and the port. Bargains available in the low season.

Very Expensive (€€€€)

****Hotel Hoyuela, Avda de los Hoteles 7, **t** 94 228 2628, *www. gruposardinero.com*. Perhaps the prettiest hotel overlooking El Sardinero's beach, in a turn-of-the-20th-century mansion.

****Gran Hotel Sardinero, Plaza de Italia 1, **t** 94 227 11 00, *http:// hotelsardinero.es*. Lavishly renovated and reopened in 2011, this occupies a splendid Belle Époque mansion near the beaches of Sardinero and the casino.

Expensive (€€€)

****Silken Rio Hotel, Avenida Reina Victoria 153, **t** 94 227 43 00, *www.hoteles-silken.com/hotel-rio-santander*. A grand hotel with a perfect location on Avda Reina Victoria, the main street facing the Sardinero beachfront.

Las Brisas, C/La Braña 14, **t** 94 227 50 11, *www.hotellasbrisas-santander.com*. Refurbished in 2011, this charming boutique hotel occupies a turn-of-the-20th-century villa by the Sardinero beaches. Look for online packages that can drop the price considerably.

Moderate (€€)

****Hotel Vincci Puerto Chico, C/Castelar 25, **t** 94 222 52 00, *www.hotelvincci puertochico.com*. With an excellent location in the old town, the best rooms here enjoy sea views, although they cost extra.

***Hotel Central, General Mola 5, **t** 94 222 24 00, *www.elcentral.com*. Good summer choice with spacious terraces and sea views.

***Piñamar, C/Ruiz de Alda 15, **t** 94 236 18 66, *www.hotel-pinamar.com*. Modern, functional and located near the train station.

Hs Rocamar, Avda de los Castros 41, **t 94 227 72 68, *www.hostalrocamar. com*. Classic 1960s-style *hostal* located on a street in El Sardinero where there are several other inexpensive places to choose from.

Jardín Secreto, C/Cardenal Cisneros 37, **t** 94 207 07 14, *www.jardinsecreto santander.com*. Well located in the old city, this has individually decorated rooms full of style and character and a 'secret garden'. A delight.

Inexpensive (€)

Hs La Mexicana, C/Juan de Herrera 3, **t 94 222 23 50, *www.hostalla mexicana.com*. Good-value choice in the centre, with friendly management and comfortable rooms. Big enough to have space when others in this price range are full.

HR San Glorio, C/Ruiz Zorrilla 18, **t 94 231 29 62, *www.sanglorio.com*. Well located by the Barrio Pesquero, with simple rooms and a restaurant.

* La Porticada/BBB, C/Méndez Núñez 6, **t** 94 222 78 17, *www.hlaporticada. com*. Sparkling dorm--style rooms sleeping between 4 and 8, all brightly refurbished in 2011. Some have balconies.

Camping Cabo Mayor, **t** 94 239 15 42, *www.cabomayor.com*. Near the Cabo Mayor lighthouse, with pool, supermarket and launderette. *Closed mid-Oct–mid-April.*

Eating Out in Santander

Santander is hardly known for its cuisine. The seafood, however, is always good, and the traditional place to get it is at the rather piquant Barrio Pesquero, an area rebuilt after the fire, just behind the stations. Around the beaches, the restaurants are more elaborate.

(★) Jardín Secreto >>

El Serbal, C/Andrés del Río 7, t 942 22 25 15, *www.elserbal.com* (€€€; *menu de degustación* €66). The swankiest restaurant in town, with elaborate contemporary cuisine in elegant surroundings. Winner of numerous awards, so it is always worth booking in advance.

Restaurante Cañadio, C/Gómez Oreña 15, t 94 231 41 49, *www.restaurante canadio.com* (€€€–€€). For that special seafood moment – one of the best in town. Good tapas bar, too: try the *croquetas de bacalao* (croquettes filled with cod).

Bar del Puerto, Hernán Cortés 63 (in the Puerto Chico), t 94 221 30 01, *www.bardelpuerto.com* (€€). The seafood here is worth stopping off for.

Bodega del Riojano, Río de la Pila 5 (north of the Jardines de Pereda), t 94 221 67 50 (€€). One of Santander's typical *bodegas* in the old quarter, offering healthy servings of tapas. Specialities are *rabo de buey* (oxtail), *morcillo estofado* (a blood sausage stew), and stuffe d peppers. *Closed Sun eve and Mon.*

Puerta 23, C/Tetuan 23, t 94 227 10 35 (€€). White linen and wooden furnishings make this an elegant spot, where you'll find imaginative ren-derings of traditional dishes and beautifully fresh fish. *Closed Sun eve and Wed eve, except in summer.*

Bodega Cigaleña, C/Daoiz y Velarde 19, t 94 221 30 62 (€€–€). A typical dark *bodega* which harbours a wine museum; come here to get a feel for traditional fare. If you don't want a full meal, they serve excellent tapas at the bar area. *Closed Sun, Mon lunch.*

⭐ La Gaviota >

La Gaviota, C/Marqués de la Ensenada 32, t 94 222 11 32 (€€–€). A favourite in the *barrio pesquero*, where you can try the seafood *menú del dia* for around €10 or, for a little more, you can order a plate of whatever delicacy has come home with the fishermen.

El Diluvio, C/General Mola 14, t 94 221 85 63 (€). One of the best bars in town for mouthwatering canapés and tapas; always packed with locals.

Entertainment and Nightlife in Santander

Nightlife in Santander is concentrated in two places: first the proper *marcha* grounds in the old town, with a vast number of bars and clubs around C/de la Pila and Plaza de Cañadio. This is the place where you're most likely to find live music and a raucous good time. Somewhat more staid entertainment can be had around El Sardinero; the Plaza de Italia attracts the older set, while the overdressed young in search of fun head for the numerous bars and discos in Calle Panamá.

Festival Internacional de Santander. Since 1951, this August festival has showcased an extraordinary variety of music, dance and spectacle from around the world. Along with all the big-league culture, popular Spanish and Latin American song, dance, magic shows and fireworks take place every night throughout August at the Auditorium and the Finca Altamira. For information contact the Oficina del Festival, Palacio de Festivales de Cantabria, C/Gamazo s/n, 39004, t 94 221 05 08, *www.festivalsantander.com*. Tickets are on sale in advance from the ticket booth at the Palacio de Festivales, from any branch of the Caja Cantabria bank (where half-price tickets are on sale 5–8pm on the day of the performance), or from the special Festival booth in the Jardines de Pereda, near the library, t 94 222 34 34 (*open 11–2 and 5–8*).

Bodega La Montaña, San Fernando 28 (the park boulevard northwest of the RENFE and FEVE train stations), t 94 223 10 39. A typical wine *bodega*, with restaurant, full of big old barrels.

Canela, Plaza de Cañadio. One of many bars on this buzzy late-night square.

La Conveniente, C/Gómez Oreña 9. An 18th-century *bodega* resurrected into an evocative, cavernous bar, lined by 8,000-plus bottles, with live piano nightly. *Closed Sun.*

Gran Casino, Plaza de Italia s/n, t 94 203 05 00. You can risk your euros at this lavish night-time haunt (dress up and bring your passport).

South of Santander: The Heart of Cantabria

South of the capital the land gradually rises to the Montañas de Santander, a pretty, hilly region that supports only a handful of villages. There are plenty of wide open spaces along these high roads of the old County of Castile, but there are a few attractions besides the solitude: caves of prehistoric art, untouched forests, the source of the Ebro and one of the sexiest churches in Europe.

The Caves of Puente Viesgo

Visitors may no longer be able to see the caves of Altamira (*see* p.201), but you can at least get into Cantabria's second most spectacular set of prehistoric grottoes just outside **Puente Viesgo**. There are five caves altogether, but the only one open to the public is the **Cueva del Castillo**. Decorated with graceful line drawings of stags, horses and other animals, this ensemble is believed to predate the even more eloquent art at Altamira.

Cueva del Castillo
25min signposted walk from Puente Viesgo; open mid-June–mid-Sept 9.30–2.30–2 and 3.30–7.30; Mar–mid-June and mid-Sept–Oct 9.30–2 and 3.30–6.30 Nov–Feb 9.30–3.30; adm by 45min guided tour only; last tours depart 50mins before closing time; book visits at reservascuevas@culturadecantabria.es, or call t 94 259 84 25

Reinosa, on the rail line and just off the A67 motorway, is the main hub in this part of the Cantabrian mountains, with most of the area's hotels and restaurants. The source of northern Spain's longest river, the **Nacimiento del Ebro**, is signposted to the northwest in **Fontibre**; you can clamber down in the trees to stick your toes in the stream gurgling out of the ground. The river has barely begun when, just on the other side of Reinosa, it is dammed to form the massive **Embalse del Ebro**, the grass on its jagged shore cropped by horses and dairy cows, following the outline of a prehistoric lake. **Corconte**, on the eastern end of the lake, bottles mineral water next to an old spa.

The most beautiful part of the region lies west of Fontibre, in the virgin valleys of the **Saja National Reserve**, where beech, oak and birch forests follow the courses of clear streams. Real explorers can make for **Suano** and the **Población de Suso**, villages that figure on few maps but can claim a large number of dolmens, a huge cromlech and the ruins of a Templar castle. The region's most important ski installation, **Alto Campóo**, lies to the west.

Alto Campóo
www.altocampoo. com for ski resort information; also phone t 94 277 92 23 or t 699 906 220

A Trinity of Romanesque Churches

South of Reinosa you'll find good Romanesque churches – in **Bolmir** and more significantly in **Retortillo**. Retortillo is near the scanty remains of the Roman city of **Julióbriga**, once the most important city of Cantabria. Set amidst the low walls is the church, with a unique sloping stair leading up to its campanile. Over the door, note the carving of two animals shaking hands.

Julióbriga
open Wed–Sun 10.30–12.30 and 4–7; adm

But the most extraordinary Romanesque church of all is south in **Cervatos**: the singular 12th-century **Colegiata**, at the top of a newly

 Colegiata

Getting around South of Santander

Reinosa's **bus station**, t 94 275 40 67, at the south end of town, is served from Santander by García, t 94 289 16 40, and Alsa, t 902 422 242. Donato, t 97 912 20 47, links Reinosa to the Alto Campóo. There are two **trains** a day from Santander to Reinosa, t 902 320 320, *www.renfe.com*.

cobbled lane. It has a tympanum with an oriental design, a frieze of lions and, carved on to the corbels and capitals in the apse, unabashedly erotic figures that a respectable guidebook hesitates to describe. This unique medieval tantric temple probably survived clerical prudishness over the centuries because of its remote location and the explanation that such exhibitionism was meant to frighten rather than tempt parishioners with the horrors of sin.

South of Cervatos, the narrow CA272 soon meets up again with the Ebro. It's a lovely road, with lots of trees and local swimming holes by tiny villages. One of the largest is **Polientes**, with a roadside statue of a spotted dog and one of Cantabria's 'rupestrian churches' in a cave, although here little old ladies have set up a table by the altar to play cards. Follow the road and Ebro east to an even more remote region and the 12th-century church at **San Martín de Elines**, with a lofty cylindrical tower, keyhole windows, more modillions and carvings by the same school as Cervatos but without any bawdy flashers or sexual contortionists. The kindly caretaker lives in the house nearest the church and will take you around the cloister, with a 9th-century wall and tombs excavated from the garden in the centre; the most impressive is the fancy sepulchre of a pilgrim who died along the route.

Markets South of Santander

Reinosa: *Mon.*

Where to Stay and Eat South of Santander

Puente Arce ✉ 39478

One of the best restaurants in Cantabria can be found at this village, 12km inland from Santander on the road to Torrelavega.

⭐ El Nuevo Molino ›

El Nuevo Molino, Barrio Monsignor 18, t 94 257 50 55, *www.elnuevomolino.es* (€€€–€€). In a beautifully refurbished old mill on the river, this awardwinning restaurant is the perfect place to treat yourself, with exceptional modern Spanish cuisine, a superb wine list, and great service. *Closed Sun eve and Tues.*

Puente Viesgo ✉ 39478

★★★Gran Hotel Balneario, C/Manuel Pérez Mazo s/n, t 94 259 80 61, *www.balneariodepuenteviesgo.com* (€€€€€). If you have come to see the caves, you can stop at this sumptuous modern establishment connected to a spa that's good for your rheumatism and neurological troubles; swimming pool, sauna and all the amenities. Great online deals available.

★★★Casona Azul de Toranzo, C/General Díaz de Villegas 5, Corvera de Toranzo, t 94 259 64 00, *www. casonaazul.com* (€€€). A pair of elegant *indiano* villas 3km from Puente Viesgo have been converted into a stylish small hotel set in gardens with a croquet lawn.

★★Posada Los Lienzos, north of Puente Viesgo at Villar, t 94 259 81 80, *www. posadaloslienzos.com* (€€). A cheaper option, also in an *indiano* villa surrounded by gardens with delightful hosts.

Mesón El Cazador, Ctra General s/n, t 94 259 42 50 (€€–€). A good country restaurant in San Vicente de Toranzo, south of Puente Viesgo; offers boar and other game dishes.

Reinosa ›
Avenida Puente Carlos III 23, t 94 275 52 15, www.ayto-reinosa.es

Reinosa ✉ 39200

****Casona de Naveda de Campóo**, Plaza del Medio Lugar 37, t 94 277 95 15, *www.casonadenaveda.com* (€€).

An immaculate country hotel in an old stone house, with elegant rooms and friendly staff.

Posada La Lobera, C/Arroyo 63, Las Rozas (6km from Reinosa), t 94 275 17 00 (€). Appealing, rustically decorated hotel-restaurant by the lake.

*La Casona, C/Campóo 3, in Nestares, t 94 275 17 88, *www.lacasonanestares. com* (€). With bedrooms in an 18th-century mill, this is a scenic place to stay if you're driving.

The Coast West of Santander

This lush and lovely seaside stretch has been spared any Laredo toadstools, and what tourist development there is remains fairly discreet. When the summer hordes have vanished and the little winding roads belong to you alone, it is haunting and strange in a fairylike way. Even in the rain.

Santillana del Mar

Santillana del Mar

Jean-Paul Sartre, who had always wanted to be a guidebook writer but couldn't get a break, practised on Santillana del Mar, pronouncing it 'the most beautiful village in Spain'. Sooner or later someone in town will remind you of this, and it's best not to argue. The tour buses disgorge their hundreds daily upon this tiny village (which despite the 'del Mar' is not on the sea), and in summer it can be a ghastly tourist inferno, with no place to put your car for a mile around. If you come at all, do it out of season, or spend the night after the day-trippers have all gone.

Santillana is both an evocative medieval town of grand palaces and a country village of dairy farmers, whose pastures lie on the hills just beyond the mellowed stone and half-timbered houses that line Santillana's patchwork of ancient streets and squares. Its past distinctions come from great wealth in medieval times, which was earned from wool and linen. By 1600 nearly every man in town was a noble, or *hidalgo* (from *hijo de algo*, 'son of somebody'), courtesy of easily purchased titles of nobility in the time of Charles V (1516–56) and his son, Philip II (1556–98). So they stopped doing any work, and Santillana has changed little since. In the 1920s Juan Antonio Güell López, grandson of the famous Marquis of Comillas (*see* box, p.203), became minister for tourism under the dictatorship of Primo de Rivera. He took a special interest in Santillana, and began the restoration of its old buildings.

The village is famous as the birthplace of Spain's favourite fictional rogue, Gil Blas, and home of the real Marqués de Santillana, Íñigo López de Mendoza, the Spanish Sir Philip Sidney,

Getting along the Coast West of Santander

FEVE **trains** from Santander go to Torrelavega, with frequent bus connections to Santillana. Another FEVE station is 3km from San Vicente – a lovely walk if you're not carrying a lot.

Suances, Santillana, Comillas and San Vicente are linked around six times daily to Santander by La Cantábrica de Comillas or SA Continental **buses**, from Santander's main bus station.

a warrior and poet and courtly lover whose house still stands on the Calle del Cantón. Other houses have equally noble pedigrees; an archduchess of Austria owned the one across from the

Colegiata
open April–Oct daily 10–1.30 and 4–7.30; Nov–Mar Tues–Sat 10–1.30 and 4–6.30; adm

Colegiata. The latter is a 12th-century masterpiece, dedicated to St Juliana (or Iliana), an Anatolian martyr under Diocletian whose remains have lain here since the 6th century, and who gave her name to the town; the monks who built the cloister for themselves owned most of the town and ran its affairs until the 1400s.

The church has a fine weatherbeaten façade, rebuilt in the 1700s with bits and pieces of the Romanesque original tacked on; inside, the impressive altar is made of silver from Mexico – plenty of the *hidalgos'* younger sons went off to America to make their fortune, and many of the family mansions in the village are *casas de indianos*. There is a beautiful, ivy-draped **cloister**, with capitals carved with biblical and hunting scenes. The ticket to the cloister will also get you into the **Museo Diocesano**, which is installed in

Museo Diocesano
El Cruce, s/n (across town near the car park), t 94 284 03 17, www.santillanamuseo diocesano.com; open June–Sept Tues–Sun 10–1.30 and 4–7.30; Oct–May Tues–Sun 10–1.30 and 4–6.30; adm

the 17th-century Convento de Regina Coeli. It is Gothic in style and displays an exceptional collection of ecclesiastical artefacts from all over Cantabria, some Templar in origin, and all perfectly restored by the nuns.

In the eloquent Plaza Ramón Pelayo, the tower house of Don Borja holds the **Fundación Santillana**, which organizes temporary exhibitions on local themes – particularly on the region's seafaring past and its relationship with the Americas. This makes up in a way for the town's anomalous name 'del Mar' when it's 3km from the sea. On the same *plaza* stands the **Ayuntamiento**, rebuilt in 1770, and, from the same century, the **Palacio de Barreda-Bracho**, now the Parador Gil Blas (*see* p.201).

Twenty or so years ago, residents of Santillana still kept cattle on the ground floors of their homes and sold delicious rich milk by the glass and tasty *bizcocho* (cake) by the piece to tourists. You'll see less of that today, but there are still plenty of souvenirs to buy. If you're in a hurry to get to the promised *mar*, the closest beaches are at **Suances**, just 5km away; it's a fishing village and a small resort. Although the sea here isn't the cleanest, people come here for water sports, including surfing. Suances began life as Portus Blendium, the chief Roman port on this part of the coast, though there's nothing Roman to be seen.

The Caves of Altamira

🔆 Altamira

¡Mira, papa!
¡Bueyes!
(Look, papa!
Oxen!)
María de Sautuola,
discoverer of the
paintings at Altamira

From Santillana you can walk up to Altamira, one of the sublime masterpieces of Upper Palaeolithic art, in 20 minutes. Although the caves are closed to the public, an extraordinary number of people show up at the caves anyway, pilgrim-like, to pay homage to the genius of the artists of c. 12,000 BC who covered the undulating ceiling with stunningly exuberant, vividly coloured paintings of bison, horses, boars and stags. Only at Lascaux, up at the northern end of the Franco-Cantabrian arc of Magdalenian cave painting, will you find such powerful, masterful technique; the movement and strength in the coiled, startled and galloping bisons, the attentive deer, the frisking horses are awesome. As they say, 'This is the infancy of art, not an art of infancy.'

The story of the discovery of Altamira, however, is a parable of perceptions. As at Lascaux, an ancient landslide sealed the entrance of the caves and tunnels (and more or less vacuum-packed the paintings) until it was rediscovered by a hunter and his dog in 1868. In 1875, Don Marcelino de Sautuola, an amateur prehistorian, was intrigued by the black drawings on the walls in the outer rooms and, over the years, explored them, in 1879 taking his nine-year-old daughter María along. The child wandered a little deeper into the caves, and lifted her eyes to find the superb polychrome paintings. Although no one had ever seen the like, the marquis at once recognized the ceiling for what it was: a ravishing work of genius from the Stone Age. Excited, he published a description of Altamira but, rather than receiving the expected response of awe and wonder from the 'experts' in the field, Sautuola was mocked, ridiculed, viciously attacked, and even accused of forging the paintings; the scholars simply refused to believe that people who used stone axes were capable of painting, one of the 'civilized arts'.

Undaunted, the marquis held his ground, insisting Altamira was for real, and died heartbroken in 1888, vilified and as forgotten as the caves themselves. Fifteen years later, the discovery of a dozen painted caves in the Vézère Valley in the Dordogne led to a change of mind, beginning in 1902 with one expert, E. Cartailhac, making a public apology to Sautuola's memory in his *Mea Culpa d'un sceptique.*

Although the 'white disease' caused by the moisture in the breath of visitors has prevented admission to the caves, you can do the next best thing at Altamira: visit an exact replica, including videos and a holographic tableau detailing the history of the caves and offering explanations of the stunning reproductions of the paintings. Picasso, for one, would not have approved – he visited the caves back in the 1920s, declaring that 'not one of us is capable of painting like this' – but his posthumous hand-wringing is

Altamira museum

*t 94 281 88 15,
www.museodealtamira.
mcu.es; open May–Oct
Tues–Sat 9.30–8,
Sun 9–3; Nov–April
Tues–Sat 9.30–6, Sun
9.30–3; adm; ticket
office shuts 30mins
before closing time*

 Comillas

unlikely to deter the extra 400,000 tourists who show up annually to visit the fascinating **museum**. You can also explore a small stalactite **cave** which is prettily lit to emphasize nature's wonders as compensation for the inaccessibility of the more fragile works of man.

Comillas, with a Little Modernista Madness

Definitely *the* place to be on this stretch of the coast, the seaside resort of Comillas offers a bit of Catalan quirkiness in a gorgeous setting, framed by two endearing beaches – the Playa Comillas and the longer Playa de Oyambre. Comillas's old town, with its rough cobbled streets and arcaded mansions, has been a quiet watering hole for the Madrid and Barcelona aristocracy for a long time; the latter brought along their favourite architects in the 19th century to add a Modernista flair.

The peculiar legacies of the robber barons are up on the hills to the west of the village centre. There you will see Gaudí's **El Capricho**, built for a relation of the Marquis de Comillas, and now restored and open for visits. Though not one of the architect's more ambitious works, it is a delightful house, exciting the envy of the crowd of Spanish tourists usually milling about it. The main feature is an eccentric, perfectly non-functional tower, half-lighthouse and half-minaret. The decorative theme, held together by lovely ceramic tiles in green and gold and by extravagant wrought-iron balconies and cornices, has a repeated sunflower motif. There's a shop full of Gaudí-inspired gift items.

Next to El Capricho you can have a peek into the vanished lifestyle of Comillas' rich and shameless at the summer palace of the Marqués de Comillas, the **Palacio de Sobrellano**. A work of another Catalan, Gaudí's friend Joan Martorell, this ponderous palace in a quirky Modernista neo-Gothic style is protected by an imitation castle wall with oubliettes. It's worth taking the guided tour to see Gaudí's grinning Modernista dragons, which adorn the walnut fireplace in the marquis' old billiard room; more wicked specimens lurk on the arms of his fireside chairs. Next door, the marquis's **chapel** adds the perfect touch of discreet surrealism to the ensemble. It's bigger than Comillas' parish church, and inside there are furnishings by Gaudí himself and marble sepulchres of the marquis and his family.

The third member of this singular trio stands on the opposite hill, across the main road through Comillas, but it commands the views for miles around. Construction of the **Universidad Pontificia** began in 1883, with a plan by Martorell and some financial help from Antonio López. The pope's university moved to Madrid in 1964, leaving a huge complex of buildings with no specific use; still the people of Comillas maintain the site and give tours of the

El Capricho

*t 94 272 03 65
www.elcapricho
degaudi.com;
open summer daily
10.30–1 and 3–8.30;
check website for winter
opening hours; adm*

**Palacio de
Sobrellano**

*t 94 272 03 39; open
July–early Sept daily
10.30–1.30 and 4–7.30;
mid-Sept–June
Wed–Sun 10.30–1.30
and 4–7.30; adm*

**Universidad
Pontificia**

*opening times vary –
check at tourist office*

The Instant Marquis

The Spain of the Industrial Revolution is a land not very well known, but if the nation's capitalists never could match the mills of the Midlands or Massachusetts in the 19th century they certainly produced some marvels, and some incredible robber-baron careers. Antonio López was a local boy who went off to Cuba and made a fortune in shipping and slaves (slavery wasn't abolished in Spanish-run Cuba until 1886), and then moved out and made another pile running a monopoly, the Philippine National Tobacco Company. He came back home, and purchased the title of Marquis of Comillas.

The new marquis' son married the daughter of Joan Güell, the richest man in Barcelona, who had also started in Cuba and ended up as Spain's biggest textile magnate. If the name is familiar, you're thinking of Antoni Gaudí's famous surreal Güell Park in Barcelona. Like Cosimo de' Medici in old Florence, this robber baron had a talented aesthete to succeed him, whose sponsorship of Gaudí sparked the golden age of Modernista architecture in Catalunya. It was the Güell connection that brought Gaudí to Cantabria, where he helped with the López family palace in 1878 and came back to build El Capricho in 1883. The centre of the López interests was Barcelona, where they ran factories, banks and the Transatlántica shipping line (which later fell into the grasp of the greatest of all Spanish robber barons, Juan March, and still runs most of the Spanish island ferries). The Lópezes lived on the Ramblas in Barcelona, but they spent their summers here, bringing along their Catalan friends and making Comillas a genteel upper-class resort; locals called them the 'Transatlánticos'.

López's castle-like summer mansion, on the hill overlooking the town, was one of the most spectacular private homes in its day, and the centre of the glittering social season Comillas knew at the turn of the 20th century. But modern capitalist glories never seem to last more than a generation or two, and today López's palace stands as empty and weird and forlorn as *Citizen Kane*'s Xanadu.

sumptuous main building containing decorations by a third major figure of Catalan Modernism, Lluis Domenech i Montaner. There are frescoed rooms and a chapel, but the best features are the figures carved in wood over the main stairway in the form of gargoyles: fearsome monsters share space with, among others, a house cat, a chicken and a fly.

If you like Domenech i Montaner there's a wonderfully florid **Monument to Antonio López** by him near the beach, within sight of Comillas' peculiar **cemetery**, built in a Gothic ruin and topped with a huge marble angel. Domenech i Montaner is responsible for some of the funerary statues inside too, and it isn't difficult to guess which ones are his.

San Vicente de la Barquera

The next resort to the west, San Vicente de la Barquera is still as much a fishing port as a holiday retreat, though it's hugely popular with Madrileños in summer – you won't find a place to park your car. Marvellously sited on a hill in the last elbow-bend of the wide and marshy Río Escudo (arriving on the coastal road from the west provides the best view), it is linked by a long causeway to the eastern coast, near the town beach. The older, upper town is dominated by the rose-coloured parish church **Nuestra Señora de los Ángeles**, a 13th-century transitional work containing the finely sculpted Renaissance tomb of the Inquisitor Antonio Corro. Below, interwoven branches of plane trees add a French touch to the main *plaza*. Every quarter of an hour the belltower of the San Vicente church booms out a recording of the first phrase of Schubert's *Ave María*, guaranteed to drive you nuts. The locals claim an enemy of their town had it installed – with any luck it will be a bad memory by the time you get there.

If you want to take a dip inland in this western end of Cantabria, the first town south of San Vicente is **Cabezón de la Sal**, a town where the *pozos de sal* – 'salt wells' – have been mined since before the Romans came. Cabezón is little more than an industrial centre, but nearby both the landscapes and the area's modest attraction remind you of Cantabria's more rural side: at **Carrejo**, the **Museo Regional de la Naturaleza** has exhibits of local flora and fauna in an 18th-century *palacio*.

Museo Regional de la Naturaleza
open April–Oct Tues–Sat 11–2 and 4–7, Sun 11–2; Nov–Mar Tues–Sat 11–2 and 4–6

Beyond that come two rather refined villages, each with a number of fine mansions and other works: **Ruente** and **Bárcena Mayor**. Bárcena especially, on a back road in the mountains, retains a medieval ambience, with arcaded streets, wooden balconies and woodworkers' shops. Legend claims it as one of the first towns of Cantabria and a stronghold of the *foramontanos*, as they call the mountaineers who resisted the Moors in the Dark Ages; the village has a fountain that goes back to Visigothic times.

⭐ **La Casa del Organista >>**

ⓘ **Santillana del Mar >**
C/Jesús Otero 20, t 94 281 82 51, santillana@ cantabria.org

Markets on the Coast West of Santander

Suances: Tues.
Torrelavega: Wed.
Comillas: Thurs.
San Vicente and **Cabezón**: Sat.

Where to Stay and Eat on the Coast West of Santander

Santillana ✉ 39330

There's plenty of choice in Santillana del Mar, from luxury properties to inexpensive *hostales*. If you're driving, you'll find lots of *casas rurales* in the area, which usually offer great deals, and are especially good if you're travelling with kids.

*****Casa del Marqués, C/Canton 24, t 94 281 88 88 (€€€€–€€€). Magnificent boutique hotel in a 15th-century building with a stone and beam interior, set around a beautiful, flower-filled patio. *Closed mid-Dec–Mar.*

***Parador de Santillana Gil Blas, Plaza Ramón Pelayo 11, t 94 281 80 00, *santillana@parador.es* (€€€€–€€€). Wonderfully atmospheric, with medieval rooms and an elegant dining room; reserve well in advance in season; request a room on the first or second floor.

La Casa del Organista, C/Los Hornos 4, t 94 284 03 52, *www.casadel organista.com* (€€€–€€). Gorgeous wood-panelled rooms with sloping ceilings, in a medieval mansion overlooking fields on the edge of town. The nicest have balconies.

***Hotel Altamira, C/Cantón 1, t 94 281 80 25, *www.hotelaltamira.com* (€€). A good choice, in a palace with a patio and garden; its elegant dining room with wooden beams serves big plates of roast meats and is one of the best restaurants in town.

***La Casa de Güela, C/Los Hornos 9, t 94 281 82 50 (€€). A pretty boutique-style hotel with just 10 rooms in a handsome old stone palace. With pool, tennis and gardens.

Camping Santillana, t 94 281 82 50, *www.campingsantillana.com* (€€). Just

north of the village, this is a pricey campsite, but it has all amenities, including a pool and tennis courts.
Pensión El Cantón, C/Carrera 3, t 94 284 02 74 (€). A lovely and welcoming *posada*, boasting the cheapest rooms with bath in Santillana's old quarter.

 Posada Rural Rioturbio >>

Posada La Cerrá de San Roque, t 94 284 00 65, *www.posadalacerra.com* (€). A charming inn set in lovely countryside halfway between Suances and Santillana del Mar. A good family option, set in gardens.

La Joraca, C/Los Hornos 20, t 94 284 0137 (€€). An atmospheric restaurant in the Hotel Colegiata, serving fine traditional cuisine prepared with flair: try the duck confit with apricots.

Los Blasones, Plaza de la Gándara 8, t 94 281 80 70 (€€). Feast on local and mountain specialities here – from *fabada* to grilled *langostinos* (crayfish). *Closed mid-Dec–mid-Mar.*

Casa Uzquiza, C/Escultor Jesús Otero 5, t 94 284 03 56 (€). Come for the set lunch, which offers plenty of choice for around €15. Prices jump a price bracket if you go *à la carte*.

ⓘ **Suances** >
C/Ceballos 12,
t 94 281 09 24,
www.suances.es

ⓘ **San Vicente de la Barquera** >>
Avda Generalísimo 20,
t 94 271 07 97,
www.sanvicentedel
barquera.org

ⓘ **Torrelavega**
C/Juan José Ruano 9,
t 94 289 29 82,
www.torrelavega.es

ⓘ **Comillas** >
Bayos del Joaquín del
Ayuntamiento Piélago 1,
C/Aldea 6,
t 94 272 07 68

Suances ✉ 39340

*****Castillo de Suances**, C/Acacio Gutiérrez, t 94 281 03 83, *www. turismosuances.com* (€€€). This 19th-century crenellated folly by the beaches offers interesting, individually decorated rooms, some with TV. Prices plummet out of the high season, with rooms available for €50.

Casa Sito, Pso de la Marina Española, 3, t 94 281 15 08, *www.restaurante sito.com* (€). This seafood restaurant is as popular with the locals as the tourists; it offers a good-value menu (including a Wednesday special for €6) and dishes like paella with lobster (*paella bogavante*) for a splurge.

Comillas ✉ 39520

*****Marina de Campíos**, C/General Piélagos 14, t 94 272 27 54, *www. marinadecampios.com* (€€€–€€). A handsomely renovated villa with elegant, individually styled rooms and suites and a piano-bar.

****Hotel Josein**, C/Manuel Noriega 27, *www.hoteljosein.com* (€€). Modern hotel which hangs over the beach: all

rooms have sea views, but some have wonderful private terraces.

****Hs Esmeralda**, C/Antonio López 7, t 94 272 00 97, *www.hostal esmeralda.com* (€). A good cheaper choice in a pretty stone building in the old quarter; close to the beach and with a pleasant bar/restaurant.

Posada Rural Rioturbio, Rioturbio 13, 5km from Comillas, t 94 272 04 11, *www.posadarioturbio.com* (€). Delightful B&B in a traditional stone house surrounded by the breathtaking countryside of the Oyambre nature reserve. Home-cooked dinners for guests.

Adolfo, Avda Las Infantas, t 94 272 20 14 (€€). A good choice, with traditional cooking including plenty of fresh seafood. *Closed Tues and Nov.*

La Lonja, C/del Muelle s/n, t 94 272 24 58, *www.lalonjadecomillas.com* (€€). This restaurant serves wonderfully fresh fish out on the terrace overlooking the fishing boats. *Open daily in summer, in winter closed Tues, plus Sun–Thurs eves.*

La Aldea, C/Aldea 5, t 94 272 03 00 (€€). A local favourite, thanks to its copious servings of traditional cuisine and fair prices. Also does good tapas and *raciones.*

San Vicente de la Barquera ✉ 39540

******Miramar**, Pso de la Barquera 20, t 94 271 00 75 (€€). On the edge of town, with great views of the bay and the Picos de Europa, but the décor is overdue for an update.

Posada Rural Punta Liñera, Barrio de Boria, t 94 271 22 25, *www.puntolinera. com* (€) Delightful guesthouse near the lighthouse, overlooking a small bay. Immaculate rooms, tranquillity and charming hosts. It's about a 20-minute stroll into the centre.

Camping El Rosal, Playas de San Vicente, t 94 271 01 65, *www. campingelrosal.com* (€). Conveniently located near the beaches, on the main road just outside San Vicente.

Boga-Boga, Pza José Antonio 9, t 94 271 01 35, *www.bogabogasvb.com* (€€). Expect more seafood at this place, where the chef turns out delicious Cantabrian favourites along with a

---

very good *solomillo con verduras*. The upstairs hotel (€€€) is good. *Closed Tues in Oct–May*.

Maruja, Avda Generalísimo s/n, t 94 271 00 77, *www.restaurante maruja.es* (€€). For a less serious seafood attack, you can do well here for under €30, and there's a bargain menu for €16.

Bárcena Mayor ✉ 39500

Posada La Franca, C/La Franca, t 94 270 60 67, *www.lafrancaposada rural.com* (€€€). Come here for the village's famed mountain cuisine –

stuffed haunch of venison and other game in season. The comfortable **rooms** (€) are inexpensive.

Cabezón de la Sal ✉ 39500

El Jardín de Carrejo, Carrejo (1km from Cabezón de la Sal), t 94 270 15 16 (€€). An enchanting stone-built inn set amid extensive gardens, with a river and shady corners. A kitchen garden provides fresh produce for breakfasts and dinners, available to guests. For romance, choose one of the two special suites in the garden. Online packages are available.

ⓘ **Cabezón de la Sal »**
C/Botín 1,
t 94 270 03 32,
www.cabezondelasal.net

The Picos de Europa

⭐ **Picos de Europa**

They are not the highest mountains in Spain, or even in the Cantabrian-Pyrenean *cordillera*, but the Picos de Europa have a certain cachet. So many peaks, closely packed in a small area of Cantabria, Asturias and León, make a memorable landmark for Spain's north coast. No one knows the origin of the name, though it may have been that they were the first sight of the continent for Atlantic sailors. To the Asturians they are known as the Urrieles.

Thank Asturian ecologists for their efforts in keeping Spain's most beautiful mountains enchanting and unspoiled: what development there is (ski resorts, hotels) is mostly in western Cantabria. The Picos are divided by rivers into three tremendous massifs – **Andara**, mostly in Cantabria, **Urrieles**, in the middle, and **Cornión**, to the west. The highest peak, **Torre de Cerredo**, stands 8,606ft. But for sheer beauty and rugged grandeur, for the contrast of tiny rural villages in fertile green valleys against a backdrop of sheer, twisted stone peaks snow-crested year round, the Picos de Europa are hard to beat.

The range seems to have been dropped from heaven, especially for hikers; there are trails for Sunday walkers and sheer cliffs for serious alpinists. Hiking boots, however, are universally recommended because of frequent patches of loose shale on the trails and slopes. If you're going for an extended holiday in the Picos, get the detailed maps published by the Federación Española de Montañismo, generally available at Potes, the main base for visiting the mountains. Up-to-date detailed information on guides, itineraries and mountain *refugios* (the overnight shelters, which range from little more than huts to simple inns) is available from the **Federación Asturiana de Montañismo**, the **Federación Cántabra de Montaña**, and the **Delegación Leonesa de Montaña**.

Federación Asturiana de Montañismo
C/Julián Clavería 11,
Oviedo, t 98 525 23 62,
www.fempa.net

Federación Cántabra de Montaña
C/Sánchez Díaz 1,
Reinosa, t 94 275 52 94,
www.fcdme.es

Delegación Leonesa de Montaña
Paseo de la Facultad 3, León, t 98 725 00 52

Hiking in the high Picos is practical only from the end of May to October, but even then you may get a soaking – the Picos are only 32km from the rainy Atlantic seaboard. Low-level walks can be done at any time of year. Bring warm clothes and a lightweight plastic poncho, a sleeping bag and a food supply for any nights you may spend in the *refugios*, and a pair of binoculars to take in the wonderful array of wildlife and birds.

The Eastern Picos de Europa

Potes and the Valley of Liébana

The eastern mountains of the Picos are the most visited and the most accessible. The main entrance from the coast begins at **Unquera** (a FEVE stop on the coast to the west of San Vicente de la Barquera); the N621 from here climbs up through the **Desfiladero de La Hermida**, a dramatic, high, narrow gorge walling in the River Deva, and the hamlet of **La Hermida**, famous in sunny Spain for not seeing *el sol* at all from 26 October to 8 March.

The road climbs up from here into the idyllic little **valley of the Liébana**, more happily fated by geography to have an unusual 'Mediterranean' microclimate. Vines and even olives grow here, though you'll see mostly apple orchards with the vineyards around the first village, **Lebeña**, with its parish church – the 10th-century Mozarabic **Santa María** – signposted south of the village on the

Getting to and around the Eastern Picos de Europa

By Bus

Palomera buses, t 94 288 06 11, *www.autobusespalomera.com*, serve Potes up to four times daily from Santander, via Unquera, San Vicente and Torrelavega. There are two buses (one in the winter) daily between Santander and León that stop at Potes and Lebeña. From Potes there are three buses in high season from the central square to Fuente Dé and the *teleférico* (times change according to the season, so check in advance).

By Jeep, Horse and Bike

Jeeps make the link between the upper station of the *teleférico* to the *refugio de Áliva*. Arenas de Cabrales (in Asturias) is the main hub in the northern Picos, with Land Rover services to Poncebos and Sotres and daily buses to Cangas de Onis and Panes. **4WD jeeps** can be hired in Potes for journeys deeper into the mountains with **Europicos**, *www.europicos.com*, t 94 273 07 24, or with **Picostur**, *www.picostour.com*, t 94 273 00 05, two of several companies offering adventure activities in the region. Also, a stable in Turieno next to Potes offers several guided riding excursions in the Picos. If you want to do it yourself, Viajes Wences and other firms in Potes rent **mountain bikes**.

N621. This is one of the finest pre-Romanesque churches, a little jewel in the middle of nowhere that is the perfect expression of the strange little mountainous state of Asturias and, perhaps, its dreams of future greatness. Built in 925 for a Count Alfonso, Santa María is as impressive a work as any of the more famous churches around Oviedo. Most of the exterior was restored a century ago, but the original roof corbels and decorated parts of the exterior are carved with originality, and inside the simple Greek-cross plan – with horseshoe Visigothic arches and not too much regard for precision – is a delight. A few years ago, the stone step up to the altar was raised and found to be carved with geometric symbols, along with a human figure apparently painted on the stone in blood. The information card the caretaker hands out claims that the stone is 2,000 years old, and carved with Celtic sun symbols; the symbols may be that old, but the stone probably came as the original altar when the church was built. You'll see a photo of a lovely carved wood Virgin, the work of the great Renaissance sculptor Gil de Siloé. Unfortunately the picture is all Lebeña has left; someone nicked the icon in 1993. Two venerable companions, an olive and yew tree, stand next to the church; they were both planted at the time the church was built – over 1,000 years ago.

Potes, the capital of the Valley of Liébana, is the metropolis of the Picos, where you can garner information, catch buses, change travellers' cheques and stock up on supplies. For all the tourist traffic Potes is still a gracious town, with stone arcades to shelter the cafés on the main street and a warren of medieval lanes behind. There are also a number of jeep excursions on offer. The main monument in Potes itself is the 15th-century **Torre del Infantado**, a massive, square defensive-residential work in the centre of town.

Monasterio de Santo Toribio de Liébana

www.santotoribio deliebana.com; open daily 10–1 and 4–7, Sunday mass at 12 and 1

The most popular excursions from Potes include the 4km trip up to the **Monasterio de Santo Toribio de Liébana**. Don't miss it, because this is the only place in Cantabria where a visit will earn you an indulgence – time off from purgatory. It is a long-established pilgrimage site, allegedly the home of the world's largest chunk of the True Cross. In the early days of the Kingdom of Asturias the Liébana was a kind of monastic preserve, and this monastery was its centre, founded early in the 8th century. What you see today, though, is mainly Romanesque and Gothic. The 'world's largest sliver of the True Cross' is kept in an ornate Baroque chapel where masses are said daily. In its earliest days the monastery was ruled by the Abbot Beato de Liébana, whose *Commentaries on the Apocalypse* were popular in Spain throughout the Middle Ages. Girona and El Burgo de Osma have beautiful 10th-century illuminated editions of the manuscript, but in the cloister here you can see a full set of copies of one of them – mad and brilliant pictorial prophecies from an age when people were convinced the world would soon be meeting its end.

The nearby **Mirador de Santo Toribio** takes in splendid views over the Andara massif. Another, longer walk south will take you through **Cabezón de Liébana**, where some of the houses have coats of arms, and two medieval bridges cross over to the lovely church of **Santa María de Piasca**, built in 1172 with fine Romanesque carvings on the capitals within. The monastery was shared by monks and nuns, which was typical for the mountains but unusual elsewhere.

Beato de Liébana Defends the Faith

Back in the grim 8th century, when the heathen Normans were attacking from the north, the godless Magyars from the east and the infidel Moors from the south, and the Faith was in gravest peril, just what were the Christians up to? Well, they were arguing amongst themselves as usual. Christian Spain in that age may not seem to have been really big enough to generate a proper theological controversy, but somehow it managed. At issue was something called Adoptionism, the doctrine that Jesus the man was only the 'adopted son' of God. In the far corner, wearing the black trunks, we see Bishop Helipandus of Toledo, then under Muslim rule, who argued for Adoptionism. In the near corner, in the white trunks, stands Beato de Liébana, who isn't about to let anybody say his Saviour does not participate fully in Godhood.

Like all such controversies, this brouhaha masked some more mundane conflicts – between the mountaineer Asturians and the more sophisticated Mozarabic Christians of the south, over who was boss in matters of faith and politics. This particular conflict caught the attention of all Western Christianity, though, and it found a solution, surprisingly, not with the pope in Rome but at the court of Charlemagne. In those days, if you were lucky enough to find someone with the necessary wisdom and erudition to decide on such a case, he would probably have been (another surprise) an Englishman. The king of the Franks was fortunate enough to have in his services the greatest doctor of Christendom, Alcuin of York, who was busy trying to reform the Carolingian educational system and, with less success, to teach Charlemagne how to write his name. In 799 Alcuin pronounced that Adoptionism was just a rehash of the old Nestorian heresy, and awarded a clean decision to Beato, who thereupon retired from the ring of Church politics and went home to write about the End of the World.

From Fuente Dé to Arenas de Cabrales

The classic excursion from Potes is to take the bus west up to the stunning old village of **Espinama** and, 1.6km beyond, to **Fuente Dé**. Here you can catch the *teleférico* for an awesome, vertigo-inducing ride 2,568ft up the sheer cliff to the **Mirador del Cable**.

Once at the top, walk 4km (2½ miles) up to the **Hotel-Refugio Áliva**, a modern version of the old mountain refuge; a path from here leads down to Espinama – a pleasant day's circuit, and very popular with gnarly mountain bikers, who consider this one of the best rides in Europe.

From Espinama or the hotel, you can make a longer, more serious hike through the eastern and central massifs north to Sotres, a pleasant mountain village in spectacular scenery (Jeep excursions also available from Espinama). **Sotres** has a couple of basic *pensiones* and places to eat, and makes an excellent base for walks deeper into the mountains; a good one is the 11km (7-mile) haul up to **Tresviso** on the eastern edge of Andara massif, where there's a magnificent view 3,000ft down into the Desfiladero de la Hermida. Most people head west, though, across the Pass of Pandébano and into the majestic central cirque of Los Urriellos; the big landmark in this area is **Naranjo de Bulnes** (Pico Urriellu on some maps), a distinct sheer-sided tower-like pinnacle, loved and hated by daredevil alpinists. Below the Naranjo, **Bulnes** is a classic mountain village, set in a steep green valley surrounded by towering cliffs; until 2001, the only way to get there was to walk, but finally – to the delight of locals and the despair of environmentalists – a **funicular** was completed which links the village with **Poncebos**.

The most important village in the area is **Arenas de Cabrales**, connected by Land Rover with Poncebos and Sotres and the centre of an area renowned for its stinking mountain cheese – 'never matured in manure, never contains worms', the tourist literature boasts. *Raciones* of the stuff are served everywhere, and almost everyone finds themselves trying it before they can get out of town. Hikers will be more interested in the classic traverse of the Divine Gorge from Poncebos, more commonly approached from the south by way of Posada de Valdeón in León province (*see* p.215).

Mirador del Cable
t 94 273 66 10; teleférico runs July–Sept daily 9–8; Oct–June daily 10–6; in peak season arrive very early or you'll get stuck waiting, maybe for hours

Funicular
runs Easter week and July–Sept daily 10–8; rest of year daily 10–12.30 and 2–6; trains leave every 30mins; adm

Markets in the Eastern Picos de Europa

Unquera: Wed.
Potes: Mon.

Where to Stay and Eat in the Eastern Picos de Europa

It may be paradise for hikers, but there's no need to rough it. Nearly every village in the Picos has at least one *casa particular* or *fonda* or a place to camp, and you can purchase

(i) **Unquera**
(Val de San Vicente),
Ctra N-639 Km.279,
t 94 271 96 80,
www.aytovaldesan
vicente.com

(i) **Potes >**
C/Independencia 12,
t 94 273 07 87,
www.potes.es;
also try Bustamente,
C/Capitán Palacios 10,
a photo and bookshop
specializing in the Picos
de Europa with a wide
range of maps and
guides; also check out
www.liebanaypicosde
europa.com

(i) **Turieno**
National Park Office,
Urb. La Molina, t 94 273
05 55; the National Park
runs free daily guided
walks in summer in the
Liébana valley and
Cabrales, covering
various routes

(i) **Arenas de**
Cabrales >>
Ctra General, t 98 584
64 84, turismo@
cabrales.org
(summer only)

supplies or dine out in a traditional restaurant. Every village has its specialities, and the shops under the arches on the main street of Potes are treasure-houses of the mountains' finest; you can buy local cheeses and *charcuterie*, honey in various original flavours and *orujo*, the Cantabrian firewater sold in dangerous-looking bottles all over town. It's made from the stems and pulp of grapes after the wine harvest, like French *marc* or Italian *grappa*.

Potes ✉ 39570

Potes has by far the most accommodation in the region, most of it very affordable.

**Hotel & Spa Arha, C/Amapola s/n, t 94 273 10 54, *www.arhahoteles.com* (€€–€). Modern mountain hotel, with a tiny spa area, and crisp rooms with white furnishings.

**Infantado, Ojedo (1km from Potes), t 94 273 09 39, *www.hotel infantado.com* (€€–€). Modern, stone-built and comfortable.

**Picos Valdecoro, C/Roscabado 5, t 94 273 00 25 (€€–€). Modern, well-equipped rooms, and a restaurant.

*Casa Cayo, C/Cántabra 6, t 94 273 01 50, *www.casacayo.com* (€€–€). A charming mountain hotel, with simple but comfortable rooms overlooking the river and a very popular *comedor* downstairs that serves huge portions.

**Picos de Europa, C/Arco Iris 3, t 94 237 10 15, *www.hotelpicosdeeuropa.net* (€). A simple, cosy place which also arranges all kinds of outdoor activities, from hiking to canoeing.

La Casa del Frama, Frama (8km from Potes), t 94 273 04 65, *www.casadeframa.com* (€). A lovely stone mountain house with just six pretty rooms and friendly owners.

**Hs La Serna, C/La Serna 9, t 94 273 10 44, *http://lasernahostal. blogspot.com* (€). A budget choice, with a good restaurant downstairs.

Posada Bistruey, La Vega (9km south of Potes), t 94 273 60 95 (€). If Potes is too hectic, head for this peaceful roadside *posada*, run by a friendly family who provide a hearty breakfast, free sweets, and spotless rooms with bath at bargain prices.

Camping El Molino, La Vega, t 94 273 60 09, *www.campingtranquilo.com* (€). Offers pitches and bungalows in a leafy setting.

El Fogon de Cus, Plaza Capitán Palacios 2, t 94 273 00 60, *www. elfogondecus.com* (€€). Has the best name in town for local dishes and Basque cooking. It also has six comfortable **rooms** (€).

El Bodegón, C/San Roque 4, t 94 273 047 (€€–€). Old-fashioned local favourite, serving reliable *tapas* and traditional cuisine.

Los Camachos, C/El Llano, t 94 273 00 64 (€). For dinner, this place has an honest menu with *fabada*, trout and other local treats.

Fuente Dé ✉ 39588

***Parador Río Deva, t 94 273 66 51, *www.parador.es* (€€€). Since 1965, this magnificently sited hotel has been a part of the Picos experience. A modern building at the end of the *teleférico*, many of its rooms have grand views; the hotel organizes Jeep excursions into the peaks, and its restaurant specializes in mountain dishes. *Closed mid-Nov–Mar.*

***Hotel del Oso, Cosgaya (12km from Fuente Dé), t 94 273 30 18, *www. hoteldeloso.com* (€€). Amid stunning mountain scenery, this modern but traditionally stone-built place is owned by the famously welcoming Rivas family and the restaurant is perhaps the best in the area. There's a pool in the gardens.

Espinama ✉ 39500

Refugio de Áliva, about 7.5km up from Espinama, t 94 273 09 99, *www.cantur.com/aliva.asp* (€). Has a restaurant (€) and rooms for 2, 4 and 6. Ring in advance; a Land Rover from Espinama will take you up (or take the *teleférico* – they offer packages that include the fare). *Open June–mid-Oct. (For other refugios in the Picos, ask at the Potes tourist office.)*

Arenas de Cabrales and around ✉ 33554

***Picos de Europa, C/Mayor s/n, t 98 584 64 91, *www.hotelpicosde europa.com* (€€€–€€). The poshest choice here, with smart rooms, a pool and a good restaurant.

Casa Cipriano, Sotres, t 98 594 50 24, www.casacipriano.com (€€). This simple pensión is an excellent base for outdoor activities; the staff can arrange Land Rover taxis and climbing guides. Good hearty stews and raciones are served in the bar.

Pensión La Perdíz, Sotres, t 98 594 50 11, www.laperdizsotres.com (€€). Has doubles with bath; two rooms have private balconies and fantastic mountain views.

**Hotel Villa de Cabrales, Carretera General s/n t 98 584 67 19, www. hotelcabrales.com (€). Large, bright rooms with views of the Picos.

La Casa del Chiflón, Bulnes, t 98 584 59 43, www.casadelchiflon.com (€). The only places to stay in Bulnes are in casas rurales or hostales – this traditional stone-built house has attractive, if simple, rooms and can also arrange guided tours and excursions.

The Asturian Picos de Europa: Cangas and Covadonga

The salmon-filled Río Sella defines the west edge of the western Massif de Cornión. Most easily reached from Ribadesella on the Asturian coast, or through the stunning narrow **Desfiladero de los Beyos** gorge (N625) from León and Riaño, the region lacks the high drama of the mountains further east, but is nonetheless green and tranquil, and for Spaniards constitutes a pilgrimage.

Desperately Seeking Pelayo

Cangas de Onís claims to be the first capital of Christian Spain, where the Asturian kings set up shop right after their victory at nearby Covadonga. The most beautiful things in Cangas are the high **medieval bridge** (erroneously called Roman) with its great arch spanning the Río Sella, and the **Capilla de Santa Cruz**, where the kings worshipped. It was built over a dolmen, and according to legend its founder was Favila, the successor of Pelayo. The original building may really be as early as the 5th century, though it was completely rebuilt in the 15th (get the key at the Ayuntamiento, and they might also let you have the key for the cave of Buxu). On a pillar near the entrance, an old relief shows a cross over a crescent moon, symbolizing the Christians' victories over Islam. As for the dolmen, it is still clearly visible in the chapel's crypt, carved with religious symbols.

From Cangas it's 3km north to **Villanueva**, where Alfonso I founded the **Monasterio de San Pedro** in 746. Now restored and converted into a parador (see p.214) it has a 12th-century doorway, with capitals carved with bear-hunting scenes. East of Cangas, the AS114 follows the narrow valley of the Río Güeña, providing the northern part of the circuit around the Picos. In Cardes, the **cave of Buxu** contains rare, very abstract paintings from the Solutrian era (20,000–15,000 BC).

Capilla de Santa Cruz
open Easter Week and June –Sept Tues–Sun 11–2 and 4–7.30; closed rest of year, but contact the tourist office for guided visits t 98 584 80 43

Cave of Buxu
Call in advance to book a visit, t 608 175 467; open all year, Mon–Wed 10.30, 11.30, 12.30, 3.15, 4.15; max 25 visitors per day; adm, free Wed

Getting to and around the Asturian Picos de Europa

ALSA buses, t 902 42 22 42, *www.alsa.es*, serve Cangas de Onís several times daily from Oviedo and Gijón with a less frequent service from Llanes and one daily from León. There's a direct bus from Oviedo to Covadonga, or change at Cangas de Onis for services to Covadonga and Arenas de Cabrales. The ALSA website lists seasonal timetables. ALSA also run buses from Arenas de Cabrales to the Bulnes **funicular** at Poncebos. There are no bus services to Ponga, where you will need your own transport to explore properly. **Taxis** can be hired in San Juan de Beleño on **t** 98 584 30 17.

From here it's 10km to **Covadonga**, dominated by an enormous, kitschy 19th-century basilica. Here Pelayo, supposedly the son-in-law of Roderick, the last Visigothic king, and 300 followers managed to ambush a small Moorish expedition and defeat them, according to legend. The Moors, who didn't much care for the climate to begin with, made the mistake of letting the Christians stay and consolidate their power, preferring to seek richer spoils in France. Next to the basilica is the **cave** where Pelayo fought with his back to the wall and now rests in peace in a sarcophagus next to his wife.

From Covadonga it's a beautiful 12km drive through the national park to the mountain lakes of **La Ercina** and **Enol**, with the huge Peña Santa mountains as a backdrop. In response to the huge summer traffic jams, a **shuttle bus** service now ferries the endless surge of families up to the lakes. On sunny weekends the lakes pack out with day-trippers, but a stroll around the shore of La Ercina should see you well away from the picnicking throng, and surrounded instead by wild flowers. There are plenty of longer walks from the lakes; try the four-hour descent into the gorgeous **forest of Pome**, home to eagle owls and capercaillie.

Shuttle bus operates end July–early Sept every 15mins 10–6.30; outside these times you can drive up; call the Cangas de Onis tourist office for information, t 98 584 80 05

A more serious proposition is to hike right across the Cornión massif to 6,340ft Jultayu, beyond which the mountains collapse precipitously into the Garganta Divina. In summer there is a frequent bus service from Cangas and Covadonga; the rest of the year there's just one a day. Back on the AS114, the next village east is **Corao**; nearby, at a place called Abamia, the church of Santa Eulalia has parts going back to the 8th century, along with fragments of medieval frescoes.

Ponga and the Desfiladero de Los Beyos

South of Cangas de Onís the N625 follows the crystalline Rio Sella towards León, passing some hidden swimming holes that most people drive straight past; the best one is near **Ceneya**, a deep ice-blue pool reached by way of a tiny bridge across the gorge.

A couple of miles before Ceneya, in the hamlet of **Santillán**, the AS261 turns off to the west and makes its narrow and sinuous way through the *concejo* of **Ponga**, a little-known and rarely visited land of sparkling brooks, enchanting green valleys and tiny villages plastered to steep hillsides. A good overview of the area can be had from the *mirador* of **Les Bedules**, a short walk off the main road 3km beyond Beleño; to the east, the central ranges of the Picos heave their crests skyward in a crescendo of limestone extravagance, and to the west the tranquil Valle de Ponga is dominated by massive, craggy **Tiatordos**. An easy trail continues from Les Bedules into the beautiful **forest of Peloño**; die-hards can tackle the ascent of Tiatordos itself, a tough uphill grunt from the village of Taranes for which a guide must be hired. Beyond Les Bedules the road passes through raggle-taggle **Viego** before narrowing to a single lane and dropping steeply to rejoin the main road at Puente La Huera. This is the start of the **Desfiladero de los Beyos**, a narrow cleft through the mountains which Spain's engineers are pleased to announce is the narrowest motorable gorge in Europe. It's an exhilarating piece of highway, threading between cliffs that rise vertiginously to 3,000ft above the canyon floor, with plenty of pullouts and tantalizing views; snow finch and wallcreepers can be spotted flitting around the walls. After six twisting kilometres the road emerges into the wide open **Valle de Sajambre**, and León province.

Markets in the Asturian Picos de Europa

Cangas de Onís: Sun.

Where to Stay and Eat in the Asturian Picos de Europa

(i) **Cangas de Onís** ⟩
Jardines del Ayuntamiento, t 98 584 80 05, www.cangasdeonis.com; free guided walks daily from the car park at Lago de La Ercina to areas of the Peña Santa range

National Park information: *Casa Dago, t 98 584 86 14, in summer*

Cangas de Onís ✉ 33550

*****Parador de Cangas de Onís, in Villanueva (2km from Cangas), t 98 584 94 02, www.parador.es (€€€€). The 12th-century Monasterio de San Pedro de Villanueva is now one of Spain's most luxurious *paradores*, with palatial guest quarters. The views over the river and Picos are superb, as is the traditional Asturian cuisine.

****La Cepada, Avda Contranquil s/n, t 98 584 94 45, www.hotellacepada.com (€€€€–€€). Elegant, spacious classically decorated rooms with classic decoration in a modern hotel built in traditional style. There's a good restaurant (€€€–€€), serving creative Asturian cuisine.

***Nochendi, C/Constantino Gonzalez 4, t 98 584 95 13, www.hotelnochendi.com (€€). A charming hotel in a new building in the centre of town, full of attractive designer touches, and with delightful staff.

*Plaza, La Plaza 7, t 98 584 83 08, www.hotelplazacangasdeonis.com (€€). Small, friendly, and well located in a 16th-century building in the middle of town.

Piloña, San Pelayo 19, t 98 594 71 56 (€€). Cangas has pricey hotels and a score of *hostales* where the going rate is about €75 in high season, considerably less the rest of the year; this is one of the more central ones.

Casa Juan, Avda de Covadonga 20 (1km west of the centre), t 98 584 80 12 (€€). *Fabada* and other Asturian dishes are to be had at this *sidrería* and restaurant, open since 1942. *Closed Tues and Wed eves and June.*

El Molín de la Pedrera, C/Rio Güeña 2, t 98 584 91 09, www.elmolin.com (€€). An attractive mixture of modern and rustic decoration, this serves good tapas and *raciones* at the bar, and has a well deserved reputation for its imaginative interpretations of traditional Asturian cuisine.

Sidrería El Polesu, C/Ángel Tárano s/n, t 98 584 9248 (€). A traditional old *chigre*, full of locals and easily identified by the stench of cider wafting from the doors, with good *raciones* of local meats and cheeses.

Covadonga ✉ 33589

★★★★Arcea Gran Hotel Pelayo, t 985 84 60 61 (€€€). A bland chain hotel, redeemed by a magnificent setting between the sanctuary and the holy cave. Online bargains available – otherwise it's overpriced.

★ **La Casona de Con** >>

Casa Priena, Santuario de Covadonga, t 98 584 60 70 (€€). A delightful B&B close to the sanctuary, with four small, stylish rooms, hearty breakfasts and a decent traditional restaurant, open to the public.

El Colladín, in Llerices, t 98 584 90 97 (€€). A traditional, antique-filled country house close to the Santuario de Covadonga. Simple rooms and lavish home-cooked breakfasts.

El Huerto del Ermitaño, Cruce a los Lagos, t 98 584 60 97, *www.elhuerto delermitano.com* (€). Surrounded by trees and mountains with a real alpine feel. Excellent *fabada* and home-made desserts.

Hospedería del Peregrino, 200m below the sanctuary in Covadonga, t 98 584 60 47, *www.picosdeuropa.net* (€€). Has a well-deserved name for its *fabada*, seafood and mountain dishes. Rooms (€) are without bath.

Ponga ✉ 33557

La Casona de Con, Mestas de Con, t 98 594 40 74, *www.lacasonadecon. com* (€€). A wonderful rural retreat in a tiny village 10km east of Cangas de Onís, in a typical 18th-century farmhouse with stylishly furnished bedrooms and delicious breakfasts. *Closed Nov–Feb.*

Pensión Fonda de Ponga, San Juan de Beleño, t 98 584 30 04 (€). A simple *pensión* above a good restaurant (€).

The Leonese Picos de Europa

At the southern end of the *desfiladero*, pyramidal Pica Ten dominates the Sajambre valley and its main village, **Oseja de Sajambre**, a pretty place that sees few visitors. Most people pass through on their way to the isolated mountain hamlet of **Soto de Sajambre**, high above Oseja and bang in the middle of the Picos's most pristine forest. Soto attracts plenty of hikers, who come to tackle the **Senda del Arcediano**, an epic high-altitude traverse of the Sierra de Beza. The trail can also be walked from its Asturian end in **Amieva**; this used to be the main route between Cangas de Onís and the *meseta*, and traces of the original paving remain. It takes less effort to wander out through densely wooded territory to **Vegabaño**, where a lonely *refugio* looks out over spectacular views of the central Picos.

Posada de Valdeón

From Oseja it's a short drive across the Puerto de Pontón to Posada de Valdeón, chief village of the high valley of Valdeón and a serenely magnificent place to rest up in before or after the Cares Gorge; here tiny farming villages and their rustic granaries, or *hórreos*, built on stilts to protect their contents from moisture and mice, look like mere toys under the loftiest mountains in the Picos. One of the most stupendous views of these is from the **Mirador del Tombo**, 1.6km from Posada de Valdeón towards Caín, framed by a

Getting to and around the Leonese Picos de Europa

Buses (about five weekly, more in high season) from Cangas de Onís to Madrid pass through Oseja de Sajambre, as does the summer-only service from Cangas to Posada de Valdeón; Posada is also served by daily buses from Riaño, where there is a twice-daily service to León.

Beyond the main villages the only transport is by **taxi**; in Oseja **t** 98 774 03 59, or in Posada (for Land Rovers to Caín), **t** 98 774 26 09 or **t** 609 569 647/661.

statue dedicated to the chamois goat, an animal occasionally seen in the flesh frisking over the steep slopes. The **Chorco de los Lobos** nearby was used to trap the mountains' most fearsome predator, the now-rare wolf. Across the river is the tiny hermitage of **Corona**, according to Leonese legend the true site of Pelayo's coronation after the battle of Covadonga.

The Divine Gorge

Between Caín and Poncebos, the **Cares Gorge** (better known as simply the 'Garganta Divina') extends north-to-south across the Picos. It is a spectacular 12km (7-mile) walk over sheer drops down to the Río Cares, made relatively easy by a footpath sculpted into the mountainside (although 80 per cent of all accidents in the Picos de Europa happen here, so make sure you are well prepared for the trek). The classic approach is from **Caín** in the south, itself linked to Posada de Valdeón by a regular four-wheel-drive service. Walking south from **Poncebos** isn't much more strenuous – but you risk either spending the night in Caín, which has limited lodgings, or walking the 9km (5½ miles) further south to sleep in Posada de Valdeón.

ⓘ Posada de Valdeón **>>**
tourist information at www.valdeon.org; construction of a new Visitor Centre and Park Information Office in Posada de Valdeón began in 2011

Where to Stay and Eat in the Leonese Picos de Europa

Oseja de Sajambre ✉ 24916

*Hostal Pontón, Ctra Nacional 625, **t** 98 774 03 16 (€). Has great views and a good value *menú del día*.

Soto de Sajambre ✉ 24916

*Hostal Peñasanta, C/Principal s/n, **t** 98 774 03 95 (€). A lovely traditional *hostal*, with flowers on the balconies. The restaurant (for guests only) serves up slabs of *cabrito asado* (roast goat) for a minimum of six people, and Asturian stews; information about hiking trails is available next door in the *albergue*.

Posada de Valdeón ✉ 24915
Hostal Casa Abascal, El Salvador, **t 98 774 05 07 (€). Posada has several *casas particulares* and some fine *fondas*: this offers the most comforts.

Hostal Campo, Amador Campo Pérez, **t 98 774 05 02 (€). Has good-value modern rooms with bath, and wonderful views from the terrace. The cafeteria serves decent stews and *fabadas*.

Pensión Begoña, Amador Campo Pérez, **t** 98 774 05 16 (€). Offers an authentic mountain experience – small and spartan rooms with goatskins on the floor, terrific meals and a warm welcome.

Camping El Cares, Santa Marina de Valdeón, **t** 98 774 26 76 (€). Has 400 pitches and plenty of facilities, including horse-trekking. *Open June–Oct.*

Asturias

The principality of Asturias is the Spanish Wales, a rugged country of stupendous mountains, mines and a romantically beautiful coastline. The inhabitants have traditionally been a hardy lot, beginning with the Iberian tribe of Astures, after whom the province is named, who defied both the Romans and Visigoths. One of the last areas to be touched by tourism, it is fighting to maintain its integrity and environment against big developers who would exploit the magnificent Picos de Europa and the coast; instead, Asturias would have you stay in a rural village, to learn something of its culture and architecture.

10

Don't miss

🌟 **The capital of cider country**
Villaviciosa **p.222**

🌟 **Unique 9th-century churches**
Near Oviedo **p.231**

🌟 **Lammergeyers, eagles and bears**
Somiedo National Park **p.235**

🌟 **The perfect seaside hideaway**
Cudillero **p.240**

🌟 **In the footsteps of dinosaurs**
Lastres **p.222**

See map overleaf

p.302

Don't miss

① Villaviciosa p.222
② Near Oviedo p.231
③ Somiedo National Park p.235
④ Cudillero p.240
⑤ Lastres p.222

The proudest date in Asturian history is 718, when a band of Visigoths, led by the legendary Pelayo, defeated the Moors in the mountain glen of Covadonga, officially beginning the Reconquista and founding the first tiny Christian kingdom in Muslim Iberia. Their beautiful churches are Asturias's chief artistic heritage; the language they spoke, *el Bable*, or 'Babel', survives only as a dialect against the modern dominance of Castilian, its direct descendant.

Since the 14th century, the Spanish heir-apparent has borne the title of 'Prince of Asturias', a practice initiated by John of Gaunt when his daughter married the son of Juan I. Not long after that,

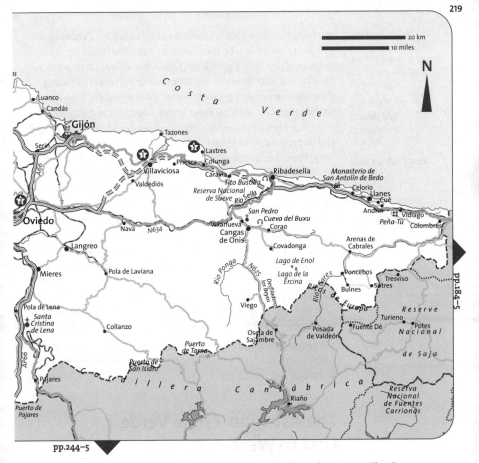

pp.184–5

pp.244–5

Asturias fell into an obscurity that lasted centuries. The discovery of iron ore and coal in the 19th century rapidly transformed its traditional agricultural economy into a mining one with radical tendencies. These brought about the second great date in Asturian history: an epic miners' revolt in October 1934 that served as a prelude to the Civil War. Even after the war, resistance to Franco continued in the wild mountains of the province.

The modern autonomous region of Asturias is, in its quiet way, one of the most progressive in Spain. In 1985, the Asturian wildlife protection fund received the European Preservation of Nature (FAPAS) prize for its efforts to preserve the rare Cantabrian bear and the capercaillie from extinction: their efforts seem to be paying off, and a 2010 survey counted approximately 200 bears in the region. One of the gentlest ways to get acquainted with the Asturian countryside is on a **pony trek**, especially along the Roman road of Lamesa, between the districts of Somiedo and Teverga. **Cyclists** can get advice on the best routes by visiting the useful official website or calling their information line, which also has tips

Pony trekking
*www.aventuraviesca.com
or call* **t** *98 535 73 69*

Cycling
*www.infoasturias.com
(also in English) or
information line*
t *902 300 202*

Fishing
www.infoasturias.com
for general information
including where to
get permits

**Surf and
Bodyboard
Federation**
www.surfasturias.com

**Real Club de Golf
Castiello**
t 98 536 63 13,
www.castiello.com

La Barganiza
t 98 574 24 68,
www.labarganiza.com

on the national parks and countless other activities. **Canoeing** to suit all standards can be found all over, from the tumbling rapids of the mountains to the gentle streams in the valleys – Asturias has a full national and international programme. Asturias is a **fishing** paradise; the waters teem with trout, salmon and eel. If you like your watersports with a flavour of salt, head for the gusty Bay of Biscay for sailing and windsurfing. Surfers should contact the **Surf and Bodyboard Federation** based in Gijón. Finally on the outdoor front, there are several golf courses in the region, including those at Gijón (**Real Club de Golf Castiello**) and Siero (**La Barganiza**).

At least once, visit an old Asturian *chigre* or *sidrería* to taste the local poison, *sidra* (cider) – natural but dangerous stuff, always poured at arm's length to give it the proper bounce. If you drink enough of it, it even begins to taste good. In recent years the principality has promoted rural tourism by way of a network of '*casas de aldea*' or country homes. These houses, some of historical interest, usually have between two and four rooms for rent, with meals also available. An official guide to these homes is put out each year and is available at any tourist office. The word ***pola*** in this chapter is the local Asturian word for *pueblo* (village).

Note that, although the Picos de Europa are partly in Asturias, the whole range has been grouped together in **Cantabria and the Picos de Europa** *(see pp.212–15).*

The Asturian 'Costa Verde': East to West

Although the Picos de Europa attract mountaineers and hikers from all over the world, the very attractive coast of Asturias sees relatively few foreigners. There are over 50 sandy beaches, most of them on unmarked roads just off the main coastal highway; some have spectacular locations, and a few can offer relative peace and quiet even in the middle of August. It's a mountainous and rugged coast for the most part, and the lack of a good road along it (until recently) has kept development to a minimum.

Llanes to Villaviciosa

Llanes

This eastern section of the coast is well endowed with beaches and quiet coves, especially around Llanes, the first sizeable town. Llanes gets busy in summer – in fact when this agreeably funky old town becomes loaded with *madrileños* it becomes charmingly anarchic. Llanes is so popular because the coast around it contains

Getting around from Llanes to Villaviciosa

By Train and Bus

FEVE **trains** along the coast take in much of the marvellous scenery. Two trains a day run between Santander and Oviedo, with stops at Unquera, Colombres, the beaches at Nueva and Villaharmes and Ribadesella; a further three a day go from Oviedo to Llanes.

To continue west up the coast from Ribadesella, you take a Gijón-bound **bus**. FEVE has frequent connections between Gijón and Avilés, and west to Cudillero, Luarca, Soto de Luiña and Ortigueiro. ALSA (**t** 902 422 242, *www.alsa.es*) buses link all these towns with Oviedo as well, while RENFE links Gijón with Oviedo, Madrid, Barcelona and the rest of the peninsula.

FEVE timetables and information can be found at *www.feve.es*, **t** 94 220 95 22 (Cantabria), and **t** 98 598 23 81 or **t** 98 598 23 80 (Asturias).

By Car

The big A8 motorway has been the biggest road project in this region for some years, and is now complete across the entire length of the coast except for a few very short sections.

some of the best beaches in Asturias: the town beach, El Sablón, is a pretty arc of golden sand, but it's small and quickly fills up in summer. Head east for bigger beaches near two pretty villages. At **Cué**, signs point to the less frenetic Playa de Toró, set among pinnacle-like rock formations; at **Andrín**, 3km further, you can find two good beaches not yet crowded and commercialized: Playa de Andrín and Playa de Ballota.

The area's two antiquities lie east of Llanes: near Vidiago and the Playa de France, there's a peculiar Bronze Age monument called **Peña-Tú** or the 'Cabeza del Gentil' (Gentile's Head). Even older are the cave drawings in the **Cueva del Pindal** near **Colombres**, featuring the only known painting of a mammoth in Spain.

West of Llanes, at **Celorio**, the unspoiled Playa de Borizu faces a small islet you can swim to, and you can find another string of beaches, some ideal for children, around the charming village of **Niembro**, along with the ruins of a 12th-century monastery, San Antolín de Bedo. For more isolation, try the **Playa de Torimbia**, situated in a perfect crescent of cliffs and accessible from a path down the rock face.

Cueva del Pindal
open Wed–Sun 10–5; adm; there are six tours a day, each with a maximum of 20 people; from Oct–Mar, visits must be booked in advance by calling t 608 175 284

Ribadesella

The next town, Ribadesella, at the mouth of the meandering Río Sella, makes an excellent base for forays along the coast or into the western Picos. Split in two by the river and bridge, with a picture-postcard backdrop of mountains, Ribadesella has a handful of old streets, a long protected beach, and plenty of chances for hiking, pony trekking, canoeing and fishing. The beaches lie just across the Sella to the west of town. Just outside town are the stalactitic **Tito Bustillo Caves,** where some 15–20,000 years ago the residents painted the walls with stylish animals and humans in the Altamira fashion, worth a visit although their burnt sienna, purple and black tones have faded.

Tito Bustillo Caves
open April–Oct Wed–Sun 10–4.30; adm; free Wed; admission by guided tour only; reserve in advance by calling t 98 586 12 55

Farther west, into what is officially known as the 'Costa Verde', you'll find quiet beaches in the tiny hamlets of **Caravia** (Baja and Alta), and near **Colunga**: La Isla, La Griega and Lastres. You'll also find evidence of Asturias' Jurassic inhabitants – fossilized shells, tree trunks, and dinosaur tracks – all along the coast between Ribadesella and Villaviciosa. The best-preserved remains are around **Playa de la Griega** near **Lastres**, including footprints left in the coastal mud by giant sauropods. Overlooking the beach, you can find out more in the slick modern **Museo del Jurásico de Asturias**, with huge bones and dinosaur skeletons, models and plenty of interactive exhibits. Equally renowned for its clams and *sidra*, Lastres' stack of red-tile-roofed houses and noble mansions overlooks one of Asturias' most picturesque fishing harbours. The setting for *Doctor Mateo*, a Spanish remake of British TV series *Doc Martin*, it has been overrun with Spanish tourists asking perplexed locals to point them in the direction of the doctor's house.

There is a small beach at the village, but a better one just to the west at **Rodiles**. Some rare Asturian horses, descendants of the hardy creatures used by the Romans for mountain duty, survive in the **Reserva Nacional de Sueve**, 3km south of Colunga, where you'll also find the **Mirador del Fito** with splendid views of the Picos de Europa and the coast. There is a small pre-Romanesque church, built in 921, in the village of **Priesca**, just west of Colunga.

Villaviciosa

Apple orchards line the coast around Villaviciosa, and as you enter the town you'll pass a sign welcoming you to the 'Apple Capital of Spain'. They grow every sort of apple around here, but most common are the ones that feed the town's dozen cider manufacturers. No town makes more of Asturias's favourite sauce, and none seems more devoted to drinking it – particularly during the Fiesta de la Manzana, held every year in mid-October. Every warm evening the tables go out from *chigres* (cider bars) onto the streets, and the noise goes on half the night. Children run around; cider is splashed everywhere. You can visit some of the cider manufacturers, including **El Gaitero**, one of the oldest.

O villa más viciosa, as an old drinking song chides it, is really a quite pleasant place, with a lively centre built around the Parque Vallina, and a small collection of old streets and palaces, including the attractive 13th-century **Santa María de la Oliva**. Not much has changed since 1517, when Villaviciosa became the first town in Spain to see the handsome but all-too-intense face of their new king, Charles V, who was sailing to Santander from his home in Flanders and was blown off course. There is a plaque on the house where the king stayed to mark the biggest surprise in Villaviciosa's history. If you want to swim, there are two beaches near

⭐ Museo del Jurásico de Asturias
t 902 306 600, www.museojurasico. com; open July–mid-Sept daily 10.30–2.30 and 4–8; Easter–June and last 2 weeks Sept Wed–Sun 10–2.30 and 4–7; Oct–Easter Wed–Fri 10–2.30 and 3.30–6, Sat–Sun 10-30–2.30 and 4–7; adm, free Wed

⭐ Villaviciosa

Villaviciosa: long **Rodiles**, facing the sea and the *ría*, and, across the *ría*, **Tazones**, a picturesque fishing village on a little cove.

Villaviciosa was a more important town a thousand years ago than it is today, and, although nothing from that time survives in the place, its surroundings have a number of early Asturian churches that can serve as an introduction to the better-known pre-Romanesque churches around Oviedo. One kilometre south, the Romanesque **San Juan de Amandi** is noted for its beautiful sculpture: graceful geometric patterns on the portal and the usual vigorous but mystifying scenes on the capitals. The lovely rounded portico was added in 1796. On the night of San Juan, celebrated across Spain with fireworks and bonfires, it's the focus of fiery celebrations. Other churches can be sought out in the nearby villages of Ambás and La Piñeda.

San Juan de Amandi
open Tues–Sun 11.30–1.30 and 5.30–7.30; closed Mon

Valdediós was probably an ancient site from the earliest times, and in the days of the Kingdom of Asturias it was the religious centre of the region. Nine kilometres southwest of Villaviciosa, in the pretty Puelles valley, it contains two separate churches. The oldest is the oratory of **San Salvador**, built in 893 by Alfonso III. It's an interesting building, one that shows some of the influences behind Asturian architecture. The top still shows a memory of Roman times with its neat classical pediment, though below this has been amplified into a basilican-style three-aisled church. The windows have stone latticework and *ajimeces* (mullioned windows) derived from al-Andalus. A Cistercian monastery was later built nearby, around the 11th-century basilica of **Santa María** (better known as El Conventín); the glorious Romanesque portal and the apse survive from the original building, though most of the interior is much later. The monastery is still in use, and the church interior, usually shut off behind an iron *reja*, glitters like a cave of mystery with its gilt Baroque *retablo* and other furnishings – an effect heightened when the organist monk is practising.

San Salvador
open Tues–Sun 11–1 and 4.30–6; closed Mon; adm

Santa María
open Tues–Sun 11–1 and 4.30–6; closed Mon; adm

10

Asturias | The Asturian 'Costa Verde': Llanes to Villaviciosa

Markets from Llanes to Villaviciosa

Llanes: Tues.
Ribadesella and **Villaviciosa:** Wed.

Where to Stay and Eat from Llanes to Villaviciosa

Llanes ✉ 33500
★★★Posada de Babel, La Pereda (4km from Llanes), t 98 540 25 25, *www. laposadadebabel.com* (€€€). An elegant country house in its own tree-filled grounds, with stylish rooms (including the glassy ultra-modern 'Cube') and a wonderful restaurant for hotel guests only. *Closed winter.*
★★★La Posada del Rey, C/Mayor 11, t 98 540 13 32, *www.laposadadelrey. com* (€€€). One of the nicest places to stay in the old quarter, its stylish rooms occupy a converted 16th-century town house. Charles V stayed next door on his way to Santander, hence the 'del Rey'.
★★★Don Paco, Parque Posada Herrera 1, t 98 540 01 50, *www.hoteles montemar.com* (€€). In a graceful

ⓘ **Llanes >**
Alfonso IX, La Torre
t 98 540 01 64,
www.venallanes.com
and www.llanes.as/guia

17th-century palace; it's quiet, with a garden, and elegant restaurant, serving mostly seafood.

***Hotel Sablón, El Sablón, t 98 540 07 87, www.hotelsablon.com (€€). Modern, perched on the rocks above the Playa El Sablón, with comfortable rooms and a restaurant with terrace.

***Arcea Hotel La Arquera, s/n Llanes, t 98 540 24 24, www.arquera.com (€€). A beautifully renovated traditional house set in extensive gardens just south of Llanes. A special treat is the breakfast room located in the former 'hórreo' (a raised granary) and the cider press. Self-catering apartments, ideal for families, are also available.

(★) La Huertona >>

(★) La Quinta Esencia >

**La Quinta Esencia, La Pereda de Llanes, t 98 540 27 06, www.hotelquintaesencia.com (€€–€). A lovely stone house, with views over the mountains, located just 3km south of Llanes. Breakfast is included, but there's no restaurant.

**Hotel Cantábrico, C/Gutiérrez de La Gándara 10, t 98 540 30 69, www.llaneshotelcantabrico.com (€). A modest hotel, with simple rooms, in a turn-of-the-20th century townhouse with original details and a patio.

**Pensión La Guia, Pza de Parres Sobrino, t 98 540 25 77 (€). Decent rooms for a bargain price in a lovely old building in the centre of town.

Casa Morán, at Puente Nuevo, t 98 540 60 93 (€€). Not far from Llanes, try this popular place with a traditional menu featuring items like fabada asturiana and roast lamb.

El Cuera, Plaza Parres Sobrino 9, t 98 540 00 54 (€€). Part-restaurant and part-sidrería on the main square, serving beautifully fresh seafood.

Mesón El Galeón, C/Mayor 24, t 98 540 16 50 (€€–€). Good food, but even better pintxos – which locals have voted the best in town.

Ribadesella ✉ 33560

****Gran Hotel del Sella, La Playa, C/Ricardo Cangas 17, t 98 586 01 50, www.granhoteldelsella.com (€€€€). A posh, air-conditioned beachside hotel in a converted palace, once belonging to the Marquesses of Argüelles. With a pool, tennis courts and garden.

***Ribadesella Playa Hotel, C/Ricardo Congas 3, t 98 586 07 15, www.hotel

(i) Villaviciosa >>
La Casina de La Oliva, t 98 589 17 59, www.villaviciosa.es

(★) La Corte de Lugás >>

(i) Ribadesella >
El Muelle, t 98 586 00 38 (summer only), www.ribadesella.com

ribadesella.com (€€). A grand residence from the turn of last century, this hotel has a lovely waterfront location on the peninsula and rooms with all modern luxuries.

Hotel El Carmen, s/n Ribadesella, t 98 586 12 89, www.hotelcarmen.com (€€–€). Inside, the meticulously chosen antique furniture creates the feel of a traditional Asturian casona. Set in large gardens facing the Santianes mountain range, this is difficult to beat at the price.

*Boston, C/El Pico 7, t 98 586 09 66, ww.ribadesella.com/hotel-boston (€). Good-value doubles with bath.

La Huertona, C/de la Piconera 2, t 98 586 05 53 (€€€–€€). This delightful restaurant sits on the banks of the river and serves superb local cuisine, including seafood and a fine fabada.

La Parrilla, Avda Palacio Valdés 33, t 98 586 11 84 (€€). Ribadesella's favourite restaurant: wonderfully fresh fish and shellfish is served simply grilled. Reservations essential.

Sidrería Carroceu, Marqueses de Arguelles 25, t 98 586 14 19, facing the harbour (€). The place to go for tapas and cider; noisy and convivial.

Lastres ✉ 33330

**Hotel Eutimio, C/San Antonio s/n, t 98 585 00 12, www.casaeutimio.com (€€). This lovely old stone residence has individually decorated rooms with views over the sea. Its restaurant, Casa Eutimio (€€), is something of a tradition round these parts, serving a marvellous sopa de marisco.

Tazones ✉ 33330

*Hotel El Pescador, San Miguel 6, t 98 589 70 77 (€€–€). Pleasant rooms in an old stone house with port views.

Villaviciosa ✉ 33300

****La Corte de Lugás, Lugás, t 98 589 02 03, www.lacortedelugas.com (€€€€). A beautiful stone country manor, with large, elegant rooms (some with four-poster beds) and a superb restaurant.

La Casona de Amandi, at Amandi, C/San Juan 6, t 98 589 01 30, www.lacasonadeamandi.com (€€€). A casa de indiano (a house built by a returned emigrant to the Americas); now a very charming nine-room hotel in a lovely formal garden.

***Casa España**, Plaza Carlos I, t 98 589 20 30, *www.hcasaespana.com* (€€). Occupies a converted *casa de indiano* in the monumental centre of town, with antique-furnished rooms and a pleasant café on the plaza.

Carlos I, Plaza Carlos I, t 98 589 01 21 (€€). A very charming hotel in a 17th-century *palacio* in the centre.

*El Manquín**, Plaza Santa Carla 2, t 98 589 05 06, *www.hotelmanquin.com*

(€€). Has quiet rooms and a restaurant on a pretty square with fountain; seafood and properly poured cider.

Hostal Café del Sol, C/Sol 27, t 98 589 11 30 (€). Pleasant rooms at bargain rates with spit 'n' sawdust bar below.

Sidrería La Oliva, C/Eloisa Fernández 6 (€). A friendly and atmospheric *sidrería* (one of many), full of local families, couples and friends knocking back cider and filling up on *raciones*.

Gijón and Avilés

With some 275,000 people, Gijón (pronounced Hee-Hon) is the largest city in Asturias and a major industrial centre and port, a salty, slightly gritty town with few sights but plenty of personality. Built on a rock projecting from the sea called the Cimadevilla, Gijón goes back to the Romans and possibly the Phoenicians – Cimadevilla is often referred to as the '*atalaya*'. When coal began to boom it grew into one of Spain's biggest ports. It was the home of the Enlightenment reformer Jovellanos, whose bicentennial was celebrated in 2011. Parts were totally rebuilt after the Nationalists devastated it in the Civil War. Lately, regionalists have painted over the road signs to remind us that the Asturian spelling is *Xixón*.

What sets Gijón apart are the excellent beaches stretching east from the Cimadevilla. Lined with the slick *urbanizaciones* of the newer town, they give the industrial city a carnival air in the warm months – hordes of locals, mostly red as lobsters, decorate the beaches in a way reminiscent of Reginald Marsh's famous caricatures of Coney Island.

Museo Casa Natal Jovellanos

open Tues–Fri 9.30–2 and 5–7.30, Sat–Sun 10–2 and 5–7.30; closed Mon

Almost everything worth seeing in Gijón is within walking distance of Cimadevilla, starting with the birthplace and home of the city's most famous reformer, the 16th-century **Museo Casa Natal Jovellanos**. As well as a collection of Jovellanos' belongings, the museum has a good cross section of 19th- and 20th-century Asturian painting and a selection of sculptures by José María Navascués. However, what everyone comes for is the *Retablo del Mar* by local woodcarver Sebastian Miranda, a misty-eyed evocation of a fishing port that takes up a whole wall. Old photographs next to the *retablo* suggest that Miranda mellowed with age – his original, carved in the 1930s and destroyed in the Civil War, was full of leering faces and grotesque posture, a stark contrast to his 1970s version.

There's not much else to see in Cimadevilla, which suffered greatly in the Civil War. The *atalaya*, also called the hill of Santa Catalina, has a park overlooking the sea, with the obligatory sculpture by Eduardo Chillida; this one's called *Elogio al Horizonte*,

Getting to and around Gijón and Avilés

By Air

There is an **airport** (the Aeropuerto de Asturias) 14km west of Avilés, t 91 321 10 00, *www.aena.es*, with flights to several Spanish cities including Madrid, Barcelona, Seville and Málaga with Iberia, Vueling, Spanair and Air Nostrum; flights to London Stansted and Geneva with easyJet; and to Paris with Air France. ALSA (t 902 422 242, *www.alsa.es*) buses link the airport with Gijón, Avilés and Oviedo, €15 return; a taxi from the airport to Gijón is around €45.

By Train and Bus

There are frequent FEVE **trains** to Avilés and Cudillero, t 98 598 23 81 or t 98 598 23 80, or *www.feve.es*, hourly RENFE services to Oviedo, and less frequent long-distance RENFE trains to León and Madrid (t 902 320 320 for timetables and reservations). The FEVE and RENFE stations are close together on the Avda de los Telares on the edge of town. The main **bus station** is also here, with services (ALSA, *see above*, is the main bus operator) to Oviedo, into the mountains of Asturias, and along the coast.

By Car and Taxi

Finding a place to **park** can be a problem in the centre of Gijón. If your hotel doesn't have parking, there is a convenient garage under Plaza 6 de Agosto.

For a **taxi**, try Radio Taxi Gijón, t 98 514 11 11, or Radio Taxi Jovellanos, t 98 516 44 44.

Termas Romanas
http://museos.gijon.es
open Tues–Fri 9.30–2 and 5–7.30, Sat–Sun 10–2 and 5–7.30; closed Mon; adm

Muséu del Pueblu d'Asturies
Paseo Dr Fleming 877, bus 10; open April–Sept Tues–Fri 10–7, Sat–Sun 10.30–7; Oct–Mar Tues–Fri 9.30–6.30, Sat–Sun 10–6.30; closed Mon; adm

Aquarium
Playa de Poniente, www. acuariodegijon.com
t 98 518 52 20; open daily 10am–dusk; adm

Talasoponiente
t 902 404 704
www.talasoponiente.com

Museo del Ferrocarril
t 98 530 85 75; open April– Sept Tues–Fri 10–7, Sat–Sun 10.30–7; Oct– Mar Tues–Fri 9.30–6.30, Sat–Sun 10–6.30; adm

Laboral Ciudad de Cultura
www.laboralciudadde lacultura.com

'Tribute to the Horizon'. The rest of the hill is taken up with an abandoned cigar factory where *farias*, the most noxious of smokes, used to be made. The centre occupies the isthmus leading to the newer quarters; there you will find the enclosed and arcaded **Plaza Mayor**, surrounded with restaurants and cafés. Behind it, and cleverly landscaped underground, are the **Termas Romanas**, part of a 2nd-century baths complex notable for its underfloor hypocaustal central heating. Computer animations explain how the baths worked. This is the start of the main beach, the **Playa de San Lorenzo**. At the other end, in the **Muséu del Pueblu d'Asturias** on the far side of the Río del Piles, there is a display of traditional Asturian architecture, from *sidrerías* and *hórreos* (raised granaries) to 18th-century farmhouses: one contains the **Museo de la Gaita**, which displays a host of bagpipes from Celtic northwestern Spain and around the world, as well as a workshop.

The **Playa de Poniente**, next to the marina, has an **Aquarium** (Acuario de Gijón), and a spanking new thalassotherapy centre, **Talasoponiente**, with pools, health and beauty treatments, and a play area for kids with slides and a cave with a water curtain.

If you have children, you'll probably end up at the **Museo del Ferrocarril**, in the old Estación del Norte, home to over 50 pieces of rolling stock and other memorabilia from the Steam Age. On some Saturdays in July and early August (*Sábados de Vapor*), the steam engines are fired up and you can pile into the original wooden carriages for short journeys.

About 3km east of the city centre, the **Laboral Ciudad de Cultura** is Gijón's most ambitious new arts and entertainment complex, which occupies a boldly remodelled neo-Gothic former university. It offers a varied programme of events, including art exhibitions,

**Jardín Botánico
Atlantico**
*t 985 13 07 13,
http://botanico.gijon.es;
open June–Sept daily
10–9; Oct–May
daily 10–6, adm*

opera and theatre performances, workshops, plus a café. You can climb the tower for fabulous views. Nearby, the blissful **Jardín Botánico Atlantico** is perfect for picnics and summer concerts.

Up to Cabo Peñas and Down Again

Between the industrial centres of Gijón and Avilés the Asturian coast juts northwards for a bit; the coastal road from Gijón will take you out beyond the new port district to **Candás**, an old tuna-fishing village once famous for its *corridas marineras* – bullfights on the beach that were unique in Spain, but are no longer practised. **Luanco**, just up the coast, had similar beginnings, but has now become much more of a resort; acres of holiday cottages surround the tidy, small centre. Luanco is famous for lace and embroideries, and there is a small **Museo Marítimo** in Calle Gijón, with model ships and old maps. Luanco has two beaches close to the centre, but there are quieter ones around the tip of the peninsula, at **Cabo Peñas**: the prettiest, Playa de Ferrero and Playa de Llumere, are found on either side of the cape.

Museo Marítimo
*t 98 588 01 01;
http://museomaritimo
deasturias.com; open
July–Aug Tues–Sun 11–2
and 5.30–8.30; Sept–June
Tues–Sat 11–2 and 5–8,
Sun 11–2; closed Mon; adm*

At the opposite side of the peninsula is **Avilés**, another large and friendly industrial town with disheartening sprawl. Once the most polluted city in Europe, Avilés is reinventing itself, reclaiming its blighted river banks. The spectacular **Centro Cultural Internacional**, designed by Brazilian architect **Oscar Niemeyer** and inaugurated in 2011, is an architectural *tour de force* composed of vast white domes and towers, which is now one of Europe's leading arts centres. Unlike Gijón, Avilés has a beautiful and well-preserved historic centre: this medieval town still has a copy of its *fueros*, its charter of rights, kept proudly in the Ayuntamiento. Look especially for the arcaded **Plaza de España**, and the expressively sculpted 16th-century fountain, **Caños de San Francisco**, in Plaza San Nicolás, next to the 13th-century church of **San Nicolás de Bari**. Inside, note the tomb to favourite son Pedro Menéndez de Avilés, who founded St Augustine, Florida, the oldest city in the USA. Avilés can be lively at night, especially in the *chigres* and clubs around Calle Galiana, on the western side of the lovely **Parque de Ferrera**. This was the garden of the Marqués de Ferrera, whose refined 17th-century palace still stands at the edge, across from the Ayuntamiento.

**Centro Cultural
Internacional
Oscar Niemeyer**
*www.centro
niemeyer.org*

Just north of Avilés, an old lighthouse guards the entrance to the *ría*, at **San Juan de Nieva**, and a long, gorgeous beach at **Salinas**.

10

Asturias | The Asturian 'Costa Verde': Gijón and Avilés

ⓘ **Gijón >**
*General information
on **Asturias**: C/Marqués
de San Esteban 1,
t 98 534 60 46*

***InfoGijón**, in the port,
t 98 534 17 71,
www.gijon.info*

Tourist Information and Services in Gijón and Avilés

Gijón **tourist office** organizes free daily walking tours in summer, and also sell the **Gijón Card**, valid for one day (€10), two days (€12) or three days (€15), which offers free entry to museums, plus unlimited local bus travel and discounts in shops and restaurants.

The **post office** is on Pza 6 de Agosto.

For internet access, try **Piles 6 Ciber**, C/Piles 6, *www.piles6ciber.com*, or use the free city-run WiFi service, available at hotspots around the city.

Markets in Gijón and Avilés

Gijón: La Camocha, C/La Camocha s/n, Mon, and a Sun am flea market in the car park of Estadio El Moliñón, in Gijón's eastern suburbs.
Avilés: Mon.

(★) Hostal Cimavillaroom >>

Where to Stay and Eat in Gijón and Avilés

Gijón ✉ 33200

****Parador Molino Viejo, in the pretty Parque Isabel La Católica, t 98 537 05 11, *www.parador.es* (€€€). An old mill with a modern annexe, it has the best rooms in town and all the usual facilities (except a pool, but the beach is a 10min walk). It serves Asturian food in its restaurant.

(★) Hotel Quinta Duro >

***Hotel Quinta Duro, Camino de las Quintas, Cabueñes, t 98 533 04 43, *www.hotelquintaduro.com* (€€). Beautifully set in a park; Carlos Velázquez-Duro and his family have converted their old country house into an intimate, smart hotel with modern amenities. Close to the botanical gardens and university.

***Asturias, Plaza Mayor 11, t 98 535 06 00, *www.hotelasturiasgijon.es* (€€). A handsome old building with plain rooms but grand public spaces in the historic centre.

***La Casona de Jovellanos, Plazuela de Jovellanos 1, t 98 534 20 24, *www.lacasonadejovellanos.com* (€€–€). Offers history along with modern comforts: built to house the great reformer's Asturian Institute of Navigation and Mineralogy, renovation work turned up remains of Cimadevilla's original Roman walls, which can now be seen in the fancy restaurant. Next door is one of the city's most popular *chigres*, a good place to begin the festivities.

**Hotel Miramar, C/Santa Lucía 9, t 98 535 10 08, *www.hotelmiramar*

gijon.com (€€–€). Gracious town house bang in the centre with tasteful revamped décor.

**La Ermita de Deva, C/San Antonio, Deva (3km from Gijón), t 98 533 34 22, *www.laermitadeva.com* (€€–€). A lovely country hotel, with just a handful of pretty rooms, a café-bar and welcoming owners.

**Castilla, C/Corrida 50, t 98 534 62 00, *www.hotelcastillagijon.com* (€€–€). Smart modern rooms with bath on the classiest street in Gijón; good out-of-season rates.

**Hostal Cimavillaroom, C/Vicaria 29, t 98 534 99 32, *www.cimavillaroom.com* (€). This immaculate little *hostal* offers six delightful rooms, and is probably the best bargain in town.

Casa Gerardo, in Prendes (8km from Gijón), t 98 588 77 97, *www.casa-gerardo.com* (€€€). This Michelin-starred restaurant breathes new life into traditional Asturian cooking, with innovative dishes, like *bacalao blanco y negro* (cod with truffles) along with updates of old favourites. *Closed Mon.*

Las Delicias, Camino de las Dalias 50 (in the suburb of Somió), t 98 536 73 78, *www.restaurantelasdelicias.com* (€€€–€€). This long-established upmarket eaterie mixes surf and turf – *lubina al horno* (oven-baked sea bass) and *ternera a la sidra* (veal in cider) – and very good service. Kids' playground in the garden. *Closed Tues.*

El Centenario, Plaza Mayor 7, t 98 534 35 61, *www.sidreria elcentenario.com* (€€). Old-fashioned restaurant and *sidreria*, serving classic Asturian fare out on the square.

La Pondala, Avda Dionisio Cifuentes 58, Somió, t 98 536 11 60, *www.lapondala.com* (€€). La Pondala has existed for over a century. Specialities are the rice and seafood dishes – try the *arroz con almejas* (rice with clams) and the *delis merluza rellena de mariscos* (hake filled with shellfish).

Torremar, C/Ezcurdia 120 (one block back from the beach), t 98 533 01 73 (€€–€). Come here for something kinder on the pocket but just as interesting to the taste buds; offerings include seafood and Asturian dishes such as *fabes con almejas*. Good-value set menus.

La Galana, Plaza Mayor 10, t 98 517 24 29 (€€–€). A fine old *sidrería* and restaurant with dark wooden beams and huge barrels.

Sidrería Plaza Mayor, Travesía Jovellanos 10, t 98 535 0938 (€). One of several convivial places around Plaza Mayor; good for a basic dinner.

ⓘ Avilés >
C/Ruiz Gómez 21,
t 98 554 43 25

Avilés ✉ 33400

***Hotel de la Villa-Arga**, Plaza Domingo Álvarez Acebal 4, t 98 512 97 04 (€€). A good, central option in a much-modernized old building.

***Hotel Don Pedro**, C/La Fruta 22, t 98 551 22 88, *www.hdonpedro.com* (€€–€). Handily located between the old city and the Niemeyer cultural centre, this is a pretty hotel with charming staff.

Casa Tataguyo, Plaza del Carbatedo 6, t 98 556 48 15, *www.tataguyo.com* (€€). Long-established classic, serving traditional stews and casseroles.

La Capilla, Plaza de España 9, t 98 551 06 84 (€€). Inventive cuisine from an up-and-coming young chef in the sumptuous Hotel Palacio de Ferrera (€€€), which occupies a stunning 17th-century palace.

La Fragata, C/San Francisco 18, t 98 555 19 29 (€€–€). Pause at the bar with the locals, or head to the *comedor* for a wide range of tasty local dishes.

Oviedo

The modern capital of Asturias, Oviedo is an elegant and delightful town wrapped around a charming old centre of crooked, tavern-lined streets opening into unexpected squares. Not long ago, the historic core was grimy and neglected, but a determined city council have cleaned it up beautifully, restricting traffic and restoring many of its graceful palaces and churches. It has a fine cathedral, a university almost 400 years old, and two of Europe's most exquisite pre-Romanesque churches, built when the rest of the continent was still living in the Dark Ages. Founded by Fruela I in 757 as a fortress guarding the key road over the mountains to the coast, Oviedo became the capital of Christian Spain when Alfonso II 'el Casto' (the Chaste) built himself a palace in 810, and stayed capital until the Asturian kings conquered León in 1002.

The city suffered terribly in the insurrection of 1934 and during the Civil War. It used to earn a living from the surrounding coal and iron mines, but today Oviedo has its sights firmly set on the tourist euro. It continues to take up a variety of causes – walls are covered with graffiti encouraging the revival of *el Bable*; a helter-skelter mix of pro-choice, 'Viva la Virgen' and 'Europa Blanca' rally posters are pasted side by side on the walls of the numerous *chigres*.

The shining results of the clean-up and new focus have not gone ignored by the outside world. When world-renowned film director Woody Allen visited Oviedo in 2002 to pick up an arts prize at the annual Prince of Asturias Awards (Spain's most prestigious awards), he described the city as 'delicious, exotic, beautiful and pedestrianized: it's as if it didn't belong to this world... Oviedo is like a fairy tale.' He later shot parts of *Vicky Cristina Barcelona* (2008) here, and the city paid back the compliment by erecting a life-size statue of him in C/Milicias Nacionales.

Getting to and around Oviedo

All **trains** leave from the station at the head of C/Uria in the centre of town. RENFE, **t** 902 320 320, has hourly connections to Gijón and fewer links to Barcelona, Zaragoza, Burgos, León, Pamplona, Madrid, Valladolid and Palencia. FEVE trains, **t** 98 529 76 56, run east to Santander and Bilbao, and west along the coast to Ferrol.

The new **Estación de Autobuses** is next to the train station, info **t** 98 596 9696, *www.estaciodeautobuses deoviedo.com*. ALSA, the biggest company, **t** 902 422 242, *www.alsa.es*, serves destinations throughout Asturias and Northern Spain, as well as Madrid, Seville, Barcelona, Valladolid and Valencia; international buses go as far as Paris, Geneva, Zurich and Brussels.

Parking and getting around can be a pain in Oviedo. Almost all of the old centre is closed to traffic; as a last resort there is a parking garage underneath the Campo de San Francisco.

For a **Radio Taxi**, call **t** 98 525 00 00.

The Cathedral

The middle of Oviedo (take C/Uría, the main shopping street, from the station) is occupied by the tranquil, shady **Campo de San Francisco** – a typically lavish Spanish city park with fervent memorials to past literati, grand promenades, carefully labelled exotic trees, ducks to feed, and children getting ice cream all over their best clothes. From here C/San Francisco leads to the oldest part of the city, and the asymmetrical **cathedral**, an attractive Gothic temple from the 14th century; its lovely tower with its delicate stone latticework is Oviedo's landmark. King Fruela began the first church on this site when he founded the city, and Alfonso el Casto enlarged it, but the current incarnation, handsomely restored, is a high Gothic work begun in 1388. In the Capilla Mayor, look for an enormous florid 16th-century *retablo* of the *Life of Christ* sculpted by Giralte of Brussels.

Best of all, a door in the right transept leads to the original church of Alfonso el Casto, now known as the **Cámara Santa**, strange and semi-barbaric, with fine carvings of the Apostles attributed to Master Mateo on the capitals of the outer chamber and disembodied heads on the walls. The Capilla de San Miguel was built by el Casto in 802 to house the relics of Visigothic Toledo rescued after its capture by the Moors, and largely rebuilt in the 12th century. Today it contains the cathedral's treasures: the *Cruz de la Victoria*, supposedly borne by Pelayo at Covadonga, and today on Asturias's coat of arms; the *Cruz de los Angeles* (808), a golden cross embedded with huge rubies and carved gems, reputedly made by the angels themselves and donated by Alfonso II; a beautiful, silver-plated reliquary chest of 1073; as well as a phial of the Virgin Mary's milk and one of Judas's 30 pieces of silver.

Cámara Santa
*open July–Sept
Mon–Fri 10–8, Sat 10–6;
Oct–June Mon–Fri 10–1
and 4–6, Sat 10–6;
closed Sun; adm to the
Cámara Santa only,
or combined adm to
Cámara Santa,
museum and cloister*

Oviedo cathedral was always famous for its collection of relics, although none has attracted as much attention of late as the Sudarium, a bloodstained cloth reputedly used to cover Jesus's head after he was crucified. In recent years, it has been put forward as supporting evidence for the authenticity of the Shroud in Turin –

unlike the Shroud, the Sudarium is documented back to the 1st century AD, and laboratory studies have shown the two were used to wrap the same body and are stained with same rare AB blood group (*see www.shroud.com/guscin.htm*). The **museum** includes Romanesque sculptures and glittering liturgical plate, and the **cloister** is pale and lovely. Just off the cloister, the Crypt of Santa Leocadia contains the plain tomb of the 3rd-century martyr-saint from Toledo. The crypt is part of the ancient cathedral under the Cámara Santa, with a pair of carved Visigothic stone reliefs.

Behind the cathedral the old convent of San Vicente houses the

Museo Arqueológico
t 98 520 89 77, www. museoarqueologico deasturias.net; open Wed–Fri 9.30–8, Sat 9.30–2 and 5–8, Sun and public hols 9.30–3; closed Mon and Tues

Museo Arqueológico, which reopened in 2011 after extensive renovations and the addition of a striking new extension by Pardo and García. The glossy new galleries display finds from the Palaeolithic era to the days of the Asturian kingdom, backed up with plenty of 21st-century audiovisuals. There are a few attractive old streets to the south of the cathedral around the **Plaza del Fontan**, an enclosed square that was starting to fall down before restoration works were started.

The Asturian Pre-Romanesque Churches

🍵 Pre-Romanesque churches

Oviedo has the finest of Asturias's post-Visigothic pre-Romanesque churches. Enjoying the patronage of its kings, this little capital can claim the beginnings of sophisticated medieval architecture at a time when most of Christian Europe was still scratching its carrot rows with a short stick. The two most important churches were built on Mount Naranco as part of the palace that Alfonso el Casto built for himself and Ramiro I (842–50) expanded, and it's fascinating to think of these pocket potentates throwing up a summer pleasure-dome in the hills in imitation of the great sultans of al-Andalus.

Some scholars have found a Carolingian influence in their structures, although this is hard to see. The major influence clearly comes from North Africa or the Middle East, via Christian refugees from those newly Islamized countries. The classical pediment common atop Asturian churches was also common there; it goes back to the origins of Christian building, to the basilicas of Constantine and Theodosius in the Greek east. Hints of later Byzantine elements can be seen in many of the details, but this is all – Byzantium was 2,700km away. The only building that has anything in common with Santa María de Naranco and its unusual plan is a unique, mysterious little chapel in central Italy called the Tempio del Clitunno, built a century earlier. Even with these influences, much in these provocative prototypes that never made it to the assembly line is original and beautiful. In 1985 UNESCO declared them the best architecture produced in 9th-century Christian Europe, protected as part of the 'Heritage of Humanity'.

San Julián de Los Prados
open summer Mon–Fri 10–1, Sat 9.30–12.30 and 2.30–5.30; winter Tues–Sat 9.30–11.30, Mon 10–12.30; closed Sun; adm

Alfonso el Casto built the oldest of these, **San Julián de Los Prados** (also called Santullano), northeast of the centre; C/de Martínez Vigil from the back of the cathedral takes you there. This is a simple, solid building with three square apses, a secret compartment in the wall, and interesting murals by an artist influenced by Roman monuments.

If you're pressed for time, head in the opposite direction up the **Cuesta de Naranco**, a hill overlooking the town (facing the RENFE station, turn left to the sign at the bridge over the tracks and continue 3km (2 miles); city bus no.10 makes cameo appearances on the hour. Pick it up from C/Uría and get off by the car park at La Cruce). The two churches here, Santa María de Naranco and San Miguel de Lillo, can be found halfway up the mountain with a view over Oviedo. Both of these churches were built by Alfonso el Casto's successor, Ramiro I; incredibly, the perfectly proportioned

Santa María de Naranco
open Tues–Sat 9.30–1 and 3.30–7, Sun and Mon 9.30–1; adm, free Mon

Santa María de Naranco is believed to have been part of the king's summer palace. Built of a fair golden stone and set in a small clearing, it is an enchanting building, supported by unusual flat buttresses and flanked by two porches. The lower level is believed to have been a waiting chamber and bath; the upper, with a rough-hewn altar on the porch, was the main hall. Inside are blind arches of subtly decreasing height, topped by round medallions. An **Interpretation Centre** is nearby in an old schoolhouse, where you can organize guided visits and pick up information.

San Miguel de Lillo
open summer Tues–Sat 9.30–1 and 3.30–7, Sun and Mon 9.30–1; winter Tues–Sat 10–1.30 and 3–5, Sun 10–1; adm

Just up the road, **San Miguel de Lillo** is a more traditional cruciform church, although of stunted proportions after an ancient amputation removed two-thirds of the original length. Its round windows are adorned with beautiful stone traceries, and what the guides claim to be a circus scene is carved on the door jamb, along with some Visigothic arabesques.

Facilities in Oviedo

The **post office** is on C/Alonso Quintanilla 1.

Cheap **internet** access is available at **Laser**, C/San Francisco 9; there are several other cybercafés, including the **Café Oriental**, C/Jovellanos 8.

(i) **Oviedo** ›
Plaza de La Constitución 4
t 98 408 60 60

'El Escorialín',
C/Marqués de Santa Cruz s/n, t 98 522 75 86,
www.ayto-oviedo.es

 Hotel de la Reconquista ›

Markets in Oviedo

Oviedo: There is a beautiful wrought-iron covered market on Plaza del Fontán, *www.mercafontan.es*, with an astonishing variety of fresh local produce piled up inside. A flea market is held outside on Sundays.

Where to Stay in Oviedo

Oviedo ✉ 33000

*****Hotel de la Reconquista, C/Gil de Jaz 16, t 98 524 11 00, *www. hoteldelareconquista.com* (€€€€–€€€). A couple of blocks from the Parque de San Francisco, this lovely 17th-century palace has been converted into a super-luxury hotel. Scenes from Woody Allen's *Vicky Cristina Barcelona* were shot here.

****Ayre Hotel Oviedo, Policarpo Herrero s/n, t 98 596 47 77, *www. ayrehoteles.com* (€€€€–€€€). In Oviedo's new convention centre, this stunning white minimalist hotel was designed by starchitect Santiago

Calatrava. It's about a 15-minute stroll into the centre.

****Gran Hotel Regente**, C/Jovellanos 31, t 98 522 23 43, *www.granhotel regente.com* (€€€€–€€€). This offers traditional elegance opposite the Monastery de San Pelayo. It is geared towards business travellers, hence good website deals.

****Libretto Hotel**, C/Marqués de Santa Cruz 12, t 98 520 20 04, *www. librettohotel.com* (€€). An elegant Modernista building, now a stylish hotel, with a chic mixture of the contemporary and antique.

****M Hotel**, C/Comandante Vallespín, t 98 527 40 60, *www.mhotel. es* (€€). An ultra-modern hotel by the Palacio de Congresos, with quirky contemporary rooms and a small spa area. Good weekend deals.

****Palacio de la Viñona**, C/Julián Clavería 14, Barrio Colloto, t 98 579 33 99, *www.palaciovinona.com* (€€). A graceful 18th-century stone manor on the outskirts, with a garden and beautiful rooms (most with Jacuzzi).

***Hotel Fruela**, C/Fruela 3, t 98 520 81 20, *www.hotelfruela.com* (€€). The late 19th century façade, painstakingly restored, couldn't be more different from the sleek, minimalist interior valued by trendy boutique hotels. The central location is also excellent.

Hotel Favila, C/Uría 37, t 98 525 38 77, *www.hotelfavilaoviedo.com* (€€). A good family-run option close to the bus and train stations, with immaculate rooms and a decent restaurant (€) downstairs.

***Hotel Vetusta**, C/Covadonga 2, t 98 522 22 29, *www.hotelvetusta.com* (€€–€). An excellent central option, in a traditional building with slick, modern décor and Jacuzzis in some rooms.

Santa Clara, C/Santa Clara 1, t 98 522 27 27, *www.hsantaclara.com* (€€–€). In the centre, this friendly, well-equipped place offers weekend discounts.

Room Mate Marcos, C/Caveda 23, t 98 522 72 72, *www.room-matehotels. com* (€€–€). For style on a budget, you can't do better than this hotel, which is part of a small Spanish chain. Cheap, chic and central.

El Ovetense, C/San Juan 6, t 98 522 08 40, *www.hotelovetense.com* (€). A welcoming little hotel close to the cathedral, with its own *sidrería* and restaurant.

Hostal Arcos, C/Magdalena 3 (just off Plaza de la Constitución), t 98 521 47 73 (€). One of the cheapest central options, with rooms with or without bath and very friendly staff.

Pensión Riesgo, C/9 de Mayo 16, t 98 521 89 45 (€). Cheap and cheerful rooms with shower, on a pedestrianized street near the centre.

Eating Out in Oviedo

For tapas and cider, take a stroll down C/Gascona where there are lots of atmospheric *sidrerías*.

Casa Fermín, San Francisco 8 (near the park), t 98 521 64 52 (€€€). Although there are plenty of restaurants and tapas bars in Oviedo, this remains the oldest and the best, offering award-winning Asturian cuisine and seasonal Spanish regional dishes in a refined atmosphere. *Closed Sun.*

La Corrada del Obispo, C/Canóniga 18, t 98 522 00 48, *www.lacorradadel obispo.com* (€€€). A romantic spot in an elegant 18th-century townhouse, where you can dine on good local specialities, including seafood and game in season. *Closed Sun.*

Ca Suso, C/Marqués de Gastañaga 10, t 98 522 82 32, *www.ca-suso.com* (€€€). Inventive contemporary cuisine and delightful staff make this the perfect choice for a special night out. Try the juicy scallops with pumpkin purée, or the tender lamb with caramelised onions and rosemary.

La Goleta, C/Covadonga 32, t 98 521 38 47, *www.lagoleta.com* (€€). A classic *marisquería*, with beautifully fresh seafood served up in an interior decked out like a ship.

La Mar del Medio, C/Mon 18, t 98 522 55 75 (€€). Has excellent fish and seafood in a suitably nautical ambience; arrive early as it fills up quickly during lunch times, or pop in and try the tasty *pintxos. Closed Sun night and Mon.*

Casa Ramón, Plaza Daoíz y Velarde, t 985 20 14 15 (€€). One of several good

⭐ Hotel Fruela >

⭐ Ca Suso >>

eaterries near the Fontán market, this is a great spot for tapas or set meals.

Villaviciosa, C/Gascona 7, t 98 520 44 12 (€). Hearty Asturian stews and good *fabadas* bubble away at this *sidrería*.

Entertainment and Nightlife in Oviedo

Oviedo is a lively university town, and there is always plenty of action, particularly on and around bar- and club-lined C/Mon.

Cervecería Asturianu, C/Carta Puebla 8. A huge range of beers and spirits, and eccentric décor that includes pieces of the Berlin Wall.

Danny's Jazz, La Luna 11. Funky café/bar with live jazz.

El Pigüeña, C/Gascona 2. On this street of *sidrerías*, one of the best.

Salsipuedes. A lively disco-bar.

Café Canela, C/Fuertes Acevodo 54. Buzzy café-bar, popular with students.

La Maniega, C/Rosal 45. Central bar, with tapas and an upbeat crowd.

Southern Asturias

The principality, beyond the coast and the Picos, is *terra incognita* for most foreigners: a hilly, wooded land of small mining towns and agricultural villages, crisscrossed with walking paths. Much of it is protected, especially in the national hunting preserves that cover the northern slopes of the Cordillera Cantábrica. The coast is excellent – rugged cliffs, few tourists, and plenty of shellfish and beaches. Public transport is limited here, and you'd do well to rent a car – and pack a big lunch – before setting out. Be sure to pick up one of the large, detailed maps at the tourist office in Oviedo.

Around Oviedo: Miners' Valleys and More Churches

Museo de Minería y Industria
www.mumi.es; open July–Aug Tues–Sun 10–8; Oct–June Tues–Sat 10–2 and 4–7, Sun 10–2; closed Mon; adm

Puerto San Isidro
in the province of León, see www.san-isidro.net for information

Southeast of Oviedo, the AS17 passes **Langreo** and **Pola de Laviana**, both typical Asturian copper-mining towns. Langreo is home to the **Museo de Minería y Industria**, with exhibits on the history of mining; there are scale models of old machinery, a recreated explosives laboratory, and a replica of a copper mine.

Beyond Pola de Laviana the road continues to Reres National Reserve and the beautiful mountain pass, **Puerto de Tarna**. The next pass to the west, **Puerto San Isidro**, has a major ski installation. Both passes can be reached by bus from Pueblo de Lillo in León province. **Collanzo**, some 12km below the pass, is set near an idyllic little gorge, the **Hoces de Río Aller**.

Directly south of Oviedo, along the train route and recently built highway to León (an engineering feat Spain is not a little proud of), the views become increasingly magnificent as you ascend to the dramatic **Puerto de Pajares**, another ski spot on the border with León. But before you get there, look for the signs 6km south of the grim industrial town of **Pola de Lena** for another of Ramiro I's lovely churches, the hilltop **Santa Cristina de Lena**, a cruciform temple built around 845, with blind arches similar to Santa María de Naranco, Visigothic decorations and an intricate iconostasis of Mozarabic inspiration.

Santa Cristina de Lena
open summer Tues–Sun 11–1 and 4.30–6.30; winter Tues–Sun 4.30–6

Getting around Southern Asturias

The RENFE **train** between Oviedo and León stops at Pajares and Pola de Lena; Pola de Lena is linked by frequent *cercanías* (local trains). Call **t** 902 320 320 for information and reservations.
All the main towns in southern Asturias can be reached by **bus**. ALSA buses from Oviedo's main bus station, **t** 902 422 242, *www.alsa.es*, go to Salas, Puerto de Somiedo, Cangas del Narcea, Tineo and Pola de Allande. Empresa Fernández, **t** 98 523 83 90, has buses to Mieres, Pola de Lena and Turón; there are also a half-dozen or so daily buses down the western coast to Cudillero and Luarca, and as many from Gijón. Alcotán, **t** 98 521 76 17 and **t** 98 560 02 68, runs buses to Pola de Laviana.
If you're **driving** when the snow is flying, it's essential to call ahead for road conditions, **t** 98 525 46 11. To **rent a car**, the main companies in Oviedo are along C/Ventura Rodríguez.

The landmark in this part of the Cantabrian mountains is the jagged 7,855ft **Peña Ubiña**, which sturdy walkers can tackle in around 4–5hrs from **Tuiza de Arriba** for incomparable views over the Picos de Europa and Somiedo (to reach Tuiza, take the side road from the highway at Campomanes). From Pajares, you can make the much shorter climb up the 5,580ft **Pico de los Celleros**.

Up to the Cordillera, and Somiedo National Park

Southwest of Oviedo, in the highest part of the Cantabrian mountains, is the **Parque Natural de Somiedo**. This vast wild area stretches from Puerto de Pajares in the east to Pola de Somiedo in the west, encompassing 7,000ft peaks, dense beech and oak forests, and several *brañas*, ancient villages of straw-roofed huts built by the *vaqueros* (*see* p.240). Although not a true National Park – much of Somiedo is protected as a hunting reserve – this is the Cordillera Cantábrica's great wildlife stronghold; it has the healthiest population of brown bears in Spain, and the Iberian wolf is so successful it is considered common. For birdwatchers too it is a paradise: middle-spotted and black woodpeckers make their home in the forests, ultra-colourful bee-eaters reach the northern limit of their range on the lower slopes, and wallcreepers flit around the vertical crags. The very fortunate may get a glimpse of the rare lammergeyer or bearded vulture, the largest bird of prey in Europe – a startling sight, with its black wings, fierce expression, and habit of dropping bones on rocks to get access to the marrow inside; the Spanish call it *quebrantahuesos*, the 'bone-breaker'. There's a **park information office** in Pola de Somiedo.

One approach to Somiedo is by way of **Trubia**, a village known mostly for its enormous armament works (*see* box, overleaf). Ten kilometres south of Trubia on the road to the park you can stop at **Tuñón** for one of the last of the 'Asturian' churches, **Santo Adriano**, built by Alfonso III (866–910). Sombre in design and Mozarabic in style, it features clerestory windows and pretty latticework crosses. Inside are some of the oldest frescoes anywhere in Spain, traces of what seem to be sun symbols over the altar and zigzag motifs

ⓘ Parque Natural de Somiedo

Park Information Office
*Pola de Somiedo,
t 98 576 37 58; open mid-June–mid-Sept 10–2.30 and 4–9; rest of year 10–2 and 4–7*

The Dress Rehearsal

The event of the 20th century in Asturias was the epic miners' revolt of 1934, a full-scale battle that eerily prefigured the Spanish Civil War. Because of the large numbers of workers in mining and industry, Asturias was politically the odd man out, an island of belligerent Marxists in the middle of the arch-conservative northwest. Mining and metalworking go way back in Asturias, but really took off at the beginning of the 20th century, when *indianos* forced home by Spain's loss of Cuba and the Philippines began to invest their money here. In the First World War, Spanish neutrality made for a boom in the mining areas, one which collapsed in the 1920s, leaving Asturias with the angriest proletariat in Spain.

Along with the Basques and Catalans, Asturians were strong supporters of the Republic when it appeared in 1931 but, for many of their leaders, the new regime was only a stepping-stone to Socialism. The depression increased popular discontent, but what really set the workers boiling was the radical right-wing national government elected in 1934. Under prime minister Gil Robles, it began dismantling all the reforms of its leftist predecessors and openly postured for the restoration of the monarchy. On 4 October 1934 the trade unions declared a general strike in Asturias in protest. Barcelona and Madrid also rose up but failed to follow through, leaving the Asturians on their own and in a fighting mood. The main centres of the revolt were Mieres, Sama and Oviedo, but it was the munitions works at Trubia, near Somiedo, that turned the strike into a war. The workers occupied it and seized some 30,000 rifles inside. Soon there was a 30,000-man 'Red Army', and a revolutionary committee was formed to govern the province.

The government sent in a dependable general named Mola, leading a force made up mainly of Moroccan troops – northern Morocco was still a Spanish protectorate. The Moors were mercenaries who had fought against their own people, but they were fiercely loyal to their commander, one Francisco Franco. Franco, a Galician married to an Asturian woman, felt right at home. He had already led troops, using the Spanish Foreign Legion, to crush a general strike in Asturias in 1917. The Legion was also present in 1934. An outfit not much like the romantic French version, this one was now led by a fascist psychopath named Millan Astray, famous for his missing arm and eye-patch. As for the Moors, some of them must have enjoyed the irony of a Spanish commander, an heir to Pelayo, bringing them to a place where they hadn't set foot for a thousand years. The government had to make its point, and the revolt was crushed quickly and with the utmost ferocity. Many of the mining towns were thoroughly wrecked, and the troops slaughtered nearly 1,300 Asturians in reprisals after the surrender on 19 October. A year and a half later, after new elections brought the leftist Popular Front to power, the coup that began the Civil War started with the same cast of characters: General Mola, who was to be the new dictator, but who died in an air crash at the start; the Foreign Legion; and the inevitable Francisco Franco, whose Moroccans won him the title of *caudillo* (leader). The best-equipped and -trained forces in Spain, they used their practice in Asturias to get the jump on the disorganized government and citizens' militias, and gained control of much of Spain within a month, an advantage that helped assure the Nationalists' final victory.

taken straight from the Grand Mosque of Córdoba. Get the key from the house next door, or call **t** 98 576 12 73 in advance.

Further south, **Proaza** has a number of medieval buildings; it is separated from the next village, **Caranga**, by a pretty gorge you can walk through, the **Desfiladero del Teverga**. The road continues south through **La Plaza**, site of the 12th-century **Colegiata de San Pedro**, where elements of Asturian pre-Romanesque combine with early French Romanesque; on the capitals are sculpted local animals, and there are two 18th-century mummies.

From La Plaza, the road south cuts through a magnificent forest to the **Puerto Ventana**, perhaps the least-used Asturian mountain

the Estaca de Bares, the northernmost point in Spain, an incredible 112km away in Galicia.

Luarca, with its sheltered harbour at the mouth of the Río Negro, is a little more tourist-orientated, but it is still a satisfactory place for a stay on Spain's northern coast. The village was an important place in medieval times, first as a whaling port and then from trade with the Americas. The best way to see it is to follow the first signposted road in from the east – a back road that will take you to the cemetery, high on a cliff with a stunning view over the village below. Luarca is still an important fishing port, mostly for tuna, and the harbourfront ensemble makes a pretty photograph. Old Luarca stretches inland from there, with some stately palaces from the 17th and 18th centuries, and some old quarters with narrow alleys climbing up the steep hills. There is a quite acceptable beach right in the centre of Luarca, but for something special head for **Playa del Barayo**, a beautiful natural area to the west of Luarca.

Continuing westwards, **Navia** is the next fishing village. Southwest of here at **Coaña** you can visit the extensive remains of another Celtic *castro* – foundations of stone walls, paved streets and the foundations of houses. The similarity between these and the *vaquero* huts led some to believe that the *vaqueros* were a lost Celtic tribe.

The Asturian coast ends with Figueras del Mar and then **Castropol**, another attractive fishing port sheltered on the broad Ría de Ribadeo. Inland, south beyond Vegadeo, tiny **Taramundi** up in the mountains has long been famous for the manufacture of knives which have become popular Asturian souvenirs.

Markets on Asturias' Western Coast

Cudillero and **Navia**: Fri.
Tapia de Casariego: Mon.

⭐ **La Casona de la Paca** >>

Where to Stay and Eat on Asturias' Western Coast

ⓘ **Cudillero** >
Puerte del Oeste,
t 98 559 13 77,
www. cudillero.org

Cudillero ✉ 33150

La Casona de Pio, C/Río Frío 3, **t 98 559 15 12, *www.lacasonadepio.com* (€€). Sympathetically designed to fit into the old port, this traditional stone establishment provides style and comfort in the centre of Cudillero.

Hotel Restaurante El Pescador, Tolombreo de Arriba s/n, **t** 98 559 09 37, *www.hotelrestaurante*

elpescador.com (€€). Charming, old-fashioned hotel with rustically decorated rooms and a superb seafood restaurant which has its own fishing boat.

La Casona de la Paca, El Pito, **t 98 559 1303, *www.lacasonadelapaca. com* (€€–€). A charming hotel in a converted *indiano* mansion, surrounded by flower-filled gardens. Choose from stylish rooms and suites or equally elegant self-catering apartments.

Azpiazu, Playa de Aguilar, **t 98 558 32 10, *www.azpiazu.com* (€€–€). Well-known hotel at Playa de Aguilar; the restaurant specializes in seafood and has a breezy terrace where you can tuck into shellfish soup, hake and cider-marinated dishes.

Pensión El Camarote, C/Garcia de la Concha 4, **t** 98 559 12 02, *www.*

(★) **Hotel 3 Cabos** >>

(i) **Navia**
Plaza del Ayuntamiento,
t 98 547 37 95,
www.ayto-navia.es

(i) **Castropol**
C/La Fuente 15, t 98
563 51 13, www.ayto-
castropol.com

(i) **Taramundi**
Avda de Galicia,
t 98 564 68 77,
www.taramundi.net

(i) **Luarca** >
Olavarrieta 27,
t 98 564 00 83, www.
luarcaturismo.com;
open summer only

(★) **Villa**
La Argentina >

(★) **Palacete**
Peñalba >>

elcamarote.es (€€–€). Has impressively large rooms with baths, and is run by a friendly family. Free wifi.

Casa Mariño, t 98 559 11 88, *www. concha-artedo.com* (€€–€). In a lovely setting with a view of the sea and mountains, Concha de Artedo has one of the many pretty beaches in the area (off the coastal road west of Cudillero). The restaurant (€€) serves top-class seafood, and a memorable *zarzuela de mariscos y pescados* (shellfish and fish casserole).

**Hotel Casona Selgas, Avda Selgas s/n, El Pito, t 98 559 01 13 (€). A charming hotel with a pretty sky-blue façade, set 1.5km from the port. The friendly owners offer a wealth of activities.

Pensión Alver, C/García de la Concha 8, t 98 559 00 05, *www.pensionalver. com* (€). Colourful paintings adorn the breezy rooms in this welcoming and eco-friendly central *pensión*. Discounts for pilgrims.

Taberna del Puerto, C/Ribera 4, t 98 559 04 77 (€€). Excellent seafood is served at this restaurant, one of many that line the tiny harbour.

Los Arcos, Plaza de la Marina, t 98 559 00 86 (€). Popular restaurant with scrubbed wooden tables overlooking the harbour, and offering an excellent seafood tapas (and menu) choice.

Luarca ✉ 33700

El Gurugú, C/de la Peña 93, t 98 547 06 13 (€€€). A lovingly restored 18th-century *casona*, with ten individually decorated rooms. All comforts are catered for, including a small swimming pool and a large terrace.

Villa La Argentina, Villar de Luarca s/n, t 98 564 01 02, *www.villalaargentina. com* (€€€). A charmingly if eccentrically refurbished *indiano* villa, with cosy rooms and suites (some with Jacuzzi) plus an outdoor swimming pool and gardens.

**Casa Consuelo, at Otur (6km west of town on the N634), t 98 547 07 67, *www.casaconsuelo.com* (€€€–€€). One of the best hotel-restaurants in the area, where the food attracts people from miles around with classic Asturian *fabada* and cider. The wine list is exceptional.

Hotel Rural Tres Cabos, Ctra de El Vallín s/n, Km4,, t 98 547 06 13, *www.hotelrural3cabos.com* (€€). This wonderful hotel occupies a striking building which imaginatively combines the remnants of a century-old *casona* with striking contemporary design. Huge windows look out over terraced gardens to the three headlands – Busto, Vidio and Peñas – which give the hotel its name. The stylish bedrooms have traditional stone walls and wooden beams, along with modern furnishings, and staff will provide bicycles and beach umbrellas. Market-fresh cuisine is available to guests only.

**Hotel La Colmena, C/Uría 2, Valdés, t 98 564 02 78, *www.lacolmena.com* (€). A reliable and friendly budget option, with bright, well-equipped rooms, a café and plenty of charm.

*Hotel Rico, Pza Alfonso X 6, t 98 570 05 59, *www.hotel-rico.com* (€). A pleasant, comfortable choice in the centre of town.

Los Cantiles, at Villar, Ctra 634, Km502.7, t 98 564 09 38, *www .campingloscantiles.com* (€). On the cliffs above Luarca, with amazing views, and a small shop and bar.

La Mesón del Mar, Paseo del Muelle 32, t 98 564 09 94, *www.meson delamar.com* (€€). As at Cudillero, for dinner in Luarca you need look no further than the row of seafood restaurants on the harbour; nearly all have outside tables, allowing you to enjoy the view. This restaurant on the far end offers a wonderful range of seafood selected from the day's catch.

La Dársena, Paseo del Muelle 11, t 98 564 11 60 (€). One of the cheaper options on the harbour (with a tiny terrace), also good for fish and seafood. *Closed in winter.*

Figueras del Mar ✉ 33793

***Palacete Peñalba, C/Granada s/n, t 98 563 61 25, *www.hotelpalacete penalba.com* (€€€€–€€€). At the farthest western limit of Asturias, near Castropol, you'll find the region's loveliest hotel. Set in a pair of glorious Art Nouveau mansions designed by a follower of Gaudí, it is a listed monument, and retains its gardens and much of its original furnishings.

Old Castile and León

Old Castile and León encompasses two ancient kingdoms of Spain and the meseta *– a flat, semi-arid table-top 2,300–3,300 feet above sea level, where the climate, summed up in an old Castilian proverb, is 'nine months of winter and three months of hell'. It looks like no other place in Europe: endless rolling dun-coloured plains, spotted with scrub and patches of mountains, but few trees; during the mindless free-for-all of the Reconquista nearly all of the forests were axed. Depending on your mood you will find the* meseta *romantic and picturesque, or brooding and eerie, but you'll never forget it.*

11

Don't miss

⭐ **Lace-like Gothic spires**
Burgos cathedral **p.256**

⭐ **The perfect Romanesque church**
Frómista **p.271**

⭐ **Haunts of the mysterious Maragatos**
Near Astorga **p.294**

⭐ **Spain's refined ancient capital**
León **p.283**

⭐ **Benedictine Gregorian chant**
Santo Domingo de Silos **p.265**

See map overleaf

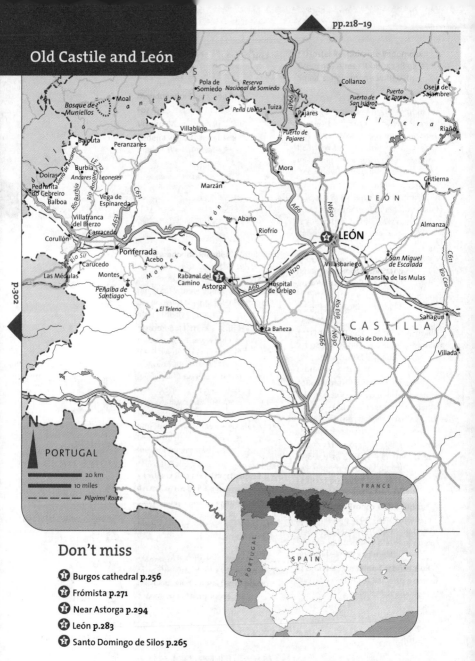

Old Castile and León

p.302

PORTUGAL

20 km
10 miles
Pilgrims' Route

SPAIN

PORTUGAL

FRANCE

Don't miss

⭐ Burgos cathedral **p.256**
⭐ Frómista **p.271**
⭐ Near Astorga **p.294**
⭐ León **p.283**
⭐ Santo Domingo de Silos **p.265**

From this unlikely land came the culture, language and people who would dominate in their day not only the nations of Iberia, but a good part of two continents. Even today Burgos, seat of the first counts of Castile, is the headquarters of all that is pure Castilian and *castizo*, down to the proper lisping pronunciation of the name of Castile's hero, the Cid, or 'El Theed'.

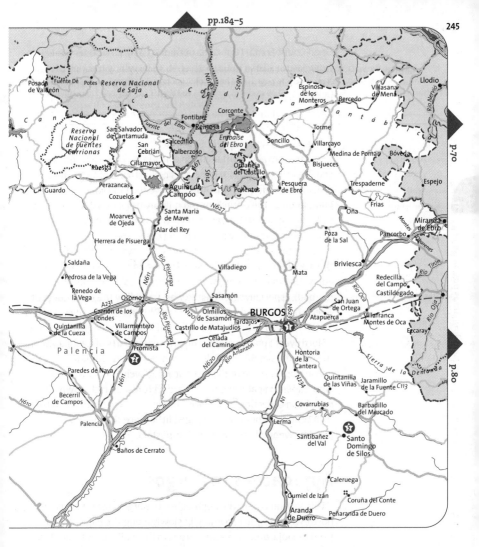

In early times Castile not only resembled America's Far West, but played the same kind of frontier role twice in European history. After the Romans whipped the native Iberians, retired legionaries were given land to raise wheat (any place named Quintanilla recalls one of their settlements, as in *quinta*, a rural villa or farm). The Visigoths followed in their tracks, but the Moors found little to like in Old Castile and conquered it without settling it. The Christian kingdoms to the north erected a string of border fortifications that gave the region its name Castile ('Land of Castles') some time around 800. In 882 the first part of Castile was reconquered by Alfonso III of Asturias; two years later, Diego Porcelos founded Burgos and became the first count of Castile. According to the medieval *Romance de Fernán González*, the

Good Count Fernán González obtained Castile's independence from Asturias-León in the 10th century by selling the king of Asturias a horse and goshawk. The king, lacking any handy cash, promised Fernán González he'd pay him double the price for every day that he didn't pay. The king forgot his promise, and by the time Fernán González reminded him the sum was so vast that all the king could do was give him Castile.

Fernán González formed his fledging state politically into seven counties, the Antiguas Merindades de Castilla. Unlike the feudal Christian kingdoms to the north, where the land was owned by great lords, or the Church, or the military orders, Castile was settled by free men or *hidalgos*, each of whom owned their farms and bore the responsibility for defending them. The difficulties in repopulating vast expanses of empty land was greatly eased by the development of the Camino de Santiago (the medieval road equivalent of the Union Pacific, America's first transcontinental railroad), especially after Castile was 'tamed' by the reconquest of Toledo by Alfonso VI and the Cid in 1085. It set off a medieval boom: settlers moved in and towns sprouted along the length of the road.

Northwest Spain includes only the oldest parts of Castilla y León, the provinces of Burgos, Palencia and León, a region that encompasses some of the most striking, weird and unknown landscapes in Spain. In between are picturesque little towns that have been collecting dust since Charles V sucked them dry in the 16th century; others have changed little since the medieval pilgrims wended their way to Compostela.

Approaches to Burgos

This section covers the approaches to Burgos from the east and north, whether you're coming in slowly along the pilgrims' road from La Rioja, quickly on the *autopista* from Bilbao, or through the mountain scenery of the Cantabrian range from Santander.

Along the *Camino*, from Redecilla to Burgos

The pilgrimage road follows the N120 from Santo Domingo de la Calzada (*see* p.122) and enters Castile at medieval **Redecilla del Campo**, built like an old strip frontier town along the road. Houses still bear their *hidalgos*' crests, but as usual the main focus is the church, Virgen de la Calle, not much in itself but notable for its sublime 12th-century baptismal font, intricately carved with the towers and windows of a city presumed to be Jerusalem. The

Getting around on the Approaches to Burgos

There are four or five **buses** a day from Burgos to Belorado, fewer to Miranda de Ebro, a major **rail** junction. At least one bus a day goes to Oña and Briviesca; services are less frequent to Frías, Espinosa de los Monteros and Poza de la Sal.

church in the next town, **Castildelgado**, has interesting Gothic *retablos*; while beyond, **Viloria de Rioja** preserves the font where Santo Domingo de la Calzada was baptised. Further west, the much larger, leather-making town of **Belorado** (the Belfuratus of the *Codex Calixtinus*) attracts a different kind of pilgrim these days with its factory outlets. The ruins of a monastery and a hospital recall its former vocation, along with two churches, San Pedro and Santa María, built in the 1500s in the wide, airy Catalan Gothic style. Hermits lived in the caves by **Tosantos**, around the church of the Virgen de la Peña, built into a cliff, while to the west in **Espinosa del Camino** you can see the 9th-century ruins of the Mozarab monastery of **San Félix de Oca**, where the first count of Castile, Diego Porcelos, was buried.

Just west of the Sierra de la Demanda, the deeply forested **Montes de Oca** (Mountains of the Goose) mark the traditional border of Castile. At their foot, **Villafranca Montes de Oca**, a town settled by Franks, was once a major pilgrims' halt; today both Franks and pilgrims have gone, leaving a church and the 14th-century Hospital de San Antón to recall its glory days. A path leads up to the **Hermitage of the Virgen de Oca**, a pretty, leafy place with plenty of picnic tables. At Villafranca the N120 and the walking path split; the latter, heading up the pine-forested slopes (enjoy it: it's the last shade before the mountains west of León) eventually emerges at **San Juan de Ortega**.

San Juan de Ortega is named after Santo Domingo's architecturally minded sidekick, who, after a pilgrimage to Jerusalem, came back to Spain determined to build chapels, bridges and hostels along the *camino*, especially in places like this, where wolves devoured more than a few pilgrims. A couple of miles from the N120, the hamlet he founded is all but abandoned, although, unlike the hostel (now *parador*) built by Santo Domingo de la Calzada, San Juan's still serves its original purpose, thanks to the local priest who feeds and lodges pilgrims. In 1142 the saint designed the church, of which most notably the apse survives, an original, elegant design of slender round columns and three receding arches around alabaster windows. Inside, San Juan is buried in a magnificent tomb, with an effigy and delightful cartoon-like scenes from his life carved in the base and crowned by an Isabelline Gothic baldachin, paid for by Isabel the Catholic herself, who got pregnant for the first time in 1477 after praying by the

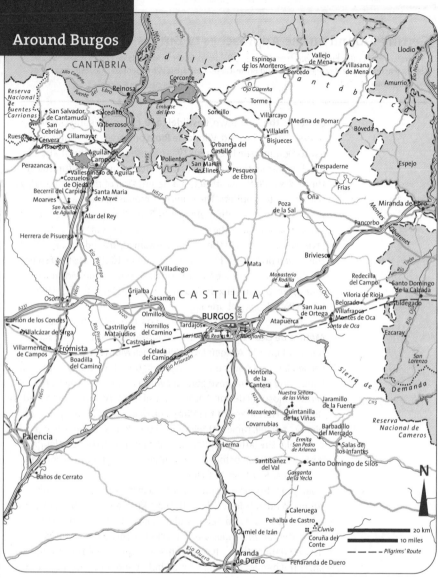

saint's Romanesque tomb (now down in the crypt). At 5pm on the day of the spring and autumn equinoxes (21 March and 22 September), pilgrims come to see the *Milagro de la Luz*, when a sunbeam illuminates the womb of the Virgin of the Annunciation, carved on a triple capital in the crossing. Isabel also paid for the chapel of San Nicolás, designed to hold the tomb now removed to the old church; in exchange the Renaissance grille from the old church has been installed in the chapel. Just to the west, the walking path continues to one of San Juan de Ortega's bridges in the tiny hamlet of **Agés**.

Atapuerca area tours
www.atapuerca.com;
*tours daily between 9–2
and 4–6; adm;
book in advance on
t 902 024 246, or
through the website
www.visitasatapuerca.
com (Spanish only);
see also the tours run
by the Museo de la
Evolución Humana,
p.260; visitor centre
open April–Oct and
3.30–8; Nov–Mar 10–2
and 4–6.30 9.30–2.30*

In **Atapuerca**, the next town (13km east of Burgos), excavations since 1990 in a complex of limestone caves and railway cuttings have thrown up incredibly important palaeontological finds, including, in 2008, the oldest human remains ever found in western Europe – a jawbone and teeth dated 1.1 to 1.2 million years, that resemble the even earlier human remains recently found in Dmanisi, Georgia – suggesting an immigration out of Africa far, far earlier than anyone previously thought, by a species generally known as *Homo antecessor* or Pioneer Man. Current studies are under way to see if *Homo antecessor* was the missing link between Neanderthals and *Homo sapiens sapiens* (Cro-Magnons), our direct ancestors. The area has been designated a UNESCO World Heritage site, and can be visited by **guided tour**. Finds are displayed in the new **Museo de la Evolución Humana** in Burgos (*see* p.260), and in the visitor centre.

Beyond the Sierra of Atapuerca are the sprawling eastern suburbs of Burgos (*see* p.255).

To Burgos from Bilbao: The Gate of Pancorbo

The Bilbao–Madrid motorway A1 runs into Castile near **Miranda de Ebro**, a major town surrounded by dreary industrial suburbs with little to see besides the glass balconies of its old houses hanging over the river. It grew up around a medieval bridge, which was replaced in 1777 by the Puente de Carlos III. The 16th-century church of **Santa María** is Miranda's most beautiful monument, while the Ebro itself sculpted the stunning gorge, the **Hoces del Sobrón**, through the nearby Montes Obarenes.

The road, the *autopista* and the train funnel dramatically through the pass at **Pancorbo**, for V.S. Pritchett 'a place of horror, for the rock crowds in, comes down in precipitous, yellow shafts, and at the top has been tortured into frightening animal shapes by the climate'. A ruined Moorish **castle** and an 18th-century **fort** that played a role when Wellington's army chased the French through the gorge in 1813 survive above the homely old town. Most of the Pancorbans work in the big truck stops, where drivers tuck into a bowl of *sopa castellano* to prepare themselves for their long ride in the night to beat the heat of the *meseta* beyond. Or, as Pritchett put it: 'Pancorbo is the moment of conversion. Now one meets Spain, the indifferent enemy.'

Between Pancorbo and Burgos, **Briviesca** on the River Oca was on the *camino francés* until the 11th century, before Sancho the Great prompted a change of route through Nájera. The regular rectangular plan of Briviesca, with its pleasant Plaza Mayor, was the model for several towns founded in South America; its octagonal church, **Santa Clara** (1565), has star vaulting and a florid carved *retablo mayor* (a rare, unpolychromed one, with a central figure dreaming of the tree of Jesse); another fine 16th-century *retablo* is in the Capilla de Santa Casilda in the **Colegiata de Santa María**. In 1388, the Cortes Generales of King Juan I were held in Briviesca, and here he bestowed on his eldest son Enrique the title of 'Prince of Asturias' for his wedding to Catherine of Lancaster, a title, like the Prince of Wales, that has been held ever since by the heir to the Spanish throne.

Farther west towards Burgos, the Benedictine Monasterio de Rodilla has vanished, leaving only its lovely Romanesque church, **Nuestra Señora del Valle**, set in a meadow with picnic tables.

Northeast Approaches

Oña

Briviesca is the chief town of the Bureba, where the foothills of the Cantabrian mountains begin. This bulge of the map in northeast Burgos province, the cradle of Old Castile, is full of curiosities and remarkable scenery; a good place to start is medieval Oña, 'La Villa Condal', north of Briviesca. Founded by the Romans on the River Oca, Oña had one of the first castles of Castile and was granted its *fueros* or privileges in 950 by Fernán González, Castile's first king. In the early days, the king's travelling court often stayed here; in 1033, Sancho the Great of Navarra, heir of Castile, ordered the old royal stronghold replaced by the Benedictine **Monasterio de San Salvador**. He meant this to serve as a royal pantheon, a status he encouraged by spending his dying days in Oña.

Oña's main *plaza* is picturesquely laid out on three different levels. Behind an old pilgrims' cross, the monastery, rebuilt in 1640 and decorated with four squat kings who would look perfectly at home on a deck of cards, is now a psychiatric hospital. However, the

Monastery church
tours Tues–Sun 10.30, 11.30, 12.45, 4, 5, 6, Sat 10.30, 11.30, 12.30, 1.15, 4, 5, 6.15; adm

town offers guided tours of its **church**, atop a flight of steps. The entrance is through the 15th-century Pórtico de los Reyes, carved with figures of kings and counts, leading into an open atrium; beyond is the oldest Romanesque façade in Castile (1072), with Flemish-Gothic paintings just inside, and a *mudéjar* door. Although the walls of the long narrow church date from the 11th century, the interior was redone in the 15th by Fernando Díaz. The second Baroque *retablo* on the right marks the tomb of Santa Tigridia, San Salvador's first abbess; its expressive Romanesque *Cristo de Santa Tigridia* is attributed to sculptors from the Toulouse school.

Further up, charming 14th-century Gothic frescoes depict the legend of St Mary of Egypt (really Isis, they say, dressed in Christian clothing). Fernando Díaz's starry dome measures 4,300sq ft and is the second largest in Spain after Tarragona; below are filigree choir stalls in walnut, and flanking the ultra-florid 18th-century Baroque *retablo* is the magnificent **Panteón Real**. Sancho the Great (d.1035) and his wife are here, among others, their tombs arranged by Fernando Díaz into charming little temples, richly carved and decorated with elaborate tracery and Hispano-Flemish paintings by Fray Alonso de Zamora. Behind the *retablo*, the **Capilla de San Íñigo** contains the 16th-century silver reliquary of Íñigo (Eneco), persuaded to be first abbot of Oña by Sancho the Great and whose death, they say, grieved Christian, Jew and Saracen alike. The **museum** in the sacristy contains the alabaster tomb of Bishop López de Mendoza by Italian Mannerist master Leone Leoni, a fragment of 10th-century cloth once belonging to Sancho the Great, with Arabic writing, the figures of an alchemist, and the horse and goshawk of Castile's independence.

The **cloister**, built by Simón de Colonia in 1508, is a rich piece of Isabelline Gothic. Presiding over the door is the Gothic statue of Santa María de Oña, whom the poet-king Alfonso the Wise praised in his *Cantiga 221*; when his son Fernando, the future saint, was given up for dead by his doctors, the statue, brought into his presence, restored him. She was also known as sovereign against worms in Infantes. One wing of the cloister holds the tombs of the counts of Bureba, cousins to the counts of Castile and the granddaughters of the Cid. One of their epitaphs translates:

> Gómez, who defended the Spanish coasts
> Like Hector you guarded them, while your faithful wife Urraca
> Remained here, and contemplated how the cold winters
> and pleasant springs passed
> And how nothing under heaven endures.

Down towards the river, you can see a little more of Oña's past: the last of its medieval gates, the **Arco de la Estrella**, and the Gothic church of **San Juan**, with a carved portal under the porch.

Up the Ebro: Frías and Medina de Pomar

East of Oña, built high over the banks of the Ebro, medieval **Frías** looks beautiful on postcards: a ruined 12th-century castle spirals up a rocky outcrop known as 'the Molar' high above the hanging whitewashed houses, arcaded lanes and intimate vegetable gardens. Because it's on the way to nowhere, few people ever visit, and if it's hot you can join the locals for a dip in the Ebro in the shadow of Frías' magnificent **medieval bridge**, complete with its mighty gate and central guard tower. Between Oña and Frías, turn north 16km to **Trespaderne** for 12th-century **San Pantaleón de Losa**, site of a curious hermitage set over the village on a boulder like a capsized boat. Odd carvings decorate the capitals (dragons' heads, masks and a speak-no-evil figure). Further up the valley, by the **Orduña pass**, is one of the highest waterfalls in Europe.

Another road north of Trespaderne leads to **Medina de Pomar**, site of a powerful two-towered castle containing a museum, the **Museo de las Merindades**, built in the 14th century by the Velasco family, the hereditary Constables of Castile; a *mudéjar* stucco frieze in the main hall is decorated with inscriptions in Gothic and Arabic letters. The Constables founded the **Monasterio de Santa Clara** in 1313, and lie buried in tombs with alabaster effigies in its early Gothic church with an octagonal star-vault; Santa Clara's lovely 16th-century Capilla de la Concepción has a Renaissance grille and *retablo* by Diego de Siloé and Felipe de Vigarni. In the convent **museum**, you'll find paintings attributed to Rogier van der Weyden, an ivory Christ of Lepanto, a dead Christ by Gregorio Fernández, and goldwork. Medina de Pomar is also proud of Juan de Salazar, who went to the New World in 1547 and founded Asunción, the capital of Paraguay.

Museo de las Merindades
open June–Sept Mon–Sat 12–2 and 6–8.30, Sun 12–2; Oct–May Tues–Sat 12.30–2 and 5.30–7.30, Sun 12–2; adm

Monasterio de Santa Clara
open daily 11.30–1.30 and 5.30–7.30; adm

The Canyons of the Ebro

Up the Ebro from Oña, just outside Puentearenas, **San Pedro de Tejada** is one of the province's finest Romanesque churches, its portal carved with a Last Supper and Ascension of Christ. Its other carvings are flagrantly erotic, in the same vein as the church at Cervatos, just over the mountains in Cantabria (*see* p.197). Further up, above Incinillas, **Villarcayo** (due west of Medina de Pomar) was the capital of the Merindad de Castilla la Vieja, one of Fernán González's original counties, but it was burned in the First Carlist War. Only bits of its medieval past survive, especially in the **Museo-Monasterio de Santa María la Real de Vileña**, founded to hold the treasures and fragments of the 13th-century Cistercian monastery that burned down in 1970.

San Pedro de Tejada
open July–Aug daily 11.30–1 and 4.30–7.30; June and Sept Sat–Sun 11–30–2 and 4-30–7.30

Museo-Monasterio de Santa María la Real de Vileña
open daily 10.30–12.30 and 4.30–6.30

Villarcayo is in easy striking distance of a pair of sites associated with the archaic judges of Castile who, in this isolated pocket in the 8th and 9th centuries, played a role somewhere between chieftain, lawmaker and general sage. One of them, *juez* Laín Calvo, was buried in the Romanesque **Hermitage of the Virgen de la Torrentera** in **Villalaín**; when disinterred, the chronicles write, all were amazed at the giant stature of his body, which turned to dust on contact with the air. The church, with a square apse and inscription dated 1130, has a lovely portal and interesting murals inside. Sculptures of the five judges of Castile decorate the elegant doorway of the large Renaissance church in nearby **Bisjueces**.

North of Villarcayo in **Torme**, the 12th-century Romanesque church of Butrera is one of the best preserved in the province; one judge, Nuño Rasura, wears a striking Chinese hat.

To the northwest, you can pick up the C6318 into the mountains (*see* below). For the Ebro Canyons, however, cut over to **Soncillo**, then drive southwest through the Puerta de Carrales towards **Rúerrero**, at the beginning of the **Canyons of the Ebro**. The cliffs grow increasingly majestic and fantastical as you drive towards **Orbaneja del Castillo**: vultures and eagles circle high over the ruddy canyon walls, sculpted by aeons of wind and rain to form a bizarre natural roof line of soaring bridges, castle walls, haunted towers or hollow snaggle-toothed caves. In Orbaneja an enchanting, lush waterfall cascades, even in August; from here the road does a semicircle through the canyon before climbing up to the N623, which links Santander and Burgos. This is not an unattractive route, but for something even better pass it by and cross the Ebro at **Pesquera de Ebro**, make your way east to Pesadas de Burgos and turn right onto the CL629.

For the next 14km the road is surreal – perfectly straight, in the middle of absolutely nowhere, yet each kilometre is systematically marked off with an impressive 10ft monument in stone, all identical, all bearing no identification whatsoever. The sensation of wandering across the middle of a bizarre games table for giants is confirmed when, after the last monument, you turn east and it's as if the world has suddenly dropped out beneath your feet, leaving you to wind down the edge of the table, with tremendous views across to the **Castillo de las Rojas**, an impressive ruin piled high on a rocky outcrop. The castle, where Charles V imprisoned the ambassadors of Pope Clement in 1528, defends **Poza de la Sal**, a town founded by the Romans, who first extracted salt from its marshes along the Río Torca Salada. Fortified in the 10th century, the town and its salt were so important that in 1530 its lord was made Marqués de Poza. In its web of tiny lanes there's a Gothic church with a Baroque façade, the 18th-century salt administration offices, a pair of old gateways and a panoramic view from Plaza Nueva; along the river, the old salt works, abandoned in the mid-19th century, are near an interesting Roman aqueduct. From here the road continues south towards Briviesca.

The Far Northeast Corner: in the Cordillera Cantábrica

Cave complex of Ojo Guareña
visitor centre in Merindad de Sotoscueva, t 94 713 86 14: caves and hermitage of San Bernabé open for guided visits weeekends and public holidays 11–1 and 5–7.30; adm

Near Soncillo the C6318 leads into the secret corner of Burgos province; if you're coming from the north, the N629 from Laredo will take you straight there. The most extraordinary attraction is the massive karstic **cave complex of Ojo Guareña** by **Quintanilla-Sotoscueva**, which extends some 100km underground and has prehistoric paintings and Upper Palaeolithic footprints. The visit includes the subterranean **Cave and Hermitage of San Bernabé** set on a panoramic esplanade with the façade built into the cliffs; inside are 17th- and 18th-century paintings and wax *ex votos*.

The C6318 continues east to medieval **Espinosa de los Monteros**, the local market town, with its 14th-century **Castillo de Los Condestables** on the far bank of the river Trueba, and the Constables' Baroque palace in town; there are several tower houses, and a good 15th-century *retablo* by Fray Alonso de Zamora in the church of **San Nicolás**. The fifth of August is the best time to come, when the citizenry indulge in what the tourist office describes with trepidation as 'strange dances of pagan origin'.

Portillo de Lunada
ski info at www.luna-da.info

Some 15km north there's a small ski station at **Portillo de Lunada**, where the old Roman road once passed between the *meseta* to Cantabria; the incredible views down the valley of the Miera are well worth the trouble of visiting at any time of year. On the other hand, if you venture east, interesting Romanesque churches are your reward: San Miguel at **Bercedo**, with a good portal and beams carved into animals; a 12th-century Templar church of Santa María at **Siones**, with an elegant double archway in the apse, strange and beautiful capitals and other carvings, a 12th-century statue of the Virgin and a Visigothic baptismal font; and the church of San Lorenzo at **Vallejo de Mena**, founded by the Knights of St John with a gallery of arcades along the top of the south façade and a handsome apse. The parish church of the big town in these parts, medieval **Villasana de Mena**, has a good relief of the Three Magi.

Markets on the Approaches to Burgos

Oña: Fri.
Medina de Pomar: Thurs.

Where to Stay and Eat on the Approaches to Burgos

Villafranca Montes de Oca
✉ 09240

***Hotel San Antón Abad**, C/Hospital 4, t 94 758 21 49, *www.hotelsan antonabad.com* (€€). A 14th-century *hospital* for pilgrims, now a handsomely renovated country hotel.

La Alpargatería, C/Mayor 2, t 94 758 20 29 (€). A sweet little *casa rural* in the centre; B&B or rent the whole place.

Pancorbo/Briviesca ✉ 09240

****Hotel Isabel**, C/Santa Maria Encimera 2, Briviesca, t 94 759 29 59, *www.hotel-isabel.com* (€€). A modern, central hotel with comfy rooms.

ⓘ **Villarcayo**
*C/Laín Calvo 22,
t 94 713 04 57, www.vil-larcayo.org*

ⓘ **Medina de Pomar >>**
C/Mayor 14, t 94 714 72 28, www. medinade-pomar.org

Hotel El Vallés, Ctra Madrid–Irún, Briviesca, t 94 759 00 25, *www. hotelelvalles.com* (€€). Glossy modern hotel with good-value weekend packages and an excellent Michelin-starred restaurant (€€€–€€).

Casa Rural El Ferial, C/San Nicolás 59, Pancorbo, t 947 35 42 76 (€). This place, on the edge of the old town, fronted by a gallery, is really a cheap bed and breakfast overlooking a garden, but the best thing about it is the charming and hospitable owners, Vicente Cardiñanos and his wife.

El Concejo, Plaza Mayor 14, Briviesca, t 94 759 16 86, *www.restauranteel con-cejo.com* (€€). Prettily set in a 15th-century mansion in town, this restaurant serves modern cuisine and imaginative desserts; good value *menú del día* (€15).

Medina de Pomar ✉ 09500

***Ciudad de Medina**, Pza Somovilla, t 94 719 08 22, *www.hotelciudad demedina.com* (€€). In a pretty, historic building with the village's best, moderately priced restaurant.

Burgos

First it must be said that Burgos is a genteel and pleasant town. Its river, the Arlanzón, is so filled with frogs in the spring and early summer that they drown out the traffic with their croaking; and the favourite promenade, the Paseo del Espolón, is one of Spain's prettiest, adorned with amazing topiary hedges. Burgos contains one of the greatest collections of Gothic art and monuments in southern Europe, and it is the city in Spain where you are most likely to see a nun riding a bicycle.

Yet throughout much of its history Burgos' role has been that of a stern military camp, from the days of El Cid Campeador to Franco el Caudillo who, during the Civil War, made it his temporary capital, the city where, it was said, 'the very stones are Nationalist'. Here, in 1970, Franco held the infamous Burgos trials in which 16 Basque separatists (two of them priests) were tried in a kangaroo court; six were sentenced to death but their sentences later commuted.

The Kingdom of Castile was born in Burgos, and it is fitting that the city itself began as a castle erected on the Moorish frontier in 884. In 926 it took its first step away from Leonese rule, electing its own judges; in 950, one of the judges' successors, Fernán González, declared his independence as Count of Castile. His descendant, Ferdinand I, elevated the title to king and married the heiress of León. Burgos remained sole capital of Castile until 1087, when Alfonso VI moved to Toledo (perhaps to put some distance between himself and the overbearing Cid). The frontier was moving south and this city that had done so much to create the ethos of Spain now found itself a backwater. But Burgos has always remained true to the cause. It is still Spain's most aristocratic, pious, polite and reactionary city. Franco rewarded it with a programme of state-financed expansion, an attempt to drag it into the 20th century that may well succeed some day.

Arco de Santa María

Burgos' glistening white, fairytale front door, the **Arco de Santa María**, was originally part of the medieval walls, but after the Comunero revolt it was embellished to appease Charles V; triumphal arches like this were a Renaissance conceit (the first one was made at Naples for a Spanish king), and they were especially favoured by the vainglorious and ambitious Charles. The Emperor himself is portrayed in a Burgos pantheon that includes its first judges, King Fernán González, and El Cid. The arch was designed by Francisco de Colonia and Juan de Vallejo, two artists you are going to know well before you leave Burgos – along with Francisco's father Juan, responsible for the great openwork spires of the cathedral, looming just behind the arch.

Getting to Burgos

By Train

RENFE is on Avda Conde Guadalhorce, across the river from the cathedral, **t** 902 320 320, *www.renfe.com*. Burgos is on the main rail line from Irún to Madrid (connections to Pamplona, Vitoria-Gasteiz, Bilbao, Valladolid, etc.), with less frequent links with Zaragoza, Palencia, León, and La Coruña; also high-speed links to Salamanca, Barcelona, Málaga, Madrid, Córdoba and Vigo.

By Bus

The **bus terminal** is on C/Miranda, across the river from the Arco de Sta María, **t** 94 728 88 55. There are daily buses to León (4), Santander (at least 10), Madrid (12), San Sebastián, Soria, Bilbao and Vitoria (4 or more), and the provincial villages. Even if there may be only one bus a day to places not on a main route, such as Frías, they're often conveniently timed for a day trip but check in advance to avoid being stranded.

The Cathedral

🟊 Burgos cathe-
dral
*www.catedralde
burgos.es;
main entrance for
mass only on Plaza
Santa María; visitor
entrance and ticket
office on Plaza Rey
San Fernando; open
Mar–Oct daily
9.30–7.30, last adm
6.30; Nov–Mar daily
10–7, last adm 6; adm
for tourist visits, free for
mass and prayer*

Along with León and Toledo, Burgos has one of Spain's greatest Gothic cathedrals. Yet while León's has an instant, sublime appeal, Burgos' power lies in its awesome number of master works and details from the tiniest carving in the choir stalls to its beautiful star-vaulted domes. In 1221, in honour of his marriage to Beatrice of Swabia, Ferdinand III and the English bishop Maurice laid the first cornerstone. On the north side, a stair leads up to the **Puerta del Sarmental**, its 13th-century tympanum showing Christ and the four Evangelists (sitting studiously at their desk, writing the Gospels). The first portal to be finished, the south-side **Puerta Alta de la Coronería** (1257) is the most interesting, with its Apostles, the Almighty, and a peculiar row of mere mortals, the Blessed and the Damned, in between. Around the corner of the transept, the **Puerta de la Pellejería** is part of the original 13th-century work.

These doors are rarely opened; Burgos is prey to a biting wind in the late afternoon, and the cross-current would blow the congregation away. From up here, though, you can get a good view of the forest of spires, especially on the lantern, adorned with scores of figures. Three generations of the Colonia family devoted themselves to moulding the soft grey stone of Burgos into the cathedral's intricate towers and pinnacles. Colonia is Cologne, in Germany; Hans of Cologne began the works in the late 1400s, and his son Simón and grandson Francisco carried on, followed by Juan de Vallejo, who built the Plateresque crossing tower. These, and the **Arco de Santa María**, are illuminated at night.

The **west façade** incorporates two Stars of David, an unintentional reminder that more than one of Burgos' bishops hailed from a Jewish family before 1492, as did the city's greatest sculptors, Diego and Gil de Siloé, the undisputed masters of Isabelline Gothic. Their work inside is one of the cathedral's main attractions. Tragically, the three portals of the west façade were 'improved' in the 'Age of Enlightenment' of the 18th century, and replaced with pallid substitutes. But around the back, another monument of late

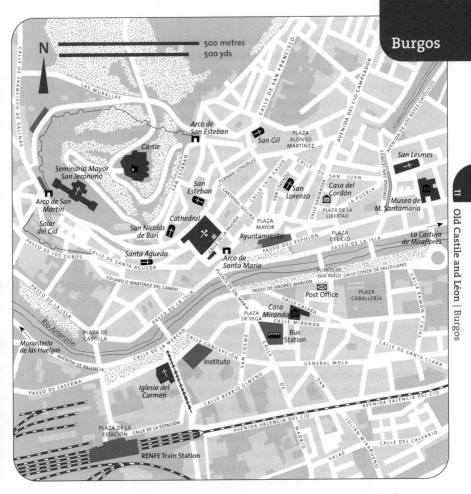

Gothic excess survives, the huge Capilla del Condestable (*see* overleaf), attached to the apse.

Along with the cathedral of Santiago, this is one of the two great treasure houses of Spain. De Vigarni, who also designed the choir, carved the tomb of Don Gonzalo de Lerma in the 16th-century **Capilla de la Presentación**, the largest and most beautiful of the chapels on the southern aisle. Look out for the famous 15th-century mechanical clock across the nave (look up in the dim corner by the rose window), the **Papamoscas** ('Flycatcher'), a grinning devil who pops out of a hole in the wall to strike the hour. The extravagantly Baroque Capilla de Santa Tecla on the northern aisle can be glimpsed through glass doors – it, like the celebrated Capilla de Santo Cristo (*see* p.259) is reserved for services. Next, the lovely **Capilla Santa Ana** has a *retablo* of the Tree of Jesse by Gil de Siloé and a fine bishop's tomb by his son Diego. One of Diego de Siloé's masterpieces, the diamond-shaped, drippingly Plateresque

Golden Stair (1523), is the most strikingly original feature of the interior, the perfectly proportioned solution to the **Puerta Alta**, 30ft above the floor of the cathedral. The idea of stairways as architectural showpieces was just beginning in 1523; Michelangelo was working on his famous one at the Laurentian Library in Florence at the same time.

The enclosed **choir** is almost entirely shut off from the rest of the church, but nonetheless accessible to the visitor. Lift your gaze above the grille work to see the magnificent gold-trimmed star vault of Juan de Vallejo's **lantern**, under the central tower, which Felipe II declared couldn't have been built by men but only by angels. Four stately round piers support a profusion of intricate carved decoration – a Spanish twist on Renaissance styles, married harmoniously into a Gothic building. Underneath its majestic beauty a simple slab marks the **tomb of the Cid and his wife Ximena**, their bones relocated here with great pomp in 1921. The other tomb in the *coro* belongs to Bishop Maurice, topped by his enamelled copper effigy; try to get in to see the magnificent carving on the wood and inlaid stalls – unabashed pagan figures on the seats, New Testament scenes above. They were done by Felipe de Vigarni, who also sculpted the dramatic scene on the ambulatory behind the main altar.

The most spectacular chapel, the octagonal **Chapel of the High Constable of Castile** (**Capilla del Condestable**), was built by Simón de Colonia for Pedro Hernández de Velasco in 1482–94. The tomb, accompanied by that of the Constable's wife, Doña Mencía de Mendoza, faces the elaborate altar by Vigarni and Diego de Siloé. The constable, the head of the Castilian army, clutches his sword even after death; his lady's little dog sleeps at her feet. Velasco was constable during the conquest of Granada, whose Moorish craftsmen inspired the great, geometric star-vaulting that crowns

---

A Building Trying to Disappear

If you have the time, take a good long look at the exterior of this cathedral (preferably from up the stairs on the edge of the *plaza*). This is the Gothic idea stretched to its wildest extreme – in its day it must have looked as outrageous as Gaudí's Sagrada Família when its first parabolic towers went up in the 1900s.

In the first blossoming of Gothic building in the Île-de-France, they concentrated on the interior – soaring arches and acres of stained glass to make the walls disappear and create a kind of spiritual union of inside and outside. Spain, the land of extremes, naturally had to take the principle a step further. The virtuoso stone lace spires, finished to Juan de Colonia's design in the 19th century, are only the crowning glory of the most diaphanous church ever built. Note how the windows in the bell towers were made so wide that from most points of view you can actually see through the towers. Hundreds of pinnacles, as electric as any of Gaudí's, pattern out the sky, while between the towers hangs an equally transparent, thoroughly over-the-top gallery of statues of Spanish kings, under the biggest, most delicate stone traceries ever perched over a façade. Imagine the master mason directing the works in the 1200s, dreaming of a building that would be built half of stone, half of light and air.

the chapel. Among the works of art within the chapel is a wonderfully voluptuous auburn-haired *Magdalen* by Giampetrino, a pupil of Leonardo da Vinci.

The nearby **Sacristía Mayor** – the cathedral's sacristy – is adorned with one of the cathedral's lighter scenes, a Baroque bubble bath of a heaven. Off the cloister, the **Museo Diocesano** is housed in a series of Gothic chapels: the Capilla de Corpus Christi contains the famous leather-bound coffer the Cid filled with sand and locked tight, then passed off as gold as security to Raquel and Vidas, two Jewish money-lenders, who made him a sizeable loan; another prized possession is the Cid's marriage agreement in the next-door chapel of Santa Catalina. The most prized possessions, including a series of vivid paintings from a medieval reliquary, are gathered in the adjoining chapels of San Juan and San Diego.

The cathedral's main draw, however, is just inside the west door, in the part of the cathedral kept separate for religious services only. To the right is the glass-doored **Capilla de Santo Cristo**, where ladies gathered to worship one of the strangest cult idols of any religion – the 13th-century Cristo de Burgos, a figure made of buffalo hide (long reputed to be human skin), real hair and fingernails (according to an old tale, both had to be trimmed regularly), in a green frock and warm to the touch. The head and arms can move, like a doll's; these were probably somehow manipulated to impress the faithful, back in the golden age of miracles. Still the focus of enormous veneration, the only way to get a glimpse is to re-enter the cathedral via the west door and peer through the chapel's glass doors, or else attend a service.

Museo Diocesano
adm included in ticket
to cathedral

11

Old Castile and Léon | Burgos

Around the Cathedral

Just to the northwest of the cathedral on Calle Fernán González, **San Nicolás de Bari** contains an incredible wall-sized alabaster *retablo* by Francisco de Colonia (1505), depicting 36 scenes from the Bible and more angels than could dance on a head of a pin. **Santa Águeda**, a plain 15th-century church on Calle Santa Águeda, is the successor of the church where the Cid forced Alfonso VI to swear on a silver lock that he had nothing to do with the assassination of his brother Sancho – an iron copy of the lock is hung over the door inside. The Cid's ancestral mansion, the **Solar del Cid**, was demolished in 1771, though two obelisks mark the site. Between his two banishments and innumerable campaigns, he probably had little leisure to enjoy it anyway.

San Nicolás de Bari
open mid-July–Sept Mon–Sat 12–1.30 and 5–7, Sun before and after mass; adm, free Mon

Santa Águeda
open before and after mass

The **castle** was blown up by the French in 1813 – an explosion that shattered most of the cathedral's stained glass – and little remains to be seen up here besides the fine view of the city. In its day, however, the castle saw many important events – Edward I of England and Leonora of Castile were married here. It is reached

Museo del Retablo
*open Tues–Sat 10–2
and 5–8; adm*

**Museum of
Human Evolution**
*open July and Aug
Tues–Sun 10–8;
Sept–June Tues–Fri
10–2.30 and 4.30–8,
Sat–Sun 10–8; closed
Mon; adm; shuttle
buses for La Atapuerca
archaeological site usu-
ally depart Tues–Sun at
11am; on Sat–Sun,
there's a return bus at
5pm; timetables are
subject to change, so
check with the muse-
um; it is highly recom-
mended to book seats
on the shuttle bus well
in advance*

Museo de Burgos
*open June–Sept
Tues–Sat 10–2 and 5–8,
Sun 10–2; Oct–May
Tues–Sat 10–2 and
4–7, Sun 10–2; closed
Mon; adm*

**Monasterio de
Las Huelgas**
*t 94 720 16 30;
open Tues–Sat 10–1
and 4–5.30, Sun
10.30–2; adm, free Weds
and Thurs afternoons;
closed Mon*

through the horseshoe **Arco de San Esteban**; also near the arch are two 14th-century Gothic churches: **San Esteban** and **San Gil**, both with fine interiors. San Esteban also houses a museum of altarpieces, the **Museo del Retablo**.

Near San Gil, in Plaza Alonso Martínez, you'll notice a grim little building called the **Capitanería**, guarded by military police and adorned with commemorative plaques dedicated to Franco and Mola. This was the Nationalist capital during the Civil War; here Franco assumed total power among the rebels and directed his campaigns in the north. Calle Santander is Burgos' main shopping street; at its head is the **Casa del Cordón**, named after the rope (really a Franciscan monk's belt) carved over the door in honour of St Francis. This palace was built by the Condestable de Velasco in 1485. Ferdinand and Isabel received Columbus here after his second voyage, and 18 years later, an ageing Ferdinand sent Ponce de León off to discover the Fountain of Youth.

Nearby, the attractive, arcaded **Plaza Mayor** has been refurbished and pedestrianized, although the shady **Paseo del Espolón** along the riverfront is the city's real centre; at the far end, a mighty equestrian **statue of the Cid** seems ready to fly off its base and attack any enemy crossing **San Pablo bridge** towards the Plaza Primo de Rivera. The bridge is embellished with stone figures of the Cid's wife, his companions and a Moorish king.

Across the bridge, the vast **Museum of Human Evolution** (**Museo de la Evolución Humana**) opened in 2010 in a spectacular contemporary building designed by Juan Navarro Baldeweg. Inside, superb high-tech exhibits focus on the finds at Atapuerca (*see* p.249), where the earliest hominids in Europe lived. There are shuttle buses linking the museum with the archaeological site at Atapuerca, and the website lists special events and activities.

Nearby, two elegant 16th-century palaces, the **Casa Miranda** and the **Casa de Íñigo Angulo**, together form the **Museo de Burgos**: the lovely Casa Miranda has an extensive archaeological collection, while the Casa de Íñigo Angulos picks up the story with finds from the Visigothic period and a large painting collection spanning the 12th to the 20th centuries. The best is the medieval art in the first gallery, which includes some exquisite treasures from the Monasterio de Santo Domingo de Silos (*see* p.265).

Monasterio de Las Huelgas

On the outskirts of Burgos lie two of Spain's richest monasteries, both well worth a visit. A 20-minute walk to the west will take you to the Cistercian monastery of Las Huelgas, founded by Alfonso VIII in 1187 at the behest of his wife Leonor, daughter of England's Henry II (*huelga* in Spanish means a strike now, but, back then *Las Huelgas Reales*, the monastery's true name, meant 'The Royal

Repose'). The abbess of Las Huelgas had more power and influence than any other woman in Spain except the queen herself, until her powers were revoked in the 19th century. In 1219 Ferdinand III 'the Saint' began the custom of Castilian kings going to Las Huelgas to be knighted into the Order of Santiago by Santiago himself; in the cloister you can see the statue of the saint with a moveable arm holding out a sword made for this purpose. Guided tours (in Spanish) will take you through the English-Gothic church: statues of Alfonso VIII and Leonor kneel before the altar, and there's a curious painted iron pulpit of 1560 that gyrated to allow the priest to address the nuns in the choir or congregation. The church also serves as a royal pantheon of Castilian kings and royal ladies. The French, as usual, desecrated the tombs, though the one they missed, that of Alfonso X's son Ferdinand de la Cerda, produced such a fine collection of goods as to form the nucleus of Las

Museo de Telas Medievales

same hours as monastery

Huelgas' **Museo de Telas Medievales**, a fascinating collection of fabrics and medieval dress with considerable Eastern influences.

These are not the only Moorish touches in Las Huelgas: note the geometric tomb of the Infanta Doña Blanca, the peacock and stars in the *mudéjar* **cloister**, and the **Capilla de Santiago**. The grandest chamber, the **Sala Capitular**, contains a trophy from Alfonso VIII's great Battle of Las Navas de Tolosa – the silk flap of the Moorish commander's tent – and Don Juan's banner from Lepanto, which he gave to his daughter Ana, abbess of Las Huelgas. If the guide's in a good mood, he'll play a scale on the well-tuned columns in the halls. Noble and wealthy pilgrims would receive a fair welcome at Las Huelgas, but for the needs of poor pilgrims Alfonso VIII also built the **Hospital del Rey**, a short walk from Las Huelgas, facing the road to León. Most impressive here are the 16th-century Plateresque gateway and the court.

La Cartuja de Miraflores

Cartuja de Miraflores

open Mon–Tues and Thurs–Sat 10.15–3 and 4–6, Sun 11–3 and 4–6; closed Wed

Burgos' second great monastery is a 3.5km walk to the east, through a lovely park of shady trees. Miraflores was founded by Juan II in 1441 and is still in use, so you can see only the church, built by the Colonia family; yet this alone contains more great art than many cathedrals. Here Isabel la Católica commissioned the great Gil de Siloé to sculpt the **tomb of Juan II and Isabel of Portugal** as a memorial to her parents and, after four years' work, he created the most elaborate, detailed tomb of all time, 'imprisoning Death inside an alabaster star' as a local guidebook poetically put it. Instead of a chisel, it looks as if Siloé used a needle to sew the robes of the effigies – Juan pensive, his wife reading a book. Isabel owed her succession to her brother's death and, as a posthumous thank you, had Siloé carve his memorial too. The tomb of the Infante Don Alfonso shows the young prince (1453–68) kneeling at prayer among a playful menagerie of animals, *putti* and birds entwined in vines. Master Siloé also did most of the gilt *retablo* of the high altar, said to be made with the gold Columbus had presented to the Catholic Kings at the Casa de Cordón.

Other works of art include a lovely painting of the Annunciation by Pedro Berruguete; carvings on the stalls of the lay brothers' choir (the middle section of the Carthusian church's traditional three divisions – the monks' choir is in the front, the general public at the back), a painting of the Virgin sending the infernal spirits packing and a wooden polychrome **statue of St Bruno** in the side chapel by the Portuguese Manuel Pereira, so lifelike 'it would speak if it weren't a Carthusian monk', as the *burgaleses* like to say.

Below Miraflores, 10km further down the road is the abbey of **San Pedro de Cardeña**, founded in 899 and now a Trappist monastery. Here the Cid left his family when banished by Alfonso VI, and here he was buried beside his wife Ximena. The French stole the bones and when the Spanish government finally got them back it was to inter them in the more secure precincts of the cathedral. You can visit the tombs with their effigies in a chapel off the **Cloister of Martyrs**, where 200 Benedictines were beheaded in a 10th-century Moorish raid. The Cid's faithful charger Babieca is buried just outside the gate.

San Pedro de Cardeña
*www.carena.org;
open April–Oct
Mon–Sat 10–1 and 4–6,
Sun 12–1.30 and 4–6;
Nov–Mar Mon–Sat
10–1.30 and 3.30–5.30,
Sun 12–1.30 and
3.30–5.30; adm*

Facilities in Burgos

The **post office** is on Plaza Conde de Castro, across the river from Paseo del Espolon; **Ciber Café Cabaret**, C/La Puebla 21, has **internet access**, at €4 per hour (*open 12pm–1am, Sat 5pm–4am, Sun 5pm–1am*).

Where to Stay in Burgos

(i) Burgos ›
*municipal offices:
both t 94 728 88 74;
Teatro Principal, Paseo
del Espolón s/n; also
Plaza del Rey de
San Fernando*

*provincial office:
Plaza Alonso Martínez 7,
t 924 720 31 25*

www.turismoburgos.org

Burgos ✉ 09000

*****Landa Palace, just outside the city, off the A1 motorway, t 94 725 77 77, *www.landa.as* (€€€€€). A member of the prestigious Relais et Châteaux, offering a memorable stay in an over-the-top pseudo-medieval tower full of antiques, with an indoor atrium, fine restaurant, and pool.

***Meson del Cid, Pza Santa María 8, t 94 720 87 15, *www.mesondelcid.es* (€€€). Magnificent location opposite the cathedral, with well-equipped modern doubles, garage space and a secret tunnel to their excellent restaurant next door. They also offer self-catering apartments.

**Norte y Londres, Plaza Alonso Martínez 10, t 94 726 41 25, *www. hotelnorteylondres.com* (€€€). Charmingly old-fashioned hotel, offering a whiff of elegance right in the middle of town.

****AC Hotel Burgos, Paseo de la Audencia 7, t 94 725 79 66, *www.mar-riott.com* (€€). A well-equipped chain hotel next to the cathedral, with ultra-modern rooms, free mini-bar, and efficient service.

****Abba Burgos, C/Fernán González 72, t 94 700 11 00, *www.abbahoteles. com* (€€). Luxury hotel in a converted palace with all the extras, including a gym and swimming pool.

***Cordón, La Puebla 6, t 94 726 50 00, *www.hotelcordon.com* (€€). A classic Spanish hotel with glass balconies on a quiet street. It has triples and rooms with private sitting room. Good deals at weekends.

***La Puebla, La Puebla 20, t 94 720 00 11, *www.hotellapuebla.com* (€€). A truly delightful little boutique hotel in the centre with chic décor. There are special discounts for pilgrims.

Hotel Entrearcos, C/La Paloma 4, **t 94 725 29 11, *www.hotelentrearcos. com* (€€). A modern hotel with just 14 rooms behind a historic façade near the cathedral, this has sleek designer rooms, and a smart restaurant serving creative cuisine.

*Hotel España, Paseo de Espolón 32, **t** 94 720 63 40, *www.hotelespana.net* (€€). Pleasant, good-value hotel on a tree-lined pedestrian street. It also has a restaurant.

Hostal Manjón, Gran Teatro 1, **t 94 720 86 89, *www.hostal-manjon.com* (€). Has good budget rooms close to the river; most have private bath. Run by two friendly sisters.

*Hostal Hidalgo, Almirante Bonifaz 14, **t** 94 720 34 81 (€). A well-kept, old-fashioned *hostal* on a relatively quiet street off the Plaza Mayor. Shared baths only.

*Hostal Evolución, C/Santa Clara 28, **t** 94 725 60 77 (€). A trim, well-equipped *hostal* with en suite bedrooms near the Museo de la Evolución Humana.

★ Acuarela
Hostal >

Acuarela Hostal, C/Guardia Civil 7, **t** 94 720 50 50 (€). The best choice in Burgos for style on a budget, with bright, designer rooms individually decorated with artworks, and each equipped with a laptop. Splash out on the gorgeous attic suite with a private terrace.

Eating Out in Burgos

Casa Ojeda, Vitoria 5, **t** 94 720 90 52, *www.restauranteojeda.com* (€€). The most popular place in town, with the best tapas in its bar and good local cuisine in its dining room. *Closed Sun.*

Mesón del Cid, Plaza Santa María 8, **t** 94 720 87 15 (€€). For a medieval atmosphere in a 15th-century building facing the cathedral, and delicious roast suckling lamb, this is the place to go. *Closed Sun.*

Mesón de los Infantes, just inside the Arco de Santa María, **t** 94 720 59 82 (€€). Offers Castilian specialities like *olla podrida* and 'medieval lentils'; outdoor summer dining.

El 22, C/La Paloma 22, **t** 94 727 95 74 (€€–€). This serves creative tapas and fine wines, or you can dine on good contemporary cuisine at the stylish **El 24 restaurant** (€€€) next door.

Gaona, C/La Paloma 41, **t** 94 720 40 32 (€€–€). Basque cooking in a glassed-in terrace near the cathedral.

Mesón de Los Herreros, C/San Lorenzo 20, **t** 94 720 24 48 (€). Fill up on delicious tapas and *raciones* at this popular local favourite.

La Favorita, C/Avellanos 8, **t** 94 720 59 49, *www.lafavoritaburgos.com* (€). Fabulous range of tapas, and well executed local classics in the charming, brick-walled restaurant.

Southeast of Burgos

The most popular corner for a day out from Burgos is the mountainous region to the southeast, on or off the N234 towards Soria, where it's hard to tell where one *sierra* begins and another ends. Covarrubias and Santo Domingo de Silos are firmly marked on the tourist map, but you'll need a car to take in the prizes just off the beaten track such as San Quirce or the Visigothic church of Quintanilla de las Viñas.

A Scatological Abbey and a Visigothic Beauty

Abadía de
San Quirce
*inside open only the
first Tues of each
month, 9.30–6*

The **Abadía de San Quirce**, just off the N234, is not easy to find; signposts guide you from **Hontoria de la Cantera**. Set in a quiet wooded valley, it was founded by Count Fernán González after his defeat of the Saracens on this spot in 929. Abandoned in 1835, the church conserves its original structure, with a stout fortified tower in the centre; the west door has 11 modillions showing the Creator,

Getting around Southeast of Burgos

Transport here is sketchy. There are several **buses** daily from Burgos to Aranda de Duero, and usually one a day to Santo Domingo de Silos (except on Sundays) and Caleruega, and about three a day to Lerma and to Covarrubias. Services are reduced at weekends. Otherwise you'll need to hire a **car** (all the main rental firms are represented in Burgos, including Hertz, *www.hertz.com*, National Atesa, *www.atesa.es*, and Avis, *www.avis.es*) to get around. For a taxi, call **t** 94 727 77 77 or **t** 94 748 10 10.

Adam and Eve, Cain and Abel and, in between, earthy reliefs of men squatting and defecating, with inscriptions reading *io cago* and *mal cago* ('I shit', and 'I shit badly'). Other reliefs decorate the north door and modillions supporting the charming bubble of an apse, unusually illuminated by two round bull's-eye windows and a regular Romanesque window, which was probably originally a bull's eye as well; inside, the capitals are carved with the legend of San Quirce and a naked woman who suckles serpents.

Further south on the N234, there's an unusual corridor-dolmen at the ghost town of **Mazariegos**, where the big stones are engraved with what could be horses. Aim your next stop for **Quintanilla de las Viñas**, where 4km up, under the steel-toned Montes de Lara and the ruins of the Castilla de Lara, the gold-stoned Visigothic **Nuestra Señora de las Viñas** drinks up the sun. This is the last Visigothic basilica in Spain, dated as 7th-century or just before the invasion of the Moors. Made of large blocks incised with Christian graffiti, only the square apse and part of the transept have survived the past 1,300 years. The exterior of the former is girdled with three friezes, the lowest band of vines and grapes, the middle band decorated with plants and birds – ducks, peacocks, doves, and what are thought to be the monograms of the founders, in round medallions of curling tendrils. The upper band has a Persian air with griffons, leopards, lions, bulls and rams. Inside, on the triumphal arch, there's another bird frieze and a rare example of Visigothic syncretism: angels with rocket wings, Byzantine in style or perhaps even more like the winged figures on Roman tombs, holding up portraits identifying Christ with the moon (a bearded figure, with a crescent moon LVNA on his head like horns) and the Virgin (or Church) with the sun SOL, topped by a Latin inscription: 'I, modest Flammola, offer this modest gift.' Blocks in the apse show heavily coiffed, symmetrical but inexplicable 'astral' figures, sculpted by another artist who had trouble getting the arms and hands right.

Nuestra Señora de las Viñas
t 94 728 15 00; open May–Sept Wed–Sun 10–2 and 4–7; Oct–April Wed–Sun 10–5; closed Mon, Tues and last weekend of month

Fernán González Country: San Pedro de Arlanza and Covarrubias

South of Quintanilla de las Viñas, the Arlanza river runs east–west through a valley known in the 10th century as the Valley of Towers, the frontier of old Castile, pushed this far south by 'the Good Count' Fernán González, the founder of the realm. His

San Pedro de Arlanza
t 94 728 15 00; open May–Sept Wed–Sun 10–2 and 4–8; Oct–April Wed–Sun 10–5; closed Mon, Tues and last weekend of month

exploits are described in an epic poem, written in the 13th century by a monk in the large, romantically ruined abbey of **San Pedro de Arlanza** founded in 912 by the count's father, Gonzalo Fernández, below a cave where the hermit Pelagio predicted the illustrious destiny of his line.

Medieval **Covarrubias** is Old Castile's half-timbered showcase of porticoed squares and lanes, guarded by the only surviving 10th-century Mozarab tower in the Valley of Towers, the sturdy **Torreón de Doña Urraca**, whose countess was walled up inside in 965 and left to die. The **Ayuntamiento** has a Romanesque doorway that once belonged to Fernán González's palace. Behind this, the ex-Colegiata, **San Cosme y San Damián**, was rebuilt in 1474 as the pantheon for the count's descendants, the Infantes de Covarrubias, whose tombs line the nave; in 1848, the remains of Fernán González and his wife Sancha were brought from San Pedro de Arlanza and placed next to the altar in a 4th-century Roman sarcophagus. The 17th-century organ, one of the most beautiful in Spain, still works, although you'll have to attend mass to hear its sweet antique sound. The cloister contains the tomb of a 13th-century Norwegian princess, promised to Alfonso the Wise but married to his ex-bishop brother Ferdinand (*see* p.272). The prize in the museum is the Flemish-inspired *Triptych of the Magi*.

San Cosme y San Damián
open Mon and Wed–Fri 10.30–2 and 4–7, Sun 10.30–12 and 4–7; closed Tues and Sat; adm; mass with organ music at noon on Sun at noon

Santo Domingo de Silos and its Sublime Cloister

South of Covarrubias at **Santibáñez del Val**, the road to Barrios leads 2km to the River Ura and the 10th-century Mozarabic hermitage of **Santa Cecilia de Barriosuso**, with a square apse and window made of five rings and a horseshoe arch inside. The attraction in these parts, though – one that brings many pilgrims down on a special detour – is **Santo Domingo de Silos**, a Benedictine monastery founded in 954 by Fernán González and ruled in the 10th century by the abbot who gave it its name. Rebuilt after al-Mansur razed it to the ground, the monastery was re-founded in the 19th century by French Benedictines from Solesmes, who have made it famous for Gregorian chant. They inherited the most beautiful Romanesque **cloister** in Spain, elegant, two-tiered and ivory-coloured, built around an ancient cypress tree. The lower section dates from the late 11th–early 12th centuries and has fascinating capitals on twin columns carved by a sculptor so well versed in animals and other motifs of the Córdoba caliphate and Middle East that he may have been a Moor. On the corners of the cloister, eight large reliefs on the life of Jesus are in a similar style; one shows the only known representation of Christ in pilgrim's garb. The cloister's *mudéjar* ceiling, painted with scenes of everyday life in the Middle Ages, has been restored. Off the cloister, the **museum** houses Mozarabic illuminations (Santo Domingo is a

✪ **Santo Domingo de Silos**
www.abadiasilos.es; open for guided visits only Tues–Sat 10–1 and 4.30–6; adm; Gregorian chant sung six times a day: times on the website, or call t 94 739 00 49

study centre of Mozarabic art, liturgies and manuscripts), the Romanesque tympanum from the first church, a 12th-century paten with Roman cameos, an 11th-century chalice and the 18th-century **pharmacy** (*botica*) with big jars. After all this, the church, rebuilt in the neoclassical style in the 18th century, seems dull.

A mere 2.5km from Santo Domingo towards Caleruega, a narrow gorge, the **Desfiladero de la Yecla**, has been fitted with some rather battered wooden walkways, making for an easy and spectacular walk; the stair descends just before the tunnel and the end of the walkway emerges just after it. The gorge is part of a nature park with colonies of vultures, hawks and buzzards, the largest *sabina* (shrubby juniper) forest in the world, and remains of a Celtic *castro*. Beyond hilltop **Hinojar de Cervera**, the Cueva de San García has even older traces of civilization, dating back to the Upper Palaeolithic era. **Caleruega**, further south, was the birthplace in 1170 of yet another canonized Domingo, the one who went into the heavenly big time, Santo Domingo de Guzmán. It was his theological battles against the heretical Cathars in Toulouse that led, in 1216, to Domingo's founding of his preaching order, the Dominicans or Black Friars, who took on the job of the Inquisition. The Guzmán tower house is still intact, and the exact spot of the saint's birth is marked in the crypt of the church of Dominican Madres.

The Bloody Cucumber of Vengeance

The seven sons of Gonzalo Gustios, the Lord of Salas, were known for their chivalry and prowess, in no small thanks to their tutor, the judge Nuño Rasura. In 986 their troubles began at the splendid wedding of their uncle Ruy Velázquez to Doña Lambra, when the youngest of the seven brothers quarrelled with a kinsman of the bride. Doña Lambra took the quarrel as a personal insult and, as the brothers rode away, she ordered her slave to heave a bloody cucumber at them. This was the ultimate deadly insult in 10th-century Castile (discretion forbade the romancers to explain exactly why); the outraged brothers slew the slave, even though he tried to 'hide even in the folds of her garment'.

Now it was Ruy Velázquez's turn to feel insulted by the brothers, and he schemed to avenge himself on the whole family. First he sent the father to Córdoba with a message in Arabic for the king, asking him to slay the bearer; but the Moorish king took pity on Gustios and merely put him in prison, where the king's sister fell in love with him and bore him a son named Mudarra. Meanwhile, Ruy Velázquez plotted an ambuscade with another Moorish king, so that when he sent the seven brothers and Nuño Rasura out to fight the Moors they were headed off at the pass by a far superior force and killed. The Moorish king sent Velázquez their eight heads, and he forwarded them to Gustios as a homecoming present. After 14 years, Mudarra came north to find his father and promised to avenge the deaths of his seven brothers. When Ruy Velázquez heard of Mudarra, he thumpingly declared, in Lockhart's translation of the Spanish Ballads:

Oh, in vain have I slaughter'd the Infants of Lara,
There's an heir in his halls – there's the bastard Mudara.
There's the son of the renegade – spawn of Mahoun:
If I meet with Mudara, my spear brings him down.

Of course it was Mudarra who brought down Velázquez instead. He then stoned and burned Doña Lambra at the stake for the bloody cucumber insult, and became lord of Salas. The parish church of Salas de los Infantes keeps the heads of the Seven Infantes and Nuño Rasura in a reliquary; their trunks are stored in the weird old tombs at San Millán de la Cogolla (*see* p.120).

East of Santo Domingo de Silos, **Salas de los Infantes** is named after the legend of the Siete Infantes de Lara, a favourite subject of Spanish ballad and romance (*see* box, left). There are some strange things around Salas, including a Visigothic hermitage covered with weird symbols on a hill just south of **Barbadillo del Mercado** (on the N234), under cliffs where you can see lammergeyers. East, in **Palacios de la Sierra**, the parish church has a collection of indecipherable Palaeochristian tombstones. **Jaramillo de la Fuente**, towards the Sierra de la Demanda, has a fine 12th-century Romanesque church.

Way Down South in Burgos Province

The A1 motorway south of Burgos to Madrid passes through **Lerma**, another town on the Arlanza river, founded by the son of Fernán González in 978. It owes its impressive appearance to the unusually successful Dukes of Lerma, one of whom (Francisco Gómez de Sandoval y Rojas) ruled Spain between 1598 and 1618 for Felipe III. It was the duke's idea to expel the *moriscos*, and devote a part of the proceeds from their expropriated property into making Lerma (effectively, the capital of Spain during his lifetime) a unique monumental complex, with at least six monasteries and a four-towered **Palacio Ducal**, recently converted into a luxurious *parador*. This is linked by a flying walkway (so the duke could attend mass without mingling with the commoners) to the **Colegiata de San Pedro**, bearing the duke's crest over the door. Inside, the church contains its original organ of 1616 and a statue in bronze of the archbishop of Seville, the uncle of the duke. The tourist office (*see* p.268) offers daily guided tours of the town.

Much further south, **Gumiel de Izán** has a fine 15th-century parish church with monumental stairs and a beautiful Renaissance *retablo* by an unknown master; the adjacent museum, open when the priest is around, has Romanesque capitals salvaged from its long-gone monastery. Gumiel marks the northern limits of DO Ribera del Duero, the largest and finest wine region in Castile, producing a variety of reds, especially from a local grape known as *tinto del país*; mixed with garnacha, malbec, merlot and cabernet sauvignon, it becomes a fresh rosé, a purplish young wine or a mellow well-aged wine; '99, 2001, 2004 and 2009 are excellent, and Vega Sicilia is the most illustrious name. **Aranda de Duero**, the third town of the province, has a number of old *bodegas* and a pair of good churches: Santa María has a beautiful portal attributed to Simón de Colonia and an excellent Renaissance *retablo*.

Downriver, the Augustinian **Monasterio de la Vid**, 'of the vine', boasts an 18th-century Baroque façade with spiraling leaves and roses on the sides of the elegant belfry and octagonal dome. East of Aranda, picturesque **Peñaranda de Duero** is built around the

Monasterio de la Vid

t 94 753 05 10; www. monasteriodelavid.org; guided tours all year Tues–Sat 10.30, 11.30, 12.30, Sun 11.30, 12.30; plus winter 4.30, 5.30, 6.30, summer 5, 6 and 7; closed Mon sprawling castle of its medieval lords, the Avellaneda, who in the safer 16th century decided to move down into the arcaded Plaza Mayor. A fine Plateresque portal marks their **Palacio de los Zúñiga y Avellaneda**, built around an elegant two-storey patio; rooms are adorned with superb *artesonado* ceilings and plasterwork. Around the corner, the 18th-century **Botica de Jimeno** is the oldest functioning pharmacy in Spain, and has been in the same family for eight generations; of its original fittings, there are some 230 pharmaceutical jars, stills and books.

North of Peñaranda, the half-ruined silhouette of a castle tops **Coruña del Conde**, where in the 18th century a local inventor named Diego Marín made the first manned flight in Spain. The equally isolated 11th-century **Ermita del Santo Cristo** is made out of stones cannibalized from the Roman city of **Clunia**, just north, near **Peñalba de Castro**. Founded under the reign of Augustus, it counted 30,000 inhabitants at its peak. In AD 69 Galba, governor of Nearer Spain, rose up here against Nero and was proclaimed emperor by his legionaries; the Senate concurred, leaving Nero to run himself through. He was the first ruler to come from outside the Julian and Claudian families, although he adopted the names Caesar and Augustus. Managing to displease nearly everybody by the time he got to Rome, he was brutally murdered the next year by Otho, his successor – another, more ominous precedent. Clunia was abandoned with the fall of Rome, leaving the forum, a large if eroded rock-cut theatre, baths, temples, and houses with mosaics dusty and mute.

Palacio de los Zúñiga y Avellaneda
open Tues–Sun 10–1.30 and 4–7; closed Mon

Clunia
t 94 739 12 50 *(only April–Sept); open summer Tues–Sun 11–2 and 4–8; winter Tues–Sun 11–2 and 3–5; closed Mon; adm*

ⓘ **Santo Domingo de Silos** >>
C/Cuatro Cantones 10, t 94 739 00 70; *open April–Oct*

ⓘ **Covarrubias** >
Monseñor Vargas s/n, t 94 740 64 61, *www.eco-varrubias.com; open Mar–Dec Tues–Sun, closed Mon*

★ **Doña Sancha** >

ⓘ **Lerma**
C/Audiencia 6, t 94 717 70 02, *www.citlerma.com*

Where to Stay and Eat Southeast of Burgos

Covarrubias ✉ 09346

***Nuevo Arlanza, Plaza de Doña Urraca 11, t 94 740 05 11, *www.hotelnuevoarlanza.com* (€€–€). Occupies a handsome old mansion in the town centre; its restaurant holds medieval banquets on Saturday nights with music and ancient Castilian dances; book ahead.

**Doña Sancha, Avda Victor Barbadillo 31, t 94 740 64 00, *www.hoteldonasancha.com* (€€–€). A welcoming rural hotel, built in traditional style. Every room has a balcony with lovely views.

Restaurante de Galo, C/Monseñor Vargas 10, t 94 740 63 93, *www.degalo.com* (€€). Atmospheric restaurant with medieval open chimney, serving typical Castilian fare. Try the house speciality: roast lamb.

Santo Domingo de Silos ✉ 09610

***Tres Coronas, Pza Mayor 6, t 94 739 00 47 (€€). In a charming 18th-century stone house, with 15 simple rooms. There's a classic restaurant which serves a filling *menú del día*.

***Santo Domingo de Silos, C/Santo Domingo 14, t 94 739 00 53 (€). Choose from the 3* hotel or the *hostal*; all rooms are flouncy in classic Spanish style, but those in the hotel are better equipped. The restaurant serves hearty Castilian classics and a good-value lunch menu.

Mesón Casa de Guzmán, Plaza Mayor 9, t 94 739 01 25, *www.mesoncasadeguzman.com* (€). Six simple rooms and an old-fashioned restaurant.

**Posada Villa de Silos, Plaza Mayor, 9, t 94 739 00 74, *www.posadavilladesilos.com* (€). Cosy, inexpensive rooms over a popular local restaurant.

Hospedería de Monasterio, t 94 739 00 49, *www.abadiadesilos.es/ hospederia.htm* (€). Men only can eat and sleep for a song (well, almost) in the monastery.

(i) Aranda de
Duero >
Plaza Mayor s/n,
t 94 751 04 76

Aranda de Duero ✉ 09400

Aranda gets plenty of business travellers en route to Madrid and concentrates its functional hotels near the highway; most have cheap weekend rates.

****Torremilanos**, Finca Torremilanos s/n, t 94 751 28 52, *www.torre milanos.com* (€€€€). A pastel-painted *bodega*-hotel set in its own gardens just outside the centre of town. Elegant bedrooms, and a fine restaurant featuring their own highly respected wines.

**Hotel Julia, San Gregorio 2, t 94 750 12 50, *www.hoteljulia.es* (€€). A modest, but conveniently central hotel, with comfy rooms and a decent old-fashioned restaurant.

Mesón de la Villa, C/La Sal 3, t 94 750 10 25 (€€). Serves some of the best food around, including a fine *lechal asado* (roast lamb), accompanied by the finest bottles of Rioja.

Rafael Corrales, C/Carrequemada 2, t 94 750 02 77 (€€). An *asador* that opened in 1902, serving lamb baked in a wood oven, washed down with Ribera del Duero. *Closed Thurs eve.*

West from Burgos along the Pilgrim Route

If the medieval pilgrim survived the storms, cut-throats and wolves at Roncesvalles, the Navarrese who exposed themselves when excited and the dupers and fleshpots of Burgos, then they faced the dustiest, flattest, hottest and most monotonous landscape in Europe. The idea is that, with nothing to look at, one becomes introspective and meditative, altogether in a proper state to receive enlightenment. On the other hand, its easy to escape the highway between Burgos and León, choosing paths and lonely back roads where 21st-century intrusions are rare; their straggling hamlets of humble adobe houses, church towers crowned with storks and huge dovecotes (pigeon was the only meat country folk could afford) evoke the Middle Ages as powerfully as any cathedral.

From Burgos to Frómista

After Burgos, the pilgrims' path goes straight to Castrojeriz, leaving the N120 in Tardajos; by car the first important stop is **Sasamón**, 33km west of the capital. This was the Celtiberian Segisamo, where Augustus camped with his Macedonian legions, en route to pummel the Cantabrians. The town's pride is its church of **Santa María la Real**, with an exact 12th-century copy of the Sarmental door on the cathedral of Burgos (*see* p.256); it has a good, if damaged, cloister and a statue of St Michael attributed to Diego de Siloé. The **Ermita de San Isidro Labrador** has a superb 16th-century cross, the Cruz del Humilladero. Of the third church, the 15th-century **San Miguel**, only the portal survives with its seven archivolts isolated in a field like a lost triumphal arch.

Getting along the Pilgrim Route West of Burgos

Daily **buses** run from Burgos to Aguilar de Campóo and Cervera de Pisuerga (twice a day on Thurs and Sat), to Palencia, Frómista, Sahagún, Saldaña and Carrión (on the Burgos–León route), to Sasamón and Grijalba. Frómista can also be reached by **train** on the Palencia–Santander line.

In nearby **Olmillos**, the stately 15th-century castle belonged to the Leví, a noble family of *conversos*; the current owner has converted it into a hotel (*see* p.272). A few kilometres northwest, at **Grijalba**, the 13th-century Gothic church of **Santa María de los Reyes** has plenty of gargoyles and carved capitals with New Testament themes; inside, the ribs of the vaults are painted with alligators with sharp teeth. The font is a pretty 12th-century work carved with interlacings, and supported by a lion and a serpent.

The main road, however, heads south of Tardajos, passing through the village of **Hornillos del Camino**, home to an old pilgims' hospital, the Espíritu Santo. After Hornillos the road passes through the haunting, ravaged remains of the 14th-century **Monasterio de San Antón**, its once-magnificent vaults hanging miraculously in the void. Its monks were famous for treating pilgrims afflicted with 'St Anthony's fire' or erysipelas, inflammations on the body, associated with leprosy. What really went on is a medieval mystery. The Order of St Anthony was founded in France in 1093, named after a 5th-century anchorite in the Egyptian desert, often depicted holding fire in his hands, symbolic of spiritual force and energy. His followers went about dressed in blue with the Greek **T** or *tau*, the cross of St Anthony, sewn on their habits, bearing a staff and bell; they would not only give passing pilgrims a meal but little *tau*-shaped amulets holding 'St Anthony's fire'. As St Anthony was also the patron of domestic animals (when not shown with fiery hands, he is accompanied by his pet pig), his monks kept pigs, or rather let them run wild, a practice that ended when one jaywalking porker in Paris tripped up the horse bearing the dauphin and caused him to break his neck.

West is the medieval castle and village of **Castrojeriz**, an old Iberian settlement that once had seven hospitals and a residence of Pedro the Cruel along its long Calle de los Peregrinos. In 974 Fernán González wrote down its privileges in a charter, giving equal rights to Christians and Jews. Its finest monument is at the village entrance: the Gothic church of **Santa María del Manzano**, named after the apple-tree trunk where its statue of the Virgin was found when Santiago, on his white horse, leapt from the castle to the tree; note the horseshoes on the door. Inside there are 16th-century tapestries and a *retablo* by Mengs; other tapestries, 17th-century and Flemish, are displayed in the parish museum of **Santo Domingo**; **San Juan**, built next to a 12th-century tower, conserves a half-ruined 14th-century cloister with an *artesonado mudéjar* ceiling. An 8km detour to the south leads to **Celada del Camino**, which recalls a former pilgrimage role in its name and in its late Romanesque church, with striking Gothic tombs. Closer to Castrojeriz, **Castrillo de Matajudíos** (apparently not 'Kill Jews' but 'Hill of Jews') was the birthplace of the great Spanish composer of the Renaissance, Antonio de Cabezón.

West of Castrojeriz the ruthless horizons of the *meseta* come into their own. The last hill for miles, the windswept **Alto de Mostelares** (2,950ft), looks over the Pisuerga river, the traditional frontier between Castile and León, although these days it just delimits the dotted line between Burgos and Palencia provinces. It is spanned by the handsome **Puente de Fitero** with 11 arches, built in the 11th century by pilgrimage-promoter Alfonso IV. Just before the bridge are the ruins of a 13th-century hospital of San Nicolás; just across it begins the Tierra de Campos, the high plains of the Visigoths. Little **Boadilla del Camino**, the first village (9km), has a beautiful 15th-century Gothic column in its *plaza*, decorated with scallops. The parish church has a curious Romanesque baptismal font on 12 baby columns and decorated with swastikas and solar symbols.

Frómista

Six kilometres west, Frómista has been a key pilgrims' stop since the days of the *Codex Calixtinus* for its 'perfect Romanesque church', golden **San Martín**, founded in 1035 by the widow of Sancho the Great. Restored in 1893 with no little controversy by the arch-restorer of France, Viollet-le-Duc, San Martín is now a national monument stripped of all its trappings. Two slender turrets buttress the west door; inside, the proportions of the three-aisled, three-apsed, barrel-vaulted interior crowned by an octagonal tower satisfy the soul, and delight every architect who has ever entered. But just as noteworthy is the extraordinary amount of sculpted detail inside and out, on the modillions and capitals; the original 11th-century carvings are superb and easy to distinguish from the fond fancies of the restorers, who based their work on medieval sarcophagi and marked their work with an R. The whole is a tantalising but ultimately inaccessible book of hundreds of medieval symbols and occult messages; a pair of binoculars comes in handy and a crick in the neck is probably unavoidable. The dedication to Martin, the 4th-century bishop of Tours, is also meaningful, for he was a strong defender of the Priscilianists when they were persecuted and their leader, Prisciliano, executed for heresy (*see* p.313); not that he supported their gnostic-Celtic beliefs as much as he fought the Church's use of civil means and persecutions to put down heresies. Of Frómista's other churches, note the 16th-century **Santa María del Castillo** with its elaborate

🐂 San Martín
open summer daily 10–2 and 4.30–8; winter daily 10–1.30 and 4–6; adm

11 Old Castile and León | West from Burgos along the Pilgrim Route: From Burgos to Frómista

Vestigia
*t 689 031 605,
www.vestigia.es; shows
May–mid-Oct Tues–Sat
12, 1 and 6, Sun 12 and 1;
mid-Oct–May Fri–Sat 12,
1, 5 and 6, Sun 12
and 1; adm*

painted Hispano-Flemish *retablo* with 29 panels. The church houses **Vestigia**, a lavish audiovisual exhibit describing the history of Frómista and its role in the Camino de Santiago.

Near Frómista, you can visit four sets of locks of the Castilian Canal, dug in the 18th and 19th century and the inspiration for Lesseps' rather bigger ditch in Panama.

West of Frómista

Beyond Frómista, the tawny little villages of Palencia merge into the tawny earth. **Villarmentero de Campos** has a delightful picnic ground, with a lawn for a siesta to prepare yourself for the next stop at **Villalcázar de Sirga**, once a thriving town and key Templar possession. The Knights, at the start of the 13th century, built the enormous church of **Santa María la Blanca** with what must be the tallest porch in Spain, to shelter a richly decorated double portal with a double frieze. Pilgrims made a beeline for the Capilla de Santiago and its miraculous Virgin (now a little the worse for wear), to whom Alfonso X the Wise dedicated his *Cantigas*, but modern visitors tend to head to the beautifully carved tombs sculpted by Antón Pérez de Carrión of the Infante Don Felipe (son of Ferdinand III the Saint) and his second wife, Leonor Ruiz de Castro, curiously gagged. Don Felipe, fifth of 14 children, was pursuing a meteoric ecclesiastical career and had just been made archbishop of Seville when he reversed course and married the Norwegian princess promised to his brother, the future Alfonso X. The princess died after four years and is buried in Covarrubias; Felipe soon remarried, but not long after, in 1271, was murdered by Alfonso, the next in line to the throne, who got away with it (no wonder he celebrated the Virgin's miracles). Here too is the tomb of a Knight Templar, with his hawk and sleeping lion: a rare burial, as most Templars were buried face-down in the earth without a casket. The magnificent *retablo mayor* was painted by the school of Berruguete.

**Santa María
la Blanca**
*open May–mid-Oct
daily 10.30–2 and 5–8;
mid-Oct–April Sat–Sun
12–2 and 4–6*

ⓘ **Frómista** ❯❯
*Paseo Central 11,
t 97 981 01 80,
www.fromista.com*

Where to Stay and Eat from Burgos to Fromista

Olmillos ✉ 09123

****Hotel Señorío de Olmillos**, Camino Santa Lucía s/n, Olmillos de Sasamón, t 94 737 40 09, *www.hotelolmillosdesasamon.com* (€€€€). Stay in a 15th-century castle built by Don Pedro de Cartagena, a converted Jew of Burgos, now transformed into a traditional hotel with a banquet hall-like restaurant.

Castrojeriz ✉ 34440

****Mesón de Castrojeriz**, C/Cordón 1, t 94 737 86 10 (€). This place offers a handful of rooms in a lovely old stone building with a peaceful setting. Simple traditional fare in the restaurant (€€).

Frómista ✉ 34440

***Hotel San Martín**, Plaza San Martín 7, t 97 981 00 00 (€). Modern, but built in traditional style, this is a friendly, central spot.

Fonda Marisa, Plaza de San Martín 3, t 97 981 00 23, *http://pensionmarisa*.

com (€). Costs even less and cooks up good menus.

Hostelería de Los Palmeros, Plaza San Telmo 4, **t** 97 981 00 67, *www.hosteria delospalmeros.com* (€€). Fine restaurant that began as a *hostal* for pilgrims, although the medieval décor has undergone several style changes since.

Villalcázar de Sirga ✉ 34440

There's limited accommodation here, besides a pilgrims' shelter behind the town hall and a couple of *casas rurales* nearby.

Hostal Infanta Doña Leonor, C/Condes de Toreno 1, **t** 97 988 80 48 , *www. hostalinfantaleonor.com*(€€–€). A delightful little *hostal* with café-bar. They also run the cosy **Las Cantigas** (€) geared towards pilgrims.

Mesón Los Templarios, Plaza Mayor, **t** 97 988 80 89 (€€–€). This charming former grainhouse offers Castilian favourites, including baked suckling pig with almonds.

North of Frómista: The Románico Palentino

If you've the time or inclination, you could wander off the beaten track into the northern part of Palencia province, into the foothills of the Cantabrian mountains, known as the Románico Palentino for its rare collection of some 200, mostly untouched, never remodelled Romanesque churches (nothing less than the greatest concentration in Europe). It seems that the masons who built churches along the *camino* came up here to build churches in the new villages, founded to repopulate the region. Aguilar de Campóo, linked by bus from Burgos or Palencia, or train from Santander, makes the best base, although you really need a car and patience, and that most elusive object of desire: a good map of Spain.

North to Aguilar

San Andrés de Arroyo
t 97 914 20 03, www. sanandresdearroyo.es; open for guided visits Tues–Sun 10–12.30 and 3.15–6; closed Mon; adm

Iglesia de San Juan
get the key from the warden across from the entrance

Northwest of **Alar del Rey** (just off the A67) you can easily see two of the finest Romanesque works in the region. **San Andrés de Arroyo** is a Bernardine convent founded in 1190 with an small, interesting museum; the chapterhouse entrance is beautiful and the cloister has extraordinary twin columns and capitals, decorated with fretwork, zigzags and exotic flora. The second church, the golden-stone **Iglesia de San Juan** at **Moarves de Ojeda**, has a superb portal, with a Christ in a mandorla, four Evangelists and 12 Apostles; the capitals are crowded with people and inside there's a 13th-century baptismal font and a Gothic Virgin and Child. Other prime stops on the Romanesque trail are north of Moarves: **Cozuelos**, with a simple early 12th-century church; **Vallespinoso de Aguilar**, home to a fortified 12th-century hermitage on a rock with a cylindrical tower and pretty door; and **Barrio de Santa María**, a handsome village where the **Ermita de Santa Eulalia** is a pristine example of a 13th-century church with a lovely apse, the narrowest windows in Spain and murals. Its parish church underwent a Renaissance remodelling and has good 15th-century paintings inside and a finely carved Renaissance *retablo mayor*. From Vallespinoso the road skirts the Aguilar reservoir to Aguilar de Campóo (*see* below).

Alternatively, if you stick to the N611, north of Alar del Rey, you'll find (just to the left) **Becerril del Carpio** with two Romanesque churches: one in Barrio de San Pedro with a fine portal; one in Barrio de Santa María, amid the Baroque mansions, where they had enough *pesetas* to remodel the church and give it some fancy *retablos*. In nearby **Santa María de Mave**, the monastery founded in 1208 has a fine portal, an octagonal lantern and some Renaissance murals in one of its three apses; the monastery building itself has been converted into a charming hotel (*see* opposite). The church in **Olleros de Pisuerga** to the west is some 300 years older, a rare example of a Spanish church carved into the living rock.

Aguilar de Campóo

Set in the green mountain valley of the Río Pisuerga and next to a large man-made lake, Aguilar de Campóo is a picturesque town of cookie-bakers and leaning medieval houses with big bold coats of arms, founded in the 10th century during the Reconquista resettlement scheme. The Aguilar, or eagle, of its name refers to its rocky limestone outcrop, its eagle's nest crowned by a ruined but still mighty five-towered **castle** built in the 11th century. At the foot of the castle, the **Hermitage of Santa Cecilia** was founded in 1041, and has a fine 12th-century tower and excellent capitals: one shows the Massacre of the Innocents, by 11th-century knights in fishscale armour. The town walls were built in the 1300s by Pedro I of Castile; one of the surviving six gates has an inscription in Hebrew and Spanish, a unique souvenir of Aguilar's once sizeable Jewish population. On the arcaded Plaza de España, Charles V once spent a week at the **Palacio de los Marqueses**; the Gothic **Colegiata de San Miguel** has the Renaissance mausoleum of the marquises of Aguilar and a **museum** full of tombs, *retablos* and sculptures. Another square is named after Aguilar sailor Juan Martín.

Colegiata museum
open June and 1st half Oct Fri–Sun 10.30–1.30 and 5–8; winter daily 12–1, other times call t *97 912 26 88*

Museo del Románico
open July–Aug daily 10.30–2 and 4–8; Sept–June Tues–Fri 4–7, Sat and Sun 10.30–2 and 4.30–7.30; adm

Two kilometres west of Aguilar, the Cistercian monastery of **Santa María la Real** (1213) has more excellent capitals and a good cloister; in 1988 it won a Europa Nostra award for its restoration and now shelters a **Museo del Románico**, with plenty of information on, and a unique collection of, models of the region's churches. Tradition has it that Bernardo de Carpio is buried in a cave nearby; offended by Charlemagne's invasion of Spain in the *Chanson de Roland*, Castilian troubadours invented Bernardo as their own hero, a doughty warrior who along with the Castilians joined up with the Saracens and personally slew Roland, the brutish Frank invader. But after the battle of Roncesvalles Bernardo was betrayed by his own king and joined the Moors for good.

Romanesque Routes North of Aguilar

The minor road directly north of Aguilar takes in more Romanesque charmers: the 12th-century church at **Matalbaniega**, with two decorated portals, carved modillions and caryatids. **Cillamayor**'s Romanesque church has a funerary hypogeum; at **Revilla de Santullán**, the church has a handsome portal with 15 figures, sitting at desks like members of the board, and other sculptures that verge on the pornographic. Further along, **Valberzoso's** church has 15th-century frescoes, and the village of **Brañosera** claims to be one of Spain's oldest municipalities, with its charter dating back to 824; its Romanesque church has a good 12th-century portal. **Salcedillo's** church also has a 12th-century portal; medieval **Villanueva de la Torre** has a 14th-century tower and church. **San Cebrián de Mudá**'s 12th-century church has Renaissance paintings and murals.

West of Aguilar, **Cervera de Pisuerga** was once an important frontier settlement, but has retired to its meadows and old family manors, proud of its elegantly restored 16th-century Gothic church, **Santa María del Castillo**

open Easter week and July–Sept daily 11–1.30 and 5–8; last 2 weeks June and first 2 weeks Oct Fri–Sun J11–1.30 and 5–8; rest of year call t 97 987 01 79; adm

Santa María del Castillo, built on the medieval citadel, with a fine Hispano-Flemish *retablo* by Felipe de Vigarni and a beautiful painting of the *Adoration of the Magi* by Juan de Flandres, both in the Capilla de Santa Ana.

Three kilometres away, by the **Ruesga** reservoir, there's a *parador* from which to enjoy the huge views across the mountains. At the northernmost point of Palencia province, **San Salvador de Cantamuda** is a graceful church with a pretty steeple and altar table. Southeast of Cervera de Pisuerga, **Perazancas de Ojeda** has a Romanesque parish church, and the 12th-century Lombard Romanesque hermitage of **San Pelayo** with contemporary murals.

11 · Old Castile and León | West from Burgos along the Pilgrim Route: The Románico Palentino

Where to Stay and Eat in the Románico Palentino

Aguilar de Campóo >
Pza de España 30, t 97 912 36 41, www. aguilardecampoo.com

Cervera de Pisuerga >>
Plaza Modesto Lafuente 1, t 97 987 06 95

Aguilar de Campóo ✉ 34800

***Valentin, Avda Generalísimo 21, t 97 912 21 25, *www.hotelvalentin.com* (€€). A classic mountain hotel with chintzy room and a good restaurant.

**Posada El Convento, in Santa María de Mave (12km from Aguilar de Campóo), t 97 912 36 11 (€€). Serene and part of a lovingly restored Benedictine monastery. Its restaurant (€€) is one of the best in the region.

Posada Santa María La Real, Avda de Cervera s/n, t 97 912 20 00, *www. posadasantamarialareal.com* (€€). Part of the 13th-century monastery

buildings now house this charming *posada*, with a lovely garden.

Cortés Poza, C/El Puente 39, t 97 912 30 55 (€€). Simple rooms and satisfying food awaits here: try the huge seafood stew for two.

**Villa de Aguilar, C/José Antonio 15, t 97 912 22 25 (€). For those on a tighter budget; all rooms with bath.

Cervera de Pisuerga ✉ 34840

***Parador de Cervera Pisuerga, Ctra de Resoba, t 97 987 00 75, *cervera@ paradors.es* (€€€). On the edge of the Picos, this modern place is a plush spot for nature-lovers.

**El Roble, General Mola 6, t 97 987 44 29, *www.hotelelroble.com* (€€). Stylish, modern hotel with well decorated rooms and a bright café-bar.

Along the Carrión River

West of Frómista, into the *campos góticos*, the Visigothic plains, the pilgrims' route continues to Carrión de los Condes, which occupies one of Old Castile's chief north–south arteries. Palencia and environs were more important in Roman and Visigothic times than now; among the things to see are two Roman villas and Spain's oldest dated church.

Back on the Pilgrim Track: Carrión de los Condes

West of Villalcázar de Sirga, Carrión de los Condes is named after the River Carrión and not for putrefying nobility, although it can't be denied that the Infantes or Counts of Carrión, who married the Cid's two daughters, were genuinely rotten villains; after picking up their big, glittering dowries, they beat their wives and tied them to oaks and left them for dead. The outraged Cid gathered up a posse, killed the counts, and found his daughters new, even more princely husbands. The wicked Infantes are buried in the lovely Renaissance cloister of **San Zoilo**, a Benedictine monastery that now also contains a luxury hotel by the river, founded in 1047 when the Emir of Córdoba sent the 4th-century relics of Zoilo to the Count of Carrión. The lower gallery of the cloister is the work of Juan de Badajoz, who began in 1537; the upper was added in 1604.

Over the 16th-century bridge from San Zoilo, the heart of Carrión has two worn 12th-century Romanesque churches that preserve interesting portals. **Santiago**, in the Plaza Mayor, has a fine Christ in Majesty and apostles and representatives of 22 medieval guilds, including an armourer, scholar, musicians, cooks, tailor, smith, soldiers bashing each other, and contortionists. On the edge of town, **Santa María del Camino** has a capital on the portal depicting the Tribute of 100 Maidens that the Castilians sent yearly to the Moors (probably because they had nothing else the Moors could possibly want); other figures are of Samson fighting the lion and women riding beasts. The interior is out of kilter, although whether it was done so intentionally (like Getaria, *see* pp.151–2) is hard to discern; it could just be falling over. Lastly, the **Convent of Santa Clara** has a small museum, with religious art and a 17th-century organ. During the great days of the pilgrimage, the town produced two men of genius: Rabbi Shem Tov Ardutiel (Sem Tob), author of the *Danza General de la Muerte*, who died in 1370, and Íñigo López de Mendoza, the Marqués de Santillana, the Renaissance poet, not to be confused with the tycoon who bought the title (*see* p.203). Lastly, just off the road before the province of León, you can visit the 3rd-century AD **Roman villa** at **Quintanilla de la Cueza** for its colourful mosaic floors and the heating system or hypocausts, protected by a shelter; there's a small museum on the site.

San Zoilo
visiting times April–mid-Oct daily 10.30–2 and 4.30–8; mid-Oct–Mar Tues–Sun 10.30–2 and 4.30–7; now also contains a luxury hotel, see p.279

Santiago
open summer daily 11–1.30 and 5–7.30; other times of the year call t 97 988 00 72

Convent of Santa Clara and Museum
t 97 988 08 37; open Mar–Oct Tues–Sun 11–1.30 and 5–7.30; Nov–Feb Tues–Sun 11–1.30 and 4.30–7; adm

Roman villa
open April–Sept Tues–Sun 10–2 and 5–8; Mar and Oct Tues–Sun 10.30–1.30 and 4–6; closed Nov–Feb; adm

Getting along the Carrión River

There are frequent **trains** between Palencia and Burgos, Valladolid, Ávila, Madrid and Santander (via Frómista and Aguilar de Campóo); trains to León call at Paredes de Nava. Palencia's RENFE station is at Plaza de los Jardinillos, **t** 902 320 320, *www.renfe.com*.

Carrión de los Condes is connected by **bus** with Frómista and Palencia; there are at least two buses a day. Palencia's bus station is next to the train station, on Plaza de los Jardinillos, **t** 97 974 32 22.

South along the Carrión to Palencia

Paredes de Nava was the birthplace of two influential Castilian artists, painter Pedro Berruguete (d.1504), who worked in Urbino and introduced the Renaissance style to Spain as court painter to Ferdinand and Isabel, and his son Alonso (d. 1561), a pupil of Michelangelo, who brought Mannerism back with him and served as court painter to Charles V, although sculpture was his real love.

A few of the Berruguetes' paintings, including a *retablo mayor* by Pedro, remain in **Santa Eulalia**. The adjacent **museum** has an impressive collection of works by other Renaissance masters (Gil de Siloé, Juan de Valmaseda, Juan de Flandres, Juan de Juni, among others) brought in from little churches in artsy Paredes de Nava. You'll find more paintings by Pedro Berruguete inside the church of **Santa María** in **Becerril de Campos**, 10km south.

Santa Eulalia
t 97 983 04 69; open July–Sept Tues–Sun 11–1.30 and 5–8; Oct–June Fri–Sun 11–1.30 and 5–6

Santa María
t 97 983 40 88; open Mon–Sat 11.30–1.30 and 5–8, Sun 11–1.30 and 5–8

Palencia

Once a thriving centre, Palencia remains one of the bigger wallflowers in the garden of Spain's provincial capitals; in 1185 Alfonso VIII made it the site of Spain's first university, though in 1239 it was removed to Salamanca. Charles V is partly responsible for Palencia's failure to thrive in later centuries, having not only sucked the city dry to pay the bribes he gave to be elected as Holy Roman Emperor, but also rubbed out the city's prospects and privileges in revenge for its leading role in the Comunero revolt.

The one thing they couldn't take away from Palencia is its Gothic **cathedral**, nicknamed *La Bella Desconocida* ('The Unknown Beauty'), in Plaza San Antolín. The exterior is magnificent; don't miss the gargoyles. Juan de Flandres' Renaissance *retablo mayor* is the prize in an interior that has remained more or less unchanged – a lack of Baroque curlicues and rolling eyeballs is a telltale sign of decline in a Spanish town. The oldest part of the crypt (673) is the only known surviving example of a Visigothic martyrium, built by King Wamba before he was shuttled off to a monastery (in the 7th century, the Visigothic kings lived in nearby Pampliega, a little village that time forgot). The clock in the transept has a lion and knight. Among the highlights of the **Museo Diocesano**, across the square in the Palacio Episcopal, are an early *San Sebastián* by El Greco and a fine *Virgin and Child* by Pedro Berruguete.

Palencia cathedral
open daily 9–2 and 4–8; adm to crypt and museum

Museo Diocesano
C/ General Mola o Mayor Antigua 34, t 97 974 59 00; open Mon–Sat 10.30–12.30, afternoon visits by prior arrangement; adm

The bridge over the Carrión, the **Puentecillas**, is contemporary with the cathedral; 11th-century **San Miguel**, further south, is a fine little ogival Romanesque church, where the Cid married his Ximena. Around the corner, the **Museo de Palencia** occupies the 16th-century Casa del Cordón, containing archaeological souvenirs of Palencia's illustrious past. There are also some well-preserved mosaics.

Museo de Palencia
*t 97 975 23 28;
open Tues–Sun 10–2
and 4.30–8.30,
Sun 10.30–2.30;
closed Mon; adm*

East of Calle Mayor, the 16th-century **Santa Clara** has a famous Cristo Yacente that elicited the comment from the ultra-pious Felipe II: 'If I had faith, I would believe that this was the real body of Christ.' Nearby, the 13th-century **Convento de San Francisco** has a magnificent *mudéjar* coffered ceiling in the sacristy.

Ten kilometres south of Palencia in the village of **Baños de Cerrato** (2km from Venta de Baños), the Visigothic King Recesvinto (he of the famous golden crown with dangling letters spelling his name) founded its own **Iglesia de San Juan Bautista** back in 661, the purest extant example of Visigothic architecture. Fretwork windows like impossible key holes and a carved doorway (and a belfry, added by restorers) relieve the simple stone exterior. Inside, the nave is divided by rows of horseshoe arches, and the capitals, the doorways and the apse are decorated with finely carved eight-pointed crosses (*croix pattées*), leaves, scallop shells, solar spirals and palms. Recesvinto's rather complex dedicatory inscription survives on the triumphal arch. In its use of pleasing, robust architectural volumes and the concentration of intricate detail in a few places, San Juan has been called 'the first Spanish church'. Recent excavations uncovered 58 7th-century tombs and the original plan of the church, with its three apses standing out separately like prongs on a fork; in the Middle Ages it was converted into a more ordinary rectangle. The Baños of its name refers to a nearby curative spring, closed in by two Visigothic arches and restored in 1941.

North of Carrión de los Condes: Saldaña and a Roman Villa

From Carrión de los Condes, the CL615 follows the River Carrión up to **Renedo de la Vega** and the ruins of the monastery of **Santa María de la Vega**, a *mudéjar* work of 1215; the parish church has a fine Renaissance cross.

Villa of Olmeda
*t 97 911 99 97; www.
villaromanalaolmeda.
com; open Tues–Sun
10.30–6.30; closed Mon;
adm, free Tues pm;
includes adm to
Saldaña museum*

Further north, towards Lobera, a sign points the way to **Pedrosa de la Vega** (1.5km), where the 3rd–4th-century Roman **Villa of Olmeda** was discovered in 1968 with its perfectly preserved polychrome mosaic floors, including not only geometric designs, but also mythological and hunting scenes. Nearby, in the pretty medieval village of **Saldaña**, the church of **San Pedro** houses finds from the ongoing excavations.

Where to Stay and Eat along the Carrión River

ⓘ **Carrión de los Condes >**

*Plaza Santa María,
t 97 988 09 32; open
weekends only May and
June, daily July, August
and Easter week*

★ **Estrella del Bajo Carrión >**

ⓘ **Palencia >**
*provincial office:
Plaza Abilio Calderón
s/n, t 97 971 51 30*

*municipal office:
C/Mayor 105,
t 97 974 00 68*

Carrión de los Condes ✉ 34120

***San Zoilo**, C/Obispo Souto, t 97 988 00 49, *www.sanzoilo.com* (€€€–€€). Monastery (*see* p.276) with attractive rooms (the nicest are in the original building) and a decent restaurant.

****Estrella del Bajo Carrión**, Ctra Palencia-Riaño, Km 29 (south of Carrión in Villoldo), t 97 982 70 05, *www.estrellabajocarrion.com* (€€). A gracious country hotel with a garden and excellent restaurant (€€€).

***Hs La Corte**, C/Santa María 34, t 97 988 01 38, *www.hostallacorte.com* (€). Rooms with or without bath along with an inexpensive restaurant.

Convento de Santa Clara, C/Sta Clara 1, t 97 988 0134 (€). Austere convent rooms with baths: an extension is planned for 2013.

Palencia ✉ 34000

****Rey Sancho de Castilla**, Avenida Ponce de León, t 97 972 53 00, *www.*

reysancho.com (€€€). Modern hotel with a pool and garden.

*****Palencia**, Avda de Cuba 25, t 97 916 57 01, *www.ac-hotels.com* (€€€). Stylish, modern hotel on the outskirts of town.

***Castilla Vieja**, Avda Casado del Alisal 26, t 97 974 90 44, *www.hotel husacastillavieja.com* (€€€). A reliable modern chain hotel, with good online deals.

Asador La Encina, C/Casañé 2, t 97 971 09 36, *www.asadorlaencina.com*(€€). Traditional Castilian dishes such as suckling pig, hearty stews, wild mushrooms plus fish. Their tortilla has been awarded the prize for the best in Spain. *Closed Sun eve and 1st 2 weeks Aug.*

La Fragata, C/Pedro Fernández del Pulgar 4–6, t 97 974 95 91 (€€–€). Delicious, affordable contemporary cuisine in a slick modern restaurant in an old building.

Bar Aparicio, C/Gaspar Arroyo 6, t 97 974 12 39 (€). Local favourite; good range of tapas and *raciones*.

Saldaña's ruined 11th-century castle was the residence of Doña Urraca, sister and advisor of Alfonso VI; the 15th-century Gothic **San Miguel** has a *retablo* attributed to Gil de Siloé and effigy tombs of the Counts of Saldaña. The holy of holies in these parts is an 8th-century statue of the Virgin in the **Ermita de la Virgen del Valle**.

West to León

The Camino de Santiago continues its flat way towards León, imperceptibly rising as it crosses 236km of the largest province in Castile. Framed by the Cordillera Cantábrica to the north and the lower, softer Montes de León to the west, the province was a refuge for Mozarabs from Andalucía in the first days of the Reconquista, and what remains of their monasteries are among the finest monuments along the whole road.

Sahagún and its *Mudéjar* Bricks

Sahagún started out as the site of a Roman villa and an early Christian basilica dedicated to San Facundo, a martyred legionary. During the 12th century, when it was the seventh official stop of the *Codex Calixtinus*, it had a population of 12,000 and artificially concentrated so much wealth in the middle of nowhere that it subsequently earned the nickname 'the Las Vegas of the Middle

Getting to Sagahún

Sahagún is reached by **trains** between Palencia and León and by **buses** between León and Carrión.

Ages'. Today a mere 2,800 souls try to fill up the dusty Plaza Mayor, the darkened old porticoes and forlorn houses.

Sahagún's rise and fall went hand in hand with that of Spain's most powerful Benedictine abbey, San Benito. In 904, the old Roman road had just begun its transformation into the pilgrims' way when the site was purchased by Alfonso III the Great of Asturias for a community of Mozarab refugees from Andalucía. Although it was twice burned by the Moors, the seeds of its future glory were sown in the 11th century when Sancho III of Castile snatched León, the inheritance of his brother Alfonso, and locked Alfonso up in the abbey. He was about to tear out Alfonso's eyes for good measure when their sister Urraca intervened. Urraca managed to save his eyes by promising nasty Sancho to become a nun. With both siblings locked away, Sancho felt safe on the throne. But Alfonso made a secret pact with the abbot of San Benito, who helped him escape and take refuge with the Moors in Toledo.

In 1072 Sancho was assassinated and Alfonso was crowned king of Castile and León. Like Henry VIII, Alfonso VI married his way through six wives; those from Aquitaine and Burgundy put him into contact with Cluny – the great promoter of the Santiago pilgrimage. Never forgetting the help he received at Sahagún, the king refounded San Benito in 1080 under the new Cluniac reforms and made his personal confessor, Bernard de Sédirac (the future primate of Spain), its first abbot. Alfonso poured money into the abbey, gave it vast estates and founded a huge pilgrims' hospital. In its heyday San Benito even minted its own coins; in 1534 its theological school had the status of a university. Philip II brought it low by moving the school to Navarra's Monasterio de Irache in 1596 and constraining the abbey to pay nearly all its rents to the crown.

In the 18th century two fires finished off what remained, leaving only a 17th-century portal by Felipe Berrojo, now a decorative city gate at the west end of town, an ungainly clock tower and the adjacent ruins of the 12th-century Gothic **Capilla de San Mancio** with its brick arches. Smaller bits of San Benito are in the **Monasterio de las Madres Benedictinas de Sahagún**: the tombs of Alfonso VI and some of his wives are in the church, and the museum contains the great silver custodia by master Enrique de Arfe. They also run a pilgrims' *hostal*.

What Sahagún never had was a ready supply of building stone, which led the craftsmen who immigrated here from the Moorish lands to develop an architecture in brick, a medium that permitted new decorative patterns and delicacy. The first example, **San Tirso**,

Monasterio de las Madres Benedictinas de Sahagún
t 98 778 00 78, www. monasteriosantacruz. com; open Tues–Sat for visits at 10, 11, 12, 4 and 5, Sun 10, 11 and 12; closed Mon; adm

was built near the monastery in the first decade of the 12th century, with its squat, tapering skyscraper tower rising out of three round apses; restoration work unearthed two sculpted Mozarab imposts with floral reliefs from the original monastery. **San Lorenzo** is just a little later and more obviously Moorish in design, but has suffered more changes over time, its interior redone in the 18th century (the chapel has Renaissance reliefs by Juan de Juni); both churches have porticoes along their sides for the famous markets Sahagún held in its boom period. In 1259 the Franciscans founded another monastery and the recently restored **Santuario de La Peregrina**, just outside the town, the third and latest *mudéjar* church, applying the new brick techniques to Gothic; inside, bits of original stucco work survive.

Near the medieval bridge that crosses the Río Cea stands a grove of poplars. According to the *Codex Calixtinus*, these are the lances of Charlemagne's paladins who, awaiting battle with the Moor Aigolando, planted them in the ground before going to sleep. Overnight some of the lances took root and flowered, a sign of impending martyrdom. Thinking to spare the men whose lances had taken root, Charlemagne let them stay in camp when he went off to fight the Moors. But when he returned, victorious, he found that all the men he had left behind had been massacred by a Moorish raiding party.

Five kilometres south, on the Cea's bank, two sisters founded **San Pedro de las Dueñas** in the 10th century, which has a Renaissance crucifix by Gregorio Fernández and 18 top-notch Romanesque capitals from the church's 1109 rebuilding, begun in stone and continued in brick by *mudéjar* craftsmen. Another road from Sahagún, the CL611, leads in 7km to the mighty, well-preserved 16th-century castle (private) at **Grajal de Campos**.

San Miguel de Escalada

After Sahagún the pedestrian *camino* parts from the highway, to meet again at **Mansilla de las Mulas** on the River Esla, which has preserved only the atmospheric ruins of its 12th-century walls, monasteries and *hostales*. Nearby, between Villamoros and Villasbariego, **Lancia** started out as an *oppidum* (fortified settlement) of the Astures; in 25 BC they were soundly defeated by the Romans after a fierce resistance: a few ruins remain and to this day farmers uncover antiquities in the surrounding fields.

This was the new frontier back in the early days of the Reconquista, when the kings of Oviedo had just added León to their title. Among the first pioneers on the scene were Abad Adefonso and his companions, refugees from Córdoba, who in 913 founded the beautiful church of **San Miguel de Escalada**. The site, a gentle hill overlooking a valley, previously had a Palaeochristian

San Miguel de Escalada
open April–Sept Tues–Sun 10–2 and 4–8; Oct–Mar Tues–Sun 10.40–2 and 4–5.50; closed Mon; donations gratefully accepted

11

Old Castile and León | West from Burgos along the Pilgrim Route: West to León church dedicated to the archangel. A lovely portico of horseshoe arches, an *ajímez* window and a heavy 11th-century tower mark the exterior, while the interior is proof in golden limestone that the Cordobans never forgot the classic symmetrical Roman basilica form and its proportions. Delicate horseshoe arches divide the three aisles, and separate the transept and triple apse from the main body of the basilica (like the Byzantines, the Mozarab liturgy called for a screen between the holy precinct and the parishioners). The capitals have simple palmette designs; luxuriant floral and geometric reliefs with lions and peacocks eating grapes decorate the chancels and friezes, and over the door you can make out the highly elaborate if faint dedicatory inscription. The ceiling, a later *mudéjar* addition, bears the arms of León and Castile.

Valencia de Don Juan

Southwest of Mansilla, **Valencia de Don Juan** was named after its first duke, son of Alfonso the Wise, and is worth a detour for a theatrical 15th-century **castle** that rises from the banks of the Río Esla and is featured on all León's tourist brochures, with its massive walls (on one side only, like a stage set) broken by a series of turrets and crenellations.

The surrounding Esla *vega* is one of the most fertile swaths of the province, producer of Valdevimbre-Los Oteros, a light, fruity rosé wine with an orangeish rose colour, fermented in curious bunker-like *bodegas*. Its gentle sparkle comes from a technique called *madreo*. Only small quantities are produced; hunt down a bottle in Valencia de Don Juan or Villamañán to the west.

Where to Stay and Eat West to León

(i) **Valencia de Don Juan >>**
Avda Carlos Pinilla,
t 98 775 07 01,
www.aytovalenciade
donjuan.org; open
July–Sept only

(★) **Hostal El Palacio >>**

Sahagún ✉ 24320
El Jardín de la Huerta, Galleguillos, 5km south of Sahagún, **t 98 778 02 76, *www.eljardindelahuerta.es* (€€–€). This farmhouse has rustic rooms, a restaurant, a covered pool (*summer only*), garden, billiards, and mini-golf. Fishing and birding along the river.
Hostal La Codorniz, Avda Constitución 97, **t 98 778 02 76, *www.hostallacodorniz.com* (€€–€). A classic Spanish *hostal*, with plain rooms above a simple restaurant.
Hostal El Ruedo II, Plaza Mayor 1, **t** 98 778 18 34, *www.restauranteelruedo. com* (€€–€). Double rooms decorated in pastel colours above a restaurant. The *menú del día* is a bargain.

*Hospedería Monástica, C/Mayor 12, **t** 98 778 01 50 (€). In summer, the Benedictine nuns at San Pedro de las Dueñas (5km from Sahagún) offer tasty meals at this place over the weekends. Reserve in advance.

Valencia de Don Juan ✉ 24200
Hostal El Palacio, C/Palacio 3, **t 98 775 04 74, *www.hostalelpalacio.com* (€). This charming inn, decorated with antiques and a document saying that King Philip III once slept here (in the bed of the missus) is the oldest house in town. Run by Asturians, it also has an excellent *sidrería* serving good home cooking.
Villegas II, C/Palacio 17, **t 98 775 01 61 (€€). Family hotel with just five rooms and a garden, in the centre of town.

León

⭐ León

León tuvo veintecuatro reyes antes que Castilla leyes

(León had 24 kings before Castile even had laws)

Radiant under the famous spires of its cathedral, León is a singularly happy city of clean boulevards shaded by horse-chestnut trees – one of the few places in Spain to achieve *urbanización* with grace and elegance. Part of the credit for this must go to its hyperactive City Hall (Ayuntamiento), which blankets the city with posters depicting itself as a friendly lion, advising the Leonese to ride the bus, recycle their glass and not blaspheme in front of children. The founding of a university has given the old city a transfusion of young blood and keeps the bars full.

History

Although the lion has long been the city's symbol, its name actually comes from Legio Septima Gemina, the Roman Seventh Legion, established here in AD 68 when Galba built a fort to guard the plain and the Roman road from Zaragoza. Reconquered from the Moors in the 850s by Ordoño I of Asturias (850–66), León changed hands several times more before King Ordoño II (914–24) moved his capital here. Even then, factionalism in the royal family left the city weak and prey to Moorish re-reconquests; in 981 al-Mansur grabbed it and his son reoccupied it from 996 until Alfonso V's victory at the Battle of Calatañazor in 1002. After this last Moorish hurrah, León, rebuilt and refortified, reconquered Castile. But just as León eclipsed Asturias, Castile – first a county, then a separate kingdom – eclipsed León. In 1252, under Ferdinand III 'el Santo', the on-again, off-again union of the two kingdoms was finalized. Castile never looked back, but for León, then one of the largest cities in Spain, the marriage spelt nothing but decline and marginalization: the nobles went off to the court in Burgos and the people left to settle the new frontiers gained by the Reconquista.

Into this vacuum of power and influence stepped the Church: the pilgrims' road became the chief source of income. Medieval pilgrims eagerly looked forward to León, with its Hilton of a *hostal*, where they could shake the dust off their wide-brimmed hats and catch their breath for the last leg of their journey. Broken and crushed during the Comunero revolt against Charles V, León sank into oblivion until the invention of the railway made its mines viable once again. These in turn declined, leaving León its share of modern autonomy atavists who, remembering the good old days of the 10th and 11th centuries, preach '*León sin Castilla*' ('León without Castile'). As yet their movement has little support.

León cathedral
www.catedraldeleon.org; open July–Sept Mon–Sat 8.30–1.30 and 4–8, Sun 8.30–2 and 5–8; Oct–June Mon–Sat 8.30–1.30 and 4–7, Sun 8.30–2.30 and 5–7

The Cathedral

The Spaniards call this the most splendid articulation of French Gothic in Spain *La Pulchra Leonina* ('Belle of León'), a cathedral so remarkable that it would stand out even in France for its daring

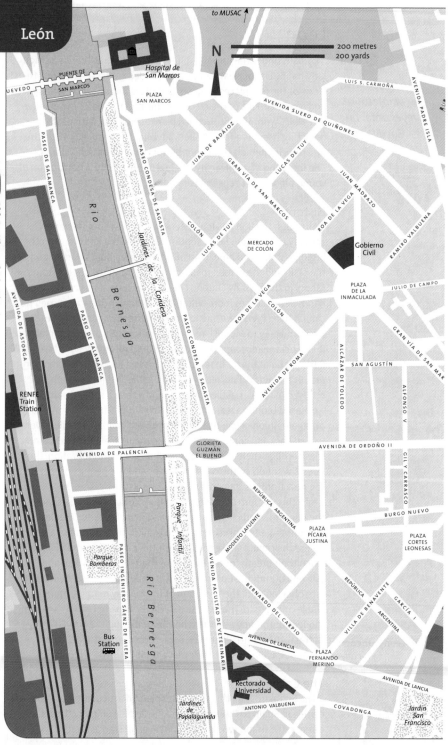

to MUSAC

N

200 metres
200 yards

UEVEDO

PUENTE DE
SAN MARCOS

Hospital de
San Marcos

PLAZA
SAN MARCOS

LUIS S. CARMOÑA

AVENIDA PADRE ISLA

AVENIDA SUERO DE QUIÑONES

PASEO DE SALAMANCA

R í o

Jardines de la Condesa

PASEO CONDESA DE SAGASTA

JUAN DE BADAJOZ

GRAN VÍA DE SAN MARCOS

LUCAS DE TUY

JUAN MADRAZO

RAMIRO VALBUENA

COLÓN

LUCAS DE TUY

LUCAS DE TUY

ROA DE LA VEGA

MERCADO
DE COLÓN

Gobierno
Civil

PLAZA
DE LA
INMACULADA

JULIO DE CAMPO

B e r n e s g a

PASEO DE SALAMANCA

PASEO CONDESA DE SAGASTA

ROA DE LA VEGA

COLÓN

AVENIDA DE ROMA

ALCÁZAR DE TOLEDO

SAN AGUSTÍN

GRAN VÍA DE SAN MAR

ALFONSO V

AVENIDA DE ASTORGA

RENFE
Train
Station

AVENIDA DE PALENCIA

GLORIETA
GUZMÁN
EL BUENO

AVENIDA DE ORDOÑO II

GIL Y CARRASCO

Parque
Infantil

REPÚBLICA ARGENTINA

MODESTO LAFUENTE

PLAZA
PÍCARA
JUSTINA

BURGO NUEVO

PLAZA
CORTES
LEONESAS

Parque
Bomberos

PASEO INGENIERO SÁENZ DE MIERA

R i o   B e r n e s g a

AVENIDA FACULTAD DE VETERINARIA

BERNARDO DEL CARPIO

REPÚBLICA

VILLA DE BENAVENTE

ARGENTINA

GARCÍA I

Bus
Station

AVENIDA DE LANCIA

PLAZA
FERNANDO
MERINO

AVENIDA DE LANCIA

Rectorado
Universidad

Jardines
de
Papalaguinda

ANTONIO VALBUENA

COVADONGA

Jardín
San
Francisco

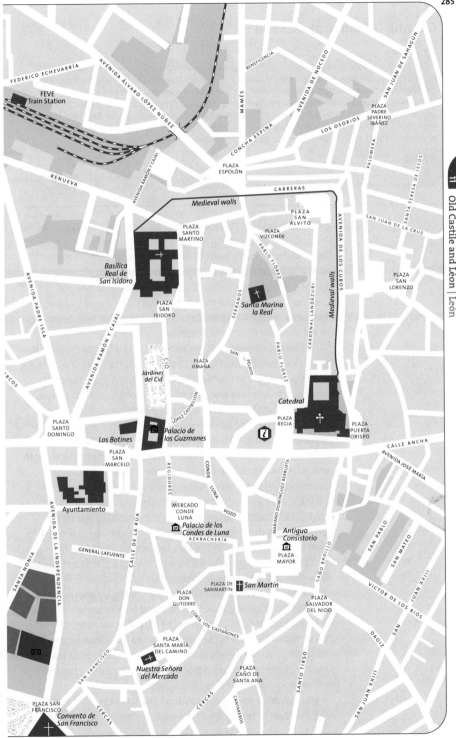

Getting to and around Léon

By Train

The RENFE station is at Avda de Astorga 11 (**t** 902 320 320, *www.renfe.com*). There are frequent trains to Burgos, Palencia, Medina del Campo, Madrid, Astorga, Ponferrada, Ourense and Lugo; regular trains depart for Oviedo and Gijón, travelling through magnificent mountain scenery and some 500 tunnels.

The **Transcantábrico** makes the journey to Santiago de Compostela from April to November. It's a 7-day trip, which costs from €2,400. Info at *www.eltranscantabricoclasico.com*. There are also daily FEVE trains from León to Bilbao (journey time 7½ hrs), which take in the scenery of the Picos de Europa. More information from the FEVE station, Avda Padre Isla 48, **t** 98 727 12 10, *www.feve.es*.

By Bus

Buses (**t** 98 721 10 00) depart from the bus terminal just south of the RENFE station, on Paseo Ingeniero Sáenz de Miera, for the villages in the province and for Oviedo, Burgos, Santander, Salamanca and Madrid.

---

and superb walls of stained glass. A similar amount of glass caused Beauvais, its closest rival in window-acreage, to collapse, a disaster León has managed to avert so far by increasing support to the walls and maintaining a continual campaign to keep it vertical in the face of subsidence; expect some scaffolding. Although Calahorra in La Rioja claims the most storks' nests, León comes in a close second with some 100 families, to the extent that droppings on the stone have become a problem.

The first church was built by Ordoño II, who donated part of his estates for the construction of Santa María de la Regla. It was twice destroyed before 1204, when Alfonso IX began a new church of warm golden stone in unheard-of dimensions, modelled on the soaring Gothic cathedrals of Chartres and Reims. His successor, Ferdinand III, worried by the expense, tried to limit its size, but the Leonese responded by putting up their own money for the construction. The cathedral was more or less completed by the 15th century – the date of the openwork tower of the west façade by Joosken van Utrecht, linked rather oddly to the main body of the cathedral with visible buttresses. Outstanding 13th-century sculptures decorate the north, south, and especially the **west portal** with its three finely carved tympana – the one in the centre illustrates a lively scene of the Last Judgement, the devils boiling the sinners. In between the doors, a pillar with a statue of Solomon was where the king or his representative sat in judgement.

The exterior, however, pales before the soaring **interior**, stripped of its Baroque frosting, leaving it bare and breathtaking, especially when the sun streams in, igniting the 19,400 square feet of vivid greens, reds and golds of the richest stained glass imaginable. The oldest glass, in the chapels around the apse and the great rose window of the 12 Apostles, dates from the 13th century; the latest is 19th-century and made by Spanish artists.

If you can draw your eyes away from the soaring walls of glass, note the **choir** in the centre of the nave, set behind an ornate triumphal arch of a façade and embellished with 15th-century alabaster carvings by Juan de Badajoz the elder; its midsection of glass was added fairly recently so you can see straight through to the altar, swimming in reflections of the windows. The *retablo mayor* contains an excellent Renaissance painting *Christ's Burial* by Nicolás Francés. The chapels in the ambulatory house beautiful Gothic tombs, and there's an altar to Nuestra Señora del Dado, at which a disgruntled gambler allegedly once flung his dice, hitting the Christ Child on the nose and making it bleed.

Cathedral museum and cloister
open July–Sept Mon–Fri 9.30–2 and 4–7.30, Sat 9.30–2 and 4–7; Oct–June Mon–Fri 9.30–1.30 and 4–7, Sat 9.30–1.30; adm

Through the Plateresque Puerta del Dado, the **cathedral museum and cloister** has one of the largest collections of Romanesque Virgin Marys in Europe, as well as a *Crucifixion* by Juan de Juni and a Mozarabic Bible. The cloister was damaged in the 14th century and reworked with classical motifs by Juan de Badajoz the elder.

Around the Cathedral: The Barrio Húmedo

Alongside the cathedral run León's **walls**, built by Alfonso XI in 1324 over the Roman and early medieval fortifications; nearly half of the original 80 bastions remain intact. To the east extend the narrow lanes of the old town, where so many Leonese come to wet their whistles that everyone calls it the **Barrio Húmedo**, the 'Humid Quarter'. The elegant **Old Consistorio** (1677) presides in the arcaded **Plaza Mayor**, where Roman walls have been unearthed. A tower here belonged to the Ponce family, one of whom went to Florida seeking the Fountain of Youth; the adjacent **Plaza de San Martín** is the most humid corner of the humid quarter. By the market in Regidores, another famous family, the Quiñoneses, had their 14th-century **Palace of the Condes de Luna**, of which only the tower and

Nuestra Señora del Mercado
t 98 725 11 59; open summer daily 7.30am–8.30pm; winter daily 11–12 and 7–8

façade remain. The best church is Romanesque **Nuestra Señora del Mercado** in the serene and lovely Plaza Santa María del Camino.

From the cathedral, busy Calle Ancha (the old Roman *decumanus*) leads up to Plaza de Botines and Plaza San Marcelo, where you suddenly come upon **Los Botines** ('The Spats'), León's version of Sleeping Beauty's castle. Antoni Gaudí's most conventional work, it was built in 1891 – 'in a moment of doubt', according to one of his

Palacio de los Guzmanes
now the provincial Diputación, open July–Sept daily 10–2 and 4–8; Oct–June Mon–Fri 9–2.30 and 4.30–6.30

biographers – as a private residence, with turrets, swirling Gaudí-esque ironwork and a statue of St George (patron of Gaudí's native Catalunya) overhanging the door, where, by the look on the dragon's face, the saint is scratching him in just the right spot.

Two fine Renaissance palaces (and two incongruous modern sculptures) share the *plazas*: the arcaded **Ayuntamiento** and the **Palacio de los Guzmanes**, with a sumptuous façade designed by

Museo de León
www.museodeleon. com; open Tues–Sat 10–2 and 4–7, Sun 10–2; closed Mon; adm

Rodrigo de Hontañón in 1559. Plaza Santo Domingo holds the **Museo de León**, with a small but prize collection: the 11th-century ivory Carrizo crucifix, enamels from Limoges, a Mozarab cross given by King Ramiro II in 940 to Santiago de Peñalba, the Corullón calvary, three pairs of beautiful capitals from the first Mozarab church at Sahagún, made by the same craftsmen as at Escalada, medieval weapons of the Roman Seventh Legion, portraits of the knights of Santiago, and artefacts discovered in a Punic necropolis near the Maragato village of Santa Colomba de Somoza – a key discovery in unravelling the origins of the Maragatos (*see* p.294).

San Isidoro and the Panteón de los Reyes

Real Colegiata
de San Isidoro
de León
www.sanisidoro
deleon.org; open
July–Aug Mon–Sat 9–8,
Sun 9–2; Sept–June
Mon–Sat 10–1.30 and
4–6.30; church free,
adm to museum and
pantheon which
are visited by guided
tour only

If León's cathedral is one of the best in Spain, the city can claim a similar pedestal for the Romanesque frescoes in its **Real Colegiata de San Isidoro de León**, north of Plaza de Botines in Plaza San Isidoro. Founded in the 9th century, razed to the ground by the iconoclast al-Mansur, it was rebuilt by Ferdinand I, the first to unify León and Castile in 1037 and the first to call himself 'King of the Spains'. In 1063 León bagged the relics of St Isidoro of Seville, that 6th-century, encyclopedia-writing Visigothic nobleman and doctor of the Church whose bones, upon hearing of the Reconquista, started to speak, asking to be transferred to Christian territory. These chattering bones must have driven the Moors in Seville crazy, so they packed them off to León; the basilica was at once rededicated to him, enlarged and given its lofty bell tower. Once here, the gentle Isidoro, like half a dozen other saints along the road, was conscripted into Reconquista duty; you can see him over the side door, on horseback in his bishop's gear, whacking the Moor with John Wayne gusto. Specifically, he helped Alfonso VIII reconquer Baeza, and to this day a confraternity from Baeza, in theory, maintains a 24-hour vigil by his relics in the church.

The façade has two entrances. The church is entered through the right-hand, 11th-century Puerta del Perdón topped by a tympanum sculpted with the Descent from the Cross, the Three Marys and the Ascension. This is the first Door of Pardon along the Camino de Santiago; if a pilgrim was too ill or weak to carry on, they could touch the door and receive the same indulgence and absolution as someone who had walked all the way to Compostela. The barrel-vaulted interior with its foiled arches, desecrated by Soult's French army in the Peninsular War, is something of a heavily restored disappointment; of the 12th-century original only the transept capitals and chapel remain.

The more ornate Puerta del Cordero, its tympanum carved with the Sacrifice of Isaac, leads into the original narthex of the church, the **Panteón de San Isidoro**, founded by Ferdinand I to house his simple stone sarcophagus and those of his descendants (now visitors enter on the guided tour via a tiny stone spiral staircase). Its two small groin-vaulted chambers are supported by elaborately carved capitals (Daniel in the Lions' Den and the Resurrection of Lazarus), and the ceiling and walls are covered with extraordinary

11

Old Castile and León | León

vivid frescoes from the 12th century, among the best-preserved Romanesque paintings anywhere still in their original setting. Stylistically similar to the 5th-century frescoes and mosaics in Santa Costanza (which all the pilgrims on their way to Rome would have visited), Christ Pantocrator and the Evangelists, with human bodies and animal heads (Luke looks like the Minotaur) reign over scenes of the shepherds, the Flight into Egypt, the Last Supper, the Tears of St Peter, the Seven Cities and Seven Lamps of the Apocalypse. Best of all, there's an allegory of the months, starting with the two-headed Janus, Roman god of the door, who looks both backward and ahead at the 'hinge' of the old and new years.

Although the French desecrated the tombs and burned the library, they somehow missed the treasures displayed in the **museum** on the first floor, which originally formed part of Ferdinand I's palace: St Isidoro's original silver reliquary, the gem-studded chalice of Doña Urraca (made from two Roman cups), and lovely Mozarab caskets covered with ivories and enamels. The library, rebuilt in the 16th century by Juan de Badajoz, has an illuminated Bible of 960 that somehow escaped the French firebugs.

Hospital de San Marcos and MUSAC

León's third great monument lies at the end of the garden along the riverside Paseo Condesa de Sagasta. The **Hospital de San Marcos** was built in 1173 as headquarters for the Order of the Knights of Santiago, charged with the pilgrims' protection; at their hospital the weary, blistered pilgrim could rest and prepare for the rigours ahead. In 1514, when the powerful knights were more devoted to their own pleasure and status, they set about rebuilding their headquarters thanks to an enormous donation by Ferdinand the Catholic – something of a pay-off for electing him to the post of Grand Master and surrendering their semi-autonomy to the Crown. Over the 16th to 18th centuries the monastery was given its superb 330ft Plateresque façade, first designed by Pedro de Larrea but altered by many hands afterwards, including those of Juan de Badajoz the younger; its frieze of busts, niches (the statues were never completed), swags and garlands, scallop shells, pinnacles, and intricate lacy reliefs culminating in the portal topped by Santiago Matamoros and the arms of Charles V, who inherited the title of Grand Master from his grandfather Ferdinand. Used after 1837 as a barracks, the building went quickly to rack and ruin and was several times condemned by the city until 1961, when the government purchased it and invested a fortune to create Spain's most beautiful luxury hotel. Non-guests as usual can partake at the bar, and visit the upper choir of the adjacent church of **San Marcos** with its cockleshell façade as part of daily guided tours (ask in the *parador*). The chapterhouse and sacristy are by

Hospital de San Marcos museum
open July–Sept Mon–Sat 10–2 and 5–8, Sun 10–2; Oct–June Tues–Sat 10–2 and 4–7, Sun 10–2

MUSAC
Avda de los Reyes Leoneses 24, http://musac.es; open Tues–Sun 10–3 and 4–8; buses 7, 11,12

ⓘ **Leon >**
Plaza de Regla 4, t 98 723 70 82, www.aytoleon.com

★ **Parador San Marcos >**

★ **La Posada Regia >**

Juan de Badajoz the younger. The Hospital houses a **museum** dedicated to the cult of Santiago and the pilgrim's road.

To prove it isn't a city stuck in the past, León established the glossy **MUSAC** (Museo de Arte Contempóraneo de Castilla y León) in a remarkable block of multicoloured cubes north of here. There is a good programme of temporary exhibitions: check the website.

Facilities in Léon

The **post office** is on Jardín de San Francisco. The **Locutório La Rúa**, C/de la Rua 8, has public telephone and **internet** facilities.

Where to Stay in Léon

León ✉ 24000

★★★★★Parador San Marcos, Plaza San Marcos 7, t 98 723 73 00, *leon@parador.es* (€€€€–€€€). This is not only Spain's best hotel, it is a veritable antiques museum. There are less expensive rooms in the modern building behind, with views over the river and pretty gardens.

★★★★NH Plaza Mayor, Plaza Mayor 15, t 98 734 43 57 (€€€). Part of a reliable chain, this is a crisp, modern hotel behind a neoclassical façade in the Barrio Húmedo. Excellent facilities.

★★★La Posada Regia, C/Regidores 9–11, t 98 721 31 73, *www.regialeon.com* (€€€). Perhaps the most charming choice in the old city, this lovely inn has original wooden beams, quirky works of art, a great restaurant and delightful staff.

★★★París, C/Ancha 18, t 98 723 86 00, *www.hotelparisleon.com* (€€€–€€). A stylish hotel with all the usual facilities, including a spa (a visit is included in the price); close to the cathedral. Good weekend deals.

★Hotel QH, C/Padre Isla 1, t 98 722 09 00, *www.hotelalfonsov.com* (€€). Chic little hotel right behind the cathedral, with comfortable rooms and a small spa (extra charge). Choose rooms on the upper floors if you're a light sleeper.

★★★Toral, Cuesta de Las Carbajalas 4, t 98 720 77 38, *www.toralhotel.com* (€€). Smart, friendly hotel in the heart of the Barrio Húmedo with minimalist rooms, a *vinoteca* serving delicious

tapas with a good range of wines, and a fashionable restaurant.

★Hostal Guzmán El Bueno, C/López Castrillon 6, t 98 723 64 12, *http://hostalguzman.es* (€) One of the best inexpensive choices in León – brightly painted rooms with bath in a restored old house, around the corner from Los Botines.

★Hostal Casco Antiguo, C/Cardenal Landázuri, 11, t 98 707 40 00, *www.h-cascoantiguo.com* (€). How many *hostales* can boast a mix of Roman remains and medieval burial ground in their cellar? (Can be viewed by guests.) This *casona Leonesa* has been elegantly updated. Unbeatable at the price.

★Pensión Blanca, C/Villafranca 2, t 98 725 19 91, *www.pensionblanca.com* (€). Excellent budget option, in a turn-of-the-20th-century building with bright, modern rooms and internet access.

Eating Out in Léon

León is famous for sweetbreads and black puddings (*morcilla*), game dishes and garlic soup with trout. In the Barrio Húmedo, Plaza San Martín is the bopping headquarters for bars, tapas and inexpensive restaurants.

Cocinandos, C/Campanillas 1, t 98 726 07 60, *www.vivaldi.com* (€€). Book weeks in advance for a table at this small, minimalist restaurant. It serves a single set menu, which changes weekly, and showcases the very best seasonal produce. Signature dishes include a terrine of *morcilla* with pistachios and chestnut purée, and a luscious artichoke and lentil soup.

Vivaldi, MUSAC, Avda de los Reyes Leoneses, t 98 726 07 60, *www. vivaldi.com* (€€). Newly ensconced in the glassy surroundings of León's contemporary art museum, Vivaldi continues to create elaborate cuisine based on fresh market produce, accompanied by a good selection of regional wines. There's a cheaper bistro downstairs.

Bodega Regia, C/Regidores 9–11, t 98 721 31 73 (€€). Specializes in well-cooked traditional dishes at reasonable prices. *Closed Sun, plus second 2 wks Jan and first 2 wks Sept.*

Restaurante Zuloaga, Sierra Pambley 3, t 98 723 78 14 (€€). Fabulous former palace skilfully redesigned as bar and restaurant with an interior courtyard.

Adonías del Pozo, C/Santa Nonia 16, t 98 720 67 68 (€€). Rustically decorated, with an excellent menu of traditional Leonesa and Maragato dishes prepared with fresh local produce and a hint of creativity. *Closed Sun.*

Palacio Jabalquinto, C/Juan de Arfe, t 98 721 53 22, *www.palaciojabalquinto. com* (€€). Refined cuisine and stylish surroundings in a sumptuously restored 17th-century palace. *Closed Sun eve and Mon.*

Casa Pozo, Plaza San Marcelo 15 (near the Ayuntamiento), t 98 722 30 39 (€€–€). Long-established classic, specializing in typical local dishes, including juicy *morcilla*, roast lamb, and *ceci-*

na – wafer-thin strips of smoked, air-dried beef. *Closed Sun eve.*

El Besugo, C/Azabachería 10, t 98 725 69 95 (€). An old-fashioned spot with good tapas and *raciones* including delicious grilled sardines. The slightly pricier restaurant upstairs serves classic Leonese dishes like roast lamb.

La Competencia, C/Conde Rebolledo 17, just off Plaza San Martín, t 98 721 23 12 (€). Very popular for good pizza. There are a handful of branches.

El Gaucho, C/Plegarías 16 (€). Just off Plaza San Martín, the *patatas bravas* at this bar are worth stopping off for.

Mesón El Llar, Plaza San Martín 9 (€). One of the very best tapas bars on the popular Plaza San Martín.

El Nuevo Racimo de Oro, Plaza San Martín 8, t 98 721 47 67 (€). Great Leonese cuisine is served in this 12th-century building; there's a good bar as well and plenty of atmosphere.

La Poveda, C/Ramiro Valbuena 9, t 98 722 71 55 (€). Track this place down for delicious home cooking at the best price. *Closed Sun.*

La Ruta Jacobea, C/del Cid, t 98 723 28 07 (€). *Campo*-style brick and stone bar fronting restaurant specialising in traditional fare and tapas. *Closed Sun.*

⭐ La Poveda >>

North of León

Northern León encompasses the southern slopes of the Cordillera Cantábrica and the Picos de Europa and one of Spain's best caves, the **Cueva de Valporquero**, 46km from León through the spectacular gorges of the Torio river. The caves have no prehistoric art, but 2.5km of colourful galleries with little lakes, esplanades, a stalactite 'cemetery', and a chamber of wonders. Another beauty spot is the **Puerto de Pajares** (4,525ft), the lofty pass in the Cordillera Cantábrica used since antiquity as the main gate between León and Oviedo. The Leonese gateway to the Picos de Europa is **Riaño**, from where you can visit the **Valle de Valdeón** and **Valle de Sajambre** (*see* pp.215–16).

Cueva de Valporquero
t 98 757 64 08, *www.cuevade valpor-quero.org; open mid-May–Sept Thurs–Sun 10–6; Oct–mid-May Thurs–Sun 10–5; adm by guided visit only; bring non-skid shoes and a jacket*

West of León

Two distinct regions fill the area between León and Galicia: between Astorga and Ponferrada is **La Maragatería**, the homeland of the Maragatos, one of Spain's marginal peoples; and west of

Getting around West of Léon

RENFE **trains** link Astorga and Ponferrada with León, Lugo and beyond, four times a day – although note that for Astorga the station is a long hike, while **buses** go to the centre. Astorga is the point of departure of buses for La Maragatería; Ponferrada for El Bierzo; and León for the villages in the south. The Cueva de Valporquero is accessible only by **car**, although there are often excursions organized from León.

ALSA has frequent **buses** to Cacabelos and Villafranca del Bierzo from León and Ponferrada; a less regular service calls in at Villafranca on the way to Galicia. AUPSA serve Vega de Espinareda from Ponferrada and Cacabelos. To continue into Los Ancares from here you'll need to have transport, or take a **taxi**.

Ponferrada is **El Bierzo**, a unique mountainous region, with some of the province's prettiest wooded valleys, distorted and eroded by mining and a favourite abode for 10th-century hermits.

Along the Pilgrimage Road to Hospital de Órbigo

On the N120, not far from the industrial sprawl west of León, is, for better or worse, the only modern chapel along the Camino de Santiago: **La Virgen del Camino**, a concrete box built in 1961 by Brother Coello de Portugal which houses a much-venerated 16th-century statue of the Virgin, set in a Baroque *retablo*; the stained-glass workshop at Chartres produced the ugly windows and Catalan sculptor Subirachs contributed the weird emaciated bronze figures of the Virgin and the Apostles that cover the front. One of the bridges the pilgrims crossed, 13th-century Puente del Paso Honros, still stands parallel to the N120, 23km west of León.

Astorga, Gaudí and the Maragatos

Astúrica Augusta was an important administrative centre for the Romans, close to the mines and a main station along their *Vía de la Plata*, the 'Silver Road' that ran down to Zamora and Seville and across to Galicia, to transport the gold of the Bierzo, the silver of Galicia and the copper of Asturias. Like León, Astorga had its own bishopric by the 3rd century; like León it was important in the Middle Ages because of the pilgrimage. It has declined genteelly ever since, helped along by a bit of sacking in the Peninsular War.

The best way to approach Astorga is to circle the centre, still belted by half of its robust Roman-medieval **walls**, and enter on the

Catedral de Santa María
open Mon–Sat 9–10.30, Sun 11–1; at other times, entrance to the cathedral is through the museum with admission fee

northwest side of town, where the **Catedral de Santa María** and Bishop's Palace looming over the walls make a startling impression. Begun in 1451, the cathedral was not completed until the 18th century, with too many cooks along the way; even the colour of the stone in the towers doesn't match. The façade with its flying buttresses between the towers was inspired by the cathedral in León, only here the ornamentation on the façade is floridly Baroque: intricate garlands, cherubs, columns with plump rings of vegetation and reliefs of the Descent from the Cross, the Adulterous Woman, and the Expulsion of the Merchants from the Temple. The interior suffers from a clammy ecclesiastical anomie,

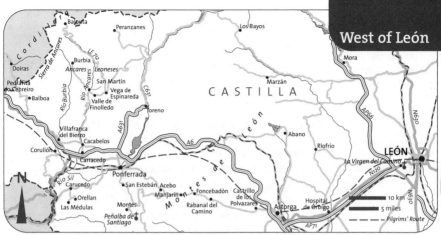

with all the interest concentrated in the *retablo mayor*, in marble high relief, by Gaspar Becerra (1520–70), an Andalucian who studied with Michelangelo. Off the neglected classical cloister, the **Museo Catedralico** houses some fine medieval pieces. Before leaving, look at the top of the cathedral apse, decorated with the figure of a Maragato named Pero Mato, who fought with Santiago at the legendary battle of Clavijo in 844.

Astorga seemed like a dusty, declining nowhere to Juan Bautista Grau y Vallespinós when he arrived as its new bishop. In 1887, hoping to give his see a dynamic jump-start into the 20th century, he commissioned the most imaginative architect he knew, his good friend and fellow Catalan, Antoni Gaudí of Barcelona, to build him a new **Palacio Episcopal**. The rest of Astorga had deep reservations about the Modernista fairytale castle that began to sprout on the edge of town and, once the bishop died in 1893, the public's hostility to the project burst open so violently that Gaudí quit and refused ever to return to Astorga. Without his input, this pale asymmetrical castle (completed only in 1963), lacks the extraordinary detail and colour that characterize the works of Gaudí, who usually designed everything down to the furniture. Instead of a bishop, the palace now houses the **Museo de los Caminos**, a collection of pilgrimage paraphernalia. For a hint of Gaudí's intentions, don't miss the magnificent atmospheric throne room with its discreet stained glass and chapels.

The only Maragatos you're likely to notice, other than those carved into the cathedral apse (*see* above), are the two figures Zancudo and Colasa, who bang the hour atop the attractive 17th-century **Ayuntamiento** at the east end of Astorga; in front of it you can descend into the Roman slaves' prison, the **Ergástula**, where the Maragatos' ancestors languished. The top two floors have been converted to house the **Museo Romano**; inside are ceramics and bronze artefacts from archaeological sites around Astorga, and

Museo Catedralico
open summer daily 10–2 and 4–8; winter daily 11–2 and 4–6; adm, combined adm with Palacio Episcopal (Museo de los Caminos)

Museo de los Caminos
open summer Tues–Sat 10–2 and 4–8, Sun 10–2; winter Tues–Sat 10–2 and 4–6, Sun 10–2; closed On; adm, combined adm with Museo Catedralico

Museo Romano
Plaza de San Bartolomé 2; open June–Sept Tues–Sat 10.30–2.30 and 5–7.30, Sun 10.30–2.30,; Oct–May Tues–Sat 10.30–1.30 and 4–6, Sun 10.30–1.30; closed Mon; adm, combined adm with Museo de Chocolate

Museo de Chocolate
*C/José María Goy 5
open June–Sept Tues–
Sat 10.30–2 and 4.30–7,
Sun 11–2; Oct–May
Tues–Sat 10.30–2 and
4–6, Sun 11–2; adm,
combined adm with
Museo Romano*

Villages of the Maragatos

some spectacular murals from the 2nd century BC. In Plaza Roma you'll find ruins of Roman houses, some with pretty mosaics.

Chocoholics will be more interested in the **Museo de Chocolate**, a thinly veiled excuse to sell some of Astorga's finest product. If you're buying, the dark chocolate is tooth-rottingly delicious.

West of Astorga: Villages of the Maragatería

The mostly ruined villages of the Maragatería have been in decline ever since the railway took over the Maragatos' ancestral occupation, but **Castrillo de los Polvazares** (6km from Astorga, just off the Camino de Santiago) has been restored to the verge of being twee, with old stone houses now mostly holiday homes, a score of roadside crosses and a main cobbled street built wide for mule trains. Further west, only a handful of people remain at **Santa Catalina de Somoza**, with its monument to a Maragato musician, while, up from El Ganso ('The Goose'), down-at-heel **Rabanal del Camino** was the ninth stop on the pilgrimage in the *Codex Calixtinus*, a spot safeguarded by the Templars: now only a few people remain to tend its little Romanesque church.

After Rabanal, pilgrims tackled the wild Montes de León, climbing up to **Foncebadón**, abandoned for decades but slowly being rebuilt

Maragato Mysteries

Astorga is the 'capital' of the Maragatos, who have lived here and in the villages to the west for as long as anyone can remember. Until the 19th century they were muleteers and carriers, transporting nearly all the goods between Castile and Galicia, a line of work forced on them by their stubborn, almost uncultivatable land; their name has been traced back to the Latin *mercator*, or merchant. Grave and dry in manner, their honesty and industry were proverbial and no one hesitated to trust them with huge sums of money. Until recently they still wore their ancient costumes: huge slouched hats, very broad-bottomed breeches called *zaraguelles* (from the Arabic word for kilts) and red garters for the men; for the women, a crescent-shaped cap covered with a mantle and heavy earrings. They kept very much to themselves, marrying only other Maragatos. Twice a year, at Corpus Christi and the Ascension, they would gather in Astorga, and at exactly 2pm all would begin a dance called 'El Canizo', finishing at exactly 3; if any non-Maragatos attempted to join in, the dance would stop immediately. In the kitchen, they are known for their cakes called *mantecadas* (available in every Astorga pastry shop) and for the odd custom of eating their Maragato stew backwards: first they would eat the meat, then the vegetables, then the soup.

Who were the Maragatos? The common beliefs that they were Celts, Visigoths or Berbers, who came over in the 8th century and managed to hold on to this enclave after converting to Christianity, have been called into question by Dr Julio Carro, who in the late 1950s discovered a Punic necropolis near the village of Santa Colomba de Somoza, west of Astorga – hardly where you'd expect to find one, because the Phoenicians were sailors and León isn't exactly on the coast. Among the finds were figurines nearly identical to those found at Punic sites in Ibiza and dressed in a style very similar to the Maragatos. Carro's conclusion, based on his discoveries and on Maragato cultural traditions, was that the Maragatos were descended from Phoenicians and Iberians enslaved by the Romans to work the gold mines of El Bierzo. The Maragatos themselves agree, and to thank Carro for discovering their true origins they put up a stone plaque to him in the village of Quintanilla de Somoza. These days the Maragato traditions and insularity have practically vanished, although you can still recognize a Maragata at once by her lime-green stretch slacks and horn-rimmed glasses.

Where to Stay and Eat in Astorga

ⓘ **Astorga** ›
Plaza Mayor s/n,
t 98 761 68 38,
www.ayuntamientode
astorga.com

⭐ **Viejo Molino Cela** ›

Astorga ✉ 24700

Viejo Molino Cela, Nistal (5km from Astorga), t 98 760 05 02, *www.viejo molinocela.com* (€€€). A lovely riverside mill, now a romantic rural hotel with a garden with white geese and dining room (*guests only, book*).

****Posada Real Casa de Tepa**, C/Santiago 2, t 987 60 32 99, *www.casadetepa.com* (€€€). Enchanting renovated mansion, with ten immaculate rooms set around a patio garden and charming staff.

****Hotel Vía de la Plata**, C/Padres Redentoristas 5, t 98 761 90 00, *www.hotelviadelaplata.es* (€€€–€). Tasteful rooms in the centre, with a spa and panoramic rooftop terrace.

***Hotel Gaudí**, Pza Eduardo de Castro 6, t 98 761 56 54, *http:// gaudi-hotel.es* (€€–€). A comfortable choice,

across from the Palacio Episcopal; its restaurant has tasty Maragato dishes.

Casa Coscolo, El Rincón, 1, Castrillo de Los Polvazares (5km from Astorga), t 98 769 19 84, *www.casacoscolo.com* (€). Delightful, rustic guesthouse in a charming village. The restaurant serves traditional Maragato *cocido*.

****Hs La Peseta**, Plaza San Bartolomé 3, t 98 761 72 75 (€). Central, and with a good old-fashioned restaurant (€€) where you can sample the wines of El Bierzo with cod *confitado* or ox stew.

Serrano, C/Portería 2, t 98 761 78 66 (€€). Classic Castillian fare, prepared with the freshest local produce.

Guts Muths, C/Matanzas s/n, Santiago Millas, t 98 769 11 23, *www. gutsmuths.com* (€€). Characterful and cosy, with a good restaurant serving succulent stews.

Casa Maragata, C/Húsar Tiburcio 2, t 98 761 88 80, *www.casamaragata. com* (€). Dedicated purely to serving the local staple *cocido de maragato* in its *menú del día*.

thanks to the steady trickle of pilgrims. Just beyond, at the top of the 4,935ft pass, stands the spindly **Iron Cross**, planted by a pilgrim untold years ago. Later pilgrims have added, one by one, the huge mound of slate stones at its foot. To the left rises **El Teleno** (7,179ft), one of the two holy mountains of the Celts in El Bierzo.

El Bierzo

In the old days the Romans dug for gold in these hills; the modern Leonese extract the iron and cobalt. El Bierzo has bleak mining towns, lovely mountain scenery, vineyards, orchards and tobacco fields, charming villages that time forgot, and ancient hermitages. Its inhabitants feel closer to their neighbours in Galicia than to León, and make half-serious murmurs about autonomy. After the Iron Cross the pilgrims' road descends into the fertile valleys of El Bierzo by way of **Manjarín**, another abandoned hamlet, and **Acebo**, with its still-flowing pilgrims' Fountain of the Trout along its one street. From Acebo it's 5km south to **Compludo**, a tiny isolated hamlet, where San Fructuoso, the first holy man in El Bierzo, founded his first monastery in 614. Although this is now long gone, San Fructuoso's forge, the remarkable **Herrería de Compludo** (now a national monument) still works as well as it did in the 7th century, using the stream to turn its great wheel.

Ponferrada

Both the easy A6 and the dramatic, lonely (but well-signed) pilgrims' track over the Montes de León lead to Ponferrada. It is the largest town of El Bierzo, and sums up the region's split personality, part of it mine-blackened, slag-heaped and shabby, the other half medievally pretty. The town's name comes from a long-gone bridge with iron balustrades, erected over the Río Sil for the pilgrims by the local 11th-century pontifex, Bishop Osmundo.

Castillo de los Templarios
open July–Aug Tues–Sun 10–2 and 4.30–8.30; Mar–April Tues–Sun 11–2 and 4–7; May–June Tues–Sun 11–2 and 4.30–8.30; Sept–Oct Tues–Sun 11–2 and 4.30–7.30; Nov–Feb Tues–Sun 11–2 and 4–6; closed Mon; adm

On the east bank of the Río Sil stands Ponferrada's proudest monument, the 12th-century **Castillo de los Templarios**, its triple ramparts built to defend the pilgrims from the Moors; its fairytale gate and towers were added later, in 1340. In 1811 the French went out of their way to vandalize it, resulting in heavy restoration. Here and there you can see Templar crosses and *taus* carved on the walls. While building the castle, the Templars discovered a statue of the Virgin in the heart of a holm oak tree, now enshrined in the **Basilica de Nuestra Señora de la Encina** (1577), with a good *retablo mayor* by the school of Gregorio Fernández. Elsewhere in the old town, look for the medieval gate, the **Puerta del Reloj**, and the early 17th-century **Ayuntamiento**. Nearby is the **Museo del Bierzo**, which displays bronzes retrieved from the mountain *castros* in Los Ancares and the original workings of Ponferrada's clock tower. Sitting on a hill, 2km south on the Madrid road, the minute church of **Santo Tomás de las Ollas** ('St Tom of the Pots' – there used to be a pottery workshop next door) is a curious Mozarabic church built by the monks of San Pedro de Montes, with horseshoe arches and, best of all, an elliptical 10-sided apse encircled with blind arcading.

Museo del Bierzo
open summer Tues–Sat 11–2 and 5–8.30, Sun 11–2; winter Tues–Sat 11–2 and 4–7; adm

Into the Valley of Silence

South of Ponferrada, the Oza river winds through the beautiful **Valle del Silencio** where, from the 7th century to the 10th, hermits took up their abode under the dramatic white flanks of Monte Aquiana, a mountain sacred to the Celts. Most of the hermits were Visigoths from Andalucía, come to spread the writings of San Isidoro of Seville. One of these was San Fructuoso, founder of the monastery of **San Pedro de Monte** in the village of **Montes**. To get there, take the road to San Esteban de Valdueza for 8km, then turn left for 14km on a narrow, hairpinning road that follows the River

DO El Bierzo

After Ponferrada the pilgrimage route enters the Valley of Bierzo, the bed of a dried-up lake, surrounded by a ring of mountains and crisscrossed by trout streams. Its microclimate is warm and damp, with few frosts – ideal for cultivating vines, both on steep slopes and on the riverbanks. The finest, DO El Bierzo reds, are made entirely from the native mencía grape and have a personality all their own, although this is diluted when prieto picudo and garnacha are added. The less interesting whites are made from malvasia and valenciana. Three of the top producers are Valdeobispo, Casar de Valdaiga and Palacio de Arganza (try their Almena del Bierzo).

Oza; at the end of the road, it's a steep 500m walk up. Reinhabited in 890 by St Genadio of Andalucía and his monks, the ruins are mostly 12th century, although Genadio's 919 dedication is still embedded in the wall and some of the original Asturian-style capitals are intact. Despite an 18th-century restoration, the whole complex is on the verge of collapse. The real jewel of El Bierzo, the little Mozarabic church of **Santiago de Peñalba**, is a bit farther on in a spectacular setting at the head of the valley. Founded by San Genadio and dedicated in 913, its perfect proportions are reminiscent of Palaeochristian basilicas in Africa, as is its shape: rectangular with three cupolas and two apses rather oddly facing one another. The rough stone and slate exterior doesn't prepare you for the refinement and fine craftsmanship inside. A track leads up to the hermit's cave of **San Genadio** for the magnificent view down on to the church and its tower, surrounded by a huddle of slate roofs.

Fifteen kilometres southwest of Ponferrada, the ruined **Castillo de Cornatel** was built in the 12th century by Ferdinand II to protect the pilgrim route between Ponferrada and Villafranca del Bierzo. The castle itself looks more impressive from the valley than it does close up, but its dominant position affords wonderful sunset views across the Lago de Carucedo to the mountains of Galicia.

Just beyond, **Carucedo** is the point of departure for an unusual journey through an ancient ecological disaster, **Las Médulas**. In the 1st century AD, the Romans noted that the soft red soil was sprinkled with gold and minium (or red lead, used for painting), but to extract it meant sifting through thousands of tons of earth. Some 60,000 slaves were brought in to dig a complex network of galleries, wells, dams and canals to erode the soil. The work was gruelling and dangerous, and thousands died over the next two centuries in moving an estimated 300 million tons of earth to extract 90 tons of gold. Whole hills collapsed, and new ones of leftover tailings were piled up by the slaves, leaving behind a landscape like a row of jagged red spinal cords – or *medullas*. There's a natural balcony over Las Médulas from Orellán; from the village of Las Médulas, 4km from Carucedo, you can take a stroll (bring sturdy shoes) past the ancient canals, galleries, rock needles and surreal caves – a natural disaster perhaps, but a strangely beautiful one. It was recognized as a World Heritage Site in 1998.

Northwest of Ponferrada: the Ancares Leoneses

North of Ponferrada, a lonely road heads north to Vega de Espinareda and the beautiful, densely forested, mountainous **Ancares Leoneses**, now under the jurisdiction of the Reserva Nacional. Although sections are reserved for hunting, the park also protects a number of endangered species – a few brown bears,

Santiago de Peñalba

take the left turning over the river, and leave your car at the entrance of the little medieval hamlet; open April–Sept Tues–Sat 10.30–1.45 and 4.30–8, Sun 10–1.45; Oct–Mar Tues–Sat 10.30–1.15 and 4.30–6, Sun 10.30–1.15; closed Mon

11

Old Castile and León | West of León: El Bierzo

Iberian wolves, roe deer and capercaillie – as well as a dying way of life in its 27 remote mountain hamlets, with their traditional *pallozas*, straw-topped round stone huts first built by the Celts.

Nestled snugly at the confluence of three valleys, **Vega de Espinareda** is the modern metropolis of Los Ancares; many of the emigrants from tiny mountain villages get their first taste of urban life here. The action is centred around a narrow pedestrian **Puente Romano**, but Vega's proudest monument is the ruined 16th-century **Monasterio de San Andrés**, on the western outskirts of town, founded in 923 by El Bierzo's home-grown saint, San Genadio. The attached church, built in 1778 in neoclassical style, contains a 13th-century crucifix, while behind the monastery the Fuente de la Vida offers a lifetime of good health to anyone who drinks seven draughts of its water.

North and west of Vega the Ancares begin in earnest, rising steeply above the villages of **Valle de Finolledo** and **San Martín**, before dropping smoothly into the wide green valley of **Burbia**, and, simultaneously, into the Middle Ages. The majority of the people here continue to live in rough stone huts, tend their rows of beans, herd sheep through the dirt streets, and regale visitors at great length with intimate family histories. From Burbia a dirt track leads to the abandoned village of **Campo del Agua**, which preserves the best collection of straw-roofed *pallozas* anywhere in Los Ancares. Serious hikers can tackle the full-day ascent of 5,880ft **Pico de los Tres Obispos**, one of the tallest mountains in the region.

More *pallozas* can be found in the next valley to the west, **Valle de los Ancares**, although there's no direct way across the mountains other than to walk (take LE712 north from Vega if you're driving). The best-preserved are in **Balouta**, and include what is believed to be the only permanently inhabited example in León. Roads lead onwards from Balouta through gorgeous mountain scenery to the Galician village of **Doiras**, from where it's possible to descend back into León via Balboa, or press on west to the main NVI, or the fast A6 highway, at Becerreá.

Further east, the **Castro de Chano** is a superbly preserved Celtiberian hill fort, just outside Peranzanes in the Valle de Fornela. The *castro* consists of several circular turrets, spectacularly positioned on a long spur, and is considered so valuable that access is restricted to archaeologists and dignitaries; an **interpretation centre** with replica turrets has been constructed nearby to satisfy lesser mortals.

Castro de Chano interpretation centre
open Oct–April Tues–Sun 10–2 and 3–4; May–Sept Tues–Sun 10.30–1 and 4–8; closed Mon

Carracedo

Cacabelos, 12km west of Ponferrada, was another important stop on the *camino*, although these days it's best known for its wines and its **Santuario de las Angustias**, where there's a famous scene of

Santa María de Carracedo
open summer Tues–Sun 10–2 and 5–8; winter Tues–Sun 10–2 and 4–6; closed Mon; adm

baby Jesus floating on a cloud playing cards with St Anthony. Don't miss a brief detour 3km south to the **Monastery of Santa María de Carracedo**, founded in 990 in a pastoral setting, this time by Bermudo II the Gouty of León. In 1138 it came under the patronage of Doña Sancha, sister of Alfonso VII, who built a new church and monastery. At the end of the 18th century the monks decided it was time for a change and began a large neoclassical church. It was only partially finished in 1811 when the French marched through and effectively put an end to the project, leaving half of a new church and much of the old intact, pieced together, restored and roofed over for the monastery's 1,000th birthday. By the church are the remains of a little **palace** built by Alfonso IX in the early 1200s to house his wife and two daughters when the pope annulled his marriage. The claims of the princesses to the throne were a reason behind the union of León and Castile declared by Ferdinand III el Santo – Alfonso IX's son from his second marriage.

Villafranca del Bierzo

The *Codex Calixtinus'* 10th stop on the Camino de Santiago, Villafranca del Bierzo, is one of the most attractive small towns along the whole road, embraced on all sides by mountains, built at the confluence of the Burbia and Valcarce rivers. As its name suggests, the town was founded by the French in the 11th century and in its heyday it had eight monasteries and six pilgrims' hospitals; today it makes wine and lodges visitors to the region.

On the hill where pilgrims entered Villafranca is the preserved 16th-century **Castillo de Villafranca** (private, no admission) and the 12th-century **Santiago**, a simple Romanesque church but an important one, with the second Puerta del Perdón along the road. Pilgrims too weary or ill to continue had only to touch the door to achieve the same indulgences as they would at Compostela. Some then keeled over dead and were buried in the adjacent cemetery. All of the church's unfortunately eroded decoration is concentrated around the Puerta del Perdón. The pilgrims would descend from the church and castle to walk along wide, atmospheric **Calle del Agua**, 'Water Street', lined with blazoned 16th- and 17th-century palaces with iron balconies that often looked over a real street of water, so frequently has the Burbia flooded it. The Plaza Mayor was set higher up away from danger, and near this you'll find the 13th-century church of **San Francisco**, all that remains of a monastery founded by St Francis himself during his pilgrimage. It has a magnificent 15th-century *mudéjar artesonado* ceiling. Down on the banks of the Burbia, the **Colegiata de Santa María** stands on the site of the 11th-century monastery founded by the monks of Cluny. It fell into ruins and was rebuilt from scratch in 1544 to designs by Rodrigo Gil de Hontañón. Construction continued into the 18th

Colegiata de Santa María
open Mar–Oct daily 10–2 and 4–7; Nov–Feb Sat and Sun 10–2 and 4–7; the tourist office organizes guided visits at weekends

century, when the money ran out, leaving the nave cut short and the west façade closed by a simple wall, although what was completed of the part-Gothic and part-Renaissance interior is uncommonly grand.

Just to the south of Villafranca, the 13th-century **San Juan de San Fiz** was built over a Roman cistern; the walls can still be seen under the raised presbytery. **Corullón** has two more lovely Romanesque churches: San Esteban and the recently restored San Miguel. Corullón's ivy-smothered castle affords a lovely view of the Bierzo valley. West of Villafranca, the pilgrims' road passes through the narrow valley of the Valcarce dotted with tiny villages. At **Herrerías**, with its old Hospital de los Ingleses (English Hostel), the road and pilgrims' route divide; the latter, rising to the pass at Cebreiro and hence into Galicia, was as dangerous and dreaded as it is beautiful.

ⓘ Ponferrada >
C/Gil y Carrasco 4,
t 98 742 42 36,
www.ponferrada.org

ⓘ Villafranca
del Bierzo >>
Avda Diaz Ovelar 10,
t 98 754 00 28, www.vil-
lafrancadel bierzo.org

★ Posada Las
Doñas del
Portazgo >>

ⓘ Vega de
Espinareda >
Casa Consistorial,
Avenida de Ancores,
t 98 756 86 19

Where to Stay and Eat in El Bierzo

Ponferrada ✉ 24400

★★★Aroi Bierzo Plaza, Plaza del Ayuntamiento 4, t 98 740 90 01, *www.aroihoteles.com* (€€€–€€). In an arcaded historic building on the main square, with crisp, modern rooms, most with balconies. It has a traditional tavern, and a charming restaurant, **La Violeta** (€€).

★★Hotel El Castillo, Avda del Castillo 115, t 98 745 62 27, *www.hotel-elcastillo.com* (€€). Castle-gaze from your room at this modern hotel in a historic building across the way.

★★Hostal Rio Selmo, C/Rio Selmo 22, t 98 740 26 65, *www.hostalrioselmo.es* (€). Simple, spotless rooms and a café-bar in a modern building a ten-minute stroll from the centre.

La Fonda, Pza Ayuntamiento 10, t 98 742 57 94 (€€–€). A long-established favourite, which uses local ingredients to create interesting dishes. *Closed Sun eve.*

Las Cuadras, Tras la Cava 2, t 98 741 93 73 (€). Located right by the castle walls and serving tasty tapas and fish.

Vega de Espinareda ✉ 24430

Casa Rural Valle de Ancares, Pereda de Ancares (30km north), t 98 756 86 19 (€). A few comfortably rustic rooms in a traditional house, with heavy wooden shutters. Meals are served, and mountain bikes can be rented.

★★HR Piñera, C/La Conchera 18, t 98 756 46 12, *www.hotelpinera.com* (€). Pleasant and modern, it makes a good base for exploring the valleys – the owners can help to arrange 4WD rental. The restaurant, **El Jardín**, serves a reasonable *menú del día*.

Villafranca del Bierzo ✉ 24500

★★★★Parador de Villafranca del Bierzo, Avda Calvo Sotelo 28, t 98 754 01 75, *www.parador.es* (€€€). Spanking new *parador* (opened end 2010) on the outskirts of town: ultra-modern, with a good restaurant.

Posada Las Doñas del Portazgo, C/Ribadeo 2 (C/del Agua), t 98 754 27 42 ,*www.elportazgo.es* (€€–€). A magical guesthouse in a 300-year-old stone house in the heart of the village. Each of the ten rooms and suites is filled with antiques and beautiful objects.

★Hostal Casa Méndez, C/Espíritu Santo 1, t 98 754 24 08, *www.casamendez.es* (€). Family-run with good home cooking, to go with its well-priced rooms with bath.

★Hostal Ultreia, C/Puentecillo 8 (in the Pasaje del Carmen), t 98 754 03 91, *www.hostalultreia.com*. Newly built, but in traditional stone, this offers four simple but attractive double rooms with large bathrooms at a good price. There's also a wine bar and shop showcasing the local wines.

Galicia

If Asturias is Spain's Wales, then Galicia is in many ways its Ireland, for many years so far removed from the mainstream of Spanish life and history that it might just as well have been an island. Here the Celtic invaders of 1000 BC found their cosiest niche, in the same kind of rainswept, green land facing the setting sun that their brethren had settled farther north in Brittany and Cornwall. The Moors left no mark in Galicia, having been expelled in the 8th century by the kings of Asturias – who promptly turned their attention to the richer spoils of the south.

12

Don't miss

⭐ **The pilgrimage site at the end of the world**
Santiago de Compostela p.315

⭐ **Rugged cliffs**
Costa da Morte p.336

⭐ **Glass balconies in a maritime 'Crystal City'**
A Coruña p.331

⭐ **Spectacular seafood**
Vigo p.353

⭐ **A lovely granite border town**
Tui p.352

See map overleaf

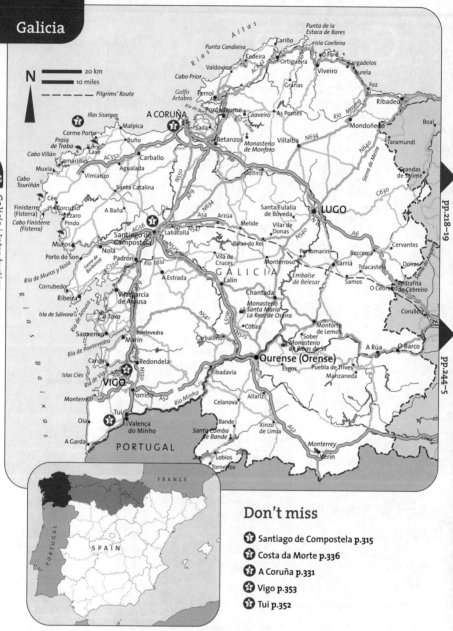

Galicia

PP.218-19

PP.244-5

20 km
10 miles
Pilgrims' Route

Don't miss

⭐ Santiago de Compostela p.315

⭐ Costa da Morte p.336

⭐ A Coruña p.331

⭐ Vigo p.353

⭐ Tui p.352

While the rest of the north expanded into the newly won lands of the Reconquista, the Galicians, or Gallegos, were hemmed in by Portugal and forced to turn inwards, dividing their land into ever smaller holdings with every generation. Famines were common and, as soon as the New World was discovered, people emigrated in droves – there are more Gallegos in Buenos Aires alone than in all of Galicia. Even today Galicia is one of the poorest regions in Spain. Yet few places in Spain have such a lasting charm. The coastline is pierced by a dozen estuaries, or *rías*, wild and scenic in the north, and, in the south, sheltering serene beaches (Galicia has some 800 of these) and tiny coves, perfect for the smuggling that has long been a mainstay of the economy. Rivers in deep, narrow valleys with fantasy names – the Éo, the Ulla, the Lor, the Sil and Jallas – spill down wild mountains on their way to the sea. Bright green gardens cover every inch of cultivatable land, although a third of the acreage is wasted by the granite walls each Gallego has erected around his own little plot. Each farm, though, however small, has a sturdy, self-sufficient air, with its cow and conical hayrack, its trellis of vines (producing excellent white wines similar to Portugal's 'green' wines) and tiny plots of turnips, peppers, maize, cabbage, peas and Spain's finest potatoes. Many cottages have granaries (*hórreos*), monumental pieces of granite set up on pillars to protect the grain from rodents and damp, with window-like vents to permit air to circulate, topped by a gabled roof with crosses. Early travellers mistook them for hermitages.

Because of the endless division of land, much of Galicia is covered higgledy-piggledy with farms and houses in some 31,000 'villages' (most with populations of 100–200), sprinkled with the showy bungalows of the *indianos* who made fortunes in Argentina. Many older houses, especially in A Coruña, have balconies closed in by glass 'crystal galleries', adorned with white mullions. Another distinctive feature of Galicia is the sculpted granite crosses at the crossroads. Some seem to have guided pilgrims, or marked out the high roads, or fulfilled vows, or perhaps even served the same geomantic organization as Neolithic menhirs and dolmens, only carved into Christian forms. In the Rías Baixas, especially along the rivers leading into them, you'll see the stately manor country villas the Gallegos call *pazos*, from the Roman *palatio*.

Galicia's language, Gallego, is chock-full of 'x's (pronounced 'sh') and closely related to Portuguese, and spoken by a greater percentage of the population than Basque or Catalan are in their respective regions. Even García Lorca penned verses in Gallego, inspired by the language of Alfonso the Wise's masterpiece the *Cantigas de Santa María* and the evocative poetry, reminiscent of Emily Dickinson's, by Rosalía de Castro (1837–85), especially her *Cantares Gallegos*. Rosalía was a key figure in the *Rexurdimento* (literary renaissance), inspired by the Catalans and, like theirs, a forerunner of Spain's nationalist movements. After decades of decline, Gallego (like Basque and Catalan) is now on the rise among young people: a 2001 survey found that 91 per cent speak it, 69 per cent read it and 58 per cent write it.

Culturally, Galicia has always looked to its ancient roots. The national instrument, the *gaita*, is very similar to Breton or Irish bagpipes, and Gallegos like nothing better than to blow it at festivals. Galicia's festivals (many associated with death, witches and evil spirits) are also strong in Celtic influences; you can buy a 400-page book that lists every one of them. Irish immigrants in the 16th century introduced lace-making (*camarinhas*), still done by older women all along the coast.

In 2002, the Bahamas-registered oil tanker, *Prestige*, ran into heavy seas off Cape Fisterra in Galicia. The 3,000-tonne oil spill devastated wildlife in the region and the fishing industry along a 400km stretch of coast was entirely shut down. After a massive two billion-euro clean-up Galicia now boasts more Blue Flag beaches than ever before, but the long-term effects of the disaster remain a cause for concern.Don't let this put you off trying Galician cuisine (*see* pp.48–9): strict food controls are in place, and Galician seafood is considered by some to be the best in the world. The fresh, fruity Galician wines from the Rías are the perfect accompaniment. Although the Galician fishing industry is still in crisis, other industries – notably tourism and traditional farming – are on the rise.

The Coast West of Asturias: As Mariñas de Lugo

In the Spanish drive to leave no coast unchristened, this wild Atlantic-thundered northernmost stretch of Galicia is known as As Mariñas de Lugo after the provincial capital, Lugo. It surrenders every so often to admit sandy beaches decorated with storm-chiselled cliffs and rocks; until very recently, deplorably slow roads conspired to keep it a secret.

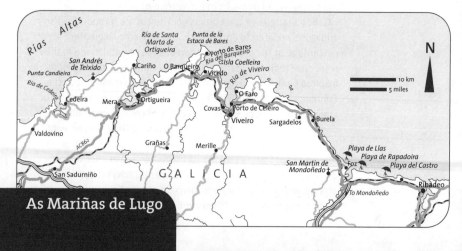

As Mariñas de Lugo

Getting along the Coast West of Asturias

Besides **buses** originating from Lugo, Gijón and A Coruña, the slow FEVE **train** *www.feve.es* follows the coast from Gijón to Ferrol, stopping at Ribadeo, Foz, Burela, Viveiro, Covas, O Barqueiro and Ortigueira.

Ribadeo and Foz

Galician *rías*, or estuaries, are usually named after their largest towns. The first *ría* west of Asturias, **Ribadeo**, is named after a piquant old fishing town that staggers up to a dusty main **Praza de España**, where palm trees and the delightfully eclectic **Casa Morena** of 1905 lend it a lost Californian air. The 18th-century town hall was built as the home of the Marqués de Sargadelos, a liberal-minded reformer and philanthropist who was tied to the tail of a horse and dragged to his death for his beliefs. The hermitage atop **Monte de Santa Cruz**, 2km south of Ribadeo on LU133, offers splendid views of the Galician-Asturian coastline, guarded by a folksy monument to the Galician bagpiper; in early August Santa Cruz pipers from across Galicia gather here in an ear-splitting *eisteddfod*, the *Xira a Santa Cruz*. West, the tiny lobster-fishing village of **Rinlo** is the gateway to the sandy beach known either as the **Praia del Castro** or **As Catedrais**, after its rock formations in the sea. Other pretty beaches dwarfed by towering cliffs, **Praia de Rapadoira** and **Praia de Llas**, lie further west by **Foz**, an industrial fishing port at the mouth of the Río Masma. Only a lonely pile of stones, the **Peña do Altar**, recalls Foz's Celtiberian origins.

Inland: Mondoñedo

If Foz is no prize, Mondoñedo, 18km to the south up the Masma valley, offers some consolation. Mondoñedo was founded in 1117, when the diocese of San Martín de Mondoñedo (*see* overleaf) was relocated inland; it received a second boost in its fortunes in the 15th century, when it became capital of its own little province, a distinction that lasted until 1834 and witnessed the construction of many proud houses of provincial barons, some with the glassed-in balconies or *solanas* typical of Galicia. Mondoñedo's granite **cathedral** was begun in 1219, and when the time came to add a Baroque façade it was done with surgical discretion, preserving the Romanesque portal and Gothic rose window in harmonious blind arches. The interior is still late Romanesque and decorated with remarkable 14th-century frescoes of the Massacre of the Innocents; there's a wonderful organ with trumpets (1710), and a painted Gothic statue known as the *Virgen Inglesa*, brought over from St Paul's in London for safekeeping during the Reformation.

Museo Diocesano
t 98 252 10 06; open daily 11–1.30 and 4.30–7.30; adm

The 17th-century cloister's **Museo Diocesano** displays paintings from Seville, furniture, and fancy liturgical bric-a-brac. The cathedral square is Mondoñedo's best, particularly colourful during the Sunday morning market, and there's a pretty *alameda* before the Baroque church **Os Remedios**, decorated with grand Churrigueresque *retablos*, 'that sculpture of emblazoned tripes' as Pritchett calls it, and lots of candles, too, for the remedies in its name are said usually to be granted. Between Mondoñedo and Foz, the Benedictine **Monasterio de Vilanova de Lourenzá** dates from the 10th century, but became wealthy enough in the 17th and 18th centuries to finance a major rebuilding programme so ambitious that the fancy façade of the church by granite wizard Fernando de las Casas y Novoa was never quite finished. The graceful interior gives the lie to the idea that Spanish Baroque means dark, gloomy and heavy. Don't miss the exquisitely carved altarpiece in the sacristy (1680); in the chapel of Santa María de Valdeflores you can make a wish while stroking the bones of the monastery's founder.

Monasterio de Vilanova de Lourenzá
*t 98 212 21 04;
open for guided visits
mid-June–mid-Sept
Mon–Sat 11 and 12; mid-
Sept–mid-June Mon–Fri
11, 12, 5, 6, and 7, Sat 11
and 12; adm*

Las Rías Altas: West of Foz to Viveiro, O Barqueiro and Ortigueira

From Foz, a brief inland detour will take you to the impressive, mightily buttressed 11th-century **Basílica de San Martín de Mondoñedo**, a rare Romanesque church left untampered with over the centuries, mainly because it was abandoned by its parishioners, leaving intact fine 13th-century murals and the original capitals and the tomb of San Gonzalo, who sank a Norman fleet with a single prayer. Heading west on the coast, you can pay your respects to the **Citanía de Fazouro**, a well-preserved Celtic *castro*; the similar Castro do Chan, near the pretty fishing port of **Burela**, yielded the unique golden torques in the Lugo museum.

Basílica de San Martín de Mondoñedo
open 10–1 and 4–8

Just inland, **Sargadelos** had one of Spain's earliest ironworks and a famous Royal Ceramics factory, which closed in 1860, but re-opened in 1970 as the **Antigua Fábrica de Cerámica de Sargadelos**, making traditional blue and white jugs and avant-garde works.

Beyond Cervo and Sargadelos, the Rías Altas, or Upper Estuaries, begin in earnest, offering some of the best wild and windy coastal scenery in Iberia. Fragrant eucalyptus groves dot the coast around **Viveiro**, at the head of its lovely *ría*. Viveiro is the choice place to stay in the Rías Altas, sheltered by its partly ruined medieval walls from the ravages of the Atlantic, automobiles, and time itself. In the 18th century it imported linen from the Baltic in exchange for Galician agricultural goods but these days its outer fishing port Celeiro, on the opposite side of the estuary, deals mostly in sardines. Three medieval gates survive, along with the fancy **Puerta de Carlos V** (1548) on Avenida Galicia, erected to curry favour with Charles V. Inside, the narrow lanes and pretty Praza de Pastor Díaz are paved in granite and lined with medieval houses sucking in light through their *solanas*, while the austere but pure 12th-century Romanesque **Santa María del Campo** provides a town

Antigua Fábrica de Cerámica de Sargadelos
*call t 98 255 78 41 for
opening hours; see
www.sargadelos.com
for information on
the ceramics courses
held in summer*

centrepiece. Viveiro has some ravishing beaches: the sand plain of **Covas** sweeping out to a treetop rock 'castle', **O Faro** facing the ocean, and **Xilloi** and **Ares** near Celeiro, where legend has it an ancient city sank into the sea for refusing to hear the preaching of St James. You can get a good overview from the *mirador* atop **San Roque**, the mountain just behind Viveiro. To the west, the rugged **Isla Coelleira** – 'Rabbit Island' – has been forlorn and desolate ever since the Templars, who took refuge there from the pope's pogrom, were massacred one night in 1307 by the lord of Viveiro.

The next estuary west, the Ría do Barqueiro, provides a magnificent setting for the hamlet of **Vicedo** and its pretty azalea gardens, the wide beach at **Arealonga** and, over the *ría*, **O Barqueiro**, a picture-postcard amphitheatre of white, slate-roofed houses round a lobster port, in a landscape of piney fjords. A road leads down the *ría* to more beaches and to the tiny fishing hamlet and curling sandy beach of **Bares**, the northernmost settlement in Spain, marked by a lighthouse and blocks of walls from the days when it was a port for Phoenician ships en route to tin mines in Cornwall.

The next estuary, Ría de Santa María de Ortigueira, takes a veritable network of rivers. **Ortigueira** on the pine-wooded east bank is a peaceful, unremarkable town (except during its July *Festival del Mundo Celta*) with narrow streets running down to the waterfront. On the west bank of the *ría* (cross at Mera), the long toes of the Sierra de Capelada extend to Cape Ortegal, where the fishing village of **Cariño** is the last to look over the Cantabrian sea.

Festival del Mundo Celta
www.festivalde ortigueira.com

Cliffs, Lizards and Cedeira

West of Cariño the road takes in spectacular views of the 2,008ft (612m) cliffs of the **Garita de Herbeira** en route to the village and tiny sanctuary of **San Andrés de Teixido**, perched on savage, wave-battered cliffs. Wild horses roam here, and pilgrims flow in year-round for, as the saying goes, '*A San Andrés de Teixido, vaí de morto o que no foi de vivo*' ('If you don't go while alive, you'll go dead') – reincarnated as a lizard or toad, creatures that are never harmed in the village. On 8 September, the dead are given a formal invitation to the festival, when colourful, archaic dough figures are baked to be consumed before Mass, and pilgrims who over the past year had a close brush with the Grim Reaper are carried to the church in coffins. Buy an amulet or *santera* of the saint, or enquire about San Andrés' famous love herb, which was consumed after mass as a prelude to a general orgy. A corniche road continues to the lovely town and port of **Cedeira**, which marks a series of stunning beaches, dunes and lagoons that stretch all the way to Ferrol. The Ría de Cedeira is lined with beauty spots: the lofty **Mirador de Peña Edrosa**, the lighthouse at **Punta Candelaria** and, to the west, the gorgeous setting of the hermitage of **San Antonio de Corveiro**.

Markets on the Coast West of Asturias

Mondoñedo: Thurs and Sun.
Foz: Tues.
Viveiro: Mon, Thurs and Sat
Cedeira: daily fish market; food market Wed and Sat.

(★) Pazo da Trave >>

(i) Ribadeo >
Praza de España,
t 98 212 86 89,
www.ribadeo.org

(i) Viveiro
Avda Ramón Canosa,
t 98 256 08 79

(★) Hotel Mi Norte >

(★) Nito >>

Where to Stay and Eat on the Coast West of Asturias

Ribadeo ✉ 27700

****Parador de Ribadeo**, C/Amador Fernández, **t** 98 212 88 25, *www. parador.es* (€€€). Lacks atmosphere but comfortable and in a scenic spot overlooking the *ría*; the restaurant offers the day's catch.

****Hotel Balastrera**, C/Carlos III, **t** 98 212 00 21, *www.balastrera.es* (€€–€). A delightful blue and white *indiano* villa with pretty rooms, garden and excellent restaurant.

Hotel Mi Norte, **t** 98 212 30 34, *www.minortehabitaciones.com* (€€–€). Enchanting rural hotel, 2km from the famous Playa de las Catedrales, with beautiful rooms inspired by famous films or movie stars.

***Hostal Galicia**, C/Virgen del Camino 1, **t** 98 212 87 77 (€). The cheapest decent place in Ribadeo.

San Miguel, Puerto Deportivo s/n, **t** 98 212 97 17 (€€). Dine on wonderful fresh seafood overlooking the port.

Mondoñedo ✉ 27740

***Montero II**, C/Lence Santer 8 (across from the cathedral), **t** 98 252 10 41 (€). Old-fashioned, characterful place decorated with antiques.

****Hostel Restaurante Padornelo**, C/Buenos Aires 1, **t** 98 252 18 92 (€). Small, simple rooms with bath.

Viveiro ✉ 27850

*****Ego**, Praia de Area, (3km from the centre), **t** 98 256 09 07, *www.hotelego. com* (€€€). Modern, overlooking the beach, with all creature comforts including a spa and a great restaurant (*see* below).

Pazo da Trave, C/A. Trave s/n, Galdo, **t** 98 259 81 63, *www.pazodatrave.com* (€€€). A luxurious 15th-century stately home in the countryside, with pools, gardens and an excellent dining (restaurant open to the public).

****Las Sirenas**, Sacido Coras, **t** 98 256 02 00, *www.hotel-apartamentos lassirenas.com* (€€). Among a clutch of hotels along Covas beach, this one is smart and offers rooms, flats and studios.

*****Orfeo**, C/J. García Navia Castrillón 2, **t** 98 256 21 01, *www.hotel-orfeo.com* (€€). Respectable, if characterless, rooms near the centre.

****Boa Vista**, Ctra Viveiro-Ribadeo 32, **t** 98 256 22 90, *www.boavistahotel. com* (€€–€). Light, bright rooms with views over the coastline, and a good seafood restaurant.

Nito (in the Hotel Ego), Praia de Áreas, **t** 98 256 09 87 (€€€–€€). This attractive hotel-restaurant offers fresh seafood prepared to traditional local recipes and is justly famous.

A Taberna do Tronco, C/Eucaliptos de Chavín s/n (2km from Viveiro), **t** 98 259 84 92 (€€). Charming tavern, serving up steaming plates of *pulpo* and grilled fish and meat.

El Laurel, C/Melintón Cortiñas, **t** 98 256 00 23 (€€–€). A bar with a dining room serving excellent seafood.

The Galician Interior: The Road to Santiago

Pilgrims who made it as far as Villafranca del Bierzo (*see* p.299) had to gird their loins for one last trial: the Puerto Pedrafita in the Sierra de Ancares. This is Galicia at its wildest, driest and bleakest, deceptively covered with blooms in the spring, but the haunt of werewolves and witches in the evening – a zone apart, bound in

Getting around on the Road to Santiago

Lugo and the junction at Monforte de Lemos are linked by **train** to León, A Coruña, Ourense and Vigo, with speedy Talgos to Zaragoza, Barcelona, Bilbao and Irún. Lugo's station is on Pza Conde de Fontao; info at *www.renfe.com*, t 902 320 320. Lugo's **bus** station is on Praza de Constitución, t 98 222 39 85; buses from Lugo to León pass through Becerreá and Pedrafita.

---

dreams and legends. The regional government, the Xunta de Galicia, has restored the atmospheric old *camino francés* and put yellow scallop-shell markers every 500m. The *camino* itself rarely coincides with the highways, making this last leg of the journey especially pleasant for walkers; to maintain the medieval mood, Galicia's fierce sheepdogs are still in place with medieval sheepdog attitudes, just asking for a buffet from a stout pilgrim's staff.

O Cebreiro, Os Ancares, and the Pilgrim's Road

After Villafranca, the *camino* (and the road) pass through the narrow valley of the River Valcarce, ascending to the 3,609ft pass at **Pedrafita**, the boundary between Léon and Galicia. Here, in 1809, Sir John Moore's troops – fleeing to A Coruña, with Marshal Soult's terrible army in hot pursuit – nearly rebelled. Discipline had vanished in Villafranca, where the soldiers had sacked, raped and looted the homes of their Spanish allies; at Pedrafita and at **O Cebreiro**, another 650ft up, hundreds of men froze to death. Such was their haste that the soldiers threw thousands of pounds in gold – the army's pay – over the cliff, along with hundreds of horses, while the women and children camp followers were abandoned in the icy wilderness. It was one of the blackest pages in the history of the British army, and it was almost miraculous that Moore was able to restore order and continue to the coast. Today O Cebreiro has a huge car park to allow everyone to enjoy the views and have a look at the village's Celtic *pallozas*, oval stone huts topped with conical straw roofs where man and beast lived side by side. Two have been set aside as a Spartan pilgrim's refuge, while another pair house a small **ethnographic museum**.

O Cebreiro
ethnographic
museum
*open Tues–Sat
11–2 and 3–6*

A Benedictine monastery, **Santa María del Cebreiro**, contemporary with the Asturian churches of the 9th century (*see* p.231), was built over an old Celtic temple (note the carved stone re-used in the entrance). Pilgrims never failed to pay their respects in its squat slate church, where one of the greatest miracles of the road took place: in the late 13th century an old priest, tired of celebrating mass for just one shepherd in the winter, was grumbling away during the Transfiguration when he and his parishioner were astonished to see the host transformed into flesh and the wine into blood. The chalice in which this miracle happened is a fine example of Romanesque goldwork and displayed in the right aisle; legend identifies it with the Holy Grail, left here by a pilgrim. Next to it in the case are the miraculous paten and a silver reliquary for the blood and flesh donated by Ferdinand V and Isabel I in 1489.

O Cebreiro and the mighty mountains to the north form part of the **Reserva Nacional de Os Ancares**, part refuge of the rare capercaillie (especially around Degrada) and part hunting reserve of roebuck and boar. Several of the tiny villages lost in the range also have *pallozas*, a few still inhabited by die-hards – **Villarello, Cervantes, Doiras** and, best of all, **Piornedo**, at the top of a twisting mountain road. **Becerreá**, on the Lugo road, is the main base for excursions into Os Ancares. From O Cebreiro, the *camino* ascends vertiginously to **O Poio** pass (4,387ft/1,337m), but from here it's all downhill through mountain meadows, chestnut groves and tiny hamlets, where most of the pilgrims' chapels and *hostales* have survived only in name. The exception, **Triacastela**, huddled under an old *castro*, still has its Romanesque church of Santiago, with a simple Baroque tower, and by the River Ouribio a pilgrims' fountain and monument. During the construction of the cathedral of Santiago at Compostela, every medieval pilgrim would pick up a chunk of limestone in the quarries outside Triacastela, and carry it 100km to the Castañeda kilns to be melted into mortar. Modern pilgrims sometimes continue the custom, but now that the cathedral is finished they leave their stone atop Monte de Gozo.

At **San Xil**, the *camino* splits, the right branch heading prettily over hill and dale, while the other, longer one passes down the wooded Ouribio valley to the huge Benedictine **Abadía de San Xulián** at Samos, where the hospitable old monks seem glad to see visitors. Founded in 655, abandoned with the arrival of the Moors but rebuilt a few years later, the abbey had a famous library in the Middle Ages. The intellectual tradition continued in the 1700s, when Samos was the home of Padre Feijóo, the 'Spanish Voltaire', a major figure in the Spanish Enlightenment. The tiny slate chapel of San Salvador is from the 9th century, but the medieval monastery burned down in the 16th century and so did its replacement in 1951, leading to the reconstruction of the two cloisters, one late Gothic and the other, larger, very strict and buttoned-down Spanish Baroque. In the centre flows the lovely Fountain of the Nereids, said to be the work of Velázquez.

Abadía de San Xulián
t 98 254 60 46; www.abadiade samos.com; adm by guided tour only, tours every 30mins Mon–Sat 10–12.30 and 4.30–6.30, Sun 12.45– 1.30 and 4.30–6.30; adm

The two branches of the *camino* meet in **Sarria**, a cement-making town on the rail line. In its quietly aloof medieval core there's a ruined castle, the little Romanesque church of San Salvador and a pilgrims' hostel in the **Convento de los Mercedarios**, where the church has Isabelline Gothic frills. Ten kilometres west, **Portomarín** was a pilgrims' halt protected by the Templars, but even they couldn't have fended off the waters of the Minho, when the river was dammed in the 1960s to form the Embalse de Belesar, submerging the medieval bridge and village. Old Portomarín's porticoed main street plan was salvaged in a new Portomarín, along with the pretty façade of **San Pedro** and the Romanesque tower church of **San Nicolás**. The latter has a rose window like a telephone dial and Romanesque portals so fine that they were long attributed to Master Mateo, one decorated with the 24 Elders playing their *rebecs* and the other with the Annunciation; step inside to see the single-aisled interior. The adjacent monument is to the electrical engineer who helped the villagers with their request to relocate rather than simply receive an indemnity for their property. And they continue to do what they've always done best: supply Galicia with excellent *aguardiente* – firewater which they not only distil but drain during the nightly *marcha*.

The Last Leg of the *Camino*

At **Vilar de Donas**, 'Ladyville' (just off the pilgrim's road, 15km west of Portomarín), the 13th-century granite church of **San Salvador** merits a detour. From the exterior you can see the ruined Gothic cloister of the long-gone monastery and the pretty Romanesque-Gothic portal, decorated with reading and praying monks; inside, the tall granite walls are emerald-green from the damp, while those in the rounded apse are embellished with 15th-century paintings: of the Resurrection, Annunciation, the queen of heaven and the noble ladies who gave their name to the village. The altar stone is carved with the miracle at O Cebreiro, with Jesus in person emerging out of the chalice; the 15th-century baldachin in the transept is one of the few to survive intact in Galicia. San Salvador was once the seat of the Knights of Santiago in Galicia (note the crossed swords, the symbol of the order, on the tombs).

If it weren't for the proximity of Santiago itself, the last two days' march along the *camino* would be disappointing, especially for the modern pilgrim. The *Codex Calixtino* advised pilgrims to say the rosary at **Palas do Rei**, the penultimate stop. The old road passes over a medieval bridge at **Furelos**, before arriving in **Melide**, where the church of Sancti Spiritus decorates the endearing Praza do Convento; the roadside cross, marking the geographic centre of Galicia, is one of the oldest. Just outside Melide, you'll find a dolmen, the **Pedra de Raposo**, and the crumbling church of Santa María with 15th-century murals in the apse. **Arzúa** was the traditional last overnight stop, 30km (19 miles) from Compostela.

These days Santiago's airport is the dominant feature of **Labacolla** ('Wash Arse'), 8km from Compostela, where 'for the love of the Apostle' the pilgrims bathed in the stream flowing by the church. Sentries were posted to ensure they did this, as much against lice as for the sensibilities of St James. Another 5km would take them up to the now rather desolate hill (Km.717 along the *autopista*) of **Monte del Gozo** or Mountjoy, and the tremendous,

12
Galicia | The Galician Interior: The Road to Santiago

long-awaited sight of the towers of Santiago. The first member of each pilgrimage band to sight the cathedral towers was called the 'king', a proud title that was passed down as a surname; if yours is King, Leroy or Rey, chances are you had a sharp-eyed ancestor. These days you barely make them out; Santiago's sprawl and traffic make the last few kilometres a hellish welcome to a heavenly goal.

Lugo: a Detour off the *Camino*

Many pilgrims made the detour to Lugo, the capital of Spain's poorest province but happily dozing away in retirement on the banks of the Minho after a career of some consequence. Its Celtic name *lug* means either the sun god or sacred forest, and when the Romans took it over in the 2nd century AD they renamed it Lucus Augusti, made it the capital of the province of Gallaecia and endowed it with a remarkable dark slate corset of walls, the best-preserved ancient fortifications in Spain, just over 2km long and 28ft (8.5m) high and interspersed with 85 rounded towers. For all that, Lugo was grabbed by the Suevi in the 5th century, the Visigoths in 585, and the Moors in the 8th century. The bastions now defend historic Lugo from its own modern sprawl.

Four ancient gates (and six modern ones) pierce the dark fastness of Lugo's fortifications. Pilgrims would enter the southern Santiago gate to visit Lugo's **cathedral**, built in 1177 and encased in a Baroque skin that offers a modest prelude to the great façade and three towers at Santiago de Compostela. On the west front, note the figure of Lugo's patron San Froilán with his wolf: the story goes that the saint was travelling with a well-laden mule when a ferocious wolf ambushed him and killed the mule. The angry saint scolded until the beast repented and agreed to bear the mule's load himself. Only the north, 14th-century, Gothic portal survived the Baroquers, with its fine Romanesque Christ in Majesty and a capital carved with a Last Supper. Inside there are fittings from every century: a Romanesque chapel and another from 1735, lavish and Baroque in the shape of a rounded Greek cross, dedicated to the Virgen de los Ojos Grandes, 'Our Lady of the Big Eyes', designed by Fernando de las Casas, master of the Obradoiro façade at Compostela. Glass protects a beautiful walnut *coro* carved with a proto Art Nouveau flair by Francisco Moure (1590–1621). The Renaissance *retablo mayor* survives in two bits, filling the transepts; there's a pretty Baroque cloister off the south transept. Since the miracle of O Cebreiro, the cathedral has had the rare privilege of *manifestado* (having the Host on permanent display).

Next to the cathedral, elegant Praza Santa María holds the handsome 17th-century **Bishop's Palace**, built in the style of a typical *Gallego pazo*. Just west, **Praza do Campo** with its fountain was the Roman forum; Lugo's medieval neighbourhood, **La Tinería**, extends here around Rúa Cruz and Rúa Nova. Just north of Prazo do Campo, the formal **Alameda Gardens** give on to the Praza Maior, site of Lugo's rococo **Ayuntamiento**. Rúa da Raiña heads north to busy Praza de Santo Domingo, dominated by an eagle on a column, dedicated to Augustus. The square has two Gothic churches: 14th-century **Santo Domingo** and 16th-century, *mudéjar*-influenced **San Francisco**, formerly part of a 12th-century monastery founded by St Francis on his return from pilgrimage to Santiago. The delicate cloister and refectory house the interesting **Provincial Museum** containing Celtic and Roman finds, including the biggest collection of sundials in Galicia, plus ceramics and folk art; if you like what you see, don't miss the Sargadelos shop in the square.

Lugo's beauty spots are along the Río Minho, the most beautiful of Galicia's rivers; in the **Parque Rosalía de Castro**, outside the Santiago gate and popular during the evening *paseo*, the *mirador* has magnificent views of the valley. Nearby are the brick vaults of the **Termas Romanas**, or Roman hot baths, now part of a hotel-spa.

Provincial Museum
t 98 224 21 12; www. museolugo.org;open July–Aug Mon–Fri 11–2 and 5–8, Sat 10–2, Sun 11–2; Sept–June Mon–Fri 10.30–2 and 4.30–8.30, Sun 11–2

Santa Eulalia de Bóveda, and a Mystery

Some 16km southwest of Lugo (take the Ourense road for 4km, then bear right to Friol and follow the signs) is the extraordinary 4th-century subterranean chapel of **Santa Eulalia de Bóveda**, built over a Celtic temple as a Roman nymphaeum, and later used as a mausoleum. Discovered in 1962, steps lead down to what must have been an antechamber. A horseshoe arch with reliefs of female dancers on one side and the healing of a man on the other leads into a vaulted room with a shallow pool (perhaps used for immersion baptisms by the early Christians), decorated with colourful, winsome murals of birds and trees, dated 4th and 8th century – just predating the pre-Romanesque churches of Asturias. The columns by the pool were found nearby and re-erected; under the pavement, a drainage system kept the water clear. The only similar known building is in the Ukraine, and just as mysterious.

Santa Eulalia de Bóveda
call to check opening times, t 98 229 42 97; usually open Mon–Fri 8–3

Heresy, Galician Style

According to popular belief, the right wall of Santa Eulalia once contained the tomb of Galicia's first 'saint', Prisciliano, whose doctrines, a syncretism of old Celtic and Christian beliefs, attracted many followers in Galicia and León but upset the Church. For one thing, Prisciliano believed works of the spirit obliterated sexual differences, and that monks and nuns should live together. His followers walked barefoot to stay in contact with the earth's forces, were vegetarians, did sun-worshipping on the side and retreated to hermitages in the holy mountains of the Celts. The council of Zaragoza (380) interdicted him, and, when that had no effect, the bishop of Triers had him beheaded five years later – making Prisciliano one of the first holy men to be martyred by the Church instead of by the Romans. His death only increased the popularity of what became known as Priscilianism in Galicia until the early 9th century, when, by an extraordinary coincidence, the head and body of St James were discovered in Santiago. Galician nationalists know they really belonged to Prisciliano...

**Sobrado
dos Monxes**
*t 98 178 75 09; open
Mon–Sat 10–1 and
4.30–7.30, Sun 12.15–1
and 4.30–7.30; adm*

Another rewarding excursion from Lugo and a popular detour for pilgrims is northwest to the ruins of **Sobrado dos Monxes**, Galicia's greatest monastery, founded by the Cistercians in 1142. Although the original building (by an architect from Clairvaux specially sent over by St Bernard) hasn't survived, efforts are being made with government funds to preserve the massive towered Baroque church, the lovely, if rotting, choir stalls and the monumental, ogival kitchen; also intact are the 13th-century chapel dedicated to the Magdalen, a sacristy (1571) by Juan de Herrera, a 12th-century chapterhouse or Sala Capitular, and three 17th- and 18th-century cloisters. The monks now run a livestock-breeding centre and their own milk business as well as a basic pilgrim's *hostal*.

A Detour South: Monforte de Lemos

If you're driving, consider a detour south to **Monforte de Lemos**, dominated by a homage tower, all that remains of the medieval castle of the Counts of Lemos. It had two important monasteries: Benedictine **San Vicente del Pino**, founded in the 10th century, with a late Romanesque church sheltering a 15th-century statue of St Anne; and, near the medieval bridge, the huge 16th-century Jesuit **Colegio de la Compañía**, inspired by the geometric Baroque of Herrera. Look in the chapel for a Renaissance *retablo* in walnut carved with the Life of the Virgin by de Moure, two El Grecos and a lovely triptych attributed to Hugo van der Goes. The area south of here towards the River Sil contains the vineyards of Amandi, one of Galicia's finest reds, grown in a village named, of all things, **Sober**.

Where to Stay and Eat on the Road to Santiago

O Cebreiro and Becerreá
✉ 27600

*Hotel Piornedo, east of Cervantes, t 98 216 15 87, *www.hotelpiornedo.com* (€). A modern building constructed from traditional pale stone with lovely mountain views.

**Hostal San Giraldo de Aurillac, near the *pallozas*, t 98 236 71 25 (€). Now a *mesón* and *hostal* in a former convent founded by French monks.

**Hostal Rivera, Piornedo de Ancares, t 98 236 01 85 (€). Roadside *hostal* with café, pool and parking.

*Hostal Herbón, C/Gómez Giménez 8, in Becerreá, t 98 236 01 34, *www. pensionhostal herbon.com* (€). Immaculate, if basic, rooms, plus cosy apartments for rent.

Casa Catuxa, Ouselle (6.5km from Becerreá), t 98 236 03 15 (€). A lovely old stone house offering simple B&B.

Sarriá ✉ 27600
***NH Alfonso IX, Rua do Peregrino 29, t 98 253 00 05, *www.nh-hoteles.es* (€€). Modern chain hotel, well placed for the old town.

Casa A Rectoral de Goián, C/Cabezares 8 (10km from Sarriá), t 98 253 3813, *www.rectoraldegoian.com* (€€). An 18th-century rectory houses this tranquil rural hotel, with gardens, and delicious breakfasts.

Casa Nova de Rente, Barbadelo, t 98 218 78 54 (€). Simple rooms in an old stone house in lovely countryside; a cheap home-cooked dinner is available on request.

Lugo ✉ 27000
Although Lugo boasts of quirky delicacies such as pancakes with pig's blood, it also has good seafood

ⓘ **Lugo >>**
*Praza Maior 27,
t 98 223 13 61, www.
concellodelugo.org*

restaurants. Ask the tourist office about the annual tapas competition.

****Gran Hotel Lugo, Avda Ramón Ferreiro 21, **t** 98 222 41 52, *www.gh-hoteles.com* (€€€). Top of the scale: a pool, piano bar, spa and a good seafood restaurant (**Os Marisqueiros**).

****Hotel Monumento Pazo de Orban, Travesía do Miño 6, **t** 98 224 02 17, *www.pazodeorban.es* (€€), In an 18th-century mansion within the walls, with traditional rooms and pleasant staff. There's a terrace café.

***Méndez Núñez, C/de la Reina 1, **t** 98 223 07 11, *www.hotelmendeznunez. com* (€€). Large, comfortable and well located, this has been run by the same family since it opened in 1861.

Casa Grande de Nadela, Nadela (6km from Lugo), **t** 98 230 59 15, *www.casagrandenadela.com* (*restaurant and hotel* €€). Elaborate contemporary cuisine, and ten comfortable guest rooms.

Hostal Mar de Plata, Ronda Muralla 5, **t 98 222 89 10 (€). You can have a view of the walls here – one of several budget choices just outside the walls, not far from the bus station.

Hostal San Roque, Praza Comandante Manso 11, **t 98 222 27 00 (€). One of the best budget choices outside the walls, in a quiet location set back from the main road.

Restaurante España, Rua do Teatr 10, **t** 98 224 27 17 (€€). Currently the city's best option, serving inventive cuisine by a rising young chef in a century-old restaurant. Surprisingly affordable.

Campos, Rúa Nova 4, **t** 98 222 97 43, *www.restaurantecampos.com* (€€). For traditional Gallego suckling pig, octopus and seasonal game dishes.

Mesón de Alberto, Rúa da Cruz, **t** 98 222 83 10, *www.mesondealberto.com*

(€€). Classic and modern Galician dishes, with good tapas at the bar.

Restaurante La Barra, San Marcos 27, **t** 98 225 29 20, *www.restaurantela barra.com* (€€). Mouthwatering meat and fish dishes, with a tapas bar.

Verruga, Rúa da Cruz 12, **t** 98 222 95 72, *www.verruga.es* (€). Seafood restaurant with a good-value lunch *menú*. Closed Sun eve and Mon.

Pulperia Palmira, Praza Comandante Manso 17, **t** 98 225 39 22 (€). Share a table and feast on octopus at this basic but friendly *comedor*.

Vilalba ✉ 27400

***Parador Condes de Vilalba, Valeriano Valdesuso, **t** 98 251 00 11, *www.parador.es* (€€€). A crenellated fortress with 3m-thick walls and slit windows. Book early for one of the six rooms in the old tower. The modern annexe is comfortable. Baronial dining in the restaurant.

***Villamartín, Avda Tierra Llana, **t** 98 251 12 15, *www.hotelvillamartin.net* (€€). This modern, functional place comes complete with disco and pool.

Monforte de Lemos ✉ 27400

****Parador de Monforte de Lemos, Praza Luis de Góngora, **t** 98 241 84 84, *ww.parador.es* (€€€). Plush *parador*, with a fine restaurant, formerly an 11th-century monastery and the 16th-century palace of the Counts of Lemos.

Hs Río, Rúa da Baramonde 30, **t 98 240 18 50 (€). Basic but fine.

O Grelo, Campo da Virxe s/n, **t** 98 240 47 01 (€€). Delicious Gallego cuisine.

Castroverde ✉ 49110

Pazo de Vilabade,Vilabade, **t** 98 231 30 00, *www.elpazo.com* (€€). One of the nicest *pazos* in Galicia, with antiques and a lovely garden.

(★) Pazo de Vilabade >>

Santiago de Compostela

(✪) Santiago de Compostela

The original European tourist destination, Santiago de Compostela still comes up with the goods. Not only does it boast a great cathedral where pilgrims are promised 50 per cent off their time in Purgatory, but the moss-stained Baroque city is pure granite magic, a rich grey palette of a hundred moods crowned with curlicues. Any tendency towards atrophy into a Euro-tourist

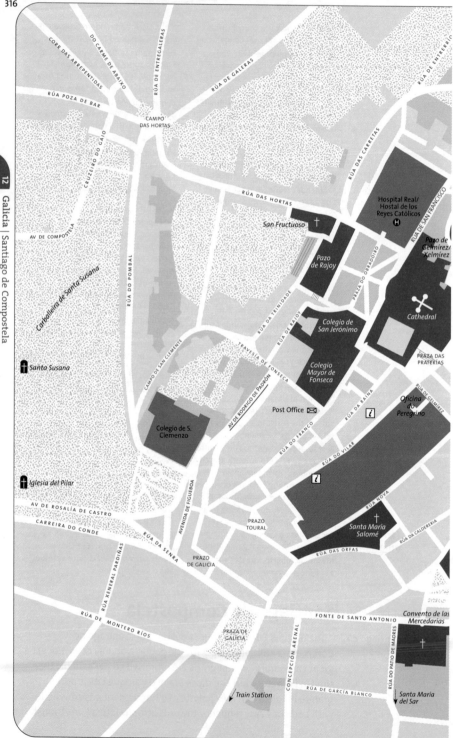

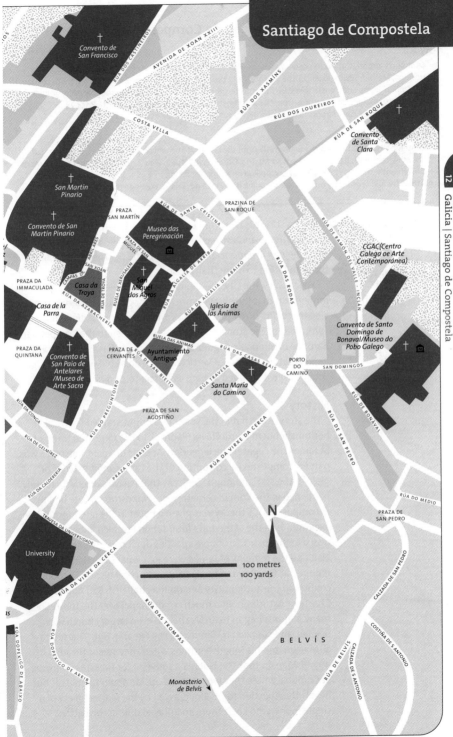

Convento de
San Francisco

AVENIDA DE XOAN XXIII

RÚA DOS CASTIÑEIROS

RÚA DOS XASMÍNS

RÚE DOS LOUREIROS

RÚA DE SAN ROQUE

COSTA VELLA

Convento
de Santa
Clara

San Martín
Pinario

PRAZA
SAN MARTÍN

RÚA DE SANTA CRISTINA

PRAZINA DE
SAN ROQUE

Convento de San
Martín Pinario

Museo das
Peregrinación

PRAZA DE SAN
MIGUEL

RÚA DE RAMÓN DEL VALLE - INCLÁN

CGAC(Centro
Galego oe Arte
Contemporánea)

CAMPAS DE
SAN XOÁN

RÚA DE ABRIL ARES

RUELA DE XERUSALÉN

RÚA DA ALCALÍA DE ARRIBA

RÚA DAS RODAS

PRAZA DA
IMMACULADA

Casa da
Troya

San
Miguel
dos Agros

RÚA DA ALCALÍA DE ABAIXO

Casa de la
Parra

RÚA DE TROYA

RÚA DA AZABACHERÍA

Iglesia de
las Ánimas

Convento de Santo
Domingo de
Bonaval/Museo do
Pobo Galego

PRAZA DA
QUINTANA

RUELA DAS ÁNIMAS

Convento de
San Paio de
Antelares
/Museo de
Arte Sacra

PRAZA DE
CERVANTES

RÚA DE SAN BIEITO

Ayuntamiento
Antiguo

RÚA DAS CASAS REAIS

PORTO
DO
CAMINO

SAN DOMINGOS

RÚA TRAVESA

Santa María
do Camino

RÚA DE BONAVAL

RÚA DA CONGA

PRAZA DE SAN
AGOSTIÑO

RÚA DA PREGUNTOIRO

RÚA DE SAN PEDRO

RÚA DE GELMÍREZ

PRAZA DE ABASTOS

RÚA DA VIRXE DA CERCA

RÚA DA CALDERERÍA

RÚA DO MEDIO

TRAVESA DA UNIVERSIDADE

PRAZA DE
SAN PEDRO

University

N

CALZADA DE SAN PEDRO

RÚA DA VIRXE DA CERCA

100 metres
100 yards

COSTIÑA DE SANTONIO

RÚA DAS TROMPAS

BELVÍS

RÚA DE BELVÍS

CALZADA DE SANTONIO

RÚA DOPEXIGO DE ABAIXO

RÚA DOPEXIGO DE ARRIBA

Monasterio
de Belvís

Getting to and around Santiago de Compostela

By Air

Santiago's airport, **t** 91 321 10 00, *www.aena.es*, is at Labacolla, 11km to the east. It has regular flights to Barcelona, Madrid, Seville, Valencia, the Balearics and the Canary Islands, as well as direct flights to London, Paris, Dublin, Rome and Zurich. There are buses to the airport from the bus station roughly every 30mins from 6am to midnight (bus returns from the aiport between 6am and 12.45am); call **t** 98 154 24 16, *www.empresafreire.com*. Airport taxi stand, **t** 98 159 15 75.

By Train and Bus

Santiago's **train station** is a 15-minute walk from the centre at the end of Rúa do Hórreo, **t** 902 320 320, *www.renfe.com*, with daily connections to Madrid, Ourense, A Coruña, Vigo, Zamora and other points. More inconveniently, the **bus station** is way out on Rúa de Rodríguez de Viguri, **t** 98 154 24 16, *www.tussa.org*, north of the old centre; city bus nos. 5 and 10 link it to Praza de Galicia. **Buses** go to most points in Galicia.

See the rain on the streets,

a moan of glass and stone,

See in the failing wind

The dust and ashes of your sea.

Federico García Lorca

museum shrine is thwarted by the university, which keeps the ancient streets and especially the bars full of life year-round and fuels the raw *urbanización* that engulfs the perimeters, swelling the population to more than 95,000.

Expect rain – the city, the 'Urinal of Spain', never fails gently to remind you that the showers are good for granite, fostering the elegant patina on its monuments and the micro-gardens that sprout out of the stone, an appropriate flourish to the Competelan Baroque of Simón Rodríguez and Fernando de Casas y Novoa with its 'vegetative impulse of verticality'. But on a cold winter's twilight you may see it stripped as bare as García Lorca did.

History

The story goes that in the year 813, a bright star led Pelayo, a hermit shepherd of Iria Flavia (Padrón), to the forgotten tomb of St James the Greater, the legendary Apostle of Spain. The place was named Compostela, a corruption of the Latin *campus stellae* or 'field of the star', although some say that Pelayo's discovery merely happened in the Roman cemetery, or *compostum*, where bodies decomposed. This theory was given a boost in the late 1940s when excavations in the cathedral's foundation revealed Roman graves over a Celtic *castro*. Of course apostles don't compost like everyone else, and the remains of James were just what Christian Spain required at the dawn of the Reconquista. Local bishop Theodomir confirmed the authenticity and built a chapel; in 829 Alfonso II the Chaste of Asturias built a much larger chapel over the tomb. So many pilgrims began to arrive that an even larger church was needed, and supplied by Alfonso III the Great in 896. This fell to al-Mansur and his Moorish armies when they swept through in 997; al-Mansur took the bells as a souvenir for the Great Mosque at Córdoba, where they were turned upside down to hold oil, but he left the Apostle's tomb alone, awed by the fearless piety of a single monk, who knelt there and prayed during the battle.

Some time in these early days James, the humble fisherman with a voice of thunder, was given a new posthumous role as Santiago Matamoros, a fierce Moor-thumping *Generalísimo*, the hero of the entirely apocryphal Battle of Clavijo of 844. This legend was 'confirmed' in a 12th-century document known as the *Privilegio de los Votos de Santiago*, purporting to be by Ramiro I of Asturias, the grateful victor of Clavijo, vowing a tax in perpetuity to the saint's church in Compostela (a tax imposed in Spain until 1834).

After al-Mansur, church and town were soon rebuilt, this time with walls. In 1075, thanks to the new tax, the present cathedral was begun, to accommodate the massive flow of pilgrims from all over Europe. By 1104, Compostela was made an archbishopric, under the feisty Diego Gelmírez; in 1189, Alexander III decreed it a Holy City, on a par with Jerusalem and Rome. In 1236, Ferdinand III the Saint brought back Santiago's bells from the Great Mosque. In 1589, with Drake (a pirate and, worse, a Protestant) ravaging the coast, Santiago was tucked away for safekeeping but, in a fit of amnesia, no one could remember where. Still, the pilgrims came, and only in the 19th century, when numbers declined drastically, did a cathedral workman stumble across the most important relics in Spain (1879). How to make sure they were genuine? An authenticated apostolic bone chip from Pistoia was sent over, and it fitted the notch in the skull like a hand in a glove.

On years when 25 July, Santiago's feast day, happens to land on a Sunday, a Holy Year is proclaimed and the city launches into a year's worth of festivities. The last one was in 2010, when hundreds of thousands of visitors enjoyed music, dance and street activities celebrating all things Gallego, and Pope Benedict XVI visited the cathedral. For the next one, you'll have to wait until 2021. Santiago de Compostela was named European City of Culture for the year 2000, and gained some significant public works out of the deal, including a new communications port on Monte Pedroso designed by Norman Foster, and a generous park by architect J.P. Kleihues.

Praza do Obradoiro

All roads in Compostela lead up to the towering granite magnet of the cathedral of Santiago, the town's *raison d'être* and culmination of the pilgrim's journey. Approach it from the huge Praza do Obradoiro, the 'Square of Works', also known as Praza de España, where for centuries the cathedral's stonemasons liberated the soul of Galicia's stone and made it sing and blaze like a Baroque bonfire. In the rain and mists, at morning or sunset or the heat of the day, the cathedral façade changes its tune; it cries out for a new Monet to paint its moods or, perhaps even better, a composer.

Before going in, pause for a look over the Praza do Obradoiro itself, where a colourful carnival of pilgrims, students, Gallegos holding demonstrations, vendors of postcards and plastic birds with flapping wings all play out their roles before a prize collection of civic monuments, erected over the last six centuries. Left, and adjacent to the cathedral, the rather plain **Pazo de Xelmírez** was built in the 12th and 13th centuries by the two archbishops whose worldly aplomb helped make Santiago great: Diego Xelmírez, the first to hold the job, who received a licence to mint money when he oversaw the forgery of the *Votos de Santiago* and used the funds to build the cathedral, and Arias, reputedly 'one of the great ecclesiastical pirates of 13th-century Spain'. They didn't build their own palace as well as they might have: new walls had to be added between the 16th and 18th centuries to keep it from collapsing.

Archbishop's Palace medieval rooms
used for special exhibitions; check what's on at the tourist office

Although the upper section is still the archbishop's palace, you can visit the lower **medieval rooms**, especially the huge Romanesque dining hall, where the corbels under the vaults are carved with delicious scenes of a medieval feast, complete with musicians; one trencherman is tucking into an *empanada*. Although often open for temporary exhibitions, you can also visit the palace as part of a guided tour which includes the cathedral's **rooftop**.

Cathedral rooftop
www.catedralde santiago.es; visits by guided tour only, must be booked in advance on t 98 155 44 03; open Tues–Sun 10–2 and 4–8; closed Mon; adm exp

Continuing around the square, the Plateresque **Hospital Real** (1501–9) was built for poor pilgrims by Ferdinand and Isabel with the booty from taking Granada in 1492. Based by Enrique de Egas on Filarete's design for the Ospedale Maggiore in Milan, its façade, typical of Plateresque, concentrates its embellishments in a few key spots, in its long Baroque balconies added in 1678 and in the crowded triumphal Gothic Renaissance altarpiece of a doorway. The building was used as a hospital until 1953, when it was converted into a five-star *parador*: at least have a drink down in the bar and try to visit the four courtyards and late Gothic chapel.

Tucked at the bottom of the stairway to the left of the hospital, the little church of **San Fructuoso** by Lucas Caaveiro (1757) is a good introduction to Compostela's special Baroque and its fondness for heavy geometrical forms. The enormous 18th-century **Pazo de Rajoy**, designed as a seminary and now the town hall, is pure Parisian neoclassicism, by French architect Charles Lemaur; on top note the proud figure of Santiago Matamoros.

Next, the 16th-century **Colegio de San Jerónimo** was founded as a university, where priests learnt languages to hear the pilgrims' confessions; classes were held just behind in the **Colegio Mayor de Fonseca**, built by Juan de Álava (1546) around a peaceful cloister with a beautiful *mudéjar* ceiling; the college is used as a library.

The Cathedral of Santiago

Back to that Baroque firecracker, the Obradoiro façade of the cathedral, where the two towers shoot like huge flames to heaven. On the right, the **Tower of the Bells** was built by José Peña de Toro in the 1600s, while the left-hand one was added by Fernando Casas y Novoa in the 1750s, when he tackled the main façade. A lively triple-ramp stair leads to a pair of doors, arranged to form a cross in stonework; stacked above are two calm windows in a shallow arch like the eye of a hurricane just before the front peaks in a flickering crest of granite fire. At the foot of the steps a door leads into the delightful **crypt of Master Mateo** or 'Catedral Vieja', built by the great master builder to distribute the weight of his Romanesque façade, but so elaborately, with ancient columns, capitals, and fine sculpture under the vaults, that people used to think this was the first cathedral.

Crypt of Master Mateo
www.catedralde
santiago.es; open
June–Sept Mon–Sat
10–2 and 4–8, Sun 10–2;
Oct–May Mon–Sat
10–1.30 and 4–6.30, Sun
10–1.30; adm; keep your
ticket for the treasury,
cloister, museum and
Pazo de Xelmírez

Inside the Cathedral: the Pórtico de la Gloria

Perhaps the most startling surprise awaits just within the busy Baroque doors up the staircase, where the original 12th-century façade of the cathedral survives perfectly intact. This is the sublime **Pórtico de la Gloria**, the greatest single piece of Romanesque sculpture, anywhere. Sculpted in warm brown granite between 1168 and 1188 by Master Mateo (dated and signed on the lintel of the central arch) its three doorways are dedicated to the Triumph of the Apocalypse, a theme that decorated many churches along the *camino*, but here, at the very end of the road, it reaches an apogee of joy and mirth, full of movement, life and rhythm; if the end of the world is like this, you want to be there. Nearly all the 200 or so figures are smiling or laughing, beginning with St James himself, welcoming you from his perch on the central pillar, carved with the Tree of Jesse; so many pilgrims have touched the pillar while bending to kiss the base in thanksgiving that the stone has five worn indentations from their fingers. It was originally brightly painted, and traces of a 17th-century touch-up remain.

Above St James in the central arch, Christ in Majesty appears 'like jasper and carnelian' according to the text in *Revelations*, raising both hands in blessing, surrounded by the four Evangelists, Apostles and angels. 'And round the throne was a rainbow that looked like an emerald', an ogival rainbow of musicians – the 24 Elders of the Apocalypse (plus a few stand-ins), each with a different instrument on his lap. On the two side pillars, apostles and prophets chat pleasantly, among them the famous laughing Daniel, who is said to owe his good humour to the loveliness of Queen Esther, whom he eyes across the way. The door on the right is dedicated to heaven and hell, mostly, and depicts children suffering the torments of the damned with their parents – on the surface a powerful psychological trick to make parents toe the line – while the scenes above the left door are more elusive and food for all kinds of interpretations; note the benign portrayal of Jews waiting for the Messiah and the twins, recalling the tradition that

*Thou shield
of that faith
which in Spain
we revere*

*Thou Scourge
of each foeman
who dares to
draw near*

*Whom the
Son of the God
whom the
elements tames,*

*Called Child of
the Thunder,
Immortal
Saint James!*

Pilgrims' hymn,
translated by
George Burrows

St James was Jesus' mortal twin (*see* p.347). After drinking in this eloquent draught of medieval happiness, pilgrims – then as now – lined up behind the central pillar before the curly-haired figure of Master Mateo, who is humbly kneeling to offer the cathedral to God; his nickname, '*O Santo dos Croques*', 'Saint Bump-on-the-Head', comes from the millions who have bowed their heads to touch Mateo's in the hope that some of his genius would rub off.

The **Romanesque interior** of the cathedral is essentially as Master Mateo left it, a long, majestic, barrel-vaulted nave lined with galleries; it takes a while to get used to the gloom, the cathedral's Baroque additions blocking out much of the light that once poured through an unusual nine-sided rose window over the Pórtico de la Gloria. The huge, silver high altar glimmers, visible since the 1940s when the enclosed Baroque choir was removed. Of the chapels along the nave the most important is the first on the right, the 16th-century **reliquary chapel** and **Royal Pantheon**. Next on the right is the cathedral **treasury**, aglitter with the silver hammer used to pound open the Holy Door in Holy Years, silver scallop shells, a score of other religious trappings and a 16th-century monstrance with scenes from the lives of Jesus and St James.

Actually, when you get close up, the glow-in-the-dark 17th-century **high altar**, lavishly covered with Mexican silver, turns out to be a piece of tomfoolery, its cast of characters borrowed from a giant's Christmas tree. On top Santiago Matamoros cuts down the Moors. Just over the altar itself sits a stiff idol, a 12th-century statue of Santiago, patron saint of Spain, his clothes and throne later tricked out lavishly by a Mexican archbishop. The thing to do is climb the narrow stairway behind the altar, kiss the statue's robe and receive a holy card (for the certificate of indulgence, the *compostellana*, pilgrims should apply with their documents to the *oficina arzobispal*, in the back of the cathedral). Below the altar you can pay your respects to the saint's bones in the 19th-century silver crypt; the outer, rounded wall here survives from Alfonso III's 9th-century church, while the inner wall is believed to be Roman.

In front of the high altar, notice the ropes and pulleys suspended from the octagonal dome or *cimborio*, from which, on high feast days, the **botafumeiro**, the world's largest censer, is suspended and swung with terrifying force across the entire length of the transept in a comet-like arc of perfumed smoke and sparks. Weighing in at 119lb, the *botafumeiro* is a smaller brass version of the original silver model made in 1602 and pilfered by Napoleon's troops: it takes eight men, the *tiraboleiros*, to swing it on a system invented in the Middle Ages. Don't miss it if you're in town on a holy day, and try not to think about the time when Catherine of Aragón attended mass and the *botafumeiro* broke loose and flew out of the window. The *botafumeiro* sweetened the air in the cathedral, where many medieval pilgrims slept at night (until a few behaved scandalously and doors were added to the previously wide-open Pórtico de la Gloria); others say the *botafumeiro* was invented as a public relations gimmick to upstage the pilgrimage to Rome.

The ten **chapels** radiating like petals from the ambulatory are all worth a look, especially the one straight behind the altar, the Romanesque **Capilla de San Salvador**, where pilgrims received Communion. Off the north transept, a doorway topped with a 13th-century relief of the Magi leads into the church-sized three-aisled Romanesque **Capilla de la Corticela**.

**Cloister/
Cathedral Museum**
*open June–Sept
Mon–Sat 10–2 and 4–8,
Sun 10–2; Oct–May
Mon–Sat 10–1.30 and
4–6.30, Sun 10–1.30;
single adm ticket*

Off the south transept, a 16th-century Gothic-vaulted **cloister** big enough for a football match was designed by Juan de Álava and Gil de Hontañón to replace Master Mateo's Romanesque original, and holds the **Cathedral Museum** and **Library**. The highlight here is a faithful but incomplete restoration of Master Mateo's original granite *coro*, torn down in the overenthusiastic spring-clean of the late 16th century. The carvings show the new Zion descending from heaven, but the computer-designed modern facsimiles can't match the delicacy of the few original pieces that survive.

Elsewhere, the museum has an illuminated 12th-century *Codex Calixtinus*, while the library contains the *botafumeiro* when it's not in use. The archaeological section is of special interest for the fragments of Master Mateo's cloister, while the lavish 18th-century **Sala Capitular** contains some of the cathedral's impressive collection of tapestries, some remarkably insipid even if designed by the likes of Rubens and Goya. There are pretty views from the gallery off the upper rooms across the Praza do Obradoiro.

Around the Cathedral

Although low-key after the Obradoiro façade, the cathedral's other entrances each deserve a look. Heading anticlockwise from the Pazo de Gelmírez, you'll come first to the split-level **Praza das Praterías**, named after the silversmiths whose shops once filled the arcades of this jewel-like square. The double **Puerta de las Praterías** is the only one to remain essentially unchanged from the Romanesque cathedral. Some of the figures were salvaged from the demolished French door and the cathedral's Romanesque stone choir. Locals use the doors as a short cut across town, as their ancestors did in the Middle Ages, when cathedrals were covered public squares as much as religious shrines. From here you can gaze up at the cathedral's highest tower, the ornament-laden 260ft **Berenguel** designed by Galician humanist Domingo de Andrade in the 1710s to hold the town clock. The *praza*'s geometric Baroque **chapterhouse** and fountain were designed by Fernández Sarela.

Continuing past the bulk of the Berenguel is the enclosed **Praza da Quintana**, an inviting place to sit on the steps and linger.

The Gallop to the Scallop

The very first thing a medieval pilgrim did upon arriving in the city was stop in the Barrio de los Conchieros, buy a scallop, eat it (this is where French pilgrims learned to make *coquilles St-Jacques*, after all) and stick the shell on the turned-up brim of his or her hat – visible proof that they had made it at last; strict laws forbade the selling of scallops anywhere else along the *camino*. By the 16th century, the real shell was replaced by a fancy souvenir replica, either in silver or in jet (*see* below).

The scallop, that tasty bivalve that thrives in the *rías* of Galicia, has been associated with the Santiago pilgrimage since the early Middle Ages. In Compostela, as usual, they can explain it with a miracle: a young Gallego, on the eve of his wedding, was spirited into the sea by his wayward horse and believed drowned, although in truth the horse was running along the waves to meet the stone boat bringing the body of St James to Galicia. When the bridegroom returned, escorting the boat, his body was covered with an armour of milk-white shells, so amazing the locals that they converted at once to the new faith. Its Spanish name, *venera*, calls up associations with the vagina and Venus, the goddess of love, who was born of the seafoam and surfed ashore on a giant scallop shell. For pilgrims, the shell also symbolized the end of the journey, the resurrection and unity in the world – the sea from which it came, the earth in its stony hardness, and the sun in its radiant lines. It's hard to think of another symbol so polyvalent, embracing sex, death, dinner and spiritual wholeness – not to mention a multinational company peddling the diesel or unleaded souls of the dead dinosaurs that fuel the way.

The upper level is named 'of the living' and the lower 'of the dead', recalling the Roman cemetery that once occupied the spot. In the Middle Ages this was the square of cheap food, ladled out from the stalls. Alongside the square runs the stern façade of the **Convento de San Paio de Antelares**, 'Pelayo before the Altars', containing a

Museo de Arte Sacra
Praza de Feixo 2–4, t 98 158 31 27; open April–Dec Mon–Sat 10.30–1.30 and 4–7; closed Jan–Mar; adm

Museo de Arte Sacra, where the Virgin holds the Child in one hand and thumps a devil with the other. The cloistered nuns keep up the square's culinary tradition with their famous almond and coconut tarts. In the lower square is the **Puerta Santa**, opened only during a Holy Year, or Año Xacobeo, when St James' Day – 25 July – falls on a Sunday. The doorway of 1611 consists of 24 compartments, each pigeonholing a carved figure from the Romanesque choir, which may have been the work of Master Mateo. In the upper level of the square, the handsome 17th-century **Casa de la Parra** is one of the prettiest in Santiago, decorated with stylized bunches of grapes.

The north façade faces **Praza de la Azabachería** ('of the Jet-makers'), where pilgrims bought souvenirs such as a little black figure of St James with you praying at his feet. The use of jet (hard black polished lignite) is said to be in memory of a local coal-worker, Contolay, who helped St Francis of Assisi on his pilgrimage. Two jet-makers are still in business, although they now specialize in jewellery and works of art: **Regueira**, at Azabachería 9, and **Mayer**, Platerías 6. In the Middle Ages, the square was the favourite rendezvous for French pilgrims.

Another attraction in Praza de la Azabachería was the chance for destitute pilgrims to hang their rags on an **iron cross**, the *crus d'os farrapos*, and pick up new clothes from the Benedictines around the corner at **San Martín Pinario**. San Martín, one of the most venerable monastic institutions in the city, was founded in 912 as the special protector of the Apostle's tomb. In the 1400s, the two other Benedictine houses in Santiago joined San Martín to form an institution powerful enough to challenge the Inquisition. In spite of complaints that it would compete with the cathedral, they commissioned an elaborate top-heavy façade by Gabriel Casas in the 18th century; note on top the monks' vocation reflected in the statue of St Martin of Tours sharing his cloak with a poor man. Inside, the vast **Claustro de la Portería** with its elegant fountain was completed by Casas' more famous follower, Casas y Novoa, while just beyond is an extraordinary, floating 17th-century staircase with Aztec decorations under a Baroque dome. Beyond, the huge barrel-vaulted **church** is the stage for Casas y Novoa's *retablo mayor*, one of the most over-ripe pieces of flummery ever produced, a feverish blast of intricate gilded detail. Casas y Novoa was also responsible for the **Capilla del Socorro** on the right side of the nave, and the rather more restrained sacristy; the elaborate 17th-century choir stalls are also well worth a look. The stately, colonnaded 18th-century façade facing Praza San Martín grows like an altarpiece above a sunken Baroque staircase designed by a Dominican named Manuel de los Mártires, all granite ribbons squirming below the level of the pavement.

In Praza San Miguel (in front of Praza San Martín) the 14th-century Gothic Pazo de Don Pedro contains the **Museo das Peregrinacións**; opposite, **San Miguel dos Agros** is another product of Santiago's 18th-century boom. But for a real eyeful of local Baroque continue along to Rúa da Algalía de Arriba and walk north to Rúa de San Roque, where the startling façade of **Santa Clara** by Simón Rodríguez almost jumps out at you, its fat, abstract volutes culminating in a trio of huge cylinders that look as if they could roll off the roof any second, altogether more 1930s in effect than 1730s.

Museo das Peregrinacións
www.mdperegrinacions.com; open Tues–Fri 10–8, Sat 10.30–1.30 and 5–8, Sun and hols 10.30–1.30; closed Mon; adm

Elsewhere in Santiago

Like any natural, organic medieval city, Santiago is a delight to wander in, its narrow, arcaded streets and intimate squares paved with granite flagstones, lined with old palaces, churches and monasteries, tinged with green and gold from moss and lichens.

The founders of the two great mendicant orders of the 13th century both made pilgrimages and personally founded monasteries. In 1214, St Francis founded the **Convento de San Francisco**, in Rúa Campiño de San Francisco, northeast of the Hospital de los Reyes Católicos; the Benedictines were impressed enough with Francis's preaching to give him the land, in return for an annual basket of fish. Rebuilt in the 18th century, the convent has a fine granite cross sculpted by Caaveiro with scenes of Francis' life. St Dominic's rather larger **Convento de Santo Domingo de Bonaval**, founded during his pilgrimage in 1220, is due east on the Puerto del

Camino at the end of Rúa das Casas Reais. Behind the Baroque façade hides a handsome Gothic church from the 1300s and the Chapel of the Pantheon of Illustrious Gallegos, last resting-place of poet Rosalía de Castro and the caricaturist Castelao (d. 1950), the Goya of the Civil War. The convent and cloister house the **Museo do Pobo Galego** with a collection of folk items and rural tools, though most memorable of all is the triple spiral staircase, a stunning architectural *tour de force* by Domingo de Andrade, where three different, unsupported granite stairways interlace almost as if by magic in a single tower, each leading to different doors.

Museo do Pobo Galego
open Tues–Sat 10–2 and 4–8, Sun 11–2; closed Mon

Off the Azabachería, Rúa de Troia is named after the venerable **Casa-Museo da Troia**, base for the local *tunas*, not fish but bands of student minstrels in capes and ribbons, who play Galician-Celtic music around the Praza da Immaculada. The Azabachería leads into Praza Cervantes and a street called Preguntoiro ('Questioning') after all the pilgrims who asked for directions here. This curves around to arcaded Rúa Nova, site of the little church of **Santa María Salomé** with a Romanesque door under a Gothic arcade. Parallel extends **Rúa do Vilar**, Santiago's delightful, arcaded main shopping street, where the **Casa do Dean** has a fine Baroque portal; at the Confitería Mora (No.60), pick up a delicious *tarta de Compostela*, made with chocolate bumps in honour of the Santo dos Croques.

Casa-Museo da Troia
www.lacasade latroya.org; open mid-July–end-Sept Tues–Sat 11–2 and 4–8, Sun 11–2; closed Mon; adm

For the classic view of Santiago's towers and roofs, walk along the **Paseo da Ferradura** just east of the cathedral, a leafy 19th-century park where old men will take your photo with cameras nearly as old as themselves.

Santa María del Sar

After all the Baroque in the centre of Santiago, take a break at the Romanesque 12th-century Santa María del Sar, a mile south of the Convento de las Mercedarias, another stately Baroque confection. Set alone in its meadow, Santa María is an architectural jewel with a different slant – literally. The piers and arches along the high barrel-vaulted nave have leant backwards from time immemorial; although the common explanation for it is subsidence, it may have been done intentionally – like the campanile of Pisa or the leaning towers of Bologna, along with other pieces of crooked bravura of the same period. The buttresses were added after the Lisbon earthquake of 1755. Don't miss the remarkable carvings by Master Mateo along one gallery in the **cloister**.

Santa María del Sar cloister
open Mon–Sat 10–1 and 4–7, Sun 10–1

ⓘ Santiago de Compostela ›
Municipal: Rúa de Vilar 63, t 98 155 51 29, www.santiago turismo.com

Tourist Information in Santiago de Compostela

The **tourist office** arranges guided walks (usually €15) with different themes, including gastronomy, old city, churches, cloistered convents, artists' workshops, magical, contemporary architecture and musical tours. There are daily walking tours at 10am in English during the summer. All can be booked at the **municipal tourist office** or on the website *www.santiagoreservas.com*.

ⓘ Santiago de
Compostela >
*Provincial: Rúa de Vilar
43, t 98 158 40 81,
www.turgalicia.es*

*Pilgrim Information
Centre: Rúa de Vilar
30–32, t 98 157 20 04,
www.archicompostela.org*

★ Costa Vella >>

★ Hostal Alfonso >>

They also offer a wide range of activities, from city audioguides to hop-on hop-off tourist bus tickets.

The **post office** is on Travesía de Fonseca, near the Praza do Obradoiro; most hotels and hostels offer internet access, and the tourist office can provide a list of *cibers*. The **m* Café e Copas**, Rua Fonte de Santo Antonio 15, has WiFi.

There is a **market** from Monday to Saturday in the covered market in Praza de San Félix.

Where to Stay in Santiago de Compostela

Santiago ✉ 15705

Finding a place to stay at any price is easy; even during the high holy day of 25 July you may be met at the bus or train station by landladies luring you to their *hostales* or *casas particulares* for around €20 a head.

*****Hostal de Los Reyes Católicos, Praza del Obradoiro, t 98 158 22 00, *www.parador.es* (€€€€€). Poor pilgrims used to stay in this magnificent 15th-century building, but since 1954 it has been the luxurious *nec plus ultra* of Spanish *hostales* and one of Europe's best hotels – but it's probably the priciest *parador* in Spain.

*****Palacio del Carmen, Oblatas s/n, t 98 155 24 44, *www.ac-hotels.com* (€€€). A much-restored convent just outside the old centre, but with every amenity including a heated pool, fine restaurant and gardens.

***Rua Villar, Rúa do Villar 8–10, t 98 151 98 58, *www.hotelruavillar.com* (€€€–€€). A chic hotel in an ancient building; the stone walls and wooden beams ooze charm, while the contemporary art and designer gadgets add pizzazz. Smaller rooms are cheaper.

***Virxe da Cerca, Rúa Virxe da Cerca 27, t 90 240 58 58, *www.pousadasde compostela.com* (€€€–€€). Stylish serenity and beautiful gardens in an 18th-century Jesuit residence. The extension is slightly cheaper.

**Hotel Airas Nunes, Rúa do Vilar 17, t 90 240 58 58, *www.pousadasde compostela.com* (€€). An elegant

pousada in an early 18th-century building. The interior is delightful, all honey-coloured stone and wood.

**Hotel Avenida, Fuente de San Antonio 5, t 98 156 84 26, *www.sino-compostela.com* (€€–€). Friendly, family-run hotel, with pretty, stone-walled rooms and wicker furniture.

*As Artes, Trav. de Dos Puertas 2, t 98 155 52 54, *www.asartes.com* (€€–€). A charming old stone house, with seven individually decorated rooms inspired by famous artists. It's by the *parador*, a stone's throw from the cathedral.

*Hotel Rosa Rosae, C/La Rosa, 7, t 98 152 83 00, *www.rosarosae.es* (€€–€). A modern stylish place with friendly service outside the old centre.

Costa Vella, Rúa Porta da Peña 17, t 98 158 36 37, *www.costavella.com* (€€). A beautiful, very peaceful place, located on a traffic-free street above the Convento de San Francisco. It's worth paying more for a sunny room overlooking the city; part of Santiago's old walls can be seen in the lovely garden. Their glossy sister hotel, **Altair (€€€), is nearby, with chic urban décor, WiFi and café-bar.

**Hotel San Clemente, Rúa San Clemente 28, t 90 240 58 58 (€). A simple hotel in another listed building with original stone and polished wood interior.

*Hotel Oca Avenida, Fonte de San Antonio 5, t 98 157 80 07, *www. ocahotels.com* (€). Provides character and comfort, with polished wooden floors in a restored 18th-century house.

*Hotel Moure, Rúa dos Loureires 6, t 98 158 36 37 (€). Newly refurbished hotel, with pristine white rooms, some with private terraces.

**Hostal Alfonso, Praza de Fonseca 5, t 98 158 56 85 (€), *wwwhostal alfonso.com*. You'll need to book early for a room at this wonderful *hostal*, with immaculate rooms and welcoming hosts.

**Pensión Barbantes Libredón, Praza de Fonseca 5, t 98 157 65 20 (€), *www.libredon barbantes.com*. Good views of the square and *palacio* from sparkling pine and white rooms.

**Hostal Mapoula, Entremurallas 10, t 98 158 01 24, *www.mapoula.com* (€).

Just inside the *casco viejo*, this old-fashioned *hostal* has simple rooms.

Hostal Suso, Rúa del Vilar 65, **t 98 158 66 11 (€). Located on Santiago's prettiest street, this pilgrims' favourite is run by a jovial fellow who knows everything and probably has something to do with the tasty tapas in the excellent bar downstairs.

*Hostal Badalada, Rúa Xelmírez, **t** 98 158 38 67, *www.badalada.es* (€). Another charming choice, in a prettily renovated stone house on a narrow street. They also have an apartment.

*Pensión da Estrela, Praza San Martín Pinario 5, **t** 98 157 69 24, *www.pensiondaestrela.com* (€). A simple, immaculate *pensión*: book early for a room with views over the old city.

Eating Out in Santiago de Compostela

Eating in Santiago is a pleasure – competition is keen and the food has to be good to succeed. Rúa do Hórreo has the biggest concentration of restaurants – one window of tempting seafood after another.

⭐ O Curro da Parra >>

Casa Roberto, San Xulián de Sales 17, **t** 98 151 17 69 (€€€). For a special treat, drive out 8km to Vedra in the Valle de Ulla, where Roberto prepares some of the most delicious, imaginative dishes in all Galicia in a lovely country villa. *Closed Sun eve and first 2 weeks Aug.*

⭐ Pedro Roca >

Pedro Roca, Rúa Domingo Garcia Sabel 1, **t** 98 158 57 76, *www.pedroroca.es* (€€€; set menus from €45–80). Exquisite cuisine from one of the city's most outstanding chefs; no deconstructed, molecular cuisine here, just the finest, locally sourced produce prepared to perfection. *Closed Sun eve.*

Tacita d'Juan, Rúa Hórreo 31, **t** 98 156 32 55 (€€€). Offers elegant cuisine made from fresh Galician ingredients. *Closed Sun and 3 weeks Aug.*

Don Gaiferos, Rúa Nova 23, **t** 98 158 38 94 (€€€–€€; set menu €22). For tradition mixed with international, seasonal dishes, try this beautiful vaulted dining room. *Closed eves Sun and Mon, except in summer.*

Casa Marcelo, Rúa Hortas 1, **t** 98 155 85 80, *www.casamarcelo.net* (€€€–€€). An utterly charming restaurant on a

pretty old street; there are no menus: the daily offerings vary according to what's in season and Marcelo Tejedor's remarkable imagination. *Closed Sun–Tues.*

Vinoteca Descorche, Rúa Hórreo 96, **t** 98 197 60 12, *www.monchovilas.com* (€€). Small restaurant and wine bar, serving a delicious tapas as well as a set lunch menu, and a few market fresh dishes from a changing menu. They have one of the best wine selections in the city.

Casa Vilas, Rosalía de Castro 88, **t** 98 159 21 70 (€€). A bastion of Gallego cuisine in a century-old restaurant. *Closed Sat eve and Sun.*

Don Quijote, Rúa Galeras, 20, **t** 98 158 68 59, *www.quijoterestaurante.com* (€€). If you ever tire of Gallego cuisine, come here to sample some traditional Castilian staples like *cochinillo* at this well-established restaurant.

A Curtidoria, Rúa Conga 2–3, **t** 98 155 43 42, *www.acurtidoria.com* (€€–€; set lunch €13). Light, modern cuisine in an elegant dining room. *Closed Sun.*

O Curro da Parra, Rúa Travesa 20, **t** 98 155 60 59, *www.ocurrodaparra.com* (€). Simple but charming restaurant, serving fresh, creative cuisine including an excellent set lunch menu (€11). *Closed Mon.*

María Castaña, Rúa Raiña 19, **t** 98 156 01 37 (€). Traditional, Gallego home cooking in a cosy setting. Hugely (and justly) popular, so get there early.

Casa Manolo, Praza Cervantes, **t** 98 158 29 50, *www.casamanolo.es* (€). Roomy restaurant, where a colossal menu drags in the crowds.

Bars and Nightlife in Santiago de Compostela

The area around Rúa Franco is the focus of the evening *marcha*.

Bodeguilla de San Roque, San Roque 3 (near Santa Clara). Serves fine wines with plates of delicious *tetilla* cheese and all kinds of gourmet titbits.

La Borriquita de Belém, San Paio de Antealtares 22. For jazz with your drinks, try here, near the cathedral.

Café Casino, Rúa do Villar 35. This 150-year-old café provides sink-into sofas and armchairs, piles of newspapers and a vast sitting-room space for drinking coffees and cocktails.

Café Iacobus, Rúa Azevacheria 5. Claims the widest selection of exotic coffees, infusions, and sinful chocolate concoctions. One of a chain of four.

Café Literarios, Praza Quintana 1. With a perfect terrace at the top of the steps of this lovely square.

Casa das Crechas, Via Sacra 3, t 98 156 07 51. Live music and other happenings can be taken in here. When you can't eat or drink any more, you can dance it off.

Pub Modus Vivendi, Praza Feixoo 98, *www.pubmodusvivendi.net*. One of the veterans in the Old Quarter's circuit

that likes to play funk and soul music. Occasional live music.

Dado Dada, Alfredo Brañas 19, t 98 159 15 74, *http://jazzclub.dadodada.com*. Santiago's classic jazz joint, with occasional live gigs.

Garigolo Café-Teatro, Praza Algalia de Arriba 1. All kinds of performances – film screenings, cabaret, theatre, etc. – take place in this café.

Liberty, Alfredo Brañas 6. A popular place with plenty of action.

Metate, Colexón de San Paio. Don't miss the hot chocolate and chocolate cocktails at this former factory.

Tupperware Lounge Café, Frai Rosendo Salvado 28. A hip hang-out, with tongue-in-cheek retro décor.

Back to the *Rías*: Golfo Ártabro

Two of Galicia's most important ports, Ferrol and A Coruña, occupy either end of the 20km Golfo Ártabro, savagely bitten out of the northwest coast, with four teeth marking the four estuaries that flow into it. You can get there by dawdling west along the Rías Altas (*see* p.306) or by racing up the A9 motorway from Santiago.

Ferrol and Pontedeume

Plump on the big fat Ría de Betanzos, swollen by four rivers, the salty city of **Ferrol** was named after its lighthouse (*faro*) and counts some 74,000 souls, many of whom work for or depend on the Spanish navy. Gently, slowly, the port city has dropped the article 'El' from the front of its name and the 'del Caudillo' stuck on the back in honour of Francisco Franco, born here in 1892, son of a naval supply officer, who grew up to be the youngest general in Spanish history before his career as dictator, never losing his Gallego roots in his maddening stubbornness and inscrutability – earning himself the nickname 'the Sphinx without a secret'. Besides the enormous docks, navy yards and sailors' red-light gauntlet, Ferrol has a pretty enough medieval core, a large planned 18th-century geometric, neoclassical quarter, the legacy of Philip V who greatly boosted Ferrol's fortunes, and a modern quarter that looks like SimCity. The best thing is to just wander among the pretty houses with 'crystal galleries' and the casino and gardens. A pair of castles on the slender waist of the *ría* defend the naval base.

At the bottom of the estuary, 5km from Ferrol, **San Martín de Xubia** was founded as a monastery in the 9th century. It was the only one in Galicia adopted by Cluny (1113), but all that survives is the Cluniac church with its three apses and carved capitals.

Getting around the Golfo Ártabro

By Air

A Coruña's **airport** is 8km away at Alvedro, t 90 240 47 04, *www.aena.es*, with connections to Madrid, Barcelona and Seville, as well as London, Amsterdam and Paris. There's an airport bus to the main bus station roughly every 30mins Mon–Fri 7.15am–9.45pm, hourly on Sat 7.30am–10.30am, and hourly on Sun 9am–10pm; bus information t 98 123 12 34. A taxi costs around €15–18.

By Boat

Three boats daily ply the *ría* between Ferrol and A Coruña, arriving next to A Coruña's tourist office; from the same spot, summer-only launches go to Praia de Santa Cristina.

By Train

RENFE (*www.renfe.com*, t 902 320 320) connects Ferrol and A Coruña with Pontedeume and the main junctions at Betanzos, Santiago, Lugo, Vigo, Padrón and Villagarcía de Arousa. In A Coruña the San Cristóbal station is a bit out of the way on Avda Joaquín Planelles; take bus no.1 from the nearby bus station to the historic centre. In Ferrol, RENFE (see above) and FEVE share the same station.

By Bus

A Coruña's bus station is on C/Caballeros, t 98 118 43 35 (near the RENFE station), with connections to the Costa da Morte and all major points in Galicia; ALSA (*www.alsa.es*) provide services to Madrid, León, and the Basque country.

Ferrol's buses depart from next to the train station, t 98 132 47 51, and go to Betanzos, Viveiro, Foz, Ribadeo and Lugo.

South of Ferrol, the charming medieval town of **Pontedeume** was once the preserve of the Counts of Andrade, who built and collected the tolls from their great bridge over the Ría Eume, once supported by 58 arches; some 15 arches still remain, as well as a 14th-century palace and tower emblazoned with the family's huge crest. The tolls financed the Andrades' hunts; note the weathered stone boars standing guard by the bridge. The parish church, the late-Gothic Santiago, is a trove of minor art. There are a couple of **beaches** along the *ría* (the **Praia Perbes** is a good one) and, off the NVI to Betanzos, **San Miguel de Breamo** (1137), with its façade pierced by a window in the shape of an 11-point star and capitals to warm the cockles of any Romanesque diehard's heart.

If you have a car, two ruined monasteries beckon inland from Pontedeume, as much for their architecture as for their lovely settings. Up the Eume river, the Benedictine **Monasterio de Caaveiro** was founded in 934 by San Rosendo, who became a bishop at 18 and defended Compostela from the Normans and Saracens. Although renowned as a stickler for the rules, Rosendo could hardly have founded Caaveiro in a more evocative place. Twenty kilometres south of Pontedeume, the 12th-century Cistercian **Monasterio de Monfero** with its two cloisters is equally derelict, even if more recently rebuilt in the 17th century, unabashedly grandiose for its remote setting; only the church, with a chequerboard façade of granite and slate blocks, is still in use.

Betanzos

Rising steeply over the head of yet another small estuary, lovely Betanzos is a far more ancient place, a Celtic village that grew into the Roman port of Brigantium Flavium. It thrived into the 18th century, when the Mandeo and Mendo rivers washed in so much silt that they stole Betanzos' sea coast. Progress stopped, leaving a time capsule: houses and mansions of all sizes with wrought-iron balconies, or *solanas*, line the narrow lanes that wind up the hill from the harbour's medieval gates. Life revolves around the charming, monumental **Praza de García Hermanos**, its central ornament a statue of two *indianos* and a replica of Versailles' Fountain of Diana. Most of the surrounding buildings are from the 18th century, including a neoclassical palace now used as the National Archives of Galicia; this runs a small but interesting historical **Museo das Mariñas**. The town's three attractive churches are just off the square: the 14th-century **Santa María del Azogue**; 15th-century **Santiago**, with a figure of Santiago Matamoros on the tympanum; and Gothic **San Francisco**, inspired by the basilica at Assisi and its door topped with a bizarre figure of a boar with a cross rising out of its back. Inside, don't miss the delightful 14th-century tomb of Fernán Pérez de Andrade O Boo (the Good), who paid for the church and whose sarcophagus, supported on the backs of a boar and a bear, is covered with hunting scenes, perhaps in the hope that there'd be plenty of game in heaven. Take time to walk along the Ría Mandeo, one of Galicia's prettiest *rías*.

Rather than take the NVI or the AP9/E1 motorway directly to A Coruña, follow the pretty scenery along the Ría de Betanzos up to the local resort of **Sada**, to see its boardwalk and **La Terraza**, the finest Modernista building in Galicia, designed by López Hernández, a curious pavilion made of glass and giant music stands. The road to A Coruña passes the **Pazo de Meirás**, residence of Galicia's greatest novelist, Countess Emilia Pardo-Bazán, and later Franco, whose descendants still own it; further along, offshore on a wooded islet, the 17th-century **Castillo de Santa Cruz** once defended A Coruña.

Museo das Mariñas
open Mon–Fri 10–2 and 4–7, Sat 10.20–1; adm

12 | Galicia | Golfo Ártabro: A Coruña

A Coruña

 A Coruña

Occupying the length of the Ría da Coruña and the southwest fringe of the Golfo Ártabro, A Coruña is the liveliest city in Galicia, a big (pop. 246,000), exuberant, commercial capital with character to spare. Sprawling over a peninsula and attached to the mainland by a thin neck of land, it has windswept beaches facing the Atlantic and a magnificent sheltered harbour in the estuary that has made its fortune and paid for all of its hypnotic wall of windowed balconies or *solanas* that gave A Coruña its nickname, 'Crystal City'.

Philip II and the Invincible Armada

The pious royal bureaucrat Philip II had more than one bone to pick with Queen Elizabeth's England in the 1580s: Elizabeth had recently invented the Bloody Mary by lopping off the head of Mary Queen of Scots, Philip's favourite candidate for the English throne, and England was helping the Protestants of the Netherlands in their revolt against Spain; Spanish trade routes were threatened but, worst of all, Elizabeth had confirmed the country's Protestant orientation.

To solve all his problems and force England back into the Catholic fold, Philip decided on what seemed to be a foolproof plan: to build up the biggest fleet of warships in Spanish history, and co-ordinate this invincible Armada with an invasion of England by his army in the Netherlands. Francis Drake got wind of Philip's plans and in 1587 sailed into Cádiz 'to singe the king's beard' by burning the parked fleet and setting the invasion date back by a year. Finally, on 22 July 1588, an Armada of 130 enormous galleons, manned by 10,000 sailors and 19,000 soldiers, set sail from A Coruña.

After some difficult sea battles, England's first stroke of luck came when the Armada set anchor near Calais, where it was to meet with the invasion fleet from the Netherlands. Lord Howard sent fireships against the Armada, which panicked the Spaniards into breaking formation; soon after, on 8 August, in a battle that raged along the Channel, the quick English defeated the lumbering Armada at Gravelines. When the Spaniards tried to sail home to regroup, the English forced them home the long way around Scotland, where storms wreaked havoc; by the time the Invincible Armada limped back to Spain, only 76 half-wrecked galleons pulled into port, minus 15,000 soldiers. Although the war between England and Spain dragged on until 1604, the repercussions of the defeat of the Armada endured for centuries. Philip's treasury was empty, but in cocky Elizabethan England the party had just begun.

A Coruña's relationship with Britain goes back to its first settlers, Phoenician merchants who imported tin from Cornwall. The Romans called it Ardobicum Corunium, and tenuously associated it with Hercules, who performed one of his Twelve Labours (stealing the cattle of Geryon) in Cádiz on the other side of Spain and reputedly had a hand in building the lighthouse. The Suevians and the Moors took turns running the show until 1002; in the Middle Ages, English pilgrims to Santiago often landed here, among them Chaucer's Wife of Bath and his patron John of Gaunt. Some 200 years later it was Spain's turn to invade England; see box, above.

In the 'Groyne'

The classic view of A Coruña is of its harbour along Avenida de la Marina, lined with a solid wall of crystal galleries set in white balconies, a window cleaner's vision of hell. It is magical to sail into, just as Drake fearlessly did in 1589, swooping down in the night with 30 ships to rub salt in Philip's wounds. Only a young girl named María Pita stood in the way, not only raising the alarm to save the city but somehow swiping Drake's flag in the process. In gratitude A Coruña gave her name to its biggest, busiest square, Praza María Pita, where the bars under its porticoes stay packed until the wee hours of the morning. One side is taken up with the city hall, the eclectic Modernista **Palacio Municipal** (1907) by Pedro Mariño, decorated with symbols of A Coruña.

The older part of A Coruña – what old British seadogs called 'the Groyne' – begins at Praza María Pita, a labyrinth of winding streets squeezed around a hill. Near the harbour at Rúa Tabernas 13, Countess Emilia Pardo-Bazán was born in 1851; the mansion now houses the **Casa Museo de Emilia Pardo-Bazán**, a small museum dedicated to the novelist.

Casa Museo de Emilia Pardo-Bazán
open Sept–July Mon–Fri 10–1.40 and 4–6.30; closed Sat, Sun and Aug

Nearby Rúa Santiago leads into little Praza A Fariña (or de Azcárraga), its bright flowerbeds covering the spot where gallows once stood. For pilgrims who sailed into A Coruña, the over-restored 12th-century Romanesque church of **Santiago** was their first stop; one door has a carving of Santiago Matamoros at Clavijo, another the Lamb of God; its 16th-century tower once defended the city from English pirates. The **Colegiata de Santa María del Campo**, begun in the 1210s and finished in the 1400s, stands at the top of the square. Its sculptors were star-struck: star decorations run along the roof and on the west façade; the triple portal has a carving of the Three Magi. Over the north door two angels stand by as someone seems to fall out of the sky with star symbols, or perhaps Ezekiel's wheel of fire, whirling up in the cosmos. Inside are some fine Romanesque tombs, polychrome statues and, just to the left of the altar, another star, carved on a capital.

Just down from here, the little Plazuela de Santa Bárbara is A Coruña's most charming, site of the **Convento de Santa Barbara** (1613), where cloistered Poor Clares live behind the portal. Behind this, the **Convento de Santo Domingo** has two excellent Baroque chapels from the 17th century, especially the Capilla de la Virgen del Rosario, sheltering the city's patroness.

Santo Domingo stands on the edge of the evocative little **Jardín de San Carlos**, set in the walls of the old fortress of San Carlos. It contains the granite tomb of Sir John Moore, who in 1809 led the routed, dispirited British army across Galicia with the French on his tail. At Elviña, just before A Coruña, he sent most of his troops ahead to board ships for home, just as Marshal Soult launched into a vicious attack; Moore managed to stall the French long enough for 15,000 of his men to embark under Soult's nose, an operation that has been called a precursor to Dunkirk. Casualties were high on both sides (Moore died pierced by a cannonball) and the British lost at Elviña, only to return under the Duke of Wellington.

Just opposite, A Coruña's busy military history is remembered in the **Museo Militar** in the old church of San Francisco. From here, bus no.3 will take you out 2km to the northernmost tip of the peninsula and the 431ft **Torre de Hércules**, A Coruña's proudest symbol, and a UNESCO World Heritage Site since 2009. Built in the 2nd century AD in the time of Trajan, it's the oldest continuously working Roman lighthouse, but with an external skin from 1791. Bring a pep pill: you'll have to climb the 242 steps to the top for the splendid view of the city and ocean. The Paseo do Parrote leads out to **Castillo de San Antón**, last rebuilt in 1779. It now defends

Museo Militar
open Mon–Sat 10–2 and 4–7, Sun and hols 10–2; adm

Torre de Hércules
open July and Aug daily 10–8.45; April–June and Sept daily 10–6.45; Oct–Mar daily 10–5.45; adm

Museo Arqueológico
open July–Aug Tues–Sat 10–9, Sun and hols 10–3; Sept–June Tues–Sat 10–7.30, Sun and hols 10–3; adm

Museo de Bellas Artes
open Tues–Fri 10–8, Sat 10–2 and 4.30–8, Sun 10–2; adm

Casa de las Ciencias
http://mc2coruna.org/ casa; open July and Aug daily 10–8; Sept–June daily 10–7; adm, combined adm with Aquárium and Domus available; check planetarium showings on the website

Domus
http://mc2coruna.org/ casa; open summer daily 11–9; winter daily 10–7; adm

Aquárium
http://mc2coruna.org/ casa; open daily 10–9; adm with Domus and Casa de las Ciencias available

artefacts from the Iron Age, the Celtic *castros*, the Roman era and the Middle Ages in the **Museo Arqueológico**.

In the newer part of A Coruña (beyond Praza de María Pita) the **Museo de Bellas Artes** has a collection of European paintings, sculptures, ceramics and coins dating from the 17th century. Near the **Mercado San Agustín**, the old Praza dos Ovos has been converted into a charmingly goofy square devoted to comedians. A completely different atmosphere reigns in spooky Praza de España, a block up from the market; it was only in 2010 that the city hall dismantled the monument to José Millán Astray, the one-armed, one-eyed psychopath who led the Spanish Foreign Legion and taught his troops to cry '*¡Viva la Muerte!*' in the Civil War. The **Casa de las Ciencias** in Parque de Santa Margarita has a planetarium and museum dedicated to the world of science, technology and nature. Nearby, the **Casa Museo Picasso** recreates the artist's studio in a house occupied by Picasso's family between 1891 and 1895, and displays reproductions of the young adolescent's paintings of the Torre de Hercules. On the other side of the isthmus lie A Coruña's beaches: the **Praias de Ríazor** and **Orzán** fill up in summer and are backed the Paseo Marítimo. Heading up towards the headland is the ultra-modern **Domus**, or **Museum of Man**, designed by Arata Isozaki to look like an upturned boat and dedicated to the human body. A little further up, just below the Torre de Hércules, is the entertaining **Aquárium**, with a vast subterranean tank of wheeling fish, a pool with six friendly seals, and an Octopus Garden.

If the summertime crush along the city beaches is unappealing, there are quieter, cleaner and prettier strands are outside the city at **Santa Cristina**, **Bastiagueiro**, **Santa Cruz**, **Mera** and **Lorbe** (this last is the farthest from town, 16km away).

Markets on the Golfo Ártabro

Pontedeume: Sat.
Betanzos: Tues, Thurs and Sat.
A Coruña: Mon–Fri (Mercado San Agustín).

Where to Stay and Eat on the Golfo Ártabro

(i) Ferrol >
Praza Camilo José Cela, t 98 131 11 79, www.ferrol-concello.es

Ferrol ✉ 15400
★★★★Pazo Libunca, Lugar de Castro, Castro (10km from Ferrol), t 98 138 35 40, www.pazolibunca.eu (€€€). A small, romantic hotel in a sumptuous Modernista villa surrounded by gardens. Excellent restaurant (€€€).

★★★Parador do Ferrol, Almirante Fernández Martín, t 98 135 67 20, www.parador.es (€€€). The ageing, nautically decorated rooms have handsome views over the *ría*.

Casa do Castelo de Andrade, Lugar do Castelo de Andrade s/n, 7km from Pontedeume, t 98 143 38 39, www. casteloandrade.com (€€). Handsome stone mansion, with ten elegant, individually decorated rooms (some with Jacuzzi) and a pretty garden.

★★★Pazo da Merced, Camiño da Merced, Neda, t 98 138 22 00, www.pazodamerced.com (€€–€). If you're driving, this is a pretty little place to stay, a 17th- and 18th-century manor with *ría* views and a pool. *Closed Oct–Easter week.*

ⓘ Pontedeume
Avda do Torreón 2,
t 98 143 02 70

⭐ Hotel Cabo
Ortegal ›

***Hotel Suizo**, Dolores 17, **t** 98 130 04 00, *www.hotelsuizo.net* (€€–€). In a Modernista building with a café.

O'Parrulo, Avda Catabois 401, **t** 98 131 86 53 (€€). A classic, serving local seafood like grilled clams from the *ría*, along with succulent meats. There's a garden in summer, and a good wine selection. *Closed Wed eve, Sun.*

****Hotel Cabo Ortegal**, C/Santos 8–12, Cariño (50km north of A Coruña), **t** 98 142 02 01, *www.hotelcaboortegal.com* (€€). A trio of turn-of-the-20th-century villas, now an enchanting little hotel overlooking the *rías*.

Casa Rivera, Galiano 57, **t** 98 135 07 59 (€; set lunch €9). A popular local favourite, with traditional dishes like *caldeirada de pescados* (fish stew) and a great-value lunch *menú*. *Closed Sun.*

Pataquiña, Dolores 35, **t** 98 135 23 11 (€). Offers heaps of good, well-prepared Gallego specialities; try their *salsa Pataquiña*, a delectable mixture of shrimp and crab in brandy and garlic.

Sur, C/Magdalena 50, **t** 98 135 08 70 (€). Old-fashioned bar with great tapas and good wine.

Betanzos ✉ 15300

***Los Ángeles**, Los Ángeles 11, **t** 98 177 15 11 (€€–€). Modest but well-equipped rooms, an excellent local restaurant downstairs and private parking.

La Casilla, Ctra de Castilla 90, **t** 98 177 01 61 (€€). Packs out, especially at weekends, with crowds enjoying the famous local tortilla. *Closed Sun eve, Mon (except July–Aug), 3 wks in Nov.*

Casanova, Pza García Hermanos 15, **t** 98 177 06 03 (€€). Rustically decorated, with traditional dishes such as *callos* (tripe), stews and roast meats; also has a lively tapas bar.

ⓘ A Coruña ›
Municipal: Rua Sol,
t 98 118 43 44, www.
turismocoruna.com

Regional: Avda de la
Marina s/n, t 98 122 18
22, www.turgalicia.es

A Coruña ✉ 15000

A Coruña fills up in the summer. The bar area around Rúa Franja and Praza Maria Pita goes on well into dawn when the fishing fleet pulls in and everyone watches the Muro, the auctioning of the catch.

*****Finisterre**, Pso del Parrote 2, **t** 98 120 54 00, *www.hesperia-hotels.com* (€€€€). Well located and luxurious, overlooking the sea, with pools, tennis courts, a nursery, playground and a health and wellness centre.

***Riazor**, Avda Pedro Barrié de la Maza 29, **t** 98 125 34 00, *www.riazor hotel.com* (€€). A pleasant, less costly alternative, with a fine beachside location and acceptable rooms.

****El Pescador**, Avda Che Guevara 81c (Ctra Santa Cruz), **t** 98 163 95 02, *www.hotelelpescadorgalicia.com* (€€). A pebble's throw from the sandy beach of Santa Cristina.

****Sol**, Sol 10, **t** 98 121 00 19, *www.hotelsolcoruna.com* (€€–€). Pleasant, welcoming *hostal* despite the disconcerting flashing sign.

***Hostal Centro Gallego**, Rúa Estrella 2, **t** 98 122 22 36 (€€–€). One of the best budget options: central, welcoming and clean. All rooms with private bath.

***Hostal Alborán**, Ruego de Agua 14, **t** 98 122 25 62, *www.hostalalboran.es* (€). Near the main *praza* with adequate rooms; clean and cheap (under €40 even in high season).

****Hotel Maycar**, C/San Andrés 159, **t** 98 122 60 00, *www.hotelmaycar.com* (€). This modern hotel is centrally located and offers excellent value for money. Parking available.

***Hostal Palacio**, Pza de Galicia 2, **t** 98 112 23 38, *www.hostalpalacio.com* (€). Delightfully old-fashioned, with cabinets full of knick knacks .

A La Brasa, Juan Flórez 38, **t** 98 127 07 27, *www.gasthof.es* (€€). True to its name, this place specializes in meat (including huge steaks) and fish sizzling from the grill.

Coral, Callejón de la Estacada 9 (near the port), **t** 98 120 05 69 (€€). This is one of the best seafood places; exceptional, delicate shellfish dishes are served in a classy setting. *Closed Sun except mid-July–mid-Sept.*

Montecarlo, General Sanjurjo 90, **t** 98 113 75 39 (€€). A delightful *casa de vinos*, with a wonderful wine selection accompanied by good *raciones*.

Casa Pardo, Novoa Santos 15, **t** 98 128 00 21 (€€). This long-established place offers lovely seafood and grilled meats; it also has a stylish branch (where the son is chef) in the Domus, with wonderful views over the bay. *Closed Sun.*

La Penela, Praza María Pita 12, **t** 98 120 92 00 (€€). A reliable and popular place on the main square. *Closed Sun.*

West of A Coruña: A Costa da Morte

Before tourism invented the Costa del Sol and the Costa Blanca, the Galicians dubbed this region down to Finisterre the 'Coast of Death' after its number of drownings, shipwrecks and ancient Celtic memories; from the end of the west, from the end of the Milky Way, Celtic warriors would sail out to their reward in the seven-towered castle of Arianhrod. The scenery along this wild land of the setting sun is romantic, the waves are dramatic and the beaches pale and inviting, but the water is icy cold.

Ría de Corme e Laxe

Heading west of A Coruña and Carballo, **Buño** is Galicia's traditional pottery town par excellence, manufacturing yellow and brown earthenware plates and crocks in the shape of pigs for as long as anyone can remember. The road north of Buño ends up at **Malpica**, where the granite cliffs west of A Coruña first relax their vigilance. A former whaling port, Malpica is partly sheltered by the windswept Sisargas islets, populated only by a large seabird nursery (*boteros*, marine taxis, will take you out for a small fee). Appropriately enough, the Costa da Morte has some fine dolmens, or Neolithic tombs, beginning with Malpica's **Pedra de Arca**. Malpica has a beach, pounded with surf, or you can head to the sheltered **Praia de Niñons**, passing by way of the romantic little ivy-shrouded castle known as the **Torres de Mens**, next to a tiny Romanesque chapel decorated with erotic figures.

Corme Porto, a picturesque fishing village to the west, has a reputation for being a law unto itself, a nest of resistance to Franco's *Guardia Civil* goons even into the 1950s, perhaps because they tried to get in the way of Corme's main industry: smuggling. Ask directions to the **Pedra da Serpe** at Gondomil, a snake carved in the stone believed to date from the Phoenicians and connected to the legend of St Adrian, the local St Patrick, who is said to have gathered all the snakes in Galicia here and given them a mighty kick into the ground, where they disappeared. It has a fine white beach and dunes and a more sheltered strand, the **Praia de Balarés** just before the medieval bridge to **Ponteceso**, birthplace of poet Eduardo Pondal (1835–1917). **Laxe**, a pleasant fishing village across the estuary from Corme, has a white beach, safe even for children; for something more remote, continue south along the coast past Pedreira to the enormous **Praia de Traba** (one of the worst affected beaches after the *Prestige* disaster, but now cleaned up). There's a 14th-century church dedicated to Santiago and two intriguing dolmens on the road to Bayo, 5km inland: signs point to the **Dolmen of Dombate**, with engravings of a ship inside on the right, and the **Pedra Cuberta**, another 1km south, with a 20ft chamber.

Getting around West of A Coruña

A Coruña and Santiago are the main bases for transport to the Costa da Morte, but **buses** are not very frequent. If you plan to visit more than one place in a day, study the bus schedules first. Carballo, 35km southwest of A Coruña, is the main bus junction for the coastal villages.

Ría de Camariñas

After some rugged coast, the rocks relent to admit another *ría* shared by the remote fishing hamlets of **Camariñas** and **Muxía**, both renowned for intricate bobbin lace (Camariñas has a little museum dedicated to the art). From small, white and increasingly trendy Camariñas you can walk 5km (3 miles) to **Cabo Villán** and its lighthouse, a wild piece of savage, torn coast, which makes you feel small and far away from civilization, although perhaps less so now that a set of experimental windmills have been erected to harness the wild winds that whip the cape. **Muxía** has always been a bit more important, as the proud escutcheons on the houses testify. It is also the holy city of the Costa da Morte, with its seaside sanctuary of **Nostra Señora de la Barca**, where the Virgin Mary herself is said to have sailed in a stone ship when Santiago was preaching in these parts (it wasn't her only Spanish holiday: she made a similar appearance riding a stone pillar in Zaragoza). Ship-shaped votive offerings dangle in the church. Parts of the Virgin's own magic boat may be seen around the church, including the hull, the Pedra de Abalar, which moves whenever someone free of sin stands on it. If you suffer from colic or gastritis, a walk under the stone keel, the Pedra dos Cadrises (the stone that looks like a stylized dinosaur) should fix you up nicely. Four kilometres from Muxía, in **Moraime**, the Benedictine church of **San Xián** (Julian) is mostly from the 12th century, but was founded in the 900s as a shelter for pilgrims; although humidity has destroyed most of the frescoes, 26 (again, two extra) Elders of the Apocalypse survive on the main portal. Inland, along the AC432, the 16th-century **Castillo de Vimianzo**, once home to the cruel Álvaro Pérez de Moscoso, has been restored to house a collection of paintings, photos and crafts.

Castillo de Vimianzo

open Tues–Sun 10–2 and 4–6.30; closed Mon; offers workshops and demonstrations of traditional crafts, check times with the tourist office in Vimianzo, t 98 171 72 88

Ría de Corcubión and the End of the World

Further south, a byroad off the AC432 leads up to the lighthouse at **Cabo Touriñán**, where, as the plaque states, and notwith-standing Finisterre, you are standing on the westernmost point of continental Europe. Another branch of the road leads to the huge (and hugely exposed) beach, the **Praia do Rostro**, before continuing south to the little industrial port of **Cée**, defended by the 18th-century Castillo de Cardenal. Cée has practically merged with **Corcubión**, an old fishing village sprinkled with manor houses and *solanas*. The parish church has a curious statue of St Mark, brought from Venice by a ship that refused to budge until the saint was

12

Galicia | West of A Coruña: A Costa da Morte

taken ashore. White beaches are sprinkled under the pines, among them **Praia Sardiñeiro** with a few bars and restaurants.

Finisterre (Fisterra)

Beyond lies the traditional westernmost point of Europe, the granite houses of Finisterre huddled on the rocks around the church of the miracle-working Christ of the Golden Beard, who came out of the sea. According to tradition, these same waters contain the city of Duyo (Dugium), which sank beneath the waves at the same time as Pompeii went under the lava; but sunken cities are a wide-ranging Celtic conceit, like Ys in Brittany, that hark back to the Hesperides, the Blessed Isles beyond the West.

Two kilometres beyond is **Cabo Finisterre** with its lighthouse, the World's End, where the Roman legions and pilgrims from Santiago came to gaze at the sun setting. Often at other times the cape is bleak and wrapped in fog, when it's easy to imagine wandering souls flitting along the savage coast before taking their last step into the Beyond. At the foot of the cape, pilgrims would visit the Romanesque church and the **Ara Solís**, evoking the mysteries of life, death and resurrection. For the best overviews, take the road up to **Vista Monte do Facho** where sterile women used to rub up against a menhir until an 18th-century bishop ordered it destroyed.

From **Cée**, the road follows the coast around to **Ezaro**, a wild, picturesque place where massive granite boulders on **Mount Pindo** (1,968ft/600m), 'the Celtic Olympus', have mysterious engravings and ruins of ancient shrines. Unable to erode an estuary of its own through the mountain, the Río Xallas instead tumbles down in a dozen shimmering waterfalls to the sea, polishing the multi-coloured stones as it flows over them. Some of its wild charm has been sacrificed to a hydroelectric plant, but a wander upstream reveals the tumbling Xallas in a more pristine state. South, beyond the cute granite port of **Pindo**, the dune-backed beach of **Carnota** is the longest in Galicia (it also holds a more gloomy record for drownings: even if you think you're a strong swimmer, beware). Carnota also claims Galicia's largest *hórreo*, about 100ft long and made entirely of granite. Although the surrounding valley is fertile, this 18th-century *hórreo* was moved here from elsewhere and extended to win the title, which doesn't seem quite fair.

Where to Stay and Eat West of A Coruña

The gastronomic prize of the the Death Coast is barnacles, or *percebes*, which cost a fortune; the people who gather them are washed away so often that they can't buy insurance.

(★) As Garzas >>

Malpica ✉ 15113

***Fonte de Fraile**, Praia de Canido s/n, t 98 172 07 32, *www.hotelfontedo fraile.com* (€€–€). Pretty seaside hotel on the beach, with Jacuzzi and café.

As Garzas, in Barizo, t 98 172 17 65, *www.asgarzas.com* (rooms €€–€, restaurant €€€). In a fine location, with four lovely rooms and a justly famous restaurant with huge windows overlooking the coast.

Hostal JB, Rueiro da Praia 3, by the beach, **t 98 172 19 06 (€). Family-run and delightful, right on the beach.

*Hostal Panchito, Pza Villar Amigo 6, **t** 98 172 03 07, *http://hostal panchito.com* (€). A good little *hostal* in the centre; rooms under €45.

San Francisco, Rúa Eduardo Pondal 5–7, **t** 98 172 04 89 (€). Good for reasonably priced fresh seafood.

Camariñas ✉ 15123

4 Ventos, C/Molino de Viento 71, **t** 98 173 60 64 (€€). Come here for comfortable, basic rooms and a restaurant.

*Hostal Scala, Paseo Marítimo 6, **t** 98 173 71 09 (€). Friendly, on the seafront, with frilly rooms (some with terraces).

⭐ **Puerto Arnela** ⟩   **Puerto Arnela**, Pza del Carmen 2, **t** 98 170 54 77, *www.puertoarnela.net* (€). An enchanting hotel, with lovely rooms (the best with a private terrace) a simple restaurant, and warm, friendly service.

Corcubión ✉ 15100

***Praia de Quenxe, Lg. Praia de Quenxe 43, Corcubión, **t** 98 174 74 50 (€€), *www.praiadequenxe.com*. Right

on the beach, with clean rooms, friendly service and a restaurant.

Casa Lestón, Ctra Finisterre (at Sardiñeiro), **t** 98 174 35 99 (€€). Can't be beaten for fresh fish.

Finisterre/Fisterra ✉ 15155

O Semáforo, Faro s/n, **t 98 172 58 69, *www.osemaforo.com* (€€). The famous lighthouse at Cabo Finisterre is a delightful little hotel, where you can enjoy the spectacular sunsets.

Insula Finesterrae, A Insula 76, **t 98 171 22 11, *www.insulafinisterrae.com* (€€). Rusticity and contemporary style are combined in this charming hotel by the lighthouse. With pool.

Hotel Pardo da Viña, Camino Barcia s/n, **t** 98 174 03 26, *www.hotelrural pradodavina.com* (€). Charming *casa rural*, with wooden beams and a pool.

Pensión Casa Velay, C/La Cerca 1, **t** 98 174 01 27 (€). Just off the main square; good-value basic doubles with bath.

Tira do Cordel, Praia de San Roque s/n, **t** 98 174 06 97 (€€–€). Some of the best seafood on this stretch of coast, famous for *navajas a la plancha* (razor clams from the *ría*).

Los Tres Golpes, C/Huertas 2, **t** 98 174 00 47 (€€–€). A good simple restaurant, serving excellent shellfish.

Into the Rías Baixas

The Lower Estuaries, or Rías Baixas/Bajas, almost at once have tamer, greener scenery than their wild cousins to the north; here the ocean is predictably warm enough to maintain a regular holiday trade. These less exposed, less continuously 'flushed' *rías* can, however, get a bit dirty if you swim in the innermost coves.

Muros to Vilagarcía

Ría de Muros e Noia

Under Monte Costiños on the north edge of the *ría*, **Muros** is a fine, old-fashioned granite town, with narrow, arcaded lanes, a market, and a fountain with a stone turtle, all stacked under its Gothic church. This contains a startling crucifix that was found in the sea, the Cristo de la Agonía, with long, flowing hair like that of his counterpart in Burgos; and a stone serpent coiled in the basin of the holy water stoup. There's a good beach at **Louro**, 'the golden',

1.6km from Muros on the tip of the cape. Inland, past Ponte-Outes, **Entines** has the shrine of miracle-working San Campio. After making the ritual walk round the crucifix (six times clockwise, three times anti-clockwise) you can pay a visit to Campio, or so it seems – the skeleton of an Christian martyr brought from Rome in the 18th century by a bishop of Santiago has been lovingly covered with wax and dressed in a centurion's costume and a garland so that he looks as if he is sleeping.

To reach Noia, cross the medieval **Ponte Nafonso**, named after its master builder who lies buried under the 14th-century cross at the end, having laboured 30 years without seeing it completed. **Noia** (or Noya) is full of legends, beginning with its name, after Noah, whose dove is said to have found the olive branch here while his ark came to rest on the holy Celtic mountain of Barbanza just south. This local Mount Ararat is adorned with dolmens and in Noia you can visit the mysterious cemetery next to the Gothic **Santa María a Nova** (1327), where guildsmen between the 10th and 16th centuries left headstones carved with symbols more pagan than Christian; some 200 have designs relating to the trades of the

Getting around from Muros to Vilagarcía

RENFE (*www.renfe.com*, **t** 902 320 320) **trains** between A Coruña and Vigo pass through Padrón and Vilagarcía. There are hourly **buses** (7am–9pm) from Santiago to Noia, from where connections can be made to Porto do Son and beyond. From Vilagarcía, buses leave for the Isla de Arousa.

deceased. Others are a total enigma. Another church, the early 15th-century **San Martín**, has a good rose window carved into its fortress-like façade, and fine carvings on the portal; opposite, the **Pazo de Tapal** dates from the same period.

Often windy beaches and lagoons dot the coast of the *ría* south from Noia. The main village, **Porto do Son**, lies between the state-of-the-art defensive outpost of NATO atop Mount Iroite and its rather more picturesque Celtic equivalent at the **Castro de Baroña**, located on an outcrop over the sea. From **Oleiros** you can drive up to a pair of *miradores* (1,633ft/500m) on the Montes Barbanza, for great views from Cabo Finisterre to Vigo on a clear day. Oleiros also has an exceptional dolmen, **Axeitos** – an enormous rock measuring nearly 172 sq ft, supported by eight smaller ones. At the tip of the headland, **Corrubedo** has a proud set of dunes, the highest in all Galicia, constantly sculpted by the wind.

Ría de Arousa to Pádron

The shore-hugging highway first runs into the Ría de Arousa, touristically the most developed of all Galicia's estuaries, although this hardly means anything remotely like Torremolinos or Benidorm. The first town you come to, **Santa Uxia** (or **Eugenia**) **de Ribeira** (often known simply as Ribeira), combines tourism with its status as Spain's top coastal and underwater fishing port. The remains of a Phoenician port are nearby at **Aguiño**, while further south the **Isla de Sálvora** is a haunt of mermaids; a 16th-century *hidalgo* married one, and gave birth to a dynasty named Mariños de Lobeira. Locally a whole science has evolved to distinguish mermaids in case of doubt: they have smooth soles on their feet and no belly buttons. The rest of this shore has quiet beaches.

At the head of the estuary, at the mouth of the blood-sucking lamprey-rich River Ulla, **Padrón** is the raggle-taggle capital of Galicia's favourite vegetable tapa, midget-green *pimientas de Padrón*, roasted in oil and salted and astonishingly tasty, although occasionally one packs the same wallop as a jalapeño. Padrón has plenty of legendary baggage to accompany its peppers: it is ancient Iria Flavia, the port where Santiago's disciples sailed with their precious cargo, anchoring their stone boat to a stone 'memorial pillar' (*pedrón*), now displayed under the altar in the 17th-century church of **Santiago**. The stone boat was met by a pagan queen, Lupa, who mockingly gave the Christians two wild bulls to transport the coffin. When yoked the bulls became peaceful oxen; astonished, Lupa converted at once and was baptized by St James himself, who popped out of his coffin in the ox cart to do the job. On the Carretera de Herbón on the fringes of town, the **Casa-Museo de Rosalía de Castro** was the home of Galicia's favourite poet Rosalía de Castro (1837–85), the illegitimate daughter of a priest, who unhappily married historian Manuel Murguía, had six children, wrote beautiful poetry in Gallego and died young of cancer. Another house nearby is covered from top to bottom in bleached scallop shells. The bridge over the Ulla to Puentecesures is attributed to Master Mateo.

Casa-Museo de Rosalía de Castro
www.rosaliadecastro. org; open June–Sept Tues–Sat 10–2 and 4–8, Sun 10–1.30; Oct–May Tues–Sat 10–1.30 and 4–7, Sun 10–1.30; adm

Vilagarcía to Isla A Toxa

From Padrón the PO548 continues south past **Catoira** and the romantic remains of Alfonso V's Towers of the West, part of the front-line defences of Santiago against the Normans (and scene of the annual *Fiesta Vikinga*). The big town on the south bank is **Vilagarcía de Arousa**, the glossy base for Galicia's drug-smuggling barons. After a drink and a look at all the suspicious types in a fancypants café, perhaps the best thing to do is leave and drive up to the home of the pagan queen, **Castro Lupario**, atop **Monte Lobeira** (5km from Vilagarcía) for the extraordinary views, or visit the woodsy, sand-fringed **Isla de Arousa**, reputedly the chief drop-off point for Colombian cocaine in Europe.

All this nefarious underworld activity seems far away in charming **Cambados**, an atmospheric, noble town with plenty of old family crests and a lovely granite-paved square; note the

The Perfect Accompaniment to Fish

As if seafood-lovers didn't have enough to rave about in Galicia, the *rías* also supply Albariño, the ideal dry, fruity white wine to go with their heaving plates of *mariscos*. Cambados is the capital of Albariño, and the first Sunday of every August the lovely gardens of its *parador* hosts a wine festival.

Burgundian monks at the Cistercian monastery of Armenteira (*see* p.346) introduced Albariño vines in the 12th century and they thrived; if most other vineyards in dry hot Spain produce red wines, the humid Atlantic coast and sunnier sheltered slopes of the *rías* provide the ideal climate for aromatic whites. In 1988, the growing region DO Rías Baixas was given its demarcation status, divided into the subzones of O Rosal, Val do Salnés (around Cambados), Condado de Tea (which also produces some reds) and the Zona del Albariño. Like its cousin, Portuguese *vinho verde*, Albariño is ever so slightly sparkling, sending a gentle trail of bubbles to the top of your glass (for lots of suds, go for the Albariño del Palacio). Although usually best drunk as young as possible, Cambados' Albariño Fefiñanes is stored in oak barrels for a few months to give it more flavour. Other recommended Albariños are Lagar de Cervera, Castelo de Fornos (from Bodegas Chaves) and Martín Codax, from Valariño-Cambados. Nothing goes to waste: the stems, seeds, and other leftovers (*oruja*) are distilled into fiery *aguardiente*.

Galicia has two other demarcated wine regions: DO Ribeiro, the largest, is just west of Ourense, where production is dominated by the large Bodega Cooperativa do Ribeiro, producer of whites (light Viña Costeira, or the rare, celebrated Brandomín) and some reds; the newly popular Armandi and Telura reds come from Ribeiro's new Bodegas Lapatena. The third region, DO Valdeorras, is out east of Ourense and produces as many red wines as whites. The latter are of interest for their recent revival of the native godella grapes (Viña Guiran and Viña Abad are two leading labels). The best reds probably come from Bodegas Jesús Nazareno, with Valdoura its most reputed wine.

Italianate details on the balconies around the 17th-century Praza de Fefiñanes. The cemetery church, **Santa Mariña Dozo**, on Camino de la Pastora has carvings on its vault of the allegory of the man who ate his own excrement; if you know where that comes from, please drop us a line.

From Cambados, the PO550 circles down to the overblown family resort of **O Grove**, linked by a bridge to **Isla A Toxa** (de la Toja), a sand-rimmed, pine-clad islet that first became famous when a donkey left for dead was miraculously restored after a few days. Now adorned with a casino (one that Franco always turned a blind eye to), shell-coated church, spa, nouveau-riche estates, sports complex, nine-hole golf course and watched by security guards, A Toxa is designed for people with bags of money, leaving O Grove for those who don't, but know how to have a good time.

An Excursion Inland: From Vilagarcía to the Manor of the Goose

From Vilagarcía, the N550 leads in 12km to the old spa town of **Caldas de Reis**, founded by the Romans. If you decide to forgo drinking the waters, which promise marriage within a year, at least take a walk through the charming *alameda* and botanical gardens.

Farther along, 8km east of the centre of **A Estrada** (the largest rural municipality in Spain), you can visit the exterior of the most lavish country villa in all Galicia, the sumptuous 18th-century **Pazo da Oca** with its ancient trees, arcaded patio, pond and chapel.

Pazo da Oca
gardens open daily
9am–dusk; adm

Markets from Muros to Vilagarcía

Noia: Thurs.
Vilagarcia de Arousa: Tues and Sat.
Cambados: Thurs.

Where to Stay and Eat from Muros to Vilagarcía

Muros ✉ 15250

**La Muradana, Avda Castelao 99, t 98 182 68 85, *www.hotelmuradana. com* (€). A friendly, comfortable place to eat and sleep.

*Hostal Ría de Muros, Rua Castelao 53, t 98 182 60 56 (€). Charming owner and good value for money; go for the panoramic room 36 if possible.

*Convento Padres Franciscanos Muros, t 98 182 61 46 (€). The Franciscan brothers run an austere but atmospheric *hostal* (June–Sept).

Noia ✉ 15250

Pesquería del Tambre, Santa Maria de Roo (4km from Noia), t 98 176 94 25, *www.pesqueriadeltambre.com* (€€€). An unsual and charming rural hotel with restaurant, in a cluster of Modernista buildings used a century ago to produce electricity.

**Hostal Ceboleiro, Avda Galicia 15, t 98 182 44 97 (€€). Friendly, with a decent restaurant.

Porto do Son ✉ 15250

*Hostal Arnela II, Travesía 13 de Septiembre 4, t 98 176 73 44 (€). Modern and friendly, with baths in all rooms, and a good restaurant.

Padrón ✉ 15900

Casa Antiga do Monte, Boca do Monte, Lestrove, t 981 81 24 00, *www.susavilaocio.es* (€€). An elegant

(i) **Cambados >>**
Praza do Concello,
t 98 652 07 86,
www.concello-
combados.com

(★) **La Casa Grande**
de Cornide >

(i) **Vilagarcía**
de Arousa >
Avda Juan Carlos I, 37,
t 98 651 01 44

(i) **O Grove >>**
Praza de O Corgo,
t 98 673 09 75,
www.turismogrove.com

stone hotel in charming grounds just outside Padrón, with an 18th-century *hórreo* and stylishly decorated rooms. Also offers pool, gym and all kinds of outdoor activities.

***Escala**, Pazos, t 98 181 13 12, *www.hscala.com* (€€). Modern and central, with a decent restaurant.

La Casa Grande de Cornide, in Cornide, t 98 180 55 99, *www.casagrandede cornide.com* (€€). A *pazo-hosteria* from the 18th century with elegant suites, a library, a pool, and three family-friendly 'cabins' in the gardens.

Pensión Jardín, Salgado Araujo 3-1, t 98 181 09 50 (€). A sweet little stone house, with fussy but cosy rooms.

Casa Ramallo, C/Castros in Rois, t 98 180 41 80 (€€). Don't miss this favourite restaurant of Spanish novelist and Nobel Prize-winner Camilo José Cela. Family-run and rustic. *Closed Mon.*

Chef Rivera, Enlace Parque 7, t 98 181 14 54, *www.chefrivera.com* (€). This is your chance to try José Rivera Casal's fresh seasonal dishes (if you're not squeamish, the lamprey *empanada* is exquisite) and a mix of traditional Gallego and international cuisine. Also has traditional **rooms** (€).

Vilagarcía de Arousa ✉ 15900

***Castelao**, Arzobispo Lago 5, t 98 651 24 26, *www.hcastelao.com* (€€€). Comfortable doubles and apartments in the centre.

Hotel Playa Compostela, Av. Rosalía de Castro, 134, t 98 650 40 10, *www.galinor.es/playacompostela* (€€€). This is a comfortable option along the Arousa estuary, with modern amenities like WiFi, whirlpools and air-conditioning. The top-floor rooms have terraces.

****Pazo O Rial**, O Rial 1, Ctra Vilagarcia-Cambados, t 98 650 70 11, *www.pazorial.com* (€€€–€€). Set in a pine wood, this 17th-century *pazo* is quiet and near the sea, with a pool and good seafood restaurant.

***Hostal 82**, Pza de la Constitución 13, t 98 650 62 22 (€). Small and pleasant, well located in the centre.

Loliña, Alameda 1, in Carril, t 98 650 12 81 (€€). The day's catch gets the home-cooked treatment here, served in a

sun-baked courtyard. *Closed Sun eve and all day Mon.*

Cambados ✉ 36630

***Parador de Cambados**, Paseo de Cervantes, t 98 654 22 50, *www. parador.es* (€€€). Occupies an old country *pazo* (manor house) with a beautiful garden and a restaurant featuring seafood.

***Europa**, Ourense 12, t 98 654 37 25 (€€). Simple, modern hotel with neat rooms with bath.

****Casa Rosita**, Avda de Villagarcía 8, t 98 654 28 78, *www.hrosita.com* (€). Light, airy rooms in a sumptuous villa, with covered pool in the gardens, and a good restaurant.

***El Duende**, Ourense 10, t 98 654 30 75 (€). Offers a nice, cheaper alternative by the sea. With or without bath.

Pazos Feijoo, Rúa Curros Enríquez 1, t 98 654 29 10 (€). Spick and span *hostal* in the centre of town.

Maria José, Rúa San Gregorio 2, t 98 654 22 81 (€). Surrender to the tender loving culinary care of Maria José, who makes a mean *sopa de mariscos*.

Ribadumia ✉ 36980

Pazo Carrasqueira, in Sisán, t 98 671 00 32, *www.perfectplacespain.com* (€€–€). A lovely 18th-century manor, with a handful of comfortable rooms, and a pool and gardens.

O Grove/A Toxa ✉ 36980

*****Gran Hotel La Toja**, Isla A Toxa, t 98 673 00 25, *www.granhotelhesperia-latoja.com* (€€€€). In summer, in a park setting, you can enjoy golf, tennis, a spa, and a heated pool in a park setting.

****Mar Atlántico**, Pedras Negras San Vicente do Mar, t 98 673 80 61, *www.hotelmaratlantico.com* (€€€). Another large, elegant hotel, with a pool in the gardens and a spa.

***Bosque Mar**, Reboredo, t 98 673 10 55, *www.bosquemar.com* (€€). In O Grove proper, a pleasant family place with a garden and a swimming pool.

***Maruxia**, Luis Casais 14, t 98 673 27 95, *www.hotelmaruxia.com* (€€–€). A good, modern choice, with well-equipped rooms in the centre.

***Hotel Puente de la Toja**, Rua Castelao 206, t 98 673 07 61, *www.hotelpuentedelatoja.com* (€€–€). An excellent choice, with beautiful rooms and a restaurant just a stone's throw from the beach.

*Hs Isolino, Avda Castelao 30, **t** 98 673 02 36 (€). One of the best deals in town, offering good-value modern rooms at the heart of O Grove's nighttime scene.

Restaurant D'Berto, Avda Teniente Dominguez 84, **t** 98 673 34 47, *www.dberto.com* (€€€). Fabulously fresh seafood at one of the city's top restaurants, with a superb wine selection: book in advance.

Beira Mar, Avda Beiramar 30, **t** 98 165 05 49 (€€€). Serves delicious oysters plucked straight from the *ria*, in elegantly modern surroundings with views of the port.

O Crisol >

O Crisol, Rúa Hospitál 10, **t** 98 673 00 29 (€€€). A long-time favourite for its excellent seafood and fine service. *Closed Mon.*

Casa Pepe, Rúa Castelao 149, **t** 98 673 02 35 (€€). Slightly cheaper than O Crisol, though with a similar pedigree, again specializing in local seafood.

Posada del Mar, Rúa Castelao 202, **t** 98 673 01 06 (€€). Fine views from its dining room and fabulous *empanada* with *zamburiñas* (Galician clams), now served by its third generation.

Caldas de Reis ✉ 36650

Acuña, Herrería 2, **t 98 654 00 10 (€€–€). Attached to the spa, this hotel has a charming Modernista air, with *solanas* overhanging the river.

Sena, Juan Fuentes 99, **t** 98 654 05 96, *www.hotelsena.com* (€). A cheaper option on the outskirts of the centre, with a pool and decent restaurant.

Casa Baltar, Alhóndiga 9, **t** 98 654 00 41 (€). An attractive dining room with a lovely summer terrace serving surprisingly contemporary local cuisine.

Ría de Pontevedra

Although nothing in the southern Rías Baixas is as touristorientated as the Ría de Arousa, the hotels of the Ría de Pontevedra fill up fast enough in the summer with vacationing Spaniards and Portuguese. The scenery is domesticated, green and pretty, while most of the beaches are safe even for the kids. Pontevedra, the provincial capital, is a handsome confection of granite, the best urban architecture in Galicia after Santiago itself.

The end of the Salnés peninsula, dividing the Arousa and Pontevedra estuaries, is occupied by the great sweep of the **Praia da Lanzada**, one of Galicia's finest beaches, the delight of windsurfers and, in the old days, of family planners: hoping to get pregnant, women would flock to Lanzada and wade into the sea, lifting up their skirts and letting nine waves (one for each month of gestation) rush against them.

Nearby **Portonovo** and its neighbour **Sanxenxo** are jumping little resorts, with beaches like sugar and a Chamber of Commerce claim that they get more sun than the rest of Galicia; on summer evenings everyone for miles around descends on their clubs for a bop. Sanxenxo is also the departure point for ferries to the **Isla de Ons** (which along with the Islas Cíes, Isla Sálvora and Isla Cortega forms part of the Parque Nacional de las Islas Atlánticas de Galicia), whose romantic gorse-covered hills and immaculate beaches suggest a lost Scilly Isle, stranded off Galicia. Aside from the

Getting around the Ría de Pontevedra

In Pontevedra the RENFE **train station, t** 902 320 320, *www.renfe.com*, and **bus station, t** 98 685 24 08, *www.autobusespontevedra.com*, are next to each other, but a long walk along Avda Vigo; buses C1 and C2 can take you into town, except on Sundays. Frequent buses serve the main *ría* villages.

Up to eight **ferries** a day run from Portonovo and Sanxenxo to the Isla de Ons, from July to mid-September. Three boats make the longer journey out from Marin.

gorgeous sand and crystalline water of **Praia de Melide**, the big attraction here is the **Buraco del Infierno**, a blowhole 16ft across and 130ft deep, through which the ocean explodes.

Continuing along the *ría*, pretty little **Combarro** has a famous view of its *hórreos* lined up along the shores of the *ría*. Roads from Sanxenxo or Combarro go up to the abandoned medieval **Monasterio de Armenteira**, where the Virgin favoured a monk named Ero: one morning, while listening to the song of a bird, he was granted a look into eternity. To him the ecstasy lasted but a few minutes, but upon returning to the monastery he found that centuries had passed (if the story sounds familiar *see* Leyre, in Navarra, p.100). The story is the subject of King Alfonso the Wise's *Cantiga CIII*, and of the carvings on the entrance to Armenteira. The rose window on the main façade of the church is believed to have been a mandala for meditation, the carved archivaults around the door are *mudéjar*, and the guardian will show you the unusual octagonal cupola inspired by Islamic architecture. Look for the peculiar masons' marks left on the walls.

Monasterio de Poio

*www.mercedarios.com; although still home to a community of Mercedarian monks, it is open for visits May–mid-Oct Mon–Sat 10–1.30 and 4–6, Sun 4–6; mid-Oct–April Mon–Sat 10–1, Sun 4–6; adm; **hostal** open Easter–mid-Oct, **t** 98 677 00 00, hospederia monasteriopoio@terra.es, or book online*

Just before Pontevedra, the **Monasterio de Poio** was founded in the 7th century by San Fructuoso, a member of the Visigothic royal family, who caused a sensation by walking across the water to the islet of Tambo to rescue a sinking boat. In the oldest part of the church is the tomb of yet another unorthodox Galician saint, Santa Trahamunda, whose body floated to Galicia in a stone boat from Córdoba; note her statue, clutching an Andalucían palm tree. The modern annexe is a *hostal* and the orchards contain an enormous 18th-century *hórreo* – the monks say it's also the oldest ever built.

Pontevedra

Pontevedra is nothing less than the perfect genteel granite Gallego town. Its streets are shaded with arcades, its squares marked with stone crosses. Ancient tradition states that it was first called Helenes, founded by Teucer (Teucro), who fought at Troy. *Teucro* means 'Trojan' in Castilian, and there is, in fact, a Teucro who fits the bill, a son of Scamander and a nephew of Priam, who is recorded as leading a band of Cretans to western Spain to found a colony. It's also significant that Teucro named the city after Helen, the sister of the twins Castor and Pollux, the favourite gods of Roman warriors. The cult of the warrior twins inspired the soldiers of the Reconquista in the apocryphal tradition that St James was the twin brother of Jesus. As if this weren't enough, Pontevedra (along with Mallorca, Barcelona and Corsica) also claims to be the birthplace of Columbus; there's a statue to him at the west end of the Alameda looking towards the ocean and the distant Americas.

Pontevedra's promising mythological progress was stymied back in the Middle Ages, when the Río Lérez silted up the port. By the time of Columbus, all the marine business had moved south to Vigo, leaving a compact, endearing and vibrant **Zona Monumental**, its showcases all within a stone's throw of the Praza da Peregrina. Here is the tall, twin-towered 18th-century **Virgen La Peregrina** church, built in the shape of a scallop to house a statue of the city's patroness. It was one of the few instances where the Virgin had any role at all to play in the pilgrimages (Pontevedra lies on the *camino* from Portugal); in August her feast day is celebrated with folk dances and a procession of hundreds of revellers before a crowd so thick you can scarcely breathe.

Behind the Virgen La Peregrina, there's a lovely 16th-century fountain in a small garden and the 13th- and 14th-century church of **San Francisco** with some good tombs, while across the street arcaded **Praza da Ferrería** is a favourite hang-out for Pontevedrans. From here, Calle Pasantería descends to Pontevedra's most perfect little granite square, the **Praza da Leña**, with its granite porticoes and an ancient cross as its centrepiece. On one side two old houses have been joined to form the main body of the charming **Museo de Pontevedra**, which holds an excellent collection of jet figures from Santiago, Celtic goldwork, ancient headstones, paintings by the likes of Zurbarán and Murillo, and works by the talented Gallego caricaturist Alfonso Castelao. The buildings are joined by an enchanting little stone courtyard, with trailing roses and ancient fountains. Almost next door, another section of the museum is housed in the Férnando López building, with a gallery of 19th-century painters, including works by Goya. The fourth section is the Baroque Sermiento building, around the corner, with a beautiful stone staircase and fine vaulting.

There are other pretty little squares tucked in the streets to the northwest, among them **Praza de Teucro** with its crystal galleries, named after the city's putative father. Just below, where Rúa Isabel II intersects with four other streets, there's a fine stone cross portraying Adam, Eve and the serpent – the numerous tapas bars in the vicinity are also tempting. Rúa Isabel II cuts across the Zona Monumental to the **Basílica de Santa María la Mayor**, constructed in the 16th century by the local Seafarers' Guild, with a Plateresque façade by Cornelis of Holland, with scenes of the Assumption and Death of the Virgin; two cannons still defend the church from incursions up the river. Inside there's a wooden Gothic *retablo* and

Museo de Pontevedra

with three other locations around the town; open Tues–Sat 10–9 Sun 11–2; closed Mon

12

Galicia | Into the Rías Baixas: Ría de Pontevedra

Convento de Santo Domingo
also part of the Museo de Pontevedra; open May–Sept Tues–Sat 10–9, Sun 11–2; Mar–April and Oct Tues–Sat 10–2 and 4–7, Sun 11–2; closed Mon and Nov–Feb

some relief comic-strip-like carvings on the back wall. On the corner with Praza de España and the Alameda are the romantic, ivy-draped late 13th-century ruins of the **Convento de Santo Domingo**; the leafy Alameda and adjacent **Jardines de Vincenti** are favourite spots for the evening's *paseo*.

Out on a little promontory, a granite statue called the 'Emigrant's Wife', looking out forever across the *ría*, was put up by the people, for the people, honouring the earthy, independent, hardworking women who ran families and farms on their own for years.

Along the South Bank of the Ría de Pontevedra

If Pontevedra has a drawback it tends to be olfactory: a strong pong that wafts in when the wind's up from the massive paper mill to the south. Usually it doesn't hit you until you start down the *ría*, and usually it puts people off from exploring further; this coast, in spite of its garden charm and sandy coves, has scarcely any tourist facilities. Persevere. One of the chief curiosities is just past **Marín** and its naval academy, by the newish fishing hamlet and beach of **Mogor**: here are some of the most important **petroglyphs** in Spain, a labyrinth and spirals carved by the Celts. They inspired a local retiree to carve his own petroglyphs, some less than perfect spirals and symbols of God and Country.

Another 15km further south along the PO551 you'll find **Bueu**, a sleepy fishing village with a couple or so *hostales*, a great base from which to explore the surrounding beaches (it's also one of the departure points for boats to the Isla de Ons). The sands continue 12km west, down towards the tip of the cape, **Hio**, site of Galicia's most elaborate stone crucifix, sculpted out of a single block of granite in the 19th century by José Cerviño of Pontevedra, with a Descent from the Cross and souls in Purgatory.

Tourist Information on the Ría de Pontevedra

ⓘ Sanxenxo »
Avda Generalísimo,
t 98 672 02 85,
www.sanxenxo.org

⭐ Antiga Casa de Reis »

As well as the **main tourist office**, Pontevedra's **tourist information booths** are located in the Alameda and the Jardines de Castro Sampedro. **Walking tours** (only in Spanish) are available during July, August and September.

Pontevedra's **post office** is on Rúa La Oliva 19, t 98 685 16 77.

There are several WiFi hotspots in Pontevedra, including at the **Café Continental**, at Rúa Castelao 10; ask at the tourist office for *cibercafés*.

There is a **market** in Pontevedra in the Mercado by the river (*daily except Sunday*).

Where to Stay and Eat on the Ría de Pontevedra

Sanxenxo/Sangenjo ✉ 36000
There are scores of places to stay, but just try to get one in the summer without a reservation.

***Hotel Minso, Avda do Porto 1, t 98 672 01 50, *www.hotelminso.com* (€€). Modern, seafront hotel, attractively renovated. *Closed Oct–Mar.*

***Rotilio, Arda del Puerto 7–9, t 98 672 02 00, *www.hotelrotilio.com* (€€). Some of the best hotels are along Praia de Silgar, like this modern place (with superb seafood restaurant).

Antiga Casa de Reis, Reis 39, Padriñán (2km from Sanxenxo), t 98 669 05 50, www.antigacasadereis.com (€€). A beautiful 19th-century stone house in lovely gardens, with rooms furnished with antiques, offering complete tranquillity. Wonderful breakfasts with home-made jam and a genuine welcome from the owners.

⭐ **La Casa de 5 Puertas** >>

***Pazo el Revel**, Revel 15, Villalonga (5km from Sanxenxo), t 98 674 30 00 (€€–€). An ivy-clad 18th-century *pazo*, with gardens, pool and restaurant.

*****Hostal San Roque**, Anebados 6, t 98 672 40 82 (€). A good, central budget option – near the beach and the marina at Portonovo.

ⓘ **Pontevedra** >
Gutiérrez Mellado s/n,
t 98 685 08 14, www.
visit-pontevedra.com
and www.riasbaixas.org

Pontevedra ✉ 36000

***Parador Casa do Barón**, Barón 19, t 98 685 58 00, www.parador. es (€€€). Sleep in an 11th-century Gallego *pazo* with a magnificent stone staircase and a garden.

***Virgen del Camino**, Virgen del Camino, t 98 685 59 04, *www. hotelvirgendelcamino.com* (€€–€). Modern, comfortable business hotel, with excellent online deals.

*****Hotel Rúas**, Sarmiento 37, t 98 684 64 16, *www.hotelruas.net* (€). In the Zona Monumental; the nicest rooms have balconies overlooking the pretty Praza da Verdura. It also has a delightful, stone-walled **restaurant** serving a good *menú del día* for €12.

*****Comercio**, Avda González Besada 3, t 98 685 12 17 (€). Adequate and central; restaurant.

Monasterio de Poio, 2km from Pontevedra, t 98 677 00 00 (€). The Mercedarian monks run a guesthouse (*see* p.346). *Closed mid-Oct–Easter.*

Casa Solla, Avenida Sineiro 7, San Salvador de Poio (2km out of town),

t 98 687 28 84 (€€). One of the best and prettiest restaurants in Galicia, with two Michelin stars; famous for its traditional recipes, the freshest seafood and meat dishes and excellent service. *Closed Thurs and Sun eves, and all day Mon.*

La Casa de 5 Puertas, Santa María 8, t 98 685 19 48 (€€). A restaurant, bar and *vinoteca* serving creative modern cuisine, tapas (including an award-winning *tortilla*) and a superb selection of wines. *Closed Sun eve.*

Casa Román, Avda Augusto García Sánchez 12 (south of the centre), t 98 684 35 60 (€€). Prides itself on select ingredients, especially shellfish. *Closed Sun eve and Mon (except Aug).*

Alameda de Doña Antonia, Soportales Herrería 4-1 (on the first floor), t 98 684 72 74 (€€). Has a well-deserved reputation for imaginative dishes – including duck breasts, baked honeyed lamb and seafood salads. *Closed Sun.*

Bar El Pitillo, Rúa Alta 3, t 98 687 23 22 (€). This popular spot is always full, especially with students, and offers cheap simple meals cooked in garlic: try the heavenly *zamburiñas* (bay scallops), and mop up the sauce with fresh bread. Good local wines, too.

La Navarra, Princesa 13 (€). Evocative old *bodega* where locals help themselves to wine from the barrels, accompanied by thick slices of chorizo and cheese.

Do Pincho Taberna, Rúa Sarmiento, 15, t 98 686 24 72 (€). Friendly spot for coffee, wines, and a huge range of tapas; in summer, there's a terrace.

O Merlo, Santa María 4, t 98 684 43 43 (€). Great tapas. *Closed Mon.*

Ría de Vigo

The Ría de Vigo is the economic star of Galicia's estuaries: where all the others get narrower and shallower as they cut into land, the Ría de Vigo narrows at Rande (site of a huge suspension bridge), then widens again to form the sheltered inlet of San Simón, site of one of Europe's largest oyster beds. At the mouth of the estuary, the enchanting Cíes islets (part of the national park of Atlantic Islands, *see* p.345) protect the port from tempests off the Atlantic and enable mussel-farmers to moor their wooden platforms or

Getting to and around the Ría de Vigo

By Air

Vigo's airport, t 91 321 10 00, *www.aena.es*, is 9km away, with flights to major Spanish cities, London, Brussels and Paris.

By Bus and Train

There are plenty of buses, and several **trains** daily between Vigo and Pontevedra and beyond. A regular regional train plies between Vigo and A Coruña. The train station is at the top of Rúa Alfonso XIII, a 15min walk uphill from the port, t 902 320 320, *www.renfe.com*. **Buses** (to Tui, A Garda, Baiona, Pontevedra, O Grove, Vilagarcía, Santiago and A Coruña) depart frequently from the bus station near Praza de España, a few blocks from the train station; for information, call t 98 637 34 11. Bus C4C links the centre with the bus station.

By Boat

On weekdays 6am–10pm and Sundays 9am–10.30pm, **ferries** (foot passengers only) sail every 30mins to Cangas, every hour to Moaña and up to 10 times daily from mid-June to mid-Sept to the Islas Cíes from Vigo's Estación Marítima near El Berbés (*port information t 98 622 52 72*). For the Cíes, buy your ticket early in the day so you can choose your return boat – the latest sailings fill up first. The islands are also accessible from Cangas and Baiona in summer.

---

bateas safely in the estuary, where the little molluscs incubate on long ropes suspended in the water. Vigo itself has grown to become the largest city in Galicia, with a population of 297,000.

The North Bank of the Ría and the Islas Cíes

From Hio (*see* p.348) the road crosses the dolmen-dotted promontory for the pleasant small resort of **Cangas**, stretching along the coast with a lively port in its centre and a pleasant beach at the end. In a pirate raid in the 17th century, nearly the entire male population was massacred, leaving the women, they say, to go mad, slowly; accused of witchcraft, they would meet on Areas Gordas beach on St John's Eve, and get into trouble; many ended up in the Inquisition's dungeons, including María Soliña, the subject of a famous Gallego nationalist song. Five kilometres east, **Moaña** is another if quieter resort in the Cangas mould, with an even better beach.

From Cangas, Vigo or Baiona the summer-only excursion to the two **Islas Cíes** (the third is off-limits as a bird sanctuary) is a delight. Linked by a lick of sand that forms a sheltered lagoon of calm crystal water, the islands offer a perfect lazy day out on the beach, with a couple of cafés and restaurants; or take a picnic and wander along the oceanside paths. As it is a national park, the only place to stay is a **campsite** with limited space; book online, or ring ahead .

Campsite
www.campingislascies. com; t 98 668 76 30; open Easter week and summer only; they also have tents for rent

Vigo

Nothing less than Spain's premier fishing port, bringing in more fish than anywhere in the world except Tokyo, Vigo occupies a privileged hillside spot that attracted both ancient Phoenician and Greek seamen. Its name comes from the Roman Vicus Spacorum, but the city claims that its true founder was an early 12th-century troubadour, Martín Codax, who, as he describes in his most famous poem, liked to hang out with the boys where Vigo stands today and watch their lady-loves bathe in the estuary. The city's history is full of unwanted English visits: two by Sir Francis Drake (1585 and 1589) and in 1702, when the English surprised a joint Spanish and French treasure fleet just back from the New World, in the Battle of Rande. The English captured some of the ships but 11 were sunk or run aground near the tiny islets by the suspension bridge, the Puente de Rande; some sources say the silver had already been unloaded, but they haven't stopped treasure-seekers from looking.

For all that, there's not much to 'see' in Vigo beyond the fine views towards the sea, although the old part of town hugging the fishing port, the **Barrio del Berbés**, is thick with atmosphere and rough, cobbled streets. As in A Coruña, there's a lively fish auction by the waterside at the crack of dawn; if you've had a rough night you'll have no problem finding a dozen supremely fresh oysters on the half-shell from the fishwives along Rúa Teófilo Llorente or in the **Rúa da Pescadería** morning market. Look at the noblemen's palaces in López Puigcerver (**Calle Real**); from **Parque del Castro**, on top of the city, enjoy a great view of the *ría* from the modern monument to the Galeones de Rande.

The municipal museum **Quiñones de León** is in the 17th-century Pazo de Castrelos in the southwest of town, in the geometric gardens of the **Parque Quiñones de León**. The museum has antique furniture and paintings by some of Galicia's most important artists, and funerary stelae from archaeological excavations around the city. Vigo also has a magnificent **Contemporary Art Museum** on Rúa Príncipe in what was once in the old prison. Overlooking the Ría at the Punta de Muíño, the sleek modern **Museo da Mar de Galicia** offers an interesting glimpse into the region's maritime history. Vigo is home to Galicia's sole **zoo**, situated along the road to the airport.

Quiñones de León
www.museodevigo.org; open Tues–Fri 10–1.30 and 5–8, Sat 5–8, Sun 10–1.30; closed Mon

Contemporary Art Museum
www.marcovigo.com; open Tues–Sat 11–9, Sun 11–3; closed Mon; adm

Museo da Mar de Galicia
www.museodomar.com; open mid-June– mid-Sept Tues–Fri 11–2 and 5–8, Sat–Sun 11–9; mid-Sept–mid-June Tues–Fri 10–2, Sat–Sun 11–7; closed Mon; adm

Zoo
www.vigozoo.com; open April–Oct daily 10–8.30; Nov–Feb daily 11–6.30; Mar daily 11–7.30; closed Mon in Mar and Nov; adm

South of Vigo to the Ría de Baiona

Vigo's main beaches, white **Praia de Canido** and **Praia Samil**, are just west and often crowded, but the main lure here is **Baiona** (Bayona), down the coast, one of Galicia's choice resorts, topped by the walls of the medieval **Castillo de Monterreal**. The grounds are occupied by a ravishing *parador*; fork out to tour the grounds and walls. The coast is embellished with little beaches of soft sand, namely **Ladeira**, **Santa María** and the magnificent crescent of **Praia América**. The latter was named after the fact that Baiona was the first place in Europe to learn that Columbus had discovered a New World, on 10 March 1493, when the little *Pinta* sailed into its port. A replica sits on a floating jetty in the harbour, complete with ship's cat, ropes of garlic, and dummy sailors.

Santa María
open Mon–Sat 9.30–
12.45 and 5.30–8.30,
Sun 9.30–1.30

The 13th-century church of **Santa María** is a good example of transitional architecture; more contemporary religious art is 1km south of town in the form of a huge granite sculpture of 1910, a sailors' *ex voto* to the **Virgen de la Roca**. Wild horses have a free rein in the hills here, rounded up once a year in a *rapa das Bestas*, or *curros*, when Gallego cowboys tame them, run a race or two, then let them go again. In **Oia**, 16km south along the pretty and wild coastline, there's a lonely 18th-century Baroque monastery, where the monks run a charming little *hostal* (*see* p.354).

To the south, **A Guarda**, at the mouth of the Río Minho, may look more intriguing on the map than it does in reality, with its clutch of nouveaux-riches *americanos*' bungalows. However, a 40-minute walk (or shorter drive) up, in the excavated Celtic *castro* on **Monte Santa Tegra**, is one of Spain's most important *citanías*, or fortified hill settlements, inhabited from the 7th century BC up to the Roman period. It has over 100 houses, some reconstructed, others mere foundations, linked by cobbled lanes and encircled by walls.

Monte Santa Tegra
open summer daily
11–8; winter daily
11–5; adm

From the top of Monte Santa Tegra there are fine views over the valley of the Minho into Portugal. Farther up there's a cromlech, or Neolithic stone circle, and at the very top a church with a small **museum** where you can find out about the strange carving discovered on the site, believed to be a map; if so, one of the oldest found in the West. The nearest beach is at **Camposancos**, 3km from A Guarda, overlooking the mouth of the wooded Río Minho, the frontier between Spain and Portugal.

Tui

✪ **Tui**

From A Guarda the best thing to do is follow the course of the River Minho up to Tui (or Tuy, pronounced *twee*), a rare frontier town worth visiting in its own right. One of the seven ancient capitals of Galicia, Tui is picturesquely piled upon its acropolis; like Pontevedra, it claims to have been founded by wandering Greeks after the Trojan War. It was the capital of the Visigoth King Witiza in 700, and has seen many battles and border skirmishes with Portugal, defended by the walled city of Valença.

Tui's granite lanes and houses are crowned by the military profile of the **Catedral de Santa María** with its powerful walls and keep; until the 13th century it did double duty as Tui's castle. Construction began in 1120 but was not completed until much later; the stone has mellowed into a grey, vertical garden of wild flowers. There is a fine Romanesque porch and a portal from 1225, carved with the Adoration of the Magi by French-trained sculptors, one of the first and finest Gothic works in Galicia; be sure to note the lovely but strange coat of arms on the side wall, which has five stars and a crescent moon, said to symbolize the burning of the town by al-Mansur. The inside of the cathedral is also heavily fortified – against earthquakes – and contains the relics of San Telmo, also known as Pedro González of Astorga (confessor of King Saint Ferdinand of Castile), who also worked among the seafolk of Galicia in 1246. He is the patron saint of Spanish sailors, who confused his name with their first patron St Elmo (or Erasmus), who sends them his lucky fire to light upon their masts, igniting even their fingers without burning them. His tomb, accredited with miracles, oozes a vinegary gunk prized as a cure-all.

Among Tui's smaller churches are **Santo Domingo** (1415) – inside is a mix of Gothic and pre-Romanesque with finely carved effigies on the tombs and the stone pulpit – and the circular **San Telmo** (1803), the only example of Portuguese Baroque in Galicia.

In 30 minutes, you can walk from the centre of Tui to the lovely Portuguese walled town of **Valença do Minho**, crossing an iron bridge built by Gustave Eiffel. The views from Valença to Tui are lovely, as is Valença itself, blanketed in bright towels that Spaniards flock to buy. If it's hot, there are a couple of small river beaches.

Markets on the Ría de Vigo

⭐ Hotel Puerta Gamboa >>

Cangas: Fri.

Baiona: Mon.

Tui: Gallego/Portuguese market Thurs.

ⓘ **Cangas**
Paseo Castelao,
t 98 639 20 23

Where to Stay and Eat on the Ría de Vigo

Vigo ✉ 36200

ⓘ **Vigo** >
Municipal: Rúa Teófilo Llorente 5, t 98 622 47 57, www.turismo devigo.org; also summer booths in the city centre; has a guide book In English of walking tours in the countryside

Regional: Rúa Cánovas del Castillo (in the port), t 98 643 05 76

 Seafood in Vigo

Eating out is an excellent reason for staying in Vigo. To every kind of seafood and shellfish and the delicacies from the River Minho: salmon, lamprey and baby eels. Don't miss the fresh oysters, served straight from the shell, at the market.

****Bahía de Vigo, Canovas del Castillo 24, t 98 622 67 00 *www. hotelbahiadevigo.com* (€€€–€). A tall, modern block, offering rooms and apartments, with great views of the port and the *ría* (especially from the top floor); its restaurant serves up colossal *parrilladas* of grilled seafood. Great deals available online.

***Ensenada, Alfonso XIII 7, t 98 644 74 40 (€€). Modern and central, with a small gym and helpful staff.

**Hotel Puerta del Sol, Puerta del Sol 14, t 98 622 23 64, *www.alojamientos vigo. com* (€€). Brightly furnished

rooms and apartments in a charming old stone building with glassed-in balconies in the upper floors.

**Hotel Puerta Gamboa, Rúa Gamboa, 12, t 98 622 86 74, *www.hotelpuerta gamboa.com* (€€–€). Eleven elegant rooms in a gracefully restored mansion in the old centre, with a good restaurant.

*Hotel Águila, C/Victoria 6, t 98 643 13 98, *www.hotelaguila.com* (€). This pretty hotel is in a historic building by the Praza da Compostela.

**Hostal La Nueva Colegiata, Praza da Igrexa 2, t 98 622 09 52 (€). All rooms have bath, and double glazing to muffle the wake-the-dead tolling of the bells across the *praza*.

El Mosquito, Pza da Pedra 4 (near the port), t 98 643 35 70 (€€€). For seafood or roast leg of lamb, the people's choice in Vigo is a classic place with a family atmosphere. *Closed Sun and 2nd fortnight in Aug.*

Timón Playa, Cánido 8, Corujo, t 98 649 08 15, *www.restaurantetimon playa.ws* (€€€). Perfectly prepared seafood, rice dishes and *empanadas* at this attractive beachfront restaurant, with views of the Cíes. *Closed Sun.*

Casa Esperanza Luis Taboada 28, t 98 622 86 15 (€€). Delightfully old-fashioned little restaurant, which has been serving up delicious traditional dishes since 1949.

(i) Tui >>
*Edif. Área
Panorámica,*
t 98 660 17 89,
www.concellotui.org

(★) Pazo da Touza >

La Oca, Avda Purificación Saavedra 8, t 98 637 12 55 (€€). Award-winning cuisine at very reasonable prices, prepared with whatever's freshest at the Teis market nearby. *Book well ahead. Closed Mon eve, Tues eve, Sat eve and Sun eve and 3 weeks Aug.*

Marisquería Bahía, Avda Cánovas Castillo, t 98 644 96 56, *www. marisqueriabahia.com* (€€–€). Another catch-of-the-day restaurant – but one of the best, with outside tables on seafood street and oysters hawked by fishermen's wives. *Closed Wed.*

Cocedero Bar La Piedra, Pescadería 3, t 98 643 12 04 (€). A classic in A Pedra, with stalls of oysters to eat on the street or on the terrace.

Baiona ✉ 36300

****Parador Conde de Gondomar**, Monte Real, t 98 635 50 00, *www. parador.es* (€€€). Galicia's finest, housed in a modern reconstruction of a typical Galician *pazo* within the medieval walls of Monterreal, in a lovely park; it offers a pool, tennis and children's recreation area, and it's just a short walk to the beach.

**Pazo de Mendoza, Elduayen 1, t 98 638 50 14, *www.pazodemendoza.com* (€€). A tastefully restored 18th-century *casona*, with a restaurant (€€€), where the best Gallego traditions and ingredients are prepared with plenty of imagination.

Pazo da Touza, Rúa dos Pazos 119, Nigrán (8km from Baiona), t 98 636 69 89, *www.pazodatouza.info* (€€). A beautiful 18th-century *pazo* set in orchards and gardens. Spacious rooms and wonderful breakfasts.

**Hotel Tres Carabelas, Ventura Misa 61, t 98 635 54 41, *www.hoteltres carabelas.com* (€). A fine old inn on a narrow cobbled lane right in the middle of town; renovated in 2010.

*HR Carabela la Pinta , C/Carabela La Pinta, t 98 635 51 07 (€). Reliable budget option in the centre.

Paco Duran, Igrexa 60, t 98 635 50 17 (€€). Wonderful sea views from the huge windows, and a big selection of (mostly live) crustaceous goodies.

Taperia Parrillada O Muino, As Fontiñas 1, t 98 635 11 08 (€). Good for tapas and grilled meats at reasonable prices: it gets very busy, so arrive early to secure a table.

A Guarda ✉ 01300

**Convento de San Benito, Pza de San Benito, t 98 661 11 66, *wwww.hotelsan benito.es* (€€). Set in a 16th-century monastery with a garden, antique-furnished rooms, and a collection of old *azulejos* in the cloister.

*Hostal Martirrey, José Antonio 8, t 98 661 03 49 (€). A spotless *hostal* with rooms with or without bath.

**Hotel Vila de Guarda, Rúa Pontevedra 4, t 98 661 00 02 (€). Pristine little hotel near the port, with old-fashioned rooms, a minimalist lobby, and its own parking.

La Pizzicata, Rúa Galicia 55, t 98 661 15 34 (€). There's something for everyone at this local favourite, from platters of fresh fish and succulent grilled meats, to pizzas and pasta for the kids. Good set lunch menu.

Tui ✉ 36700

***Parador de Tui, Avda Portugal, t 98 660 03 00, *www.parador.es* (€€€). Overlooking the Minho, and located in a large reproduction of a typical Gallego *pazo* 1km below town, with a garden, tennis and pool; very refined.

Abadía do Pelouro Axeito, at Caldelas de Tui (12 km from Tui), t 98 662 90 24, *http://abadia.opelouro.org* (€€). If you're looking for something special, this is a magical rural hotel in an 18th-century abbey with rooms and apartments set among old stone buildings half-lost in woodland.

*Hostal San Telmo 91, Avda de la Concordia 88, t 98 660 30 11 (€). A good cheapie, with pretty rooms.

Hostal Cruceiro do Monte, Carretera de Baiona 23, t 98 660 09 53 (€). Simple and family-run, in a country setting; good home-cooked food.

O Novo Cabalo Furado, Pza do Concello, t 98 660 22 63 (€€). Good home cooking, with the emphasis on fish from the *rías. Closed Sun eve; closed all day Mon, Sun in summer.*

Viñoteca de García, Rúa Seixas 6, t 630 824 498 (€). A wide selection of wines accompanied by freshly prepared tapas and *raciones*.

Up the Minho to Ourense

Galicia's least known and only landlocked province is an introspective place, with more valleys, they say, than towns. The province is famous for wine (DO Valdeorras, DO Ribeiro, Verín and Monterrey), hot springs, and Julio Iglesias.

From Tui to Ribadavia

Both the train and road follow the wooded banks of the Minho, offering one more chance to cross into Portugal on the ferry from Salvaterra do Minho to the delightful walled city of Monção. To the east, past the first dam, the river becomes wider and more elegiac, around the start of the wine-growing region of Ribeiro.

Ribeiro's charming 15th-century capital, **Ribadavia**, has the best-preserved Jewish *barrio* in Galicia; even after the expulsion of the Jews by the Catholic Kings, many remained here, hidden with the help of the Christian population. Ribadavia has a beautiful **Praza Maior** and some interesting Romanesque churches: a tree grows out of the bell tower of the **Oliveira** church, **San Juan** has a 13th-century *cruceiro*, while the **Convento de Santo Domingo**, occasional residence of the kings of Galicia, has a fine Gothic church and a cloister. The **Museo Etnológico de Ribadavia** offers information on local trades, including wine and textiles, and the ruined **Castillo de los Condes de Ribadavia** is an impressive pile of walls, gates, towers, and rock tombs.

Museo Etnológico de Ribadavia
open Tues–Sat 9.30–2.30 and 4–8, Sun 10–2; closed Mon; adm, except Sat pm and Sun

The Minho and its tributary, the Sil, are the 'holy rivers' of Galicia, their banks thick with churches and hermitages. South of Ribadavia, the village of **Celanova** is built around a vast **Praza Maior**, with a fountain in the middle (where you mustn't drink from the north spout, because of the risk of going mad) and a Cecil B. de Mille Baroque façade of 1681, pasted on to the venerable Benedictine monastery of **San Salvador**. The church's Capilla Mayor holds a gargantuan *retablo* of 1697 and the choir is a masterpiece of Gothic carving. Although the monastery itself is occupied by a school, you can pick up the key to see the elegant Renaissance cloister, a Baroque cloister, and the garden at the back, the setting for the diminutive (25ft by 10ft) chapel of **San Miguel**, a Mozarabic jewel with a roof that looks like a Chinese hat.

An even older church is further south on the OU540 near **Bande**: the rural Visigothic chapel of **Santa Comba**, overlooking the reservoir of Limia. Built with a Byzantine plan around the year 700, Santa Comba is remarkably well preserved with its borrowed late Corinthian marble columns supporting a horseshoe arch. The rest of the decoration is quite sober, but there are traces of frescoes, including a man in the moon. A few kilometres further south around **Lobios** are monuments that pre-date Santa Comba;

monolithic Roman *miliarios*, or milestones, standing from the days when this was the main Roman route between Astorga and the newly conquered territory of Gallaecia. The best can be found way up in the hills on the Portuguese frontier, south of **Torneiros**. The surrounding glacial valleys and granitic peaks are home to wolves and wild boar, and enjoy protection as a natural park.

East of Celanova (and south of Ourense just off the A52 motor-way), the medieval town of **Allariz** is a monument in itself and site of two more Romanesque churches: **Santiago** with an unusual round apse and **San Esteban**, on the way to the ruins of the castle. The **Convento de Santa Clara** was founded in 1282 by Violante, the wife of Alfonso X, who is buried in the huge Baroque cloister. Between Allariz and Ourense, the ruined 12th-century **Santa Mariña das Aguas Santas** (a 15min walk from the village; bring a flashlight) has steps down to its crypt – actually a corridor dolmen.

Ourense (Orense)

Continuing up the Río Minho, Ourense greets visitors with a graceful **Ponte Romano**, its seven ogival arches striding over 100ft above the Minho. The footbridge was built by the Romans and rebuilt on the ancient piers in the 13th century. It's now been upstaged by a vast modern bridge, built for the millennium.

Traffic is Ourense's day-in, day-out nightmare, funnelled down the discouraging main street, Rúa do Progreso, cut through the city in the 19th century. Equally discouraging *urbanizaciones* housing Ourense's 108,000 souls take up most of the rest of the space.

If you can find a place to park, or don't mind walking a mile in from the bus or train stations, you can see what first attracted the Romans: the steaming hot springs, *Aquae Urentes*, known by the Visigoths and Suevi as Warm Sea (hence *Ourense*). The main source, **As Burgas**, still steams out of the neoclassical fountain midway down Rúa do Progreso. The locals have invented many a use for the hot water – put a dead chicken in it, they say, and you can pluck it in two minutes. During 1386–7, when Ourense was John of Gaunt's capital when he tried to claim the throne of Castile, many Englishmen here had the first hot baths of their lives.

Up from here, the arcaded **Praza Maior** and its charming little annexe, **Praza de la Magdalena**, is Ourense's historic core and hub of its social life. The old episcopal palace in Praza Maior houses the **Museo Arqueológico Provincial**, with a collection of finds spanning from the Neolithic era to the Bronze Age, as well as *retablos* and other bits of art salvaged from the province's numerous churches.

In the Praza Maior, the **cathedral** was begun in the 12th century and is entered through the Pórtico del Paraíso, a 13th-century (and rather naïve) brightly painted reproduction of Santiago's great

Museo Arqueológico Provincial
www.musarqourense. xunta.es; some rooms may be closed owing to ongoing renovations, so check website; open Tues–Sat 9.30–2.30 and 4–9, Sun 9.30–2.30; closed Mon; adm

Getting to and around Ourense

Ourense is the main hub here, with **trains** to Santiago, Lugo, A Coruña, Vigo, Ribadavia, León and elsewhere. RENFE's Estación Empalme is across the river, **t** 902 320 320, *www.renfe.com*; tickets are also on sale at Rúa do Paseo 15, **t** 98 821 46 04. The **bus station** is 1km from the centre on the Vigo road, **t** 98 821 60 27, with frequent services to Vigo and all major points in Galicia.

Pórtico de la Gloria. The high altar contains the reliquary of St Martin of Tours, while the florid Baroque chapel by Francisco Castro Canseco houses Ourense's oddest attraction, the Santísimo Cristo who, like the Christ of Burgos, has real hair and a beard and a wood and fabric body; according to legend it was made by Nicodemus and floated ashore near Finisterre. The **Museo Catedraliceo**, off the 12th-century cloister, has one of the first books printed in Galicia and the 'Treasure of San Rosendo' – rare 10th-century chesspieces carved from rock crystal.

Museo Catedraliceo
open Mon–Sat 12–1 and 4.30–7, Sun 4.30–7; adm

Around Ourense

From Ourense, drive north to the monumental Cistercian monastery of **Oseira**, where Graham Greene spent time with his heretical thoughts on Catholicism and wrote *Monsignor Quixote* (1982). He came to the right spot: founded in 1137 by four hermits, Oseira was famous for monks who dabbled in alchemy and magic cures. The monastery façade has a gigantic Churrigueresque doorway and the odd crest of two bones with the tree of knowledge. The massive church dates from the 12th century, and has seven chapels around its altar, with the Virgen de la Leche, supposedly an alchemist's idol, in the main one. Don't miss the curious faces carved in the Claustro de los Medallones.

Oseira
www.mosteirodeoseira. org; guided visits only, April–Sept Mon–Sat 10, 11, 12, 3.30, 4.30, 5.30, 6.30, Sun 12.30, 3.30, 4.30, 5.30, 6.30; Oct–Mar same times except 6.30; adm

The most majestic scenery in these parts begins just east of Ourense, heading up the Minho along the N120, where the cliffs over the river rise ever steeper. At **San Esteban**, dominated by its Romanesque **Monasterio de Ribas de Sil**, the Sil flows into the Minho, and along the latter are wild gorges to walk along.

The nearly-as-dramatic OU536 east of Ourense goes up to **Esgos**, where a small by-road leads to the ruined monastery and church of **San Pedro de Rocas**, founded in 573 by followers of Prisciliano (*see* p.313), its three apses excavated in the rock. Abandoned in the Muslim invasion, the spot was rediscovered in the 10th century. The road continues to rise up higher and higher to **Puebla de Trives** (**Pobra de Trives**), where there's a ski resort, **Manzaneda**. If you're heading southeast from Ourense towards Bragança or Zamora, consider stopping in the old walled town of **Verín**, capital of the wine-growing Monterrey valley; high on one side of the valley looms the **Castle of Monterrey**, built in the 16th century, part of it converted into a *parador*. Try a bottle of Verín red – as long as you aren't driving; this Galician wine can pack 14 per cent alcohol.

Manzaneda
www.manzaneda.com

Markets around Ourense

Ourense: 7th and 17th of month.
Allariz: 1st and 15th of month.
Ribadavia: 10th and 25th of month.
Verín: Wed and Fri.

Where to Stay and Eat around Ourense

(i) **Ribadavia >**
Praza Maior 7,
t 98 847 12 75,
www.ribadavia.travel

Ribadavia ✉ 32000

****Mosteiro de San Clodio**, Praza
Eladio Rodríguez 1, Leiro (10km from
Ribadavia) t 98 848 56 01, *www.
monasteriodesanclodio.com* (€€). A
beautiful, luxurious hotel in a lovingly
restored 16th-century monastery;
four-poster beds, gardens, pool and
restaurant.

Hotel Rural Doña Blanca, San Clodio,
Leiro (10km from Ribadavia) t 98 848
56 88, *www.casadedonablanca.com*
(€€). A stylish fusion of old and new
characterize this chic rural hotel in
Leiro, with an outdoor pool for
summer and tiny spa for winter.

****Pazo de Esposende**, t 98 849 18 91,
www.pazodeesposende.com (€€–€).
This early 16th-century manor house
with a handful of doubles has been
restored with simple elegance to cater
for modern comforts including
disabled facilities.

****Hostal Oasis**, Ctra N 120, t 98 847
16 13 (€). Modern place a couple of km
out of town, with pleasant rooms,
views and a no-frills but perfectly
acceptable budget restaurant.

***Hostal Evencio**, Avda R. Valcárcel 30,
t 98 847 10 45 (€). Has a swimming
pool and garden to delight its guests.

(i) **Verín >>**
*Casa del Escudo, t 98
841 16 14, www.verin.net*

(i) **Ourense >**
*Municipal: Burgas 12,
Bajo, t 98 836 60 64,
www.turismode
ourense.com*

*Regional: Ponte
Romana, t 98 837 20 20,
www.turismourense.com*

Lobios ✉ 32868

****Lobios Caldaria**, Rio Caldo s/n,
t 98 801 00 50, *www.caldaria.es* (€€€).
Modern spa hotel, with all kinds of
treatments and good amenities.

***Lusitano**, Ctra Concejal 312 (Mayeta
Portela), *www.lusitanohotel.com*, t 98
844 80 28 (€). A stone-built inn, with
cosy rooms and a restaurant.

Ourense ✉ 32000

Ourense has plenty of business
hotels but nothing with much charm.
However, this does mean great
bargains at weekends and in August.

****Gran Hotel San Martín**, Curros
Enríquez 1, t 98 837 18 11, *www.gh-
hoteles.com* (€€€). Modern, business-
orientated hotel with all mod-cons.

***Eurostars Auriense**, El Cumial, t 98
823 49 00, *www.eurostarsauriense.
com* (€€€). Another modern business
hotel a few minutes from the centre,
with pool, tennis and disco.

***Hotel Princess**, Avda de la Habana
45, t 98 826 95 38, *www.hotelprincess.
net* (€€€). Central, off the main square.

Martín Fierro (Casa Ovidio), Sáenz
Díez 17, t 98 837 20 26, *www.
restaurantemartinfierro.com* (€€).
Tuck in to the surf or turf delicacies
from the grill, or try the tasty
pilgrims' menu. *Closed Sun.*

San Miguel, San Miguel 12, t 98 822 12
45, *www.restaurante-sanmiguel.com*
(€€). One of Ourense's best restaurants, specializing in seafood fresh
from the coast, accompanied by
Galicia's finest wines. *Closed Tues.*

Pena Vixía, Hernán Cortés 29, t 98 824
69 69 (€€–€). A traditional *tasca*,
offering gourmet tapas and *raciones*.

Puebla de Trives/Pobra de Trives ✉ 32600

***Casa Grande de Trives**, Marqués
de Trives, t 98 833 20 66, *www.
casagrandetrives.com* (€€). Set in a
lovely 18th-century building with
seven rooms plus private chapel.

***Pazo Paradela**, Ctra de Barrio Km.2,
t 98 833 07 14 (€€). Another equally
charming *pazo*, in a rural setting.

****As Maceiras**, Manzaneda (near the
ski resort), t 98 833 00 34, *www.
asmaceiras.com* (€€). Offers pool,
sauna, gym, horse-riding.

Verín ✉ 32600

***Parador de Verín**, 4km outside
Verín, t 98 841 00 75, *www.parador.es*
(€€€). Part of the 16th-century Castle
of Monterrey has been converted into
this *parador*, with lovely views across
the valley; its restaurant offers
seafood and Gallego dishes.

***Dos Hermanas**, Avda de Sousas 106,
t 98 841 02 80 (€). Literally, a lower-
range option, from where you can
look up at the castle.

Index

Main page references are in **bold**. Page references to maps are in *italics*.

7th American edition published 2012 by

CADOGAN GUIDES USA
An imprint of Interlink Publishing Group, Inc
46 Crosby Street, Northampton, Massachusetts 01060
www.interlinkbooks.com
www.cadoganguidesusa.com

Text copyright © Dana Facaros and Michael Pauls 1996, 1999. 2001, 2003, 2006, 2008, 2012
Copyright © 2012 New Holland Publishers (UK) Ltd

Cover photographs: front cover Santillana del Mar, Cantabria, Spain, © Robert Harding Picture Library Ltd / Alamy; back cover © Mountain sunrise on the Picos de Europa, © istockphoto.com.
Photo essay photographs: © istockphoto.com.
Maps © Cadogan Guides, drawn by Maidenhead Cartographic Services Ltd
Publisher: Guy Hobbs
Cover design: Jason Hopper
Photo essay design: Sarah Gardner
Editor: Mary-Ann Gallagher
Proofreading: Linda McQueen
Indexing: Isobel McLean

Printed in India by Replika Press Pvt Ltd
Library of Congress Cataloging-in-Publication Data available
ISBN: 978 1 56656 878 4

To request our complete full-color catalog, please call use toll free at 1-800-238-LINK, visit our website at www.interlinkbooks.com, or send us an email: info@interlinkbooks.com.

Northern Spain
touring atlas

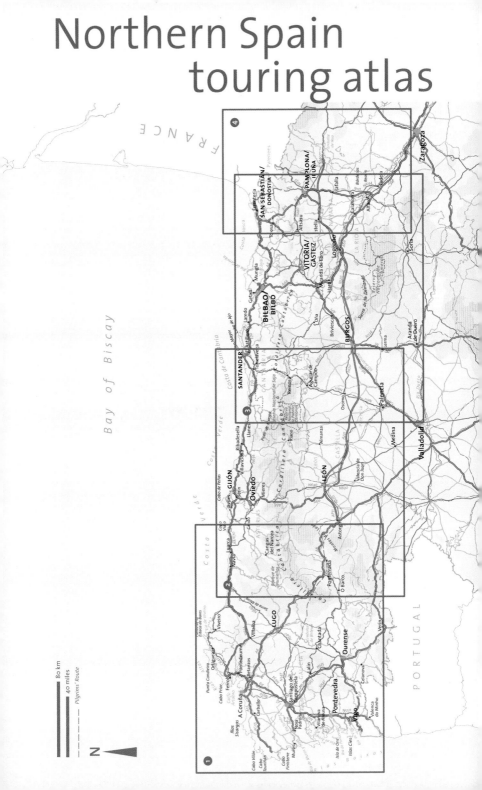

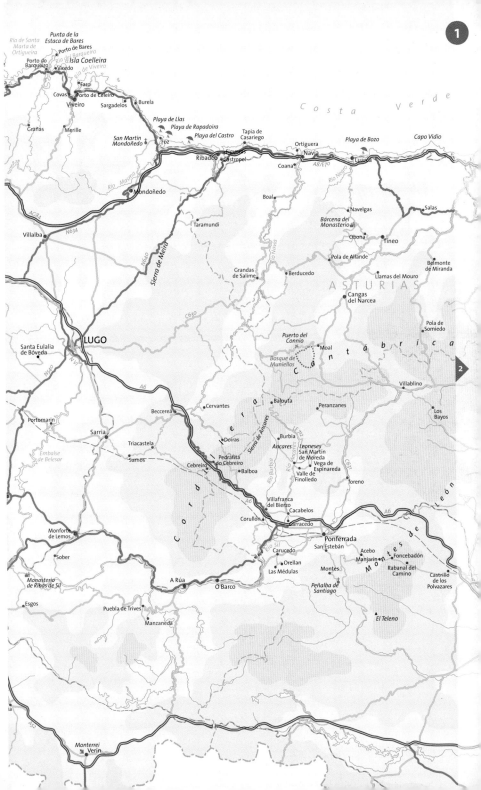

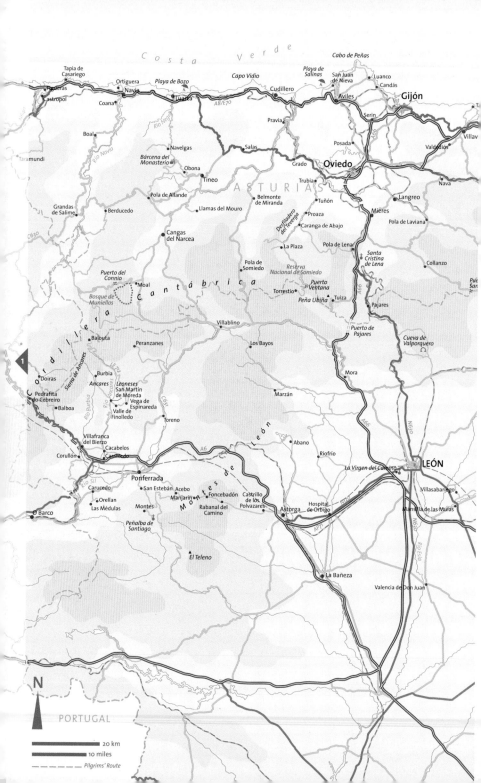

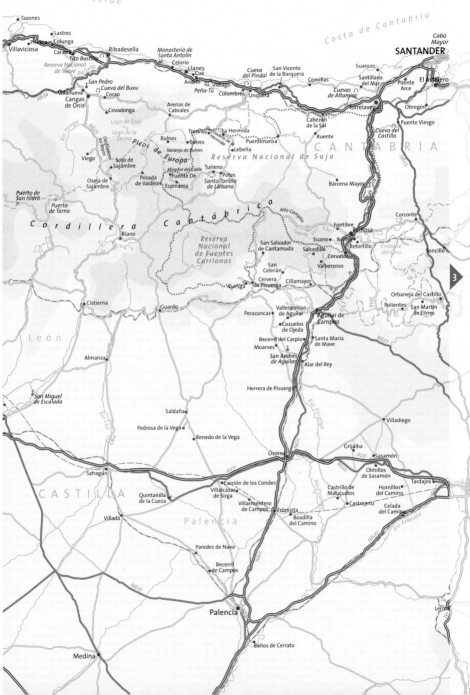

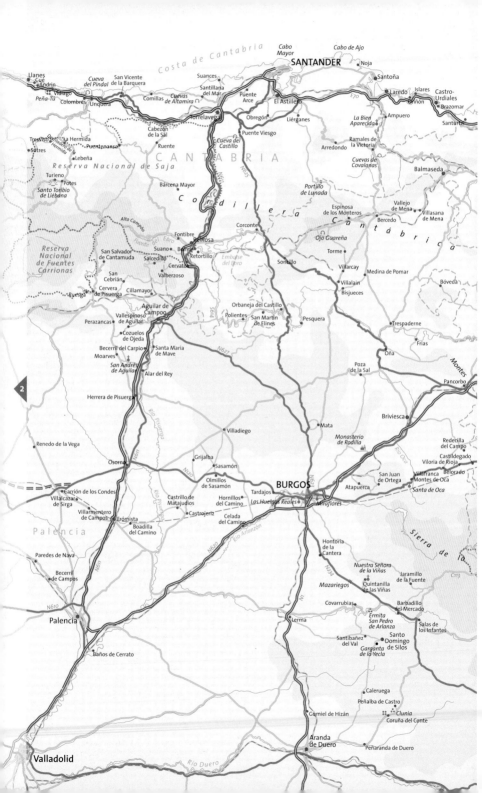

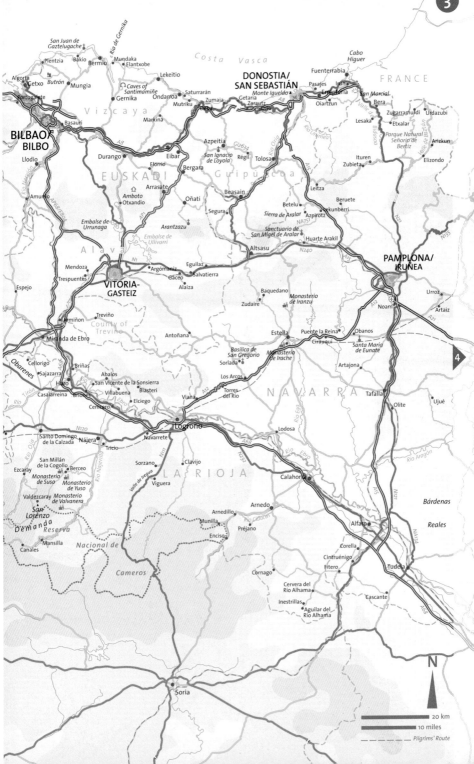